ORIENTALIA CHRISTIANA ANALECTA
273

THE HOMILIES OF ST JOHN CHRYSOSTOM — PROVENANCE

Reshaping the Foundations

ORIENTALIA CHRISTIANA ANALECTA

EDITOR

Edward G. Farrugia, S.J.

WITH

The Professors of the Pontifical Oriental Institute

SECRETARY

Bernardo Arruti, S.J.

MANAGING EDITOR

Jarosław Dziewicki

All correspondence concerning manuscripts should be addressed to the Editor;
all other correspondence to the Managing Editor.

ORIENTALIA CHRISTIANA ANALECTA
273

Wendy Mayer

THE HOMILIES OF ST JOHN CHRYSOSTOM — PROVENANCE

Reshaping the Foundations

PONTIFICIO ISTITUTO ORIENTALE
PIAZZA S. MARIA MAGGIORE, 7
I-00185 ROMA
2005

ISSN 1590-7449
ISBN 88-7210-347-9

Finito di stampare nel mese di febbraio 2005
dalla Tipolitografia 2000 s.a.s. di De Magistris R. & C.
00046 Grottaferrata (Roma); via Trento, 46
tel.-fax 06/9410437

TABLE OF CONTENTS

PART ONE
THE DISTRIBUTION AND DATING OF THE HOMILIES:
THE EIGHTEENTH CENTURY TO THE PRESENT

PART TWO

THE CRITERIA ON THE BASIS OF WHICH HOMILIES HAVE
BEEN ASSIGNED TO ANTIOCH OR CONSTANTINOPLE

PART THREE

TOWARDS AN IMPROVED METHODOLOGY

LIST OF TABLES

PREFACE

In the field of Patristics, the last quarter of the twentieth century has seen an increasing move away from research on theological and doctrinal controversies towards an interest in the social aspect of religion, a move particularly noticeable in the area of the liturgy. A similar shift away from the history of great people, events and ideas towards the everyday is observable in the field of Late Antiquity. As a result of the efforts to access the day-to-day life of early Christian communities, increasing attention is being paid to the information provided by the early Christian homilies. Due to the large numbers in which they survive and to the circumstances of their author's career, the homilies of John Chrysostom are among the most widely exploited. In eliciting material from the corpus, however, scholars have largely been selective and have often failed to distinguish carefully between the locations at which the various homilies were preached.

A secure knowledge of the physical setting of a homily is fundamental to the socioliturgical, sociocultural and sociohistorical approaches. It is thus important not only that the place of preaching is determined with care, but that care is taken also to acknowledge cases where such detail is less than certain or is impossible to retrieve. Failure to make careful distinction inevitably distorts the interpretation of any data which a homily contains. In the case of John Chrysostom, whose career spanned both the cities of Antioch and Constantinople and involved more than one preaching place at each location, certainty regarding the status of the provenance of each sermon is vital, if an accurate and nuanced interpretation is to be achieved. An examination of the criteria which underpin the current assessment of where his homilies were preached reveals a number of inadequacies. This study is devoted to a reassessment of those criteria and the development of a more cautious and rigorous approach.

Thanks are due to the Australian Research Council and to the Australian Postgraduate Award scheme. The funds granted Pauline Allen in 1991-1993 enabled much of the research for this project to be carried out, while concurrently investigating the use of early Christian homilies as a source for social history. The Australian Postgraduate Award scheme generously provided funding in 1994 and early 1995 for the completion of this research. The continued funding provided by an Australian Research Council Postdoctoral Fellowship 1998-2000 has enabled me to update and revise my doctoral dissertation into the present work. Thanks are due also to the Australian Federation of University Women — A.C.T.

Inc. who assisted with accommodation in February 1994, while I was accessing materials held at the Australian National Library in Canberra. It is with deep gratitude that I acknowledge the kind assistance of Bronwen Neil and the Kathegoumenos of the Holy Monastery Stavronikita on Mount Athos in supplying photographs of the folios of Stav. 6 missing from the microfilm supplied by the Patriarchal Institute in Thessaloniki. Without Bronwen's mediation and the monastery's generosity the case study of the *Novae homiliae* presented in Part Three could not have been completed.

The comments of the examiners of the original dissertation, Frans van de Paverd, Wolfgang Liebeschuetz and Philip Rousseau, and their ongoing support of my research are gratefully acknowledged. The suggestions of Frans van de Paverd, in particular, have been incorporated into the present volume. Any errors which remain are my own. I am also deeply grateful to my doctoral student, Silke Trzcionka, for her assistance with proofreading towards the end, when I was beyond seeing the errors and inconsistencies. The assistance over the lengthy course of this project of Fran Wilkinson, secretary in the School of Theology, and Elaine Mortimer, Interlibrary Loans Librarian, both at McAuley Campus, Australian Catholic University, must not pass unacknowledged, as also the support and encouragement of Dan Corbett, my long-suffering husband. Above and beyond his own work at the more obscure cutting edges of computer science, he now has a greater familiarity with the thoughts of Bonsdorff, Tillemont and Montfaucon and a deeper understanding of the intimate details of fourth-century Antiochene and Constantinopolitan life than he would perhaps have liked. Finally, the rigorous training and the encouragement and support offered by my doctoral supervisor and colleague, Pauline Allen, are beyond expression. This book is dedicated to her.

ABBREVIATIONS

A = Antioch.

AB = *Analecta Bollandiana*.

a.i. = *ab imo*.

cat. = catechesis/catecheses.

CP = Constantinople.

CPG = M. Geerard, *Clavis Patrum Graecorum*, 4 vols, Turnhout 1974-1983; (Suppl.) M. Geerard and J. Noret, Turnhout 1998.

CSCO = Corpus Scriptorum Christianorum Orientalium, Louvain 1903-.

CSEL = Corpus Scriptorum Ecclesiasticorum Latinorum, Vienna 1866-.

DOP = *Dumbarton Oaks Papers*.

EEC = A. di Berardino (ed.), *Encyclopedia of the Early Church* (Eng. trans. of *Dizionario Patristico e di Antichità Cristiane*), 2 vols, Cambridge 1992.

EO = *Échos d'Orient*.

ep. = *epistula/epistola*

GCS = *Die griechischen christlichen Schriftsteller der ersten Jahrhunderte*, Leipzig – Berlin 1897-.

hom. = *homilia/homiliae*.

JbAC = *Jahrbuch für Antike und Christentum*.

JECS = *Journal of Early Christian Studies*.

JRS = *Journal of Roman Studies*.

JThS = *Journal of Theological Studies*.

LSJ = H. G. Liddell and R. Scott, *A Greek-English Lexicon*, with Supplement, revised and augmented by H. S. Jones with R. McKenzie, Oxford 1983⁹.

ms. = manuscript.

MSR = *Mélanges de science religieuse*.

NMS = *Nottingham Mediaeval Studies*.

NF = Neue Forschung, Neue Folge.

NS = New series, Neue Serie, Nouvelle série.

OCA = *Orientalia Christiana Analecta*, Rome 1935-.

OCP = *Orientalia Christiana Periodica*.

ODB = *The Oxford Dictionary of Byzantium*, 3 vols, edd. A. P. Kazhdan et al., New York – Oxford 1991.

or. = oratio.

PG = *Patrologia cursus completus, series graeca*, acc. J.-P. Migne, Paris 1857-1886.

PLRE I = A. H. M. Jones, J. R. Martindale, and J. Morris, *The Prosopography of the Later Roman Empire* I. *A.D. 260-395*, Cambridge 1971.

PLRE II = J. R. Martindale, *The Prosopography of the Later Roman Empire* II. *A.D. 395-527*, Cambridge 1980.

PO = *Patrologia orientalis*, éd. F. Graffin, R. Graffin et F. Nau, Paris 1903-.

Praef. = *Praefatio.*

RE = *Paulys Realencyclopädie der classischen Altertumswissenschaft*, neue Bearbeitung begonnen von G. Wissowa, Stuttgart 1894-.

REB = *Revue des Études byzantines.*

SC = *Sources Chrétiennes*, Paris 1941-.

Socr., HE = Socrates, *Historia ecclesiastica.*

Soz., HE = Sozomen, *Historia ecclesiastica.*

Stav. = Stavronikita

STC = *A Short-Title Catalogue of Books Printed in England, Scotland, & Ireland and of English Books Printed abroad 1475-1640*, W. A. Jackson, F. S. Ferguson and K. F. Pantzer, 2 vols, London 1976[2].

StP = *Studia Patristica. Papers presented to the International Conference on Patristic Studies held in Oxford.*

Theod., HR = Theodoret of Cyrrhus, *Historia religiosa.*

ThQ = *Theologische Quartalschrift.*

TU = *Texte und Untersuchungen zur Geschichte der altchristlichen Literatur*, Leipzig – Berlin 1882-.

VC = *Vigiliae Christianae.*

ZKG = *Zeitschrift für Kirchengeschichte.*

ZNW = *Zeitschrift für die neutestamentliche Wissenschaft und die Kunde des Urchristentums.*

LIST OF WORKS CITED IN ABBREVIATED FORM

De Aldama, *Repertorium* = J. A. de Aldama, *Repertorium Pseudochrysostomicum* (Documents, études et répertoires publiés par l'Institut de Recherche et d'Histoire des Textes 10) Paris 1965.

Allen – Mayer, "A New Approach" = P. Allen and W. Mayer, "Chrysostom and the Preaching of Homilies in Series: A New Approach to the Twelve Homilies *In epistulam ad Colossenses* (CPG 4433)", OCP 60 (1994) 21-39.

——, "A Re-examination" = P. Allen and W. Mayer, "Chrysostom and the Preaching of Homilies in Series: A Re-examination of the Fifteen Homilies *In epistulam ad Philippenses* (CPG 4432)", VC 49 (1995) 270-289.

——, "Hebrews: The Last Series?" = P. Allen and W. Mayer, "The Thirty-Four Homilies on Hebrews: The Last Series Delivered by Chrysostom in Constantinople?", *Byzantion* 65 (1995) 309-348.

Ameringer, *Stylistic Influence* = T. E. Ameringer, *The Stylistic Influence of the Second Sophistic On the Panegyrical Sermons of St. John Chrysostom. A Study in Greek Rhetoric*, diss. Catholic University of America, Washington, DC 1921.

Antioch On-the-Orontes II = R. Stillwell (ed.), *Antioch On-the-Orontes* II. *The Excavations 1933-1936*, Princeton 1938.

Aubineau, "Restitution" = M. Aubineau, "Restitution de quatorze folios du codex hierosolymitain, Photios 47, au codex Saint-Sabas 32. Prédications de Chrysostome à Constantinople et notamment à Sainte-Irène", JThS NS 43 (1992) 528-544.

Bardenhewer, *Geschichte* = O. Bardenhewer, *Geschichte der altkirchlichen Literatur*, 5 vols, Freiburg 1913², repr. Darmstadt 1962. All references are to the 1962 reprint.

Batiffol, "Quelques homélies" = P. Batiffol, "De quelques homélies de s. Jean Chrysostome et de la version gothique des Écritures", *Revue Biblique* 8 (1899) 566-572.

Baur, *Chrysostome et ses oeuvres* = C. Baur, *S. Jean Chrysostome et ses oeuvres dans l'histoire littéraire*, Louvain 1907.

——, *Chrysostom and His Time* = C. Baur, *Johannes Chrysostomus und seine Zeit*, 2 vols, Munich 1929-1930 = *John Chrysostom and His Time*, 2 vols, Westminster, Maryland 1959-1960. All references are to the English translation.

Bingham, *Antiquities* = J. Bingham, *Origines Ecclesiasticae; or the Antiquities of the Christian Church*, 8 vols, rev. by R. Bingham, London 1834.

Bonsdorff, *Zur Predigttätigkeit* = M. von Bonsdorff, *Zur Predigttätigkeit des Johannes Chrysostomus, biographisch-chronologische Studien über seine Homilienserien zu neutestamentlichen Büchern*, diss., Helsinki 1922.

Brottier, *Sermons* (SC 433) = L. Brottier, *Jean Chrysostome. Sermons sur la Genèse* (SC 433) Paris 1998.

Brown, "Rise and function" = P. Brown, "The rise and function of the Holy Man in late antiquity", JRS 61 (1971) 80-101.

Cameron, "Earthquake 400" = A. Cameron, "Earthquake 400", *Chiron* 17 (1987) 343-360.

——, "A misidentified homily" = A. Cameron, "A misidentified homily of Chrysostom", NMS 32 (1988) 34-48.

Cameron, Long & Sherry, *Barbarians and Politics* = A. Cameron and J. Long, with L. Sherry, *Barbarians and Politics at the Court of Arcadius*, Berkeley 1993.

Clinton, *Fasti Romani* = H. F. Clinton, *Fasti Romani. The Civil and Literary Chronology of Rome and Constantinople from the Death of Augustus to the Death of Heraclius*, 2 vols, Oxford 1845, 1850.

Costanza, "Waar predikte Chrysostomus?" = M. Costanza, "Waar predikte Sint Chrysostomus zijn vier en twintig homilieën als commentaar op Sint Paulus' brief aan de Ephesiërs?", *Studia Catholica* 27 (1952) 145-154.

Dagron, "Les moines et la ville" = G. Dagron, "Les moines et la ville. Le monachisme à Constantinople jusqu'au concile de Chalcédoine (451)", *Travaux et Mémoires* 4 (1970) 229-276.

——, *Naissance* = G. Dagron, *Naissance d'une capitale. Constantinople et ses institutions de 330 à 451* (Bibliothèque Byzantine Études 7) Paris 1974.

Devine, "Manuscripts" = A. Devine, "The Manuscripts of St. John Chrysostom's *Commentary on the Acts of the Apostles*: A Preliminary Study for a Critical Edition", *Ancient World* 20 (1989) 111-125.

Devos, "Quatre homélies baptismales" = P. Devos, "Saint Jean Chrysostome à Antioche dans quatre homélies baptismales (dont *BHG* 1930w)", AB 109 (1991) 137-156.

Downey, *Antioch* = G. Downey, *A History of Antioch in Syria from Seleucus to the Arab Conquest*, Princeton 1961.

Dumortier, *Homélies sur Ozias* (SC 277) = J. Dumortier, *Jean Chrysostome. Homélies sur Ozias (In illud, Vidi Dominum)* (SC 277) Paris 1981.

Eltester, "Die Kirchen Antiochias" = W. Eltester, "Die Kirchen Antiochias im IV. Jahrhundert", ZNW 36 (1937) 251-286.

Festugière, *Antioche païenne et chrétienne* = A. J. Festugière, *Antioche païenne et chrétienne. Libanius, Chrysostome et les moines de Syrie* (Bibliothèque des Écoles Françaises d'Athènes et de Rome 194) Paris 1959.

Foerster = R. Foerster, *Libanii opera*, 8 vols, Leipzig 1903-1915.

Grillet-Guinot, *Homélie sur Babylas* (SC 362) = M. A. Schatkin, avec la collab. de C. Blanc et B. Grillet, *Jean Chrysostome. Discours sur Babylas* suivi de l'*Homélie sur Babylas*, B. Grillet et J.-N. Guinot (SC 362) Paris 1990.

Grillmeier, *Christ in Christian Tradition* = A. Grillmeier, *Christ in Christian Tradition I. From the Apostolic Age to Chalcedon (451)*, Engl. trans., London-Oxford 1975².

Handbook of Classical Rhetoric = S. E. Porter (ed.), *Handbook of Classical Rhetoric in the Hellenistic Period 330 B.C.-A.D. 400*, Leiden 1997.

Henry = R. Henry, *Photius. Bibliothèque*, 9 vols, Paris 1959-1977, 1991.

Janin, *Géographie ecclésiastique* = R. Janin, *La géographie ecclésiastique de l'empire byzantin. Première partie. La siège de Constantinople et le patriarchat oecuménique III. Les églises et les monastères*, Paris 1969².

Jones, LRE = A. H. M. Jones, *The Later Roman Empire 284-602. A Social Economic and Administrative Survey*, 2 vols, Oxford 1964, repr. 1973.

Jones, VI = W. H. S. Jones, *Pliny. Natural History*, vol. 6 (Loeb Classical Library), London 1961.

Kelly, *Golden Mouth* = J. N. D. Kelly, *Golden Mouth. The Story of John Chrysostom — Ascetic, Preacher, Bishop*, London 1995.

Kinzig, "Greek Christian Writers" = W. Kinzig, "The Greek Christian Writers", Ch.21 in *Handbook of Classical Rhetoric*, 633-670.

Lampe = G. W. H. Lampe, *A Patristic Greek Lexicon*, Oxford 1961.

Lassus, "L'Église cruciforme" = J. Lassus, "L'Église cruciforme. Antioche-Kaoussié 12-F", in *Antioch On-the-Orontes* II, 5-44.

Liebeschuetz, *Antioch* = J. H. W. G. Liebeschuetz, *Antioch. City and Imperial Administration in the Later Roman Empire*, Oxford 1972.

——, "The Fall" = J. H. W. G. Liebeschuetz, "The Fall of John Chrysostom", NMS 29 (1985) 1-31.

——, *Barbarians and Bishops* = J. H. W. G. Liebeschuetz, *Barbarians and Bishops. Army, Church, and State in the Age of Arcadius and Chrysostom*, Oxford 1990.

Lietzmann, *Apollinaris* = H. Lietzmann, *Apollinaris von Laodicea und seine Schule*, Tübingen 1904.

——, "J. Chrysostomos" = H. Lietzmann, art. "Johannes Chrysostomos", RE 9 (1916) 1811-1828.

Mahler, "Zur Chronologie" = E. Mahler, "Zur Chronologie der Predigten des Chrysostomos wegen der Weihnachtsfeier", *Orientalistische Literaturzeitung* 24 (1921) 59-63.

Malingrey, *Sur le sacerdoce* (SC 272) = A.-M. Malingrey, *Jean Chrysostome. Sur le sacerdoce (Dialogue et Homélie)* (SC 272) Paris 1980.

——, *Sur l'égalité* (SC 396) = A.-M. Malingrey, *Jean Chrysostome. Sur l'égalité du Père et du Fils. Contre les Anoméens homélies VII-XII* (SC 396) Paris 1994.

——, *Sur l'incompréhensibilité* (SC 28ᵇⁱˢ) = A.-M. Malingrey, avec J. Daniélou et R. Flacelière, *Jean Chrysostome. Sur l'incompréhensibilité de Dieu*. I (*Homélies I-V*) (SC 28ᵇⁱˢ) Paris 1970².

Mango, "Development" = C. Mango, "The Development of Constantinople as an Urban Centre", in *The 17th International Byzantine Congress. Main Papers*, New Rochelle, NY 1986, 117-136.

Mathews, *Early Churches* = T. F. Mathews, *The Early Churches of Constantinople: Architecture and Liturgy*, University Park 1977.

Auf der Maur, *Mönchtum* = I. Auf der Maur, *Mönchtum und Glaubensverkündigung in den Schriften des hl. Johannes Chrysostomus* (Paradosis 14) Freiburg 1959.

Mayer, "Pargoire's sequence" = W. Mayer, "'Les homélies de s. Jean Chrysostome en juillet 399'. A second look at Pargoire's sequence and the chronology of the *Novae homiliae* (CPG 4441)", *Byzantinoslavica* 60/2 (1999) 273-303.

Mayer – Allen, *John Chrysostom* = W. Mayer and P. Allen, *John Chrysostom* (The Early Church Fathers) London 2000.

Meyer, *Jean Chrysostome* = L. Meyer, *Saint Jean Chrysostome. Maître de perfection chrétienne*, Paris 1933.

Miller, *Birth of the Hospital* = T. S. Miller, *The Birth of the Hospital in the Byzantine Empire* (The Henry E. Sigerist Supplements to the Bulletin of the History of Medicine NS 10) Baltimore 1985.

——, "Sampson hospital" = T. S. Miller, "The Sampson hospital of Constantinople", *Byzantinische Forschungen* 15 (1990) 101-136.

Montfaucon = B. de Montfaucon, *Sancti patris nostri Ioannis Chrysostomi archiepiscopi Constantinopolitani opera omnia quae exstant, uel quae eius nomine circumferentur*, 13 vols, Paris 1718-1738.

Nägele, "Homilien zu d. Timotheusbriefen" = A. Nägele, "Des Johannes Chrysostomus Homilien zu den Timotheusbriefen des hl. Apostels Paulus und die Zeit ihrer Abfassung", ThQ 116 (1935) 117-142.

Olivar, *La predicación* = A. Olivar, *La predicación cristiana antigua* (Sección de teología y filosofía 189) Barcelona 1991.

Opelt, "Das Ende von Olympia" = I. Opelt, "Das Ende von Olympia. Zur Entstehungszeit der Predigten zum Hebräerbrief des Johannes Chrysostomos", ZKG 81 (1970) 64-69.

Palladius, *Dial.* = Palladius, *Dialogus de vita s. Ioannis Chrysostomi*; A. M. Malingrey avec P. Leclercq, *Palladios. Dialogue sur la vie de Jean Chrysostome*, 2 vols (SC 341-342) Paris 1988.

Pargoire, "Les homélies en juillet 399" = J. Pargoire, "Les homélies de s. Jean Chrysostome en juillet 399", EO 3 (1899-1900) 151-162.

van de Paverd, *Messliturgie* = F. van de Paverd, *Zur Geschichte der Messliturgie in Antiocheia und Konstantinopel gegen Ende des vierten Jahrhunderts* (OCA 187) Rome 1970.

——, *Homilies on the Statues* = F. van de Paverd, *St. John Chrysostom, The Homilies on the Statues. An Introduction* (OCA 239) Rome 1991.

Petit, *Libanius* = P. Petit, *Libanius et la vie municipale à Antioche au IVe siècle après J.-C* (Institut Français d'Archéologie de Beyrouth. Bibliothèque archéologique et historique 62) Paris 1955.

Photius, *Bibl.* = Photius, *Bibliotheca*.

Piédagnel, *Panégyriques de S. Paul* (SC 300) = A. Piédagnel, *Jean Chrysostome. Panégyriques de S. Paul* (SC 300) Paris 1982.

——, *Trois catéchèses* (SC 366) = A. Piédagnel, *Jean Chrysostome. Trois catéchèses baptismales* (SC 366) Paris 1990.

Pliny, *Nat. hist.* = C. Plinius Secundus, *Naturalis historiæ*.

Quasten, *Patrology* = J. Quasten, *Patrology*, 4 vols, Utrecht-Antwerp 1950-1960; Westminster, Maryland 1986.

Rauschen, *Jahrbücher* = G. Rauschen, *Jahrbücher der christlichen Kirche unter dem Kaiser Theodosius dem Grossen. Versuch einer Erneuerung der Annales Ecclesiastici des Baronius für die Jahre 378-395*, Freiburg im Breisgau 1897.

Savile = H. Savile, *Τοῦ ἐν ἁγίοις πατρὸς ἡμῶν Ἰωάννου ἀρχιεπίσκοπου Κωνσταντινουπόλεως τοῦ Χρυσοστόμου τῶν εὑρισκομένων τόμος (ἀ - ἠ) - Δι' ἐπιμελείας καὶ ἀναλωμάτων Ἑρρίκου τοῦ Σαβιλίου ἐκ παλαιῶν ἀντιγραφῶν ἐκδοθείς*, Eton 1612-1613 (= STC [2nd ed.] — 14629a).

Schwartz, *Ostertafeln* = E. Schwartz, *Christliche und jüdische Ostertafeln* (Ahandlungen der königlichen Gesellschaft der Wissenschaften zu Göttingen. Philologisch-historishe Klasse NF 8 Nr. 6) Berlin 1905.

Seeck, "Studien zu Synesios" = O. Seeck, "Studien zu Synesios", *Philologus* 52 (1894) 442-483.

Stilting, *Acta SS. Sept.*, IV = J. Stilting, art. "De S. Joanne Chrysostomo, episcopo Constantinopolitano et ecclesiae doctore, prope comana in Ponto, commentarius historicus", 401-700 in *Acta Sanctorum Septembris*, IV, Antwerp 1753.

Tillemont, *Mémoires*, XI = L. S. Lenain de Tillemont, *Mémoires pour servir à l'histoire ecclésiastique des six premiers siècles* XI, Paris 1706.

Usener, *Weihnachtsfest*[2] = H. Usener, *Religionsgeschichtliche Untersuchungen* I. *Das Weihnachtsfest*, Bonn 1911[2].

Vinson, "Maccabean Martyrs" = M. Vinson, "Gregory Nazianzen's Homily 15 and the Genesis of the Christian Cult of the Maccabean Martyrs", *Byzantion* 64 (1994) 166-192.

Voicu, "I confini del corpus" = S. J. Voicu, "Pseudo-Giovanni Crisostomo: I confini del corpus", JbAC 39 (1996) 105-115.

Wenger, "La tradition des oeuvres" = A. Wenger, "La tradition des oeuvres de saint Jean Chrysostome", REB 14 (1956) 5-47.

——, "Homélie «à son retour»" = A. Wenger, "L'homélie de saint Jean Chrysostome «à son retour d'Asie»", REB 19 (1961) 110-123.

——, *Huit catéchèses* (SC 50bis) = A. Wenger, *Jean Chrysostome: Huit catéchèses baptismales inédites* (SC 50bis) Paris 1985[3].

——, "Restauration" = A. Wenger, "Restauration de l'*Homélie* de Chrysostome sur Eléazar et les sept frères Macchabées (PG 63, 523-530)", in *Texte und Textkritik. Eine Aufsatzsammlung* (TU 133) Berlin 1987, 599-604.

Wilken, *Chrysostom and the Jews* = R. L. Wilken, *John Chrysostom and the Jews: Rhetoric and Reality in the Late Fourth Century* (The Transformation of the Classical Heritage IV) Berkeley 1983.

Zincone, "Le omelie" = S. Zincone, "Le omelie di Giovanni Cistostomo 'De prophetiarum obscuritate'", StP 32 (1997) 393-409.

Zincone, *Omelie sull'oscurità* = S. Zincone, *Giovanni Crisostomo, Omelie sull'oscurità delle profezie* (Verba seniorum NS 12) Rome 1998.

INTRODUCTION

THE SCOPE OF THE PROBLEM

In 1991, with the assistance of the Australian Research Council, Pauline Allen embarked on a project titled "Early Christian Homilies as a Source for Everyday Life in the Mediterranean World and the West to 700 C.E.". In the course of preparing an edition of the homilies of Leontius of Constantinople with Cornelis Datema, Allen had observed that homilies, by virtue of their ethical exhortation and exempla, can prove a useful source of information concerning everyday life. This circumstance is particularly true of the homilies prior to the seventh century.[1] This body of literature had hitherto been tapped only incidentally for such information. Allen thus set out to examine the homilies from this period systematically and methodically, beginning with those delivered in the city of Constantinople, as the recent addition of Leontius' homilies to those of Proclus and John Chrysostom provided a large body of material spanning the critical fourth to sixth centuries.[2] As Research Assistant to the project, I was intimately involved in the reading of homilies and the accumulation and analysis of data from the beginning.

When we came to the homilies of Chrysostom we began by examining those series and individual sermons which common opinion assigns to Constantinople. This undertaking was not as simple as it might seem, as in some cases, most notably that of the fifteen homilies on the Letter to the Philippians, the consensus was not as strong as might at first appear. Such hints of disagreement among the original investigators led us to question the provenance of the Constantinopolitan homilies more closely. The preliminary results of three of those investigations were subsequently published.[3] It became clear as we progressed, however, that these problems were not restricted to the small group of homilies in which we were interested, but were part of a wider problem that spanned the corpus as a whole. A reassessment of the issue of how one deter-

---

[1] On the changes which affected preaching in the seventh to eighth centuries see M. Cunningham, "Preaching and the Community", in R. Morris (ed.), *Church and People in Byzantium*, Birmingham 1990, 29-47.

[2] For an outline of the original project see P. Allen – W. Mayer, "Computer and Homily: Accessing The Everyday Life Of Early Christians", VC 47 (1993) 260-280.

[3] Allen – Mayer, "A New Approach"; eaed., "A Re-examination"; and eaed., "Hebrews: The last series?".

mines the provenance of homilies and how the methodology employed affects the distribution of Chrysostom's homilies between Antioch and Constantinople were clearly necessary, if the project was to achieve its goal. That reassessment became the focus of my own research. It is the initial results of what has subsequently proved to be an extensive re-investigation of Chrysostom's homiletic corpus in relation to sequence and chronology, as well as provenance, that are presented here.

The problems associated with accessing and using in a sound manner data contained in the homiletic corpus can be outlined in the following way. A cursory glance at the literature on the topic of the provenance of John's sermons reveals an overwhelming interest in the chronology of his preaching. Inherently there is nothing wrong with this approach. Given the significant role which Chrysostom played in late antiquity and early Christianity, it is natural for historians from a range of disciplines to wish to tie individual items of his homiletic output to specific events or periods in his life and ecclesiastical career. The data thus localised have long been of value to those investigating liturgical practice and development, the function of ecclesiastical and political structures, social practices and beliefs, leisure and entertainment and a wide variety of other areas. The value of such data is necessarily dependent, however, upon the security of the foundation upon which the chronological distribution of the homilies that contains them is based.

The homilies have been distributed in large part on the basis of establishing the date of certain sequences of sermons and homiletic series. These larger building blocks have been distributed around small clusters of sermons or individual homilies of supposedly certain date. Once they have been slotted into place, these building blocks have in turn been used as a means of distributing the remaining sermons or series which in themselves contain no useful chronological information. This technique in turn rests upon a singular premise — that the order in which homilies are arranged in the manuscript tradition faithfully reproduces the order in which the homilies within a particular series were originally preached. Recently the validity of this premise has been challenged by the discovery that at least one of these "series", namely that on Colossians, contains homilies that can be shown to have been delivered in two different locations.[4] More recently still we have demonstrated that the theory that the

---

[4] Allen – Mayer, "A new approach". In eaed., "Hebrews: The last series?" we conclude that the series on Hebrews (CPG 4440) probably also contains homilies which derive from Antioch as well as Constantinople.

constituent homilies in another series, the *Novae homiliae* (CPG 4441), are arranged in chronological sequence is patently false.[5]

These findings have acute consequences for the techniques used in the chronological approach to the issue of provenance. If a series proves to be a series by virtue of subsequent editing, rather than faithful replication of the order in which the constituent homilies were originally preached, then not only is the chronology and sequence of these homilies affected but also their provenance. Data contained in individual homilies can no longer be applied uniformly to the other sermons within the same "series". Instead the provenance of each homily within a series is obliged to stand or fall on the basis of the evidence which it contains alone. When it is considered that the homilies which form series constitute more than half of the genuine Chrysostomic corpus and that, by virtue of their exegetical character, such homilies contain indications of provenance which are more than usually sparse, it can be seen that the impact of the failure of this premise upon the traditional way in which the corpus has been viewed is considerable.

The interest in chronology which has consistently informed the approach taken toward the corpus in the past gives rise to a second problem. This difficulty is of equal concern. So long as provenance is treated as an independent issue and is accorded equal weight no difficulty arises. When chronology is accorded priority, however, evidence of provenance is easily overlooked or considered to be of secondary importance. In many cases provenance becomes a consequence of date, without any separate investigation of whether the implied provenance holds true. Thus, if a homily shows evidence of having been delivered between the years 386 and 397 AD, it is automatically assumed to belong to Antioch. If it is thought to have been preached between the years 398 and 404, it is assigned to Constantinople. The potential for error resulting from this approach is demonstrated in the case of *In Col. hom. 7*. There, as we have shown, the chronological evidence which was thought to point to a date following the fall of Eutropius in late 399, causing the homily to be assigned to Constantinople, is in conflict with more compelling evidence, which points to a provenance of Antioch. By giving priority to the perceived chronological data, the more substantial data had been discounted, giving rise to a false result.[6] When prioritisation of chronologi-

---

[5] Mayer, "Pargoire's sequence". F. van de Paverd, *Homilies on the Statues*, Part II, has also demonstrated that, in the case of the homilies *De statuis* (CPG 4330), although the constituent homilies were delivered at the one location (Antioch) over a short period of time, the order in which they are transmitted in the manuscripts is the result of later editing and does not correspond to the order in which they were preached.

[6] Allen – Mayer, "A New Approach", 30-36.

cal data is employed together with the mistaken assumption of the homogeneity of series, the potential for error is magnified.

It is this second finding which argues not just for a thorough reassessment of the chronology of the homilies of John Chrysostom, but for a
reassessment also of their provenance. If the emphasis on chronology
has led to evidence of provenance being overlooked or, in some cases,
misinterpreted, to what extent might it not also have influenced the
manner in which provenance itself has been assessed? A further practical
consideration lends its weight. In recent decades postmodern investigators have focused not upon the commonality of forms in the late antique
world but upon their diversity. The approaches they apply demand the
ability to locate evidence geographically as well as chronologically and,
on occasion, to match data with individual features within a single urban
landscape.[7] In the process, the homilies of John Chrysostom have frequently been culled for data supporting one or another conclusion. The
opinions offered in the secondary literature with regard to the provenance of homilies used for this purpose demonstrate an alarming degree
of confusion.[8] Although some of the peculiar opinions offered may be
due simply to carelessness, the majority can be seen to stem from the
lack of a single, comprehensive, modern reference work in which all
prior opinion regarding provenance is assembled. If nothing else, a total
revision and updating of the literature on the subject of where Chrysostom preached what is urgently required.

To sum up, there are three discrete aspects to the wider problem —
provenance, sequence and chronology. The relationship between these
three aspects is not bi- or tri-directional but uni-directional. Recognition
of the nature of their relationship to one another is essential, if the tan-

---

[7] In the liturgical field the work of John Baldovin, Thomas Mathews and, most
recently, Antoine Chavasse exemplifies this approach. See Baldovin, *The Urban Character
of Christian Worship: The Origins, Development and Meaning of Stational Liturgy* (OCA 228)
Rome 1987; Mathews, *Early Churches*; Chavasse, *La liturgie de la ville de Rome du Ve au
VIIIe siècle. Une liturgie conditionnée par l'organisation de la vie* in urbe *et* extra muros
(Studia Anselmiana 112; Analecta Liturgica 18) Rome 1993.

[8] Miller, *Birth of the Hospital*, 42 and n. 95, for instance, ascribes *In II Cor. hom. 7* to
Constantinople, a homily usually assigned to Antioch; Wilken, *Chrysostom and the Jews*,
84, cites *In Col. hom. 8* as evidence of amulet use at Antioch; the same homily is cited by
H. Maguire, "Garments Pleasing to God: The Significance of Domestic Textile Designs in
the Early Byzantine Period", DOP 44 (1990) 218, as evidence for the practice at
Constantinople. For further examples see V. Nutton, "From Galen to Alexander, Aspects of
Medicine and Medical Practice in Late Antiquity", DOP 38 (1984) 9 n. 80 (*In Matt. hom. 56*
= Constantinople); F. van de Paverd, "Anaphoral Intercessions, Epiclesis and Communion-
rites in John Chrysostom", OCP 49 (1983) 320 (*In Rom. hom. 12* = Constantinople); and
Vinson, "Maccabean Martyrs", 186 n. 61 (*De Eleazaro et septem pueris* [CPG 4441.13] =
Antioch). In none of these cases is there acknowledgement that the claim is contrary to the
consensus.

gled mass of misconceptions and false conclusions is to be unwound. That is, it follows logically that one cannot properly establish when the various homilies were delivered (chronology) unless one first addresses the problem of how the homilies interconnect (sequence). It also follows that one cannot determine how the homilies interconnect, unless one first addresses the problem of where each and every homily was preached (provenance). After all, the linking of homilies in sequence presupposes that they were all delivered at the one place. Provenance is therefore the first step in the process; the issue of sequence is the next to be addressed; while an investigation and assessment of chronology necessarily comes last. Since the literature on both provenance and chronology has overwhelmingly been addressed from the latter perspective, a reassessment of all three aspects in relation to this massive homiletic corpus is ultimately required. In this process, provenance is the obvious point at which to start. That particular investigation is addressed in Part Two. However, before one can set out confidently along this long and difficult path, one must first step back, since one cannot adequately assess the methodological approach taken towards provenance in the past, without also understanding how the approach itself and the views engendered have developed. Because chronology, sequence and provenance are at this point inextricably entwined, and since no comprehensive review of the literature on the topic has been undertaken since the mid-eighteenth century, Part One is devoted to a summary of all of the significant contributions to the debate since Tillemont in 1706, and to an analysis of their interrelationships. The *terminus ad quem* observed in Part One is July 2000. In Part Three the results obtained from the investigation undertaken in Part Two are analysed and summarised and a modified approach outlined.

Aims and Methodology

The primary aim of the present study is thus to demonstrate the instability of the foundations upon which scholars who exploit the rich data contained in this substantial and important homiletic corpus currently rely. A secondary objective is to cut a path through the mass of scholarship regarding the corpus and provide a tool for approaching the homilies of John Chrysostom that, in the first instance, will provide easy reference to significant prior opinion regarding the provenance, sequence and chronology of the homilies, and, in the second, will allow quick access to the conclusions resulting from the analysis of the reliability of that opinion in relation to the provenance of individual homilies. For that reason tables, in which results and opinion are summarised, appear at the end of almost every section, and several different indices to

the homilies are supplied. A third aim is to place future exploitation of
the contents of the homilies on a more secure footing. This objective is
achieved by stripping the dead wood away from the current approach
and by then modifying the remnants of that approach so that it produces
results that are more honest and reliable.

Various constraints — most notably that of size (the genuine homiletic corpus consists of some 800+ items of markedly varying content and
length) — play a role in shaping the manner in which the investigation
proceeds. Firstly, investigation is necessarily restricted to the corpus of
genuine homilies. The definition of that corpus, however, is not beyond
dispute.[9] In order to maintain the firmest possible base against which to
test the criteria in Part Two, the investigation is limited to the corpus defined by Geerard in the *Clavis Patrum Graecorum* (CPG 4317-4472), with
the exclusion of the fragments and so-called commentaries.[10] As an exception to this, *De capto Eutropio* (CPG 4528) is removed from among
the *dubia*, where it was placed by Geerard, and is treated as authentic.
Stylistically and in terms of vocabulary it is homogeneous with the other
genuine homilies. Further, as Alan Cameron has convincingly demonstrated, the manuscript title to this homily is erroneous,[11] a circumstance
which nullifies the reasons put forward in the past for denying it genuine
status.[12] The homily *In illud: Apparuit gratia dei omnibus hominibus* (CPG
4456), published for the first time by Wenger in 1971,[13] on the other
hand, has been excluded. Despite being listed by Geerard among the *opera genuina extra*, the style and vocabulary seem to me to be sufficiently
alien to Chrysostom to raise doubts. The homily *In poenitentiam Ninivi-
tarum* (CPG 4442) has likewise been excluded from discussion, because
its status has been considered doubtful.[14] Since it has in any case rarely
been given more than a passing glance, it seems best to set it aside for
the present. The fourth of the six homilies *In illud: Vidi dominum* (CPG

---

[9] For a more recent assessment of the boundaries of the corpus than CPG see Voicu, "Il confini del corpus".

[10] CPG 4367 (*De fato et providentia or. 1-6*) is also excluded on the basis that the form in which it survives is that of a written treatise rather than individual orally-delivered homilies.

[11] Cameron, "A misidentified homily", 34-48.

[12] See the comments of Voicu, "Il confini del corpus", 108, in regard to this homily and a number of others which, in his opinion, may also be genuine (CPG 4508, 4529 and 4536).

[13] A. Wenger, "Une homélie inédite de Jean Chrysostome sur l'épiphanie", REB 29 (1971) 117-135.

[14] See Voicu, "Il confini del corpus", 107.

4417) has been excluded from consideration in Part Two because of the doubt cast upon its authenticity by Dumortier.[15]

Several other homilies, previously among the genuine corpus, are also excluded from the body of homilies given consideration. *De paenitentia hom.* 7 (CPG 4333) has long been reattributed to Severian of Gabala[16] and is currently being edited for inclusion in the projected edition of Severian's homiletic corpus.[17] The authenticity of *De paen. hom.* 9 is also considered doubtful,[18] whereas it is now thought that *De paen. hom.* 8 (CPG 4508), once held to be of dubious authenticity,[19] may be genuine.[20] Whereas the inadmissability of *De paen. hom.* 7 is patent, the doubts surrounding the status of the latter two sermons are also sufficient to warrant their exclusion. However, where Voicu would consider the status of *In quatriduanum Lazarum* (CPG 4322), *De Christi precibus* (PG 4323), *De s. Pelagia* (CPG 4350), *De Macabeis hom.* 3 (CPG 4354), *In quatriduanum Lazarum* (CPG 4356) and *De terrae motu* (CPG 4366) questionable,[21] I would argue that the style and vocabulary of *De s. Pelagia* and *De terrae motu* are indicative of their authenticity. For that reason both CPG 4350 and 4366 are retained within the body of homilies subjected to examination.

The condition of the texts currently available to an investigator of the homilies presents a further difficulty. The manuscript tradition of very few of Chrysostom's homilies has as yet been subjected to rigorous modern scientific investigation.[22] Collation and analysis, when it does occur,

---

[15] Dumortier, *Homélies sur Ozias* (SC 277), 13-17; and id., "Une homélie chrysostomienne suspecte", MSR 30 (1973) 185-191. See, however, P. Augustin, "La pérennité de l'Église selon Jean Chrysostome et l'authenticité de la IVᵉ Homélie *Sur Ozias*", *Recherches augustiniennes* 28 (1995) 95-144, who argues, *contra* Dumortier, for a *terminus ante quem* of 422 and who seeks to demonstrate on stylistic grounds that it is in fact genuine.

[16] See C. Martin, "Une homélie De Poenitentia de Sévérien de Gabala", *Revue d'Histoire ecclésiastique* 26 (1930) 331-343; and De Aldama, *Repertorium*, 144 (no.395).

[17] See C. Datema, "Towards a critical edition of the Greek homilies of Severian of Gabala", *Orientalia Lovaniensia Periodica* 19 (1988) 107-115, esp. 108, where it is titled *De paenitentia et compunctione*.

[18] It is found translated into Latin from Slavic under the name of Ephraem. See J.S. Assemani, *S.P.N. Ephraem Syri opera omnia*, III, Rome 1746, 608.

[19] See De Aldama, *Repertorium*, 34 (no.88).

[20] Voicu, "Il confini del corpus", 108.

[21] Voicu, "Il confini del corpus", 107.

[22] To date, critical editions of CPG 4317, 4318, 4320-4325, 4344, 4347, 4410.1-8, 4417, 4460-4462 and 4465-4472 have appeared in the series *Sources Chrétiennes*, while a critical edition of 4420 has recently been published by Sergio Zincone (Zincone, *Omelie sull'oscurità*). New editions of 4327, 4330, 4426, 4438-4439 and 4441 have been announced by W. Pradels and R. Brändle, A. Valevicius, F. Gignac and A. Devine (separately), W. Pradels, and M. Aubineau, respectively. Three parts (in six volumes) of a partial edition of the shorter recension of the series on John (CPG 4425) being undertaken by M.-É.

is slow, with a number of projects already exceeding the lifetime or interest of the original investigator.[23] When the proposed editions are taken into account, the number of homilies that are currently or will eventually be available in a modern edition does not exceed twenty per cent of the full corpus. This circumstance gives rise to a major dilemma. The methodology employed in attributing the homilies, both chronologically and geographically, assumes that the text transmitted faithfully reproduces the homilist's original comments. This assumption is problematic in any circumstance but is particularly disturbing when applied to the exegetical series. The cases of the series on John (CPG 4425) and the series on Acts (CPG 4426), where close study of the mansucript tradition indicates editorial interference in each instance,[24] counsel considerable caution in regard to the adoption of this principle. The discovery of a "rough" and a "smooth" recension in the case of a number of the series on the Pauline epistles likewise gives pause, since the study of the manuscript tradition in these instances indicates that Montfaucon presents in his text a mixture of the two readings.[25] Given the condition of the majority of the published texts, all conclusions in the following investigation must be considered tentative until such time as the precise relationship between text

---

Boismard and A. Lamouille (*Un évangile pré-johannique*, Études bibliques NS 17-18, 24-25, 28-29, Paris 1993, 1994, 1996) have appeared, with other volumes still in process. Boismard and Lamouille (II.1 7), however, disclaim any intention to produce a complete critical edition.

[23] So the edition of the series on Acts (CPG 4426) has passed from E.R. Smothers to F. Gignac; and that of the series on Philemon and Titus (CPG 4438-4439) from B. Goodall to W. Pradels. Various scholars have picked up investigation of the manuscript tradition of the series on John (CPG 4425) without, however, indicating an intention to edit that lengthy series (so Boismard and Lamouille, see previous note).

[24] J. Taylor, "The Text of St John Chrysostom's Homilies on John", StP 25 (1993) 172-175, on the basis of Boismard and Lamouille's findings, argues that incongruities between the commentary and ethical parts of the homilies, as well as discrepancies between the text-type of John in each part, point to compilation of the series from disparate material by someone other than John (Boismard and Lamouille, I.2 191-205, in fact claim that the commentary part of the homilies belongs to Diodore of Tarsus). P. W. Harkins, "The Text Tradition of Chrysostom's Commentary on John", StP 7 (1966) 210-220, earlier argued for two distinct families of manuscripts pointing to editorial intervention in the case of the smoother (longer) recension. F. Gignac, "Evidence for Deliberate Scribal Revision in Chrysostom's *Homilies on the Acts of the Apostles*", in J. Petruccione (ed.), *Nova & Vetera. Patristic Studies in Honor of Thomas Patrick Halton*, Washington, DC 1998, 209-225, cites numerous examples of editorial cleaning and augmentation of the "rough" recension of the homilies on Acts, which appear throughout the "smooth" recension.

[25] On the mixed texts published by Montfaucon in general and the state of the manuscripts in regard to the series on Titus (CPG 4438) and Philemon (CPG 4439) in particular see B. Goodall, *The Homilies of St. John Chrysostom on the Letters of St. Paul to Titus and Philemon. Prolegomena to an Edition* (University of California Publications in Classical Studies 20) Berkeley 1979.

and delivery, if such a thing is possible, can be established. On the other hand, the urgency of the problem with regard to provenance is such that waiting a century or more for the appearance of scientifically established editions of every single homily in the corpus is counterproductive, since such a lengthy delay would substantially proliferate invalid results. The investigation which follows is thus conducted in the knowledge that every decision constitutes a trade-off between the need to correct entrenched errors and the possibility of creating new ones.

In an investigation which aims to address the full extent of the homiletic corpus, further difficulties are encountered in identifying individual homilies with consistency. Even in the present day, and despite the existence of the *Clavis Patrum Graecorum*, certain homilies or series can be found referred to in a variety of ways. This is particularly the case with the miscellaneous or so-called occasional homilies. In order to be clear about which homily or series is under discussion, the title employed by CPG, whether in full or in an abbreviated form, is used here without exception.[26] After the first citation, the appropriate CPG number is restated as often as necessary to maintain clarity.

The most profound constraint, however, is that imposed by the sheer size of the corpus. If the full corpus cannot be addressed in Part Two, since such an undertaking would extend well beyond the present volume, it is necessary to determine how the number can be reduced without in the process compromising the results. This is a difficult issue and one not easily resolved. An obvious place to start is with the current scholarship regarding provenance. Assuming that over the course of three hundred years most of the evidence indicative of provenance has been identified and recorded (regardless of the accuracy of the result), one can begin with a list of all of the sermons which have ever received mention in the literature. Every single one of these sermons must in any case be addressed, if one is to assess the validity of the criteria used to draw conclusions from the data. To consider these homilies alone, however, is to gain an unbalanced view of the situation. As many homilies as possible must be added in order to provide an adequate context in which to assess both the character of the original data and the validity of the criteria applied to them. In deciding what to add to this list one can further draw distinction between two basic types of sermon — the sermon which has the examination of a biblical text as its primary focus (the exegetical) and

---

[26] In the case of the homilies on the statues (CPG 4330) the alternative title supplied by Geerard (*De statuis*) is the one consistently used, since this is the more familiar. Likewise in the case of the eight baptismal catecheses (CPG 4465-4472) the more distinctive label *Cat. 1*, *Cat. 2* etc., employed by Geerard in the initial title to the series, is used, even though he proceeds to label them individually *Hom. 1*, *Hom. 2*.

everything else (catechetical, panegyric, moral etc.). On the whole, exegetical homilies contain less data which are specific to the audience or
local environment. Excluding those sermons from consideration both re-
duces the corpus considerably and, on the face of it, should reduce the
risk of excluding information which is of importance. It is to be remembered that individual homilies from the exegetical series which have been
identified in the literature as containing evidence of provenance are retained.

At this point, the corpus of homilies assembled for examination constitutes CPG 4317-4325, 4327-4347, 4349-4366, 4368-4399,[27] 4406, 4408,
4441, 4460-4472 and 4528, plus approximately 110 sermons from among
the exegetical series — in total, some 281 sermons. Since the full corpus
contains over 800 homilies, this total is not sufficiently high to ensure an
adequate sample. To the above group can be added the exegetical sermons not incorporated in series (CPG 4414-5, 4417-4423: 13 homilies)
and the smallest of the exegetical series (CPG 4410-4412, 4438-4439: 26
homilies). The increase gained by this is not substantial. Fortuitously,
however, all of the exegetical series ascribed to Constantinople had been
read for the purposes of our original investigation into the usefulness of
homilies as a source for everyday life (CPG 4426, 4432-4435, 4440: 132
homilies). Since by our own investigation we have shown that many of
the homilies contained in them do not necessarily stem from Constantinople, while a question mark must be placed over the provenance of the
homilies contained in those series which have not yet been thoroughly
investigated, the addition of these particular sermons to the base-line
study should not noticeably bias the results. The total thus derived (c.
450 homilies) is more respectable (just over fifty percent of the full corpus). The sample is also likely to be more representative. While this percentage is the bare minimum upon which it is reasonable to base a study
of this kind, it is adequate if caution is exercised at every step in the
process. A study based on this sample will not find answers for every
question, but it should determine the questions which need to be asked
and establish a sound foundation for future investigation.

It is helpful at this point to restate the objectives of the present investigation. The study which follows does not purport to present a thorough
and systematic review of the provenance of the full corpus of genuine
homilies, although that is the long-term objective to which it is intended
to contribute. Instead, the present investigation focuses upon four goals
— a systematic review of the literature on the provenance of the homilies
of John Chrysostom; a thorough examination of the validity of the criteria that have been adduced; the establishment of a base-line group of

---

[27] Excluding CPG 4395 and 4398, which survive only in Latin.

homilies that can be located at Antioch or Constantinople with certainty; and the development of a more sound and reliable methodology for determining provenance. The broader aim is to assemble and present a body of evidence to which other scholars can refer and which can be used with confidence by them as a basis for further investigation.

Finally, how can we be sure that a new assessment of the issue of provenance will not fall into the same difficulties as the old? The only answer that can be offered is that an awareness of the failings of prior approaches is a useful safeguard. There are no guarantees, however, that a newly modified approach will not fall into misguided assumptions of its own.

PART ONE

THE DISTRIBUTION AND DATING OF
THE HOMILIES: THE EIGHTEENTH CENTURY
TO THE PRESENT

CHAPTER ONE

THE STATUS QUAESTIONIS

The scholarship concerned with the location and date of the homilies of Chrysostom can be divided roughly into four phases — the work of Cardinal Baronius, Sir Henry Savile and others (c. 1590-1690);[1] that of Louis Lenain de Tillemont, Bernard de Montfaucon and Jean Stilting (1706-1753); the writings of Gerhard Rauschen, Hans Lietzmann, Max von Bonsdorff, Chrysostom Baur and others (c. 1890-1930);[2] and the small quantity of scattered articles, editions and other material which has appeared since. After so many centuries and such intensive investigation of the corpus it is reasonable to suppose that the majority of questions regarding the provenance and chronology of the homilies has been answered, and that a complete and cogent schema has been devised. But is this really the case? Just how definitive is the chronological and geographic distribution of the homilies currently being promoted? Is it free from error? Perhaps more importantly, is it comprehensive and complete?

Before we can even attempt to answer these questions, we must first discover the details of the schemas being promoted and then come to an understanding of how these have been derived. Essential to this process is both the situation of a schema within its context (upon what earlier work has the scholar relied? what arguments does the scholar address?

---

[1] For a full outline see Baur, *Chrysostome et ses oeuvres*, 224-229.

[2] In the decades prior to Rauschen there appeared several biographies of Chrysostom, most notably those of J. A. Neander, *Der hl. Johannes Chrysostomus und die Kirche, besonders des Orients, in dessen Zeitalter*, I-II, Berlin 1821-1822; E. Martin, *Saint Jean Chrysostome, ses oeuvres et son siècle*, 3 vols, Montpellier 1860; and W. Stephens, *Saint Chrysostom. His Life and Times: A sketch of the church and the empire in the fourth century*, London 1872. Toward the end of the previous century there also appeared an edition of four homilies prepared by C. Matthaei, *Ioannis Chrysostomi homiliae IV ex omnibus ejus operibus selectae graece et latine*, I-II, Misenae 1792, which was of some influence. For a full outline of the work which appeared throughout this period see Baur, *Chrysostome et ses oeuvres*, 118-139, 232-247. While each of these authors presents opinion on these matters, their opinion has usually been derivative and has had no lasting influence. For this reason, and for the sake of keeping the historical overview within manageable bounds, discussion of their work, except in so far as it impinges upon that of others, is not entered into.

whose work has the scholar ignored?) and a clear understanding of the
direction from which the corpus has been approached. In the course of
this chapter the progression of thought on the provenance and date of
the homilies from the eighteenth century through to the present day
(Phases 2-4) is set out and summarised. Care is taken to place each development within its context and to determine the method of approach
which has been employed. The scholarship of the earliest phase is not
subjected to examination, since, as will become evident, it is the investigations undertaken in the second phase which have had the greatest influence upon opinion in the present day. An exception is made in the
case of Savile, due to the particular influence of his definition of the corpus and of his thoughts regarding the exegetical series.

Keeping track of such vast bodies of information and such a large
number of homilies presents enormous difficulties. In order to assist the
reader, the opinion expressed by each individual or group of scholars is
summarised in table form at the end of each section or sub-section. Two
larger tables (13.a-b), in which the opinions of those scholars who have
addressed all or a large portion of the corpus are compared, are located
at the end of Part One. A third table (14) permits the reader to compare
the major opinions put forward in Phase Three concerning the chronology of the first two years at Antioch (386-387).

1. Savile

The history of the scholarship concerning where and when Chrysostom delivered each homily is shaped by two, not always discrete, lines of
approach — the biographic and the editorial. The latter, into which category falls the work of the Henry Savile, results more from the constraints
of preparing the corpus in full or in part for publication than from any
conscious consideration on the part of the editor. It is generally characterised by a difference in focus, although the label "editorial" is perhaps
at best a convenient way of distinguishing the work of Savile, Montfaucon and, in more recent times, Wenger and Aubineau from that of the
majority of scholars. That is to say, the necessity of dealing with the
homilies or series one by one tends to lead the editor to consider these on
a case-by-case basis. This has a tendency on the whole to militate against
a biographic (and therefore chronologically-oriented) approach, although Montfaucon, as will be seen, strove to overcome this. For Savile,
in his role as the first person to assemble and produce an edition of the

complete works of Chrysostom,[3] interest in the connections between
homilies and the location at which they were preached is incidental to
the task of defining the extent of the genuine corpus. As a consequence,
comment on the miscellaneous homilies is rare, largely uncritical and
scattered throughout the notes contained in the eighth volume.[4] He re-
serves his analytical skills for the larger of the exegetical series.

1. THE EXEGETICAL SERIES

Savile devotes several columns each to discussion of the provenance
of the series on Genesis (CPG 4409),[5] Psalms (CPG 4413),[6] Matthew (CPG
4424),[7] Acts (CPG 4426)[8] and Hebrews (CPG 4440).[9] The remaining series
on the Pauline epistles (CPG 4427-4439) are treated together in brief in
the paragraphs which preface the notes to the third volume.[10] In his
introduction to the series on the Gospel of John (CPG 4425), he refrains
from comment.[11]

In attributing these series to one location or the other Savile relies
heavily on the stylistic criterion proposed in the ninth century by
Photius.[12] In brief, this argues that the responsibilities attached to the
episcopal office interfered with the amount of time Chrysostom was able
to devote to preparing his homilies. The homiletic series which are most
elegant and polished were therefore delivered at Antioch, while those
which are less smooth and finished were delivered at Constantinople.

---

[3] For a critical appraisal of this edition see B. Goodall, *The Homilies of St. John
Chrysostom on the Letters of St. Paul to Titus and Philemon. Prolegomena to an Edition*,
Berkeley 1979, 2-3.

[4] As a general rule, of the eight volumes of the Savile edition I-IV contain the exegetical series, V the miscellaneous homilies on passages of scripture and panegyrics, VI the
polemical and thematic homilies and tracts, VII the spuria and VIII further spuria, the
biographic material and notes. For those who wish to consider its structure in greater detail an index to the Savile edition is printed at PG 64,127-142, with cross-reference to the
edition of Montfaucon. When consulting this index it should be noted that, although the
original Montfaucon volume numbers are used, the page numbers correspond rather to
the columns in Migne.

[5] Savile, VIII 3-4.

[6] Savile, VIII 95-96.

[7] Savile, VIII 145-146.

[8] Savile, VIII 623-626.

[9] Savile, VIII 227-228 and 553-554.

[10] Savile, VIII 225-228.

[11] Savile, VIII 183-184; but see 145-146: "Porro ubi scriptae vel dictae fuerint hae homiliae, de illis in Iohannem nihil mihi liquet".

[12] See Photius, *Bibl.* 172-174 (119a-119b) = Henry, II (1960) 169-170.

Savile attributes the sixty-seven homilies on Genesis (CPG 4409) to Constantinople entirely on the basis of Photius' criterion. In a rare reference to the chronology of the corpus, he also accedes to Photius' speculation that the homilies date to the second and fourth year of the episcopate (399 and 401), adding that the anonymous author of a *vita Chrysostomi* places the series amongst those derived from shorthand (excepta ὑπὸ ταχυγράφων).[13] This date requires some elucidation. The sixty-seven homilies on Genesis divide neatly into two parts.[14] From internal comment it appears that *hom. 1-32* were delivered during Lent, while *hom. 33-67*, assuming that they are homogeneous, were delivered after Pentecost. In the homily known to us as *Hom. 33 in Gen.* Chrysostom lists the sermons delivered in the interim, a list which includes certain homilies delivered on the book of Acts.[15] Photius speculates that this may refer to the homilies which constitute a full commentary on Acts (CPG 4426). If this is the case, and since, as he argues, the series on Acts took a full year to preach and can be dated to the third year of Chrysostom's episcopate, the two halves of the series on Genesis would then fall into the years which precede and follow.

Both on the basis of style and on the authority of George of Alexandria, Savile locates the collection of homilies on Psalms (CPG 4413) at Antioch.[16] In considering where the series on Matthew (CPG 4424) was delivered, Savile for the first time admits internal evidence. The homilies were delivered at Antioch because in *In Matt. hom.* 7 Chrysostom states: "Our city was the first to be credited with the name 'Christian'".[17] Savile briefly refers the reader also to *In Matt. hom. 67*, the example of a famous Phoenician prostitute who upon her conversion settled in an ascetic community near the city, as a further indication by the homilist that he is preaching at that location. He admits, however, that in several places, notably in *hom. 17, 40, 82* and *85*, Chrysostom appears to speak like a bishop. This, he states, is not strong enough to undermine the evi-

---

[13] Savile, VIII 3-4: "De loco & tempore assentior Photii conjecturis, habitas esse Constantinopoli ... & auctor ἀνώνυμος vitae Chrysostomi cap. 36. hunc librum in Genesin ponit inter excepta ὑπὸ ταχυγράφων, & annis episcopatus sui secundo & quarto, hoc est, annis Christi 399. & 401." For the probable significance of the remark regarding the series' transmission see p. 289 below.

[14] In the edition Photius had to hand there were only sixty-one. For his discussion of this division see Photius, *Bibl.* 172-174 (118b-119a) = Henry, II (1960) 167-169.

[15] PG 53,305 25-5 *a.i.*

[16] Savile, VIII 95-96: "Et quidem Antiochiae scripta esse, cum stylus ipse aperte indicat, sine salebris fluens, altior & copiosior, quam in scriptis eiusdem Constantinopolitanis, tum Georgii Alexandrini, qui opus hoc ab eo, dum presbyter esset, confectum scribit, auctoritas...".

[17] PG 57,81 23-24. For the significance of this statement see p. 290 below.

dence in *hom. 7*, unless one entertains the possibility that they were not all delivered at the same time and place.[18] With respect to the fifty-five homilies on Acts, Savile invokes both the stylistic criterion of Photius and internal evidence to demonstrate that the series was delivered at Constantinople. The style alone indicates this beyond doubt.[19] He prefers, however, to add that in *hom. 3, 8* and *9* John clearly refers to himself as bishop, with the addition that in *In Acta apost. hom. 8* the city is described as imperial (βασιλευούση), a title which could not be applied to a city other than Constantinople or Rome. Savile also invokes *In Acta apost. hom. 11*, where the population of Christians is numbered at one hundred thousand, and *hom. 42* where Chrysostom states that the city is large (μεγάλη).[20] In attributing the series on Hebrews (CPG 4440) likewise to Constantinople, Savile relies solely on the perceived episcopal tone in *In Heb. hom. 4*, adding only that the title to the homilies, in which it is stated that they were published from shorthand notes after Chrysostom's death, makes it likely that they were delivered at the very end.[21]

The other series on the Pauline epistles are in the main attributed to the one city or the other on the basis of Photius' criterion, although Savile does on occasion undertake to test the criterion's validity by introducing internal evidence. In some few instances he relies entirely on internal data.[22] In the case of the forty-four homilies on the First Letter to the Corinthians (CPG 4428), the statement in *In I Cor. hom. 21*: "And this in Antioch, where they were first called Christians",[23] is found to confirm the impression afforded by the polished style of the homilies that the series was delivered at Antioch. The six sermons on Titus (CPG 4438) were "more than probably" (*plusquam probabile*) delivered at Antioch also because in *hom. 3* Daphne, the famous suburb of Antioch, is explicitly mentioned. The series on Colossians (CPG 4433) was with certainty delivered at Constantinople because in *In Col. hom. 3* Chrysostom refers to himself as a leader (προεστώς) of the church, states that he occupies a throne and, finally, associates himself with the rank (ἀξίωμα) of a bishop.[24] Both the series on the First and on the Second Letter to the Thessalonians (CPG

---

[18] Savile, VIII 145-146: "Quae tamen coniecturae non eam vim habent, ut possint illa infirmare, quae sunt in hom. 7. nisi forte non omnes eodem loco habitas, aut eodem tempore dicamus".

[19] Savile, VIII 623-624.

[20] Savile, VIII 625-626.

[21] Savile, VIII 227-228. The issue of the title is treated in greater detail at 553-554.

[22] Discussion of all of these series is found in Savile, VIII 227-228.

[23] PG 61,178 40-42.

[24] Savile is here refuting the assertion of an earlier scholar, Andreas Dounaeus, that the series was delivered at Antioch because in *In Col. hom. 7* the city is associated with the riots of 387 AD.

4434 and 4435) were likewise delivered at Constantinople: the first, because in *In I Thess. hom. 11* Chrysostom says that he is accountable for
his authority (προστασία) over his listeners;[25] the second, because in *In II
Thess. hom. 4* he alludes to his position as leader (ἡγούμενος).[26] These
statements, asserts Savile, are appropriate only to one who is bishop. In
the case of the thirty homilies on the Second Letter to the Corinthians
(CPG 4429), the style, which is a little more polished than that of Colossians, I and II Thessalonians and Hebrews, leads Savile to hesitate. However, he concludes that if the moral exhortation with which *In II Cor.
hom. 26* closes is genuine, the statement that the body of Constantine is
buried "here" (ἐνταῦθα) clearly indicates a provenance of Constantinople.
In support of the provenance of the remaining series he can find no internal evidence and attributes the thirty-two homilies on Romans (CPG
4427) to Antioch, the series on Ephesians (CPG 4431), Philippians (CPG
4432), I and II Timothy (CPG 4436 and 4437) and Philemon (CPG 4439)
to Constantinople entirely on the basis of style.

2. MISCELLANEOUS HOMILIES[27]

On only rare occasions does Savile mention that one homily was
delivered before or after, and therefore in the same year as another. He
does assign a larger number of the miscellaneous homilies to a location.
In many instances, however, the issue of neither date nor place is raised,
while in a large percentage of cases where the provenance is stated, he
fails to indicate how he arrived at that conclusion. As a complicating factor, certain of the small groups of homilies which have come to be accepted as series, such as the eight *Sermones in Genesim* (CPG 4410) and
the four homilies *In principium Actorum* (CPG 4371), are presented by
Savile as individual homilies. This leads him to consider the evidence
found in each separately, with the result that in one instance he attributes the same homily to two different locations. On occasion the duplicate of a homily from one of the exegetical series creeps in as a miscellaneous homily, again with interesting consequences for the attribution of
provenance.

In order to represent faithfully the tenor of Savile's thoughts with regard to the miscellaneous homilies, his deductions are presented in the
same order in which they appear in the original edition.[28]

---

[25] PG 62,463 60-464 5.

[26] PG 62,490 5-7.

[27] The term refers broadly to the homilies presented in vols V and VI.

a. *Volume V*

Sermo 1 in Gen. (*t. 5 h. 1*: CPG 4410) is assigned to Antioch since, as is apparent from the end of the homily, the bishop Flavian was present.[29] *De Anna sermo 1* (*t. 5 h. 11*: CPG 4411) is found likewise to have been delivered at Antioch because in it Chrysostom makes mention of his "father", i.e., Flavian.[30] Savile is inclined to believe that the rest of the homilies on Anna (*t. 5 h. 12-15*: CPG 4411) were also preached at that location.[31] *De capto Eutropio* (*t. 5 h. 18*: CPG 4528), considered genuine by Savile, was delivered at Constantinople in the year of Eutropius' consulship. The connection with Eutropius is asserted, despite acknowledgement of the discrepancy between the homily's version of events and the evidence supplied by the church historians.[32] The two homilies *In illud: Ne timueritis cum dives factus fuerit homo (Ps. 48,17)* (*t. 5 h. 19-20*: CPG 4414) were, in his opinion, also preached at that location. With regard to the second (*h. 20*) Savile states that it seems to have been delivered by Chrysostom after one of his presbyters had preached a sermon. It is unclear whether this is by way of substantiating the alleged Constantinopolitan provenance, or is an entirely unrelated comment.[33] The claim that *In illud: Vidi dominum hom. 2* (*t. 5 h. 22*: CPG 4417) is to be assigned to Antioch is stated without accompanying evidence. Savile simply concludes: "as also the rest on Uzziah".[34] The authenticity of *De Chananaea* (*t. 5 h. 31*: CPG 4529), concerning which Savile initially expresses some doubt,[35] is defended, and on stylistic grounds the homily is included amongst those delivered at Constantinople.[36] The first four of the *Conciones de Lazaro* (*t. 5 h. 35-38*: CPG 4329) are considered to belong together.

---

[28] In the following sub-sections, the number assigned to the homily by Savile and the volume in which it is found are indicated in parentheses, alongside the appropriate CPG reference. *T. 5 h. 11*, for instance, = *tomus 5 homilia 11*.

[29] Savile, VIII 713.

[30] Savile, VIII 717.

[31] Savile, VIII 717. In Savile, V, the homilies are labelled Sermo II, III, V and VI respectively, in recognition that a further sermon, now lost, was delivered between the third and fourth extant homily.

[32] Savile, VIII 721.

[33] Savile, VIII 722. Being the last to preach in an instance where several homilies have been delivered in succession has commonly been regarded an indication of episcopal status. See pp. 284-285 below.

[34] Savile, VIII 723. The latter statement appears to refer to *t. 5 h. 21* and *h. 23-25*, which correspond to *In illud: Vidi dom. hom. 1* and *3-5* in Montfaucon's edition. It does not appear to include *t. 5 h. 26*, which Montfaucon identifies as *In illud: Vidi dom. hom. 6*.

[35] Geerard assigns it to a place amongst the *dubia*.

[36] Savile, VIII 726: "puto tamen germanam esse, quamvis languidiuscule scriptam, ut sunt multae huius Nostri Constantinopolitanae".

While Savile makes no attempt to assign these to either location, he does
state that *De Lazaro concio 1* (*h. 35*) was delivered on the day following
In kalendas (*t. 5 h. 53*: CPG 4328).[37]

   In principium Actorum hom. 2 (*t. 5 h. 42*: CPG 4371) was delivered at
Antioch because toward the end of the homily Chrysostom compares
Flavian to the apostle Peter who, he says, founded the church at Antioch.
This homily is one of four on the beginning of Acts which John preached
at Antioch in the presence of Flavian.[38] Without making us privy to his
reasons, Savile states that in his opinion the homily *In illud: Diligentibus
deum omnia cooperantur* (*t. 5 h. 45*: CPG 4374) was delivered at Constantinople.[39] Again no reason is given in ascribing *In illud: Vidua eligatur* (*t.
5 h. 62*: CPG 4386) to Antioch. Savile does add, however, that it was
delivered after the homily placed next to it.[40] By this he appears to mean
De s. hieromartyre Babyla (*t. 5 h. 63*: CPG 4347), which on its own account is assigned to Antioch, again without any accompanying evidence.[41] The connection between that city and *In diem natalem* (*t. 5 h. 72*:
CPG 4334) is likewise simply stated.[42] Savile finds a reference to *De proditione Iudae hom. 2* (*t. 5 h. 80*: CPG 4336) in the exordium to *Hom. 33 in
Gen.* (CPG 4409), as a result of which he infers that the former homily
was delivered at Constantinople.[43] *In ascensionem* (*t. 5 h. 87*: CPG 4342)
and *De s. pentecoste hom. 1* (*t. 5 h. 88*: CPG 4343) were both delivered at
Antioch, the latter, it is stated, while Flavian was present.[44] In the case of
In s. Iulianum martyrem (*t. 5 h. 92*: CPG 4360) it is simply asserted that
the homily was preached at Antioch.[45]

b. *Volume VI*

   When in his notes he refers to *Adversus Iudaeos oratio 1* (*t. 6 h. 22*:
CPG 4327) "etc." — among which he appears to include at least *Adv. Iud.*

---

[37] Savile, VIII 727.

[38] Savile, VIII 728-729. The first of the four is *In princ. Act. hom. 1* (*t. 6 h. 66*), the second undiscovered, the third *In princ. Act. hom. 2*, and the fourth *In princ. Act. hom. 3* (*t. 8
h. 17*). Savile appears to be unaware of the existence of the homily which both Montfaucon and CPG record as *In princ. Act. hom. 4*.

[39] Savile, VIII 730.

[40] Savile, VIII 734.

[41] Savile, VIII 734.

[42] Savile, VIII 737.

[43] Savile, VIII 739. For Savile's attribution of the sixty-seven homilies on Genesis to
Constantinople see p. 38 above.

[44] Savile, VIII 740.

[45] Savile, VIII 741.

or. 1 and *4-8* (*t. 6 h. 17-22*), if not *Adv. Iud. or. 2-3* (*t. 6 h. 24* and *23*)[46] —
Savile, although he nowhere explicitly states this, implies that the homilies were delivered at Antioch. His concern lies rather with the date to be assigned to the collection. He asserts that all of John's biographers locate the homilies among the first published on the grounds that he states in one instance that it is twenty years since Julian was emperor,[47] in another that he speaks in the presence of Flavian,[48] while at another that he speaks after the events surrounding the overturning of the imperial statues.[49] All of these statements cannot, Savile argues, be valid at one and the same instant, unless in fact the homilies were altered by Chrysostom himself at different points in time.[50] In the same way Savile's interest in the location of the homilies *De statuis* (*t. 6 h. 34-54*: CPG 4330) is marginal, although a provenance of Antioch is clearly implied.[51] In the case of *De Lazaro concio 6* (*t. 6 h. 60*: CPG 4329), Savile is more specific. It was delivered at Antioch not long after the overturning of the statues, perhaps at the end of Lent in that same year.[52] In a note to *In princ. Act. hom. 1* (*t. 6 h. 66*: CPG 4371), which is presented in the sixth volume as a miscellaneous homily, Savile asserts that it was preached at Constantinople,[53] apparently unaware that he had earlier assigned this homily to Antioch in the body of a note referring to *In princ. Act. hom. 2.*[54] At the same location he states that *De spiritu sancto* (*t. 6 h. 67*: CPG 4188) was delivered at Antioch in the presence of Flavian.[55] Of the two homilies *De paenitentia hom. 4* (*t. 6 h. 77*: CPG 4333) and *In I Thess. hom. 8* (*t. 6 h. 86*:

---

[46] In vol. VI Savile presents as a self-contained series of five sermons against the Jews (*t. 6 h. 17-21*) the homilies which come to be numbered 4-8 in Montfaucon's sequence. The first three homilies of Montfaucon's series Savile labels separately (*t. 6 h. 22-24*) and locates following these five homilies, in the order 1, 3, 2.

[47] This refers to *Adv. Iud. or. 5* (*t. 6 h. 18*), PG 48,900 39-42.

[48] See *Adv. Iud. or. 6* (*t. 6 h. 19*), PG 48,904 16 *a.i.*

[49] See *Adv. Iud. or. 6* (*t. 6 h. 19*), PG 48,913 23-28.

[50] Savile, VIII 797.

[51] Savile, VIII 804-809. Of the twenty-one homilies assigned to this series by Savile, the last two (*t. 6 h. 53-54*) are those which Montfaucon labels *De statuis hom. 21* and *Ad illuminandos catechesis 2* (CPG 4464) respectively. The homily which comprises *De statuis hom. 20* in Montfaucon, Savile lists separately (*t. 6 h. 55*).

[52] Savile, VIII 809.

[53] Savile, VIII 813.

[54] See n. 38 above. In the note to *t. 5 h. 42* Savile erroneously cites the location of *In princ. Act. hom. 1* as *t. 6* p. 272, which may be the source of his confusion. It is in fact found at p. 722 of that volume.

[55] Montfaucon considers the homily to be spurious. Geerard lists it among the genuine works of Severian of Gabala. See further De Aldama, *Repertorium*, 205-206 (no.551) and, most recently, C. Datema, "Towards a critical edition of the Greek homilies of Severian of Gabala", *Orientalia Lovaniensia Periodica* 19 (1988) 113.

CPG 4434) it is simply stated that the first was delivered at Constantinople,[56] the second at Antioch.[57] In the latter instance Savile again appears
unaware that the homily forms part of a series which he had earlier assigned to Constantinople.[58]

c. *Volume VIII*

Of the small number of homilies printed in this volume the seven *De
laudibus s. Pauli* (*t. 8 h. 7*: CPG 4344) are the only ones to receive comment worth mention. Savile states that they were delivered at Antioch
because in one instance Chrysostom refers to local events which are described in greater detail in *De s. hieromartyre Babyla* (*t. 5 h. 63*: CPG
4347).[59] The attribution of *In princ. Act. hom. 3* (*t. 8 h. 17*: CPG 4371) to
Antioch we have already discussed in the context of volume V.[60]

3. SUMMARY

Because of the number of homilies involved and the difficulty in
keeping track of the proposed relationships, a full view of the distribution of the corpus proposed by Savile is best obtained when the results
are presented in tabulated form. This method of summation will be useful later when considering the degree to which subsequent scholarship is
dependent upon his work.

a. *Provenance*

The following table provides a summary of Savile's distribution of the
homilies according to location alone. The proposed relationships between
homilies and comments concerning date are considered separately in
section b. Only those homilies or series regarding the provenance of
which Savile offered an opinion are listed. The order in which the homi-

---

[56] Savile, VIII 816.

[57] Savile, VIII 819.

[58] Savile, VIII 228. See pp. 39-40 above.

[59] Savile, VIII 934. He appears to refer to the account of the burning of the temple of
Apollo at Daphne and the drying up of the springs there at the time of the emperor Julian
which occurs in *In laudibus s. Pauli hom. 4*, SC 300,192 5-16. *De s. Babyla* is itself assigned
to Antioch. See p. 42 above.

[60] See n. 38 above. In the notes to volume VIII the connection earlier established between this homily and *In princ. Act. hom. 2* goes unremarked.

lies are presented is determined solely by the order in which they appear in CPG.

Table 1.a. Provenance — Savile

CPG no.	Antioch	CPG no.	Constantinople
4188	De spiritu sancto (t. 6 h. 67)	4333	De paenitentia hom. 4 (t. 6 h. 77)
4327	Adv. Iudaeos or. 1,4-8 (t. 6 h. 17-22)	4336	De prod. Iudae hom. 2 (t. 5 h. 80)
4329	De Lazaro concio 6 (t. 6 h. 60)	4371	In princ. Act. hom. 1 (t. 6 h. 66)
4330	De Statuis hom. 1-19,21 (t. 6 h. 34-53)	4374	In illud: Diligentibus deum (t. 5 h. 45)
4334	In diem natalem (t. 5 h. 72)	4409	Hom. 1-67 in Genesim (t. 1)
4342	In ascensionem (t. 5 h. 87)	4414	In illud: Ne timueritis hom. 1-2 (t. 5 h. 19-20)
4343	De s. pentecoste hom. 1 (t. 5 h. 88)	4426	In Acta apost. hom. 1-55 (t. 4)
4344	De laudibus s. Pauli hom. 1-7 (t. 8 h. 7)	4429	In II Cor. hom. 1-30 (t. 3)
4347	De s. Babyla (t. 5 h. 63)	4431	In Eph. hom. 1-24 (t. 3)
4360	In s. Iulianum (t. 5 h. 92)	4432	In Phil. hom. 1-15 (t. 4)
4371	In princ. Act. hom. 1*-3 (t. 6 h. 66, t. 5 h. 42, t. 8 h. 17)	4433	In Col. hom. 1-12 (t. 4)
4386	In illud: Vidua eligatur (t. 5 h. 62)	4434	In I Thess. hom. 1-11 (t. 4)
4410	Sermo 1 in Genesim (t. 5 h. 1)	4435	In II Thess. hom. 1-5 (t. 4)
4411	De Anna serm. 1-5 (t. 5 h. 11-15)	4436	In I Tim. hom. 1-18 (t. 4)
4413	Expositiones in psalmos (t. 1)	4437	In II Tim. hom. 1-10 (t. 4)
4417	In illud: Vidi dominum hom. 1-5 (t. 5 h. 21-25)	4439	In Philemon hom. 1-3 (t. 4)
4424	In Matt. hom. 1-90# (t. 2)	4440	In Heb. hom. 1-34 (t. 4)
4427	In Rom. hom. 1-32 (t. 3)	4528	De capto Eutropio (t. 5 h. 18)
4428	In I Cor. hom. 1-44 (t. 3)	4529	De Chananaea (t. 5 h. 31)
4434	In I Thess. hom. 8* (t. 6 h. 86)		
4438	In Titum hom. 1-6 (t. 4)		
4464	Ad illuminandos cat. 2 (t. 6 h. 54)		

* Also assigned to Constantinople. # If series accepted as homogeneous.

b. *Chronology*

Where Savile refers directly to the date of a homily or series, or where this can be inferred from an association drawn between a dated homily and another, this is recorded in the table below. As will be immediately evident, Savile's interest in the chronology of the homilies is minimal.

Table 1.b. Chronology — Savile

Year	Homily
386	
387	
388	
389	
390	
391	
392	
393	
394	
395	
396	
397	
398	
399	
date unspecified	*Hom. 1-32 in Genesim*[#] (*t. 1*: CPG 4409) *De capto Eutropio* (*t. 5 h. 18*: CPG 4528) (in the year of Eutropius' consulship)
400	
401	
date unspecified	*De prod. Iudae hom. 2*[#] (*t. 5 h. 80*: CPG 4336) *Hom. 33-67 in Genesim*[#] (*t. 1*: CPG 4409)
402	
403} 404}	*In Heb. hom. 1-34* (*t. 4*: CPG 4440) (delivered at the very end)

[#] Inferred.

c. *Sequence*

On occasion Savile points out the relationship between a small group of homilies, indicating that they were delivered in proximity to one another and therefore, it can be inferred, in the same year. Since these sequences in later phases constitute building blocks integral to the chronology applied to the corpus, it is important that they be outlined. To preserve their anonymity the series are labelled Sequence A, Sequence B and so on, progressively.

Sequence A. *In kalendas* (*t. 5 h. 53*: CPG 4328), followed on the next day by *De Lazaro concio 1* (*t. 5h. 35*: CPG 4329); *De Lazaro conciones 2-4* (*t. 5 h. 35-38*).

Sequence B (Antioch). *De s. hieromartyre Babyla* (*t. 5 h. 63*: CPG 4347), followed by *In illud: Vidua eligatur* (*t. 5 h. 62*: CPG 4386). The interval is unspecified.

Sequence C (Antioch). *De statuis hom. 1-19, 21* (*t. 6 h. 34-53*: CPG 4330) and *Ad illuminandos cat. 2* (*t. 6 h. 54*: CPG 4464); (perhaps at the end of Lent) *De Lazaro concio 6* (*t. 6 h. 60*: CPG 4329).

2. Tillemont, Montfaucon and Stilting

The extensive investigations undertaken by the French scholar Louis Sebastian Lenain de Tillemont, the Benedectine Bernard de Montfaucon and the Bollandist Jean Stilting, the results of which were published between 1706 and 1753, reversed many of the assertions made by Savile and established the foundation upon which all subsequent enquiry has been based. Many of the assumptions which are tacit in the work of Bonsdorff and Baur and of the post-1930s movement can be traced back to arguments proposed at this time. In addition, the shape which Montfaucon gave to the corpus in his edition has been decisive in determining how the homilies have since been viewed.[61]

The phase itself is characterised by a progressive move away from reliance on Photius' criterion towards a greater use of internal, combined with historical evidence. In addition, for the first time the questions of both provenance and date are addressed to the corpus as a whole. This is most noteworthy in the case of Tillemont, for whom the limits of the homilies authentic to Chrysostom were still somewhat ill-defined. Another feature of this period is the by now overwhelming interest in the life of Chrysostom, which manifests itself in a predominantly chronology-oriented approach. Tillemont and Stilting both set out their discussion of the homilies on this basis, while Montfaucon, whose arrangement is necessarily influenced by editorial concerns, nonetheless attempts wherever possible to fit the homilies into the sequence of events in Chrysostom's life. Montfaucon resolves this conflict of interest by producing at the end of his edition of the corpus his own *vita Chrysostomi*, into which he melds his proposed distribution of the homilies.[62]

---

[61] As a cursory glance at the CPG numbering of the *Chrysostomica genuina* shows, the majority of the entries (4307-4450) are laid out according to the distribution favoured by Montfaucon.

[62] Montfaucon, XIII 91-177.

1. TILLEMONT

With Savile's edition and that of Morel[63] available to him, Tillemont was one of the first scholars to attempt to distribute the bulk of the homilies between the cities of Antioch and Constantinople on the basis of a chronological analysis of the homilies and homiletic series. In approaching the corpus from this angle, not only did he lay the foundation for his immediate successors, Montfaucon and Stilting, but he also established the basic components of many of the sequences which have come down to us in the literature as an accepted datum. Although he still relies to some extent on Photius' stylistic criterion, especially with respect to determining the location of the exegetical series, Tillemont's interest in the corpus as a depository of historical data leads him to explore the possibilities afforded by internal evidence to a greater degree.

Due to his chronological approach, Tillemont's discussion of the homilies roughly follows a pattern from Chrysostom's first year of preaching through to the point of his second exile, with the homilies of relatively certain date considered first and discussion then turning to an assessment of the homilies of uncertain date considered to stem from first Antioch and then Constantinople. As the period to which the various homilies and series are assigned is not always precisely defined, the following summary of his view is not broken down according to the years between 386 and 404, but rather divided broadly into the category of homilies which belong to Antioch and Constantinople. Within these categories every attempt has been made to preserve the original order in which the homilies and series are discussed. Tillemont presents his assessment of the homilies in a series of "Articles",[64] supplemented by a number of lengthy notes which appear later in the same volume.[65] In the course of the following, the two are fully integrated. It should be noted that the primary edition used by Tillemont is that of Morel, which he supplements with homilies from the edition of Savile. The results of Til-

---

[63] Fronto Ducaeus, *Sancti Joannis Chrysostomi Opera omnia in 12 tomos distributa*, Paris 1636-1642 (referred to as the Morel edition after its printer, Charles Morel). Only six of the twelve volumes are the work of Ducaeus. The remaining six are a reprint of the Commelin text, which predates that of Savile. On this see Baur, *Chrysostome et ses oeuvres*, 84-85; and P. W. Harkins, "The Text Tradition of Chrysostom's Commentary on John", *Theological Studies* 19 (1958) 405 n. 3.

[64] Tillemont, *Mémoires*, XI 39ff (Articles XV-CXLIX). The discussion of the homilies extends a little beyond Article CXLIX. Those cited here, however, cover the genuine corpus as presently defined by Geerard.

[65] Tillemont, *Mémoires*, XI 559ff (Notes XVII-CXVIII). These tend to contain a more detailed analysis of certain chronological issues.

lemont's deliberations on the questions of provenance as well as chronology are summarised in Tables 2.a and 2.b in section c below.

a. *Antioch*

Calculating that Chrysostom's ordination as presbyter took place very early in 386,[66] Tillemont states that *Cum presbyter fuit ordinatus* (CPG 4317) was the first homily ever to be preached by Chrysostom. He finds it difficult to ascertain, however, whether it was delivered on the actual day of ordination.[67] The sermon which followed was most probably *In illud: Vidi dom. hom. 2*. Tillemont bases this suggestion on the homilist's comment that at the previous synaxis he discussed a certain passage in Ps. 148. That same passage is in part the topic of *Cum presbyter fuit ordinatus*.[68] That *In illud: Vidi dom. hom. 2* was delivered at Antioch can be established with certainty, since John says that he is concluding the homily in order to allow the "teacher" to preach. He further compares this person's preaching to an aged wine, while his own is described as a wine that has just been bottled from the press. Tillemont sees in this an allusion to the fact that Chrysostom has not been preaching long, and to the marked difference in age between the forty to forty-five year-old presbyter and his bishop Flavian.[69] *In illud: Vidi dom. hom. 1*, on the other hand, appears not to have preceded *hom. 2*,[70] but rather belongs to a later period. Tillemont infers that it belongs to a time when the empire was in crisis and most probably at war. Since the situation is widely attributed to the poor judgement of those in power, i.e., the emperor, he argues that the homily cannot refer to any point during the reign of Theodosius. Such an accusation could easily have been levelled against Arcadius, however, and most especially during 395, his first year in power.[71] *Hom. 4* also appears to have nothing in common with *hom. 3*,

---

[66] At this point it was still being argued that the event took place in 385. See Tillemont, *Mémoires*, XI 559 (Note XVI). Tillemont arrives at his own conclusion largely through identifying *In illud: Vidi dominum hom. 2* (CPG 4417) as the second homily delivered at Antioch.

[67] Tillemont, *Mémoires*, XI 39 (Article XV).

[68] Tillemont, *Mémoires*, XI 39 and 560 (Note XVII).

[69] Tillemont, *Mémoires*, XI 560. Towards the end of Note XVII he compares the humility expressed here to that found in the first two sermons *In Genesim* (CPG 4410), delivered at the beginning of Lent 386.

[70] Tillemont finds no evidence of the discussion of Ps. 148 mentioned in *hom. 2*.

[71] Tillemont, *Mémoires*, XI 560. At p. 107, however, he situates the homily following *In ps. 145* (CPG 4415) circa 396.

which leads him to consider in some detail the relationship between *In illud: Vidi dom. hom.* 2-6.[72]

Like *hom.* 2, *hom.* 3 stems with certainty from Antioch, although Tillemont does not make us privy to the grounds for this assertion. He considers that a certain interval elapsed between the delivery of the latter and the former. *Hom.* 5, although its subject matter follows naturally upon that of *hom.* 3, contains the appeal: "Don't you see this sea?", which Tillemont finds difficult to reconcile with a provenance of Antioch. Moreover, in *hom.* 5 Chrysostom reflects upon a question which he says he proposed some time ago at the beginning, but of which Tillemont can find no trace in either *homilies* 2 or 3. This leads him to suggest that John preached on Isaiah's vision at Constantinople as well as Antioch. Like *hom.* 2 and 3, *hom.* 6, which follows equally well upon either *hom.* 4 or 5, stems with certainty from Antioch,[73] and was preached a little before the Lenten fast, that is, in either January or February. It has several points in common with *hom.* 2 and 3. On this basis *hom.* 4, since it was delivered at a time when the weather was hot, is unlikely to have preceded *hom.* 6, bearing in mind also that it has nothing in common with *hom.* 5. Tillemont toys with the idea that another homily, now lost, intervened between *hom.* 3 and 4, or alternatively that *hom.* 4 was delivered some time after *hom.* 3, with *hom.* 6 falling just before Lent, not in 386, but in 387. It is not entirely certain, however, that *hom.* 4 stems from Antioch. While the homilist's comments regarding the enthusiasm of the inhabitants for the Word of God is typical of Antioch, the mention of the senate as a feature of the city gives pause. After weighing up all of these discrepancies, Tillemont suggests that, while the provenance of *hom.* 4 and 5 is uncertain,[74] *hom.* 2, 3 and 6 are to be located immediately following Chrysostom's ordination, since the style conforms to that of a person at the very beginning of his preaching career.

By identifying *Sermo 2 in Gen.* (CPG 4410) as another very early homily, Tillemont is then able to assign the first eight *Sermones in Genesim* to Lent 386. He does this on the basis of the opening to *sermo* 2, where John says that it is through the affection and prayers of the people that he has acquired the courage to embark on the exegesis of Scripture. The approach taken by the homilist in this and in *sermo 1* further confirms that they are the product of a novice preacher.[75] The Antiochene

---

[72] For the full argument see Tillemont, *Mémoires*, XI 561-562 (Note XVIII).

[73] Tillemont appears to base this on the impersonal reference to "this great highpriest" (ὁ μέγας οὗτος ἀρχιερεύς: SC 277,216 9-20).

[74] Tillemont later states, however, that *hom.* 4 was "faite apparemment à Constantinople". See *Mémoires*, XI 128.

[75] Tillemont, *Mémoires*, XI 563 (Note XX).

provenance of all eight sermons is therefore assumed, with Tillemont
making only passing reference to the fact that Flavian was present during
sermones 1 and *8*, on the latter occasion in the company of numerous
other prelates.[76] That they belong to the Lenten period is determined
from *sermo 1*, clearly delivered on the first day of Lent, and from the fact
that all eight homilies form a reasonably close-knit sequence. By calculating backwards from the date of Easter in 386 (April 5) and assuming
the observance at Antioch of a seven week Lent, Tillemont narrows the
date of *sermo 1* to Monday, Feb. 16.[77]

The next homily to receive mention is the encomium *De s. Meletio*
(CPG 4345) which, as a result of Chrysostom's statement that it is now
five years since Meletius' death (381), can also be assigned to 386. The
only query concerns the actual day of its delivery. Although one could
argue that the Antiochenes held the commemoration of their former
bishop on Feb. 12 and that therefore, since his death took place in May,
the homily was delivered in 387, Tillemont prefers to interpret the five-
year lapse in a strict sense, locating the homily in 386, either late in May
on the anniversary of Meletius' death or on the day on which his remains
were received and interred at Antioch.[78]

There then follows a rather complex series of deliberations over the
interrelatedness of a number of homilies, all of which are to be assigned
to the years 386 or 387. Throughout this section the issue of provenance
is almost entirely sidelined in favour of minutely determining sequence.
The first sequence established concerns certain of the homilies *Contra
Anomoeos* (CPG 4318-4323) and *Adversus Iudaeos* (CPG 4327) and extends from the second half of 386 into the early part of 387:

> (386) *De incompr. dei natura hom. 1* (CPG 4318); (the following Sunday, c.
> mid-September) *Adv. Iudaeos or. 1*;[79] (six or seven days later) *Adv. Iud. or. 2*;
> (after a longer interval) *De incompr. dei nat. hom. 2-5*; (Sunday, Dec. 20) *De
> beato Philogonio* (CPG 4319); (Friday, Dec. 25) *In diem natalem* (CPG 4334);
> (Dec. 26/27) *De profectu evangelii* (CPG 4385);[80] (387: Jan. 1) *In kalendas* (CPG
> 4328); (Saturday, Jan. 2) *De Lazaro concio 1* (CPG 4329);[81] (Sunday, Jan. 3)

---

[76] Tillemont, *Mémoires*, XI 43, 45.

[77] Tillemont, *Mémoires*, XI 42-46 (Article XVI).

[78] Tillemont, *Mémoires*, XI , 563 (Note XXI).

[79] Tillemont, *Mémoires*, XI 563-564 (Note XXII) argues at some length against the
location of *Adv. Iud. or. 1* and *or. 4-8* in the same year. In the Morel edition, these six
homilies were grouped together (*t. 1* pp. 385-484), while *or. 2* and *3* were located at some
distance in volume five (*t. 5* pp. 608-635).

[80] For the relationship between this homily and *De incompr. dei nat. hom. 5* see Tillemont, *Mémoires*, XI 565 (Note XXIII).

[81] For the rationale behind locating this and the preceding homily in 387 see Tillemont, *Mémoires*, XI 565-566 (Note XXIV).

De consubstantiali (CPG 4320); (Jan. 4) De petitione matris fil. Zeb. (CPG 4321); (Jan. 6) De baptismo Christi (CPG 4335); (Jan. 7) In s. Lucianum (CPG 4346); (Sunday, Jan. 10) De Lazaro concio 2; (Sunday, Jan. 17) De Lazaro concio 3; (Sunday, Jan. 24) De s. Babyla (CPG 4347);[82] (next day) In Iuventinum et Maximum (CPG 4349); (Sunday, Jan. 31) De Lazaro concio 4; De Lazaro concio 5; (next synaxis) In illud: Vidua eligatur (CPG 4386); (Saturday, before Lent) Adv. Iud. or. 3.[83]

With respect to the provenance of the extended sequence, Tillemont notes in the cases of De incompr. dei nat. hom. 1 and In kalendas that they were preached at a time when Flavian was absent,[84] while on the occasions of De b. Philogonio and In diem natalem Flavian was due to preach also.[85]

The next group of homilies to to be assigned to 387 is the series De statuis (CPG 4330).[86] Since Tillemont's arrangement of this collection of homilies has been discussed in detail by Montfaucon,[87] and most recently by Frans van de Paverd,[88] only a summary of his conclusions is provided here. Calculating from a Paschal date in 387 of April 25 and a Lent which lasted seven weeks, he arrives at the following sequence:

De statuis hom. 1; hom. 2; (Sunday before Lent, March 7) hom. 3; (Monday, March 8-Friday, March 12; first week of Lent) hom. 4-8; (c. Monday, week 2, March 15) hom. 9; (a few days later) hom. 10; (Saturday, March 20) hom. 15; (Sunday, March 21) hom. 16; (Monday-Wednesday, week 4, March 29-31) hom. 11-13; (c. end of week 4) hom. 17; (a little after mid-Lent, week 5)

---

[82] Tillemont, Mémoires, XI 57, who at this point assumes that Sunday is the only day of regular synaxis at Antioch in the month of January, notes that the festival of St Babylas (Jan. 24) falls in 387 on a Sunday, which accords well with the information provided in De Lazaro concio 4. There the homilist states that he was recently prevented from continuing on the topic of Lazarus by the festivals of St Babylas and Iuventinus and Maximus, which intervened.

[83] Tillemont, Mémoires, XI 46-61 (Articles XVII-XXII). At p. 60 Tillemont mistakenly refers to h. 55 of tome 1 (De paen. hom. 7). It is clear from Note XXV (pp. 566-567), however, that Adv. Iud. or. 3 (t. 5 h. 55) is intended.

[84] Tillemont, Mémoires, XI 46, 51.

[85] Tillemont, Mémoires, XI 49, 50.

[86] Tillemont, who was working from the Morel edition in this instance, encountered twenty-two homilies as a result of the latter's inclusion of Ad illuminandos cat. 2 (CPG 4464) (t. 1 h. 20 = Montfaucon De statuis hom. 21; h. 21 = Ad illum. cat. 2; h. 22 = De statuis hom. 20). After originally incorporating it into his chronology of this series (pp. 73-75), he was subsequently persuaded to disengage Ad illum. cat. 2 from the series and to locate it in the following year. See further Tillemont, Mémoires, XI 570 (Note XXX).

[87] See Montfaucon, II Praef., pp. 2-8.

[88] Van de Paverd, Homilies on the Statues, Part II, 205-362.

hom. 18; (next day) *hom. 14*; (c. April 11) *hom. 19*; (following Thursday or Friday) *hom. 20*; (Easter Sunday, April 25) *hom. 21*.[89]

Tillemont then determines that, after a discourse or two against the pagans, a number of martyr's festivals and a sermon against swearing,[90] Chrysostom embarked upon the following sequence of homilies:

> *De Anna sermo 1* (CPG 4411); (a little later) *De Anna sermo 2*; (next) *De Anna sermo 3*; (a homily, now lost); (Sunday, June 6) *De Anna sermo 4*; (Pentecost);[91] (Sunday, June 20) *De Anna sermo 5*; *De decem millium talent. deb.* (CPG 4368); *De Davide et Saule hom. 1* (CPG 4412); (next Sunday) *De Davide et Saule hom. 2*; (a little later) *De Davide et Saule hom. 3*; *De Christi precibus* (CPG 4323);[92] *De resurrectione mortuorum* (CPG 4340); (c. mid-September) *Adv. Iudaeos or. 4* (CPG 4327); (4-5 days before Day of Atonement) *Adv. Iud. or. 5*; (Day of Atonement) *Adv. Iud. or. 6*; (during Feast of the Tabernacles) *Adv. Iud. or. 7*; (after the Jewish Festivals) *Adv. Iud. or. 8*;[93] *Exp. in ps. 41* (CPG 4413.2).[94]

Concerning the provenance of this sequence, Tillemont mentions only that Flavian was present on the occasion at which *Adv. Iud. or. 6* was preached.[95]

To the beginning of 388 he assigns another sequence of homilies:

---

[89] Tillemont, *Mémoires*, XI 62-75 (Articles XXIII-XXVII).

[90] See Tillemont, *Mémoires*, XI 76. He bases this on information found in *De Anna sermo 1*.

[91] Tillemont, *Mémoires*, XI 568 (Note XXVI) hesitantly identifies the sermon for this day, mentioned in *De Anna sermo 5*, as *De s. pentecoste hom. 1* (CPG 4343), although the absence of any reference to the prodigal son gives him pause. The Antiochene provenance of the latter is patent from the homilist's mention of "the common father and teacher", who pronounced peace upon the whole assembly. Tillemont considers that this figure is without doubt the bishop of Antioch, Flavian.

[92] Tillemont, *Mémoires*, XI 80, states that it was possibly preceded by *In quatrid. Lazarum* (CPG 4322), although he later argues (p. 569, Note XXVII) that this homily is of doubtful authenticity.

[93] Tillemont, *Mémoires*, XI 569-570 (Note XXVIII), arguing that the Jews of Antioch are more likely to have accommodated their practice to that of the Romans and therefore followed a fixed rather than a lunar calendar, calculates that *Adv. Iud. or. 4* could have been delivered on Sunday, Sept. 5, and *or. 5* on Sept. 12. He encounters difficulties with this thesis, however, when attempting to reconcile the projected date of *or. 6* with that of the Day of Atonement, and therefore breaks off at that point.

[94] Tillemont, *Mémoires*, XI 76-84 (Articles XXVIII-XXX). At *Mémoires*, XI 619 (Note CVII) Tillemont states that *Exp. in ps. 41* was perhaps delivered in the month of October. For his argument regarding the association between *Adv. Iud. or. 7* and *Exp. in ps. 41* see *Mémoires*, XI 570 (Note XXIX).

[95] Tillemont, *Mémoires*, XI 82.

> *De prophetiarum obscuritate hom. 1* (CPG 4420); (Sunday, a little later) *De proph. obsc. hom. 2*; *De diabolo tentatore hom. 1* (CPG 4332);[96] (c. the end of Lent, two days later) *Ad illuminandos cat. 2* (CPG 4464);[97] (same day) *De diabolo tent. hom. 2*;[98] (two days later) *De diabolo tent. hom. 3.*[99]

To some point in this sequence also belongs *Ad illuminandos cat. 1* (CPG 4460) which, since it was delivered a month before Easter (i.e., in the third week of Lent), is to be excluded from 387.[100] With regard to the issue of provenance, Tillemont points out that in the case of *De proph. obsc. hom. 2* John speaks of the bishop in a manner which indicates that he himself does not hold that office,[101] while on the occasion at which *De diabolo tent. hom. 2* was delivered Flavian was among the audience.[102]

The next year to which Tillemont is able to assign a sequence with any confidence is 392, where on the 14th of April Chrysostom delivered the sermon *De ss. Bernice et Prosdoce* (CPG 4355). This assertion is based both on the argument that the festival of the Cross of twenty or so days earlier, to which the homily refers, is not the commemoration of the Cross usually identified as occurring in September, but in fact Good Friday, and that several martyrologies testify to the fact that the festival of Domnina and her daughters was celebrated at Antioch not on Oct. 4, as had previously been thought, but on April 14.[103] On the basis of the summary of the Good Friday sermon provided in *De ss. Bernice et Prosdoce* Tillemont identifies it as the homily *De coemeterio et de cruce* (CPG 4337), further calculating that 392 is the only year in which Good Friday pre-

---

[96] Regarding the connection between this homily and the preceding, Tillemont, *Mémoires*, XI 570 (Note **XXXI**) suggests that the absence in *De proph. obsc. hom. 2* of the required citation of Luke 5.8 gives pause, but is of little consequence in the face of the remaining evidence.

[97] For the grounds for disassociating this homily from the series *De statuis* (387) and locating it rather on the same day as *De diabolo tent. hom. 2* (388), see Tillemont, *Mémoires*, XI 570 (Note **XXX**).

[98] Tillemont, *Mémoires*, XI 571 (Note **XXXII**) points out that on content alone the homily of two days earlier, to which *De diabolo tent. hom. 2* refers, could as easily be *Adv. Iud. or. 8*. Since, however, the latter was delivered in September or October and the former during Lent, the sermon *De diabolo tent. hom. 1* is the preferred candidate. Even so, the subject matter of this latter homily does not accord perfectly with the summary provided in *hom. 2*.

[99] Tillemont, *Mémoires*, XI 84-89 (Articles **XXXI-XXXII**).

[100] Tillemont, *Mémoires*, XI 89. See in particular p. 571 (Note **XXXIII**), where he argues that in the third week of Lent 387 Chrysostom explicitly did not preach due to the cloud hanging over Antioch and the arrival of Caesarius and Ellebichus.

[101] Tillemont, *Mémoires*, XI 86.

[102] Tillemont, *Mémoires*, XI 88, 570.

[103] Tillemont, *Mémoires*, XI 571-572 (Note **XXXIV**).

cedes April 14 by the required number of days.[104] He suggests that the sermon *In ascensionem* (CPG 4342) could likewise have been delivered in that year, since the homilist refers to the customs observed at Antioch on Good Friday as detailed in *De coemeterio*.[105] To later that year, on the occasion of a visit to Antioch by Chrysostom's former teacher Diodore, Tillemont assigns the homily *Laus Diodori episcopi* (CPG 4406).[106] No explicit comment regarding the provenance of this group of homilies is made.

With respect to the issue of provenance, Tillemont's assertions regarding the sixty-seven homilies on Genesis (CPG 4409) represent a major contribution. Whereas Savile, adopting the arguments of Photius, had considered the series to stem from Constantinople,[107] Tillemont proposes that the homilies instead derive from Antioch. After dismissing the proof from style as not infallible, he moves immediately to address Photius' and Savile's main ground for assigning the series to the period of Chrysostom's episcopate, namely that the sermons on Acts which preceded *Hom. 33 in Gen.* are to be identified as the series of fifty-five homilies on that topic (CPG 4426), delivered with certainty in John's third year at Constantinople. Tillemont points out that not only is this not necessarily the case, but that there are certain other homilies on Acts (CPG 4371) which are more appropriate, particularly since they were delivered during the paschal period. These sermons were delivered not at Constantinople but at Antioch, as seen from *In princ. Act. hom. 2* where the homilist speaks of the Palaia or Old Church. Moreover, in the course of the series on Genesis itself, namely in *hom. 12*, Chrysostom mentions a recent sermon preached against those who fast with the Jews, a problem common at Antioch but not associated with Constantinople.[108] Having established the Antiochene provenance of the series, Tillemont then proceeds to determine its date. In the course of *hom. 6* the homilist complains about certain of his audience attending the circus, despite the fact that it is Lent. Having determined that this homily was most probably

---

[104] Tillemont, *Mémoires*, XI 572, notes that the comments in *De coemeterio* regarding the audience's behaviour during celebration of the eucharist might suggest that the homily belongs to the same period as *In diem natalem* (386) and *De baptismo Christi* (387), but points out that in these years the interval between Good Friday and April 14 does not conform.

[105] Tillemont, *Mémoires*, XI 91 (Article XXXIII). He adds that the homily was preached in a church called "la Romaine".

[106] Tillemont, *Mémoires*, XI 92.

[107] See p. 38 above.

[108] Tillemont, *Mémoires*, XI 572 (Note XXXV). For further detail regarding this criterion see pp. 303-304 below.

delivered on the Friday of the first week of Lent,[109] Tillemont points out
that the Roman calendar records no games for the beginning of March,
while it is unlikely that the Gothic games of Feb. 4-9 are the ones mentioned. In 395, however, the first Friday in Lent fell on Feb. 11, while in
396 it fell on Feb. 29, both dates for which games are recorded. Although
for various reasons he prefers 395, he admits that the calculations involve more conjecture than certainty.[110]

The sixty-seven homilies on Genesis are not the only sermons to have
been delivered in this year, however. On the basis of information contained in *Hom. 33 in Gen.* and other evidence, Tillemont constructs the
following sequence:

> (Sunday before Lent) *Hom. 1 in Gen.*; (Lent, Day 1-Wednesday, Holy
> Week) *Hom. 2-32 in Gen.*; (Maundy Thursday) *De prod. Iudae hom. 1* (CPG
> 4336);[111] (Good Friday) *De cruce et latrone hom. 1* (CPG 4338); (Easter Sun-
> day) *De resurrectione* (CPG 4341); (15 days later) *In princ. Act. hom. 1* (CPG
> 4371);[112] (homily, now lost); *In princ. Act. hom. 2*; (next day) *In princ. Act.
> hom. 3*; *In princ. Act. hom. 4*; (following synaxis, before Pentecost) *De muta-
> tione nom. hom. 1* (CPG 4372); (next day) *De mut. nom. hom. 2*; *Sermo 9 in
> Gen.* (CPG 4410); *De mut. nom. hom. 3-4*; (after Pentecost) *Hom. 33-67 in
> Gen.*[113]

Regarding the provenance of the sequence, Tillemont asserts only that in
the case of *In princ. Act. hom. 2* Chrysostom preached in the Old Church
at Antioch,[114] while in the course of *De mut. nom. hom. 1* he makes men-

---

[109] See Tillemont, *Mémoires*, XI 572-573, where he establishes the following sequence
by virtue of the homilist's comments: (Sunday before Lent) *Hom. 1 in Gen.*; (next day,
Monday, first day of Lent) *hom. 2*; (next day) *hom. 3*; (next day) *hom. 4*; (Thursday, 1st
week) *hom. 5*; (Friday, 1st week) *hom. 6*; (Saturday-Monday, 2nd week) *hom. 7-9*; (2nd
week) *hom 10*; (Saturday, 2nd week) *hom. 11*. Towards the end of p. 573, however, he confesses that although *hom. 5-9* were delivered on consecutive days, the placement of these
between the Thursday of the first week of Lent and the Friday of the second admits some
leeway.

[110] Tillemont, *Mémoires*, XI 573. At the beginning of Article XXXIV (p. 92), however,
Tillemont asserts this date with some degree of confidence.

[111] Towards the end of *Mémoires*, XI 576, in discussing the similarity between *De prod.
Iud. hom 1* and *2*, Tillemont suggests that, were there less conformity between the two,
one might consider that it was in fact *hom. 2* that followed *Hom. 32 in Gen.* and that *hom.
1* was delivered later at Constantinople.

[112] For the argument that this homily contains a clear citation of *De prod. Iud. hom. 1*
and the grounds for linking the series *In princ. Actorum* with that on Genesis see Tillemont, *Mémoires*, XI 95, 575-576 (Note XXXVII).

[113] Tillemont, *Mémoires*, XI 93-100 (Articles XXXIV-XXXVI).

[114] Tillemont, *Mémoires*, XI 96.

tion of various bishops who are among the audience, some of whom are to preach after him.[115]

To the year 396 Tillemont assigns a small number of homilies on the subject of penitence, largely because of the allusion in one of them to the ravages of war.[116] This enables him to establish the following sequence:

> (Sunday before Lent, Feb. 24) *De paenitentia hom. 5* (CPG 4333); (two homilies, now lost); *De paen. hom. 4*; *De paen. hom. 7*; *De paen. hom. 8*; (homily, now lost); (Wednesday, week 4 of Lent, March 19) *De paen. hom. 6*.[117]

Regarding its provenance, he states only that in the case of *hom. 5* Flavian was due to preach also.[118] Although *De paen. hom. 2-3* had been attached to this sequence by others,[119] Tillemont remains uncommitted on the question of whether they belong together.[120] He is, however, convinced that they belong to Antioch, since in *hom. 3* it appears that Chrysostom is preaching at this point on Sundays only, a practice which Tillemont associates with that city. In the case of *De paen. hom. 1*, he believes that it belongs to this location also, since the homilist indicates that his time is much occupied with preaching.[121] Aside from the sequence just mentioned, in relation to 396 Tillemont discusses several other homilies, in particular *In ps. 145* (CPG 4415) and *In illud: Vidi dom. hom. 1* (CPG 4417). These he attributes to c. 396 entirely on the grounds that the second can be said to follow the first and on the basis of his earlier dating of the second homily.[122] Concerning the argument that *De Lazaro concio 6* belongs to this year by virtue of the recent earthquake to which the homilist refers, Tillemont is entirely non-committal.[123]

After working on those homilies which can be assigned to a definite year or day during Chrysostom's presbyterate at Antioch, Tillemont eventually moves to consider those sermons which can be shown to stem

---

[115] Tillemont, *Mémoires*, XI 97.

[116] See Tillemont, *Mémoires*, XI 578 (Note XL), where he argues that the war mentioned in *hom. 4* refers to the activity of the Huns in the east and the Goths in Greece towards the end of 395.

[117] Tillemont, *Mémoires*, XI 101-105 (Articles XXXVII-XXXVIII).

[118] Tillemont, *Mémoires*, XI 102.

[119] For a description of the work of Godefroid Hermant (1664) and Ellies Du Pin (1689, 1690) see Baur, *Chrysostome et ses oeuvres*, 224 and 229.

[120] See Tillemont, *Mémoires*, XI 106, 578 (Note XLI).

[121] Tillemont, *Mémoires*, XI 107.

[122] See Tillemont, *Mémoires*, XI 560, where he assigns *In illud: Vidi dom. hom. 1* to the end of 395 or later.

[123] Tillemont, *Mémoires*, XI 108 (where he considers the opinion of Hermant).

from Antioch but provide no clear indication of date. The first to receive
mention is *In s. Ignatium* (CPG 4351), which he believes to have been
delivered on Dec. 20, since this is stated in several manuscripts and is the
anniversary of Ignatius' death. The sermon was delivered not long before
the homily *De s. Pelagia* (CPG 4350), since in that homily it is referred to
as having been preached recently (πρώην).[124] Tillemont asserts that the
encomium *In s. Iulianum* (CPG 4360) stems with certainty from Antioch,
where the martyr Julian's body had been translated and where there existed a church in his name. According to a certain manuscript, it was delivered on June 21, the date of Julian's festival among the Greeks.[125] With
equal assurance Tillemont locates at Antioch the homily *In illud: In faciem ei restiti* (CPG 4391), as a result of the homilist's explicit association
of the city with certain events in Acts. He further states that Chrysostom
had spent the previous day with Flavian in the New Church, while on the
present day he had returned to preach in the Old Church, his accustomed
place of preaching. Following that homily, on the evidence of the sermon
In illud: Domine, non est in homine (CPG 4419), Tillemont locates the
two encomia *In s. Eustathium* (CPG 4352) and *In s. Romanum* (CPG
4353). The first had been a former bishop of Antioch, while the second
had been martyred there on Nov. 17, 303. The homily *In illud: Dom., non
est in hom.* closes this brief sequence.[126] Drawing a close link between the
celebration of the Maccabeean martyrs and the city of Antioch, where
there apparently existed a church in their honour, Tillemont locates
there on the day of their commemoration (Aug. 1) the sermon *De Macabeis hom. 1* (CPG 4354). He points out that *De Mac. hom. 2*, delivered on
the following day, is brief by virtue of the fact that Flavian was also due
to preach on that occasion.[127]

The next homily to receive mention is *De ss. martyribus* (CPG 4357).
This, Tillemont states, was preached a little after the festival of the Maccabees, on the festival of certain martyrs celebrated amongst the rural
communities, the day after the festival of certain other martyrs celebrated at Antioch. Tillemont notes the absence of Flavian on that occasion. In the same year and only several days after this homily he locates
the sermon *Non esse ad gratiam concionandum* (CPG 4358).[128] In the case

[124] Tillemont, *Mémoires*, XI 358, where he accepts that the festival of Pelagia was celebrated at Antioch on Jan. 9. The grounds on which he assigns the two homilies to Antioch
are not made explicit.

[125] Tillemont, *Mémoires*, XI 359.

[126] Tillemont, *Mémoires*, XI 359.

[127] Tillemont, *Mémoires*, XI 359-360, where he further argues that *De Macabeis hom. 3*
is not a genuine work of Chrysostom.

[128] Tillemont, *Mémoires*, XI 360-361.

of *In s. Barlaam* (CPG 4361) Tillemont observes that the homily cannot have been delivered on Nov. 16, as stated in one of the manuscripts, since in the sermon delivered on the following day (*In dictum Pauli: Nolo vos ignorare*: CPG 4380) the weather is described as warm with a gentle breeze, which suggests rather that the two were preached in summer. In this context he notes the mention in *De Anna sermo 1* (CPG 4411) of a cluster of martyrial festivals celebrated at Antioch in the period following Easter, although no attempt is made to identify the festival of St Barlaam as one of these. As for the provenance of the two homilies, Tillemont finds John's request in the second for the prayers of the "leaders" (τῶν προεδρῶν ἀπάντων) firm proof that they stem from Antioch, since at Constantinople no-one took precedence over him. Moreover, the frequency of tombs of martyrs, particularly those which were extra-urban, was greater at Antioch than in the imperial capital.[129] Finally, the fact that Barlaam had been martyred at Caesarea in Cappadocia accounts for the celebration of his festival in the Syrian capital.[130]

Regarding the collection of some sixty homilies on various Psalms (CPG 4413.1,3-5), Tillemont states that he can find no evidence of the time at which they were delivered, except perhaps that the list of ominous events which occurred under the reign of Julian, found in *Exp. in ps. 110*, is more appropriate to Antioch than Constantinople, since that is where the majority of the prodigies occurred.[131] He further alludes to Photius' stylistic argument, asserting that the beauty of the expositions leads one to believe rather that they stem from the period of Chrysostom's priesthood.[132] The next sequence of homilies regarding which Tillemont offers any evidence of provenance are the three *In illud: Habentes eundem spiritum* (CPG 4383).[133] These were delivered at Antioch because in the first the homilist cites as an example the monks who withdraw to the mountains. All three were delivered at successive synaxes.[134] In the case of the seven panegyrics *De laudibus s. Pauli* (CPG 4344), *hom. 4* is to be assigned to Antioch because John refers to events at Antioch during the reign of Julian as having occurred locally (παρ' ἡμῖν: "among us"). Tillemont further suggests that all seven encomia can therefore be at-

---

[129] Tillemont, *Mémoires*, XI 617-618 (Note CV).

[130] Tillemont, *Mémoires*, XI 362.

[131] Tillemont, *Mémoires*, XI 619 (Note CVII).

[132] See Photius, *Bibl.* 172-174 (119a-b) = Henry, II (1960) 170.

[133] At the bottom of *Mémoires*, XI 364, Tillemont casually assigns *De eleemosyna* (CPG 4382) to Antioch, but supplies no evidence to support the attribution.

[134] Tillemont, *Mémoires*, XI 365-366.

tributed to that location, if it is the case that they were delivered in succession.[135]

Responding to an earlier suggestion that *De futurae vitae deliciis* (CPG 4388) stems from Antioch,[136] Tillemont finds himself in agreement, arguing that the comparison between the church and imperial palace would have been inappropriate at Constantinople and that in any case the manner in which Chrysostom speaks of his audience indicates that, although they represented the cream of the population, the emperor was not among them. He further points out that the synaxis was held at the extra-urban tomb of a martyr, a situation more common at Antioch than at Constantinople.[137] In the case of another homily delivered at an extra-urban synaxis (*In martyres*: CPG 4359), Tillemont believes that it was preached at Antioch, because the governor of the province (ὁ ἄρχων) was present. He argues that at Constantinople administrative officials were not singled out in that way.[138] The homily *De s. Droside* (CPG 4362) was again delivered at Antioch, during the course of an extra-urban synaxis at which Flavian was present. Tillemont identifies the church as the martyrium at which the Good Friday services were held, situated within the cemetary.[139] He further considers that the homily *In s. pascha* (CPG 4408), if genuine, belongs to the homilist's Antiochene period, since it is mentioned that lilies and roses are flowering at Easter.[140]

Having dealt with the various miscellaneous homilies which can be said to originate at Antioch,[141] Tillemont proceeds to assess the remainder of the exegetical series, in each of which the homilist treats a book from the New Testament (CPG 4424 following). With respect to the ninety homilies on Matthew (CPG 4424), he firmly asserts the Antiochene provenance of the series, on the basis of the evidence cited by Savile with regard to *In Matt. hom. 7* and *hom. 67/68*.[142] With respect to the concerns raised by Savile regarding the apparent episcopal tone displayed in *hom. 17, 40, 82* and *85*, Tillemont argues that it is difficult to suppose that a portion of the series was preached at Constantinople,

---

[135] Tillemont, *Mémoires*, XI 366.

[136] This suggestion had been put forward by Hermant (see n. 119 above).

[137] Tillemont, *Mémoires*, XI 621 (Note CIX).

[138] Tillemont, *Mémoires*, XI 367.

[139] Tillemont, *Mémoires*, XI 368.

[140] Tillemont, *Mémoires*, XI 621 (Note CXI).

[141] Later Tillemont (p. 385), referring to the homily *In Heliam et viduam* (CPG 4387), mentions that Hermant had assigned it to Antioch but states that he himself can find no evidence to support this, while in the case of the two homilies *In illud: Salutate Priscillam et Aquilam* (CPG 4376) he says (p. 388) that Hermant assigns both to Antioch, but offers no opinion of his own.

[142] See p. 38 above.

since this must relate to the latter half, in which *hom. 67/68* falls and which belongs with certainty to Antioch. Moreover, in the course of *hom. 72/73* the schism in the church at Antioch is referred to in a way which assumes that it is well known to the audience. Finally, in *In I Cor. hom. 27*, which definitely stems from that location, John refers back to material treated in *In Matt. hom. 59/60*.[143] Concerning the question of when the latter series was delivered, Tillemont states that *hom. 10* dates to around the beginning of Lent, while in *hom. 72/73* the Antiochene schism is referred to as a thing of the past. This leads him to suggest that the series as a whole dates to after the death of Paulinus (388/389) and Evagrius, who succeeded the latter for some three years.[144] The series on the Gospel of John (CPG 4425) he assigns likewise to Antioch, entirely on the basis of a reference to it found in *In I Cor. hom. 7*. Pointing out that the homilies were preached at a time of wars, earthquakes and other disasters (*In Ioh. hom. 34*), he suggests that these details could concur with the situation in 394.[145]

With respect to the thirty-two homilies on Romans (CPG 4427) Tillemont confesses that it is impossible to determine whether they were preached at Antioch or Constantinople. In *In Rom. hom. 8* John makes it clear that he and his audience have the same "shepherd", and at *hom. 31* apparently preaches at the same location at which St Paul had been imprisoned,[146] yet in *hom. 29* numbers himself among the "shepherds" in a manner which scarcely conforms to that of a simple priest. As for the time of year when the series was preached, Tillemont states only that *hom. 10* contains information which might lead one to suppose that it was delivered about a month after Easter.[147] By contrast, in the series on I Corinthians (CPG 4428) the homilist explicitly states that he is preaching at Antioch (*hom. 21*) and has already preached on the Gospels of Matthew and John (*hom. 7, 27*). In the case of the series on II Corinthians (CPG 4429), Tillemont believes it likely that since the series on I Corinthians stems from Antioch, the former belongs to that city also. He finds this conjecture supported by *In II Cor. hom. 26*, where Chrysostom speaks about Constantinople in a manner which indicates that he is not

---

[143] Tillemont, *Mémoires*, XI 622 (Note CXII).

[144] Tillemont, *Mémoires*, XI 370.

[145] Tillemont, *Mémoires*, XI 370-371.

[146] This information is in fact contained in *In Rom. hom. 30*.

[147] Tillemont, *Mémoires*, XI 371-372.

there.[148] Tillemont makes no attempt, however, to define the point at
which either of the two was preached.

Responding to the claim that the twenty-four homilies on Ephesians
(CPG 4431) stem from Constantinople by virtue of their style,[149] Tillemont devotes an entire note to demonstrating that on the contrary they
originate at Antioch.[150] First, in *In Eph. hom. 9* the homilist introduces St
Babylas without explanation, which he could only have done at Antioch,
where the whole population was familiar with the associated events. The
same approach is taken in *hom. 21*, where John cites as an example a
monk by the name of Julian, stating that those of his audience who saw
the monk at the time know whom he means. This monk is to be identified as Julianus Sabas, who aroused some excitement when he visited
Antioch in 373. Second, in *hom. 11* reference is made to divisions among
the orthodox in the local Christian community, which conforms perfectly
to the situation at Antioch, but is not something one associates with the
church at Constantinople. As for the allusion in that homily to the fact
that Chrysostom is himself the subject of attack, which had been taken
by some to indicate that he is bishop, Tillemont argues that the term "us"
could be being used here not in the personal but in the collective sense,
the term embracing the whole body of priests including Flavian. Concerning the date of the series, the war with the barbarians and other disasters alluded to in *hom. 6* and the reference to an earthquake in *hom. 10*
suggest 395. However, at *hom. 11* Chrysostom makes it clear that the
Eustathians still have a bishop, which must date the series to before the
death of Evagrius in 392. Tillemont suggests that it belongs within the
period of Evagrius' episcopate (388/389-392), but admits that this possibility is weakened by the circumstance that no historical evidence for
disasters of the kind mentioned in *hom. 6* and *10* exists for that time.

The final series assigned to Antioch is that which comprises six homilies on the Letter to Titus (CPG 4438). Here Tillemont expands upon the
argument put forward by Savile,[151] pointing out that in *In Titum hom. 3*
the homilist attacks those Christians who make a practice of fasting with
the Jews, a failing which, as Tillemont had argued earlier in relation to
the series on Genesis (CPG 4409), was specific to the community at

---

[148] Tillemont, *Mémoires*, XI 372. The same passage in *In II Cor. hom. 26* had been used
by Savile to demonstrate the Constantinopolitan provenance of this series (see p. 40
above).

[149] This had been proposed by Savile (see p. 40 above) and reiterated by Du Pin (see
n. 119).

[150] Tillemont, *Mémoires*, XI 622-623 (Note CXIII). See, however, pp. 132-133 where he
firmly attributes *In Eph. hom. 13* to Constantinople.

[151] See p. 39 above.

Antioch. The reference to the site in Cilicia and the cave of Matrona at Daphne simply confirms that John is preaching in that vicinity.[152]

b. *Constantinople*

Although the first homily preached by Chrysostom after his episcopal consecration is lost, Tillemont claims that *Contra Anomoeos hom. 11* (CPG 4324) is the next sermon to have been delivered at Constantinople. He further states that it was preached in a little-frequented church, apparently situated in the suburbs.[153] The next indication Tillemont gives as to why he has assigned a particular sermon to the period of John's episcopate occurs with respect to *In martyres Aegyptios* (CPG 4363). Here the fact that the importation of relics was more common at Constantinople than Antioch leads Tillemont to believe that the homily was delivered at the first location.[154] In the case of *De terrae motu* (CPG 4366) he is convinced of its Constantinopolitan provenance by the circumstance that, although Chrysostom makes considerable mention of the litanies observed at the time of the earthquake, he makes no reference at all to Flavian.[155] In *De Christi divinitate* (CPG 4325) Tillemont finds mention of a previous sermon, apparently *Contra Anom. hom. 11*, which leads him to suppose that it was the third homily delivered following John's episcopal consecration.[156]

While discussing the fifty-five homilies on Acts (CPG 4426), Tillemont claims that no-one doubts that the series belongs to Constantinople, since in *In Acta apost. hom. 9* the fact that Chrysostom is bishop is clearly indicated. As regards the year in which it was preached, Tillemont prefers 400 to 401,[157] arguing that the phrase τριετίαν ἔχομεν (*hom. 44*) is intended to parallel the situation of St Paul, who spent no more than two years and a few months at Ephesus. It is therefore intended to designate the third year of John's episcopate (Feb. 26 400-Feb. 26 401) and does not indicate that three full years have passed. Tillemont experiences some

---

[152] Tillemont, *Mémoires*, XI 375-376.

[153] Tillemont, *Mémoires*, XI 111. In the course of the discussion which follows (pp. 111-162) a number of homilies are associated with the imperial city in passing. Except where Tillemont's comments are relevent to the issue of provenance, they are not discussed. The titles of the homilies and their relevant details are included in Table 2.a below.

[154] Tillemont, *Mémoires*, XI 144-145.

[155] Tillemont, *Mémoires*, XI 145.

[156] Tillemont, *Mémoires*, XI 150.

[157] This date had been promoted by Baronius (1591). For an outline of his work see Baur, *Chrysostome et ses oeuvres*, 227-228.

difficulty with the earthquake of the previous year mentioned in *hom. 41*, the only tremor known to have occurred at that period being the one recorded by Synesius for the year 400, but manages to resolve this by arguing that the year at Constantinople began with the indiction on Sept. 1. Since the first homily in the series was preached during the Paschal period, it is possible that *hom. 41* was not delivered until September or later, a circumstance which would permit Chrysostom to state that the earthquake occurred in the previous year.[158]

To the year 402 Tillemont assigns the first of the two homilies *In illud: Ne tim. cum dives factus fuerit homo* (CPG 4414), since it is the last of the years spent at Constantinople by Chrysostom which was relatively free of trouble. That *hom. 1* was delivered at that location is indicated by his statement that he is "shepherd" and bishop.[159] In *hom. 2*, delivered likewise at Constantinople and in the Great Church, as indicated by the title, Tillemont finds a possible allusion to John's first deposition and exile, which leads him to locate the homily in 403 a little after John's return.[160] To the period immediately following the return from exile he further assigns *Cum Saturninus et Aurelianus* (CPG 4393), a homily which he had earlier located in the year 400.[161]

The next discussion concerning material from this city occurs in relation to the exegetical series. Referring to the criterion introduced by Photius, Tillemont acknowledges that the style of the series on Philippians (CPG 4432), I and II Timothy (CPG 4436-4437) and Philemon (CPG 4439) is a little more careless, suggesting that all four could have been delivered at Constantinople. In the case of the first, this conclusion is perhaps supported by the manner in which Chrysostom speaks of the reigning emperor (*In Phil. hom. 15*), which suggests that it dates to after the events of 399-400.[162] However, concerning the series on I Timothy, Tillemont in a footnote questions whether the reference in *In I Tim. hom. 17* to Cappadocia is not better suited to a location in Syria than Thrace.[163]

The twelve homilies on Colossians (CPG 4433) were also preached at Constantinople, since in *In Col. hom. 7* Chrysostom refers to Eutropius as deposed but still alive, suggesting a date in autumn 399. Moreover, in that same homily John refers to the riots at Antioch in a manner which

---

[158] Tillemont, *Mémoires*, XI 162-163 (Article LIX), 582-583 (Note L).

[159] Tillemont, *Mémoires*, XI 187.

[160] Tillemont, *Mémoires*, XI 188-189.

[161] Tillemont, *Mémoires*, XI 210 (Article LXXVII) and 600 (Note LXXIV). See, however, p. 155 (Article LVII).

[162] Tillemont, *Mémoires*, XI 376.

[163] Tillemont, *Mémoires*, XI 376 n. I.

indicates that he is not situated in that city and that the emperor Theodosius is no longer alive, while in *hom. 3* he explicitly states that he occupies the episcopal office. This role is further indicated in *hom. 7*, where
Chrysostom threatens to exclude the women in his congregation from
the church. In narrowing the date of this series, Tillemont notes that
hom. 2 was preached at a time of frequent earth tremors, which may or
may not refer to those which occurred in 398. In either case, the reference to Eutropius is so explicit that the homilies can only date to the latter months of 399.[164] As for the series on I and II Thessalonians (CPG
4434-4435), in these Chrysostom also speaks as bishop (*In I Thess. hom.
11*), in the first threatening to exclude sinners from the church (*In I
Thess. hom. 10*) and in the second stating that he is the head and is responsible for the entire congregation (*In II Thess. hom. 4*).[165] Tillemont
further suggests that the second series belongs to the period a little before the first occasion on which Chrysostom was sent into exile.[166] Finally, following the suggestion of Savile,[167] Tillemont assigns the thirty-
four homilies on Hebrews (CPG 4440) to the last years of the episcopate,
on the grounds that they were published from stenographic notes after
Chrysostom's death. He finds the provenance of this series confirmed by
In Heb. hom. 4, where the homilist speaks like a bishop, although he confesses himself puzzled by *hom. 26*, where John appears ignorant of the
fact that the body of St Andrew was buried at Constantinople.[168]

Finally, Tillemont turns to a small number of miscellaneous homilies
which demonstrate little or no evidence of their chronology, but which
contain information suggestive of Constantinopolitan provenance. The
first of these is *In illud: Si esurierit inimicus* (CPG 4375), which contains
a reference to the imperial court.[169] In the case of *Quales ducendae sint
uxores* (CPG 4379), he defers to the opinion of Hermant, who had argued
for the episcopal status of the "companion in harness" who had preached
at the preceding synaxis in Chrysostom's place, identifying the Maximus
named in the title as the bishop of Seleucia in Isauria.[170] Tillemont situates this homily following two others in which John treats a similar topic
(*In illud: Propter fornicationes uxorem*: CPG 4377 and *De libello repudii*:
CPG 4378).[171] With respect to the homily *In illud Isaiae: Ego dominus*

---

[164] Tillemont, *Mémoires*, XI 376-377.

[165] Tillemont here largely follows Savile (see p. 40 above).

[166] Tillemont, *Mémoires*, XI 378.

[167] See p. 39 above.

[168] Tillemont, *Mémoires*, XI 378-379 and 378 n. I.

[169] Tillemont, *Mémoires*, XI 379.

[170] Tillemont, *Mémoires*, XI 380. See n. 119 above.

[171] Tillemont, *Mémoires*, XI 381-382.

deus feci lumen (CPG 4418), he suggests that the fact that another has preached before John on that occasion may point to his episcopal rank.[172] As for the claim that *In illud: Diligentibus deum* (CPG 4374) must have been preached at Constantinople, since the sentiments expressed at the opening of the homily are similar to those with which the homilist begins *De decem millium talentorum debitore* (CPG 4368), Tillemont dismisses the assumption behind it as invalid.[173]

c. *Summary*

Within the parentheses which follow each homily listed in Table 2.a, the first reference is to the location of the homily within the relevant edition, the second to the page or pages in Tillemont on which its provenance is discussed. The reference system used in the previous section (*t.* = tome, *h.* = homily) is retained in the case of both tables, and unless otherwise stated all citations refer to the Morel edition.[174] As an alternative to *h.*, the abbreviation p. (= page/s) is used with respect to the Morel edition in instances where homilies are not individually numbered. Included in the tables are homilies attributed by Tillemont to Antioch or Constantinople or assigned by him to a particular year which have been omitted from the above discussion since no rationale for the date or attribution is supplied. Those sequences established by Tillemont which have not been clearly outlined in sections a and b are listed following Table 2.b.

Table 2.a. Provenance — Tillemont

CPG no.	Antioch	CPG no.	Constantinople
4317	Cum presbyter fuit (t. 4 p. 834; p. 39)	4324	Contra Anom. hom. 11 (t. 1 p. 698; p. 111)
4318	De incompr. dei nat. hom. 1-5 (t. 1 h. 26-h. 30; pp. 46ff)	4325	De Christi divinitate (t. 5 h. 7; p. 150)
4319	De beato Philogonio (t. 1 h. 3; p. 49)	4363	In martyres Aegyptios (t. 1 h. 70; p. 144f)

---

[172] Tillemont, *Mémoires*, XI 385-386.

[173] Tillemont, *Mémoires*, XI 387. This view had been expressed by Hermant (see n. 119).

[174] Migne (PG 64,118-126) provides a useful cross-index between the Morel and Montfaucon editions. When consulting this index it should be borne in mind that, although the original Montfaucon volume numbers are used, the page numbers correspond rather to the columns in Migne. The cross-referencing is also on occasion inaccurate.

4320	*De consubstantiali* (*t. 1 h. 32*; p. 53)	4364	*De s. Phoca* (*t. 1 h. 71*; p. 144)
4321	*De petit. matr. fil. Zeb.* (*t. 1 h. 33*; p. 54)	4366	*De terrae motu* (*Comb. 6 p. 203;** p. 145)
4323	*De Christi precibus* (*t. 5 h. 54*; p. 80)	4370	*In paralyticum demissum* (*t. 5 h. 65*; p. 150)
4327	*Adv. Iud. or. 1-8* (*t. 1 h. 34-39, t. 5 h. 55-56*; pp. 46ff, 60, 81f)	4375	*In illud: Si esurierit inimicus* (*t. 5 h. 16*; p. 379)
4328	*In kalendas* (*t. 1 h. 23*; p. 51)	4377	*In illud: Propter fornicat.* (*t. 5 h. 19*; p. 381)
4329	*De Lazaro conciones 1-5* (*t. 5 h. 2-5,30*; pp. 51-57, 59)	4378	*De libello repudii* (*t. 5 h. 20*; p. 381)
4330	*De stat. hom. 1-21* (*t. 1 h. 1-20,22*; pp. 62ff)	4379	*Quales duc. sint uxores* (*t. 5 h. 29*; p. 119, 380)
4332	*De diabolo tentatore hom. 1-3* (*t. 5 h. 63, t. 1 h. 25, t. 2 h. 85*; p. 86ff)	4392	*In Eutropium* (*t. 4 p. 481*; p. 154)
4333	*De paenitentia hom. 1-8* (*t. 1 h. 53-58, t. 4 p. 487, t. 5 h. 73*; pp. 101ff)	4393	*Cum Saturninus et Aurelianus* (*t. 5 h. 73*; pp. 155, 210)
4334	*In diem natalem* (*t. 5 h. 33*; p. 50)	4394	*De regressu* (*Sav. t. 7 h. 120*;† p. 170, 586)
4335	*De baptismo Christi* (*t. 1 h. 24*; p. 54)	4414	*In illud: Ne timueritis cum dives hom. 1-2* (*t. 3 pp. 689,705*; pp. 119, 187ff, 620)
4336	*De prod. Iudae hom. 1* (*t. 5 h. 32*; p. 93)	4417	*In illud: Vidi dom. hom. 4* (*t. 3 p. 750*; p. 128)
4337	*De coemeterio et de cruce* (*t. 5 h. 34*; p. 571)	4418	*In illud: Ego dominus deus feci lumen*b (*t. 3 p. 776*; pp. 385f)
4338	*De cruce et latr. hom. 1* (*t. 5 h. 35*; p. 93)	4426	*In Acta apost. hom. 1-55* (*t. 3*; p. 582)
4340	*De resurr. mortuorum* (*t. 5 h. 36*; p. 80)	4431	*In Eph. hom. 13*a (*t. 5 p. 974*; pp. 132f)
4341	*De resurrectione* (*t. 5 h. 37*; p. 94)	4432	*In Phil. hom. 1-15* (*t. 6*; p. 376)
4342	*In ascensionem* (*t. 5 h. 38*; p. 91)	4433	*In Col. hom. 1-12* (*t. 6*; p. 376f)
4343	*De s. pentecoste hom. 1* (*t. 5 h. 39*; p. 568)	4434	*In I Thess. hom. 1-11* (*t. 6*; p. 378)
4344	*De laudibus s. Pauli hom. 1-7* (*t. 5 p. 492*; p. 366)	4435	*In II Thess. hom. 1-5* (*t. 6*; p. 378)
4345	*De s. Meletio* (*t. 1 h. 45*; p. 46)	4436	*In I Tim. hom. 1-18*b (*t. 6*; p. 376)
4346	*In s. Lucianum* (*t. 1 h. 46*; p. 55)	4437	*In II Tim. hom. 1-10*b (*t. 6*; p. 376)
4347	*De s. Babyla* (*t. 1 h. 59*; p. 57)	4439	*In Philemon hom. 1-3*b (*t. 6*; p. 376)
4349	*In Iuv. et Maximum* (*t. 1 h. 40*; p. 57)	4440	*In Heb. hom. 1-34* (*t. 6*; p. 378f)
4350	*De s. Pelagia* (*t. 1 h. 41*; p. 358)	4528	*De capto Eutropio* (*t. 3 p. 666*; p. 154)
4351	*In s. Ignatium* (*t. 1 h. 42*; p. 358)	4529	*De Chananaea* (*t. 6 h. 28*; p. 212)
4352	*In s. Eustathium* (*t. 1 h. 52*; p. 359)		
4353	*In s. Romanum* (*t. 1 h. 43*; p. 359)		
4354	*De Macab. hom. 1-2* (*t. 1 h. 44,49*; p. 359)		
4355	*De ss. Bern. et Prosd.* (*t. 1 h. 51*; pp. 571f)		
4357	*De ss. martyribus* (*t. 5 h. 70*; p. 360)		
4358	*Non esse ad grat. conc.* (*t. 5 h. 61*; p. 361)		
4359	*Hom. in martyres* (*t. 5 h. 62*; p. 367)		

4360	*In s. Iulianum (t. 1 h. 47; p. 359)*		
4361	*In s. Barlaam* *(t. 1 h. 73; pp. 362, 618)*		
4362	*De s. Droside (t. 5 h. 71; p. 368)*		
4368	*De decem mill. tal. deb.* *(t. 5 h. 1; p. 78)*		
4371	*In princ. Act. hom. 1-4* *(t. 5 h. 51,12,53,68; p. 95f)*		
4372	*De mutatione nom. hom. 1-4* *(t. 5 h. 50, 69, 13, 52; p. 97ff)*		
4380	*In d. Pauli: Nolo vos ignorare* *(t. 5 h. 21; pp. 362, 618)*		
4382	*De eleemosyna (t. 5 h. 23; p. 364f)*		
4383	*In illud: Hab. eundem spiritum* *hom. 1-3 (t. 5 h. 24-26; pp. 365f)*		
4385	*De profectu evangelii* *(t. 5 h. 28; pp. 50f)*		
4386	*In illud: Vidua eligatur* *(t. 5 h. 31; p. 60)*		
4388	*De futurae vitae deliciis* *(t. 5 h. 58; p. 621)*		
4391	*In illud: In faciem ei restiti* *(t. 5 h. 64; p. 359)*		
4406	*Laus Diodori* *(source unknown; p. 92)*		
4408	*Hom. in s. pascha* *(t. 6 h. 72; pp. 369, 621)*		
4409	*Hom 1-67 in Gen.* *(t. 2 pp. 1-725; pp. 571f)*		
4410	*Serm. 1-9 in Gen.* *(t. 2 h. 68-76; p. 42-46, 98)*		
4411	*De Anna serm. 1-5* *(t. 2 h. 77-81; pp. 76f)*		
4412	*De Davide et Saule hom. 1-3* *(t. 2 h. 82-84; pp. 78f)*		
4413	*Exp. in psalmos*# *(t. 3 pp. 8-553; pp. 83, 619)*		
4415	*In ps. 145 (t. 3 p. 712; pp. 107)*		
4417	*In illud: Vidi dom. hom. 1-3,6* *(t. 3 p. 723; pp. 560ff)*		
4419	*In illud: Dom., non est in homine* *(t. 3 p. 789)*		
4420	*De proph. obsc. hom. 1-2* *(t. 3 pp. 799ff; p. 84f)*		
4424	*In Matt. hom. 1-90* *(t. 1; pp. 370, 622)*		
4425	*In Ioh. hom. 1-88 (t. 2; p. 370)*		
4428	*In I Cor. hom. 1-44 (t. 5; p. 372)*		
4429	*In II Cor. hom. 1-30 (t. 5; p. 372)*		
4431	*In Eph. hom. 1-24+* *(t. 5; pp. 375, 622f)*		
4438	*In Titum hom. 1-6 (t. 6; pp. 375f)*		
4460	*Ad illuminandos cat. 1* *(t. 1 h. 60; p. 89)*		

4464	*Ad illum. cat. 2* (*t. 1 h. 21*; pp. 75, 87)		

* Comb. = Fr. Combefis, *Homiliae sex*, Paris 1645 (see Baur, *Chrysostome et ses oeuvres*, 110 [152]). † Sav. = Savile. # Probably. + *hom. 13* also assigned to Constantinople. ª Also assigned to Antioch. ᵇ Possibly.

Table 2.b. Chronology — Tillemont

Year (month-season)	Homily	Cited (page)
386		
early	*Cum presbyter fuit* (*t. 4* p. 834: CPG 4317)	39
before Lent	*In illud: Vidi dom. hom. 2,3,6* (*t. 3* pp. 735ff: CPG 4417)	560-562
Feb. 16 - (Lent)	*Sermones 1-8 in Genesim* (*t. 2 h. 68-h. 75*: CPG 4410)	42-46, 563
c. end of May or later	*De s. Meletio* (*t. 1 h. 45*: CPG 4345)	46, 563
c. September -	*De incompr. dei natura hom. 1* (*t. 1 h. 26*: CPG 4318)	46f
	Adv. Iudaeos or. 1-2 (*t. 1 h. 34, t. 5 h. 56*: CPG 4327)	"
date unspecified	*De incompr. dei nat. hom. 2-5* (*t. 1 h. 27-30*)	48f
Dec. 20	*De beato Philogonio* (*t. 1 h. 31*: CPG 4319)	49f
Dec. 25	*In diem natalem* (*t. 5 h. 33*: CPG 4334)	50
Dec. 26/27	*De profectu evangelii* (*t. 5 h. 28*: CPG 4385)	50f, 565
387		
Jan. 1	*In kalendas* (*t. 1 h. 23*: CPG 4328)	51, 565f
Jan. 2	*De Lazaro concio 1* (*t. 5 h. 2*: CPG 4329)	51, 566
Jan. 3	*De consubstantiali* (*t. 1 h. 32*: CPG 4320)	53, 566
Jan. 4	*De petit. matr. fil. Zeb.* (*t. 1 h. 33*: CPG 4321)	54, 566
Jan. 6	*De baptismo Christi* (*t. 1 h. 24*: CPG 4335)	54
Jan. 7	*In s. Lucianum* (*t. 1 h. 46*: CPG 4346)	55
Jan. 10	*De Lazaro concio 2* (*t. 5 h. 3*)	55
Jan. 17	*De Lazaro concio 3* (*t. 5 h. 4*)	56
Jan. 24	*De s. Babyla* (*t. 1 h. 59*: CPG 4347)	57
Jan. 25	*In Iuventinum et Maximum* (*t. 1 h. 40*: CPG 4349)	"
Jan. 31	*De Lazaro concio 4* (*t. 5 h. 5*)	"
date unspecified	*De Lazaro concio 5* (*t. 5 h. 30*)	59
	In illud: Vidua eligatur (*t. 5 h. 31*: CPG 4386)	60
before Lent	*Adv. Iudaeos or. 3* (*t. 5 h. 55*: CPG 4327)	566f
just before Lent	*De statuis hom. 1-3* (*t. 1 h. 1-3*: CPG 4330)	62-65
Lent (March 8-)	*De statuis hom. 4-20* (*t. 1 h. 4-19,22*)	65-75
April 25 (Easter)	*De statuis hom. 21* (*t. 1 h. 20*)	75
date unspecified	*De Anna serm. 1-3* (*t. 2 h. 77-79*: CPG 4411)	76f
June 6	*De Anna sermo 4* (*t. 2 h. 80*)	77
June 20	*De Anna sermo 5* (*t. 2 h. 81*)	"
date unspecified	*De decem mill. tal. deb.* (*t. 5 h. 1*: CPG 4368)	78
	De Davide et Saule hom. 1-3 (*t. 2 h. 82-84*: CPG 4412)	78f
	De Christi precibus (*t. 5 h. 54*: CPG 4323)	80
	De resurr. mortuorum (*t. 5 h. 36*: CPG 4340)	"
c. mid-Sept. -	*Adv. Iud. or. 4-8* (*t. 1 h. 35-39*: CPG 4327)	81-83
October?	*Expos. in ps. 41* (*t. 3* p. 145: CPG 4413.2)	83, 619
388		

date unspecified	*De proph. obsc. hom. 1-2* (*t. 3* pp. 799ff: CPG 4420)	84-86
	De diabolo tent. hom. 1 (*t. 5 h. 63*: CPG 4332)	86, 570
Lent	*Ad illuminandos cat. 1* (*t. 1 h. 60*: CPG 4460)	89
	Ad illuminandos cat. 2 (*t. 1 h. 21*: CPG 4464)	87, 570
	De diabolo tent. hom. 2 (*t. 1 h. 25*)	86f, 571
	De diabolo tent. hom. 3 (*t. 2 h. 85*)	88f
389		
390		
391		
392		
March 26 (Good Friday)	*De coemeterio et de cruce* (*t. 5 h. 34*: CPG 4337)	571f
April 14	*De ss. Bernice et Prosd.* (*t. 1 h. 51*: CPG 4355)	571f
Ascension	*In ascensionem* (*t. 5 h. 38*: CPG 4342)	91
date unspecified	*Laus Diodori* (source unknown: CPG 4406)	92
393		
394		
date unspecified	*In Ioh. hom. 1-88#* (*t. 2*: CPG 4425)	370-371
395		
Feb. 6	*Hom. 1 in Gen.* (*t. 2* p. 1: CPG 4409)	572-573
Lent (Feb. 7-)	*Hom. 2-32 in Gen.*	572-574
Maundy Thursday	*De prod. Iudae hom. 1* (*t. 5 h. 32*: CPG 4336)	576
Good Friday	*De cruce et latr. hom. 1* (*t. 5 h. 35*: CPG 4338)	93
March 27 (Easter)	*De resurrectione* (*t. 5 h. 37*: CPG 4341)	94
after Easter	*In princ. Act. hom. 1-4* (*t. 5 h. 51,12,53,68*: CPG 4371)	95-96
	De mutatione nominum hom. 1-2 (*t. 5 h. 50,69*: CPG 4372)	97-98
	Sermo 9 in Genesim (*t. 2 h. 76*: CPG 4410)	98
	De mut. nom. hom. 3-4 (*t. 5 h. 13,52*)	99
after Pentecost	*Hom. 33-67 in Gen.*	577
396		
Feb. 24	*De paenitentia hom. 5* (*t. 1 h. 53*: CPG 4333)	102
date unspecified	*De paen. hom. 4* (*t. 1 h. 54*)	102
	De paen. hom. 7 (*t. 1 h. 55*)	103-104
	De paen. hom. 8 (*t. 4* p. 487)	104
March 19	*De paen. hom. 6* (*t. 1 h. 56*)	578
date unspecified	*De paen. hom. 2* (*t. 5 h. 73*)	106, 578
	In illud: Vidi dom. hom. 1 (*t. 3* p. 723: CPG 4417)	107, 560
	In ps. 145 (*t. 3* p. 712: CPG 4415)	107
397		
398		
after Feb. 26	*Contra Anomoeos hom. 11* (*t. 1* p. 698: CPG 4324)	111
	De Christi divinitate (*t. 5 h. 7*: CPG 4325)	150
date unspecified	*In paralyticum demissum* (*t. 5 h. 65*: CPG 4370)	150
399		
date unspecified	*In Eutropium* (*t. 4* p. 481: CPG 4392)	154
	De capto Eutropio (*t. 3* p. 666: CPG 4528)	154, 620
latter months	*In Col. hom. 1-12* (*t. 6*: CPG 4433)	376-377
400		
Easter -	*In Acta apost. hom. 1-55* (*t. 3*: CPG 4426)	582-583
date unspecified	*Cum Saturninus et Aurelianus* (*t. 5 h. 73*: CPG 4393)	155
401		

c. end of April	*De regressu* (Sav. *t. 7 h. 120*: CPG 4394)	170, 586
402		
date unspecified	*In illud: Ne timueritis hom. 1* (*t. 3* p. 689: CPG 4414)	187
403		
after return from exile	*Cum Saturninus et Aurelianus* (*t. 5 h. 73*: CPG 4393)* *De Chananaea* (*t. 6 h. 28*: CPG 4529) *In illud: Ne timueritis hom. 2* (*t. 3* p. 705)	210, 600 212, 601 189
404		

* Also assigned to 400. # Possibly.

Sequence A. *In illud: In faciem ei restiti* (CPG 4391); *In s. Eustathium* (CPG 4352); *In s. Romanum* (CPG 4353); *In illud: Domine, non est in homine* (CPG 4419).

Sequence B. (Aug. 1) *De Macabeis hom. 1* (CPG 4354); (Aug. 2) *De Mac. hom. 2*.

Sequence C. (shortly after Aug. 1) *De ss. martyribus* (CPG 4357); (several days later) *Non esse ad gratiam concionandum* (CPG 4358).

Sequence D. *In s. Barlaam* (CPG 4361); (next day) *In d. Pauli: Nolo vos ignorare* (CPG 4380).

Sequence E. *In illud: Propter fornicationes uxorem* (CPG 4377); *De libello repudii* (CPG 4378); *Quales ducendae sint uxores* (CPG 4379).

Sequence F. *Peccata fratrum non evulganda* (*t. 5 h. 60*: CPG 4389); (next day) *Non esse desperandum* (*t. 5 h. 59*: CPG 4390).[175]

2. MONTFAUCON

Because he presents the most complete and, due to its reprint by Migne, the most widely accessible edition of the Chrysostomic corpus, Montfaucon's opinion has shaped to a greater degree than any other the approach of the generations of scholars which succeeded him. The most notable feature of his methodology is the precedence given chronology over provenance, with the result that the conclusions reached in the first three volumes, in particular, exhibit a heavy reliance on perceived connections between homilies. In those volumes the issue of provenance is marginalised to such an extent that it is often left entirely implicit. It is only in the later volumes, where the bulk of the exegetical series are presented, that the issue of location is given prominence.

Since that is the way in which the majority of scholars access Montfaucon's opinion, the following summary is presented according to the sequence of introductory comments which preface each text or group of texts, volume by volume. The personal *vita Chrysostomi*, which he pre-

---

[175] Tillemont, *Mémoires*, XI 624 (Note CXVIII).

sents in the thirteenth volume, essentially represents a synthesis of these. Certain of the homilies listed by Montfaucon as genuine are now considered spurious. Except in cases where his comments affect issues of provenance or date with regard to the genuine corpus as currently defined by Geerard, discussion of Montfaucon's opinion regarding those sermons is not entered into here.

a. *Volume I*

Regarding the first of the homilies presented in Vol. I (*Cum presbyter*: CPG 4317), Montfaucon says little more than that it was delivered early in 386, after the homilist had been ordained presbyter by Flavian, and that it marks the beginning of Chrysostom's career as a preacher.[176] The five homilies *De incompr. dei natura* (CPG 4318) he locates among those preached in 386 at Antioch, on the basis of the following evidence. In *De incompr. dei nat. hom. 4* John refers to the conspiracy of Theodorus as having occurred some ten years earlier. That event dates to the year 374 at the latest. Further, in *Adv. Iud. or.5* (CPG 4327) it is stated that Julian was emperor twenty years earlier. Calculating from his death in 363, this brings us to 383, when the homilist was deacon. Since, as stated in *Cum presbyter*, Chrysostom did not preach before his ordination as presbyter, this locates the homilies in 386. Montfaucon adds that *De incompr. dei nat. hom. 1* was delivered in the absence of Flavian.[177]

Of the next three homilies *Contra Anomoeos* (CPG 4319-4321), the first (*De b. Philogonio*) was delivered on Dec. 20, 386. This is inferred from the statement that it is five days until Christmas, the date for this latter festival at Antioch being confirmed by the homily *In diem natalem* (CPG 4334). In the course of *De b. Philogonio* Chrysostom has occasion to refer to Flavian. The second homily (*De consubstantiali*) was preached at the beginning of 387, most probably on Jan. 5, a day on which circus games were celebrated.[178] The third homily (*De petitione matris fil. Zeb.*) was delivered on the following day.[179] To this sequence, delivered at the end of 386 and beginning of 387, Montfaucon adds a further two homilies (CPG 4322-4323), on the basis of thematic conformity.[180] A final two

---

[176] Montfaucon, I 436.

[177] Montfaucon, I 443-444. For the association drawn between this series and the sermons *Adv. Iudaeos* see the *Monitum* to the latter (I 583-586), where Montfaucon further explores the question of their chronology.

[178] Regarding this date see further the *Monitum* to *In kalendas*, Montfaucon, I 696.

[179] Montfaucon, I 492.

[180] Montfaucon, I 523.

homilies on the subject (CPG 4324-4325), however, belong to Constantinople and were delivered there in 398. It is evident from the opening of
the first of these (*Contra Anom. hom. 11*) that it is only the second homily
to have been preached by Chrysostom at that location. Montfaucon
places no great reliance, however, on the information appended to the
title to this sermon in two of the manuscripts, to the effect that it was
delivered in "the New Church". Regarding the second of the two (*De
Christi divinitate*), the homilist's comments indicate that it was delivered
only a few days after the first.[181]

The next group of homilies to be considered is that *Adversus Iudaeos*
(CPG 4327). Montfaucon points out in the introduction that he has
brought together into a new arrangement eight homilies, which were
formerly considered a separate series of five or six sermons and two or
three miscellaneous homilies.[182] He then proceeds to defend this sequence. The position of the first is secure, since it can be demonstrated
that the rest of the homilies were delivered subsequent to it. Here John
interrupts his polemic against the Anomoeans, after preaching only the
first of those homilies (*De incompr. dei nat. hom. 1*). As already demonstrated, this latter sermon belongs to the year 386. As for the time of
year, the festivals of the Jews which are said to be approaching all pertain to the month of September. In particular, the Feast of Tabernacles
began in 386 on Sept. 15. From this it appears that the first of the homilies *Adv. Iudaeos* is to be located in the month of August. From the
opening to *Adv. Iud. or. 2* it is clear that this sermon was delivered ten or
more days after the first, five days before the beginning of the Jewish
fast. Despite the fact that Savile had located it eighth, its relationship to
the first is securely established on the basis of internal evidence. On this
basis, the following sequence can be formed: *De incompr. dei nat. hom. 1*;
(August 386) *Adv. Iud. or. 1*; (beginning September 386) *Adv. Iud. or. 2*;
(end of September) *De incompr. dei nat. hom. 2*.[183]

At the opening to the third homily *Adv. Iudaeos*, the homilist mentions
that he has had occasion to interrupt his polemic against the Anomoeans
a second time. It is uncertain, however, whether this sermon follows the
second, third, or fourth homily *De incompr. dei natura*. It cannot, however, have been delivered long after September, since in the Christmas
sermon of 386 (*In diem natalem*) Chrysostom states that in that same
year he preached a number of sermons against the Jews toward the end
of September. Montfaucon takes this to be approximate and to refer to

---

[181] Montfaucon, I 540.

[182] See Montfaucon, I 583-584. For its relationship to the arrangement presented by
Savile see n. 46 above.

[183] Montfaucon, I 584-585.

the first three homilies *Adv. Iudaeos*.[184] As is clear from comment in both
or. 4 and *or. 6*, however, the last five sermons *Adv. Iudaeos* belong to the
period following the riots of early 387. Of these homilies, internal evidence indicates that *or. 4* was delivered some ten days before the Jewish
fast, *or. 5* in the intervening period, *or. 6* on the day of the fast itself, *or. 7*
when the festival had not yet been completed, and *or. 8* after both fast
and festival, such that all five occurred within a span of twenty days. Although there is no certainty as to the year in which these homilies fall,
the opening of *Adv. Iud. or. 4* seems to recall *or. 1-3*, making the next
year (387) the most probable.[185]

The next homily to be presented in this volume is *In kalendas* (CPG
4328), delivered with certainty on January 1. The year and the identity of
the recent encomium on Paul, to which the homilist alludes, however,
are less certain. Montfaucon identifies the encomium as one of the seven
homilies *De laudibus s. Pauli* (CPG 4344), in the fourth of which it is
made clear that these were delivered at Antioch. This confirms the provenance of *In kalendas*, at the opening to which John declares that the
bishop is absent. As for the year in which this homily fell, Montfaucon
dismisses Tillemont's argument for 387, on the grounds that the reasons
for the fequency of Chrysostom's preaching at one time versus another
are not so easily fathomed.[186]

The final group presented constitutes a sequence of four homilies on
the topic of Lazarus, to which a further three have been appended (CPG
4329). As the title and opening to the first sermon indicates, it was delivered on Jan. 2, the day after the Saturnalia on which the sermon *In
kalendas* was preached. The vocabulary which Chrysostom employs in
concio 1 and in *In kalendas* indicates that they belong to the same year.[187]
Although the identity of that year cannot be established, *De Lazaro conciones 1-4* were delivered in sequence within a short space of time, the
homilist having broken off between the third and the fourth to preach
encomia on St Babylas and on the martyrs Juventinus and Maximus.
This is made clear in the beginning to *De Lazaro concio 4*.[188] That the
fifth homily was delivered after the first four is made clear both by its
subject matter and by John's statement that he has already preached for

---

[184] Montfaucon, I 585. This opinion is reiterated in the *Praefatio* to the series *De statuis*
(II 2). For his lengthy refutation of Tillemont's proposal that *or. 3* belongs to early Lent
387 (p. 52 above), see I 585-586.

[185] Montfaucon, I 586.

[186] Montfaucon, I 696-697.

[187] Although it is never stated explicitly, Montfaucon assumes from this that the Antiochene provenance of *De Lazaro conciones 1-4* is confirmed.

[188] Montfaucon, I 707.

four days on the topic, which is found at its opening.[189] The sixth homily, although it does not constitute a sequence with the first four, was delivered only a modest period of time later, since in the course of the sermon the homilist states that, through his constant preaching on the topic, he has rendered his audience instructors concerning the parable. Any attempt to date the homily by identifying the earthquake mentioned, however, is fruitless, due to the frequency with which such seismic disturbances occurred at Antioch.[190] The seventh *concio de Lazaro* Montfaucon locates a little after the first four, on the grounds that Chrysostom indicates that his audience is familiar with the parable and that he himself has preached on the topic previously. Despite its location in some of the manuscripts immediately following *conciones 1-4*, the close connection between the first four and *concio 5* locates it after the latter.[191]

One further homily occurs (*De anathemate*: CPG 3430), which is now no longer assigned to Chrysostom. Montfaucon, however, considering it genuine, locates it in 386 following the third of the homilies *De incompr. dei natura*.[192]

b. *Volume II*

The second volume opens with the twenty-one homilies *De statuis* (CPG 4330). Due to the subject matter, the riots at Antioch, Montfaucon assumes throughout his introduction that the series stems from that location. It is the issues of in which year the riots occurred, which method for calculating the date of Easter was employed at Antioch, the duration of Lent at this location, and therefore the order and chronology to be assigned to the homilies which absorb his attention. Montfaucon's main criticism is directed towards the confidence with which Tillemont distributed the homilies throughout Lent and the boldness with which he defied the order presented in the manuscripts.[193] Having established that the riots occurred in 387, Montfaucon adopts the view that the Antiochenes followed a seven week Lent. He finds it difficult to accept, however, that in 387 they observed Easter on April 25. With this in mind, he

---

[189] Montfaucon, I 762.

[190] Montfaucon, I 772.

[191] Montfaucon, I 789.

[192] Montfaucon, I 691. He does this on the basis of the verbal link with *De incompr. dei nat. hom.* 3 established at the beginning of the homily. Tillemont, *Mémoires*, XI 363, also considering it on balance genuine, had located it after 388. For its current status see De Aldama, *Repertorium*, 168 (no.448).

[193] See pp. 52-53 above.

adopts a more cautious approach to the sequence and date of the homilies than Tillemont, arriving at the following chronology:

> (a little before the riots) *De statuis hom. 1*; (seven days after the riots)
> *hom. 2*; (Sunday before Lent) *hom. 3*; (Monday, 1st day of Lent) *hom. 4*;
> (Tuesday-Thursday, Week 1) *hom. 5-7*; (Saturday, Week 1) *hom. 8*; (unspec.)
> *hom. 9*; (not the next day) *hom. 10*; (Monday, Week 4) *hom. 11*;[194] (Tuesday-
> Wednesday, Week 4) *hom. 12-13*; (unspec.) *hom. 14*; (unspec.) *hom. 15*;
> (unspec.) *hom. 16*; (after the arrival of Ellebichus and Caesarius) *hom. 17*;
> (after mid-Lent) *hom. 18*; (last Sunday of Lent) *hom. 19*;[195] (Friday, last day of
> Lent, ten days before Easter) *hom. 20*; (Easter Sunday) *hom. 21*.[196]

Along with another catechesis, Montfaucon presents immediately
following the series *De statuis* a homily formerly considered to constitute
part of that series.[197] He labels the two *Ad illuminandos cat. 1* and *2* (CPG
4460, 4464), respectively. Concerning the first, Montfaucon is persuaded
by John's exhortations against swearing to locate it during Lent of 387,[198]
arguing that Tillemont's objections to this are inconclusive.[199] While the
homilist's statement that it was delivered thirty days prior to Easter
places it during the third week of Lent, and although it appears from *De
statuis hom. 11* that Chrysostom did not preach for some days prior to
the beginning of week four, the fact that he was instructing a select
group of catechumens constitutes an exception to that situation. The absence of reference to the aftermath of the riots is likewise to be explained
by the catechist's focus on the task in hand, with such comment reserved
for the occasions when he was speaking to the general assembly.[200] Although there is no evidence to link the second catechesis, delivered during Lent ten days after another, to the first, there is also nothing to prevent this. In the end, it is the reference in the second to events associated
with the riots which persuades Montfaucon to place the two together.[201]

The next homilies to be considered are the three *De diabolo tentatore*
(CPG 4332). As indicated by a comparison of the opening to *De diab. tent.*

---

[194] This opinion is later reiterated by Montfaucon, II 225.

[195] Montfaucon later assigned this homily to the Sunday before Ascension, 387. See
the *Admonitio* to *De decem mill. tal. deb.* (CPG 4368), located immediately following the
preface to vol. III, and in particular the *Praefatio* to vol. IV, pp. 8-12.

[196] Montfaucon, II *Praef.* For a more detailed discussion see van de Paverd, *Homilies
on the Statues*, Part II, 205-362.

[197] See n. 51 above.

[198] Consideration of the catechesis' provenance is entirely absent.

[199] See n. 100 above.

[200] Montfaucon, II 224-225.

[201] Montfaucon, II 225.

hom. 1 and the contents of *De prophetiarum obscuritate hom. 2* (CPG 4420), the first was delivered a few days after the Sunday on which the latter was preached. From the third of the homilies it is also clear that *hom. 3* was delivered two days after *hom. 2*. The interval between *hom. 1* and *2*, however, is by no means certain, as is the question of whether *hom. 1* actually preceded *hom. 2*. What is certain is that all three homilies stem from Antioch. In the case of the first, during the homilies *De proph. obscuritate* Chrysostom speaks of the bishop in a way that indicates that another person holds that position. With respect to *hom. 2* and *3*, in *hom. 2* John makes it clear that Flavian, the bishop of Antioch, is among the audience. As for the year of their delivery, Montfaucon argues that this is impossible to determine. In this regard, he is at some pains to dismiss Tillemont's identification of the catechesis mentioned in *De diab. tent. hom. 2* as *Ad illuminandos cat. 2*.[202]

Following *De diab. tent. hom. 1-3* Montfaucon presents a group of nine homilies loosely collected under the title *De paenitentia* (CPG 4333). Of these, he considers only the first six to be indisputably genuine and the last three to be the least suspect of a larger group, the remainder of which are more obviously spurious.[203] Because of the disparate nature of the homilies, Montfaucon is obliged to consider the question of their place of origin case by case. Although *De paen. hom. 1* contains no clear evidence for either location, he is inclined to believe that it stems from Antioch. In the case of *hom. 2*, it cannot be proven that it followed *hom. 1*. Even if it did, at least one homily must have intervened, since the summary provided in *hom. 2* does not match the contents of the first homily. *Hom. 3*, however, was delivered following *hom. 2*, as is clear from the contents of both homilies. While it is impossible to determine when the two were preached, Montfaucon is again inclined to locate them at Antioch, on the basis of the homilist's statement (*hom. 3*) that the city is adorned with suburbs and that the population is attentive to Christian teaching and assiduous about attendance at synaxis. This, he argues, is characteristic of Antioch rather than Constantinople. In the fourth homily, Chrysostom says that it is the fourth day on which he has preached on the topic of penitence. Whether the homilies which preceded are *hom. 1-3* or three entirely different sermons, is impossible to determine. That *hom. 4* was delivered at Antioch, however, is indicated by the long list of disasters mentioned by the homilist. The fact that John was himself present at these times and involved in preaching is appropriate only to the period of his presbyterate.[204] In addition, Montfaucon

---

[202] Montfaucon, II 245-246. See Tillemont (p. 54 above).

[203] See Montfaucon, II 277.

[204] Savile (see pp. 43-44 above) had assigned the homily to Constantinople.

sees no difficulty with Tillemont's identification of the "enemy incursion"
as the activities of the Huns in 395, a circumstance which locates this
homily in the final years at Antioch. That *hom.* 5 likewise stems from
that location is indicated by a reference to the monks living on the
mountains nearby. This is a characteristic feature of Antiochene homilies. *Hom.* 6, on the other hand, provides no clue as to its place of origin,
while with respect to *hom.* 7-9 Montfaucon declines all comment.[205]

There then follows a series of homilies presented according to the sequence in the liturgical calendar of the festivals on which they were
preached. The first of these is *In diem natalem* (CPG 4334), the date of
which Montfaucon had already had occasion to discuss in association
with that of *De b. Philogonio* and the first three homilies *Adv. Iudaeos.*[206]
Regarding the location of the homily in 386, he is persuaded both by an
allusion to the discourses against the Jews (i.e., *Adv. Iud. or. 1-3*), which
fell in September of that year, and by the homilist's comments regarding
the novel status of the Christmas festival, which suggests to Montfaucon
that this is the first occasion on which Chrysostom had preached on the
topic. He further demonstrates that it was delivered on Dec. 25, five days
after *De b. Philogonio.*[207] The Epiphany homily (*De baptismo Christi*: CPG
4335) belongs to 387 and was preached only a short space of time after
the latter two, as indicated by John's comments concerning those who
communicate only on liturgical festivals.[208] Of the doublet *De proditione
Iudae* (CPG 4336), Montfaucon speculates that the first homily was
preached some years before the second, the latter belonging to Maundy
Thursday of the same Lent as that in which the first thirty-two homilies
on Genesis (CPG 4409) are to be located.[209] The sermon *De coemeterio et
de cruce* (CPG 4337) was delivered in the same year as, and some twenty
days before that on the martyrs Bernice, Prosdoce and Domnina (CPG
4355), as indicated by the opening to the latter homily. Montfaucon
argues that it was preached not on the festival of the Veneration of the
Cross (Sept. 14), as had been thought, but on Good Friday. With respect
to the year to which these two homilies belong, he follows Tillemont's
suggestion that they be located in 392, in which year Good Friday fell on
March 26.[210] Accepting the date of April 14 for the festival of the three

---

[205] Montfaucon, II 278.

[206] See p. 73 above.

[207] Montfaucon, II 352.

[208] Montfaucon, II 367. Montfaucon here forgets that he has already assigned the
eighth homily *Contra Anomoeos* (CPG 4321) to this date. See p. 72 above.

[209] Montfaucon, II 375-376. By virtue of this connection he assumes, although it is
never stated, that both homilies were delivered at Antioch.

[210] See p. 54 above.

martyrs, this allows for an interval of the required duration. As a note of caution, however, Montfaucon points out that the identity of the method then used for calculating the date of Easter is by no means certain.[211]

Regarding the doublet *De cruce et latrone* (CPG 4338-4339), Montfaucon speculates that they were delivered on Good Friday in different years, although which was delivered first is uncertain. With some hesitation he also suggests that each was delivered following one of the two *De prod. Iudae*, although he admits that one could claim equally in the case of *De cruce et latrone hom. 2* that neither of the latter is to be identified as the homily of the previous day.[212] *De resurrectione mortuorum* (CPG 4340), by contrast, clearly indicates the point of its delivery. The opening of the homily refers to the first five homilies *Contra Anomoeos* (CPG 4318), delivered in 386. On this basis it can be argued that it was preached at the beginning of 387 before Lent, since the whole of Lent in that year was taken up with the discourses on the Statues (CPG 4330).[213] The homily *De resurrectione* (CPG 4341) belongs to the same year as *De prod. Iudae hom. 2*, in which year the series *In principium Actorum* (CPG 4371) was delivered, among others.[214] This is established from *In princ. Act. hom. 1*, which recalls the subject matter of *De resurrectione*, and describes the topic as recent.[215] The information that the homily *In ascensionem* (CPG 4342) was preached in the martyrium at Romanesia in Antioch Montfaucon extracts from the title. As for the year to which it belongs, this cannot be determined.[216] The series closes with two homilies on the feast of Pentecost (CPG 4343). After excluding the possibility that one of these is the homily referred to in *De Anna sermo 5* (CPG 4411), Montfaucon simply assumes, in the case of the first, that it originates at Antioch. With regard to the second, he states only that there is no means of determining its date.[217]

There are then presented a number of homilies, each delivered on the festival of a particular martyr or saint. The first constitutes a collection of seven panegyrics on the apostle Paul (CPG 4344). Montfaucon reiter-

---

[211] Montfaucon, II 396-397. Again, the Antiochene provenance of this homily is established *a priori* by virtue of the connection.

[212] Montfaucon, II 402-403. Again, although it is never stated, Montfaucon gives the impression that he is thinking of Antioch.

[213] Montfaucon, II 421-422.

[214] For the full extent of the sequence which Montfaucon establishes for this year, see Sequence D, p. 108 below.

[215] Montfaucon, II 437.

[216] Montfaucon, II 446. Montfaucon here argues against Tillemont (see p. 55 above), who wished to locate the homily with *De coemeterio et de cruce* in 392.

[217] Montfaucon, II 456-457.

ates the connection between these and *In kalendas*,[218] dismissing Tillemont's opinion that in the latter John refers rather to the homily *Quales
ducendae sint uxores* (CPG 4379), on the grounds that the homily in question must have focused entirely on the topic of Paul, and not simply mentioned him in passing. Further, all seven encomia belong to Antioch,
since in *De laudibus s. Pauli hom. 4* the homilist mentions the temple of
Apollo at Daphne, which was struck by lightning. Concerning the year of
their delivery, there is nothing that can be said, except that some of the
seven date to before the homily *In kalendas*, and some after.[219] *De s. Meletio* (CPG 4345), on the other hand, provides an indication of the day and
year of its delivery. Chrysostom says that a fifth year has passed since the
death of Meletius. As that event occurred at Constantinople towards the
end of May 381, the homily is to be located after that date. While the
tense used excludes the anniversary of his death, Montfaucon suggests as
an alternative the anniversary of the day on which the bishop's remains
were translated to Antioch (Feb. 12). As the dates provided by the Maty-
rologies are not always certain, he concludes that the homily can be assigned to either 386 (after May) or the beginning of 387.[220]

In the opening to *In s. Lucianum* (CPG 4346) Montfaucon sees a reference to *De baptismo Christi*, which is described as having been
preached on the previous day. Since, as already demonstrated, the latter
homily was delivered in 387,[221] this locates *In s. Lucianum* on Jan. 7 of
that year. Lucianus was a former presbyter of Antioch.[222] The homily *De
s. Babyla* (CPG 4347) was delivered following the third of the *Conciones
de Lazaro*, as indicated in the opening to *De Lazaro concio 4*. Montfaucon
reconciles the comment that on the day in question the three youths in
the furnace as well as Babylas were celebrated, no detail of which is
found in the homily on Babylas, by arguing that the topic may have been
covered by one of the more senior presbyters or Flavian, all of whom
John indicates were due to preach after him. As indicated in the Maty-
rologies, the feast of St Babylas fell in January, apparently on the twenty-
fourth.[223] The opening to *In Iuventinum et Maximum* (CPG 4349) indicates that it was delivered a few days after a homily on Babylas, which
can be positively identified as CPG 4347.[224] The sermon *De s. Pelagia*
(CPG 4350) stems from Antioch, since it was at that location that Pelagia

---

[218] See p. 74 above.
[219] Montfaucon, II 474-475.
[220] Montfaucon, II 517.
[221] See the discussion of CPG 4335, p. 78 above.
[222] Montfaucon, II 523.
[223] Montfaucon, II 529.
[224] Montfaucon, II 578.

was martyred. While Montfaucon quotes an earlier scholar on the question of the identity of the Pelagia whose festival is being celebrated, and therefore the day on which the homily fell, he expresses no personal opinion regarding the findings.[225]

The next genuine homily to be presented is *In s. Ignatium* (CPG 4351). This was delivered at Antioch a few days after a sermon on St Pelagia. Montfaucon finds no means of determining the year to which it belongs, although he does state that it seems that Dec. 20 was the day on which Ignatius was venerated and that his bones lay interred at Antioch in the cemetery beyond the gate to Daphne.[226] On the basis of John's comments in *In illud: Dom., non est in hom.* (CPG 4419), Montfaucon establishes the following sequence: a homily on the controversy between Peter and Paul at Antioch; *In s. Eustathium* (CPG 4352); a sermon on St Romanus; and CPG 4419 itself. All four were delivered at Antioch, although in which year is uncertain.[227] The homily *In s. Romanum* (CPG 4353) is to be identified as the one which constitutes part of this sequence, delivered a few days after the sermon on Eustathius.[228]

The next group of homilies to be considered are the three *De Macabeis* (CPG 4354). Montfaucon assigns them to Antioch, although he admits that the authenticity of the third is suspect. The evidence for Antioch he appears to derive from the second homily, where Chrysostom alludes to the bishop and indicates that that individual is due to preach after him. He finds the year in which they fell impossible to determine.[229] With respect to *De ss. Bernice et Prosdoce* (CPG 4355), Montfaucon refers the reader to his discussion of *De coemeterio et de cruce*, where there was established a firm link between the two.[230] He reiterates that the two homilies most probably belong to the year 392, the former being delivered on April 14.[231] As is evident from its contents, the homily *In quatrid. Lazarum* (CPG 4356), which Montfaucon publishes for the first time, was preached a few days before Easter, on the festival of the martyrs Bernice, Prosdoce and Domnina. This, as he has indicated in the *Monitum* to the

---

[225] Montfaucon, II 584.

[226] Montfaucon, II 592. Montfaucon here seems unaware of the possible conflict on Dec. 20 at Antioch between the veneration of Ignatius and that of Philogonius. For the day on which he locates the latter, see p. 72 above.

[227] Montfaucon, II 601-602. For the full argument regarding this sequence see the *Monitum* to CPG 4419, VI 157.

[228] Montfaucon, II 610.

[229] Montfaucon, II 622.

[230] See his comments concerning CPG 4337 (p. 78 above).

[231] Montfaucon, II 633-634.

preceding homily, fell on April 15.[232] The year, however, he is unable to determine.[233]

Montfaucon locates together the two homilies *De ss. martyribus* (CPG 4357) and *Non esse ad gratiam concionandum* (CPG 4358). The first was delivered at Antioch apparently following the homilies *De Macabeis* (CPG 4354), as is evident from the homilist's statement that he is preaching a little after the festival of the Maccabees, in Flavian's absence. The contents of the second of these two homilies make it clear that it was delivered after the first. Its contents also indicate that both followed a homily on the topic of Lazarus. Whether that sermon can be identified as one of the *Conciones de Lazaro* (CPG 4329), however, is uncertain.[234] A second homily on the martyrs (CPG 4359), as is clear from its contents, was preached in the countryside around Antioch.[235] That *In s. Iulianum* (CPG 4360) likewise stems from Antioch is indicated by the reference to Daphne and by the circumstance that the remains of the saint had been translated there. Regarding the celebration of Julian's festival on March 16 versus June 21, Montfaucon cites the work of an earlier scholar, without providing any personal comment.[236]

The sermon *In s. Barlaam* (CPG 4361), however, cannot be assigned to any of the known dates (Nov. 16 or 19), since in *In d. Pauli: Nolo vos ignorare* (CPG 4380), which was delivered on the day following the feast of St Barlaam, the homilist refers to the arrival of summer. It can be said to belong to Antioch, because the surrounding countryside held numerous tombs of martyrs, to which the urban population were accustomed to flow when celebrating their memory, a situation which entirely suits that location. Moreover, at the close to *In d. Pauli: Nolo vos ignorare* Chrysostom requests the prayers of all the leaders (τῶν προέδρων ἁπάντων). At Constantinople he himself was the supreme leader and had no-one above him.[237] *In s. Droside* (CPG 4362) was likewise delivered in the Antiochene countryside, whence the people had been led on the day by Flavian, as the homilist clearly indicates.[238] In the case of the sermon on the Egyp-

---

[232] In fact, at II 633f he states in one place that the Roman Martyrology locates the festival on April 15, while in calculating the required interval of twenty days he arrives at April 14. In the *Monitum* to CPG 4337, he follows Tillemont's location of the festival on April 14.

[233] Montfaucon, II 646. Although not stated, it is to be inferred that the homily belongs to Antioch.

[234] Montfaucon, II 649-650.

[235] Montfaucon, II 667.

[236] Montfaucon, II 670-671.

[237] Montfaucon, II 680-681. Although it is not stated, Montfaucon derives the entire argument from Tillemont (see p. 59 above).

[238] Montfaucon, II 688.

tian martyrs (CPG 4363), however, Montfaucon does little more than shrug his shoulders regarding Tillemont's suggestion that the translation of their remains indicates Constantinople, where such occurrences were more frequent.[239] There is, on the other hand, absolutely no doubt concerning the provenance of *De s. Phoca* (CPG 4364). The mention of the involvement of the emperor and his wife in the procession conveying the remains out of the city can point only to Constantinople. As for the year to which it belongs, John's comment that it is his wont to experience persecution and harrassment may indicate that it was delivered after the first exile, at the end of 403 or beginning of 404.[240] Montfaucon closes the series of encomia on saints and martyrs with a third homily *De ss. martyribus* (CPG 4365). Aside from the information that it was preached less than seven days after Pentecost on a feast of all the martyrs, the contents provide no clue as to its provenance or date.[241] There then follows the homily *De terrae motu* (CPG 4366). That this was preached at one of the churches outside the city of Antioch, frequented by the people, is indicated by the homilist's allusion to the effort and sweat involved in making the journey. However, neither the earthquake itself nor the period of ill health, to which John also alludes, lends itself to certain dating.[242]

c. *Volume III*

In the third volume Montfaucon assembles the occasional homilies — those which exegete brief passages of scripture but do not belong to one of the larger series, sermons on moral topics, and some which were preached in response to or which make allusion to contemporary historical events. None of these associates itself directly with a specific point in the liturgical year.

The first sermon presented is *De decem millium talentorum debitore* (CPG 4368). Montfaucon finds the evidence for the association between this homily and the series *De statuis*, throughout which Chrysostom prosecuted the habit of swearing, compelling. The nature of the comment, in which the latter series is reflected upon, locates the homily after Lent in 387. By taking the summary of events presented in *De Anna sermo 1* (CPG 4411), where John indicates that he has preached in the

---

[239] Montfaucon, II 698. See p. 63 above.

[240] Montfaucon, II 703.

[241] Montfaucon, II 710.

[242] Montfaucon, II 717. This is reiterated at the *Monitum* to the *Novae homiliae*, XII 319-320, where he dismisses Tillemont's argument for locating the homily in 398 (see p. 63 above).

following sequence: *De statuis hom. 21*; one or more sermons against the pagans; celebration of various martyrs (many days); homily on swearing (large number of people from the country present); *De Anna sermo 1* — and by identifying the homily on swearing as *De statuis hom. 19*, Montfaucon is persuaded to locate *De decem mill. tal. deb.* one or more days before that sermon. In *De decem mill. tal. deb.* the homilist states that it is the first occasion on which he has preached after a longer than usual bout of ill-health; in *De statuis hom. 19*, that he was unable to participate in the festivities surrounding the commemoration of the martyrs for that same reason. Since Montfaucon is now convinced that *De statuis hom. 19* belongs to the Sunday before Ascension,[243] this locates *De decem mill. tal. deb.* in 387, one or more days prior to that occasion.[244]

The date and location of the next homily (*In illud: Pater, si possibile est*: CPG 4369) are far less easily determined. However, on the basis of an allusion to the Anomoean heresy and to topics covered in the five sermons *De incompr. dei natura* (CPG 4318), he is inclined to believe that it was delivered at Antioch, not long after these.[245] In the opening to *In paralyticum dimissum per tectum* (CPG 4370), on the other hand, the homilist states that he has recently preached on the topic of the man paralyzed for thirty-eight years, a homily which can be identified as *De Christi divinitate* (CPG 4325). This locates the sermon at Constantinople, where it was delivered a few days after the latter in 398.[246]

In the case of the sermons *In princ. Actorum* (CPG 4371), Montfaucon gathers together as a series four homilies, which had previously been published separately.[247] After demonstrating that the four are interconnected and establishing their correct order, he turns to the time and year of their delivery. That they were delivered not long after Easter is indicated by the reference to the newly baptised at the close of *hom. 1* and *3*. Moreover, in *hom. 1* the sermon *De resurrectione* (CPG 4341) is referred to as having been given recently, indicating that it was delivered only a few days after Easter. This is confirmed by the mention in *hom. 1* of a sermon delivered in the past few days on the topic of Judas. That sermon can be identified as *De prod. Iudae hom. 2* (CPG 4336). From this it is clear that the series *In princ. Actorum* belongs to the same year as, and constitutes part of a larger sequence with, the sixty-seven homilies on

---

[243] Montfaucon had previously located it on the last Sunday in Lent. See p. 76 above.

[244] Montfaucon, III (1721) *Admonitio* immediately following the *Praef.*

[245] Montfaucon, III 15. This would locate the homily somewhere toward the end of 386, or a little later.

[246] Montfaucon, III 32. Montfaucon indicates that the homily was not published by Savile, but had nonetheless been available prior to his own edition.

[247] Regarding the arrangement presented by Savile, see n. 38 above.

Genesis (CPG 4409).[248] The first of the homilies *De mutatione nominum* (CPG 4372) was preached following *In princ. Act. hom. 4*, since in *De mutatione nom. hom. 1* Chrysostom explicitly states that the latter was the previous sermon delivered. He also indicates that the paschal period has not yet ended. *De mutatione nom. hom. 2* was delivered on the following day, as stated by the homilist. There then followed *Sermo 9 in Gen.* (CPG 4410), in which the previous two discourses are recalled. *De mutatione nom. hom. 3* then follows, a few days later, while some time intervened between *hom. 3* and *4*. In the latter homily Chrysostom recalls the three which preceded.[249]

In the case of *De gloria in tribulationibus* (CPG 4373), Montfaucon confesses that he can neither determine whether it stems from Antioch or Constantinople, nor in what year or at what time it was delivered.[250] The same applies to *In illud: Diligentibus deum omnia cooperantur* (CPG 4374). Montfaucon firmly rejects the arguments of those who assign the homily to Constantinople on the basis of the similarity between the comments made at the opening to this homily and that of *De decem mill. tal. debitore*. John's bouts of illness were frequent and he could easily have repeated the same comments at Antioch after an interval of several years.[251] *In illud: Si esurierit inimicus* (CPG 4375), on the other hand, stems from Constantinople, as indicated by the reference to the imperial court and the emperor's personal bodyguard. The information contained in the homily is insufficient, however, for determining the year of its delivery.[252] Montfaucon finds the provenance of the two sermons *In illud: Salutate Priscillam et Aquilam* (CPG 4376) difficult to establish, although he suspects that both were preached at Antioch. He is persuaded of this by a passage in the second, where the homilist in discussing lay criticism of the priesthood refers to "the common fathers" (τῶν κοινῶν πατέρων). Had Chrysostom already been bishop at Constantinople, he would scarcely have used this term. Montfaucon finds it more likely that he here alludes to the senior members among the priesthood at Antioch. He further sees an allusion at the beginning of *In illud: Salutate Prisc. et Aqu.*

---

[248] Montfaucon, III 47-49. For the full sequence see Sequence D, p. 108 below. Montfaucon, III 49-50, closes his discussion with a refutation of Tillemont's supposed argument (see *Mémoires*, XI 575) for locating the series *In princ. Actorum* in 387. In fact Tillemont was at this point summarising the thesis of an earlier scholar preparatory to discounting it in favour of arguing that the series belonged in sequence with that on Genesis. For his opinion see pp. 55-57 above.

[249] Montfaucon, III 96-97. Montfaucon leaves the reader to infer the provenance of these homilies and their place in the larger Genesis sequence (see previous note).

[250] Montfaucon, III 140.

[251] Montfaucon, III 149.

[252] Montfaucon, III 156.

hom. 2 to the series *In princ. Actorum* and *De mutatione nominum*. Since
the latter both stem from Antioch, he infers that the two homilies under
discussion were delivered at that same location.[253]

Montfaucon considers it evident that the three homilies CPG 4377-
4379 were delivered one after the other in the order presented, because at
the beginning of the second and third the first and second are referred to
as "recent". Moreover, in the title to the third (*Quales ducendae sint
uxores*) the person who preached in Chrysostom's place at the preceding
synaxis is identified as Maximus. This is thought by some to be the
Maximus who was at that time bishop of Seleucia in Isauria. Since at the
beginning of the homily Chrysostom implies that Maximus is his equal in
rank, and since the preaching of guest bishops in the imperial city is well
documented, Montfaucon is persuaded to identify the location as Constantinople.[254] As already suggested in the discussion on *In s. Barlaam*
(CPG 4361),[255] *In d. Pauli: Nolo vos ignorare* (CPG 4380) was preached on
the following day. This is explicitly stated by the homilist, who also indicates that it is summer. The Antiochene provenance of the homily is established by its connection with the festival of St Barlaam, which was
celebrated at Antioch.[256] As for the time and place of *In d. Pauli: Oportet
haereses esse* (CPG 4381), nothing can be said, except that the sermon
was preached after another on the disasters which struck Jerusalem, in
which the audience was reduced to tears.[257] By contrast, the homily *De
eleemosyna* (CPG 4382) indicates its Antiochene origin in at least two
places. In the first, the homilist says that he had to negotiate the forum
and various streets in order to reach the church. When bishop at Constantinople, Chrysostom was never that distant from his place of
preaching. The second, where the present location is directly associated
with the Antioch of Acts 11.30, provides much clearer proof. The year in
which it was delivered, however, is unable to be determined.[258]

Montfaucon argues that the three homilies *In illud: Habentes eundem
spiritum* (CPG 4383) were all delivered at Antioch, because of the reference to monks living a harsh existence on the peaks of the mountains.[259]

---

[253] Montfaucon, III 171-172. Although he fails to substantiate this, Montfaucon here
assumes that there is a firm link between *In illud: Sal. Prisc. et Aqu. sermo 1* and *sermo 2*.

[254] Montfaucon, III 192.

[255] See p. 82 above.

[256] Montfaucon, III 228. However, see the *Monitum* to *In s. Barlaam* (II 680-681),
where the homilist's invocation of the prayers of the *proedroi* is cited as evidence.

[257] Montfaucon, III 239.

[258] Montfaucon, III 248.

[259] Although it is not stated, Montfaucon derives this argument from Tillemont (see p.
59 above), who applies it to the first of the three homilies only.

Such comment is a common feature of Antiochene homilies, but is missing in those which stem from Constantinople. He is unable to offer any conjecture, however, concerning the year of their delivery.[260] The sermon *In illud: Utinam sustineretis modicum* (CPG 4384), on the other hand, provides no clue as to the year or location to which it belongs.[261] By contrast, it is almost certain that Chrysostom preached the sermon *De profectu evangelii* (CPG 4385) at Antioch at the same time as his homilies against the Anomoeans, since at the beginning he mentions a recent sermon, which can be identified as *De incompr. dei nat. hom. 5* (CPG 4318). Since the latter immediately preceded the sermon on Philogonius and it appears that no homily intervened between *De b. Philogonio* (CPG 4319) and *In diem natalem* (CPG 4334), *De profectu evangelii* is to be located in the very last days of 386.[262] The homily *In illud: Vidua eligatur* (CPG 4386) likewise belongs to Antioch, because in the introduction the homilist states that he recently preached on the same topic as *De Lazaro concio 5*. Montfaucon therefore locates it in the same sequence as the homilies on Lazarus (CPG 4329) and *In kalendas* (CPG 4328), reserving judgement concerning the year to which this sequence belongs.[263]

The sermon *In Heliam et viduam* (CPG 4387), on the other hand, permits no assessment as to either the place or year of its delivery.[264] Montfaucon argues that *De futurae vitae deliciis* (CPG 4388), however, stems from Antioch, as indicated by the zealousness the population displays in venerating the martyrs and the extra-urban location of the synaxis. Although John indicates that it is summer, there is no means of identifying the year.[265] In the case of *Peccata fratrum non evulganda* (CPG 4389) and *Non esse desperandum* (CPG 4390), Montfaucon agrees with Tillemont that the two belong together,[266] the second on the day following the first. Neither, however, provides any indication of the year of their delivery.[267] In the *Monitum* to *In illud: In faciem ei restiti* (CPG 4391), Montfaucon says nothing about either the provenance or date of this homily.[268] He later identifies it as the sermon on the controversy be-

---

[260] Montfaucon, III 259-260.

[261] Montfaucon, III 291.

[262] Montfaucon, III 300.

[263] Montfaucon, III 311. For a full outline of this sequence see Sequence B, p. 107 below.

[264] Montfaucon, III 328.

[265] Montfaucon, III 337. Although it is not stated, Montfaucon derives his comments regarding the provenance of this homily from Tillemont (see p. 60 above).

[266] See p. 108, Sequence F.

[267] Montfaucon, III 343-344.

[268] Montfaucon, III 361-362.

tween Peter and Paul at Antioch, which forms a sequence with the homilies on Saints Eustathius and Romanus.[269]

At this point Montfaucon presents a collection of homilies which
touch on historical events associated with Chrysostom's life as bishop of
Constantinople. The first two relate to the deposition of the consul-
eunuch Eutropius (CPG 4392, 4528). The first of these was delivered on
the day after Chrysostom had granted sanctuary to the fugitive Eutropius, the second scarcely two days later. Concerning the date of the
homilies, Montfaucon states only that the events to which they refer occurred in 399.[270] Around the beginning of 400, Chrysostom was involved
in negotiations with the Gothic general Gainas to secure the lives of Saturninus and Aurelianus. It is in associaton with this event that the homily *Cum Saturninus et Aurelianus* (CPG 4393) was delivered.[271] The sermons *De regressu* (CPG 4394) and *De recipiendo Severiano* (CPG 4395)
both date to the period following John's return from Ephesus. This locates them after the Easter of 401.[272] The next four homilies (CPG 4396-
4399) belong to the period surrounding the first occasion on which
Chrysostom was sent into exile. This locates them loosely in the year
403.[273] To that same period Montfaucon dates the homily *De Chananaea*
(CPG 4529), the first part of which he considers to be indisputably
genuine.[274]

The final two sermons presented in this volume are an encomium on
Diodore bishop of Tarsus (CPG 4406) and a homily delivered at Easter
(CPG 4408). In the first, Chrysostom indicates that Diodore is to preach
after him, a circumstance which, as Montfaucon points out, is not uncus-
tomary at Antioch. Regarding Tillemont's suggestion that the encomium
be dated to 392, he finds himself unable to either confirm or deny this.[275]
Despite the marked similarity between the homilies *In sanctum pascha*
and *De resurrectione* (CPG 4341), Montfaucon asserts that the former is
genuine, on the basis that it is not unreasonable that Chrysostom repeated himself in the course of eighteen years of preaching. He offers no
suggestion, however, regarding either its provenance or date.[276]

---

[269] See the *Monitum* to *In illud: Domine, non est in homine* (CPG 4419), Montfaucon,
VI 157. For the full sequence see Sequence E, p. 108 below.

[270] Montfaucon, III 379-380. In the *Monitum* to the eleven *Novae homiliae* (XII 321),
however, he dates the events surrounding the deposition to c. August 399.

[271] Montfaucon, III 404-405.

[272] Montfaucon, III *Praef.*, p. 3.

[273] Montfaucon, III *Praef.*, pp. 3-4.

[274] Montfaucon, III 431-432.

[275] Montfaucon, III 746-747. See p. 55 above.

[276] Montfaucon, III 750.

d. *Volume IV*

The fourth volume marks the beginning of the exegetical series. In this and in the next two volumes Montfaucon presents those series in which the homilist treats material from the Old Testament, arranging them according to the order in which the subject matter appears in the bible. As a result, the first comments to appear in volume four concern the larger of the two series on Genesis (CPG 4409).

Montfaucon begins by questioning the reliability of Photius' stylistic criterion, upon which Savile had based his attribution of the series to Constantinople. He points out that despite the less precise style characteristic of these homilies, they nonetheless stem with certainty from Antioch. This he argues from the opening to *Hom. 33 in Gen.*, on the basis of which it can be established that the sixty-seven homilies on Genesis form part of a larger sequence which incorporates, among others, the four homilies *In princ. Actorum* (CPG 4371).[277] From the opening to the second of these and from its title, we gain the information that it was preached in the Palaia or Old Church, a well-known Antiochene landmark. Moreover, at the beginning of *Hom. 12 in Gen.* John says that he broke off his exegesis to preach against those who persist in fasting with the Jews. This is an error into which certain Antiochene Christians had fallen, as demonstrated by *Adv. Iudaeos or. 3*, which was delivered in 386, but is an issue never raised in the material which stems from Constantinople. It therefore follows that the entire series on Genesis was delivered at Antioch.[278]

Montfaucon then turns to the question of the year to which the series, and therefore the larger sequence to which it belongs, can be assigned. In this respect he first addresses the argument put forward by Tillemont, that in the year in question the Friday of the first week of Lent, on which *Hom. 6 in Gen.* was delivered, coincided with the staging of circus games, and that on this basis it might be suggested that the series belongs to the year 395.[279] Tillemont had heavily qualified this conclusion with the caveat that it depended entirely upon whether the Roman calendar was in use at Antioch at the time, and whether *Hom. 6* really did fall on the Friday, neither of which is entirely certain. Montfaucon commends this caution, but points out that by the time of Theodosius it is unlikely that there was any convergence between the Roman calendar and that followed at Antioch. Furthermore there is no certainty that the

---

[277] For the full extent of this sequence see Sequence D, p. 108 below.

[278] Montfaucon, IV (1721) *Praef.*, pp. 1-3. Although it is not stated, he here adopts and expands the thesis put forward by Tillemont (see p. 55 above).

[279] See pp. 55-56 above.

Paschal tables upon which Tillemont based his calculations are reliable or indeed conform with those in use at Antioch. As a result, no pronouncement can be made concerning the date of the series, except to conclude that, since a large portion was delivered during Lent, the years 386, in which at this time the eight *Sermones in Genesim* (CPG 4410) were being preached, and 387, in which Lent was taken up by the discourses *De statuis*, can be excluded.[280]

Of the nine sermons on Genesis (CPG 4410), which are presented next, the first eight were preached at the beginning of Lent in 386. This is patent from John's comments at the opening to *Sermo 2*, where he describes himself as stripping off for the stadium and embarking on a bold enterprise, which suggest that he is entering his first Lent. Since Lent of 387 was taken up with the homilies on the Statues, this locates the series firmly in Chrysostom's first year at Antioch. Although Montfaucon acknowledges Tillemont's assertion that *Sermo 1* was delivered on the Monday, which was the first day of Lent, he prefers to avoid calculating the exact date on the basis of the uncertainty over the Paschal tables then in use at Antioch.[281] The ninth homily belongs to a period much later than the first eight, both by virtue of the passage from Genesis treated and the fact that there is little similarity between them. Rather it belongs to the major sequence associated with the sixty-seven homilies on Genesis,[282] in which it follows the second homily *De mutatione nominum* (CPG 4372). Chrysostom recalls the subject matter of the first two homilies in that series in the course of *Sermo 9 in Gen*. Montfaucon here reiterates his belief that the entire sequence belongs after the year 387.[283]

The five sermons on Anna, the mother of Samuel (CPG 4411), locate themselves firmly in 387 in the period after Easter, following the return of Flavian from Constantinople. The evidence for this is found in *De Anna sermo 1*, where Chrysostom reminds his audience of the subject matter preached in *De statuis hom. 21*. In *sermo 1* Chrysostom also sets out the festivals and homilies which have intervened: one or more sermons against the pagans; encomia on the martyrs (many days); and a homily against swearing preached in the presence of rural visitors. This latter homily Montfaucon now identifies firmly as *De statuis hom. 19*, which he had previously assigned to the last Sunday in Lent. On the basis of the sequence established on the evidence of *De Anna sermo 1*, and since *De Anna sermo 5* was delivered after Pentecost, he now accepts the argument that the Sunday τῆς ἐπισωζομένης of the title is the fifth Sunday

---

[280] Montfaucon, IV *Praef.*, pp. 3-5.

[281] Montfaucon, IV 644.

[282] See Sequence D, p. 108 below.

[283] Montfaucon, IV 687.

after Easter, that is, the Sunday before Ascension.[284] If this identification is sound,[285] the following chronology for the sermons on Anna can be established:

> (Monday before Ascension) *sermo 1*; (Friday after Ascension) *sermo 2*; (Monday of the following week) *sermo 3*; (Wednesday) a homily now lost; (Friday, before Pentecost) *sermo 4*; (after Pentecost) *sermo 5*.[286]

That the three homilies on David and Saul (CPG 4412) were likewise delivered in 387 is evident from *De Davide et Saule hom. 1*, where Chrysostom says that he had recently preached on the topic central to the homily *De decem mill. tal. deb.* (CPG 4368). The latter refers to preaching on the topic of swearing during Lent, which concurs with the situation in 387, while the homilies on David and Saul themselves develop further the theme of loving one's enemies, which had been taken up in that homily.[287]

e. *Volume V*

The fifth volume is taken up entirely by the work known as the Exposition on the Psalms (CPG 4413) and by a few miscellaneous homilies on isolated verses from psalms (CPG 4414-4415). Leaving aside the current state of the first work and the questions of whether Chrysostom ever produced commentary upon all one hundred and fifty of the psalms in the Old Testament and whether the commentary as it exists was preached before an audience,[288] Montfaucon first addresses the issue of this work's provenance by invoking the stylistic criterion proposed by Photius. If this criterion is to be relied upon, the particularly elegant nature of the expositions points strongly toward Antioch. This impression is supported by the commentary on Ps. 110, in which the homilist refers to the lightning-strike which destroyed the temple of Apollo at Daphne and the translation of the remains of St Babylas as among the more notable miracles which have occurred in the audience's lifetime. These and a later allusion to the attempted restoration of the temple at Jerusalem under Julian are all events to which an audience at Antioch was witness or

---

[284] Regarding the confusion which surrounds the interpretation of this label see Lampe s.v. ἐπισωζομένη.

[285] See Montfaucon, *Praef.*, pp. 8-12.

[286] Montfaucon, IV 697-699.

[287] Montfaucon, IV 747.

[288] For discussion of these see Montfaucon, V *Praef.*, p. 1 and 3ff.

to which Chrysostom makes not infrequent reference in the homilies which stem from that location. Another point against Constantinople, in favour of Antioch, is the size of the work. Montfaucon argues that as bishop of Constantinople John would not have had sufficient leisure in which to produce such a voluminous composition. He is further persuaded by the occasional references to monks found in the Exposition to Ps. 6 and elsewhere. Such celebration of the monastic life is customarily found in homilies from Antioch, where celebrated communities lived in close proximity. It is not germane, however, to Constantinople.[289] Concerning the period during which Chrysostom composed this massive work, Montfaucon is inclined to suggest that it was first put together in written form some time between 370 and 386, prior to John's ordination as presbyter, after which he then perhaps preached them as homilies. However, Montfaucon stresses that this is entirely conjectural.[290]

The *Expositio in ps. 41* (CPG 4413.2) represents a special case, as it clearly falls outside this series. In the opening words of this homily reference is made to a recent lengthy sermon on Melchisedec and to the passing of the festivals of the Jews, both of which point to *Adv. Iud. or. 7* (CPG 4327). *Adv. Iud. or. 8*, although lengthy, makes no mention of Melchisedec, a circumstance which suggests that *Exp. in ps. 41* may have been delivered in between. This argument is supported by the fact that in *Adv. Iud. or. 8* it is likewise indicated that the festivals of the Jews are over. On this basis, it can be established that *Exp. in ps. 41* was delivered in 387, after the month of September.[291]

Regarding the two homilies *In illud: Ne timueritis cum dives* (CPG 4414), on the other hand, Montfaucon is persuaded that both were delivered at Constantinople. In the first, reference is made to the countless local examples of wealth which has suddenly evaporated, in which John employs much the same vocabulary as that found in the homily *In Eutropium* (CPG 4392). In support of this perceived allusion to Eutropius, Montfaucon invokes another piece of evidence for Constantinople, which had previously been adduced by Tillemont[292] — namely that Chrysostom refers to himself as "shepherd", which indicates his episcopal status. The provenance of *hom. 1* is further substantiated by the fact that *hom. 2* can definitely be shown to have been delivered at that location. The title to *In illud: Ne timueritis hom. 2* not only states explicitly that it was preached at Constantinople, but the opening to the homily also indicates that Chrysostom is speaking after another has preached.

---

[289] Montfaucon, V *Praef.*, pp. 2-3.

[290] Montfaucon, V *Praef.*, pp. 7-8.

[291] Montfaucon, V 128-129.

[292] See p. 64 above.

The allusion in this second homily to current upheaval and tumult leads Montfaucon to locate it in the period leading from the deposition of Eutropius to the threat posed by Gainas, around the year 400.[293] By contrast, the last of the homilies (*In ps. 145*: CPG 4415) provides very little evidence of its place of origin and none at all regarding the year of its delivery. It can be said only that it was preached on the Saturday of Holy Week, possibly at Antioch, since in the course of the homily Chrysostom invokes the monks who live on the mountains as an example.[294]

f. *Volume VI*

Of the homilies presented in Vol. VI, the first constitute a group of six sermons assembled under the title *In illud: Vidi dominum* (CPG 4417). As Montfaucon proceeds to demonstrate, the order in which the homilies are found in the manuscripts is not the order in which they were delivered. *Hom. 1* bears no connection to *hom. 2* and indeed appears to have been preached some years later, as indicated by the allusion to the poor decision-making of the current emperor and the present wars and troubles. This, as Tillemont proposed,[295] suggests the emperor Arcadius, which dates the homily to the year 395 or later. Whether it was delivered in Antioch or at Constantinople, however, is uncertain. *Hom. 2* demonstrates that it stems from Antioch because toward the end John alludes to the necessity of finishing quickly in order to yield his place to his "teacher". As for the year in which it was preached, Montfaucon points out a piece of evidence which Tillemont had overlooked, namely that Chrysostom says that he will discuss the alteration of names such as that of Abram to Abraham at another time. On this basis, Montfaucon locates it in the same year as the series *De mutatione nominum*. For the first time, he suggests that the larger sequence to which the latter, and now *In illud: Vidi dom. hom. 2* belong, could perhaps be located in 388.[296] *Hom. 3* was delivered some time after *hom. 2*, on another occasion at which Flavian preached afterwards. *Hom. 4*, however, bears no relation to *hom. 3* and was not even delivered in the same city. Montfaucon infers this from the mention that the city contains the senate and consuls, which is cause for a comparison with Rome. This, he believes, cannot refer to

---

[293] Montfaucon, V 503-504.

[294] Montfaucon, V 534.

[295] See p. 49 above.

[296] By the time of VII *Praef.*, p. 2 (published three years later), Montfaucon has convinced himself of this. For the larger sequence to which these homilies belong, see Sequence D, p. 108 below.

anywhere other than Constantinople, for which reason he would prefer
to separate this homily from the rest of the series. *Hom. 5*, on the other
hand, follows *hom. 3*, while *hom. 6* naturally follows *hom. 5* and was delivered at Antioch.[297] The last was preached a few days before Lent.[298]

Regarding the homily *In illud Isaiae: Ego dominus deus feci lumen*
(CPG 4418), Montfaucon confesses that it is difficult to determine
whether it belongs to Antioch or Constantinople. He does not consider at
all convincing Tillemont's assertion that it stems from the latter location
because Chrysostom had preached after someone else.[299] The sermon
which follows (*In illud: Domine, non est in homine*: CPG 4419), however,
was delivered at Antioch. At the beginning of this homily Chrysostom
mentions three others which preceded, all of which can be identified and
all of which stem from that location.[300] Of the two homilies *De proph. obscuritate* (CPG 4420), it is certain that the first was delivered a few days
before the second, and that the second was delivered on a Sunday. This
latter piece of information is derived from the first of the homilies *De
diabolo tentatore* (CPG 4332), where the subject matter of *De proph. obsc.
hom. 2* is alluded to and is said to have been the topic treated on the previous Sunday. Montfaucon is unable to identify the year in which the sequence falls, but points out that both *hom. 1* and *2* stem from Antioch. In
the second Chrysostom speaks of the bishop in such a way as to indicate
that not he, but another holds that office.[301] With respect to the year of
delivery, Montfaucon is at pains to dismiss the notion that the sermon on
the topic of Melchisedec mentioned in *hom. 1*, which the homilist says
that he will preach another day, is to be identified as *Adv. Iud. or. 7*. The
aspect upon which John proposes to preach in this sermon is not dealt
with in the latter homily.[302]

In the remainder of the sixth volume Montfaucon presents a number
of miscellaneous homilies in which passages or subjects from the Old
and New Testament are treated. Of these only three are now considered
genuine. Of those three the first, the sermon *In illud: Filius ex se nihil facit* (CPG 4421=4441.12), had only recently come to light.[303] Montfaucon

---

[297] No basis for this assertion is given.

[298] Montfaucon, VI (1724) 93-94.

[299] Montfaucon, VI 144. Cf. Tillemont (see p. 66 above).

[300] Montfaucon, VI 157. For the identity of the other homilies see Sequence E, p. 108
below. In fact in none of the four *Monita* to the homilies in question does Montfaucon set
out his reasons for assigning them to Antioch.

[301] Montfaucon, VI 167.

[302] Montfaucon, VI 167-168.

[303] Montfaucon mentions an edition by Eric Benzel of Uppsala, which appeared in
1708. For further detail see Baur, *Chrysostome et ses oeuvres*, 114 (184).

now presents the homily in an improved condition, arguing that it was delivered with certainty at Antioch, where it was preached in the Great Church, as indicated by the title. He is convinced of this by a combination of factors — that the Anomoean heresy is being addressed, and that "Flavian" has cut short his own sermon in order to let John preach,[304] because of the latter's increased standing as a preacher and greater powers of persuasion. The fact that Chrysostom has gained such a reputation leads Montfaucon to suggest that the homily does not belong among the ten sermons *Contra Anomoeos* (CPG 4318-4323) of 386 and early 387, but to a slightly later period at Antioch.[305]

The next, *Contra ludos et theatra* (CPG 4422=4441.7), which had been unknown prior to its publication by Montfaucon, is particularly rich in chronological detail. That it was delivered at Constantinople, after Chrysostom had been there for a year, is indicated some way into the homily. From this information, accepting that John's ordination took place on Feb. 26, a *terminus post quem* of Feb. 26, 399 can be established. This much is certain. However, Montfaucon provides three opinions regarding the more precise location of the homily within the year 399. In the *Monitum* he suggests with some hesitation that it was delivered on Easter Sunday, on the basis of the reference to Good Friday and other factors.[306] In the preface to the volume, however, he revises that opinion, on the basis of the status of the crops which were damaged in the sudden storm of the previous Wednesday. The grain is described as having formed mature ears, a circumstance which would be impossible at the time of Easter, which in that year fell in April. This leads Montfaucon to locate the homily some time around June.[307] Yet in the *Monitum* to the eleven *Novae homiliae* (CPG 4441), published subsequently in 1735, he reiterates his former opinion, concluding that the homily was delivered on Easter Sunday 399.[308] The last of the three sermons, *In illud: Hoc scitote quod in novissimis diebus* (CPG 4423), contains little by way of evidence regarding either the time or the location of its delivery. The homilist's allusion to ill-health which has prevented him from preaching is of little use, since this was a frequent occurrence. However, Montfaucon finds one indication that it may possibly stem from Antioch, namely that John says at the beginning that he is inexperienced at preaching.[309]

---

[304] Montfaucon here contradicts his usual argument that preaching after another is indicative of the homilist's episcopal status.

[305] Montfaucon, VI 254.

[306] Montfaucon, VI 271-272.

[307] Montfaucon, VI *Praef.*, pp. 3-4.

[308] Montfaucon, XII 321.

[309] Montfaucon, VI 278.

g. *Volume VII*

From volume seven onwards, Montfaucon presents the exegetical series on books of the New Testament, again in biblical order. The whole of
the seventh volume is taken up by the series of ninety homilies on the
Gospel of Matthew (CPG 4424).
   Montfaucon declares that all ninety were preached at Antioch. He deduces this from a passage in *In Matt. hom. 7*, where the city is identified
as that in which the term 'Christian' was first used, and from the mention
throughout of the monks in the neighbouring mountains, whom Chrysostom not infrequently uses as exempla. The year of their delivery, however, is less easy to determine. Montfaucon postulates that they were not
all delivered in the one year, since the normal course of liturgical festivals must have caused other homilies to be interspersed, expanding the
length of time taken to deliver the series. He prefers to locate them in the
latter years at Antioch (390 onwards), since in the earlier years (386-388)
John had occasion to frequently admonish the Antiochenes concerning
their swearing, while in the homilies on Matthew the matter is only
touched upon lightly. Regarding the more precise location of the series
during these years, he dismisses the conjecture raised by Tillemont that
in *hom. 72/73* Chrysostom alludes to the Meletian schism in a manner
that suggests that Paulinus, and perhaps even Evagrius are dead. Instead,
Montfaucon puts forward another argument for excluding the years 386-
388. John preached such a large number of homilies in his first three
years as presbyter,[310] that there is no room in these, nor perhaps in the
year following, in which to locate the series.[311]

h. *Volume VIII*

The entire eighth volume is occupied by the series of eighty-eight
homilies on the Gospel of John (CPG 4425). Within the homilies themselves Montfaucon can find no evidence for their place of origin. The
only available data upon which to base a conjecture are the various passages against those who adhere to the Anomoean heresy. Since this heresy was prevalent at both Antioch and Constantinople, however, it is of

---

[310] Montfaucon here includes Sequence D, implying that it occupied the bulk of 388.
Prior to this, the proposal that the sequence be located in 388 had been put forward only
once and with some hesitancy. See the *Monitum* to *In illud: Vidi dom. hom. 1-6*, Montfaucon, VI 93-94.
   [311] Montfaucon, VII *Praef.*, pp. 1-2. However, in the preface to VIII p. 3, published in
the following year, he claims that he located the series on Matthew after 388, i.e., 389 onwards, and states that he now assigns it to the years 389 and 390.

no use as a criterion for distinguishing between the two cities. Instead, Montfaucon adduces a passage from *In I Cor. hom. 7*, in which Chrysostom ostensibly refers the audience to a written version of the homilies on John, and in particular to *In Ioh. hom. 50*. Since, as Montfaucon intends to demonstrate, the series on I and II Corinthians were both delivered at Antioch, and since the series on John must have been delivered prior to these, it too must stem from that location. As for the year in which this occurred, since the years 386-388 are excluded and since, as he now postulates, the series on Matthew occupied much of 389 and 390, the series on John can only be located after that period.[312] He prefers, in addition, to posit a *terminus ante quem* of 394 or 395, since there must be room for the homilies on Corinthians to follow. Finally, Montfaucon suggests, as with the series on Matthew, that the homilies on John took more than a year to preach.[313]

i. *Volume IX*

In the ninth volume, Montfaucon presents the series of fifty-five homilies on the book of Acts (CPG 4426) and the thirty-two homilies on the Letter to the Romans (CPG 4427).

That the series on Acts stems in its entirety from Constantinople is beyond question, since in more than one place Chrysostom indicates that he is bishop and occupies the episcopal throne. In the course of *In Acta apost. hom. 44* he further indicates that the homilies were delivered in the third year of his episcopacy, a circumstance which, since his ordination took place on Feb. 26, 398, ought to locate the series in 401. However, as Montfaucon admits, Chrysostom's statements regarding the lapse of time are not always accurate. With this in mind, he points to another piece of evidence which supports the proposed chronology. In *hom. 41* Chrysostom has occasion to mention an earthquake which occurred in the previous year. This could be identified as the quake recorded by Synesius, which is usually dated to 400. However, such occurrences were frequent at Constantinople, and Montfaucon prefers to follow Tillemont, who situated the earthquake in question in 399. Since "the previous year" does not have to mean that a whole year has elapsed, this leads him to locate *hom. 41* either at the end of 400 or in 401. Moreover, on the basis of statements made in the homily which begins the series (*hom. 1*) it can be inferred that it was delivered in the Paschal period, which indicates

---

[312] Montfaucon gives no indication why the series on Matthew necessarily precedes that on John.

[313] Montfaucon, VIII *Praef.*, pp. 2-3.

that Chrysostom began preaching the series on Acts at that point in 400.[314]

Despite Tillemont's indecision on the matter,[315] Montfaucon argues that the provenance of the series on Romans can be determined with equal certainty. Tillemont had found evidence pointing to Antioch in *In Rom. hom. 8*, where Chrysostom speaks of another as "shepherd", and in *hom. 30*, where the city is identified as that in which Paul stayed and was put in chains, but had come across conflicting evidence in *hom. 29*, where Chrysostom says that he himself is a "shepherd". While he commends his colleague's careful scholarship, Montfaucon argues that Tillemont has been overly cautious, since the first two pieces of data are irrefutable, while the significance of the last can be called into question. Members of the ordinary priesthood could be designated shepherd as well as bishops, as Chrysostom indicates in *De Lazaro concio 6*, a homily preached at Antioch. Even though he does not state it explicitly, John implies in this latter sermon that he is himself a shepherd. Moreover, in other Antiochene homilies he deports himself in a way which might be thought to indicate that he is bishop, as, for instance, in *De statuis hom. 20*, where he threatens his audience if they do not exhibit some improvement. It is therefore beyond dispute, claims Montfaucon, that the series was in its entirety preached at Antioch.[316] Concerning the year of its delivery, however, he is unable to say more than that it must belong to the period after 388, since the first three years are too full to accommodate it.[317]

j. *Volume X*

The tenth volume contains the two series on the Letters to the Corinthians (CPG 4428-4429). After stating that many think the first of these to have preceded the second, Montfaucon says that the first stems from Antioch, since in *In I Cor. hom. 21* this is stated explicitly and the fact that the city was the first to be named Christian is mentioned. In the case of the second, he argues that Savile poorly understood the passage in *In II Cor. hom. 26*, in which the burial site of Constantine is mentioned, when he claimed that it clearly showed that the series originated at Con-

---

[314] Montfaucon, IX *Praef.*, vi.

[315] See p. 61 above.

[316] Montfaucon is *a priori* firmly convinced of the homogeneity of the series. Why, he asks (IX 420), would Chrysostom have indicated twice that he was preaching at Antioch, if this was not the case throughout?

[317] Montfaucon, IX 417-420.

stantinople.[318] Taken in context, the passage refers rather to a location other than that at which the homilist is preaching, a circumstance which locates these thirty homilies at Antioch.[319] Montfaucon makes no attempt to define when the two series were delivered.[320]

k. *Volume XI*

In the eleventh volume, Montfaucon presents a number of smaller series, in which Chrysostom exegetes the letters sent by Paul to the Ephesians (CPG 4431), Philippians (CPG 4432), Colossians (CPG 4433) and Thessalonians (CPG 4434-4435), and to his co-workers Timothy (CPG 4436-4437), Titus (CPG 4438) and Philemon (CPG 4439).

In support of the Antiochene provenance of the twenty-four homilies on Ephesians, Montfaucon cites Tillemont's argument that the criticism of those who are dividing the church in *In Eph. hom. 11* cannot have been said about the Christian community at Constantinople, and must therefore refer to the Eustathian schism at Antioch.[321] Another circumstance which proves that the series belongs to that location is the homilist's praise of the lifestyle lived by the monks on the mountains, which is expressed throughout. Chrysostom's response to the monks who lived near Constantinople is one of consistent criticism, while he never uses negative terms when discussing those in the neighbourhood of Antioch. Montfaucon offers no opinion as to when this particular series was delivered.[322]

Where Tillemont had surmised, entirely on the basis of style, that the fifteen homilies on Philippians derived from Constantinople,[323] Montfaucon offers a different argument by which he claims to prove that they belong to that location. In *In Phil. hom. 9* Chrysostom says not only that he sits as judge between the priesthood and the laity, but that he has the status of a "father". This denotes episcopal rank, proving that the homilies were delivered at Constantinople, since at Antioch John was just a

---

[318] See p. 40 above.

[319] Montfaucon, X *Praef.*, iii-vii. With respect to the second series, this was also Tillemont's opinion (see p. 61 above.)

[320] This is in contrast to the opinion expressed by Montfaucon four years earlier (VIII *Praef.*, pp. 2-3; see p. 97 above), where he suggested that the two belong to the latter years at Antioch (394/395 onwards).

[321] See p. 62 above.

[322] Montfaucon, XI *Praef.*, i-ii.

[323] Tillemont had in fact also argued that the reference to the reigning emperor in *In Phil. hom. 15* dated the series to after the troubles of 399 and 400. See p. 64 above.

presbyter. Again, Montfaucon puts forward no opinion as to the year in which this took place.[324]

By contrast, the series of twelve homilies on Colossians provides clear information regarding both its place of origin and date. At the close of *In Col. hom. 3* Chrysostom says that he occupies a throne and that he is bishop, from which it is patent that the series belongs to Constantinople. Further, in the course of *hom. 7* he alludes to the deposition of the eunuch-consul Eutropius. Montfaucon, inferring from John's comments that the person who only yesterday sat on the tribunal was one of the eunuchs, is firm in this identification. Since Eutropius was removed from office and subsequently executed toward the end of 399, it follows that the homilies were preached in that same year. Montfaucon finds supporting evidence in *hom. 2*, where earthquakes of recent occurrence are mentioned. These he associates with an earthquake purported to have taken place in 398.[325] In arguing that both of the series on the Letters to the Thessalonians likewise stem from Constantinople, Montfaucon adduces much the same evidence as Savile and Tillemont before him.[326] In *In I Thess. hom. 8*, Chrysostom says that he is accountable by virtue of his prefecture, such that he of all people cannot avoid being answerable, while in *In II Thess. hom. 4* he identifies himself as "leader". He makes no comment, however, regarding the period at which they were preached.[327]

With regard to defining the provenance of the two series on the Letters to Timothy, Montfaucon confesses that nowhere has he experienced greater difficulty. Dismissing as of no consequence Tillemont's conclusion that they were delivered at Constantinople, since this was based upon the stylistic criterion adduced by Photius, Montfaucon is himself inclined to locate both series at Antioch. Two factors encourage him in this. The first is the praise of monks and their communities which occupies the greater part of *In I Tim. hom. 14*. As not infrequently argued by Montfaucon, such praise never appears in the homilies preached at Constantinople. The second circumstance is the discussion concerning the office of bishop which is prompted by the biblical text. Nowhere in the course of this comment does Chrysostom indicate that he himself occupies such a position, yet he does so elsewhere in cases where far less of an opportunity is provided. However, Montfaucon is careful to stress that

---

[324] Montfaucon, XI 188-189.

[325] Montfaucon, XI 321-322. The earthquake and its date are inferred from a list of portents which Claudian (*In Eutropium* II.24-45) attributes to the year preceding the consulate of Eutropius. See the *Monitum* to the *Novae homiliae*, XII 319.

[326] See pp. 40 and 65 above.

[327] Montfaucon, XI 424.

this is at best an opinion and certainly not to be taken as a definitive judgement. As a consequence of this, no discussion regarding the date of these series is undertaken.[328]

Of the remaining two series presented in this volume, the six homilies on the Letter to Titus were with certainty delivered at Antioch. Montfaucon here agrees with the conclusion reached by Tillemont on the basis of *In Titum hom. 3*, where Chrysostom refers to those Christians who fast with the Jews and who persist in visiting pagan holy places, such as those at Daphne, the cave of Matrona and a site in Cilicia dedicated to Kronos.[329] The first of these practices is characteristic of the Christians at Antioch, while the first two of the sacred sites are to be found in the suburbs of that city. Montfaucon admits that there is some difficulty, however, with *hom. 1*, which contains apparently contradictory evidence. Here John, in the process of addressing those who criticise bishops without real cause, seemingly numbers himself among those who are the object of such criticism. Convinced of the series' Antiochene provenance, Montfaucon dismisses this as the rhetorical assumption by the homilist of another's persona. No discussion as to when the homilies were preached is entered into.[330] In the case of the last series presented, the three homilies on the Letter to Philemon, Montfaucon finds no evidence that suggests either the location or date of their delivery.[331]

1. *Volume XII*

Montfaucon opens the twelfth volume with the last of the series in which Chrysostom exegetes a book of the New Testament (*In Heb. hom. 1-34*: CPG 4440). Although in the preface to these homilies he focuses much of his effort on identifying the Constantius (or Constantine) mentioned in the title to the manuscripts, Montfaucon does claim that the series originates from Constantinople, on the basis of the tone taken toward the end of *In Heb. hom. 4*. Here Chrysostom threatens those who persist in employing pagan mourners at funerals. Such a tone, argues Montfaucon, could only have been taken by one with supreme authority over the priesthood.[332] This conclusion, he continues, is supported by a passage at the close of *hom. 23*, where John identifies himself as "father

---

[328] Montfaucon, XI 546.

[329] See p. 62 above.

[330] Montfaucon, XI 728.

[331] Montfaucon, XI 771. He warns here against accepting a Constantinopolitan provenance for the homilies on the basis of their less polished style.

[332] Cf. Savile (p. 39 above).

of all". As for the point at which they were preached, he adduces the
manuscript title to argue that Chrysostom died not long after their completion.[333]

There then follows a series of eleven homilies published for the first
time (CPG 4441). Montfaucon claims, on the basis of the manuscript titles, that all eleven stem with certainty from Constantinople and were
delivered in the years 398-399. Although he stops short of asserting that
they were delivered in precisely the order in which they are presented in
the manuscript (Ottobonianus gr. 431), he is inclined to believe that this
is probable. The first (CPG 4441.3) was delivered at a martyrium or
Church of the Martyrs situated in Palaia Petra, a location as yet unidentified. The point at which it was preached is indicated shortly after the
opening, when it is said that not yet thirty days have passed since a terrible earthquake. Montfaucon identifies the tremor as one of those which
occurred in 398, preceding the consulate of Eutropius.[334] This leads him
to state that all eleven of the homilies were with certainty delivered during the period prior to the consulate of Eutropius and before his deposition, which occurred circa August 399.[335] The second (CPG 4441.1)
records the translation of a martyr's remains from the Great Church to a
martyrium of St Thomas in Drypia, at which location the homily was delivered. The third (CPG 4441.2) was preached likewise at the martyrium
of St Thomas, on the following day. The fourth (CPG 4441.4) was delivered in the Church of St Anastasia, while the Church of Eirene is the location of the fifth (CPG 4441.5). The sixth (CPG 4441.6) was delivered in
the Church of the Apostles on the anniversary of the death of the emperor Theodosius, after two other bishops had preached. Since Theodosius died on Jan. 17, Montfaucon locates the homily on Jan. 17, 399.[336]

At this point Montfaucon refers to *Contra ludos et theatra* (CPG
4441.7), which is presented following CPG 4441.6 in his manuscript
(Ottob. gr. 431). He is here obliged to reiterate his conclusions regarding
its date,[337] since in the title to the ninth of the *Novae homiliae* (CPG
4441.10) and within the ninth homily itself, clear reference is made to
this sermon.[338] Following this digression he returns to the collection of
eleven homilies. The seventh (CPG 4441.8) was preached in St Anastasia.

---

[333] Montfaucon, XII *Praef.*, iii-v. He makes no attempt to address the interval of three
years between the point at which Chrysostom was sent permanently into exile (June 404)
and his death (407).

[334] See n. 325 above.

[335] Montfaucon, XII 319.

[336] Montfaucon, XII 319-320.

[337] See p. 95 above.

[338] Montfaucon, XII 321.

Montfaucon infers that it belongs to the week following Easter from the titles to the homilies which surround it. The eighth (CPG 4441.9) was delivered in the Church of St Paul in front of a congregation of orthodox Goths, after a Gothic presbyter had preached. Again Montfaucon locates it within the week following Easter, on the basis of the title to the ninth homily. The ninth homily (CPG 4441.10) was itself delivered in the Great Church on the second Sunday after Easter. In the course of that homily Chrysostom indicates that on the previous Sunday a bishop from Galatia preached at the Great Church in his place. He also refers back to the subject matter of the homily *Contra ludos et theatra*. The tenth homily (CPG 4441.11) was delivered in the church of the Apostle, after a certain elderly bishop had preached. Montfaucon asserts that the eleventh and final homily (CPG 4441.13) was delivered on the feast day of the Maccabees, again after an elderly person had preached.[339]

m. *Summary*

A summary of the conclusions reached by Montfaucon with respect to the provenance and date of the homilies is presented in the form of two tables, one recording location and the other the chronology which he developed. This is followed by a list of the various sequences established, in addition to those clearly indicated in sections a-l.

Table 3.a. Provenance — Montfaucon

CPG no.	Antioch	CPG no.	Constantinople
4317	*Cum presbyter* (I 436)	4324	*Contra Anomoeos hom. 11* (I 540)
4318	*De incompr. dei natura hom. 1-5* (I 443)	4325	*De Christi divinitate* (I 540)
4319	*De beato Philogonio* (I 492)	4364	*De s. Phoca* (II 703)
4320	*De consubstantiali* (I 492)	4370	*In paralyticum demissum per tectum* (III 32)
4321	*De petitione matris fil. Zeb.* (I 492)	4375	*In illud: Si esurierit inimicus* (III 156)
4322	*In quatriduanum Lazarum* (I 523)	4377	*In illud: Propter fornicat. uxorem* (III 192)
4323	*De Christi precibus* (I 523)	4378	*De libello repudii* (III 192)
4327	*Adv. Iudaeos or. 1-8* (I 584ff)	4379	*Quales ducendae sint uxores* (III 192)
4328	*In kalendas* (I 696f)	4392	*In Eutropium* (III 379f)

[339] Montfaucon, XII 321-322.

4329	De Lazaro conciones 1-7 (I 707)	4393	Cum Saturninus et Aurelianus (III 404f)
4330	De statuis hom. 1-21 (II Praef.)	4394	De regressu (III 410)
4332	De diabolo tentatore hom. 1-3 (II 245f)	4395	De recipiendo Severiano (III 410)
4333	De paenitentia hom. 1-5 (II 278)	4396	Antequam iret in exsilium (III 414)
4334	In diem natalem (II 352)	4397	Cum iret in exsilium (III 421)
4335	De baptismo Christi (II 367)	4398	Post reditum a priore exsilio 1 (III 423f)
4336	De prod. Iudae hom. 1-2 (II 375f)	4399	Post reditum a priore exsilio 2 (III 424)
4337	De coemeterio et de cruce (II 396f)	4414	In illud: Ne timueritis cum dives hom. 1-2 (V 503f)
4338	De cruce et latrone hom. 1* (II 403)	4417	In illud: Vidi dominum hom. 4 (VI 94)
4339	De cruce et latrone hom. 2* (II 411)	4426	In Acta apost. hom. 1-55 (IX Praef., vi)
4340	De resurrectione mortuorum (II 421f)	4432	In Phil. hom. 1-15 (XI 188f)
4341	De resurrectione (II 437)	4433	In Col. hom. 1-12 (XI 321)
4342	In ascensionem (II 446)	4434	In I Thess. hom. 1-11 (XI 424)
4343	De sancta pentecoste hom. 1 (II 456f)	4435	In II Thess. hom. 1-5 (XI 424)
4344	De laud. s. Pauli hom. 1-7 (I 696f, II 474f)	4440	In Heb. hom. 1-34 (XII Praef., v)
4345	De s. Meletio (II 517)	4441.1	Hom. dicta post. reliq. martyrum (XII 319f)
4346	In s. Lucianum (II 523)	4441.2	Hom. dicta praesente imperatore (XII 319f)
4347	De s. hieromartyre Babyla (II 529)	4441.3	Quod frequenter conveniendum sit (XII 319)
4349	In Iuventinum et Maximum (II 578)	4441.4	Adv. eos qui non adfuerant (XII 319f)
4350	De s. Pelagia (II 584)	4441.5	De studio praesentium (XII 319f)
4351	In s. Ignatium (II 592)	4441.6	Adversus catharos (XII 319f)
4352	In s. Eustathium (II 601f)	4441.7	Contra ludos et theatra (VI 271)
4353	In s. Romanum (II 610)	4441.8	Dicta in templo s. Anastasiae (XII 319ff)
4354	De Macabeis hom. 1-3 (II 622)	4441.9	Habita postquam presb. Gothus (XII 319ff)
4355	De ss. Bernice et Prosdoce (II 633f)	4441.10	In illud: Pater meus usque modo (XII 319ff)
4356	In quatrid. Lazarum (II 646)	4441.11	In illud: Messis quidem multa (XII 319ff)
4357	De ss. martyribus (II 649f)	4441.13	De Eleazaro et septem pueris (XII 319ff)
4358	Non esse ad gratiam conc. (II 650)	4528	De capto Eutropio (III 379f)
4359	Hom. in martyres (II 667)	4529	De Chananaea (III 431f)
4360	In s. Iulianum (II 670f)		
4361	In s. Barlaam (II 681)		
4362	De s. Droside (II 688)		
4366	De terrae motu (II 717)		
4368	De decem mill. tal. deb. (III Admon.)		
4369	In illud: Pater si possibile est (III 15)		

4371	*In princ. Act. hom. 1-4* (III 47ff)		
4372	*De mutatione nom. hom. 1-4* (III 96f)		
4376	*In illud: Sal. Prisc. et Aqu. serm. 1-2* (III 171f)		
4380	*In d. Pauli: Nolo vos ignorare* (III 228)		
4382	*De eleemosyna* (III 248)		
4383	*In illud: Hab. eund. spir. hom. 1-3* (III 259f)		
4385	*De profectu evangelii* (III 300)		
4386	*In illud: Vidua eligatur* (III 311)		
4388	*De futurae vitae deliciis* (III 337)		
4391	*In illud: Faciem ei restiti* (VI 157)		
4406	*Laus Diodori episcopi* (III 746f)		
4409	*Hom. 1-67 in Genesim* (IV *Praef.*, pp. 1ff)		
4410	*Sermones 1-9 in Gen.* (III 96f, IV 644)		
4411	*De Anna sermones 1-5* (III 697)		
4412	*De Davide et Saule hom. 1-3* (IV 747)		
4413	*Expositiones in psalmos* (IV *Praef.*, 128f)		
4415	*In psalmum 145* (V 534)*		
4417	*In illud: Vidi dom. hom. 2,3,5,6* (VI 93f)		
4419	*In illud: Dom., non est in hom.* (VI 157)		
4420	*De proph. obscuritate hom. 1-2* (II 245)		
4423	*In illud: Hoc scitote* (VI 278)*		
4424	*In Matt. hom. 1-90* (VII *Praef.*, 1f)		
4425	*In Ioh. hom. 1-88* (VIII *Praef.*, 2)		
4427	*In Rom. hom. 1-32* (IX 417ff)		
4428	*In I Cor. hom. 1-44* (X *Praef.*, iv)		
4429	*In II Cor. hom. 1-30* (X *Praef.* vi f)		
4431	*In Eph. hom. 1-24* (XI *Praef.*, i-ii)		
4436	*In I Tim. hom. 1-18** (XI 546)		
4437	*In II Tim. hom. 1-10** (XI 546)		
4438	*In Titum hom. 1-6* (XI 728)		
4441. 12	*In illud: Filius ex se nihil facit* (VI 254)		
4460	*Ad illuminandos cat. 1* (II 224f)		
4464	*Ad illuminandos cat. 2* (II 225)		

* Possibly.

Table 3.b. Chronology — Montfaucon

Year (month-season)	Homily	Cited (Vol., col.)
386		
beginning	*Cum presbyter fuit ordinatus* (CPG 4317)	I 436
early Lent	*Sermones 1-8 in Genesim* (CPG 4410)	IV 644
(Aug. or earlier) date unspecified	*De incompr. dei natura hom. 1* (CPG 4318)	I 584
Aug.	*Adv. Iudaeos or. 1* (CPG 4327)	I 584
beg. September	*Adv. Iudaeos or. 2*	"
end of September	*De incompr. dei nat. hom. 2*	I 584f
date unspecified	*De incompr. dei nat. hom. 3*	I 443, 584f
	De anathemate (CPG 3430)	I 691
	De incompr. dei nat. hom. 4	I 443, 584f
	Adv. Iudaeos or. 3	"
	De incompr. dei nat. hom. 5	III 300
Dec. 20	*De beato Philogonio* (CPG 4319)	I 492
Dec. 25	*In diem natalem* (CPG 4334)	I 585
after Dec. 25	*De profectu evangelii* (CPG 4385)	III 300
387		
Jan. 5	*De consubstantiali* (CPG 4320)	I 492
Jan. 6	*De petitione matris fil. Zeb.* (CPG 4321)	I 492
	De baptismo Christi (CPG 4335)	II 367
Jan. 7	*In s. Lucianum* (CPG 4346)	II 523
early#	*In quatriduanum Lazarum* (CPG 4322)	I 523
	De Christi precibus (CPG 4323)	"
	De resurr. mortuorum (CPG 4340)	II 421f
before Lent	*De statuis hom. 1-2* (CPG 4330)	II *Praef.*
Lent	*De statuis hom. 3-18,20*	"
	Ad illuminandos cat. 1-2 (CPG 4460, 4464)	II 224-225
Easter Sunday	*De statuis hom. 21*	"
date unspecified	*De decem mill. tal. debitore* (CPG 4368)	III *Admon.*
Sunday before Ascension	*De statuis hom. 19*	IV *Praef.*, 8-12; IV 697ff
Monday before Ascen. - after Pentecost	*De Anna sermones 1-5* (CPG 4411)	IV *Praef.*, 8-12; IV 697ff
c. September	*Adv. Iudaeos or. 4-7*	I 586, IV 128f
after September	*Expos. in ps. 41* (CPG 4413.2)	IV 128f
	Adv. Iudaeos or. 8	"
date unspecified	*De Davide et Saule hom. 1-3* (CPG 4412)	IV 747
388*		
389		
	Series on Matthew (CPG 4424)	VIII *Praef.*, 2-3
390		
	Remainder of series on Matthew	VIII *Praef.*, 2-3
391		
392		
March 26	*De coemeterio et de cruce* (CPG 4337)	II 396f
April 14	*De ss. Bernice et Prosdoce* (CPG 4355)	II 396f, 633f
393		
394		

395		
396		
397		
398		
date unspecified	*Contra Anomoeos hom. 11* (CPG 4324)	I 540
	De Christi divinitate (CPG 4325)	"
	In paralyticum dim. per tectum (CPG 4370)	III 32
	Quod frequenter conven. sit (CPG 4441.3)	XII 319
399		
Jan. 17	*Adversus catharos* (CPG 4441.6)	XII 320
Easter Sunday / c. June	*Contra ludos et theatra* (CPG 4441.7)	VI 271f; VI *Praef.*, 3-4
Paschal week	*Dicta in templo s. Anastasiae* (CPG 4441.8)	XII 321
	Habita postquam presb. Gothus (CPG 4441.9)	XII 321f
second Sunday after Easter	*In illud: Pater meus usque modo operatur* (CPG 4441.10)	XII 322
(c. Aug. -) date unspecified	*In Eutropium* (CPG 4392)	III 379f
	De capto Eutropio (CPG 4528)	"
	In Col. hom. 1-12 (CPG 4433)	XI 321f
400		
early	*Cum Saturninus et Aurelianus* (CPG 4393)	III 404f
after Easter	Most of series on Acts (CPG 4426)	IX *Praef.*, vi
date unspecified	*In illud: Ne tim. cum dives hom. 2* (CPG 4414)	V 503f.
401		
after Easter	*De regressu* (CPG 4394)	III *Praef.*, 3
	De recipiendo Severiano (CPG 4395)	"
date unspecified	Remainder of series on Acts	IX *Praef.*, vi
402		
403		
date unspecified	*Antequam iret in exsilium* (CPG 4396)	III *Praef.*, 3-4
	Cum iret in exsilium (CPG 4397)	"
	Post reditum a priore exsilio 1 (CPG 4398)	"
	Post reditum a priore exsilio 2 (CPG 4399)	"
	De Chananaea (CPG 4529)	III 431f
404		

\# *Terminus ante quem* for *De s. Meletio* (CPG 4345; II 517 [after May 386-beginning 387]) * See Sequence D below.

Sequence A. (386) *De incompr. dei nat. hom. 1* (CPG 4318); (August) *Adv. Iud. or. 1* (CPG 4327); (beginning of September) *Adv. Iud. or. 2*; (end of September) *De incompr. dei nat. hom. 2*.

Sequence B. One of *De laudibus s. Pauli hom. 1-7* (CPG 4344); (Jan. 1) *In kalendas* (CPG 4328); (Jan. 2) *De Lazaro concio 1* (CPG 4329); *De Lazaro conc. 2-3*; (Jan. 24) *De s. Babyla* (CPG 4347); (a few days later) *In Iuventinum et Maximum* (CPG 4349); *De Lazaro conc. 4-5*; (not long after) *In illud: Vidua eligatur* (CPG 4386); *De Lazaro concio 7*.

Sequence C. *De proph. obsc. hom. 1* (CPG 4420); (a few days later, Sunday) *De proph. obsc. hom. 2*; (a few days later) *De diabolo tent. hom. 1* (CPG 4332).

Sequence D. (Antioch, not 386/387; prob. 388) (before Lent) *In illud: Vidi dom. hom. 2, 3, 5, 6* (CPG 4417); (Lent) *Hom. 1-32 in Gen.* (CPG 4409); (Maundy Thursday) *De prod. Iudae hom. 2* (CPG 4336); (Good Friday) one of *De cruce et latrone hom. 1-2* (CPG 4338-4339);[340] (Easter Sunday) *De resurrectione* (CPG 4341); *In princ. Act. hom. 1-4* (CPG 4371); *De mutatione nom. hom. 1-2* (CPG 4372); *Sermo 9 in Gen.* (CPG 4410); *De mutatione nom. hom. 3-4*; *Hom. 33-67 in Gen.*

Sequence E. *In illud: In faciem ei restiti* (CPG 4391); *In s. Eustathium* (CPG 4352); *In S. Romanum* (CPG 4353); *In illud: Domine, non est in homine* (CPG 4419).

Sequence F. A homily on Lazarus (unidentified); *De Macabeis hom. 1-3*(CPG 4354); *De ss. martyribus* (CPG 4357); *Non esse ad gratiam concionandum* (CPG 4358).

Sequence G. (summer) *In s. Barlaam* (CPG 4361); (next day) *In d. Pauli: Nolo vos ignorare* (CPG 4380).

Sequence H. *Peccata fratrum non evulganda* (CPG 4389); (next day) *Non esse desperandum* (CPG 4390).

3. STILTING

As with his immediate predecessors, Stilting's interest in the corpus lies with its chronology, a fact which he makes clear as he begins to discuss the homilies. Pointing out that Tillemont and Montfaucon differ considerably on the issue of when they were preached, he concludes that a careful and unbiased assessment of these scholars' arguments is due, as is also a thorough re-investigation of the homilies to see whether further chronological indicators might not be brought to light.[341] A direct consequence of his approach is the full integration into the chronological schema of a number of the sequences established by Montfaucon. Considered side by side with that of Tillemont and Montfaucon, Stilting's contribution to the field is of at least equal importance, not only for its assessment of the validity of their claims, but also since in a number of places he proposes a point of view which is substantially new. From this perspective, the failure of his schema to vie successfully with that of Montfaucon in influencing later generations of scholars is particularly noticeable. The extent to which Stilting's opinion is overlooked or disregarded in the subsequent literature will become apparent as we begin to examine Phases Three and Four.

---

[340] This is stated explicitly in the *Monitum* to *In princ. Actorum*, Montfaucon, III 49.

[341] Stilting, *Acta SS. Sept.*, IV 449.

Although Stilting's interest in the homilies is primarily chronological, his presentation falls into two parts along geographic lines, the first part detailing the material which stems from Antioch, the second the items which belong to Constantinople. This division has been observed below. Also, since his approach is to consider first the arguments put forward by Tillemont and Montfaucon and then to offer his own opinion, in instances where he concurs with both and reiterates their arguments in support the reader is referred in the footnotes to the relevant sub-sections of 2.1 and 2.2, respectively. Discussion here is reserved for cases where his arguments differ substantially from those of his predecessors. Certain individual homilies receive only passing reference in the body of the text or in the chronological summary provided by Stilting at the close of his article.[342] In these instances his opinion regarding the provenance or date of the homily is recorded only in the relevant table or tables in section c below.

a. *Antioch*

Stilting approaches his task by first running through those homilies whose date is more or less well established. With regard to the homilies preached in the first year of Chrysostom's presbyterate, Stilting accepts the opinion of both Tillemont and Montfaucon that *Sermones 1-8 in Genesim* (CPG 4410) are to be numbered among the first, on the basis of the homilist's comments early in *Sermo 2*.[343] He further states that *Sermo 1* was preached on the first day of Lent, while the remaining seven were delivered in close succession.[344] Concerning the homily *De s. Meletio* (CPG 4345), Stilting accepts the opinion of Tillemont against that of Montfaucon,[345] locating it on the anniversary of Meletius' death in May 386.[346] He then establishes the following sequence with respect to the homilies *De incompr. dei natura* (CPG 4318), *Adv. Iudaeos* (CPG 4327) and others:

> (386: Sunday) *De incompr. dei nat. hom. 1*; (following Sunday, late August/early September) *Adv. Iud. or. 1*; (September, ten or more days later) *Adv. Iud. or. 2*;[347] (November onwards) *De incompr. dei nat. hom. 2-5*; (two other

---

[342] Stilting, *Acta SS. Sept.*, IV 695-700.

[343] See Tillemont (pp. 50f above) and Montfaucon (p. 90 above).

[344] Stilting, *Acta SS. Sept.*, IV 449-450.

[345] See Tillemont (p. 51 above) and Montfaucon (p. 80 above).

[346] Stilting, *Acta SS. Sept.*, IV 450.

[347] Although this is not stated, Stilting here differs from Montfaucon (see pp. 73f and 106 above), who assigned *Adv. Iud. or. 3* to the same period.

homilies, to be identified); (Dec. 20) *De b. Philogonio* (CPG 4319); (five days later) *In diem natalem* (CPG 4334).[348]

Stilting then argues that Chrysostom resumed his polemic against the Anomoeans (CPG 4320-4323) not on Jan. 3 or Jan. 5, 387, as Tillemont and Montfaucon had proposed,[349] but in February of that year. Both had assigned the homily *De consubstantiali* (CPG 4320) to early January on the basis of Chrysostom's comment that attendance figures were down due to the concurrent secular games. Stilting points out that the identification of these games with the festivities associated with the kalends is without foundation, particularly since, on the basis of the source used by Tillemont, it is difficult to make a distinction between "circuses" and "games", while games in general were of frequent occurrence. However, from internal comment it is clear that the homily was not delivered so long after the last of the series *De incompr. dei natura* that the homilist's remarks had faded from memory. Moreover, just because at the opening to *De petitione matris fil. Zeb.* (CPG 4321) there is mention of a homily against heretics of the previous day, it does not necessarily follow, as Montfaucon had proposed, that that sermon was delivered on the day following *De consubstantiali*. Rather, Stilting points out, when John summarises the contents of the latter in the former, he does not use the term "yesterday" but "recent". He is therefore led to conclude that another homily intervened. He finds a possible candidate in *In illud: Filius ex se nihil facit* (CPG 4441.12),[350] likewise preached against the Anomoeans, in which the homilist refers to John 5.17 as a verse on which he preached at the previous synaxis. That same verse is one of several mentioned in *De consubstantiali*. While this does not prove that the latter was the sermon preached at that synaxis, it does suggest to Stilting that *In illud: Filius ex se nihil facit* belongs among the homilies preached in February 387.[351] Two further sermons against the Anomoeans (CPG 4322-4323) follow *De petitione matris fil. Zeb.* At the opening to the second (*De Christi precibus*) Chrysostom indicates that it was preached more than a few days after the rest, although later in the homily he recalls the substance of *De consubstantiali*, which he designates as recent. This leads

---

[348] Stilting, *Acta SS. Sept.*, IV 450-452.

[349] See pp. 52 and 72 above.

[350] It should be borne in mind here that it was only in the late 1800s (see pp. 157f below) that it was suggested that this homily belonged with the eleven *Novae homiliae* (CPG 4441), and only with the rediscovery of Stavronikita 6 in the 1950s that this suspicion was confirmed. See further Wenger, "La tradition des oeuvres", 32-40.

[351] Stilting considers that this cluster cannot have been delivered before February because of the large number of homilies which he later assigns to January of this year.

Stilting to locate CPG 4323 after the middle of February, but before the beginning of Lent.[352]

Following this discussion, Stilting turns to investigate the year and period to which the third of the discourses *Adv. Iudaeos* belongs. As he points out, Montfaucon had located *Adv. Iud. or. 3*, along with *or. 1-2*, in or just after September 386.[353] Stilting is inclined, however, to favour Tillemont's proposal that it belongs to the period before Lent in 387.[354] Since he finds that both scholars have failed to consider the contents of the homily properly, he undertakes to do so at some length. The title itself, he argues, has also been misunderstood. Rather than alluding to those Christians who celebrated Easter later and were therefore still fasting at the time that the rest had ceased, which had been the opinion of Tillemont, Stilting takes it to refer to the Quartodecimans, who in fact began the fast too soon. This is borne out by the contents of the homily. Moreover, within the course of the homily Chrysostom mentions that in the year in question (387) the Jewish Passover fell on a Sunday, precisely seven days before the celebration of Easter by the orthodox Christians at Antioch. Since both groups of Christians observed a forty day fast, it follows that in that year the beginning of the fast among the Quartodecimans preceded that of the orthodox Christians by as many days. Further, at the opening to the homily Chrysostom states that it has been necessary to interrupt his discourses against the Anomoeans a second time. Stilting cannot see why Montfaucon should think this matter would be urgent in the month of September. It would rather be particularly pressing, he finds, around the end of February or beginning of March,[355] when the Quartodecimans were beginning their fast. This leads him to conclude that the homily must have been delivered in 387, at least eight days before the beginning of Lent.[356]

Regarding the date of the remaining five homilies *Adv. Iudaeos* (*or. 4-8*), however, Stilting is in agreement with Montfaucon. They were all delivered in the vicinity of September 387. In *or. 4*, John says that he is again broaching the topic of those who fast with the Jews, while in *or. 6* it is made clear that it cannot have been delivered before 387, since Chrysostom has occasion to mention the overturning of the imperial

---

[352] Stilting, *Acta SS. Sept.*, IV 452-453.

[353] See pp. 73f above.

[354] See p. 52 above.

[355] Stilting, *Acta SS. Sept.*, IV 456, posits that the Antiochenes observed a six week Lent. He further bases his calculations upon Easter falling in 387 on April 25.

[356] Stilting, *Acta SS. Sept.*, IV 453-456. As a final argument against locating *or. 3* in September 386, Stilting adds (p. 455) that in the course of the homily Chrysostom recalls numerous sermons preached on the topic of Judaizing Christians in much the same way as he does in *In diem natalem*, i.e., not as recent, but as remote.

states, an event which took place before Lent in that year. At the close
of this same homily he indicates that he is preaching at the time of the
Jewish fast. *Or. 7* was delivered not much later, since at the beginning
John indicates that it was delivered around or possibly even on the day of
the Feast of the Tabernacles, while *or. 8* was preached after the festivals
of the Jews were over. It is clear, moreover, that all five belong together
and were delivered in sequence. Stilting cannot agree with Montfaucon,
however, that they occupy an interval of less than twenty days. Since the
Festival of the Trumpets (the Jewish New Year) and the Feast of the Tabernacles fell fourteen days apart, while fasting began before the first of
these, *or. 4* cannot have been delivered less than ten days before that
feast. Moreover, the last of the five homilies (*or. 8*) was preached after
the Feast of the Tabernacles was over. By this calculation, Stilting establishes a span of at least thirty days, leading him to state that this second
sequence of homilies *Adv. Iudaeos* was begun in September and completed around or after the middle of the following month.[357]

Stilting then moves to examine a number of homilies which, by virtue
of their connection to sermons whose delivery in the later months of 386
and early part of 387 has already been established, can be located also in
that time period. The first of these is *De anathemate* (CPG 3430), a homily now not considered to constitute part of the genuine corpus.[358] Although Tillemont had raised doubts about its authenticity,[359] Stilting affirms its status, citing Montfaucon in support.[360] On the same grounds as
the latter, he locates it following the third of the homilies *De incompr. dei
natura* (CPG 4318), which leads him to conclude that it was delivered at
the end of November or beginning of December 386.[361] On the basis that
In diem natalem (CPG 4334) was patently delivered on Dec. 25 and followed the sermon on Philogonius (CPG 4319), Stilting now formally assigns the Christmas homily to Dec. 25, 386.[362] To the period between
Christmas of that year and the beginning of 387 he assigns the sermon
De profectu evangelii (CPG 4385), citing the connection with *De incompr.
dei nat. hom. 5* observed by Montfaucon.[363] He also follows Montfaucon's

---

[357] Stilting, *Acta SS. Sept.*, IV 456-457.

[358] See n. 192

[359] See Tillemont, *Mémoires*, XI 363.

[360] See Montfaucon, I 691.

[361] Stilting, *Acta SS. Sept.*, IV 457. For his refutation of the arguments put forward by
Tillemont against its authenticity see sections 274-275 of Paragraph XXI (pp. 457-458).

[362] Stilting, *Acta SS. Sept.*, IV 458.

[363] See p. 87 above.

argument that the homilies *De incompr. dei nat. hom. 5, De b. Philogonio* and *In diem natalem* form an uninterrupted sequence.[364]

Stilting departs from the view held by Montfaucon, however, when he identifies *De profectu evangelii* as the recent encomium on St Paul to which John refers at the beginning of *In kalendas* (CPG 4328).[365] The establishment of this connection encourages him to locate the latter on Jan. 1, 387. Aside from the fact that it was delivered at the right time of year, Stilting argues that *De profectu evangelii* contains by far the most extensive praise of St Paul undertaken by Chrysostom, such that it outclasses any of the encomia on St Paul (CPG 4344) in this respect. It is certainly, he finds, a more likely candidate than *Quales ducendae sint uxores* (CPG 4379), the homily which Tillemont had proposed.[366] Against Montfaucon, he further argues that nowhere in *In kalendas* is it stated that the recent homily was devoted exclusively to the praise of St Paul, while in any case there was no festival dedicated to St Paul celebrated at that time of year.[367] The sermon *In kalendas* had itself been linked by Montfaucon to a number of other homilies.[368] Stilting now confirms that sequence, interleaving its components among the homilies already assigned to the earlier months of 387:[369]

(Jan. 1) *In kalendas*; (Jan. 2) *De Lazaro concio 1* (CPG 4329); (Jan. 6) *De baptismo Christi* (CPG 4335); (Jan. 7) *In s. Lucianum* (CPG 4346);[370] *De Lazaro concio 2*; *De Lazaro concio 3*; (Jan. 24) *De s. Babyla* (CPG 4347); (January, a few days later) *In Iuventinum et Maximum* (CPG 4349); *De Lazaro con-*

---

[364] Stilting, *Acta SS. Sept.*, IV 458 (sec. 278).

[365] Montfaucon had identified the encomium as one of the seven homilies *De laudibus s. Pauli* (CPG 4344). See p. 74 above. This view becomes the consensus in the subsequent literature. See pp. 142 and 235 below.

[366] Stilting here makes the mistake of confusing *De profectu evangelii* (*t. 5 h. 28* in the Morel edition) with the homily which follows (*Quales ducendae sint uxores*: *t. 5 h. 29*). It is the first, not the second, which Tillemont (see p. 51 above) had located toward the end of 386, preceding *In kalendas*. Although the error obscures the fact, Stilting's argument at this point is firmly based upon the latter scholar's opinion.

[367] Stilting, *Acta SS. Sept.*, IV 458-459. Although the view of Montfaucon prevails, nowhere in the subsequent literature are the arguments put forward by Stilting against this taken into consideration or addressed.

[368] See Sequence B, p. 107 above.

[369] In situating this sequence early in 387 he follows Tillemont (see p. 51 above).

[370] In assigning CPG 4335 and CPG 4346 to 387, Stilting, *Acta SS. Sept.*, IV 460, concurs with the arguments put forward by both Montfaucon (see p. 80 above) and Tillemont (pp. 51f above).

cio 4; (just before February) *De Lazaro concio 5*;[371] (February) various homilies *Contra Anomoeos* (see Table 4.b below).

To the month of February he adds *De resurr. mortuorum* (CPG 4340),
which he considers to have been delivered after two or more of the
homilies *Contra Anomoeos* (CPG 4320-4323).[372] In this respect he agrees
in essence with Montfaucon, who had assigned the homily to early
387.[373] To this same period he assigns, with Tillemont,[374] the sermon *In
illud: Vidua eligatur* (CPG 4386), re-affirming that it was delivered not
long after *De Lazaro concio 5*.[375] He also locates in the month of February
the remaining homilies in the sequence associated with *In kalendas*,
namely *De Lazaro conciones 6-7*, since they appear to have been preached
at a time when the earlier homilies *De Lazaro* were still fresh in the
minds of the citizens at Antioch. Stilting further identifies the earthquake
mentioned in *De Lazaro concio 6* as the tremor to which reference is
made in *De statuis hom. 3* (CPG 4330), a sermon delivered at the beginning of Lent in 387.[376]

In order to complete the list of homilies preached in Chrysostom's
first year as presbyter, Stilting then goes back to 386. With respect to
hom. 2, 3, 5 and *6 In illud: Vidi dominum* (CPG 4417),[377] he sides with the
opinion of Tillemont,[378] rejecting Montfaucon's criticism of the latter's
argument.[379] As Stilting points out, aside from the fact that the recent
sermon mentioned in *hom. 2* is clearly identifiable as *Cum presbyter fuit
ordinatus* (CPG 4317), Chrysostom alludes directly in the sermon to his
ordination (ὅτε ... διαλεχθῆναι κατηξιώθημεν: "when we were appointed to
the office of preaching"). This allusion Stilting finds reinforced towards
the end of the same homily, when John draws a comparison between the
quality of his own preaching and a wine just drawn from the press. As for

---

[371] Stilting, *Acta SS. Sept.*, IV 459-461.

[372] Stilting, *Acta SS. Sept.*, IV 461 (sec. 290).

[373] See p. 79 above.

[374] See p. 52 above.

[375] Stilting, *Acta SS. Sept.*, IV 461 (sec. 291). This connection had also been noted by
Montfaucon (see p. 87 and Sequence B, p. 107 above).

[376] Stilting, *Acta SS. Sept.*, IV 461 (sec. 292-293).

[377] Stilting, *Acta SS. Sept.*, IV 463, agrees with both Tillemont and Montfaucon that it
is only these four which form a series. For his response to the doubts raised by Tillemont
with respect to the coherence between *hom. 2-3* and *5-6*, see p. 463 (sec. 302).

[378] See p. 50 above.

[379] Montfaucon (see pp. 93f above) links the homilies rather to the sequence
incorporating the larger series on Genesis (CPG 4409). See Sequence D, p. 108 above. It is
this view which becomes the status quo. See, e.g., pp. 140, 165 and 174 below. Dumortier
(see p. 234 below), who essentially follows the view expressed by Tillemont, is a recent
exception.

Montfaucon's objection that the homilist's stated intention to speak later on the topic of biblical names that underwent change necessarily indicates that *hom. 2* was delivered in the same year as the sermons *De mutatione nominum* (CPG 4372), Stilting finds this of little consequence. The comment could have been made simply because Chrysostom intended to preach on the book of Genesis that Lent, as he indeed set out to do. Stilting is therefore led to conclude that the series was preached early in 386 and before Lent, as indicated in the last of the four (*hom. 6*). Calculating that the latter was delivered on the day before Lent and that in 386 Easter fell on April 5, while Lent lasted for six weeks, it can be determined that the four homilies (*hom. 2, 3, 5, 6*) occupied much of February, with the last being preached on Sunday, Feb. 22.[380]

In the case of the two homilies *De obscuritate prophetiarum* (CPG 4420) and the three *De diabolo tentatore* (CPG 4332), Montfaucon had noted the connection between *De diabolo tent. hom. 1* and *De proph. obsc. hom. 2*, while he had expressed some hesitation regarding whether the second and third homily *De diabolo tentatore* formed a sequence with the first.[381] In the belief that all five constitute an uninterrupted sequence,[382] Stilting now assigns them to Lent of 386.[383] That they belong to John's first year as preacher he construes from the opening comments of *De proph. obsc. hom. 1*, where Chrysostom compares both himself and the audience to inexperienced sailors. He finds further expressions of hesitation and modesty on the part of the homilist in *De proph. obsc. hom. 2*.[384] Regarding the early delivery of these homilies, their subject matter is also persuasive. In the first Chrysostom preaches at length against the Jews and to some extent against the Anomoeans, in neither instance indicating any previous discussion of these subjects. Moreover, in the eight sermons on Genesis (CPG 4410), delivered at the beginning of Lent in 386, he had preached against the Manichaeans, a polemic which is a feature of *De*

---

[380] Stilting, *Acta SS. Sept.*, IV 462-463.

[381] See Sequence C (p. 107 above) and pp. 76f and 94 above.

[382] Stilting, *Acta SS. Sept.*, IV 464, argues that the order in which Montfaucon presents the three homilies *De diabolo tent.* is incorrect. He considers them to have been delivered in the following sequence: *De diabolo tent. hom. 1*; (two days later) *hom. 3*; (two days later) *hom. 2*, on the basis that *hom. 2* contains clear reference to both *hom. 1* and *3*. Rauschen (see p. 141 below), the only scholar subsequently to discuss this sequence, draws upon both Tillemont and Montfaucon but makes no mention of Stilting.

[383] Stilting accepts as tacit Montfaucon's proofs that the homilies were delivered at Antioch.

[384] Stilting, *Acta SS. Sept.*, IV 463 (close of sec. 303), argues that expressions of modesty are a characteristic feature of the homilies delivered during Chrysostom's first year as presbyter, whereas his sermons of later years exhibit an increasing sense of authority. This thesis resurfaces several times in the ensuing literature. See, e.g., Rauschen (p. 135 below) and Bonsdorff (pp. 173, 184).

proph. obsc. hom. 1-2 also. Since *De diabolo tent. hom. 3*, which concludes the sequence, was delivered on a day on which instruction was
given to the catechumens, the sequence as a whole is to be located in
Lent.[385]

Regarding the homily *In illud: Hoc scitote quod in novissimis diebus*
(CPG 4423), Montfaucon had cautiously stated that it might have been
delivered at Antioch, since at the beginning John alludes to his inexperi-
ence at preaching.[386] Stilting takes this several steps further, claiming
that the homily was not only delivered at Antioch, but belongs firmly to
386, both on the ground already mentioned by Montfaucon and because
of the audience's alacrity. Stilting argues that not only are claims of in-
experience absent from the later homilies, but so also are generous
words of praise for the audience's attentiveness. Since in this sermon
Chrysostom mentions that he has returned to preaching after a lengthy
illness, that prolonged bout of ill-health can then be taken to account for
the vacuum in the chronology for the months from Easter to August
386.[387]

From his investigation of the first year of preaching at Antioch, Stilting then turns to Lent 387, the period occupied by the twenty-one homilies *De statuis* (CPG 4330).[388] His main concern here is to confirm Tillemont's opinion,[389] against Montfaucon,[390] that the Antiochenes followed
the Alexandrians in calculating the date of Easter, resulting in a date for
this festival in 387 of April 25.[391] He also argues, against Tillemont, Montfaucon and others, that the duration of Lent at Antioch at this time was
not seven or eight weeks but six.[392] On the basis of these calculations, he
arrives at the following sequence:

> *De statuis hom. 1*; (early March, a few days before Lent) *hom. 2*; (March
> 14, Sunday before Lent) *hom. 3*; (March 15-19, Monday-Friday of first week
> of Lent) *hom. 4-8*; (March 20, Saturday of first week of Lent) *hom. 15*; (March
> 22-23, Monday-Tuesday of second week of Lent) *hom. 9-10*; (March 26/28,
> end of week 2 or beginning of week 3) *hom. 16*; (April 2/3, Friday or Saturday

---

[385] Stilting, *Acta SS. Sept.*, IV 463-465.

[386] See p. 95 above.

[387] Stilting, *Acta SS. Sept.*, IV 465.

[388] In his recent reassessment of the chronology of these homilies van de Paverd (see
p. 246 below) makes no mention of Stilting's opinion.

[389] See p. 52 above.

[390] See p. 75 above.

[391] Stilting, *Acta SS. Sept.*, IV 467-468.

[392] Stilting, *Acta SS. Sept.*, IV 468-469. While Hermant (see n. 119) had proposed a
Lent of eight weeks, Tillemont (see p. 52 above) and Montfaucon (see p. 75 above) had
both followed a seven week Lent.

of week 3) *hom. 17*; *hom. 18*; (next day) *hom. 11*; (next day) *hom. 12*; (next day) *hom. 13*; (one or more days later) *hom. 14*; (c. April 18, on or near Palm Sunday) *hom. 19*; (during Holy Week) *hom. 20*; (April 25, Easter Sunday) *hom. 21*.[393]

Stilting then begins to fill in the remainder of Chrysostom's second year as presbyter, that is, the period from Lent 387 to Lent 388. In agreement with Montfaucon,[394] and against Tillemont, who wished to locate them in the following year,[395] he argues that the two catecheses *Ad illuminandos* (CPG 4460 and 4464) belong to the Lent of 387. Stilting resolves the problem of *cat. 1* falling during the third week of Lent, at which time Chrysostom says he did not preach,[396] by locating the baptismal instruction during the second week, on the basis that the homilist is not always precise in his use of numbers. He is moved to argue this because the lengthy exhortation against swearing convinces him that *cat. 1* must have been delivered in 387. The second catechesis falls naturally on the Saturday or Sunday after the third week of Lent, in which the trial of those who participated in the riots took place, since in the course of the instruction Chrysostom recalls that event in a manner which indicates that it was recent.[397] In this same year, beginning in May on the second or third Sunday after Easter and continuing until after Pentecost, Stilting locates the five sermons *De Anna* (CPG 4411). Except in details of chronology, resulting from his dismissal of Montfaucon's argument that *De statuis hom. 19* was delivered just prior to Ascension,[398] he here agrees with the view put forward by both Tillemont and Montfaucon.[399] Stilting distributes the homilies on the basis that in *De Anna sermo 4* John states that he is preaching only once a week (i.e., Sunday), a circumstance which leads him to locate the final homily in the series on the Sunday after Pentecost (June 20).[400] Stilting posits that for the rest of June and much of July Chrysostom was unable to preach due to ill health, a conclusion arrived at by locating the homily *De decem mill. tal. deb.* (CPG 4368) after the series on Anna and before the three homilies on David

---

[393] Stilting, *Acta SS. Sept.*, IV 465-478.

[394] See p. 76 above.

[395] See p. 54 above.

[396] See *De statuis hom. 11*, PG 49,119 13-14 *a.i.*; 120 24-25 *a.i.*

[397] Stilting, *Acta SS. Sept.*, IV 478.

[398] See p. 84 above.

[399] For the opinion of Tillemont see p. 53 above.

[400] Stilting, *Acta SS. Sept.*, IV 478-479.

and Saul (CPG 4412).[401] The reference in *De Davide et Saule hom. 1* to a recent sermon on the parable of the talents leads him to locate the three homilies on consecutive Sundays at the end of July or beginning of August.[402]

Between this cluster of homilies and the second series *Adv. Iudaeos* (*or. 4-8*) Stilting locates *In illud: Si esurierit inimicus* (CPG 4375), a homily assigned by Montfaucon to Constantinople.[403] Stilting points out that imperial *exempla* of the kind adduced by Montfaucon are not uncommon among the homilies from Antioch. He is persuaded rather that the sermon follows those on David and Saul, since Chrysostom refers extensively to the history of David in support of his exegesis of Rom. 12.20, yet does so with the kind of brevity that indicates that he has expounded on this topic before. Moreover, the sermon was delivered when it was summer and the weather very hot, which suits the time of year in question. At least one other homily intervened, however, since the contents of *De Davide et Saule hom. 3* do not match the summary of the preceding discourse supplied in *In illud: Si esurierit*.[404] To the period following *Adv. Iud. or. 4-8*, which he believes spanned the period from September to around mid-October, Stilting assigns *Exp. in ps. 41* (CPG 4413.2).[405] In this he follows the lead taken by both Tillemont and Montfaucon.[406]

As for the remainder of 387 and beginning of 388, Stilting finds himself unable to locate any homilies delivered with certainty during that period, a circumstance which leads him to look for suitable candidates among the miscellaneous homilies presented by Montfaucon in the third volume. There he finds five sermons which he considers more than suited to the months from October 387 to the beginning of Lent 388. In the first (*De eleemosyna*: CPG 4382) John indicates more than once that it is winter. Stilting promotes the second of the arguments put forward by Montfaucon, that the city is associated directly with the Antioch of Acts 11.30,[407] as proof that it stems from that location.[408] He is persuaded to

---

[401] Stilting, *Acta SS. Sept.*, IV 479-480. Montfaucon (see p. 84 above) located this homily prior to the sermons *De Anna*.

[402] Stilting, *Acta SS. Sept.*, IV 480.

[403] See p. 85 above.

[404] Stilting, *Acta SS. Sept.*, IV 480. At p. 559 sec. 794, however, Stilting forgets entirely that he has already assigned this homily to Antioch and argues that it was delivered at Constantinople, on the same basis as Montfaucon.

[405] Stilting, *Acta SS. Sept.*, IV 481.

[406] See pp. 53 and 92.

[407] See p. 86 above.

[408] Stilting, *Acta SS. Sept.*, IV 481 (sec. 391). Aside from pointing out that it was delivered in winter, Stilting does not explain why he is persuaded that this homily belongs to the second year of Chrysostom's presbyterate. He does suggest, however, that it is par-

situate the three homilies *In illud: Habentes eundem spiritum* (CPG 4383) during the same period and following *De eleemosyna*, on the basis that they deal with the same topic. He considers their Antiochene provenance to have been proved by Montfaucon,[409] and argues that they contain nothing which might exclude their having been delivered at this time.[410] Following these three Stilting locates *In illud: Utinam sustineretis modicum* (CPG 4384), since it contains nothing that indicates that it cannot have been delivered at this point and because the homilist spends considerable time praising the humility of Paul, a theme already developed in the third and last of the homilies *In illud: Habentes eundem spiritum*.[411] On the basis that he can find no other sermons with which to fill this period, Stilting posits that the whole time up until Lent 388 cannot have been occupied in preaching.

Although neither Tillemont nor Montfaucon was able to assign the major series on Genesis (CPG 4409) to a year with any confidence,[412] Stilting is convinced that it belongs to 388. He adduces three points in support of this conclusion. First, in the very first Lent of his preaching career Chrysostom began to explain the book of Genesis, which makes it most likely that he wanted to exegete this first. Second, his exposition of Genesis was interrupted by many other homilies, which makes it more likely that the series belongs to the earlier years than later. The third and most important point is that the homilies exhibit the same immature style as the earlier sermons on Genesis (CPG 4410), which leads Stilting to conclude that they were delivered before Chrysostom undertook to expound the Psalms, the gospels of Matthew and John and finally, the Pauline epistles. Stilting further points out that by style, he means the construction of the individual homilies. He finds a similarity between the longer exordia, particularly those exhibited in *Hom. 1-32 in Gen.*, and the structure of the homilies preached during the first two years. This peculiarity of style is lacking in the latter half of the series on Genesis and is rarely exhibited in the homilies of the other exegetical series.[413]

Having established the year of delivery, Stilting then turns to the distribution of the series throughout the course of 388. Allowing for the fact that Easter fell in that year on April 9 and that Lent at Antioch lasted for

---

ticularly polished and erudite. For the possible significance of this comment, see further p. 288 below.

[409] See p. 86 above.

[410] Stilting, *Acta SS. Sept.*, IV 481 (sec. 392).

[411] Stilting, *Acta SS. Sept.*, IV 481-482.

[412] See pp. 55f and 89f above. Stilting, *Acta SS. Sept.*, IV 487, considers Montfaucon's proof of the Antiochene provenance of this series definitive.

[413] Stilting, *Acta SS. Sept.*, IV 482.

six weeks, he calculates that *Hom. 1 in Gen.* was preached on Feb. 27,
which is the Sunday before Lent. The next thirty-one homilies from the
series then distribute themselves throughout Lent, with *hom. 32* being
delivered on the Wednesday of Holy Week (April 5).[414] While it is certain
that Chrysostom preached on both the Thursday and Friday of that week,
in contrast to Montfaucon,[415] Stilting finds no reason to assign either of
the two homilies *De proditione Iudae* (CPG 4336) or *De cruce et latrone*
(CPG 4338-4339) to those days.[416] From Easter Sunday onwards, however, he adopts the same sequence of homilies as Montfaucon, his conviction that the sequence belongs to 388 permitting him to establish certain chronological details:

> (April 9, Easter Sunday) *De resurrectione* (CPG 4341); (following Sunday)
> *In princ. Act. hom. 1* (CPG 4371); (homily *In princ. Act.*, now missing); *In
> princ. Act. hom. 2-4*; (midway between Easter and Pentecost) *De mutatione
> nom. hom. 1* (CPG 4372); (next day) *De mutatione nom. hom. 2*; *Sermo 9 in
> Gen.* (CPG 4410); *De mut. nom. hom. 3*;[417] (after Pentecost) *De mut. nom.
> hom. 4*; (June-September/October) *Hom. 33-67 in Gen.*[418]

Stilting confesses at this point that the further one progresses the more
uncertain the chronological traces become, a circumstance which he believes to be the natural result of the evolution of Chrysostom's career as a
homilist. It is his argument that the longer Chrysostom preaches, the less
detail concerning himself and his audience he provides, such that gradually all clues as to the year or sequence of delivery fade away.[419] This
premise leads Stilting to suggest that after finishing his exegesis of Genesis and before taking on any other book of scripture (i.e., late in 388)
John preached the two sermons *In illud: Salutate Priscillam et Aquilam*
(CPG 4376), since in both he commends the reading of Scripture at some
length, a topic which occupies his attention throughout that year.[420]

---

[414] Stilting, *Acta SS. Sept.*, IV 482-484.

[415] See Sequence D (p. 108 above) and p. 79 above.

[416] Stilting, *Acta SS. Sept.*, IV 484. Although he implies here and in the summary (p.
697) that all four stem from Antioch, at p. 503 he suggests that the second homily in each
instance was delivered at Constantinople. This suggestion is more firmly stated at p. 513
sec. 555.

[417] Stilting, *Acta SS. Sept.*, IV 486, posits that the homilies *In ascensionem* (CPG 4342)
and one of the two *De s. pentecoste* (CPG 4343) may have been delivered between *De mut.
nom. hom. 3* and *4*. He admits, however, that this is entirely conjectural. In the case of *De
s. pentecoste hom. 1-2*, he later confesses (p. 503) that neither contains sufficiently clear
information for its provenance to be ascertained.

[418] Stilting, *Acta SS. Sept.*, IV 484-487.

[419] Stilting, *Acta SS. Sept.*, IV 487 (§ XXVIII).

[420] Stilting, *Acta SS. Sept.*, IV 487.

This brings Stilting to the eighty-eight homilies on John (CPG 4425), on which he believes Chrysostom to have embarked just before the end of 388 or early in 389. While he accepts that the Antiochene provenance of both this and the series on Matthew (CPG 4424) has been proven beyond doubt,[421] Stilting points out that neither Tillemont nor Montfaucon questioned which of the two was undertaken first, both assuming that Chrysostom began with Matthew. While he confesses that he himself started out with that presupposition, he now holds on stylistic grounds that the series on John preceded that on Matthew. The most compelling evidence is the persistence, particularly in the earlier homilies of the series on John, of the use of exordia, whereas in Matthew and in all other exegetical series the homilist moves straight into his exposition of the pericope.[422] A second, more obvious reason is that in *In Ioh. hom. 9* he exhorts his listeners in a way which suggests that he has never given such advice before, whereas in *In Matt. hom. 1* John gives the same advice, but in a much more clipped manner. Since such advice is nowhere to be found in the series on Genesis, it seems likely that *In Ioh. hom. 9* is the first occasion on which this was expressed, while in *In Matt. hom. 1* the homilist is looking back to that occasion.[423] Stilting is convinced that the eighty-eight homilies took a year or less to deliver, on the basis of various pieces of internal evidence. This leads him to conclude that the series was completed somewhere between the middle and end of 389.[424]

As proof of the Antiochene provenance of the ninety homilies on Matthew, Stilting combines three arguments put forward variously by Savile, Tillemont and Montfaucon.[425] In order to fix the time of their delivery, he then resorts to the proof that they precede another Antiochene series, namely that on I Corinthians,[426] after which he dismisses, with Montfaucon, Tillemont's claim that the series belongs to the end of Chrysostom's

---

[421] Stilting, *Acta SS. Sept.*, IV 488 (sec. 428), considers the arguments of both Tillemont (see pp. 60f above) and Montfaucon (pp. 96f above) convincing.

[422] Stilting, *Acta SS. Sept.*, IV 487 (sec. 421-422).

[423] Stilting, *Acta SS. Sept.*, IV 487 (sec. 423-424).

[424] Stilting, *Acta SS. Sept.*, IV 489 (sec. 429). He concludes (sec. 430) by dismissing Tillemont's argument for locating the series circa 394, on the grounds that the calamities listed in *In Ioh. hom. 34/33* do not necessarily refer to the same year and are in any case consistent with events circa 388 and 389.

[425] That the city is that which was first named Christian (*In Matt. hom. 7*) — see Savile (p. 38 above), Tillemont (p. 60 above), Montfaucon (p. 96 above); the proximity of monks (esp. *hom. 72/73*) — Montfaucon; and that the locations mentioned in the exemplum of the prostitute (*hom. 67/68*) are closer to Antioch than Constantinople — Tillemont, who cites Savile. Stilting, *Acta SS. Sept.*, IV 490 (sec. 436-437), discounts the possibility (raised by both Savile and Tillemont) that in *hom. 82/83* Chrysostom speaks as bishop.

[426] Stilting, *Acta SS. Sept.*, IV 490. In this he follows Tillemont.

presbyterate because in *hom. 72/73* the Meletian schism is described as a thing of the past. Finally, although he finds certain of Montfaucon's arguments unconvincing, he agrees that, due to the number of homilies already assigned to the years 386-388, Chrysostom could not have begun this series until the latter part of 388 at the very earliest. Since the series on John preceded that on Matthew, Stilting concludes that the latter was begun either at the end of 389 or beginning of 390 and not completed until late in 390 or at some point in 391.[427]

With respect to the Antiochene provenance of the thirty-two homilies on the Letter to the Romans (CPG 4427), Stilting adopts the arguments put forward by Montfaucon in dismissal of the doubts raised by Tillemont.[428] He takes this one step further, however, in the case of *In Rom. hom. 30*, where he proposes that the verb ἐδέθη ("he was bound"), used in respect of Paul and his association with the location, is a corruption of ἐδεήθη ("he spoke"). If adopted, the proposed emendation removes any objection to the identification of the location as Antioch. Where Montfaucon found himself unable to determine when this series was delivered, unless perhaps not until after 388, Stilting is convinced that Romans is the first of the Pauline epistles to have been exegeted by Chrysostom and that therefore the series situates itself in 391.[429] That the series on the two Letters to the Corinthians (CPG 4428-4429) likewise stem from Antioch, he considers to have been definitively proven by Montfaucon.[430] Without stating his grounds for doing so, Stilting posits that the two were delivered following the series on Romans, a circumstance which locates them around the year 392.[431]

Stilting finds that the combined bulk of the remaining Antiochene series is sufficient to fill the years from 393-397, although the order in which they were delivered is difficult to determine. In assigning the twenty-four homilies on Ephesians (CPG 4431) to Antioch, Stilting follows both Tillemont and Montfaucon,[432] adducing the schism referred to in *In Eph. hom. 11* as evidence. Against Tillemont's argument that the series dates to the period of Evagrius' episcopate among the Eustathians at

---

[427] Stilting, *Acta SS. Sept.*, IV 490-491.

[428] See p. 98 above.

[429] Stilting, *Acta SS. Sept.*, IV 491-492. Stilting is convinced that it did not precede the series on John and Matthew on the basis of style, while he argues that it does precede the other series on the Pauline epistles because of the nature of the discussion undertaken in the Preface. He takes John's comments to be an introduction to all of the Pauline material, not just Romans.

[430] See pp. 98f above.

[431] Stilting, *Acta SS. Sept.*, IV 493. This appears to stem from a belief that the series on the Pauline epistles were preached in biblical order.

[432] See pp. 62 and 99 above.

Antioch (388/389-392), Stilting interprets the same evidence in *hom. 11* as indicating that the Eustathians are currently without a bishop and that therefore the series dates to after Evagrius' death (c. 393). He finds that this concurs well with the references to war and natural disaster which occur at the close of *hom. 6.*[433] In the case of the fifteen homilies on Philippians (CPG 4432), however, Stilting assigns these to Antioch, contrary to the opinion of both Tillemont and Montfaucon.[434] He does this on the basis of *In Phil. hom. 15*, where the homilist mentions the difficulties faced by the present emperor. Stilting finds that the description given accords well with the experience of Theodosius and that the order likewise points to this conclusion, since the emperor mentioned just prior to the current incumbent is Valens, Theodosius' immediate predecessor. Since Theodosius died early in 395, Stilting concludes that the series was delivered after that on Ephesians in either 393 or 394.[435] With respect to the series on the two Letters to Timothy (CPG 4436-4437), he agrees with Montfaucon's assessment that both stem from Antioch.[436] Although the grounds on which the latter based this conclusion apply only to the first of the two series, Stilting is convinced that Chrysostom embarked immediately upon the second after concluding the first. In any case, he argues, there is ample time in these latter years at Antioch for the preaching of the series, whereas at Constantinople Chrysostom was much occupied with administrative affairs.[437] In assigning the six homilies on Titus (CPG 4438) to the same location, he is entirely in accord with both Tillemont and Montfaucon.[438] Finally, whereas Montfaucon had remained undecided with regard to the provenance of the three homilies on Philemon (CPG 4439),[439] Stilting is inclined to believe that they were delivered at Antioch, as much because in the Constantinopolitan homilies John alludes to either his episcopal status or the imperial palace, as because it is easier to find time for them at Antioch than at Constantinople. However, he confesses that these arguments are somewhat light and that the matter must therefore remain uncertain.[440]

Before concluding his discussion of the Antiochene homilies and their distribution, Stilting turns to the collection of expositions on the Psalms (CPG 4413). Convinced that these constitute the remnants of a system-

---

[433] Stilting, *Acta SS. Sept.*, IV 494-495.
[434] See pp. 64 and 99 above.
[435] Stilting, *Acta SS. Sept.*, IV 495-496.
[436] See p. 100 above.
[437] Stilting, *Acta SS. Sept.*, IV 496 (sec. 466-467).
[438] Stilting, *Acta SS. Sept.*, IV 496 (sec. 468). See pp. 62 and 101 above.
[439] See p. 101 above.
[440] Stilting, *Acta SS. Sept.*, IV 496 (sec. 469).

atic commentary of the book of Psalms, he concurs with Montfaucon's view that the commentary was written first and only subsequently delivered before an audience.[441] In support of the Antiochene origin of this work, he then adduces Montfaucon's proof from *Exp. in ps. 110*, to which he adds the latter's argument based on the relative leisure required for such an undertaking.[442] He takes the argument from leisure one step further by arguing that although it is possible that Chrysostom could have found sufficient relief from his other commitments at Constantinople for the writing and polishing of this work, the quantity of homilies from the five series already assigned to that location more than fills the available time there and therefore definitely excludes this possibility.[443] On the point of when the exposition was undertaken, however, he disagrees with Montfaucon's attempt to locate the initial writing during Chrysostom's diaconate. Positing that John must have preached continuously throughout the twelve years of his presbyterate, Stilting confesses that he has so far filled only nine of the available years. Since the exposition of Psalms, if complete, would easily have filled a further two or three years, this leads him to argue that it was both composed and delivered during that period. On the basis of style and the belief that this commentary belongs after the series on the gospels of Matthew and John and also those on the ten Pauline epistles, Stilting concludes that Chrysostom began exegeting the book of Psalms some time in 394 or 395 and finished doing so in the last year of his presbyterate (397). This chronology conforms well with John's comments in *Exp. in ps. 119*, where he alludes to the treacherous character of the barbarians, a passage in which Stilting sees a reflection of the situation with the Goths subsequent to the death of Theodosius.[444]

Finally, in the course of discussing numerous individual homilies which contain insufficient indication of their chronology, Stilting firmly assigns the encomium *In martyres Aegyptios* (CPG 4363) to Antioch, against the opinions of both Tillemont and Montfaucon.[445] As he points out, the homily does not commemorate the translation of relics, as Tillemont had assumed, but talks of Egyptians condemned to work in the mines of Syria. This leaves him in no doubt that the homily was addressed to an Antiochene audience.[446] He further assigns the sermons *Peccata fratrum non evulganda* (CPG 4389) and *Non esse desperandum*

---

[441] Stilting, *Acta SS. Sept.*, IV 497-498.

[442] See p. 92 above.

[443] Stilting, *Acta SS. Sept.*, IV 498-499.

[444] Stilting, *Acta SS. Sept.*, IV 499-500.

[445] Where Tillemont (see p. 63 above) had suggested Constantinople, Montfaucon (p. 83 above) had argued that the homily contained insufficient evidence to decide.

[446] Stilting, *Acta SS. Sept.*, IV 505 (sec. 512-513).

(CPG 4390) to this location, by identifying the homily of the previous day, the contents of which are summarised in the first of these, as *De incompr. dei nat. hom. 5* (CPG 4318). Since he has already demonstrated that the latter belongs to December 386, this permits him likewise to situate the two homilies in that month and year.[447]

b. *Constantinople*

Accepting the view that the sermons *Contra Anom. hom. 11* (CPG 4324), *De Christi divinitate* (CPG 4325) and *In paralyticum demissum per tectum* (CPG 4370) were the second, third and fourth preached there,[448] Stilting finds that the homilies of this first year at Constantinople exhibit the same characteristics as those of the first few years at Antioch, the most noticeable of which is the familiar way in which John speaks to his audience.[449] Despite Montfaucon's reservations regarding its provenance,[450] to this same year Stilting assigns *In illud: Pater, si possibile est* (CPG 4369), arguing that Chrysostom had already refuted this aspect of the Anomoean argument at Antioch in the seventh of the homilies *Contra Anomoeos* (CPG 4320). Moreover, the content of this homily conforms to the intention stated in the first homily preached at Constantinople and reiterated in the second, namely to refute the Anomoeans on the basis of the Old as well as New Testament, in order to dispute the Marcionites, Manichaeans and Valentinians at one and the same time.[451]

Turning to the eleven *Novae homiliae* (CPG 4441) edited for the first time by Montfaucon, Stilting questions the latter's assertion that all eleven were delivered in the years 398-399 and before the fall of Eutropius.[452] He finds this position untenable, since the very first homily (*Quod frequenter conveniendum sit*: CPG 4441.3) refers to the latter event and was therefore delivered after Eutropius was sent into exile.[453] Stilting argues that the word σεισμός does not in this instance necessarily indicate an earthquake,[454] and points out that the event is directly associated with

---

[447] Stilting, *Acta SS. Sept.*, IV 561.

[448] See Montfaucon (pp. 73 and 84 above).

[449] Stilting, *Acta SS. Sept.*, IV 511-512.

[450] Montfaucon (see p. 84 above), although hesitant, was inclined to locate the homily in the first few years at Antioch.

[451] Stilting, *Acta SS. Sept.*, IV 512-513.

[452] See p. 102 above.

[453] Stilting, *Acta SS. Sept.*, IV 513 (sec. 553).

[454] Montfaucon , following that view, had identified the "quake" as one of those which purportedly occurred toward the end of 398.

the consequences of greed. As the "upheaval" is clearly to be identified as the deposition of Eutropius and is said to have occurred some thirty days before, this locates the sermon in February 399.[455] If there is a homily which refers to the earthquake of 398, it is rather *De terrae motu* (CPG 4366). Arguing against Montfaucon's assertion that Chrysostom could well have repeated himself at Antioch after an interval of one or two years, Stilting locates the homily *In illud: Diligentibus deum* (CPG 4374) at Constantinople, on the grounds that the exordium is almost identical to that of the Antiochene homily *De decem mill. tal. deb.* (CPG 4368). He further situates it in 398, since the homilist still exhibits a friendly attitude towards his audience and has not yet begun to attack their vices. From the exordium to this homily he posits that Chrysostom suffered from an extended period of ill-health throughout part of 398, to which circumstance *De terrae motu* conforms.[456]

To the period from the latter part of 398 to after the fall of Eutropius in January 399 Stilting assigns the twelve homilies on Colossians (CPG 4433). He does so on the same basis as Montfaucon[457] — that is, the allusion to the deposition of Eutropius contained in *In Col. hom.* 7 and the reference to earthquakes in *hom.* 2. Stilting believes, however, that his dating of the first event produces a more acceptable chronology for the series, since this requires that only a month or two elapse between the preaching of the second and the seventh homily. In support of the Constantinopolitan provenance of the series he adduces not only *hom.* 3,[458] but also points out that in *hom.* 10 Chrysostom alludes to the empress Eudoxia.[459] Also in 399 Stilting locates the two homilies *In illud: Ne timueritis cum dives* (CPG 4414). He believes that the second of the two, preached after another person had spoken briefly, was probably delivered first. Both, he argues, belong to the period immediately after the coup struck by Gainas, but before Chrysostom was sent to negotiate.[460] In this he differs from Montfaucon, who located both homilies in the interval between the fall of Eutropius and the coup.[461]

---

[455] Stilting, *Acta SS. Sept.*, IV 540. There was some dispute at this time as to whether Eutropius had been deposed in January or August 399, due to the ms. dating of *Codex Theodosianus* IX.40.17, which suggested that it had taken place on c. Jan. 17.

[456] Stilting, *Acta SS. Sept.*, IV 505 and 513.

[457] See p. 100 above.

[458] See Savile (p. 39 above).

[459] Stilting, *Acta SS. Sept.*, IV 539-540.

[460] Stilting, *Acta SS. Sept.*, IV 542. He sees in *hom. 1* an allusion to the fact that Gainas has been shut out of the city and declared an enemy. In *hom.* 2 the "tumult and upheaval" is taken to refer to the coup itself. As a result of placing the fall of Eutropius in January 399, the coup and related events are moved forward to July 399.

[461] See p. 93 above.

By telescoping the deposition of Eutropius and the insurrection led by
Gainas into 399,[462] Stilting is led to argue, against the consensus,[463] that
Chrysostom departed for Ephesus in February or March 400, returning
in mid to late summer of that year.[464] Since the chronology applied to
these three events is crucial to the distribution of the Constantinopolitan
homilies in the period from the end of the first year up to the first exile,
the view presented by Stilting diverges somewhat at this point from that
of his predecessors. An example is his location in 400 of the series on I
and II Thessalonians (CPG 4434-4435), interrupted in part by the journey
to Asia Minor.[465] In this instance, Stilting takes the same arguments put
forward by Tillemont and applies them to the period when relations between the bishop and the empress Eudoxia were beginning to disinte-
grate.[466] In the case of the fifty-five homilies on Acts (CPG 4426), his particular dating of the journey to Ephesus leads him to locate the series in
401, since he agrees with Tillemont's judgement that *In Acta apost. hom.
1* was delivered in the period immediately following Easter.[467] He finds
confirmation of this in the two statements regarding an earthquake of
the previous year (*hom. 7, 41*), which he identifies as the quake of 400,
arguing at some length in this respect against the opinion of Tillemont.
Believing that the series was delivered without interruption, on which
basis he calculates that it would have taken ten months or so to deliver,
Stilting concludes that the preaching of this series must have extended
into the following year (402).[468] This leads him to locate the thirty-four
homilies on Hebrews (CPG 4440) in 402, following the last of the homilies on Acts, since this is the last of the exegetical series undertaken and

---

[462] Stilting, *Acta SS. Sept.*, IV 534-539.

[463] Both Tillemont (see Table 2.6 p. 71 above) and Montfaucon (Table 3.6 p. 107
above) locate the pastoral visit in the first half of 401.

[464] Stilting, *Acta SS. Sept.*, IV 545-546.

[465] Tillemont (see p. 65 above) had assigned the second to the period leading up to
Chrysostom's deposition and exile.

[466] Stilting, *Acta SS. Sept.*, IV 551. In particular, he argues that *In II Thess. hom. 5* is
more appropriate to the period just before the close of 400 or beginning of 401, than to
any other time. He finds that the arguments of Tillemont and Montfaucon (see p. 100
above) regarding the provenance of the series are convincing and therefore does not enter
into discussion on that issue.

[467] Stilting, *Acta SS. Sept.*, IV 557. Because of their dating of the pastoral visit to 401
and the statement in *hom. 44* that it is Chrysostom's third year at the location, Tillemont
(see p. 63 above) and Montfaucon (pp. 97f above) both located the series in 400, prior to
the journey to Ephesus.

[468] Stilting, *Acta SS. Sept.*, IV 557-558. Regarding the provenance of the series, he
claims (p. 557 sec. 781) that in *hom. 8* Chrysostom makes it clear that he is bishop, while
in *hom. 11* the homilist speaks of the emperor in such a way as to indicate that he is at
Constantinople.

there is ample space in that year for the preaching of it.[469] He claims to have the support of both Tillemont and Montfaucon, who believed that it belonged to the later years of John's episcopate.[470]

c. *Summary*

Stilting's opinion is summarised in the form of two tables, one detailing his view regarding provenance, the other his thoughts with respect to chronology. Sequences not clearly indicated in sections a-b are listed following Table 4.b.

Table 4.a. Provenance — Stilting

CPG no.	Antioch	CPG no.	Constantinople
4317	*Cum presbyter fuit ordinatus* (p. 696)	4324	*Contra Anomoeos hom. 11* (pp. 511f)
4318	*De incompr. dei nat. hom. 1-5* (pp. 450ff)	4325	*De Christi divinitate* (p. 512)
4319	*De beato Philogonio* (p. 452)	4336	*De proditione Iudae hom. 2* (p. 513)
4320	*De consubstantiali* (p. 452)	4339	*De cruce et latrone hom. 2* (p. 513)
4321	*De petitione matris fil. Zeb.* (p. 452)	4364	*De s. hieromartyre Phoca* (p. 528f)
4322	*In quatriduanum Lazarum* (p. 453)	4366	*De terrae motu*† (pp. 505, 513)
4323	*De Christi precibus* (p. 453)	4369	*In illud: Pater, si possibile est* (pp. 512f)
4327	*Adv. Iudaeos or. 1-8* (pp. 450-457)	4370	*In paralyticum demissum per tectum* (p. 512)
4328	*In kalendas* (pp. 458f)	4374	*In illud: Diligentibus deum* (p. 513)
4329	*De Lazaro conciones 1-7* (pp. 459-461)	4375	*In illud: Si esurierit inimicus*# (p. 559)
4330	*De statuis hom. 1-21* (pp. 465-478)	4377	*In illud: Propter fornicationes* (pp. 559f)
4332	*De diabolo tentatore hom. 1-3* (pp. 463f)	4378	*De libello repudii* (pp. 559f)
4333	*De paenitentia hom. 1-9* (p. 697)	4379	*Quales ducendae sint uxores* (pp. 559f)
4334	*In diem natalem* (pp. 452, 458)	4392	*In Eutropium* (pp. 532-536)
4335	*De baptismo Christi* (p. 460)	4393	*Cum Saturninus et Aurelianus* (pp. 536-539)

---

[469] Stilting, *Acta SS. Sept.*, IV 558-559. In asserting the Constantinopolitan provenance of this series, he resorts (p. 559 sec. 790) to the usual argument that in *In Heb. hom. 4* Chrysostom speaks in an episcopal tone. See, e.g., Savile (p. 39 above).

[470] See pp. 65 and 101f above. Montfaucon is particularly vague in this respect. It is Tillemont who in fact makes this statement.

4336	*De proditione Iudae hom. 1* (p. 697)	4394	*De regressu* (p. 548)
4337	*De coemeterio et de cruce* (p. 503)	4396	*Antequam iret in exsilium* (p. 698)
4338	*De cruce et latrone hom. 1* (p. 697)	4398	*Post reditum a priore exsilio 1* (p. 698)
4340	*De resurrectione mortuorum* (p. 461)	4399	*Post reditum a priore exsilio 2* (p. 698)
4341	*De resurrectione* (p. 484)	4414	*In illud: Ne timueritis hom. 1-2* (pp. 542f)
4342	*In ascensionem* (p. 486, 503)	4417	*In illud: Vidi dominum hom. 1,4* (p. 560)
4343	*De sancta Pentecoste hom. 1-2†* (p. 486)	4426	*In Acta apost. hom. 1-55* (p. 557)
4344	*De laudibus s. Pauli hom. 1-7* (p. 502)	4433	*In Col. hom. 1-12* (pp. 539f)
4345	*De s. Meletio* (p. 450)	4434	*In I Thess. hom. 1-11* (p. 551)
4346	*In s. Lucianum* (p. 460)	4435	*In II Thess. hom. 1-5* (p. 551)
4347	*De s. hieromartyre Babyla* (p. 460)	4440	*In Heb. hom. 1-34* (p. 558)
4349	*In Iuventinum et Maximum* (p. 460)	4441.1	*Dicta postquam reliquiae martyrum* (pp. 528f)
4350	*De s. Pelagia* (p. 503)	4441.2	*Dicta praesente imperatore* (pp. 528f)
4351	*In s. Ignatium* (p. 503)	4441.3	*Quod frequenter conveniendum sit* (p. 513)
4352	*In s. Eustathium* (p. 504)	4441.4	*Adversus eos qui non adfuerant* (p. 540)
4353	*In s. Romanum* (p. 504)	4441.5	*De studio praesentium* (p. 540)
4354	*De Macabeis hom. 1-2* (p. 504)	4441.6	*Adversus catharos* (pp. 540f)
4355	*De ss. Bernice et Prosdoce* (p. 503)	4441.7	*Contra ludos et theatra* (pp. 541f)
4356	*In quatriduanum Lazarum* (p. 503)	4441.8	*Dicta in templo s. Anastasiae* (p. 541)
4357	*De ss. martyribus* (p. 504)	4441.9	*Habita postquam presb. Gothus* (p. 541)
4358	*Non esse ad gratiam conc.* (p. 504)	4441.10	*In illud: Pater meus usque modo op.* (pp. 541f)
4359	*Hom. in martyres* (p. 505)	4441.11	*In illud: Messis quidem multa* (p. 542)
4360	*In s. Iulianum* (p. 505)	4441.13	*De Eleazaro et septem pueris* (p. 542)
4361	*In s. Barlaam* (p. 505)	4528	*De capto Eutropio* (pp. 532f)
4362	*De s. Droside* (p. 505)	4529	*De Chananaea* (p. 698)
4363	*In martyres Aegyptios* (p. 505)		
4368	*De decem mill. tal. debitore* (pp. 479f)		
4371	*In princ. Act. hom. 1-4* (pp. 484f)		
4372	*De mutatione nom. hom. 1-4* (p. 485)		
4375	*In illud: Si esurierit inimicus** (p. 480)		
4376	*In illud: Salutate Prisc. et Aquilam hom. 1-2* (p. 487)		
4380	*In dictum P.: Nolo vos ignorare* (p. 505)		
4382	*De eleemosyna* (p. 481)		
4383	*In illud: Habentes eundem spir. hom. 1-3* (p. 481)		

4384	*In illud: Utinam sustineretis* (pp. 481f)		
4385	*De profectu evangelii* (p. 458)		
4386	*In illud: Vidua eligatur* (p. 461)		
4389	*Peccata fratrum non evulganda* (p. 561)		
4390	*Non esse desperandum* (p. 561)		
4391	*In illud: In faciem ei restiti* (p. 504)		
4406	*Laus Diodori episcopi* (p. 506)		
4409	*Hom. 1-67 in Genesim* (p. 482)		
4410	*Sermones 1-9 in Genesim* (pp. 449, 485)		
4411	*De Anna sermones 1-5* (pp. 478f)		
4412	*De Davide et Saule hom. 1-3* (p. 480)		
4413	*Exp. in psalmos* (pp. 481, 498f)		
4417	*In illud: Vidi dom. hom. 2,3,5,6* (pp. 462f)		
4419	*In illud: Dom., non est in homine* (p. 504)		
4420	*De obsc. prophetiarum hom. 1-2* (p. 463)		
4423	*In illud: Hoc scitote* (p. 465)		
4424	*In Matt. hom. 1-90* (p. 490)		
4425	*In Ioh. hom. 1-88* (p. 488)		
4427	*In Rom. hom. 1-32* (p. 492)		
4428	*In I Cor. hom. 1-44* (p. 493)		
4429	*In II Cor. hom. 1-30* (p. 493)		
4431	*In Eph. hom. 1-24* (pp. 494f)		
4432	*In Phil. hom. 1-15* (p. 495)		
4436	*In I Tim. hom. 1-18* (p. 496)		
4437	*In II Tim. hom. 1-10* (p. 496)		
4438	*In Titum hom. 1-6* (p. 496)		
4439	*In Philemon hom. 1-3†* (pp. 496f)		
4441.12	*In illud: Filius ex se nihil facit* (pp. 452f)		
4460	*Ad illuminandos cat. 1* (p. 478)		
4464	*Ad illuminandos cat. 2* (p. 478)		

* Also assigned to Constantinople. † Possibly. # Also assigned to Antioch.

Table 4.b. Chronology — Stilting

Year (month-season)	Homily	Cited (page)
386		
January	*Cum presbyter fuit ordinatus* (CPG 4317)	463, 696
February	*In illud: Vidi dom. hom. 2,3,5* (CPG 4417)	462f

Feb. 22	*In illud: Vidi dominum hom. 6*	463
early Lent	*Sermones 1-8 in Genesim* (CPG 4410)	449f
Lent	*De obsc. prophetiarum hom. 1-2* (CPG 4420)	463-465
	De diabolo tentatore hom. 1 (CPG 4332)	464f
	De diabolo tent. hom. 3	"
	De diabolo tent. hom. 2	"
May	*De s. Meletio* (CPG 4345)	450
August	*In illud: Hoc scitote* (CPG 4423)	465
	De incompr. dei natura hom. 1 (CPG 4318)	450f
end August/beg. September	*Adversus Iudaeos or. 1* (CPG 4327)	450f
September	*Adv. Iudaeos or. 2*	451
November	*De incompr. dei natura hom. 2-3*	452, 457
end of November/ beg. of December	*De anathemate* (CPG 3430)	457
December	*De incompr. dei natura hom. 4-5*	452, 457
	Peccata fratrum non evulganda (CPG 4389)	561
	Non esse desperandum (CPG 4390)	"
Dec. 20	*De beato Philogonio* (CPG 4319)	452
Dec. 25	*In diem natalem* (CPG 4334)	458
after Dec. 25 - before Jan. 1	*De profectu evangelii* (CPG 4385)	458
387		
Jan. 1	*In kalendas* (CPG 4328)	458f
Jan. 2	*De Lazaro concio 1* (CPG 4329)	459
Jan. 6	*De baptismo Christi* (CPG 4335)	460
Jan. 7	*In s. Lucianum* (CPG 4346)	"
January	*De Lazaro conciones 2-3*	459f
Jan. 24	*De s. hieromartyre Babyla* (CPG 4347)	460
late January	*In Iuventinum et Maximum* (CPG 4349)	460
	De Lazaro conciones 4-5	460f
February (before Lent)	*In illud: Vidua eligatur* (CPG 4386)	461
	De consubstantiali (CPG 4320)	452f
	In illud: Filius ex se nihil facit (CPG 4441.12)	"
	De petitione matris fil. Zeb. (CPG 4321)	"
	De resurrectione mortuorum (CPG 4340)	461
	In quatriduanum Lazarum (CPG 4322)	452f
	De Christi precibus (CPG 4323)	"
	De Lazaro conciones 6-7	461
late February/ early March	*Adv. Iudaeos or. 3*	455f
early March - March 20	*De statuis hom. 1-8,15* (CPG 4330)	469ff
c. March 22	*Ad illuminandos cat. 1* (CPG 4460)	478
March 22- c. April 2	*De statuis hom. 9-10,16-17*	469ff
early April	*Ad illuminandos cat. 2* (CPG 4464)	478
April	*De statuis hom. 18,11-14,19-20*	469ff
Apr. 25	*De statuis hom. 21*	"
May-June 20	*De Anna sermones 1-5* (CPG 4411)	478f
c. end of July	*De decem mill. talentorum debitore* (CPG 4368)	479f
late July-early August	*De Davide et Saule hom. 1-3* (CPG 4412)	480
date unspecified	*In illud: Si esurierit inimicus** (CPG 4375)	480

Sept.-c. mid Oct.	*Adv. Iudaeos or. 4-8*	456f, 480f
after mid October	*Exp. in psalmum 41* (CPG 4413.2)	481
winter	*De eleemosyna* (CPG 4382)	481
	In illud: Hab. eundem spiritum hom. 1-3 (CPG 4383)	"
	In illud: Utinam sustineretis (CPG 4384)	481f
388		
Feb. 27- April 5	*Hom. 1-32 in Genesim* (CPG 4409)	482-484
April 9	*De resurrectione* (CPG 4341)	484
	In princ. Act. hom. 1-4 (CPG 4371)	484f
Sunday after Easter - Pentecost	*De mutatione nom. hom. 1-2* (CPG 4372)	485
	Sermo 9 in Genesim (CPG 4410)	"
	De mutatione nom. hom. 3	"
after Pentecost	*De mutatione nom. hom. 4*	486
June - Sept./Oct.	*Hom. 33-67 in Genesim* (CPG 4409)	486f
date unspecified	*In illud: Sal. Prisc. et Aquilam hom. 1-2* (CPG 4376)	487
389		
(circa)	*In Ioh. hom. 1-88* (CPG 4425)	487ff
390		
(circa)	*In Matt. hom. 1-90* (CPG 4424)	490f
391		
date unspecified	*In Rom. hom. 1-32* (CPG 4427)	491ff
392		
date unspecified	*In I Cor. hom. 1-44* (CPG 4428)	493
	In II Cor. hom. 1-30 (CPG 4429)	"
393		
(circa)	*In Eph. hom. 1-24* (CPG 4431)#	494f
394		
395		
	Expositiones in psalmos (CPG 4413.1,3-5)	499f
396		
	Exp. in psalmos cont...	"
397		
	Remainder of *Exp. in psalmos*	"
398		
after Feb. 26	*Contra Anomoeos hom. 11* (CPG 4324)	511f
	De Christi divinitate (CPG 4325)	512
Lent	*In paralyticum demissum* (CPG 4370)	512
date unspecified	*In illud: Pater, si possibile est* (CPG 4369)	512f
	De terrae motu (CPG 4366)	505, 513
	In illud: Diligentibus deum (CPG 4374)	513
just before the end	Beginning of series on Colossians (CPG 4433)	539
399		
January	*In Eutropium* (CPG 4392)	533-536
	De capto Eutropio (CPG 4528)	"
February	*Quod frequenter conveniendum* (CPG 4441.3)	540
first few months	End of series On Colossians (CPG 4433)	539f
early	*Adv. eos qui non adfuerant* (CPG 4441.4)	540
	De studio praesentium (CPG 4441.5)	"
April 10	*Contra ludos et theatra* (CPG 4441.7)	541f, 557
Easter - Pentecost	*In illud: Pater meus usque* (CPG 4441.10)	541
	Habita postquam presb. Gothus (CPG 4441.9)	"

July or later	*In illud: Ne timueritis hom. 1-2* (CPG 4414)	542f
	Cum Saturninus et Aurelianus (CPG 4393)	536-539
date unspecified	*Dicta in templo s. Anastasiae* (CPG 4441.8)	541
	In illud: Messis quidem multa (CPG 4441.11)	542
	De Eleazaro et septem pueris (CPG 4441.13)	"
400		
Feb./March - late summer	*De regressu* (CPG 4394)	548
date unspecified	*In I Thess. hom. 1-11* (CPG 4434)	551
	In II Thess. hom. 1-5 (CPG 4435)	"
401		
after Easter -	*In Acta apost. hom. 1-55* (CPG 4426)	557f
402		
early	Remainder of CPG 4426	"
date unspecified	*In Heb. hom. 1-34* (CPG 4440)	558
403		
c. Sept.	*Sermo antequam iret in exsilium* (CPG 4396)	698
date unspecified	*Post reditum a priore exsilio 1* (CPG 4398)	698
	Post reditum a priore exsilio 2 (CPG 4399)	"
	De Chananaea (CPG 4529)	"
404		

* Also assigned to between 398 and first exile (403). # Followed by *In Phil. hom. 1-15* (CPG 4432) in 393/394

Sequence A. (Sunday before Lent) *De paenitentia hom. 5* (CPG 4333); (following Sunday) *De paen. hom. 2*; (following Sunday) *De paen. hom. 3*; (following Sunday) *De paen. hom. 4*; (following Sunday, second half of Lent) *De paen. hom. 6*.[471]

Sequence B. (Good Friday) *De coemeterio et cruce* (CPG 4337); (less than twenty days later) *De ss. Bernice et Prosdoce* (CPG 4355).[472]

Sequence C. *In illud: In faciem ei restiti* (CPG 4391); *In s. Eustathium* (CPG 4352); *In s. Romanum* (CPG 4353); *In illud: Domine, non est in hom.* (CPG 4419).[473]

---

[471] Stilting, *Acta SS. Sept.*, IV 502-503. On the basis of the deference accorded Flavian in *hom. 5* and the laudatory character assigned the population in *hom. 3*, it is suggested that the sequence is appropriate to the first year of preaching, 386. Stilting stresses, however, that both the sequence and the date assigned it are conjectural. Regarding the Antiochene provenance of these homilies, he adopts Montfaucon's argument regarding *hom. 3*, while in the case of *hom. 5* Stilting points out that Chrysostom clearly refers to another as bishop. Montfaucon (see p. 78 above) had somehow overlooked this point.

[472] Stilting, *Acta SS. Sept.*, IV 503. He argues (sec. 502) against the location of this sequence in 392, pointing out that the martyrologies in which the date April 14 for the festival of Domnina and her daughters is found do not indicate Antiochene practice. For the claim that the homilies belong to 392 see Tillemont (p. 54 above) and Montfaucon (p. 81 above).

[473] Stilting, *Acta SS. Sept.*, IV 504. Cf. Montfaucon, Sequence E, p. 108 above. Stilting argues, on the basis of the shift from one topic to another exhibited in this sequence, that

Sequence D. *De Macabeis hom. 1* (CPG 4354); (next day) *De Macabeis hom. 2*.[474]

Sequence E. *De ss. matyribus* (CPG 4357); (shortly after) *Non esse ad gratiam concionandum* (CPG 4358).[475]

Sequence F. (spring or early summer) *In s. Barlaam* (CPG 4361); (next day) *In d. Pauli: Nolo vos ignorare* (CPG 4380).[476]

Sequence G. (398 or 399) *De s. Phoca* (CPG 4364); *Hom. dicta postquam reliquiae martyrum* (CPG 4441.1); (next day) *Hom. dicta praesente imperatore* (CPG 4441.2).[477]

3. c. 1850-1930[478]

The stimulus for the renewed interest in the questions of the provenance and chronology of the homilies of Chrysostom after a century of relative silence can be said to derive from two quarters — the reprinting in the 1860s of Montfaucon's edition by Jacques-Paul Migne, and the revision of the chronicles of Baronius for the years 378-395, which Gerhard Rauschen completed and published towards the end of the nineteenth century.[479] The first gave greater accessibility to the homilies and the opinion expressed by Montfaucon regarding them; the second necessitated that the homilies of Chrysostom thought to belong to the years 378 to 395 be taken into consideration. A minor flood of books and articles followed. This flurry of endeavour culminated in the 1920s with Max von Bonsdorff's attempt to fix the location and chronology of the exegetical series, and with Chrysostom Baur's extensive foray into the life and times of Chrysostom.

The most prominent aspect of this period is the finalisation of the identity and sequence of the homilies to be assigned to the first two years of Chrysostom's presbyterate at Antioch. This is mirrored by the work of

---

it belongs to the first few years at Antioch. He is further convinced by Chrysostom's mention in *In illud: In faciem ei restiti* of his movements in the company of Flavian.

[474] Stilting, *Acta SS. Sept.*, IV 504 (sec. 507). He again posits that these homilies belong to the first years at Antioch, because in the second Chrysostom mentions that Flavian is to speak after him.

[475] Stilting, *Acta SS. Sept.*, IV 504 (sec. 508).

[476] Stilting, *Acta SS. Sept.*, IV 505 (sec. 510-511).

[477] Stilting, *Acta SS. Sept.*, IV 528-529. He argues (p. 529 sec. 642-643) that in addition to those of St Phocas the remains of several other martyrs were translated at this time.

[478] Regarding the works which appeared in the interim (1753-1890) see p. 35 n. 2 above.

[479] Doubtless there are other historical factors involved, but these appear to have been the most immediate.

Pierre Batiffol and Jean Pargoire regarding the *Novae homiliae*, which saw those homilies distributed between the first two years at Constantinople. The results of both areas of investigation were an enabling factor in Bonsdorff's neat distribution of the series between the two locations.

1. RAUSCHEN

It is perhaps obvious to say that Rauschen's chief interest in the homilies concerns their chronology. Yet it is precisely his interest in how they fit into the years of Theodosius' reign which prompts him to delve further into the questions of when, in what sequence, and even which homilies were delivered during the period stretching from Chrysostom's ordination as presbyter (386) to the point of Theodosius' death (395). The fact that it is the overall sequence of events, not the homilies themselves that are important, moreover, dictates the way in which the information is presented. Thus we find sporadic mention of the homilies throughout the body of his text (from p. 251 onwards), with a more intense discussion reserved for three excurses appended at its conclusion (pp. 495-529). These excurses deal with the homilies which pre-date the riots (386-Lent 387), the homilies on the statues (387), and Chrysostom's preaching activity at Antioch after 387, respectively. In order to preserve the flavour of Rauschen's approach, the overview of his arguments which follows is presented according to the same divisions. Where a homily is mentioned in the body of his text, but the date proposed is discussed neither there nor in the relevant excursus, the information is reserved for the tables which appear in the summary below. For the derivation of such data (not always acknowledged by Rauschen), the reader is referred to Table 13.b, located at the end of Part One.

a. *Preaching activity at Antioch up to the riots of 387*

As a characteristic feature of the sermons which belong to Chrysostom's first year of preaching, Rauschen points to their brevity, and to the tendency of the homilist to yield his place to his bishop.[480] As for the location of the first eight *Sermones in Genesim* (CPG 4410) soon after Chrysostom's ordination, Rauschen cites the opening of *Sermo 2* as the basis for that decision.[481] In considering that the sermon on Meletius

---

[480] Rauschen, *Jahrbücher*, 251-252, cites *De b. Philogonio* (CPG 4319) and *In diem natalem* (CPG 4334) as examples.

[481] Rauschen, *Jahrbücher*, 252 n. 4.

(CPG 4345) was delivered on the fifth anniversary of the bishop's death (c. the end of May 386),[482] he argues against Montfaucon, who wished to locate it on the day commemorating the translation of Meletius' remains to Antioch from Constantinople and therefore situated the homily in 387.[483] It is the sequence and interrelationship of three particular groups of homilies, however, which occupy Rauschen's attention and form the basis of his first excursus.

Only a few years earlier, Usener had radically reassessed the sequence, and therefore chronology, of the series of homilies *Adv. Iudaeos* (CPG 4327) and *Contra Anomoeos* (CPG 4318-4323), and of a small group of homilies associated with the Christmas sermon *In diem natalem* (CPG 4334).[484] Rauschen, unable to agree with Usener on many points, finds it necessary to go back over the whole issue. In discerning among the homilies *Adv. Iudaeos* two discrete series (*or. 1, 2, 8;* and *or. 5-7*)[485] and a homily which stands on its own (*or. 3*),[486] Rauschen does not differ from Usener. The point at which he diverges concerns the position of *Adv. Iud. or. 4,* which, on the basis of its thematic conformity, he appends to the second series just prior to *or. 5.*[487] Rauschen further extends this sequence by positioning *Exp. in ps. 41* (CPG 4413.2) immediately after *Adv. Iud. or. 7,* claiming that in the opening of the former Chrysostom makes explicit reference to the latter, further indicating that no other sermon intervened.[488] In the case of *Adv. Iud. or. 3,* while he agrees in essence with Usener's argumentation regarding the location of this homily in January 387, Rauschen is at pains to argue further that the Christians of Antioch at that time celebrated Easter not with the Alexandrians, but in accord with the Roman custom, a circumstance which would mean that Easter was celebrated in 387 on March 21 and not on April 25. This is of considerable significance for the chronology of the homilies *De statuis* (CPG 4330), delivered during Lent of that year.[489] Rauschen also disagrees with Usener's location of *Adv. Iud. or. 6* after the Jewish Day of Atonement. He considers the evidence to indicate that it was delivered on

---

[482] Rauschen, *Jahrbücher*, 252 n. 8.

[483] In fact Montfaucon (see p. 80 above) offered the alternative of just after the fifth anniversary of his death (i.e., after the end of May 386) in addition to the anniversary of the translation (early 387).

[484] See pp. 152-154 below.

[485] Rauschen, *Jahrbücher*, 496-497.

[486] Rauschen, *Jahrbücher*, 497.

[487] Rauschen, *Jahrbücher*, 501-502. In this he follows Montfaucon (see p. 74 above). Usener (see p. 152 below) had considered it to post-date the second series and had located it by itself in early September 389.

[488] Rauschen, *Jahrbücher*, 497, in particular n. 10.

[489] Rauschen, *Jahrbücher*, 497-501.

the Day of Atonement itself.[490] Without defining the chronology further, Rauschen on this basis establishes the following sequences:

> **Sequence A**. *De incompr. dei nat. hom. 1* (CPG 4318);[491] (soon after, shortly before Jewish New Year) *Adv. Iud. or. 1*; (ten or more days later, five days before the Jewish Day of Atonement) *Adv. Iud. or. 2*; (shortly after the Day of Atonement) *Adv. Iud. or. 8*.[492]

> **Sequence B**. (before Jewish New Year, ten or more days before the Day of Atonement) *Adv. Iud. or. 4*; (the day preceding the Day of Atonement) *Adv. Iud. or. 5*; (Day of Atonement) *Adv. Iud. or. 6*; (before the Festival of the Tabernacles) *Adv. Iud. or. 7*; (shortly after) *Exp. in ps. 41*.[493]

The next group of homilies to be considered is that associated with the sermon *In diem natalem*. Rauschen finds the connection between this and the homily *De b. Philogonio* (CPG 4319) firmly established,[494] as also the connection between *De baptismo Christi* (CPG 4335) and *In s. Lucianum* (CPG 4346).[495] He further concurs with Usener and Montfaucon that there is a close relationship between the Epiphany and Christmas sermons. He disagrees with Usener, however, in the definition of that relationship. Where Usener located *In diem natalem* at the end of the year in which *De baptismo Christi* occurred, Rauschen finds his grounds for doing so unconvincing and argues, moreover, that if, as he himself establishes, the Christmas homily is located in the year 386, this arrangement becomes impossible, as Chrysostom had at that point not yet been ordained. Rauschen further finds an indication within *De baptismo Christi* that this is the first Epiphany on which the homilist has preached, a circumstance which neatly locates the homily following *In diem natalem*.[496] This leads to the establishment of the following sequence:

> **Sequence C**. (Dec. 20) *De b. Philogonio*; (Dec. 25) *In diem natalem*; (Jan. 6) *De baptismo Christi*; (Jan. 7) *In s. Lucianum*.

---

[490] Rauschen, *Jahrbücher*, 497.

[491] Like Usener, Rauschen considers the connection between *Adv. Iud. or. 1* and this first of the homilies *Contra Anomoeos* to have been firmly established. See further Montfaucon (p. 73 above).

[492] Rauschen, *Jahrbücher*, 496-497.

[493] Rauschen, *Jahrbücher*, 497 and 501-502. For the actual dates assigned the individual homilies of both Sequence A and B see Table 5.b.

[494] Rauschen, *Jahrbücher*, 503.

[495] Rauschen, *Jahrbücher*, 504.

[496] Rauschen, *Jahrbücher*, 503-504.

The third group of homilies (CPG 4318-4323) prompts only a brief discussion by Rauschen, leading to the following expression of their relationship:

> **Sequence D**. (shortly before Jewish New Year) *De incompr. dei nat. hom. 1* (CPG 4318); remainder of Sequence A (see above); *De incompr. dei nat. hom. 2-4*; *De anathemate* (CPG 3430);[497] *De incompr. dei nat. hom. 5*; (Dec. 20) *De b. Philogonio* (CPG 4319); (day of circus) *De consubstantiali* (CPG 4320); (next day) *De petitione matris fil. Zeb.* (CPG 4321); *In quatrid. Lazarum* (CPG 4322); *De Christi precibus* (CPG 4323).[498]

The interrelationship of the three groups, already determined in part with respect to the fourth sequence, is the next issue to require resolution. Taking as his baseline the third group, the ten homilies *Contra Anomoeos*, Rauschen points to evidence indicating that the sequence was interrupted at three points. The first point occurs directly after the first homily (*De incompr. dei nat. hom. 1*), where the first series *Adv. Iudaeos* (see Sequence A) intervenes. The second instance occurs following *De b. Philogonio*, where the close relationship between this homily and *In diem natalem* requires that the latter closely follow the former.[499] The third instance, concerning which Rauschen argues at some length, involves the interruption of the latter part of the series *Contra Anomoeos* by *Adv. Iud. or. 3*. Since the latter homily was delivered in January 387, this establishes that the Philogonius and Christmas sermons belong to 386, the first series of homilies *Adv. Iudaeos* to September of that year likewise, and the bulk of the homilies *Contra Anomoeos* to the latter part of 386, the remainder to the beginning of 387.[500] On the basis of internal evidence the second series *Adv. Iudaeos* (*or. 4-7*) locates itself after the riots in 387 and therefore in autumn of that year at the earliest. While admitting that this same evidence suggests that they were delivered after that year, Rauschen prefers nonetheless to situate the homilies in autumn 387, arguing that, since the homilist's efforts of 386 met with little success, it would have been difficult for him to have passed over the situation in 387 in silence without in subsequent years having to take up the struggle entirely anew.[501]

---

[497] Less than a decade later, Schwartz (see p. 147 below) dismissed this homily as spurious. See further n. 541 below.

[498] Rauschen, *Jahrbücher*, 504-506.

[499] Rauschen, *Jahrbücher*, 506.

[500] Rauschen, *Jahrbücher*, 506-508. This is in sharp distinction to the schema established by Usener, the rest of the supporting evidence for which Rauschen proceeds to address (pp. 508-511).

[501] Rauschen, *Jahrbücher*, 508.

b. *The Homilies on the Statues*

Since the relationship to its antecedents of the chronology Rauschen put forward for the homilies *De statuis* has been addressed more than adequately by van de Paverd in his introduction to the series,[502] no more than an outline of the results of Rauschen's deliberations is presented here.[503] In considering the following, it should be borne in mind that against the majority of opinion, which accepted a date for Easter calculated according to the Alexandrian tradition (April 25, 387), Rauschen considers Easter to have been celebrated along Roman lines (March 21).[504] He also assumes that the duration of Lent at Antioch is six weeks.[505]

The sequence and placement of the first eight homilies bears no surprises. *De statuis hom. 1* was delivered prior to the riots, while *hom. 2* occurs a few days after the event, but is demonstrably the successor to the first homily. Both fall in the period before Lent. *Hom. 3-8* situate themselves in the first week of Lent, with *hom. 8* delivered on the Saturday. On the next day, the Sunday before the second week of Lent, *hom. 15* was preached, then *hom. 9* and *10*, while *hom. 16* was delivered on the following Saturday. The third week of Lent was entirely taken up by the arrival of Caesarius and Ellebichus, the trial and their subsequent departure. As a consequence no sermon was delivered that week. Preaching resumes in week four of Lent with *hom. 17*, delivered on the Sunday, and *hom. 11-13* preached over the next three days (Monday to Wednesday). In the fifth week of Lent Rauschen locates *hom. 18*, which was delivered after mid-Lent, but less than twenty days after the closure of the baths at Antioch. *Hom. 14* and *20* occupy a place during the sixth week of Lent, the latter towards the end of that week, while *hom. 21* was delivered on Easter Sunday (March 21). *Hom. 19*, while it bears no relationship to events following the riots, appears to be close in content to *hom. 14*. This circumstance leads Rauschen to situate it in the same year, soon after Easter.[506]

---

[502] Van de Paverd, *Homilies on the Statues*, 205-362. For van de Paverd's own findings see pp. 245f below.

[503] For the full argument see Rauschen, *Jahrbücher*, 512-520.

[504] See Rauschen, *Jahrbücher*, 500-501 and 518.

[505] This view had earlier been promoted by Stilting (see p. 116 above).

[506] Rauschen, *Berliner Philologische Wochenschrift* 30 (1911) 923-927, in response to the criticisms of R. Goebel, *De Ioannis Chrysostomi et Libanii orationibus quae sunt de seditione Antiochensium*, diss., Göttingen 1910, 51-55, later revised this schema, placing *hom. 3* on the Sunday before the first week of Lent, *hom. 4-8* on successive days in the same week (Monday-Friday), and *hom. 15* on the Saturday of that week, not the Sunday as previously suggested. *Hom. 9* and *10* he locates more firmly on the Monday and Tuesday

c. *Preaching at Antioch after 387*

Rauschen then proceeds to fill in the remainder of 387 subsequent to *De statuis hom. 21*. On the basis of *De Anna sermo 1* (CPG 4411) and the title to *De statuis hom. 19*, he establishes that the latter was in fact delivered on the Sunday before Ascension, followed by the homily *De decem mill. tal. deb.* (CPG 4368).[507] The five extant sermons *De Anna* then followed, the first four being preached before Pentecost, a homily (now lost) following on Pentecost itself, and the fifth being delivered shortly thereafter. The three homilies *De Davide et Saule* (CPG 4412) belong likewise to this year and were delivered some time later.[508] Finally, the second of the series *Adv. Iudaeos* (see Sequence B above) is to be situated in autumn of this year.[509] Rauschen argues against the location of the two catecheses *Ad illuminandos* (CPG 4460, 4464) in Lent of 387,[510] preferring to situate the first in 388 or later and the second in 388 or 389.[511]

He then turns to the group of homilies associated with the larger series on Genesis (CPG 4409) and argues, against Tillemont,[512] that the latter cannot have been delivered in either 395 or 396.[513] For the cluster of homilies attached to this series and the sermons within the series itself, Rauschen establishes the following sequence.

> **Sequence E.** (before Lent) *In illud: Vidi dom. hom. 2, 3, 5, 6* (CPG 4417); (Sunday before Lent = seventh Sunday before Easter) *Hom. 1 in Gen.*; (Monday, first week of Lent) *Hom. 2 in Gen.*; *Hom. 3-10 in Gen.*; (Saturday, week two) *Hom. 11 in Gen.*; (to before Maundy Thursday) *Hom. 12-32 in Gen.*; (Maundy Thursday) *De prod. Iudae hom. 2* (CPG 4336); (Good Friday) *De cruce et latrone hom. 2* (CPG 4339); (Easter Sunday) *De resurrectione* (CPG 4341); *In princ. Act. hom. 1-4* (CPG 4371); *De mutatione nom. hom. 1-2* (CPG

---

of week two of Lent, while admitting with Goebel that *hom. 17* belongs after the sequence *hom. 11-13*, towards the end of week four. He further reverses the places of *hom. 18* and *14*, locating *hom. 14* around the end of week four or beginning of week five. With respect to *hom. 20*, he suddenly talks of it being located in the sixth or seventh week of Lent.

[507] Rauschen, *Jahrbücher*, 520-521. In this he contradicts Montfaucon (see pp. 83f above), who had located CPG 4368 before *De statuis hom. 19*.

[508] Rauschen, *Jahrbücher*, 521.

[509] Rauschen, *Jahrbücher*, 278-279.

[510] See Montfaucon, p. 76 above.

[511] Rauschen, *Jahrbücher*, 522.

[512] See p. 56 above.

[513] Rauschen, *Jahrbücher*, 522-523.

4372); *Sermo 9 in Gen.* (CPG 4410); *De mutatione nom. hom. 3-4*; (after the second week of Easter) *Hom. 33-67 in Gen.* (CPG 4409).[514]

Although no date is assigned to this sequence in the body of Rauschen's text, the index to the volume records that the individual components were delivered in 388 or at least some time between 388 and 396.[515]

Concerning the three homilies *De diabolo tentatore* (CPG 4332), Rauschen finds himself in agreement with Tillemont and Montfaucon.[516] *Hom. 1* was delivered shortly after *De obsc. proph. hom. 2* (CPG 4420). There is no clear link between the second of the homilies *De diabolo tentatore* and the first, but it is evident that the third followed immediately upon the second. Moreover, *De diabolo tent. hom. 2* and *3*, by virtue of the reference to Flavian's absence in the former, supply clear proof of their delivery at Antioch. Both homilies were delivered during Lent, the one two days after the other.[517] The nine homilies *De paenitentia* (CPG 4333), on the other hand, neither cohere as a series, nor contain any indication of date or that they were delivered at Antioch.[518]

On internal grounds, Rauschen finds the perceived link between the homilies *De coemeterio et cruce* (CPG 4337) and *De ss. Bernice et Prosdoce* (CPG 4355) secure. The point at which he disagrees with Montfaucon concerns both the date of the festival of Bernice, Prosdoce and Domnina and the year in which the two homilies were preached. Since the former was delivered on a Good Friday, less than twenty days before the latter, while the festival which the latter commemorates fell on April 20,[519] it can be established that the homilies belong to 391.[520] The sermon deliv-

---

[514] Rauschen, *Jahrbücher*, 523-524.

[515] Rauschen, *Jahrbücher*, 582-583. This is presumably on the grounds that Lent of 386 and 387 are already occupied and on the basis of his arguments against the years 395 or 396.

[516] See pp. 54 and 77 above.

[517] Rauschen, *Jahrbücher*, 524. Stilting (see p. 115 above) had argued that the three homilies *De diabolo tentatore* did indeed form a tight-knit sequence and that therefore all five homilies were delivered at the same period. Rauschen fails to take this view into consideration.

[518] Rauschen, *Jahrbücher*, 524 n. 14, argues against Montfaucon (see pp. 77f above), who adduced two pieces of evidence in favour of their Antiochene provenance.

[519] Montfaucon (see p. 78 above) believed that it fell on April 14, leading him to locate the homilies in 392.

[520] Rauschen, *Jahrbücher*, 525. A. Wilmart, "Le souvenir d'Eusèbe d'Émèse. Un discours en l'honneur des saintes d'Antioche Bernice, Prosdoce et Domnine", AB 38 (1920) 254 n. 4, later argued, on the same grounds, that *De ss. Bernice et Prosdoce* was delivered in 394. More recently, C. Nardi, "A proposito degli atti del martirio di Bernice, Prosdoce e

ered in the presence of Diodore of Tarsus (CPG 4406) is assigned by him
to the period before 393.[521] Rauschen further explores the dates of a
number of festival homilies. *De s. Pelagia* (CPG 4350) and *In s. Ignatium*
(CPG 4351) were delivered on Oct. 8 and 17, respectively. *In s. Eustathium* (CPG 4352) was followed on Nov. 18 by *In s. Romanum* (CPG
4353), in turn followed by *In illud: Domine, non est in hom.* (CPG 4419).
In s. Iulianum (CPG 4360) was delivered at Antioch, where the martyr's
grave was located, probably on March 16. The homily *In s. Barlaam* (CPG
4361) was delivered in summer, most probably on Aug. 14, followed the
next day by *In d. Pauli: Nolo vos ignorare* (CPG 4380). Finally, Rauschen
asserts that the festival of all martyrs, at which *De ss. martyribus* (CPG
4365) was preached, was probably celebrated at Antioch on the Friday
following Pentecost.[522]

Just prior to the festival homilies, he also considers the group associated with the homily *In kalendas* (CPG 4328). While the year to which
this sequence belongs is uncertain, Rauschen points out that 388 not
387, as Tillemont had proposed,[523] is the earliest possible year for their
delivery.

> **Sequence F.** (shortly before January) one of *De laudibus s. Pauli hom. 1-7*
> (CPG 4344); (Jan. 1) *In kalendas*; (Jan. 2) *De Lazaro concio 1* (CPG 4329); *De
> Lazaro conc. 2-3*; (Jan. 24) *De s. Babyla* (CPG 4347); (Feb. 4) *In Iuventinum et
> Maximum* (CPG 4349); *De Lazaro conc. 4-5*; *In illud: Vidua eligatur* (CPG
> 4386); (three days after an earthquake) *De Lazaro concio 6*; *De Lazaro concio
> 7*.[524]

Rauschen then turns to the exegetical series delivered at Antioch. He
finds no difficulty with accepting that the series on Matthew (CPG 4424),
the explanation of the Psalms (CPG 4413), John (CPG 4425), the two Letters to the Corinthians (CPG 4428-4429), the commentary on Galatians
(CPG 4430) and the homilies on Titus (CPG 4438) were all preached at
that location. He further considers that they "most probably" belong to
the period after 390.[525] The provenance of the series on Romans (CPG
4427) and Ephesians (CPG 4431), however, is by no means as certain. In
the case of the first, after dismissing the stylistic criterion of Photius as
invalid, Rauschen turns to the argument for Antiochene provenance put

---

Domnina", *Civilta Classica e Cristiana* 1 (1980) 245, while ostensibly following Wilmart,
claims that the homily was delivered in "392 or 394".

[521] Rauschen, *Jahrbücher*, 386.

[522] Rauschen, *Jahrbücher*, 526-527.

[523] See p. 51 above.

[524] Rauschen, *Jahrbücher*, 525-526.

[525] Rauschen, *Jahrbücher*, 527.

forward by Montfaucon.[526] Although the latter had regarded a passage in *In Rom. hom. 8* as proof that, aside from Chrysostom and the audience, the bishop (ποιμήν: "shepherd") was also present, Rauschen points out that the homilist merely states that all are assembled under the one shepherd, which does not exclude the possibility that Chrysostom is here referring to himself. As for the passage, which Montfaucon had elicited from *hom. 30*, regarding the sites associated with St Paul, not only had Paul never been in chains at Antioch, but there is no indication that the homilist identifies these sites with the location at which he preaches. On these grounds, Rauschen sees the passage as referring rather to Jerusalem or Rome.[527] Instead, in *hom. 29* the homilist explicitly designates himself "shepherd". Although Montfaucon had argued that Chrysostom also called himself "shepherd" at Antioch, in neither of the instances cited by Montfaucon (*De Lazaro concio 6*; *De statuis hom. 20*) does he explicitly do so, nor do they indicate more than his office of preaching or his increased authority in the absence of Flavian. Rauschen concludes that not only is there no certainty that the series on Romans was preached at Antioch, but every likelihood that it was in fact delivered at Constantinople.[528]

The point of origin of the homilies on Ephesians is more difficult to determine. Although Tillemont and Montfaucon had both settled upon Antioch,[529] Rauschen finds that the series contains apparently conflicting evidence. In *In Eph. hom. 6* Chrysostom refers to the current state of war, a circumstance which excludes the years 388-395 and indicates that the series must belong to the period 395 or later. Everything hinges, however, on the interpretation placed upon the passage referring to a schism within the local church (*hom. 11*). Here, if the perceived association with Evagrius is set aside, it is made clear by John that the opposition is ranged against himself and, while at one point he denies holding ἀρχή, at another he makes it clear that he does in fact hold such authority. On this basis, Rauschen finds himself unable to accept that the division in question is the Meletian schism which persisted at Antioch, but finds that overall the evidence in *hom. 11* points instead to Constantinople. Yet, despite this, the references to the martyr Babylas (*hom. 9*) and to the ascetic Julianus Sabas (*hom. 21*) point to Antioch. Rauschen concludes that, if one accepts an Antiochene provenance for this series, it is certain

---

[526] See p. 98 above.

[527] Rauschen, *Jahrbücher*, 527.

[528] Rauschen, *Jahrbücher*, 528.

[529] See pp. 62 and 9 above.

that the homilies were not delivered before 395 and that the bishop
Evagrius was still alive at that juncture.[530]

d. *Summary*

With regard to the provenance of the homilies examined by Rauschen, the overwhelming impression gained is that, with the exception of
certain of the exegetical series, this issue had long since been decided.
The majority of the homilies assumed to stem from Antioch have
therefore not been entered in Table 5.a. For a list of these the reader is
referred to the relevant column of Table 13.a (pp. 255-259). As we have
seen, however, within the course of the third excursus Rauschen does
enter into a discussion of the provenance of several homilies and series.
Along with a list of the Constantinopolitan homilies which receive
mention, the conclusions reached are presented below.

Table 5.a. Provenance — Rauschen

CPG no.	Antioch	CPG no.	Constantinople
4332	*De diabolo tentatore hom. 2-3* (p. 524)	4324	*Contra Anomoeos hom. 11* (p. 506)
4431	*In Eph. hom. 1-24* (pp. 528f)*	4325	*De Christi divinitate* (p. 506)
		4417	*In illud: Vidi dominum hom. 1, 4* (p. 523 n. 3)
		4426	*In Acta apost. hom. 1-55* (p. 524 n. 1)
		4427	*In Rom. hom. 1-32* (pp. 527f)*

* Probably.

Table 5.b. Chronology — Rauschen

Year (month-season)	Homily	Cited (page)
386		
beginning	*Sermo cum presbyter* (CPG 4317)	251, 511
day before Lent	*Sermo 1 in Genesim* (CPG 4410)	252
Lent	*Sermones 2-8 in Genesim* (CPG 4410)	252
end of May	*De s. Meletio* (CPG 4345)	252
end Aug./ beg. Sept.	*De incompr. dei natura hom. 1* (CPG 4318)	252, 504f
early September	*Adv. Iudaeos or. 1* (CPG 4327)	496, 511
mid September	*Adv. Iudaeos or. 2*	496, 511

---

[530] Rauschen, *Jahrbücher*, 528-529.

shortly after Sept. 19	*Adv. Iudaeos or. 8*	496f, 511
c. late September - before Dec. 20	*De incompr. dei natura hom.* 2-4 (CPG 4318) *De anathemate* (CPG 3430) *De incompr. dei natura hom.* 5	504f,511 " "
Dec. 20	*De beato Philogonio* (CPG 4319)	253, 503
Dec. 25	*In diem natalem* (CPG 4334)	253, 503
387		
Jan. 1	*De consubstantiali* (CPG 4320)	505, 511
Jan. 2	*De petitione matris fil. Zeb.* (CPG 4321)	505, 511
Jan. 6	*De baptismo Christi* (CPG 4335)	503f, 511
Jan. 7	*In s. Lucianum* (CPG 4346)	504, 511
after Jan. 6 - before end of January	*Adv. Iudaeos or. 3* (CPG 4327) *In quatriduanum Lazarum* (CPG 4322) *De Christi precibus* (CPG 4323) *De resurrectione mortuorum* (CPG 4340)	497ff, 511 505f, 511 " 505, 511
Jan. 24 - March 21	*De statuis hom. 1-18, 20-21* (CPG 4330)	512, 519
Sunday before Ascension	*De statuis hom. 19*	278, 521
before Pentecost	*De decem mill. talentorum deb.* (CPG 4368) *De Anna sermones 1-4* (CPG 4411)	521 278, 521
after Pentecost	*De Anna sermo 5*	278, 521
c. Aug. 29	*Adv. Iudaeos or. 4* (CPG 4327)	501f, 512
Sept. 7	*Adv. Iudaeos or. 5*	497, 512
Sept. 8	*Adv. Iudaeos or. 6*	497, 512
Sept. 8 - Sept. 13	*Adv. Iudaeos or. 7*	497, 512
after Sept. 13	*Expositio in psalmum 41* (CPG 4413.2)	497, 512
date unspecified	*De Davide et Saule hom. 1-3* (CPG 4412)	521
388*		
389		
390		
391		
April 4	*De coemeterio et cruce* (CPG 4337)	525
April 20	*De ss. Bernice et Prosdoce* (CPG 4355)	525
392		
393		
394		
395		

* *Ad illum. cat. 1* (CPG 4460) = 388 or later; *Ad illum. cat. 2* (CPG 4464) = 388/389

The larger sequences established by Rauschen (Sequences A-F) have already been outlined in the course of the above discussion.[531] Several smaller sequences, however, are also confirmed.

---

[531] For Sequences A-D see pp. 137-138 above. For Sequences E-F see pp. 140 and 142.

Sequence G. *De proph. obsc. hom. 2* (CPG 4420); (shortly after) *De diabo-lo tent. hom. 1* (CPG 4332).

Sequence H. (Lent) *De diabolo tent. hom. 2*; (two days later) *De diabolo tent. hom. 3*.

Sequence I. *In s. Eustathium* (CPG 4352); (Nov. 18) *In s. Romanum* (CPG 4353); *In illud: Domine, non est in homine* (CPG 4419).

Sequence J. (prob. Aug. 14) *In s. Barlaam* (CPG 4361); (the next day) *In d. Pauli: Nolo vos ignorare* (CPG 4380).

2. SCHWARTZ

In 1905 Eduard Schwartz, who had access to the writings of Tille-mont, Montfaucon and Hermann Usener, but not of Rauschen, devoted a chapter in his treatise on Jewish and Christian Easter tables to a reassessment of the chronology of the homilies *Adv. Iudaeos* (CPG 4327). As has been seen in the work of Rauschen and those before him, the arrangement accorded these sermons is central to the fixing of the identity and distribution of the homilies delivered during the first two years at Antioch (386-387). With the appearance of Schwartz's solution to the problem, the flurry of activity regarding these years essentially comes to a halt.[532]

a. *386-387*

In contrast to Rauschen, who had approached the problem purely from the view of the interrelationship of the various groups of homilies, Schwartz's interest lies with fixing the calendar in use among the Jewish community at Antioch in the latter half of the fourth century. Based on the investigations undertaken earlier in his monograph,[533] it is Schwartz's contention that the "reformed" calendar was not yet in existence at Antioch. This permits him to dismiss out of hand the work of Usener, who had relied upon that calendar when making his calculations.[534] Rather, Schwartz's belief is that the evidence accords better with the old observance, in which the Jewish festivals were simply reckoned accord-ing to the Julian calendar. In order to prove this and in order to demon-

---

[532] Lietzmann (see p. 166 below) considers the work of Schwartz to be the final word. See, however, Mahler, p. 162 below.

[533] See Schwartz, *Ostertafeln*, Chapters VI-X.

[534] See pp. 152-154 below. Schwartz noticeably avoids addressing the conclusions reached by Usener.

strate the superiority of Montfaucon's calculations over those of Usener, he finds it necessary to establish beyond doubt the chronology of the two series *Adv. Iudaeos* (*or. 1-2*; *or. 4-8*).

Since there is insufficient evidence for securing their date within the individual homilies *Adv. Iudaeos*, Schwartz turns to the larger sequence of homilies to which they belong, namely those which fall in the first year of preaching. First of all, two secure points in the chronology can be established — that *Adv. Iud. or. 3* was delivered at the end of January 387 (prob. Jan. 31),[535] and that the riots in Antioch occurred at the beginning of that same year.[536] Moreover, if one considers the frequency with which the homilist preached at this time, aside from the daily synaxes during Lent, Chrysostom himself says that as a rule services were held three or four times a week.[537] The days on which this regular worship occurred Schwartz identifies as Sunday, Wednesday, Friday and the occasional Saturday.[538]

In the second instance, the following sequence for the first year of preaching at Antioch can be established:[539]

> **Sequence A.** (beginning 386) *Cum presbyter fuit ordinatus* (CPG 4317); (Monday, Feb. 16, 386; first day of Lent) *Sermo 1 in Gen.* (CPG 4410); (Lent) *Sermones 2-8 in Gen.*; *De incompr. dei nat. hom. 1* (CPG 4318); *Adv. Iud. or. 1-2*; (Oct. 8) *De s. Pelagia* (CPG 4350); (Oct. 17) *In s. Ignatium* (CPG 4351);[540] *De incompr. dei nat. hom. 2-5*;[541] *De profectu evangelii* (CPG 4385); (Dec. 20) *De b. Philogonio* (CPG 4319); (Dec. 25) *In diem natalem* (CPG 4334); (Jan. 6, 387) *De baptismo Christi* (CPG 4335); (Jan. 7) *In s. Lucianum* (CPG 4346); (Jan. 16) *De consubstantiali* (CPG 4320); (Jan. 17) *De petitione matr. fil. Zeb.* (CPG 4321); (Jan. 31) *Adv. Iud. or. 3*; *In quatrid. Lazarum* (CPG 4322); *De resurr. mortuorum* (CPG 4340); *De Christi precibus* (CPG 4323); (poss. Feb. 12) *De s. Meletio* (CPG 4345).

---

[535] See Schwartz, *Ostertafeln*, 120-121, in particular 121 n. 1.

[536] Schwartz, *Ostertafeln*, 170.

[537] As evidence for this Schwartz cites *Adv. Iud. or. 3*, PG 48,867 4-6.

[538] Schwartz, *Ostertafeln*, 170-171.

[539] For the basis of this sequence see Schwartz, *Ostertafeln*, 171-179. Cf. Montfaucon, p. 106 above.

[540] Schwartz, *Ostertafeln*, 173-174, identifies the festivals of Sts Pelagia and Ignatius as those to which the opening of *De incompr. dei nat. hom. 2* refers.

[541] Schwartz, *Ostertafeln*, 175 n. 1, argues against Montfaucon's insertion of *De anathemate* (CPG 3430) following *De incompr. dei nat. hom. 3* (see p. 75 above), pointing out that not only does the summary located at the opening to the former fail to concur convincingly with the contents of the latter, but the former cannot be a genuine homily of Chrysostom. For the status of this homily see De Aldama, *Repertorium*, 168 (no.448).

In addition to this Schwartz, although avoiding discussion of the chronology of the homilies *De statuis* (CPG 4330), asserts that *De statuis hom. 3* fell on Sunday, March 7, 387 (the day before Lent), a circumstance which suggests that the first two homilies in this series, as also the sermons in Sequence A from *In quatrid. Lazarum* onwards, belong to February of that year.[542]

This leads him to the question of the second sequence of homilies *Adv. Iudaeos*, which he arranges as follows:

Sequence B. *Adv. Iud. or. 4-7; Exp. in ps. 41* (CPG 4413.2); *Adv. Iud. or. 8.*[543]

While it is self-evident, from a comment in *Adv. Iud. or. 6*, that this sequence dates to after the riots and can therefore only have been delivered in autumn 387 at the earliest, there is also the point that the homilist makes reference in *Adv. Iud. or. 4* to earlier polemic on the same topic. If one takes his words at face value, their most natural point of reference is *Adv. Iud. or. 1-2*. Finding it improbable that Chrysostom would have recalled those homilies in such a way if two or more years had intervened, Schwartz finds himself strongly inclined to situate the sequence in autumn 387 itself.[544]

With the chronology of the sequence established, Schwartz is able to demonstrate the validity of his earlier premise that the old observance still persisted among the Jews of Antioch. In the Christmas sermon of 386 the homilist states that the Day of Atonement and the Feast of Tabernacles fell in that year at the end of September. Reckoned according to the "reformed" calendar, upon which Usener based his calculations, the dates for those festivals in no way suit the circumstances. When calculated according to the old observance, however, all of the evidence is in accord.[545] While the evidence concerning Sequence B is too uncertain to permit calculation, this does allow Schwartz to pinpoint the date of the first two homilies *Adv. Iudaeos*. He is led to conclude that they were delivered on Sept. 2 and Sept. 13, 386, respectively.[546]

In the course of this investigation, Schwartz has occasion to consider the date of one further sequence of homilies.

Sequence C. (prob. Dec. 28) one of *De laudibus s. Pauli hom. 1-7* (CPG 4344); (Jan. 1) *In kalendas* (CPG 4328); (Jan. 2) *De Lazaro concio 1* (CPG

---

[542] Schwartz, *Ostertafeln*, 179.
[543] Schwartz, *Ostertafeln*, 180-181.
[544] Schwartz, *Ostertafeln*, 181. Cf. Rauschen (p. 138 above).
[545] Schwartz, *Ostertafeln*, 182.
[546] Schwartz, *Ostertafeln*, 183.

4329); *De Lazaro conc. 2-3*; (Jan. 24) *De s. Babyla* (CPG 4347); *In Iuventinum et Maximum* (CPG 4349); *De Lazaro conc. 4-5*.[547]

The force of this footnote is to argue, with Montfaucon,[548] against the possibility that the homily *In kalendas* belongs to the beginning of 387.[549] Aside from the fact that the sequence of homilies already established for early 387 (see Sequence A) does not permit the inclusion of the cluster of homilies associated with this address, Jan. 1 and 2 of the year in which Sequence C occurs must both have fallen on days of regular synaxis.[550] This restricts the list of possible years to those which began with a Friday or Saturday. In the case of the latter, the years 388 or 393 are both a possibility. In the case of the former, the appropriate years (387 and 398) are both excluded, the first on the grounds already stated, the second on the basis that on Feb. 26 Chrysostom was already enthroned at Constantinople. This leaves available only the first option, 388 or 393.

b. *Summary*

Since Schwartz discusses homilies which stem exclusively from the early period of Chrysostom's presbyterate at Antioch, the table recording provenance has been dispensed with and only a summary of his conclusions regarding chronology is presented. For the three sequences which he either endorses or establishes, the reader is referred to Sequences A-C above.

Table 6. Chronology — Schwartz

Year (month-season)	Homily	Cited (page)
386		

---

[547] Schwartz, *Ostertafeln*, 176 n. 3.

[548] See p. 74 above.

[549] This view had been promoted by both Tillemont (see p. 51 above) and Stilting (p. 113 above).

[550] On the basis of his own predication of Friday as a day of regular synaxis, Schwartz, who cites Tillemont in support of the assertion, here assumes that Tillemont held the same view. In determining the year, the latter does not require, however, that Jan. 1 *as well as* Jan. 2 fall on a day of regular synaxis, since he apparently assumes that the Kalends were at this point celebrated as a Christian festival. See further Tillemont, *Mémoires*, XI 566 (Note XXIV).

beginning (before Lent)	Sermo cum presbyter (CPG 4317)	171
Feb. 16 - (Lent)	Sermo 1 in Genesim (CPG 4410) Sermones 2-8 in Genesim	" "
date unspecified	De incompr. dei natura hom. 1 (CPG 4318)	172
Sept. 2	Adv. Iudaeos or. 1 (CPG 4327)	172f, 183
Sept. 13	Adv. Iudaeos or. 2	"
Oct. 8	De s. Pelagia (CPG 4350)	173
Oct. 17	In s. Ignatium (CPG 4351)	173-174
date unspecified	De incompr. dei natura hom. 2-5 De profectu evangelii (CPG 4385)	174-175 176
Dec. 20	De beato Philogonio (CPG 4319)	176
Dec. 25	In diem natalem (CPG 4334)	"
387		
Jan. 6	De baptismo Christi (CPG 4335)	176
Jan. 7	In s. Lucianum (CPG 4346)	177
Jan. 16	De consubstantiali (CPG 4320)	"
Jan. 17	De petitione matris fil. Zeb. (CPG 4321)	"
Jan. 31	Adv. Iudaeos or. 3	121, 177f
February	In quatrid. Lazarum (CPG 4322) De resurr. mortuorum (CPG 4340) De Christi precibus (CPG 4323) De s. Meletio (CPG 4345) De statuis hom. 1-2 (CPG 4330)	178 178-179 179 " "
March 7	De statuis hom. 3	179
date unspecified	Remainder of CPG 4330	"
autumn	Adv. Iudaeos or. 4-7 Exp. in psalmum 41 (CPG 4413.2) Adv. Iudaeos or. 8	181 " "

3. MISCELLANEOUS WRITINGS[551]

The miscellaneous writings of this period demonstrate a diversity of
narrow interests. Some reflect the heightened interest in fixing the chronology of the first two years of preaching at Antioch, characterised by
lively debate concerning the date of the Christmas homily. Several, notably those of Batiffol and Pargoire, focus upon an entirely different sequence of homilies. Seeck's note on the homilies on Acts stands alone in
terms of its interest in the exegetical series.

---

[551] During this period Athanasius Papadopoulos-Kerameus, *Varia Graeca Sacra. Sbor-
nik Greceskikh neisdannikh bogoslovskikh tekstov IV-XV vekov*, St Petersburg 1909, increased the number of available catechetical instructions from two to five with his edition
of three hitherto unknown baptismal catecheses (CPG 4461-4462, 4467). In the introduction he apparently offers an opinion concerning their location and date. Regrettably, this
work has been unavailable to me.

a. *Clinton*

A propos of the debate regarding the date of *In diem natalem* (CPG 4334), which occupied the minds of Rauschen, Schwartz and Usener at this period, it would be remiss not to mention the earlier opinion of Henry Clinton. Because of the centrality of the Christmas sermon to the chronology of the first two years at Antioch, his comments, though brief in the extreme, are nonetheless important.

In a note of 1850 located in the appendix to his *Fasti Romani*, Clinton takes issue with Montfaucon over his dating of the homily to the year 386. It is Clinton's thesis that it was delivered a year later on Dec. 25, 387.[552] He proceeds by pointing to the passage in *In diem natalem* in which Chrysostom makes reference to his recent numerous discourses against the Jewish festival celebrated at the end of Gorpiaeus (i.e., September).[553] Montfaucon had identified these discourses as the first three sermons *Adv. Iudaeos* (CPG 4327), delivered in autumn of 386, and had dated the homily accordingly.[554] Clinton argues, however, that in *Adv. Iud. or. 6* the sedition at Antioch of February 387 is mentioned, dating the discourses on the Jews to September of 387 and *In diem natalem* accordingly to December 387.[555] He accuses Montfaucon of having based his identification of the discourses mentioned in the Christmas sermon on an *a priori* assumption that this latter sermon belongs to the first year of Chrysostom's preaching at Antioch. However, Clinton points out, the first three homilies *Adv. Iudaeos* were not all delivered in September as required by the statement in *In diem natalem*. The first of these was delivered in August, as Montfaucon himself admits. The five which belong to 387 were, on the other hand, all delivered within twenty days of the month of September.[556] It is far more probable, Clinton concludes, that these five are the numerous, lengthy discourses delivered in the month of September, to which Chrysostom refers.

---

[552] Clinton, *Fasti Romani*, II 238 note c.

[553] See PG 49,358 2-6.

[554] See p. 78 above.

[555] The wording I have used here is deliberately vague. Clinton appears to refer here simply to the discourses mentioned by the homilist in *In diem natalem*. It takes careful reading of the passage following this statement to determine that he intends not the full eight discourses on the Jews, but *Adv. Iud. or. 4-8*.

[556] For the evidence produced by Clinton to demonstrate this see the section of note c which is wrapped onto p. 239.

b. *Usener*

In 1889 Hermann Usener, in the course of investigating the adoption
of the feast of Christmas in the East, argued against both Montfaucon
and Clinton in favour of situating the homily *In diem natalem* (CPG
4334) on Dec. 25, 388.[557] In association with this he established a markedly different sequence and chronology for the eight homilies *Adv. Iudaeos* (CPG 4327), a circumstance which further prompted a revision of
the dates of the homilies *De b. Philogonio* (CPG 4319), *De baptismo
Christi* (CPG 4335) and *In s. Lucianum* (CPG 4346).

Because of the mention in *In diem natalem* of a series of recent discourses which the homilist preached on the Jewish New Year celebrations, Usener begins with the eight homilies *Adv. Iudaeos*. These, he argues, do not divide neatly into the two sequences (386: *or. 1-3*; 387: *or. 4-
8*) proposed by Montfaucon. While *or. 2* clearly follows *or. 1*,[558] it is *or. 8*,
not *or. 3*, which can be shown to have succeeded *or. 2*.[559] Aside from this
sequence (*or. 1, 2, 8*), a second group builds itself around *or. 5-7*. From
internal evidence, and based on their thematic cohesiveness, he argues
that the three were delivered within the space of a few days in rapid and
unbroken succession. A further homily, the contents of which are summarised in *or. 5*, is no longer available, as also a fifth sermon which followed *or. 7*.[560] Addressed against the same Jewish New Year festivities
but in a year when Chrysostom had not delivered such polemic for some
time, *or. 4* cannot be attached to either sequence. In this homily Chrysostom states that it is ten or more days before the Day of Atonement. On
this basis the discourse can only be located in the year 389, when the
Jewish New Year fell on Sept. 6 and the Day of Atonement on Sept. 15.
This fact locates *or. 4* on Sunday Sept. 2, 389.[561] *Or. 3*, addressed against
a small group of Antiochene Christians still adhering to the pre-Nicene
celebration of Easter, stands entirely on its own. The fact that Chrysostom here states that the Jewish *azyma* begins on a Sunday dates it to the
year 387, in which that festival commenced on Sunday March 21. It is
further to be observed that the homily locates itself after the announcement of the Lenten fast and the date of Easter for that year, but before

---

[557] Usener, *Weihnachtsfest*², 234-247. In so far as I can establish, throughout this
section the page numbering in the second edition (1911) is identical to that of the first.

[558] Usener, *Weihnachtsfest*², 237, in particular n. 8.

[559] Usener, *Weihnachtsfest*², 237-238. This is established on the basis of thematic
similarities.

[560] Usener, *Weihnachtsfest*², 238.

[561] Usener, *Weihnachtsfest*², 238-239.

the beginning of the Jewish Passover. This situates *or. 3* between Jan. 6 and 31, probably on Sunday Jan. 24, 387.[562]

Further, in *Adv. Iud. or. 3* we find the homilist prepared to enter into battle with the heretics on the question of the equality of the Son with the Father. This we find also in *or. 1* of the series, where the long sermon against the Anomoeans of the previous Sunday is clearly to be identified as *De incompr. dei nat. hom. 1* (CPG 4318). It was on this basis that Tillemont and Montfaucon assigned the first homilies *De incompr. dei natura* and the first sequence *Adv. Iudaeos* (*or. 1-3*) to the autumn of 386.[563] Two circumstances, however, speak against this. The details of the Jewish New Year celebrations provided in *or. 2* and *8* do not conform with the date on which the festival fell in 386, while what is stated concerning the Jews in the January 387 discourse (*or. 3*) indicates that it had not yet occurred to the homilist to take issue with the Jews.[564] There is nothing, moreover, in the homilies against the Anomoeans (CPG 4318) themselves which ties them to a specific year. Further to this, on internal grounds the second sequence *Adv. Iudaeos* (*or. 5-7*) must be situated after the Antiochene riots early in 387, albeit without specification of the length of the intervening period.[565]

It is here that we arrive at the question of the Christmas sermon (*In diem natalem*). Accepting Clinton's observation that the homily must refer to the second sequence *Adv. Iudaeos* (*or. 5-7*), Usener turns to the observation in *In diem natalem* that the Day of Atonement in that year fell towards the end of Gorpiaeus (September). On this basis the homily cannot be located in 387, as Clinton argued, since in that year the Day of Atonement fell at the beginning not the end of that month. The year 388, however, fits these circumstances exactly (Day of Atonement = Sept. 27), in which year therefore not only *In diem natalem* is to be located, but also *Adv. Iud. or. 5-7*.[566] This leaves only 387 for the first sequence *Adv. Iudaeos* (*or. 1, 2, 8*).[567] Further, accepting Montfaucon and Tillemont's observation that the homily on St Lucian (CPG 4346) necessarily follows that on the Epiphany (CPG 4335), but rejecting their argument that the Epiphany homily follows that on Christmas (CPG 4334), Usener argues in brief that *In S. Lucianum* and *De baptismo Christi* locate themselves in

---

[562] Usener, *Weihnachtsfest²*, 239-240.

[563] See pp. 51 and 73 (and 106) above. Tillemont in fact assigned only *or. 1-2* to autumn 386, arguing that *or. 3* belonged early in 387.

[564] Usener, *Weihnachtsfest²*, 241.

[565] Usener, *Weihnachtsfest²*, 241-243.

[566] Usener, *Weihnachtsfest²*, 243-244. For the precise dates assigned to these homilies see Table 7, p. 162 below.

[567] Usener, *Weihnachtsfest²*, 244.

January of 388, at a distance from *In diem natalem*.[568] As for *De b. Philogonio* (CPG 4319), as Usener had earlier established, this must necessarily be located shortly before the latter,[569] a circumstance which now allows it to be situated on Dec. 20, 388.[570]

c. *Seeck*

In 1894 Otto Seeck, arguing that Synesius of Cyrene departed from Constantinople not in 400 but in 402, dismissed the evidence of *In Acta apost. hom. 41* (CPG 4426) by relocating it, along with the homily commonly used to date that series (*hom. 44*), to Antioch.[571] Arguing that the three year period mentioned in *hom. 44* could as easily refer to Chrysostom's first three years as lector at Antioch,[572] Seeck points out that nowhere does the homilist indicate the location or his personal status.[573] In the course of *hom. 41*, moreover, John mentions a certain Theodorus. This can only refer to the conspiracy which occurred at Antioch in 372 and which is recorded by Libanius. The familiar reference to St Babylas of only a few lines earlier further speaks against Constantinople, as the audience there would scarcely have had knowledge of a local Antiochene saint. Thus, Seeck concludes, the earthquake mentioned in *hom. 41* must have occurred in Syria and has no relevance for Synesian chronology.

d. *Batiffol*

Pierre Batiffol, in an article of 1899, was the first in recent times to draw attention to the series of eleven homilies known as the *Novae*

---

[568] Usener, *Weihnachtsfest*[2], 244-246.

[569] Usener, *Weihnachtsfest*[2], 222-225.

[570] Usener, *Weihnachtsfest*[2], 247. For an outline of the full sequence see 244-245.

[571] Seeck, "Studien zu Synesios", 460 n. 44. He never actually states that the whole series was therefore delivered at Antioch, although this appears to be implied. Certainly subsequent scholarship has assumed this to be the case and has argued against Seeck's thesis on this basis. See the responses by Bonsdorff and Cameron, pp. 192 and 240 below.

[572] Seeck conveniently ignores the fact that only two orders (presbyter and bishop) had the authority to preach. Concerning the office of lector see Bingham, *Antiquities*, III.v.

[573] This is a somewhat peculiar statement. The homilist's explicit mention of his episcopal status (*In Acta apost. hom. 3* and *9*), a strong element in the arguments for the series' Constantinopolitan provenance, had been noted as early as Savile. See p. 39 above. Seeck may, however, be referring to *hom. 44* alone.

homiliae.[574] He considers that the titles to each of these initially recorded only the location at which the homily was preached, since this information is entirely independent of the contents. The brief précis of the subject matter now found in each is, he believes, a later addition.[575]

Hom. 6 (*Adv. catharos*: CPG 4441.6) is the first sermon to come under discussion. Here Batiffol affirms Montfaucon's opinion that it was delivered in the Church of the Apostles on the anniversary of Theodosius' death, the evidence for which is found in the title. Where Montfaucon had boldly assigned the homily to January 399,[576] however, Batiffol takes care to argue that as John was consecrated bishop of Constantinople in February 398, while the anniversary of the death of Theodosius falls on Jan. 17, this means that the homily can have been delivered no earlier than Jan. 17, 399.[577]

The next homily to be discussed is *Contra ludos et theatra* (CPG 4441.7). Here Batiffol points out, on the basis of the passage in which Chrysostom says it is a year since he arrived at the city, that the homily must have been preached after Feb. 25, 399. He then proceeds to the more difficult issue concerning the identity of the Friday on which the offending races were held. Here he accedes to Montfaucon's second argument in which it is observed that Good Friday, which fell in that year on April 8, is out of the question because of the mention of the recent havoc wreaked by a rainstorm upon the ripened, but as yet unharvested grain.[578] This indicates the possibility that the homily was delivered around June 399. There is no mention in the title of the location at which it was preached.[579]

Regarding the ninth homily in the series (*In illud: Pater meus usque modo operatur*: CPG 4441.10), in which Montfaucon had seen a direct reference to *Contra ludos et theatra* and which, on the basis of the original dating of the latter, had been assigned to the second Sunday following Easter,[580] Batiffol confirms the connection between the two homilies and proceeds to adjust the discrepancy in date. Since in the homily it is

---

[574] As a result of the rediscovery in 1955 of the ms. Stavronikita 6, these are now considered to number fifteen. For an account of the arrangement of the homilies found in that codex see Wenger, "La tradition des oeuvres", 32-43. This is the arrangement followed by Geerard, CPG 4441 (1)-(15). Batiffol, however, naturally follows the number and order proposed by Montfaucon.

[575] Batiffol, "Quelques homélies", 566.

[576] See p. 102 above.

[577] Batiffol, "Quelques homélies", 566-567.

[578] Montfaucon, VI *Praef*. § II, as opposed to VI 270-271, where the homily is assigned with confidence to April 10 (Easter) 399.

[579] Batiffol, "Quelques homélies", 567.

[580] See p. 103 above.

made clear that Chrysostom did not preach on the preceding Sunday because of a visiting bishop, while on the last occasion on which he did preach he lambasted the audience for their passion for the circus and theatre, the homily locates itself fifteen days after *Contra ludos et theatra*. This circumstance, on the revised dating of the latter, would place it in June or July 399. On the basis of the title it can be established that the sermon was delivered in the Great Church at Constantinople (Hagia Sophia).[581]

Hom. 4 (*Adv. eos qui non adfuerant*: CPG 4441.4) and 7 (*Hom. dicta in templo s. Anastasiae*: CPG 4441.8) both indicate that they were delivered in the Church of the Resurrection (St Anastasia), but contain no further information.[582] *Hom. 5* (*De studio praesentium*: CPG 4441.5), delivered in the Church of Holy Peace (St Eirene), is likewise devoid of further information.[583] Batiffol presumably derives the location of these homilies from their titles.

In the case of *hom. 8* (*Dicta postquam presbyter Gothus*: CPG 4441.9), the title indicates that it was delivered in the church dedicated to Paul. This building is identified by Batiffol with the church of the Goths described by Socrates (HE 6.6), as a result of which the homily must date prior to the massacre of the Goths at Constantinople on July 12, 400, since the church was burnt down on that occasion.[584]

According to the title of *hom. 10* (*In illud: Messis quidem multa*: CPG 4441.11), it was preached in the Church of the Apostle. Batiffol wishes to identify this as the Church of the Goths (St Paul), since Sozomen (HE 7.10) says that the ignorant thought that it contained the body of the apostle Paul.[585] He further disagrees with the "redactor" of the title who identifies as a bishop the elderly person who had just preached. Nothing in the homily, says Batiffol, justifies that comment.[586]

The eleventh homily (*De Eleazaro et septem pueris*: CPG 4441.13) contains no indication of its location. Batiffol mentions that, although Chrysostom has again preached after an elderly person, the redactor guards against identifying the individual as a bishop. He does suggest,

---

[581] Batiffol, "Quelques homélies", 567-568.

[582] Batiffol, "Quelques homélies", 568. Montfaucon (see p. 103 above) and Stilting, *Acta SS. Sept.*, IV 541, however, had both discovered sufficient grounds to assign the latter (CPG 4441.8) to the paschal period of 399.

[583] Batiffol, "Quelques homélies", 568.

[584] Batiffol, "Quelques homélies", 568-569, where he follows Tillemont (*Mémoires*, XI 147ff) in equating the two churches.

[585] Batiffol, "Quelques homélies", 568, indicates that Theodosius had placed there the ashes of Paul, a former bishop of Constantinople.

[586] Batiffol, "Quelques homélies", 569.

however, that it may likewise have been delivered in the Church of the Goths.[587]

Hom. 1 (*Quod frequenter conveniendum sit*: CPG 4441.3) was, according to the title, preached in the martyrium at Palaia Petra. This, says Batiffol, indicates a church dedicated to a martyr and situated in the quarter known as Palaia Petra. He finds that there exists reference to a martyrium of St Euphemia on the Rock, which had been in existence at Constantinople since the time of Theodosius.[588] It is not entirely clear, however, whether this information is offered as more than a suggestion. Further to this homily, Batiffol effectively demolishes the argument of Montfaucon that the passage referring to an upheaval in the city of thirty days previously, indicates the earthquake of 398.[589] On the other hand, Batiffol finds it difficult to accede to the hypothesis of Christian Matthaei that the event referred to is the downfall of Eutropius. According to that scholar's argument, since Eutropius was banished in late August, this dates the homily to September 399.[590] Batiffol points out that the disgrace suffered by the individual, while strongly associated with wealth, has little to do with politics.[591]

The titles to *hom. 2* (*Dicta postquam reliquiae martyrum*: CPG 4441.1) and *3* (*Dicta praesente imperatore*: CPG 4441.2) declare that they were delivered in the marytrium of the apostle and martyr Thomas in Drypia, the second adding that this site is located nine miles from the city. Batiffol states that up until now this location had never been identified but that Pargoire, in a detailed personal note, had indicated to him the opinion of another scholar who identifies Drypia as Tchifout-Bourgas (Tower of the Jews), situated to the west of Constantinople on level ground, almost as far from the base of the Golden Horn as from the Sea of Marmara. Aside from this, the second homily indicates that it was delivered on the day following the first, while the eulogistic terms in which the empress is described in the first homily indicate that the two can only belong to the early part of Chrysostom's episcopate.[592]

Batiffol's greatest contribution, however, lies in identifying the homily *In illud: Filius ex se nihil facit* (CPG 4441.12) as belonging to the series of

---

[587] Batiffol, "Quelques homélies", 569-570.

[588] Batiffol, "Quelques homélies", 570.

[589] See Montfaucon (p. 102 above).

[590] For the view of Matthaei see PG 63,461 note (a). This comment does not appear in his 1792 edition of four of the *Novae homiliae* (see n. 2) and it is with regret that I confess that I have been unable to establish its origins. This point had earlier been argued by Stilting (see p. 125 above) who, because of his dating of the fall of Eutropius to January, located the homily in February of 399.

[591] Batiffol, "Quelques homélies", 570-571.

[592] Batiffol, "Quelques homélies", 571.

Novae homiliae. This he did entirely on the basis of its title and contents, without the benefit of supporting manuscript evidence.[593] Batiffol had noted the existence in the title of a rare reference to the location at which the homily was preached, a feature typical of the titles to the homilies in this series. The title also indicates that another individual had preached before Chrysostom. Montfaucon had taken this to be the bishop Flavian, a circumstance which led him to conclude that the homily was preached at Antioch.[594] Batiffol, however, points out that nothing within the homily itself supports the identification of that person as a bishop, let alone the bishop of Antioch. Further, Chrysostom states here that he preached at the preceding synaxis on the verse: "Pater meus usque modo operatur" (Jn 5.17) and on the equality of the Father with the Son. Although Montfaucon had declared himself unable to locate any such homily on the subject at Antioch, *Nov. hom.* 9 (CPG 4441.10) deals with just such a topic. Moreover, like *In illud: Filius ex se nihil facit, hom.* 9 was delivered in the Great Church at Constantinople.[595]

e. *Pargoire*

Writing at virtually the same time as Batiffol (1899-1900), Jean Pargoire takes the homily *Contra ludos et theatra* (CPG 4441.7) as a jumping off point and then moves on to consider two or three other of the *Novae homiliae*, which he considers to be associated with that homily. As a result he secures the precise date of four of the *Novae homiliae*, determining that they were all delivered within a short space of time as a coherent sequence.

Pargoire begins by confirming that the consensus of opinion regarding the year to which *Contra ludos et theatra* belongs is beyond doubt. Within the homily Chrysostom clearly states that he has been in the city for a year. Since he was installed as bishop on Feb. 26, 398, this locates the homily after Feb. 26 of the following year.[596] In establishing that the discourse was delivered on a Sunday, Pargoire lists five pieces of evidence presented by the homilist. The offending horse races occurred on a Friday; the next day, i.e., Saturday, the people immersed themselves in the theatre; two days before the races, i.e., Wednesday, the people had divided their time between fear and prayer (there was a terrible storm in

---

[593] Stavronikita 6 subsequently provided this. See Wenger, "La tradition des oeuvres", 40.

[594] See p. 95 above.

[595] Batiffol, "Quelques homélies", 572.

[596] Pargoire, "Les homélies en juillet 399", 151 (sec. I).

the morning, a procession in torrential rain to the Church of the Apostles, then a pilgrimage to the basilica of Sts Peter and Paul); at the time of the homily the events of the Wednesday occurred three days prior (πρὸ τριῶν ἡμερῶν); and finally, the day of the homily is not the Saturday, since the way in which he admonishes the audience over their attendance at the theatre requires the space of at least one night to have intervened. As the homily cannot have been delivered on a Saturday, for the reason just given, and since to place it after Sunday would extend the interval between the homily and the events of the previous Wednesday beyond the requisite three days, it must therefore have been delivered on the Sunday. This is further confirmed by the title to the homily *In illud: Pater meus usque modo operatur* (CPG 4441.10). There it is stated that the homily against the races and theatre took place on a Sunday.[597]

Pargoire then takes the time to review the arguments against locating the homily on Easter Sunday, as Montfaucon had originally thought, in favour of Montfaucon's subsequent opinion, later approved by Batiffol, that the homily was delivered in the middle of the year, i.e., somewhere around June. On the negative side, John makes no mention of Easter Saturday nor of the resurrection itself, a circumstance which would seem impossible if he really had been preaching at Easter. The homily does, however, contain a positive indication in terms of the status of the crops at the time of the storm on the Wednesday. The damage was so severe because the ears of grain were in the latter stages of their development. This is extremely unlikely at the time of Easter, but normal for the middle of the year.[598]

Pargoire then arrives at the original section of his thesis.[599] There is a further indication, the visits to the churches of the Apostles and of Sts Peter and Paul on the Wednesday, which permits one to assign to the homily a precise date. Pargoire argues that the initial choice of the Church of the Apostles is not a random event. The day is in fact the festival devoted to the apostles Peter and Paul, and as the nearest sanctuary dedicated to the two lay at that time across the Propontis, the Church of the Apostles is the most appropriate location for their celebration within Constantinople itself. This is reinforced by the heavy rain in the morning, which would have influenced this choice, and by the events of the after-

---

[597] Pargoire, "Les homélies en juillet 399", 151-152 (sec. II). The connection drawn between the two homilies dates back as far as Montfaucon (see p. 103 above). Batiffol (p. 155 above) had just reaffirmed it.

[598] Pargoire, "Les homélies en juillet 399", 152-153 (sec. III).

[599] Matthaei, *Ioannis Chrysostomi homiliae IV ex omnibus ejus operibus selectae graece et latine*, Misenae 1792, II 82 n. 4, had come close to this solution but had failed to draw all of the threads together, preferring to argue (81 n. 3) that Chrysostom's description of crops was not always precise.

noon, after the debilitating rain had ceased. With the cessation of the rain the Propontis, too dangerous to cross during the storm, must have settled, with the result that Chrysostom and his flock hastily crossed to Rufinianes to celebrate the festival in a church containing genuine relics of the two apostles.[600] This is the only explanation which takes all of the details into consideration.[601] Pargoire then proceeds to establish the date June 29 for the feast of Sts Peter and Paul at Constantinople. This is confirmed by the fact that in the year 399 June 29 fell on a Wednesday. It can thence be determined that the following Sunday, and therefore the homily in question, fell precisely on July 3, 399.[602]

This conclusion permits Pargoire to locate the date of three more homilies. The connection between *Contra ludos et theatra* and the ninth of the *Novae homiliae* (CPG 4441.10) has already been mentioned. The title to the latter indicates that it is the first occasion on which Chrysostom has preached since the discourse against the races and theatre, since on the Sunday following that homily (i.e., July 10) he had yielded his place to a visiting bishop. In order to determine the precise date of *In illud: Pater meus usque modo operatur*, the only piece of information required is the day of the week on which the homily was delivered. As the previous two discourses were delivered on Sundays, Pargoire finds it most natural to locate it on that day likewise. The homily, he concludes, was therefore delivered on July 17, 399.[603]

Batiffol had been the first to establish the connection between the last homily and another (*In illud: Filius ex se nihil facit*: CPG 4441.12), not previously considered to have belonged to the *Novae homiliae*.[604] Pargoire reaffirms this connection and now proceeds to assign that homily a date. Since in the opening to the homily it is clearly stated that *In illud: Pater meus usque modo operatur* was preached at the previous synaxis, it remains only to establish the day on which the present sermon was delivered. Once again Pargoire considers this to have been a Sunday, a circumstance which allows him to date the homily to July 24, 399.[605]

The final sermon to be considered is the one titled *De Eleazaro et septem pueris* (CPG 4441.13). Despite Chrysostom's declaration here that he

---

[600] Pargoire, "Les homélies en juillet 399", 155 n. 1, argues that the terms employed here exclude a crossing of the Golden Horn.

[601] Pargoire, "Les homélies en juillet 399", 153-155 (sec. IV).

[602] Pargoire, "Les homélies en juillet 399", 155-157 (sec. V). Pargoire adds, 157 n. 1, that the horse races which so offended the homilist were thus held on the kalends of the month (Friday July 1), a circumstance particularly appropriate to this chronology.

[603] Pargoire, "Les homélies en juillet 399", 157-159 (sec. VI).

[604] Batiffol (p. 158 above) had failed, however, to carry this discovery to its logical conclusion.

[605] Pargoire, "Les homélies en juillet 399", 159 (sec. VII).

is "young", a circumstance which, along with the topic of the Maccabean martyrs, might suggest a provenance of Antioch, Pargoire is inclined to see in this homily indications of Constantinople. Chrysostom's
apparent youth is easily explained by the title to the homily in which it is
made clear that an individual of advanced age had just finished preaching before him. The self-characterisation is little more than relative. Two
circumstances, however, suggest a Constantinopolitan provenance.
When inviting the audience to participate the next day, the festival of the
Maccabees, in a stational journey of several stades, Chrysostom employs
the verb διαπεράω. This, declares Pargoire, has the specialised meaning of
"to cross by sea" or "to cross a strait". This connotation naturally leads
one to think of the Church of the Maccabees mentioned in the *Chronicon
paschale*,[606] situated across from Constantinople on the other side of the
Golden Horn. The second factor to convince Pargoire is circumstantial.
The homily is found situated among eleven other homilies all with certainty delivered at Constantinople. Its homogeneity with the others is indicated by the title assigned to it in the manuscripts, which is entirely in
character with the other eleven. Having convincingly established the location, it remains for Pargoire to attempt to establish a date. Three times
in the the course of the homily Chrysostom indicates that it is the day before the feast of the Maccabees. As this festival is firmly located on Aug.
1, the present homily can be assigned to July 31. The only cause for delivering a homily so close to this festival is that, in the relevant year, July
31 must have fallen on a day of regular synaxis. Thinking of a Sunday,
Pargoire finds that only two years are possible — 399 or 404. July 404 is
to be excluded, as Chrysostom was at that time already in exile. This
leaves July 31, 399 as the date of the homily.[607]

f. *Mahler*

In 1921 Eduard Mahler for the last time raised the issue of the date of
the Christmas sermon (CPG 4334), arguing against the proposed years
388[608] and 386,[609] in favour of locating it once again in 387.[610] The target
of Mahler's article is, somewhat strangely, the chronology adopted by

---

[606] PG 92,1005 and 1008.

[607] Pargoire, "Les homélies en juillet 399", 159-161 (sec. VIII).

[608] See Usener (p. 152 above).

[609] For this, the consensus, see Lietzmann (p. 164 below).

[610] See Clinton (p. 151 above).

Usener,[611] although he is at pains to point out that the year 386 is equally impossible. Recalling the homilist's statement that the Jewish Day of Atonement fell toward the end of September that year, Mahler argues that the calendar on which Usener based his calculations did not reflect the practice of the Jewish community at Antioch.[612] Nor, he finds, are the computations on which Schwartz assigned the homily to 386 accurate.[613] On the basis of his own understanding of the situation at Antioch, of the years 386-388, 387 presents the only possibility.[614]

g. *Summary*

Table 7. — Overview of miscellaneous opinion (Phase Three)

CPG no.	Place	Date	Proposed by
4318*	A	Aug. 15, 387	Usener
4319	A	Dec. 20, 388	Usener
4327	A	Aug.- Sept. 386 (*or. 1-3*); Sept. 387 (*or. 4-8*)	Clinton
"	A	387- 389: Jan. 24 (*or. 3*), Aug. 22 (*or. 1*), Sept. 4 (*or. 2*), Sept. 11 (*or.8*) 387; Sept. 28-30 (*or. 5-6*), Oct. 1 (*or. 7*) 388; Sept. 2 (*or. 4*) 389	Usener
4334	A	Dec. 25, 387	Clinton
	"	Dec. 25, 388	Usener
	"	Dec. 25, 387	Mahler
4335	A	Jan. 6, 388	Usener
4346	A	Jan. 7, 388	"
4426	A	after 372	Seeck
4441.1	CP: Church of St Thomas	early years	Batiffol
4441.2	CP: Church of St Thomas	early years	"
4441.3	CP: Martyrium of St Euphemia?		"
4441.4	CP: St Anastasia		"
4441.5	CP: St Eirene		"
4441.6	CP: Church of the Apostles	Jan. 17, 399 or later	"

[611] This had long since been disproved in favour of 386 by Rauschen (see p. 137 above), of whose work Mahler appears unaware, and Schwartz (p. 147 above), with whose chronology for the Jewish Day of Atonement in the years 386-389 Mahler takes issue.

[612] Mahler, "Zur Chronologie", 60.

[613] Mahler, "Zur Chronologie", 63.

[614] Mahler, "Zur Chronologie", 61-63.

4441.7	CP	c. June, 399	Batiffol
	"	July 3, 399	Pargoire
4441.8	CP: St Anastasia		Batiffol
4441.9	CP: Church of Paul = Church of the Goths	before July 12, 400	"
4441.10	CP: Great Church	June/July 399	Batiffol
		July 17, 399	Pargoire
4441.11	CP: Church of the Goths		Batiffol
4441.12	CP: Great Church	the synaxis following CPG 4441.10	Batiffol
		July 24, 399	Pargoire
4441.13	CP: Church of the Goths?#	(no opinion)	Batiffol
		July 31, 399	Pargoire

* *Hom. 1* only. # Batiffol's opinion only.

4. LIETZMANN

With Hans Lietzmann's abbreviated biography of Chrysostom, which appeared in Pauly-Wissowa in 1916, there are signs that the process begins to move into its mature phase. For the first time a sufficient level of consensus had been reached for it to be possible to compress into one brief article the results of some two centuries of lively debate. As a result, Lietzmann's work is to be valued less for its insights into the provenance and date of the corpus — beyond certain questions of date, he contributes little that is new to the picture — than for its delineation of the emerging status quo.

Since it is Lietzmann's intent to present as concisely as possible the consensus of opinion at the time, this often leads him to cite as lists the homilies which belong to a certain year or place. Rather than repeat such lists verbatim, the previous mode of presentation has here been altered, with an outline of Lietzmann's schema supplied first (Table 8.a). Since his approach is biographical and therefore chronologically oriented, the table follows this perspective. Lietzmann's schema is in part a composite of opinions from a number of sources. This is particularly the case with the miscellaneous homilies. It is thus important to ascertain which opinion he followed in making which assertion. However, on occasion Lietzmann also allows us insight into the reasons behind his decisions. By collecting all of this information it is possible to determine which assertions are derivative and which, if any, are original. A summary of this information is therefore provided immediately following Table 8.a. Finally, Lietzmann's distribution of the homilies between Antioch and Constantinople is summarised in the usual way (Table 8.b below).

a. *Distribution — chronology*

As will be immediately clear from the table below, Lietzmann exhibits extreme caution in assigning a date to the exegetical series. A precise fixing of their chronology has, he claims, yet to be established. In consequence, the following series do not appear in the table: Psalms (CPG 4413); John (CPG 4425); Romans (CPG 4427); I and II Corinthians (CPG 4428-4429); Ephesians (CPG 4431); Philippians (CPG 4432); I and II Thessalonians (CPG 4434-4435); I and II Timothy (CPG 4436-4437); Titus (CPG 4438); and Philemon (CPG 4439).

The final column refers to the location in the article where the assertion is made. Where sequences of homilies are delineated without precise indication of date, these are described following the table.

Table 8.a. Chronology — Lietzmann

Year (month-season)	Homily	Cited (column)
386		
beginning	*Sermo cum presbyter* (CPG 4317)	1815
Lent (Feb. 16-)	*Sermones 1-8 in Genesim* (CPG 4410)	"
autumn*	*Adv. Iudaeos or. 1-2* (CPG 4327)	"
Oct. 8	*De s. Pelagia* (CPG 4350)	"
Oct. 17	*In s. Ignatium* (CPG 4351)	"
Dec. 25	*In diem natalem* (CPG 4334)	"
date unspecified	*De profectu evangelii* (CPG 4385)	"
387		
Jan. 6	*De baptismo Christi* (CPG 4335)	1815
Jan. 7	*In s. Lucianum* (CPG 4346)	"
Jan. 31	*Adv. Iudaeos or. 3* (CPG 4327)	"
Lent	*De statuis hom. 1-21* (CPG 4330)	"
autumn	*Adv. Iudaeos or. 4-8* (CPG 4327)	"
date unspecified	*De s. Meletio* (CPG 4345)	"
	De resurrectione mortuorum (CPG 4340)	"
	De decem mill. talentorum (CPG 4368)	"
	De Anna sermones 1-5 (CPG 4411)	"
	De Davide et Saule hom. 1-3 (CPG 4412)	"
	Exp. in psalmum 41 (CPG 4413.2)	"
388#	Terminus post quem: *In Matt.* (CPG 4424)	1817
389		
390		
391		
392		
393#		
Nov. 20	Terminus ante quem: *In Matt.* (CPG 4424)	1817
394		
395		
396		

397		
398[a]		
399		
April 10	*Contra ludos et theatra* (CPG 4441.7)	1820
summer	*In Col. hom. 1-12* (CPG 4433)	1819
date unspecified	*In Eutropium* (CPG 4392) *De capto Eutropio* (CPG 4528)	1820
400		
2nd half	*Cum Saturninus et Aurelianus* (CPG 4393)	1821
401		
date unspecified	*In Acta apost. hom. 1-55* (CPG 4426)	1819
402		
403 / 404	*In Heb. hom. 1-34* (CPG 4440)	1819

* See also Sequence A below. # See Sequence B below. [a] See Sequence D below.

There are several sequences outlined by Lietzmann. Three of these are assigned to a specific period of time.

Sequence A. (autumn 386-c. February 387) *De incompr. dei nat. hom. 1-5* (CPG 4318); *De b. Philogonio* (CPG 4319); *De consubstantiali* (CPG 4320); *De petitione matr. fil. Zeb.* (CPG 4321); *In quatrid. Lazarum* (CPG 4322); *De Christi precibus* (CPG 4323).[615] Lietzmann makes no attempt to integrate these with the other homilies from this period (see shaded section of Table 8.a).

Sequence B. (388 or 393; most prob. 388) *In kalendas* (CPG 4328); *De Lazaro conc. 1-7* (CPG 4329); (Jan. 24) *De s. Babyla* (CPG 4347); *In Iuventinum et Maximum* (CPG 4349); *In illud: Vidua eligatur* (CPG 4386). *In kalendas* is preceded (Dec. 28 of the previous year) by one of the seven homilies *De laudibus s. Pauli* (CPG 4344).[616]

Sequence C. Antioch: (before Lent) *In illud: Vidi dom. hom. 2, 3, 5 and 6* (CPG 4417); (Lent) *Hom. 1-29 in Gen.* (CPG 4409); (Monday-Wednesday of Holy Week) *Hom. 30-32 in Gen.*; (Maundy Thursday — sermon on betrayal of Judas, unknown);[617] (Good Friday — sermon on the cross, unknown); (Easter Sunday) *De resurrectione* (CPG 4341); *In princ. Act. hom. 1-4* (CPG 4371); *De mutatione nom. hom. 1-4* (CPG 4372) and *Sermo 9 in Gen.* (CPG 4410); *Hom. 33-67 in Gen.*[618]

---

[615] Lietzmann, "J. Chrysostomos", 1815 29-32.

[616] Lietzmann, "J. Chrysostomos", 1816 6-16. Cf. Rauschen, Sequence F, p. 142 above.

[617] Lietzmann, "J. Chrysostomos", 1816 45-1817 22, devotes an excursus to demonstrating that neither of the two extant homilies *De prod. Iudae* (CPG 4336) is the sermon in question. In the process he concludes that neither are the homilies a stenographic doublet. They constitute distinct sermons delivered on separate occasions.

[618] Lietzmann, "J. Chrysostomos", 1816 27-44. Cf. Rauschen, Sequence E, p. 140 above.

Sequence D. (late 398-early 399) *Quod frequenter conven. sit* (CPG 4441.3); *Hom. dicta postquam reliquiae* (CPG 4441.1); *Hom. dicta praesente imperatore* (CPG 4441.2); *Adv. eos qui non adfuerant* (CPG 4441.4); *De studio praesentium* (CPG 4441.5); *Adv. catharos* (CPG 4441.6); *Hom. dicta in templo s. Anastasiae* (CPG 4441.8); *Hom. Postquam presb. Gothus* (CPG 4441.9); *In illud: Pater meus* (CPG 4441.10); *In illud: Messis quidem multa* (CPG 4441.11); *De Eleazaro* (CPG 4441.13); (April 10, Easter Sunday) *Contra ludos et theatra* (CPG 4441.7).

b. *Basis of distribution*

For Lietzmann a considerable degree of uncertainty still attaches to the provenance and date of the various series. At the time at which he writes, however, for a proportion of the miscellaneous homilies these issues are considered to have been settled. Consequently when Lietzmann surveys the homiletic output of Chrysostom, it is noticeable that the inclusion of supporting evidence is reserved almost exclusively for the series, while in the discussion of occasional homilies he feels able to rely with confidence upon the investigative efforts of his contemporaries. This is the case with the homilies which belong to the years 386 and 387.[619] Here, without further discussion, Lietzmann allegedly records the schema established by Usener,[620] Rauschen[621] and Schwartz.[622] This is also the case with Sequence B, in which he claims to follow the view adopted by Rauschen and Schwartz. Where these two had proposed a

---

[619] Lietzmann, "J. Chrysostomos", 1815 20ff.

[620] See pp. 152-154 above and Table 14. In fact the schema proposed by Usener is in conflict with that proposed by Rauschen and Schwartz, whose arguments Lietzmann personally favours. Although Lietzmann fails to make the distinction, pp. 379ff. in his citation of Usener (1815 22-23) refer to work which Lietzmann himself produced. See Lietzmann, "Über das Datum der Weihnachtspredigt des Johannes Chrysostomos", in Usener, *Weihnachtsfest*[2], 379-384. There he promotes, against Usener, the arguments of Rauschen and, in particular, Schwartz in favour of a schema centred around Christmas of 386. Any reassessment of the chronology for the years 386-387 should take this article into consideration.

[621] See pp. 135-140 above. In several important points the sequence presented differs from that proposed by Rauschen (see Table 14).

[622] See pp. 146-149 above. In general Lietzmann demonstrates a preference for the conclusions of Schwartz over those of Rauschen. This is noticeable in the case of the homily *De s. Meletio* (CPG 4345), which Schwartz, following Montfaucon, had located in 387, but which Rauschen (p. 136 above) had assigned to the end of May 386. For a full comparison of the three (Usener, Rauschen and Schwartz) see Table 14.

date of 388 or 393 for the series,[623] the suggestion that 388 is more probable is entirely his own.[624]

The first instance where supporting evidence is offered occurs when Lietzmann arrives at the seven homilies *De laudibus s. Pauli* (CPG 4344). Lietzmann, following everyone before him, states that the Antiochene provenance of these homilies is firmly established on the basis of *hom. 4*.[625] The oldest of the exegetical series is that on Genesis (CPG 4409). That it belongs to Antioch is indicated by the reference to the "old church" in *In princ. Act. hom. 2* (CPG 4371), a homily which was delivered at the same time.[626] That these two series were delivered in the same year, as also the other sermons located between *hom. 32* and *33* on Genesis (see Sequence C above), is established, as usual, from the opening of *Hom. 33 in Gen.*[627] The series on Matthew (CPG 4424), as is common, is assigned to Antioch on the basis of *In Matt. hom. 7*.[628]

Lietzmann is more expansive than usual, however, when it comes to the question of this series' date. In an entirely original excursus,[629] he points out that in *In Matt. hom. 88* John recalls a solar eclipse which occurred within the lifetime of his audience. A total eclipse in Asia Minor, which was near total at Antioch, took place on Nov. 20, 393. This, Lietzmann argues, must have been experienced by everyone. However, the eclipse in *hom. 88* is described as remote and experienced only by a small percentage of the audience, leading to the conclusion that the phenomenon could not have been described in this way if the series was delivered after that date. Previous solar eclipses at Antioch occurred on June 6, 346 (total), Aug. 28, 360 and April 15, 386. Any of these events, he finds, could be intended. Having established a *terminus ante quem* for the series, Lietzmann then seeks to establish in which of the early years it could not have been delivered. In *hom. 88* he again finds the answer. Chrysostom states later in the homily that certain of his discourses are available to the audience in published form. These discourses Lietzmann identifies as the homilies *Contra Anomoeos* (CPG 4318-4323 = Sequence

---

[623] See Schwartz (p. 149 above). Rauschen (see p. 142 above), however, stated simply that the series could only have been delivered in 388 at the earliest.

[624] Lietzmann, "J. Chrysostomos", 1816 6-16. For the basis of this assertion see 1817 23-52.

[625] Lietzmann, "J. Chrysostomos", 1816 9-11.

[626] Lietzmann, "J. Chrysostomos", 1816 20-27.

[627] Lietzmann, "J. Chrysostomos", 1816 33-43.

[628] Lietzmann, "J. Chrysostomos", 1817 23-24.

[629] Lietzmann, "J. Chrysostomos", 1817 25-52.

A) and *Adv. Iudaeos* (CPG 4327), delivered between 386 and 387, and *De s. Babyla* (see Sequence B), which he now firmly assigns to 388.[630]

After considering the homilies on Matthew, Lietzmann turns to the series on John (CPG 4425). This he assigns to Antioch also, not on the basis of any internal evidence, but because in *In I Cor. hom.* 7 (CPG 4428), a homily clearly delivered at Antioch, it is described as readily available.[631] Concerning when the series was delivered, he mentions no more than the possibility that the series distributed itself over the course of a year.[632] Lietzmann then turns his attention to the series of homilies in which Chrysostom exegetes the Pauline epistles. The majority of these series, he believes, were delivered at Antioch. Romans is, *contra* Rauschen,[633] assigned there because in *In Rom. hom.* 8 (CPG 4427) Chrysostom refers to their "common shepherd".[634] The homilies on I Corinthians (CPG 4428) belong likewise to that location because in *In I Cor. hom.* 21 this is directly stated,[635] while in the case of II Corinthians (CPG 4429) an Antiochene provenance is proved indirectly, because *In II Cor. hom.* 26 excludes Constantinople.[636] The series on Ephesians (CPG 4431) demonstrates its origins through the veiled allusions in *In Eph. hom.* 11 to a schism, a situation known to have existed in the church at Antioch. This is supported by the reference in *hom.* 9 to St Babylas and above all, *hom.* 21, to the famous ascetic Julian whom Theodoret informs us once visited Antioch. Furthermore in *hom.* 11 John states that he has no ἀρχή, an assertion which could not have been made if at the time he had been bishop.[637] The six homilies on the Letter to Titus (CPG 4438) are the only other series able to be assigned to Antioch on internal grounds. In these sermons the manner in which the homilist speaks of the obligations of a bishop in *In Titum hom.* 1 and the mention by name

---

[630] Lietzmann appears to have become confused here between the homily *De s. Babyla* (CPG 4347) and the tract *De s. Babyla contra Iulianum et gentiles* (CPG 4348), which he had earlier, "J. Chrysostomos", 1814 14-21, assigned to 382 or thereabouts. If this is the case, a *terminus post quem* of no later than 387 could be established and the now confident location in 388 of Sequence B is without ground.

[631] Lietzmann, "J. Chrysostomos", 1817 54-59. This argument was proposed by Tillemont (see p. 61 above) and subsequently promoted by Montfaucon (p. 97 above).

[632] Lietzmann, "J. Chrysostomos", 1817 64-66.

[633] Rauschen (p. 143 above) had dismissed this passage, arguing that it is unclear whether the "shepherd" referred to is a person other than the homilist.

[634] Lietzmann, "J. Chrysostomos", 1818 17-20.

[635] Lietzmann, "J. Chrysostomos", 1818 20-23.

[636] Lietzmann, "J. Chrysostomos", 1818 23-25. See Tillemont (p. 61 above) and Montfaucon (pp. 98f). This same passage had once been interpreted as a clear indication of Constantinopolitan provenance. See Savile (p. 40 above).

[637] Lietzmann, "J. Chrysostomos", 1818 33-47.

in *hom. 3* of certain localities in the vicinity of Antioch provide clear indication.[638] The series on I and II Timothy (CPG 4436-4437) and Philemon (CPG 4439) are assigned to Antioch solely on the basis that they cannot be separated from the homilies on Titus.[639]

The series of homilies on Philippians (CPG 4432), Colossians (CPG 4433) and I and II Thessalonians (CPG 4434-4435), on the other hand, are assigned to Constantinople entirely on the basis of their episcopal tone (*In Phil. hom. 9, In Col. hom. 3, In I Thess. hom. 8, In II Thess. hom. 4*).[640] Lietzmann takes *In II Thess. hom. 5*: ἅπαξ ἢ δεύτερον τοῦ μηνὸς ἢ οὐδὲ ἅπαξ ("once or twice a month, or not even once": PG 62,498 30-31), to indicate that Chrysostom found less need for such exegetical preaching in Constantinople.[641] On the question of date, *In Col. hom. 7* can be precisely located because it refers to the sudden fall of Eutropius which occurred in the summer of 399.[642] The thirty-four homilies on Hebrews (CPG 4440) Lietzmann assigns to the last year of Chrysostom's episcopate (403/404), relying on the common argument that, as stated in the title, they were published from stenographic notes after his death.[643] The fifty-five homilies on Acts (CPG 4426) were delivered in 401 on the evidence of *In Acta apost. hom. 9*, where the homilist is clearly bishop, and *hom. 44*, where John indicates that he has held that position for three years.[644]

As regards the exegesis of books from the Old Testament, Lietzmann considers all of the extant material (Psalms, Isaiah, Daniel and Job) to belong to written commentaries.[645] In the course of discussing the exegetical pieces on Psalms (CPG 4413), like Montfaucon and Stilting before him, he assigns these to Antioch on the basis of the commentary on Psalm 110 (CPG 4413.5).[646]

Of the miscellaneous homilies to be assigned to Constantinople, Lietzmann locates the eleven *Novae homiliae* (CPG 4441.1-6,8-11,13) at the end of 398 and beginning of 399. To these he adds a twelfth homily, *Con-*

---

[638] Lietzmann, "J. Chrysostomos", 1818 47-53.

[639] Lietzmann, "J. Chrysostomos", 1818 53-56.

[640] Lietzmann, "J. Chrysostomos", 1818 56-64.

[641] Lietzmann, "J. Chrysostomos", 1818 64-68. This is a highly questionable interpretation of the passage.

[642] Lietzmann, "J. Chrysostomos", 1819 1-3. Presumably the remainder of the series is likewise to be assigned to this period.

[643] Lietzmann, "J. Chrysostomos", 1819 3-8.

[644] Lietzmann, "J. Chrysostomos", 1819 9-16.

[645] Lietzmann, "J. Chrysostomos", 1819 17-57.

[646] Lietzmann, "J. Chrysostomos", 1819 34-36.

tra ludos et theatra (CPG 4441.7), delivered on April 10 (Easter) 399,[647] in which Chrysostom indicates that he has been bishop for a year. The first of the eleven *Novae homiliae* (CPG 4441.3) refers to an earthquake of thirty days earlier. This Lietzmann identifies with the portent which, according to Claudian, preceded the consulate year of Eutropius (399).[648] In 399 are to be located the homilies *In Eutropium* (CPG 4392) and *De capto Eutropio* (4528), which describe the immediate consequences of Eutropius' deposition.[649] The sermon *Cum Saturninus et Aurelianus* (CPG 4393) he dates to after the withdrawal of Gainas and his forces from Constantinople in the middle of 400.[650] The homilies *Antequam iret in exsilium* (CPG 4396), *Cum iret in exsilium* (CPG 4397),[651] *Sermo post reditum 1* (CPG 4398) and *Sermo post reditum 2* (CPG 4399), delivered one day later, all belong to the period after 400 and before the end of 403.[652]

c. *Summary of distribution - location*

Table 8.b. Provenance — Lietzmann

CPG no.	Antioch	CPG no.	Constantinople
4317	*Sermo cum presbyter* (col. 1815)	4392	*In Eutropium* (col. 1820)
4318	*De incompr. dei natura hom. 1-5* (col. 1815)	4393	*Cum Saturninus et Aurelianus* (col. 1821)
4319	*De beato Philogonio* (col. 1815)	4396	*Antequam iret in exsilium* (col. 1822)
4320	*De consubstantiali* (col. 1815)	4397	*Cum iret in exsilium* (col. 1822)
4321	*De petitione matr. fil. Zeb.* (col. 1815)	4398	*Sermo post red. 1* (col. 1822): Church of the Apostle
4322	*In quatrid. Lazarum* (col. 1815)	4399	*Sermo post reditum 2* (col. 1822)
4323	*De Christi precibus* (col. 1815)	4426	*In Acta apost. hom. 1-55* (col. 1819)

---

[647] Here Lietzmann is either unaware of Pargoire's argument against Easter or is maintaining a conservative stance in following the date proposed by Montfaucon and accepted by Stilting. Montfaucon (p. 95 above) had himself expressed doubt about this conclusion. For Pargoire's proposal of July 3, 399 see p. 160 above.

[648] Lietzmann, "J. Chrysostomos", 1820 13-27.

[649] Lietzmann, "J. Chrysostomos", 1820 41-66. This is nowhere directly stated, but is clearly to be understood from the references supplied and from the earlier discussion of *In Col. hom. 7*.

[650] Lietzmann, "J. Chrysostomos", 1821 1-4.

[651] Lietzmann, "J. Chrysostomos", 1822 16-23, records that there is some concern regarding the authenticity of this homily.

[652] To be inferred from events detailed by Lietzmann, "J. Chrysostomos", 1821 16-1823 40. Lietzmann (1822 61-1823 32) includes in this a discussion of the homily *In decollatione praecursoris* [= *In decollatione s. Iohannis*] (CPG 4570), concerning the authenticity of which he is undecided. This homily is usually considered to be not genuine. See De Aldama, *Repertorium*, 138-139 (no.381).

4327	*Adv. Iudaeos or. 1-8* (col. 1815)	4432	*In Phil. hom. 1-15* (col. 1818)
4328	*In kalendas* (col. 1816)	4433	*In Col. hom. 1-12* (col. 1818)
4329	*De Lazaro conciones 1-7* (col. 1816)	4434	*In I Thess. hom. 1-11* (col. 1818)
4330	*De statuis hom. 1-21* (col. 1815)	4435	*In II Thess. hom. 1-5* (col. 1818)
4334	*In diem natalem* (col. 1815)	4440	*In Heb. hom. 1-34* (col. 1819)
4335	*De baptismo Christi* (col. 1815)	4441	*XI Novae homiliae 1-11,13* (col. 1820)
4340	*De resurrectione mortuorum* (col. 1815)	4528	*De capto Eutropio* (col. 1820)
4341	*De resurrectione* (col. 1816)		
4344	*De laudibus s. Pauli hom. 1-7* (col. 1816)		
4345	*De s. Meletio* (col. 1815)		
4346	*In s. Lucianum* (col. 1815)		
4347	*De s. Babyla* (col. 1816)		
4349	*In Iuventinum et Maximum* (col. 1816)		
4350	*De s. Pelagia* (col. 1815)		
4351	*In s. Ignatium* (col. 1815)		
4368	*De decem mill. tal. deb.* (col. 1815)		
4371	*In princ. Act. hom. 1-4* (col. 1816)		
4372	*De mutatione nom. hom. 1-4* (col. 1816)		
4385	*De profectu evangelii* (col. 1815)		
4386	*In illud: Vidua eligatur* (col. 1816)		
4409	*Hom. 1-67 in Genesim* (col. 1816)		
4410	*Sermones 1-9 in Genesim* (col. 1815)		
4411	*De Anna sermones 1-5* (col. 1815)		
4412	*De Davide et Saule hom. 1-3* (col. 1815)		
4413	*Exp. in psalmos* (col. 1815, 1819)		
4417	*In illud: Vidi dom. hom. 2,3,5,6* (col. 1816)		
4424	*In Matt. hom. 1-90* (col. 1817)		
4425	*In Ioh. hom. 1-88* (col. 1817)		
4427	*In Rom. hom. 1-32* (col. 1818)		
4428	*In I Cor. hom. 1-44* (col. 1818)		
4429	*In II Cor. hom. 1-30* (col. 1818)		
4431	*In Eph. hom. 1-24* (col. 1818)		
4436	*In I Tim. hom. 1-18* (col. 1818)		
4437	*In II Tim. hom. 1-10* (col. 1818)		
4438	*In Titum hom. 1-6* (col. 1818)		
4439	*In Philemon hom. 1-3* (col. 1818)		

5. BONSDORFF

In 1922, in response to the caution Lietzmann expressed regarding the sequence and location of the exegetical series, and influenced by Stilting, who traced a stylistic progression in the homilies preached at Antioch and Constantinople, Max von Bonsdorff set out to determine once and for all where and when each of the exegetical series was delivered. These facts, he considered, could be firmly established if one but sifted more minutely through the evidence. His methodology, the assumptions which inform it, as well as the results of this approach have all had a marked effect upon subsequent scholarship.

Bonsdorff's approach is at the outset chronological. Although his focus is the series which exegete books of the New Testament, he does sketch an outline of the homilies located in the first two years at both locations in order to place certain events in context. In the case of Antioch he relies on Rauschen, Usener and Schwartz, as detailed by Lietzmann; in the case of Constantinople, the conclusions drawn by Batiffol and Pargoire. Rather than repeat such material, the relevant detail is set out in Table 9.b, located in the summary below. Discussion is reserved for the series themselves, with the exception of the first two years at Constantinople, where Bonsdorff briefly introduces new material. As his argument is sequential, relying in each instance on the data established in the previous section, Bonsdorff discusses the series in the order in which he believes them to have occurred. Before he can begin his discussion of the series, however, he finds it necessary to address the chronology of Lietzmann's Sequence B and C.[653]

a. *Sequence B*

Bonsdorff takes the first of the two sequences (B) and establishes on various grounds that its homilies were delivered in the following order: (Jan. 1) *In kalendas* (CPG 4328); (Jan. 2) *De Lazaro concio 1* (CPG 4329); (January, a few days later) *De Lazaro conc. 2*; (January, a few days later) *De Lazaro conc. 3*; (Jan. 24) *De s. Babyla* (CPG 4347); (Feb. 4) *In Iuventinum et Maximum* (CPG 4349); *De Lazaro conc. 4-5*; *In illud: Vidua eligatur* (CPG 4386); (three days after an earthquake) *De Lazaro conc. 6*; (concluding the sequence) *De Lazaro conc. 7*.[654] This leads Bonsdorff to conclude that the group of homilies must fall at the beginning of the year. On the basis of the reference to the bishop's absence in *In kalendas*, it also permits him to confirm that the sequence as a whole was delivered at Antioch.[655]

---

[653] See p. 165 above.

[654] Bonsdorff, *Zur Predigttätigkeit*, 5. In fact he simply restates the details already established by Rauschen (see p. 142 above).

[655] This is the standard methodology employed throughout. Bonsdorff first establishes or reaffirms provenance, then proceeds to investigate the issue of chronology.

On the basis of Tillemont's observation that in the year to which the homilies belong the first two days must have been a Saturday and Sunday (i.e., days of regular liturgical synaxis),[656] Schwartz had calculated that only the years 388 and 393 were possible.[657] Of these Lietzmann, if somewhat mistakenly, had argued that 388 was the more likely.[658] Bonsdorff sets out to demonstrate that 388 is indeed the year of delivery. In the homilies *In kalendas*, *De Lazaro conc. 1* and *De s. Babyla* he finds several passages which suggest to him that the period is earlier rather than later in Chrysostom's career.[659] Further, in *De Lazaro conc. 1* the homilist raises certain questions regarding the nature and purpose of parables, concluding that these he will save up for another time.[660] Thinking of Lietzmann's argument based on *In Matt. hom. 88* and the long-standing view that Matthew (CPG 4424) was one of the first exegetical series undertaken,[661] Bonsdorff points out that in the homilies on Matthew the issue of parables, as well as the differences to be found between the four gospels, also raised in *De Lazaro conc. 1*,[662] is dealt with in some detail. In addition, Bonsdorff finds marked similarity in thought between the discussion of Judas' betrayal in this homily and in the homily on Matthew in which the relevant verses are exegeted. The words ὅ πολλάκις εἶπον ("as I have often said") which occur in *In Matt. hom. 88*, however, point to its later delivery.[663] Since Lietzmann demonstrated that the series on Matthew must date to before Nov. 20, 393 and since the present sequence must be located before that, Bonsdorff is led to conclude that of the two years (388 and 393) 388 is the only option.[664]

---

[656] See p. 51 n. 81 above.

[657] See p. 149 above.

[658] See p. 165 and n. 630 above. Bonsdorff, *Zur Predigttätigkeit*, 6 n. 2, also makes this observation.

[659] Bonsdorff, *Zur Predigttätigkeit*, 6. Chrysostom invokes his bishop's prayers before launching into the sermon (*In kalendas*, PG 48,953 31-34), which shows lack of self confidence; *In kalendas* appears to be his first New Year's sermon (*De Lazaro con. 1*, PG 48,964 42-43); he says many will take offence at his words, accusing him of trying to introduce a new custom (ibid., PG 48,974 48-50); in *De s. Babyla* he calls himself young, after speaking of the bishop and older presbyters (SC 362,296 8-10).

[660] See PG 48,970 31-35.

[661] Montfaucon (see p. 96 above) and Stilting (p. 121 above) both located it among the earlier years at Antioch.

[662] See PG 48,970 39-50.

[663] This and similar phrases are commonly used by Bonsdorff to determine whether a homily or series was delivered earlier or later at a given location.

[664] Bonsdorff, *Zur Predigttätigkeit*, 6-7. Although it is not stated at this point, Bonsdorff assumes that the series on Matthew took a full year to deliver (see n. 689 below).

b. *Sequence C*

To the order of the second sequence (Sequence C: [before Lent] *In illud: Vidi dom. hom. 2, 3, 5* and 6; [Lent] *Hom. 1-32 in Gen.*; [Maundy Thursday] sermon on betrayal of Judas; [Good Friday] sermon on the cross; [Easter Sunday] *De resurrectione* [CPG 4341]; [between Easter and Pentecost, beginning a few days later] *In princ. Act. hom. 1-4*; *De mutatione nom. hom. 1-2*; *Sermo 9 in Gen.* [CPG 4410]; *De mutatione nom. hom. 3-4*; [soon after Pentecost] *Hom. 33-67 in Gen.*) Bonsdorff contributes little that is new,[665] except to suggest that the homilies delivered on the Thursday and Friday of Holy Week be identified as *De prod. Iudae hom. 2* (CPG 4336) and *De cruce et latrone hom. 2* (CPG 4339).[666]

Having established that the links between the homilies are firm and that they form a tight, cohesive sequence,[667] Bonsdorff then proceeds to demonstrate that they were delivered at Antioch.[668] In *In illud: Vidi dom. hom. 2* and *3* "the teacher", i.e., Bishop Flavian, is twice mentioned, while in *In princ. Act. hom. 2* not only is it the case that the synaxis is held at "the old church",[669] but in the course of the homily it is stated also that "our city", the first in the world to be honoured with the name Christian, once had the apostle Peter as its teacher. "Another Peter" is now its common father and teacher. The fact that in the homilies on Genesis little evidence of Antioch is to be found is irrelevent in the face of this evidence.[670]

Once Sequence C's Antiochene provenance has been satisfactorily established, Bonsdorff turns to the question of the year to which this large cluster of homilies is to be assigned.[671] On the basis that Genesis provided the topic for his very first homilies, that this book attaches to the

---

[665] Bonsdorff, *Zur Predigttätigkeit*, 7-9.

[666] Bonsdorff, *Zur Predigttätigkeit*, 8 nn. 6-7. In this Bonsdorff follows Montfaucon (see pp. 79 and 108 above).

[667] See in particular Bonsdorff, *Zur Predigttätigkeit*, 9 n. 9.

[668] Bonsdorff, *Zur Predigttätigkeit*, 9-10.

[669] This information is obtained from the title.

[670] Bonsdorff, *Zur Predigttätigkeit*, 10 n. 4, takes issue with Prince Max Herzog zu Sachsen who, in the course of his German translation of the homilies (2 vols, Paderborn 1913-1914), a work unavailable to me, apparently assigned the homilies to Constantinople. Bonsdorff argues that the reference to the beautiful ceiling of the church in *hom. 6* could as easily refer to the Old Church at Antioch as the Great Church at Constantinople. Moreover, the fact that the homilist threatens his listeners with the legal authority of the church does not necessarily mean that he is bishop. Further, in *hom. 4* his deference to the Syriac-speakers among the audience, as also the mention in *hom. 12* of a now lost homily chastising those Christians who celebrate the Jewish fast at Easter, both clearly speak for Antioch.

[671] Bonsdorff, *Zur Predigttätigkeit*, 10-13.

liturgy followed in Lent, and that in his later exegetical series Chrysostom repeatedly adduces exempla from the book of Genesis, at times with extreme brevity, Bonsdorff argues that the series must *a priori* be located in the earlier years of the presbyterate. He finds confirmation of this in the commentary on Galatians (CPG 4430), also originating in Antioch, where it is stated that the homilies *De mutatione nominum* are available in published form. Further in *hom.* 4 of the latter series John discusses the opening of I Corinthians in a manner which indicates that the series on I Corinthians (CPG 4428) cannot have been in existence, while the homilies on Matthew (CPG 4424), the only other serious contender, are likewise to be located after this sequence.[672] Having proved its early delivery, Bonsdorff then searches for a possible year, finding that 388 is the earliest in which it can be accommodated.[673] Despite the attraction of uniting the two sequences, the fact that this union would necessitate the delivery of ten homilies between Feb. 4, the date of the Juventinus and Maximus homily (CPG 4349), and Feb. 20, the beginning of Lent in 388,[674] makes this impossible.[675] This is confirmed by the fact that in none of the last four homilies *De Lazaro* (CPG 4329), which would under these circumstances be integrated with the four *In illud: Vidi dominum*, is there displayed any consciousness of the latter homilies. There is therefore no alternative but to place Sequence C in the following year, 389.[676]

---

[672] Bonsdorff prefers to leave the proof of the series on Matthew's later delivery until the following section.

[673] This conclusion had earlier been promoted by Montfaucon (see p. 98 above) and Stilting (pp. 141 above), and more recently by Rauschen (p. 141 above). At this point Bonsdorff, *Zur Predigttätigkeit*, 8 n. 1, had already demonstrated, against Tillemont (p. 49 above) and Stilting, that the four homilies *In illud: Vidi dominum* bear no relationship to the sermon *Cum presbyter* (CPG 4317) and that there are therefore no grounds for locating them in the year 386.

[674] This calculation is based on the assumption of a six week Lent, excluding Holy Week.

[675] Bonsdorff, *Zur Predigttätigkeit*, 13 n. 1, points out that on internal evidence none of the homilies was preached the day after another.

[676] This conclusion leads Bonsdorff, *Zur Predigttätigkeit*, 13 n. 2, to identify the martyrial festival mentioned in *In illud: Vidi dom. hom.* 3 as that of Juventinus and Maximus (Feb. 4) and into a complex set of calculations regarding the individual dates of the homilies delivered between Easter and Pentecost. For the results see Table 9.b, p. 201 below.

c. *Matthew*

The Antiochene provenance of the series on Matthew (CPG 4424), as Bonsdorff accurately states, has gone virtually undisputed.[677] The evidence usually adduced to support this attribution is *In Matt. hom. 7* where the homilist says that the city is the first to have acquired the name "Christian".[678] Bonsdorff feels obliged to reinforce this. In the same homily, when exegeting a Hebrew name, Chrysostom is moved to remark: καὶ ὅσοι τὴν Σύρων ἴσασι γλῶτταν, ἴσασι τὸ λεγόμενον ("and all those who know the Syriac language know what was said"),[679] in which Bonsdorff sees a reference to the Syriac-speakers amongst the inhabitants of Antioch. The statements in *hom. 32* that the homilist has never embarked on a major journey and that he identifies himself with the inhabitants can only have been made in the city of his birth. That Chrysostom is not bishop is clearest in *hom. 85* where reference is made to the burdens which "our bishops" carry.[680] Moreover, in numerous places the homilist tells his listeners of the monks who live in the mountains, encourages his audience to visit them and offers to take them there. In the vicinity of Antioch there lived numerous monks with whose lifestyle Chrysostom was familiar through personal experience. At Constantinople, however, colonies of that kind were unknown at the time of his episcopate.[681] Finally, the Antiochene provenance of the series is confirmed by *In I Cor. hom. 27* (CPG 4428) where John refers the listener to the more extensive exegesis provided in *In Matt. hom. 59*.[682] Regarding Savile's discovery of episcopal tone in *hom. 82*, Bonsdorff finds the evidence unconvincing, arguing that it indicates merely that Chrysostom is not in the earliest years of his presbyterate. As for Savile's location of the final homilies of the series at Constantinople, the statement in *hom. 85* which has been already adduced speaks against this.[683]

---

[677] Bonsdorff, *Zur Predigttätigkeit*, 14. Reference is made to the very early doubts raised by Savile (see p. 38 above).

[678] So Montfaucon (see p. 96 above), Stilting (p. 121 n. 425 above) and Lietzmann (p. 167 above).

[679] PG 57,74 25-28.

[680] Bonsdorff, *Zur Predigttätigkeit*, 15. This and the preceding observations are original.

[681] Bonsdorff here borrows directly from the observations of Montfaucon (see p. 96 above) and Stilting (p. 121 n. 425 above).

[682] This observation, originally made by Tillemont (see p. 61 above), had been further developed by Stilting (p. 121 above).

[683] Bonsdorff, *Zur Predigttätigkeit*, 15-16. As far as I can see, this was never intended by Savile (see p. 38 above), who found evidence of episcopal tone in homilies which fall early as well as late in the series.

Having definitively situated the homilies at Antioch, Bonsdorff turns
to investigate the year of their delivery.[684] As already shown, the series on
Matthew must date prior to that on I Corinthians. On the basis of Lietzmann's argument regarding *In Matt. hom. 88*, the series must further be
located before Nov. 20, 393.[685] Bonsdorff, however, finds evidence which
convinces him to locate it earlier still. The contents of *hom. 1* appear to
function as an introduction to the whole New Testament and not just the
gospel in question. Moreover, whereas in that homily not only the synop-
tic gospels but also that of John receive mention, the case is quite otherwise with the first of the homilies on John (CPG 4425). This leads Bonsdorff to conclude that the series on Matthew takes precedence. Comparisons between Matthew and the series of homilies on Romans (CPG 4427)
and Ephesians (CPG 4431) lead him to a similar conclusion. The
Matthean series constitutes, he argues, Chrysostom's first excursion into
the exegesis of the New Testament. As a consequence it is to be situated,
if not in the very first years, at least soon afterwards.[686]

This conclusion leads Bonsdorff to attempt to locate the series more
precisely. The beginning of the year 388 provides a secure *terminus post
quem*. Given that Sequence B locates itself only in the opening portion of
that year, it is possible that the homilies on Matthew may have filled the
remainder. This option is to be excluded, however, on the grounds that
Matthew must be placed later than Sequence C, which contains the
lengthy series on Genesis (CPG 4409).[687] Having established this fact,
Bonsdorff then turns to Baur's arguments for the early date of this series

---

[684] Unlike Baur, his contemporary, Bonsdorff nowhere discusses the issue of whether
the exegetical series as we have them stem from an oral performance or are a purely
literary production. With the exception of Galatians (CPG 4430), it is uniformly assumed
that they were delivered.

[685] See p. 167 above.

[686] Bonsdorff, *Zur Predigttätigkeit*, 16-17. Bonsdorff, *Zur Predigttätigkeit*, 18-19, argues
against the view Baur held at that time that the series spreads itself over the years 386 and
387. This was promoted by Baur on p. 6 of the introduction to his German translation of
the homilies, *Bibliothek der Kirchenväter*, NS 23, 1915. Baur later (see p. 207 below)
renounced this opinion in favour of the conclusion drawn by Bonsdorff.

[687] Bonsdorff, *Zur Predigttätigkeit*, 19-21. Bonsdorff bases this on the argument that
phrases such as ὅπερ ἀεὶ ἔλεγον ("as I constantly keep saying") and ὃ πολλάκις εἶπον ("which
I've often said") always indicate the later delivery of a series. While seven examples can be
found in Matthew, in the series on Genesis there occur none. In the brief treatment
afforded the numerous passages adduced from Genesis in the course of the homilies on
Matthew, Bonsdorff sees a further indication of its later delivery. Finally, in *De mutatione
nom. hom. 3* (CPG 4372) the homilist mentions the criticism he has received over his
lengthy introductions. In the homilies which occur afterwards, particularly in those given
after he resumed his exegesis of Genesis (i.e., *Hom. 33-67 in Gen.*), it is to be observed that
he corrects this defect. In the majority of the homilies on Matthew, moreover, such
introductions are almost entirely absent.

as proof that it must be located as soon as possible following the second sequence. In *In Matt. hom. 38* it is stated that there are still people who saw the martyrdoms of earlier that century take place; in *hom. 37* the way in which the homilist speaks of the theatre indicates that the homily is to be dated to shortly after the riots of 387; while in *hom. 88* the writings to which the audience is referred — the homilies *Adv. Iudaeos* (CPG 4327) and *Contra Anomoeos* (CPG 4318-4323) and the tracts *De s. Babyla contra Iulianum et gentiles* (CPG 4348) and *Contra Iudaeos et gentiles quod Christus sit deus* (CPG 4326) — all belong to the first two years at Antioch. This leads Bonsdorff to adopt the suggestion put forward by Bardenhewer,[688] namely that the series dates to around 390.[689]

d. *John*

In the case of the series on John (CPG 4425) it has never been suggested that the homilies were delivered anywhere other than Antioch.[690] Bonsdorff finds convincing but unsatisfying the usual proof that in *In I Cor. hom. 7* (CPG 4428), itself delivered with certainty at Antioch, the listener is referred to the series on John.[691] As with the homilies on Matthew, Bonsdorff looks for further evidence. This he finds in *In Ioh. hom. 12*, where, through a citation of Matt. 4.24, the present location (ἐνταῦθα) is identified as Syria.[692]

As for the date of this series, chronological indicators are entirely lacking. Bonsdorff rapidly dismisses Tillemont's suggestion that the wars, earthquakes and other disasters listed in *In Ioh. hom. 34* permit the series to be located in 394.[693] These calamities, Bonsdorff points out, are presented simply as signs of the apocalypse and bear no indication of the

---

[688] Bardenhewer, *Geschichte*, III 337, follows the conclusion first promoted by Stilting (see p. 122 above) and revived by Max Herzog zu Sachsen, *Des heiligen Johannes Chrysostomus, Homilien über das Evangelium des heiligen Matthäus*, I, Regensburg 1910, IV.

[689] Bonsdorff, *Zur Predigttätigkeit*, 21-22. The remaining discussion, *Zur Predigttätigkeit*, 22-25, is devoted to determining the time of year at which the various homilies were delivered in order to establish whether all ninety were delivered in the same year. Even with the exclusion of the Lenten period, Bonsdorff finds this possible.

[690] This statement is almost correct. Savile (see p. 37 above) in fact abstained because of the total lack of internal evidence.

[691] So Tillemont (see p. 61 above), Montfaucon (p. 97 above), Stilting, *Acta SS. Sept.*, IV 488 (sec. 428), and Lietzmann (p. 168 above).

[692] Bonsdorff, *Zur Predigttätigkeit*, 25. A list of different peoples cited in *hom. 2*, in which the Syrians are mentioned first (*Zur Predigttätigkeit*, 26 n. 2), is considered insignificant by comparison.

[693] See p. 61 above.

specific year of occurrence. As with Matthew, it is to a comparison with other of the exegetical series that one must look for evidence.[694] Through a comparison of the series on John with that on Matthew (CPG 4424), Bonsdorff first moves to establish that the series was delivered later than the latter.[695] This he does by pointing out several instances where the homilist assumes a knowledge of the series on Matthew. Further, in the sermons on John comments of the kind ὅπερ ἀεὶ λέγω ("as I constantly say") appear more frequently than in those on Matthew. Having established this, Bonsdorff then turns to a comparison of John with other of the New Testament series. As already discussed, the series on John must predate that on I Corinthians. For evidence that it is also to be located before the homilies on Romans (CPG 4427), Bonsdorff adduces *In Ioh. hom. 9*. As Romans is, as he will demonstrate, the first of the epistles to be exegeted, the series on John must have immediately followed that on Matthew. This situates it in the year 391.[696]

e. *Romans*

By contrast, the provenance of the series on Romans (CPG 4427) is less clear cut. As Bonsdorff points out, while the majority favours Antioch,[697] Tillemont felt unable to decide the issue,[698] while Rauschen actually assigned the series to Constantinople.[699] Bonsdorff, although he acknowledges the validity of Rauschen's arguments, nonetheless comes down on the side of Antioch. He admits that the oft-cited passage in *In Rom. hom. 8*,[700] taken to indicate that Chrysostom is not himself bishop, does not necessarily prove that the homilist and "shepherd" (ποιμήν) are mutually exclusive. However, since the same thought is repeated elsewhere in the homily,[701] Bonsdorff finds himself inclined to accept Montfaucon's arguments against those of Rauschen. If Chrysostom were

---

[694] Bonsdorff, *Zur Predigttätigkeit*, 26.

[695] Bonsdorff, *Zur Predigttätigkeit*, 26-28. This is done in order to address Stilting's proposal (see p. 121 above) that the series on John preceded that on Matthew.

[696] Bonsdorff, *Zur Predigttätigkeit*, 28-29. Bonsdorff further (pp. 29-30) devotes a brief discussion to the duration of the series and the time of year at which it is to be located. He concludes that it most likely began following Easter, with the possibility that the last few homilies ran into the early part of the following year.

[697] So Savile (see p. 40 above), Montfaucon (p. 98 above), Stilting (p. 122 above) and Lietzmann (p. 168 above).

[698] See p. 61 above.

[699] See p. 143 above.

[700] See PG 60,464 42-44.

[701] PG 60,465 27-35.

in fact bishop he might once have aligned himself with the audience in speaking of the church's "shepherd" or "leader". That he does it twice persuades Bonsdorff that the statements are to be taken at face value.[702] Rauschen had also elicited in favour of Constantinople a passage in *hom. 29* in which John states that he is "shepherd".[703] Bonsdorff dismisses this by pointing out that the distinction between shepherd and flock is in this instance not one of bishop and those beneath him, but of a spiritual leader and his flock. This is made clear at the close of the homily where it is stated that those subject to authority (ἀρχόμενοι) are themselves shepherds in their own milieu.[704] On the other hand, he agrees with Rauschen concerning the passage in *In Rom. hom. 30* where the audience is referred to the places where St Paul was bound, and sat and taught. These, he finds, could as easily be locations sanctified through the memory of the apostle as physical sites once visited by him, a possibility which renders the evidence indeterminate.[705]

This conclusion prompts Bonsdorff to look for other evidence. He first turns to a negative argument. If the homilies had been delivered at Constantinople, as Rauschen proposed, they ought to demonstrate personal experience of the imperial court and its circles.[706] Of all such exempla examined, however, not one exhibits the required level of awareness. Some, moreover, are better suited to the situation at Antioch.[707] Further, in *hom. 23* the characterisation of the ἄρχων (who may be baptised or non-baptised and who has judicial authority)[708] indicates an official of the level of *comes Orientis*, a circumstance which likewise speaks for Antioch. Had he been preaching at Constantinople, the homilist can only have used the emperor himself as his exemplum.[709] A Syrian perspective is likewise to be seen in *hom. 2* where the early missionary activity is attributed to "Syrian men" (ἄνδρες Σύροι),[710] and in *hom. 13* where the Thracians are included among the barbarian races located at the outer limits of the inhabited world.[711] In *hom. 26* Bonsdorff finds a reference to monks, which reflects the mountain-dwelling communities in the vicinity of Antioch. Moreover, in this same homily, as on several other occasions

---

[702] Bonsdorff, *Zur Predigttätigkeit*, 32-33.

[703] See PG 60,660 55-58.

[704] Bonsdorff, *Zur Predigttätigkeit*, 33-34.

[705] Bonsdorff, *Zur Predigttätigkeit*, 34.

[706] Bonsdorff, *Zur Predigttätigkeit*, 35.

[707] Bonsdorff, *Zur Predigttätigkeit*, 35, adduces *hom. 24* as an example.

[708] See PG 60,618 17-40.

[709] Bonsdorff, *Zur Predigttätigkeit*, 36.

[710] See PG 60,401 40-41.

[711] Bonsdorff, *Zur Predigttätigkeit*, 36-37.

throughout this series, the homilist contrasts the urban and rural communities, always referring to the former in the plural. In this Bonsdorff sees a further indication in favour of Antioch, since, had Chrysostom been preaching in the imperial capital, he must have betrayed it when using such expressions.[712]

As for the year in which the series is to be located, Bonsdorff points out that he has already established that it was delivered later than those on the gospels of Matthew (CPG 4424) and John (CPG 4425). This is consistent with the appearance of remarks such as ὅπερ ἀεὶ λέγω,[713] which indicate that the homilist has been preaching for a longer period of time. The introduction to these homilies, moreover, indicates that Romans is the first of the Pauline epistles to be exegeted, a conclusion supported by John's subsequent investigation into the chronology of the epistles. Here remarks concerning the letters to the Corinthians, Galatians and second letter to Timothy indicate that he cannot yet have exegeted those epistles. This encourages Bonsdorff to locate the series in the next available year, 392, an inference which he finds supported by the few available chronological indicators. By contrast with the later Antiochene series on Ephesians (CPG 4431), the homilies are delivered at a time of relative peace. Also in contrast to Ephesians, there is no evidence of schism at this time within the congregation at Antioch.[714]

f. *I Corinthians*

I Corinthians (CPG 4428), Bonsdorff states, is the only of the New Testament series in which Chrysostom openly declares (*hom. 21*) that he is preaching at Antioch.[715] This places the provenance of the series beyond doubt. He finds it necessary only to add in passing that the contents of other sermons in the series conform to this conclusion.[716]

The year of delivery is therefore the only detail which needs to be determined. As already established from *hom. 7* and *27*, I Corinthians must

---

[712] Bonsdorff, *Zur Predigttätigkeit*, 37.

[713] See Bonsdorff, *Zur Predigttätigkeit*, 38 n. 1.

[714] Bonsdorff, *Zur Predigttätigkeit*, 38-39. At *Zur Predigttätigkeit*, 39-40, Bonsdorff further attempts to establish the time of year at which the homilies were preached and the duration of the series. He concludes that the series began some time after Easter and, through twice weekly delivery, lasted some four months (p. 42).

[715] Prior to Bonsdorff this evidence had proved so convincing that all investigation of provenance ceased with this homily. So Savile (see p. 39 above), Tillemont (p. 61 above), Montfaucon (p. 98 above), Stilting (p. 122 above) and Lietzmann (p. 168 above).

[716] Bonsdorff, *Zur Predigttätigkeit*, 40. For instance, in *hom. 36* the homilist speaks of the leader of the congregation as someone other than himself.

have been preached after the series on John (CPG 4425) and Matthew
(CPG 4424). As the latter were at the time available to the audience as
books, the series cannot have been initiated immediately following them,
an inference supported by the fact that Romans (CPG 4427) has already
been securely located in that position. From points of comparison with
this latter series and from other details, however, Bonsdorff concludes
that I Corinthians came next in sequence.[717] It is "a time of peace" (*In I
Cor. hom. 3*), the gains made by Christianity in approaching far-flung
barbarian races are underscored (*hom. 6* and *7*), and although in *hom. 31*
friction within the church is mentioned, this is quite other than
schism.[718] On this basis, and since the homilies on Romans were begun
after Easter 392 and must have lasted for around four months, the present series could have been embarked upon in the latter portion of 392.
This conforms well with the numerous references to rain and cold (*hom.
11, 21, 23* and *30*),[719] as do also the allusions to frequently occurring
religious festivals (*hom. 15, 27, 28,* and *40*).[720] As a result the series can
be situated in the autumn and winter at the close of 392 and beginning of
393.

g. *II Corinthians*

Concerning the interpretation to be placed upon ἐνταῦθα in the context
of the much-adduced passage in *In II Cor. hom. 26* (CPG 4429), Bonsdorff takes the side of Tillemont and those after him against Savile,[721]
agreeing that, rather than providing positive proof that John is in Constantinople, the passage excludes the possibility that he is preaching at
that location.[722] Furthermore, that the thirty homilies stem from Antioch
is not contradicted by data found elsewhere in the series. In *hom. 10* the
unexpected nature of the emperor's entry speaks for Antioch, as also the
statement that on such an occasion the homilist would not have access
to him. The way in which the appearance of emperors on their festal
days is characterised in *hom. 12* again seems better suited to a provincial

---

[717] Bonsdorff, *Zur Predigttätigkeit*, 41 n. 6, cites the instances of ὅπερ ἀεὶ λέγω and
similar phrases in order to demonstrate that the series belongs to a period later in
Chrysostom's preaching activity at Antioch.

[718] Bonsdorff, *Zur Predigttätigkeit*, 41-42.

[719] Bonsdorff, *Zur Predigttätigkeit*, 42.

[720] Bonsdorff, *Zur Predigttätigkeit*, 43-44. The rationale behind this argument is never
actually stated.

[721] Montfaucon (see pp. 98f above), Stilting (p. 122 above) and Lietzmann (p. 168
above) all follow Tillemont (pp. 61f above). For Savile's opinion see p. 40 above.

[722] Bonsdorff, *Zur Predigttätigkeit*, 45.

city than the imperial capital. A passage in *hom. 9*, which describes the way in which the soldiers present in the city serve the ἄρχοντες,[723] does not speak against this.[724] Further, where Chrysostom makes mention of those in ecclesiastical office (*hom. 14, 15* and *18*), he does so in a way that is impersonal and objective. In none of these instances does he indicate that he himself possesses such ἀρχή.[725] Finally, in *hom. 3* and *8* Bonsdorff finds evidence of a Syrian-based perspective.[726]

Having firmly established the Antiochene provenance of the series, the next question for Bonsdorff is the relationship between this and the series on I Corinthians (CPG 4428). It is natural, says Bonsdorff, to think that the two were preached in succession, and a more minute investigation reveals that this was indeed the case. *In II Cor. hom. 1*, with its discussion of why Paul wrote a second letter after the first and its comparison of the latter with the former, speaks for this conclusion, while the character of the numerous citations of passages from I Corinthians (e.g., in *In II Cor. hom. 1-4*) indicates that the exegesis of that epistle had been carried out within recent memory of the audience. Further, the political and ecclesiastical situtation reflected in the two series appears to be the same. In *hom. 18* Bonsdorff finds a reference to *In Rom. hom. 8*, a circumstance which confirms that a time of schism is not in question and provides proof that the three series are to be located together in close succession.[727] A lack of internal chronological data leaves him unable to locate II Corinthians more precisely than to say that it was delivered after the series on I Corinthians in the first half of 393.[728]

h. *I Timothy*

Regarding the provenance of the series of homilies on I Timothy (CPG 4436), the dearth of evidence had previously caused scholars some difficulty,[729] with the result that only Montfaucon had attempted to adduce

---

[723] The term can be both technical ("archons", "magistrates") and general ("rulers", "persons in authority"). See PG 61,466 4-8.

[724] Bonsdorff, *Zur Predigttätigkeit*, 45-46.

[725] Bonsdorff, *Zur Predigttätigkeit*, 46-47.

[726] Bonsdorff, *Zur Predigttätigkeit*, 47. For the passages in question see PG 61,459 5-7 and 61,413 41.

[727] Bonsdorff, *Zur Predigttätigkeit*, 48-49.

[728] Bonsdorff, *Zur Predigttätigkeit*, 49-50.

[729] Tillemont (see p. 64 above), adopting Savile's application of the Photian criterion (see p. 37 above) had inclined towards Constantinople. Rauschen (p. 144 Table 5.a above) avoided discussion of the series altogether.

internal data in support of Antioch.[730] Bonsdorff argues that through a
closer examination of the homilies the validity of Montfaucon's view can
be firmly established. As one of the grounds on which he had based his
conclusion, Montfaucon had argued that, if Chrysostom had been bishop
at the time, he could not have spoken so frequently of the offices of priest
and bishop without letting slip that he was personally of that status.
Montfaucon had, however, neglected to cite any examples. From *hom. 5,
10, 11* and *15* Bonsdorff supplies the missing evidence.[731] In the total lack
of other than general references to the emperor and his circle Bonsdorff
sees a further indication that the series belongs to Antioch. Two passages
in particular (*hom. 12* and *14*) could not, he argues, have been so
phrased had John been speaking in Constantinople.[732] Further, as Montfaucon had argued, the monastic life described in *hom. 14* is of a kind
always associated with Antioch, never with Constantinople. Bonsdorff
points out that in that same homily the audience is exhorted to go take
alms to the monks and to do so often, advice which clearly points to
Antioch.[733] Finally, a passage in *hom. 17*, in which there is adduced as an
exemplum the relative cost of produce locally versus in Cappadocia,
would be ineffective in Constantinople but entirely natural at Antioch.[734]

As for the chronology of I Timothy in relation to the other New Testament series, there are several factors which indicate a longer period of
preaching activity. Not only is the by now usual ὅπερ ἀεί φημι to be found,
but also on one occasion μυριάκις ὑπὲρ τούτων διελέχθημεν καὶ διαλεγόμενοι
οὐ παυόμεθα ("we've preached about these matters countless times and
won't stop preaching").[735] The characterisation of the differences between presbyter and bishop as minimal (*hom. 10*) points to the growing
independence of Chrysostom as he increases in stature as a presbyter. By
contrast, however, in *In Eph. hom. 11* (CPG 4431), which Bonsdorff believes to be among the last delivered at Antioch, the bishop appears to be
altogether missing from the picture and responsibility for the situation
devolves upon Chrysostom himself. In *In I Tim. hom. 7* and *18* mention
is made of the barbarians, but in such a way that it is unclear whether
there is presently any military engagement. From this circumstance it is

---

[730] See p. 100 above. In this he was followed by Stilting (p. 123 above). Lietzmann (p.
169 above) who also located the series at Antioch, did so more on the basis that he could
not see it separated from Titus (CPG 4438).

[731] Bonsdorff, *Zur Predigttätigkeit*, 54-55.

[732] Bonsdorff, *Zur Predigttätigkeit*, 56.

[733] Bonsdorff, *Zur Predigttätigkeit*, 56-57.

[734] Bonsdorff, *Zur Predigttätigkeit*, 57.

[735] Bonsdorff, *Zur Predigttätigkeit*, 57.

also clear that the series on Ephesians came later.[736] Further, from a passage in the *argumentum* to I Timothy in which the difficult matter of circumcision is treated with otherwise inexplicable brevity,[737] Bonsdorff deduces that the series dates to after the commentary on Galatians (CPG 4430),[738] but to before that on Ephesians (i.e., some time in 394). Bonsdorff finds, moreover, that two chronological indicators support that conclusion. In *hom. 15* the reference to τοὺς βασιλεῖς τοὺς νῦν ὄντας καὶ αὔριον οὐκ ὄντας ("the emperors who exist today and tomorrow don't exist") suits better the period before the death of Theodosius (Jan. 17, 395) than shortly after, while in the statement later in this same homily that the sun does not often fail or darken, Bonsdorff sees an indication that the total eclipse of Nov. 20, 393 had taken place not long before.[739]

i. *II Timothy*

The series on II Timothy (CPG 4437) has always been treated as inseparable from that on I Timothy. This connection is confirmed by the absence of an *argumentum* and through the frequent citations of I Timothy in a manner which assumes knowledge of the homilist's exegesis of them on the part of the audience.[740] Since, however, as Stilting had pointed out, Montfaucon's arguments for provenance relate only to I Timothy,[741] Bonsdorff finds it necessary to confirm the Antiochene origin of the series on II Timothy on the basis of its internal evidence. As in the homilies on I Timothy, here too (*In II Tim. hom. 2, 3* and *4*) Chrysostom speaks of the ecclesiastical offices in a way that indicates that he personally is not a bishop.[742] The emperor and palace life are again spoken of in an entirely general way, while in *hom. 2* there occurs an exemplum of

---

[736] Bonsdorff, *Zur Predigttätigkeit*, 57-58.

[737] See PG 62,501 5-10.

[738] Bonsdorff, *Zur Predigttätigkeit*, 50-52, locates this commentary in 393 following the series on II Corinthians. Although the question of the date and place of the commentaries is not considered in the present investigation, the date Bonsdorff assigns to the commentary on Galatians is central to the overall distribution he adopts. For this reason, Galatians appears alongside the homiletic series in Table 9.b, p. 201 below.

[739] Bonsdorff, *Zur Predigttätigkeit*, 58. Bonsdorff attempts (pp. 58-59) to locate the series more precisely within the course of 394. He is able to conclude only that *In I Tim. hom. 5* appears to have been delivered some time after Easter.

[740] Bonsdorff, *Zur Predigttätigkeit*, 59. These points had originally been made by Stilting, *Acta SS. Sept.*, IV 496 (sec. 467).

[741] Montfaucon, in his *monitum* to the two series (see p. 100 above) essentially treats them as one.

[742] Bonsdorff, *Zur Predigttätigkeit*, 59-60.

this kind which could scarcely have been adduced in Constantinople.[743] Finally, several remarks of a geographic nature likewise point to Antioch. In *hom. 4*, while commenting on the ethnic background of Paul, John makes a point of mentioning the relationship between Hebrew and Syriac; in *hom. 8* he feels it necessary to identify the Antioch mentioned in II Tim. 3.11 as τὴν τῆς Πισιδίας ("the one in Pisidia"); while in *hom. 10* the Miletus referred to in II Tim. 4.20 is characterised as ἡ Μίλητος τῆς Ἐφέσου ἐγγὺς οὖσα τυγχάνει ("the Miletus that's near Ephesus").[744]

As for the year in which the series is to be located, since it follows close upon its companion little more can be said than that it belongs to around 394.[745]

j. *Titus*

The provenance of the series on Titus (CPG 4438) has never been disputed. The references in *In Titum hom. 3* to those who fast with the Jews and to Daphne, the cave of Matrona and a location dedicated to Kronos in Cilicia, all provide incontrovertible proof that it was delivered at Antioch.[746] As a further indication of his geographic perspective, in *hom. 6* Chrysostom finds it necessary to identify the Nikopolis mentioned in Titus 3.12 as "the one in Thrace".[747] Moreover, the way in which the homilist discusses the episcopal office (*hom. 1* and *2*) indicates that he himself is not at this time an incumbent.[748]

Concerning the chronology of the series, the way in which Chrysostom speaks of the distinction between bishop and presbyter indicates, as in *In I Tim. hom. 10* and *11*, a much more developed and independent sense of self. This stance is in marked contrast to the earlier years of John's presbyterate where the bishop is characterised as "teacher" and "father". The comparison with the series on I and II Timothy (CPG 4436-4437) naturally leads one to locate the series on Titus next to these, al-

---

[743] Bonsdorff, *Zur Predigttätigkeit*, 61.

[744] Bonsdorff, *Zur Predigttätigkeit*, 61.

[745] Bonsdorff, *Zur Predigttätigkeit*, 62. Bonsdorff, *Zur Predigttätigkeit*, 61 n. 1, finds several indicators (in particular, in *hom. 4*) which convince him of the series' late delivery.

[746] Bonsdorff, *Zur Predigttätigkeit*, 62. So Savile (see p. 39 above), Tillemont (pp. 62f above), Montfaucon (p. 101 above), Stilting (p. 123 above), and Lietzmann (p. 168 above). Rauschen, *Jahrbücher*, 527, also assigned it to Antioch, but without recording his grounds for doing so.

[747] Bonsdorff, *Zur Predigttätigkeit*, 62 n. 6.

[748] Bonsdorff, *Zur Predigttätigkeit*, 62-63. Bonsdorff spends some time addressing the passage in *hom. 1* in which Montfaucon (see p. 101 above) had seen an indication of episcopal status.

though, as Bonsdorff admits, there is no evidence to support this decision.[749]

k. *Ephesians*

With varying degrees of conviction,[750] the series on Ephesians (CPG
4431) has generally been assigned to Antioch.[751] Bonsdorff, arguing that
the Antiochene provenance of these homilies has never been definitively
proven, proceeds to rectify this. In the first instance, there is nothing in
the series that suggests that Chrysostom was preaching in Constantinople. Leaving aside the identity of the schism outlined in *hom. 10* and *11*,
any references to the emperor or palace are entirely general in character.
The exempla adduced in *hom. 4* and *9* tend, in fact, to speak for
Antioch.[752] Furthermore, the criticism of frivolity levelled at "our city" in
hom. 11 is likewise better suited to that location, as the citizens of the
Syrian capital, in contrast to those of Constantinople, were well known
for this characteristic. The references in *hom. 6* and *13* to men who leave
their houses, wives and children and take to the mountain tops further
elicit the style of monasticism practised in the vicinity of Antioch.[753] The
brevity with which the figure of St Babylas is introduced in *hom. 9*, on
the basis of which it might be thought that the homilist is addressing an
audience familiar with that story and is therefore preaching at Antioch
is, however, inconclusive. In *In Acta apost. hom. 41* (CPG 4426), part of a
series delivered with certainty at Constantinople, the person of Babylas
receives an even briefer mention. The passage in which the monk Julian
is adduced as an example (*In Eph. hom. 21*), on the other hand, can only
refer to Antioch. This figure has uniformly been identified as Julianus
Sabas, the Edessan ascetic who, as Theodoret records, once visited that
city.[754]

The real difficulty, however, lies with the schism alluded to in *hom. 6,
10* and *11*. After considering the details, Bonsdorff concludes, against

---

[749] Bonsdorff, *Zur Predigttätigkeit*, 63-64.

[750] Rauschen (see p. 143 above), for instance, argued that the division within the
church detailed in *In Eph. hom. 6* and *11* cannot have been the Meletian schism, but leads
one to think rather of Constantinople. The fact that the data found in *hom. 9* and *21* point
to Antioch, however, left him inclined, with some reservations, to favour the latter location.

[751] So Tillemont (see p. 62 above), Montfaucon (p. 99 above), Stilting (p. 122 above)
and Lietzmann (p. 168 above).

[752] Bonsdorff, *Zur Predigttätigkeit*, 64-65.

[753] Bonsdorff, *Zur Predigttätigkeit*, 65, here revives an argument put forward by Montfaucon (see p. 99 above).

[754] Bonsdorff, *Zur Predigttätigkeit*, 65-66.

Rauschen, that Chrysostom cannot have been bishop at the time and that further, even though Flavian receives no mention in these homilies, it can be said that he must have been quite old and that John, though a presbyter, was in reality the leader of the congregation.[755] This accords well with the idea that the series belongs to the last years of his presbyterate in Antioch, and that it marks a peak in the growing self-confidence and independence in the performance of presbyteral duties that has previously been observed. Concerning the proposal that the homilies were delivered at a time when Evagrius was still alive, Bonsdorff argues that had this been the case Chrysostom must have openly attacked him. This not being the case, the homilies must therefore have been delivered at some point after that bishop's death.[756] That the series belongs to the last years at Antioch is further confirmed by the reference to a war with the barbarians in *hom. 6*. This must allude to the war with the Goths and Huns in 395 and following, a circumstance which situates the homilies in the years 395 (or more probably 396) to 397.[757]

1. *398-399*

In the case of two of the *Novae homiliae* (CPG 4441) Bonsdorff offers more than just the status quaestionis. On the basis of the homilist's allusion to a recent homily devoted to the topic of the hippodrome and theatre, Bonsdorff wishes to place *In illud: Messis quidem multa* (CPG 4441.11) at around the same time as the four homilies (CPG 4441.7, 10,12,13) located by Pargoire in July 399.[758] He admits, however, that its location in that sequence cannot be more precisely determined. As for the homily placed first in Montfaucon's version of the series (*Quod frequenter conveniendum sit*: CPG 4441.3), Bonsdorff points out that, depending on the interpretation of the σεισμός ("quake") of thirty days earlier, two entirely separate dates can be elicited. The first, in which the catastrophe is identified as the earthquake listed by Claudian as one of a series of portents preceding the consulate year of Eutropius, locates the

---

[755] For the full argument see Bonsdorff, *Zur Predigttätigkeit*, 66-69.

[756] Bonsdorff, *Zur Predigttätigkeit*, 69-70. Bonsdorff here follows Stilting, *Acta SS. Sept.*, IV 495, in arguing that the antagonist alluded to in *hom. 11* must have been a presbyter of the Eustathian party attempting to set himself up as bishop in opposition to Flavian.

[757] Bonsdorff, *Zur Predigttätigkeit*, 70. Bonsdorff sees a further possible chronological indication in the reference to a recently occurring "threat from above" in *hom. 10*, but finds himself unable to isolate the meaning.

[758] Bonsdorff, *Zur Predigttätigkeit*, 74-75.

homily at the end of 398.[759] The second, in which the disaster is seen as the dismissal of Eutropius itself, sees the homily located during the brief period of exile which followed, variously dated to February or September 399.[760] Bonsdorff comes down on the side of this second explanation, which, since the date of Eutropius' fall had recently been fixed at c. Aug. 17, 399, permits him to locate the homily with confidence in mid-September of that year.[761]

m. *Philippians*

Despite Stilting's assertion that they belong to Antioch,[762] the homilies on Philippians (CPG 4432), Bonsdorff argues, constitute the first of the exegetical series undertaken by Chrysostom at Constantinople. Their Constantinopolitan provenance can be fully demonstrated from the adduced passages in *In Phil. hom. 9* and *15*.[763] In the former, even though John had talked of his fatherly feelings and defended himself against the attacks of his adversaries at Antioch, the chastisement of unworthy priests is more natural in the mouth of a bishop than a presbyter. Moreover, the statement πατήρ εἰμι ("I am a father") suggests the more emphatic tone of a bishop. Against this, however, it must be said that in this same homily (*hom. 9*) priests in general are characterised as fathers. Were this the only evidence for Constantinople, it could not in any way be considered definitive.[764]

The argument regarding the list of troubles which have struck the emperors and their families in recent history (*hom. 15*) lies with the identification of the last emperor to receive mention (οὗτος δὲ ὁ νῦν κρατῶν ["the one who rules now"]).[765] Is this Theodosius or Arcadius? Bonsdorff

---

[759] This was first proposed by Montfaucon (see p. 102 above) and revived by Lietzmann (p. 166 above).

[760] See Stilting (p. 126 above) who dates the fall to Jan. 16. Matthaei, whose view is expressed in PG 63,462 note (a), dates the event to before the end of August. By the time of Bonsdorff, Seeck, among others, had fixed the date in mid August 399. See, e.g., Seeck, "Arkadios 2)", RE 3 (1895) 1146-1147. Batiffol (p. 157 above), who likewise disagreed with Montfaucon, was not, however, entirely satisfied with Matthaei's explanation.

[761] Bonsdorff, *Zur Predigttätigkeit*, 75.

[762] See p. 123 above.

[763] So Tillemont (see p. 64 above), Montfaucon (p. 99 above) and Lietzmann (p. 169 above) all assigned the series to Constantinople, the first because of the reference to the problems assailing the reigning emperor in *hom. 15*, the other two on the basis of the episcopal tone perceived in *hom. 9*.

[764] Bonsdorff, *Zur Predigttätigkeit*, 77-78.

[765] For the relevant passage see PG 62,295 15-46, in particular lines 44-46.

finds it impossible that Chrysostom would have spoken of Theodosius in such a light. Moreover the phrase ἐξ οὗ τὸ διάδημα περιέθετο ("since he put on the imperial crown") requires a relatively short period of time to have elapsed. All in all, the exemplum can only refer to the weak, much-troubled Arcadius. That the location is indeed Constantinople is supported by the level of knowledge the homilist demonstrates of matters concerning palace life.[766] Although this is the only passage which provides certain evidence of the series' provenance, it can further be said that the relationship between the emperor and his highest official (ὁ ὕπαρχος, i.e., *praefectus praetorio per Orientem*), touched upon in *hom. 6*, could also be considered evidence for this location, while in the same homily Chrysostom lists among other heretics Apollinaris of Laodicea, a person not identified as a heretic in any of the series from Antioch.[767]

As for the time at which the homilies were delivered, no direct evidence is to be found. That it is currently a time of peace (*hom. 8*) is adduced in comparison to the situation in apostolic times, while the knowledge of scandals attached to the palace (*hom. 15*) indicates no more than that the homily dates to after the first few months at Constantinople. That Chrysostom has already been in the imperial capital for a while can be determined from the allusions to an earlier period of preaching.[768] That he has not been preaching for all that long, however, is indicated by a comparison between similar passages in *In Phil. hom. 6* and *In I Thess. hom. 10* (CPG 4434), the latter being from a series delivered later at Constantinople.[769] Further, at no time in the series on Philippians does John complain about the lack of results despite the length of time for which he has been preaching, as he does, however, in the series on Colossians (CPG 4433).[770] It is also appropriate psychologically that in the imperial capital Chrysostom began to strew his sermons with comments such as ὅπερ πολλάκις εἶπον at an earlier stage than at Antioch. These circumstances, Bonsdorff believes, do not permit one to locate the homilies much beyond the first year of the episcopate.

As a further point, the comment on the miserable ends experienced by the rich and powerful in contrast to the poor (*hom. 2*), as already noted

[766] Bonsdorff, *Zur Predigttätigkeit*, 78-79.

[767] Bonsdorff, *Zur Predigttätigkeit*, 80. A passage in *hom. 12* in which the crowning of athletes and charioteers by the emperor is prefaced by οὐχ ὁρᾶτε ("don't you see": PG 62,272 33-35) also receives mention. Bonsdorff admits, however, that similar passages are to be found in homilies delivered at Antioch.

[768] Bonsdorff, *Zur Predigttätigkeit*, 80 nn. 7-9, cites seven instances of ὅπερ ἀεί φημι and similar phrases.

[769] For the relevant passages see Bonsdorff, *Zur Predigttätigkeit*, 81, where Bonsdorff feels that the second more naturally postdates the first.

[770] Bonsdorff, *Zur Predigttätigkeit*, 81 n. 3.

by Neander,[771] suits the period before the fall of Eutropius. Had the homily been delivered shortly after that event, the exemplum would have
been worded quite differently.[772] The allusion to hot weather and the rich
who sweat for the sake of status and fashion (*hom. 10*), coupled with the
preaching of the homilies in close sequence,[773] points to the delivery of
the entire series at that time of year. Together all of these indicators
permit one to locate the series in spring or early summer 399.[774]

n. *Colossians*

Concerning the provenance of the homilies on Colossians (CPG 4433),
the facts leave no room for doubt. They were delivered at Constantinople.[775] The episcopal status of the homilist is clearly indicated in *In Col.
hom. 3*, while his episcopal authority is evident in the way he chastises
the women for their luxury (*hom. 7*) and for their use of heathen spells in
order to help their children recover from illness (*hom. 8*). So also at the
beginning of *hom. 8* the criticism undertaken in *hom. 7* is described by
John as originating not from his αὐθεντία or ἀξίωμα ("supreme authority"
or "rank"), so much as from his grief. The way in which the riot of 387 is
touched upon in *hom. 7* further speaks for Constantinople. From the tone
it appears that Chrysostom is no longer in the city of his birth. The mention in *hom. 9* of the homilist's intention to travel into the country in order to instruct there can also be considered to point to this location. The
metaphor of the head and body used in this context better suits the imperial capital.[776]
As for the point at which this series was delivered, Bonsdorff argues
that the comment in *hom. 9* must have been made before Chrysostom's
pastoral visit to Asia Minor, a circumstance which locates the homilies in
the earlier part of the episcopate. That he cannot be preaching in the first
months at Constantinople, however, is indicated by the several com-
plaints about the audience's lack of response despite his frequent ad-

---

[771] *Der hl. Johannes Chrysostomus und die Kirche*, II 51 (see n. 2).

[772] Bonsdorff, *Zur Predigttätigkeit*, 81.

[773] Bonsdorff, *Zur Predigttätigkeit*, 82 n. 3, points out that *hom. 6* and 7, as also *10* and
11 are closely connected to one another.

[774] Bonsdorff, *Zur Predigttätigkeit*, 82. Bonsdorff is at haste to point out, however, that
the homilies of July 399 (CPG 4441.7,10,12 and 13; see p. 188 above) establish a firm
terminus ante quem.

[775] This is the view promoted by Savile (see p. 39 above), Tillemont (p. 64 above),
Montfaucon (p. 100 above), Stilting (p. 126 above) and Lietzmann (p. 169 above).

[776] Bonsdorff, *Zur Predigttätigkeit*, 82-84.

monishment.[777] Two pieces of information in fact point to the second
year, 399. The mention of recent earthquakes in *hom. 2* suggests the
tremor which occurred at the end of 398, while the picture painted of the
folly of earthly power (*hom. 7*) fits in every circumstance the fall of the
consul-eunuch Eutropius which occurred c. Aug. 17, 399. While the χθές
("yesterday") of the exemplum is not to be taken literally, the series must
nonetheless have been preached in autumn of that year.[778]

o. *Acts*

Despite Seeck's claim that the series on Acts (CPG 4426) belongs to
Antioch,[779] the evidence for the Constantinopolitan provenance of these
homilies is as abundant as it is clear. The episcopal status of the homilist
is evident as early as *In Acta apost. hom. 3*, where it is stated that no-one
takes precedence over "the archon of the church", whether in the palace
or elsewhere, not even the *hyparchs* and *toparchs*. In *hom. 8* Chrysostom
further describes himself as an archon who sits on a throne, while in
hom. 9 people say that he is archon and bishop. In *hom. 11* he talks of
the birth pangs he has suffered for his "children". Elsewhere he talks of
his responsibility for the lives of his audience and the smooth running of
the congregation (*hom. 11, 18, 24, 27, 30*) and threatens with excommunication (*hom. 8, 9*) those who disrupt it.[780] Other statements indicate
that Chrysostom finds himself in the imperial capital. In *hom. 8* he
threatens to excommunicate those who persist in swearing, whether it be
a high official (ἄρχων) or the emperor himself. In *hom. 11* he compares
the joy he feels for his audience to that of the emperor after a successful
war, while in *hom. 21* the possibility of being summoned peremptorily to
the palace speaks of a closer than usual relationship between the community and its emperor. The exemplum of emperors and their discus-
sions with their political advisers concerning internal and external affairs
(*hom. 32*) undoubtedly refers to the period during which Arcadius was
experiencing conflict with the Germanic tribes.[781] In *hom. 8*, moreover,

---

[777] For the passages in question see Bonsdorff, *Zur Predigttätigkeit*, 84 n. 2.

[778] Bonsdorff, *Zur Predigttätigkeit*, 84-85. Bonsdorff, *Zur Predigttätigkeit*, 85 n. 5, demonstrates that the homilies were delivered in rapid succession. He further points out (p.
86) that the only indications of the season at which the series are being preached (*hom. 2*
and *7*) are appropriate to a colder time of year.

[779] Seeck (see p. 154 above) is the sole dissenter. Savile (p. 39 above), Tillemont (p. 63
above), Montfaucon (p. 97 above), Stilting (p. 127 above) and Lietzmann (p. 169 above) all
assigned the series to Constantinople.

[780] Bonsdorff, *Zur Predigttätigkeit*, 87-88.

[781] Bonsdorff, *Zur Predigttätigkeit*, 88-89.

we find a clear reference to the city of Constantinople. Here it is held up as a model for the rest of the world. On another occasion (*hom. 42*) the city is characterised as ἡλίκη and μεγάλη ("beautiful" and "large"). In any case, where the city of Antioch receives mention in the text of Acts there is no indication on the part of the homilist that he finds himself at that location, while in one instance a clear distinction is made between "those at Antioch" and the present audience.[782] The account given of events from his youth (*hom. 38*) also describes a city other than that in which he is preaching.[783]

Just as the provenance of the series has never seriously been open to dispute, the year to which the homilies are to be assigned has always been fixed at either 400 or 401 on the basis of a statement in *hom. 44* (ἡμεῖς λοιπὸν τριετίαν ἔχομεν ["we've spent three years"]).[784] This remark, Bonsdorff points out, is prompted by the relevant text in Acts and is therefore not to be taken too precisely, suggesting only that the homily in question belongs somewhere around the end of 400 or the beginning of 401.[785] Moreover, the interpretation placed by Tillemont and others on a passage in *hom. 1*,[786] in which they saw an indication that John began preaching on Acts in the paschal period and which consequently dictated whether the series was located in 400 or 401,[787] is mistaken. Bonsdorff points out that the phrase καὶ τότε καὶ νῦν ("both then and now") does not refer to Pentecost but draws a contrast between the time of the apostles and the present. He then adduces two further passages from the same homily which suggest that the time of year is quite otherwise.[788] The possibility that the series was begun the Easter following Chrysostom's visit to Ephesus, i.e., in 401,[789] is likewise to be ruled out, since in *hom. 44* the homilist states that for three years he has been preaching con-

---

[782] For the relevant passages see Bonsdorff, *Zur Predigttätigkeit*, 89 nn. 8-9.

[783] Bonsdorff, *Zur Predigttätigkeit*, 89. Bonsdorff, *Zur Predigttätigkeit*, 89-90, further briefly discusses *hom. 40*, in which he sees a personal nostalgia for Antioch on the part of the homilist, and *hom. 41* (St Babylas and the Theodorus conspiracy), adduced by Seeck as evidence for the Antiochene provenance of the series. For Bonsdorff's dismissal of this argument see *Zur Predigttätigkeit*, 96-97.

[784] See CPG 4426 (Tillemont to Rauschen), Table 13.b. From his comments concerning the date of the series on Genesis (CPG 4409) Savile (see p. 38 above), while avoiding the issue in his introduction to the series on Acts, appears to favour the opinion of Photius (see n. 9 above), who located the homilies in the third year of the episcopate, i.e., 400.

[785] Bonsdorff, *Zur Predigttätigkeit*, 90.

[786] PG 60,22 16-20.

[787] See Tillemont (p. 64 above), Montfaucon (p. 97 above) and Stilting (p. 127 above).

[788] PG 60,24 28-31 and 56-63. Bonsdorff, *Zur Predigttätigkeit*, 90-91.

[789] Bonsdorff, *Zur Predigttätigkeit*, 91-92, states here that the date assigned to the visit to Ephesus, in conjunction with the belief that the series was begun at Easter, has been a determining factor in whether earlier scholars have assigned the homilies to 400 or 401.

tinuously, every three or seven days.[790] Rather, if one accepts that the
"three years" points to the period late 400 to early 401, the fact that the
mention of this time span occurs only in the forty-fourth homily tends to
suggest that the bulk of the series belongs to 400, although it is difficult,
Bonsdorff admits, to account for the absence in the later homilies of any
allusion to the beginning of Lent (401).[791]

Setting this problem aside for the moment, Bonsdorff finds that the
evidence of date contained within the homilies points uniformly to the
year 400 and, in particular, to its second half. In the lengthy discussion of
the episcopal office and mention of Simon Magus in *hom. 3*, he sees an
allusion to the synod of twenty-two bishops held at Constantinople in
spring of that year, during which charges of simony were laid against the
Metropolitan Antoninus of Ephesus.[792] Two passages from *hom. 12* are
also seen to allude to that situation, which leads Bonsdorff to conclude
that the series must have been begun after the spring of 400.[793] Further,
at Constantinople the first half of that year was taken up with the coup
by Gainas. That this receives no mention in the course of the homilies
suggests that the series is not contemporaneous with the event. In fact
the only allusion (*hom. 37*) is to the massacre of the Goths on July 12.
Bonsdorff prefers to locate this homily some months later, which permits
him to situate the beginning of the series following July 12, 400, when
the city of Constantinople had been restored to a situation of relative
calm.[794] However, that the conflict with Gainas had not yet reached a
resolution is indicated by *hom. 11*, which suggests that Arcadius was still
at war and that the triumph of Fravitta had not yet taken place.[795]

Bonsdorff then turns to address the references in *hom. 7* and *41* to an
earthquake of recent occurrence. Stilting had been led to locate the entire series in 401 through his identification of the earthquake as the one
which occurred at the time of Synesius' departure from Constantinople.[796] Bonsdorff dismisses this possibility by drawing upon the chronology established for Synesius' visit by Seeck, which located the departure,
and therefore the earthquake, in 402.[797] With this out of the way and
bearing in mind the imprecision with which Chrysostom denotes inter-

---

[790] Although not explicitly stated, it appears that Bonsdorff is here arguing against
Stilting (see p. 127 above).
[791] Bonsdorff, *Zur Predigttätigkeit*, 92.
[792] Bonsdorff, *Zur Predigttätigkeit*, 92-93.
[793] Bonsdorff, *Zur Predigttätigkeit*, 93.
[794] Bonsdorff, *Zur Predigttätigkeit*, 94.
[795] Bonsdorff, *Zur Predigttätigkeit*, 95.
[796] See p. 127 above.
[797] Bonsdorff, *Zur Predigttätigkeit*, 95.

vals of time, the tremor can then be identified as the one which occurred at the end of 398, just prior to the consulship of Eutropius.[798]

Finally, reiterating that *hom. 1* was not delivered at either Lent or Easter, Bonsdorff points to a reference to cold weather and allusions to the approaching winter in *hom. 24, 26* and *29*, which leads him to conclude that this section of the series was delivered during autumn. Once he has established that the homilies were preached in relatively unbroken succession over a period of six or seven months,[799] this allows him to establish that the series was begun shortly after July 12, 400 and extended over the second half of that year, perhaps even occuping a few weeks at the beginning of 401.[800]

p. *I Thessalonians*

The two series on Thessalonians (CPG 4434 and 4435), notes Bonsdorff, belong among those whose Constantinopolitan provenance has never been questioned.[801] The evidence contained in the first he finds particularly convincing. In *In I Thess. hom. 5* John alludes to his episcopal status by describing the audience as his "body"; in *hom. 8* this is made more explicit when he talks of his προστασία (authority) and his accountability for the salvation of the audience; while in *hom. 9* he reiterates the latter. In *hom. 10* he talks of the responsibilities of the spiritual archon in the first person, including the authority to ban offenders from the church; while in *hom. 11* several of these themes (his προστασία, accountability and relationship to the audience) are brought together.[802] There are, moreover, numerous exempla concerning the emperor, empress and especially the palace, which point to Constantinople.[803] Finally, the reference in *hom. 3* to daily military exercises is likewise appropriate to that city, while in *hom. 8* the query whether anyone among the audience has visited Palestine is perhaps more natural there than in the more closely situated city of Antioch.[804]

As for the year to which this series belongs, beyond commenting that it appears to have been delivered at a time of peace (*hom. 3*) and there-

---

[798] Bonsdorff, *Zur Predigttätigkeit*, 97.

[799] See Bonsdorff, *Zur Predigttätigkeit*, 97-99.

[800] Bonsdorff, *Zur Predigttätigkeit*, 99.

[801] See Savile (p. 40 above), Tillemont (p. 65 above), Montfaucon (p. 100 above), Stilting (p. 127 above) and Lietzmann (p. 169 above).

[802] Bonsdorff, *Zur Predigttätigkeit*, 100.

[803] *In I Thess. hom. 5, 6, 8, 9, 10* and *11*. See Bonsdorff, *Zur Predigttätigkeit*, 101.

[804] Bonsdorff, *Zur Predigttätigkeit*, 101.

fore in the years following 400,[805] Bonsdorff prefers to delay discussion of this question until he has dealt with the second of the series on Thessalonians and the nature of the relationship between the two.

q. *II Thessalonians*

Just as the series on I and II Corinthians and on I and II Timothy were delivered one after the other, so it is with I and II Thessalonians. Bonsdorff finds clear proof of this in *In II Thess. hom. 1* where the first letter on Thessalonians receives mention and the necessity of writing a second letter is discussed.[806] As for the episcopal status of the homilist, this is again made explicit. In *hom. 4* John asks his audience to pray for him and in this context repeats the claim of the previous series, that he holds grave responsibilities as leader of such a large number of people; he further alludes to his role as leader, speaks of his fatherly feelings and, likening himself to a mother, talks of the pangs he has suffered in giving birth to many in his audience. In *hom. 3* he criticises some for coming just to hear him speak, as if God is not involved. The identification of Chrysostom with the church in this instance, Bonsdorff argues, indicates his position as bishop. The imperial *exempla* which occur in *hom. 3* and *4* can be adduced as further evidence of the Constantinopolitan provenance of this series.[807]

As for the date of the two series, the suspicion that they belong to the later years of Chrysostom's episcopate is strengthened by the contents of the second,[808] particularly by the hint (*hom. 4*) that the enmity against him has been developing for some time. Even so, Bonsdorff cannot bring himself to agree with Tillemont that the series is to be located shortly before Chrysostom was removed from office.[809] Instead, Bonsdorff finds in the reference to the fact that "another has often given birth",[810] i.e., performed the rite of baptism, an allusion to the situation described in the homily *De regressu* (CPG 4394), where it is stated that in the year of his visit to Ephesus (402),[811] John was absent from Constantinople at Easter

---

[805] Bonsdorff, *Zur Predigttätigkeit*, 101-102. In a footnote (p. 102 n. 4) he cites three instances of ὅπερ ἀεὶ λέγω and similar phrases in support of the later delivery of this series.

[806] Bonsdorff, *Zur Predigttätigkeit*, 102.

[807] Bonsdorff, *Zur Predigttätigkeit*, 103.

[808] *In II Thess. hom. 2, 4*. See Bonsdorff, *Zur Predigttätigkeit*, 103-104.

[809] Bonsdorff, *Zur Predigttätigkeit*, 104. See Tillemont (p. 65 above).

[810] *In II Thess. hom. 4*, PG 62,492 41-43.

[811] The journey is usually assigned to the winter of late 400-401, as detailed by Bonsdorff, *Zur Predigttätigkeit*, 105. In locating it in late 401-402, Bonsdorff follows the

when the catechumens were baptised. This leads Bonsdorff to locate the two series in 402, following Chrysostom's return from Asia Minor.[812] As for the duration of the series, this he finds difficult to determine.[813]

r. *Philemon*

Determining the location, let alone the date of the three homilies on Philemon (CPG 4439), as Bonsdorff points out, is a task that has proved particularly difficult.[814] He finds it easy to solve, however, establishing that they were in fact delivered at Constantinople. In *In Philemon hom. 3* Chrysostom reminds his audience of a promise, made recently when preaching on the topic of Hell, to take up the subject of God's mercy. Bonsdorff finds this promise in *In I Thess. hom. 8*, a comparison between this latter sermon and *In Philemon hom. 3* confirming that it is indeed the homily in question. Since the sermons on I Thessalonians were delivered at Constantinople, the series on Philemon must belong to that location also.[815]

This finding further permits Bonsdorff to establish a date for the series. Since the five homilies on II Thessalonians intervened and since, even so, in the series on Philemon *In I Thess. hom. 8* is referred to as πρῴην ("recent"), all three must have been delivered in close succession. It therefore follows that the homilies on Philemon likewise belong to the year 402, following Chrysostom's return from Ephesus.[816]

s. *Hebrews*

Although scholars have been unanimous in agreeing that the thirty-four homilies on Hebrews (CPG 4440) is the last of the exegetical series to have been undertaken by Chrysostom, this has been largely on the basis of the title appended to the homilies in the manuscripts.[817] Bonsdorff

---

chronology proposed by Seeck, *Geschichte des Untergangs der antiken Welt*, Stuttgart 1919, V 577.

[812] Bonsdorff, *Zur Predigttätigkeit*, 104-106.

[813] Bonsdorff, *Zur Predigttätigkeit*, 106-107.

[814] Savile (see p. 40 above) and Tillemont (p. 64 above) assigned it to Constantinople, Montfaucon (p. 101 above) remained undecided, while Stilting (p. 123 above) and Lietzmann (p. 169 above) were inclined to locate it at Antioch.

[815] Bonsdorff, *Zur Predigttätigkeit*, 108.

[816] Bonsdorff, *Zur Predigttätigkeit*, 108.

[817] See Savile (p. 39 above), Tillemont (p. 65 above), Montfaucon (p. 102 above), Stilting (p. 127 above) and Lietzmann (p. 169 above).

finds that there exists internal evidence which confirms that the series
belongs to Constantinople. The episcopal status of the homilist is clear
throughout. This is indicated above all in *In Heb. hom. 4*, where he
threatens offenders with excommunication, alludes to his position as
leader and speaks throughout with authority. In *hom. 23* he states that he
is a "loving father", while in *hom. 24* the comment that he has been appointed to the service of the Word, although not applicable exclusively to
the rank of bishop, does not speak against it. The claim in *hom. 30* that
there is only one of him (ἐγὼ μὲν εἷς εἰμι),[818] is a further sign that he holds
the highest rank within the congregation.[819] Moreover, there are a number of indications that John finds himself in the imperial capital. In *hom.
6* Bonsdorff finds three imperial *exempla* which impress him with their
cumulative effect. That one can suddenly and frequently cast aside one's
labours in order to catch sight of the emperor, a suggestion which occurs
in *hom. 28*, can only, he argues, refer to Constantinople; while in the
same homily and in *hom. 32* we find mention of the empress. In addition,
in *hom. 9, 13, 15* and *27* there occur similarly convincing *exempla* which
relate to palace life.[820]

Concerning the period spanned by the series, Bonsdorff first points to
hom. 17, where tribute is paid to the quality of the palace eunuchs. Seeing this as an indication that the memory of Eutropius is no longer fresh
in the minds of the inhabitants of Constantinople, he proposes that the
series belongs to the later years of Chrysostom's episcopate. This he finds
confirmed by comments such as in *hom. 9*, where John complains that,
although his listeners should by now be teachers themselves, he is
obliged to preach constantly on the same themes due to their failure to
learn.[821] While the homilies on Hebrews contain no direct references to
earlier Constantinopolitan series, a comparison with the series on Acts
(*In Heb. hom. 24* and *In Acta apost. hom. 8-13*, in particular) shows that
there is a less energetic prosecution of the congregation's faults in the
former, a circumstance which encourages Bonsdorff to assign it to a
later period than the latter.[822] The fact that throughout Hebrews allusions
to war or unrest with respect to the Germanic tribes are lacking, further
suggests that the series dates from after the end of 400; while the absence
of reference to church-political issues or clerical misdemeanours, such as
those found in the homilies on Acts and Thessalonians, points to a period
when memory of Severian's activities during Chrysostom's visit to Ephe-

---

[818] PG 63,211 10.
[819] Bonsdorff, *Zur Predigttätigkeit*, 109-110.
[820] Bonsdorff, *Zur Predigttätigkeit*, 110-111.
[821] Bonsdorff, *Zur Predigttätigkeit*, 112.
[822] Bonsdorff, *Zur Predigttätigkeit*, 112-113.

sus has disappeared.[823] By the same token, Bonsdorff finds no trace of the "Chrysostom-tragedy", in particular indications of strained relations between bishop and palace.[824] This leads him to explore the possibility that the series belongs to the period immediately after the first exile (autumn 403), when relations with the palace were temporarily restored. On the basis that Palladius and Socrates agree that this situation lasted for only two months, while all thirty-four homilies could scarcely have been delivered in so short a time, this possibility is dismissed, supported by the fact that there is a complete absence of any indication of recent exile.[825] Based on a chronology which locates the visit to Ephesus in 402, this leads Bonsdorff to locate the series some time in the second half of 402 and first half of 403. Two pieces of evidence regarding the time of year at which *hom. 11* and *17* were delivered (during winter; and not at Lent, Easter or following Easter) concur with that conclusion.[826]

t. *Summary*

Table 9.a. Provenance — Bonsdorff

CPG no.	Antioch	CPG no.	Constantinople
4317	*Sermo cum presbyter* (p. 3)	4324	*Contra Anomoeos hom. 11* (p. 72)
4318	*De incompr. dei natura hom. 1-5* (p. 3)	4325	*De Christi divinitate* (p. 72)
4319	*De beato Philogonio* (p. 3)	4392	*In Eutropium* (p. 76)
4320	*De consubstantiali* (p. 3)	4426	*In Acta apostolorum hom. 1-55* (p. 86ff)
4321	*De petitione matris fil. Zeb.* (p. 3)	4432	*In Phil. hom. 1-15* (pp. 77ff)
4322	*In quatriduanum Lazarum* (p. 3)	4433	*In Col. hom. 1-12* (p. 82ff)
4323	*De Christi precibus* (p. 3)	4434	*In I Thess. hom. 1-11* (pp. 100f)
4327	*Adv. Iudaeos hom. 1-8* (pp. 3, 4)	4435	*In II Thess. hom. 1-5* (p. 102f)
4328	*In kalendas* (p. 5)	4439	*In Philemon hom. 1-3* (pp. 107f)
4329	*De Lazaro conciones 1-7* (p. 5)	4440	*In Heb. hom. 1-34* (p. 109ff)
4330	*De statuis hom. 1-21* (p. 4)	4441.1	*Dicta postquam reliquiae martyrum* (pp. 73f)
4334	*In diem natalem* (p. 3)	4441.2	*Hom. dicta praesente imperatore* (pp. 73f)
4335	*De baptismo Christi* (p. 3)	4441.3	*Quod frequenter conveniendum sit* (p. 75)
4336	*De proditione Iudae hom. 2* (p. 8f)	4441.4	*Adv. eos qui non adfuerant* (p. 73)
4339	*De cruce et latrone hom. 2* (p. 8f)	4441.5	*De studio praesentium* (p. 73)

---

[823] Bonsdorff, *Zur Predigttätigkeit*, 113-114.

[824] Bonsdorff, *Zur Predigttätigkeit*, 114-115, citing *In Heb. hom. 25, 28, 32*.

[825] Bonsdorff, *Zur Predigttätigkeit*, 115-116.

[826] Bonsdorff, *Zur Predigttätigkeit*, 116-117.

4341	*De resurrectione* (p. 8ff)	4441.6	*Adversus catharos* (p. 74)
4347	*De s. hieromartyre Babyla* (p. 5)	4441.7	*Contra ludos et theatra* (p. 74)
4349	*In Iuventinum et Maximum* (p. 5)	4441.8	*Hom. dicta in templo s. Anastasiae* (p. 73)
4371	*In principium Act. hom. 1-4* (p. 8ff)	4441.9	*Habita postquam presbyter Gothus* (p. 73)
4372	*De mutatione nominum hom. 1-4* (p. 8ff)	4441.10	*In illud: Pater meus usque modo operatur* (p. 74)
4386	*In illud: Vidua eligatur* (p. 5)	4441.11	*In illud: Messis quidem multa* (p. 75)
4409	*Hom. 1-67 in Genesim* (p. 9f)	4441.12	*In illud: Filius ex se nihil facit* (p. 74)
4410	*Sermones 1-9 in Genesim* (pp. 3, 9)	4441.13	*De Eleazaro et septem pueris* (p. 74)
4411	*De Anna sermones 1-5* (p. 4)	4528	*De capto Eutropio* (p. 76)
4412	*De Davide et Saule hom. 1-3* (p. 4)		
4417	*In illud: Vidi dom. hom. 2, 3, 5, 6* (p. 9f)		
4424	*In Matt. hom. 1-90* (pp. 13ff)		
4425	*In Ioh. hom. 1-88* (p. 25)		
4427	*In Rom. hom. 1-32* (pp. 32ff)		
4428	*In I Cor. hom. 1-44* (p. 40)		
4429	*In II Cor. hom. 1-30* (pp. 45ff)		
4431	*In Eph. hom. 1-24* (pp. 64ff)		
4436	*In I Tim. hom. 1-18* (pp. 53ff)		
4437	*In II Tim. hom. 1-10* (pp. 59ff)		
4438	*In Titum hom. 1-6* (pp. 62f)		

Table 9.b. Chronology — Bonsdorff

Year (month-season)	Homily	Cited (page)
386		
Lent	*Sermones 1-8 in Genesim* (CPG 4410)	3
autumn	*De incompr. dei natura hom. 1-5* (CPG 4318)	3
	De beato Philogonio (CPG 4319)	"
	Adv. Iudaeos hom. 1-2 (CPG 4327)	"
Dec. 25	*In diem natalem* (CPG 4334)	3
date unspecified	*Sermo cum presbyter* (CPG 4317)	3
387		
Jan. 6	*De baptismo Christi* (CPG 4335)	3
before Lent	*De consubstantiali* (CPG 4320)	3
	De petitione matris fil. Zeb. (CPG 4321)	"
	In quatriduanum Lazarum (CPG 4322)	"
	De Christi precibus (CPG 4323)	"
	Adv. Iudaeos hom. 3 (CPG 4327)	"
Lent	*De statuis hom. 1-21* (CPG 4330)	4
c. Pentecost	*De Anna sermones 1-5* (CPG 4411)	4
after Pentecost	*De Davide et Saule hom. 1-3* (CPG 4412)	4
autumn	*Adv. Iudaeos hom. 4-8* (CPG 4327)	4
388		
Jan. 1	*In kalendas* (CPG 4328)	5
Jan. 2	*De Lazaro concio 1* (CPG 4329)	"

after Jan. 2	*De Lazaro conciones 2-3*	"
Jan. 24	*De s. hieromarytre Babyla* (CPG 4347)	"
Feb. 4	*In Iuventinum et Maximum* (CPG 4349)	"
after Feb. 4	*De Lazaro conciones 4-5* (CPG 4329)	5
	In illud: Vidua eligatur (CPG 4386)	"
	De Lazaro conciones 6-7	"
389		
before Feb. 4	*In illud: Vidi dominum hom. 2* (CPG 4417)	13 n. 2
Feb. 4	*In illud: Vidi dominum hom. 3*	13 n. 2
before Lent	*In illud: Vidi dominum hom. 5,6*	13 n. 2
Lent	*Hom. 1-32 in Genesim* (CPG 4409)	7-13
March 29	*De proditione Iudae hom. 2* (CPG 4336)#	13 n. 2
March 30	*De cruce et latrone hom. 2* (CPG 4339)#	"
April 1	*De resurrectione* (CPG 4341)	"
April 5	*In princ. Act. hom. 1* (CPG 4371)	13 n. 2
April 7	*In princ. Act. hom. 2*	"
April 8	*In princ. Act. hom. 3*	"
April 15	*In princ. Act. hom. 4*	"
April 21	*De mutatione nom. hom. 1* (CPG 4372)	"
April 22	*De mutatione nom. hom. 2*	"
April 29	*Sermo 9 in Genesim* (CPG 4410)	"
May 6	*De mutatione nom. hom. 3* (CPG 4372)	"
May 13	*De mutatione nom. hom. 4*	"
after Pentecost	*Hom. 33-67 in Genesim* (CPG 4409)	7-13
390		
date unspecified	*In Matt. hom. 1-90* (CPG 4424)	16-25
391		
date unspecified	*In Ioh. hom. 1-88* (CPG 4425)	26-29
392		
after Easter	*In Rom. hom. 1-32* (CPG 4427)	37-39
autumn-winter	*In I Cor. hom. 1-44* (CPG 4428)	41-44
393		
beginning	(remainder of CPG 4428)	"
first half	*In II Cor. hom. 1-30* (CPG 4429)	48-50
date unspecified	*In ep. ad Galatas comm.* (CPG 4430)	50-52
394		
date unspecified	*In I Tim. hom. 1-18* (CPG 4436)	57-59
	In II Tim. hom. 1-10 (CPG 4437)	61-62
395		
396a		
397a		
398*		
date unspecified	*Contra Anomoeos hom. 11* (CPG 4324)	72
	De Christi divinitate (CPG 4325)	"
	Postquam reliquiae martyrum (CPG 4441.1)	73-74
	Hom. dicta praesente imperatore (CPG 4441.2)	"
399*		
Jan. 19	*Adversus catharos* (CPG 4441.6)	74
spring/early summer	*In Phil. hom. 1-15* (CPG 4432)	81-82
July 3	*Contra ludos et theatra* (CPG 4441.7)	74
July 17	*In illud: Pater meus usque mod.* (CPG 4441.10)	74

July 24	*In illud: Filius ex se nihil facit* (CPG 4441.12)	74
July 31	*De Eleazaro et septem pueris* (CPG 4441.13)	74
c. Aug. 17	*In Eutropium* (CPG 4392)	76
following Sunday	*De capto Eutropio* (CPG 4528)	76
autumn	*In Col. hom. 1-12* (CPG 4433)	84-85
mid September	*Quod frequenter conveniendum sit* (CPG 4441.3)	75
date unspecified	*In illud: Messis quidem multa* (CPG 4441.11)	75
400		
second half	*In Acta apostolorum hom. 1-55* (CPG 4426)	90-99
401		
first few weeks	(remainder of CPG 4426)[#]	"
402		
after Easter	*In I Thess. hom. 1-11* (CPG 4434)	103-106
	In II Thess. hom. 1-5 (CPG 4435)	"
	In Philemon hom. 1-3 (CPG 4439)	108
second half	*In Heb. hom. 1-34* (CPG 4440)	112-116
403		
first half	(remainder of CPG 4440)	"
404		

* 398/399 — CPG 4441.4,5,8,9 (pp. 73-75). [#] Probably. [a] 396/397 — CPG 4431.

6. BAUR

In 1929 Chrysostom Baur produced the first of two volumes in which he set out his own approach to the life and writings of Chrysostom. At the opposite end of the spectrum from Bonsdorff, Baur's interest lay in establishing the definitive biography of his much-loved namesake. Information concerning the location or date of the homilies is almost entirely integrated into a fulsome and extensive narrative, requiring frequent leaps of intuition between text and footnote on the part of the reader. This makes it difficult to extract such data from all but the few chapters where the homiletic output is itself the subject. Yet, like the contributions of Lietzmann before him and Quasten after him, the work of Baur became and still remains a standard reference on the subject. Once again it is important to establish the basis of his model in order to determine where it fits against the background of earlier and contemporary scholarship.

Because of the peculiarities associated with the way in which Baur presents his information, the order usually adopted is here reversed. The schemas for provenance and date are set out in tabulated format first, with such supporting argumentation as occurs discussed below. As his opinion is presented in such an abbreviated fashion, simple detail of Baur's arguments for preferring one location or date to another is insufficient for placing them in perspective. It is nonetheless important to note where his schemas differ from those which preceded and to be aware of assertions that are inconsistent. This information is therefore detailed following the discussion of supporting evidence. From the perspective of chronology the exact dates of the festivals devoted to local saints and martyrs are significant, especially where a homily delivered on such an occasion forms part of a sequence. As the dates assigned are often speculative, it is important to detail these in order to determine whether Baur follows the consensus. Finally, Baur weaves into his text the attribution of certain homilies to local churches or martyria within the two cities. These data, which are important for establishing liturgical customs which are idosyncratic and therefore distinguish the one city from the other, are presented in Table 10.c.

a. *Distribution of homilies between Antioch and Constantinople*

In the following table the location (volume, page) at which Baur makes each assertion regarding provenance is recorded in parentheses following the title of the series or homily.

Table 10.a. Provenance — Baur

CPG no.	Antioch	CPG no.	Constantinople
4318	De incompr. dei nat. hom. 1-5[#] (I 259 n. 3)	4324	Contra Anomoeos hom. 11 (II 14 n. 31)
4319	De beato Philogonio (I 200 n. 72)	4363	In martyres Aegyptios (II 76 n. 14)[b]
4327	Adv. Iudaeos or. 1-8 (I 259 n. 4, 285)	4364	De s. hieromartyre Phoca (II 34 n. 17)
4328	In kalendas (I 285)	4392	In Eutropium (II 112-117)
4329	De Lazaro conc. 1-7 (I 285)	4394	De regressu (II 150f)
4330	De statuis hom. 1-21 (I 263ff)	4395	De recipiendo Severiano (II 160f)
4332	De diabolo tentatore hom. 2 (I 392 n. 10)	4398	Sermo post reditum 1 (II 267 n. 26)
4333	De paenitentia hom. 5 (I 392f n. 10)	4426	In Acta apost. hom. 1-55 (I 87 n. 21; II 82, 93f)
4334	In diem natalem (I 259)	4432	In Phil. hom. 9 (I 189 n. 29)[c]
4335	De baptismo Christi (I 259)	4433	In Col. hom. 1-12 (I 87 n. 21; II 93)
4336	De prod. Iudae hom. 1 (I 285)	4434	In I Thess. hom. 1-11 (II 93)
4337	De coemeterio et de cruce (I 198 n. 50)	4435	In II Thess. hom. 1-5 (II 93)
4338	De cruce et latrone hom. 1 (I 285)	4439	In Philemon hom. 1-3 (II 94)
4340	De resurr. mortuorum (I 285)	4441.1	Dicta post. reliquiae martyrum (II 34 f n. 19)
4342	In ascensionem domini (I 34)	4441.2	Dicta praesente imperatore (II 36f n. 21)
4343	De s. pentecoste hom. 1-2 (I 222 n. 64)	4441.3	Quod freq. conveniendum sit (II 53 n. 25)

4345	*De s. Meletio Antiocheno* (I 259 n. 5)	4441.4	*Adversus eos qui non adfuerant* (II 53 n. 21)
4346	*In s. Lucianum martyrem* (I 200 n. 62)	4441.5	*De studio praesentium* (II 51 n. 8)
4347	*De s. hieromartyre Babyla* (I 200, 285)	4441.6	*Adversus catharos* (II 53 n. 20)
4349	*In Iuventinum et Maximum* (I 285)	4441.7	*Contra ludos et theatra* (II 86f)
4350	*De s. Pelagia* (I 200 n. 69, 259)	4441.8	*Dicta in templo s. Anastasiae* (II 53 n. 21)
4351	*De s. Ignatium* (I 200 n. 68, 259)	4441.9	*Hab. postquam presb. Gothus* (II 53 n. 24, 77)
4352	*In s. Eustathium* (I 200 n. 73)	4441.10	*In illud: Pater meus usque modo op.* (II 84f n. 8)
4353	*In s. Romanum* (I 200 n. 70)	4441.11	*In illud: Messis quidem multa* (II 53 n. 20)
4354	*De Macabeis hom. 1-2*[a] (I 32f, 200 n. 67)	4441.12	*In illud: Filius ex se nihil facit* (I 394)
4355	*De ss. Bernice et Prosdoce* (I 200 n. 65)		
4356	*In quatrid. Lazarum* (I 200 n. 65)		
4357	*De ss. martyribus* (I 249f)		
4360	*In s. Iulianum* (I 200 n. 71)		
4361	*In s. Barlaam* (I 200 n. 66)		
4362	*De s. Droside* (I 200)		
4366	*De terrae motu* (I 209 n. 12)		
4368	*De decem mill. talent. debitore* (I 285)		
4371	*In princ. Act. hom. 1-4* (I 285)		
4372	*De mutatione nom. hom. 1-4* (I 285)		
4375	*In illud: Si esurierit inimicus* (I 31)		
4382	*De eleemosyna* (I 380 n. 40)		
4409	*Hom. 1-67 in Genesim* (I 285)		
4410	*Sermones 1-?* in Genesim* (I 259)		
4411	*De Anna sermones 1-5* (I 285)		
4414	*In illud: Ne timueritis hom. 1* (II 229 n. 5)		
4417	*In illud: Vidi dominum hom. 1-4* (I 285)		
4424	*In Matt. hom. 1-90* (I 288f)		
4425	*In Ioh. hom. 1-88* (I 289)		
4427	*In Rom. hom. 1-32* (I 297)		
4428	*In I Cor. hom. 1-44* (I 298)		
4429	*In II Cor. hom. 1-30* (I 298)		
4431	*In Eph. hom. 1-24* (I 299)		
4432	*In Phil. hom. 1-15* (I 299f)		
4436	*In I Tim. hom. 1-18* (I 299)		
4437	*In II Tim. hom. 1-10* (I 299)		
4438	*In Titum hom. 1-6* (I 299)		
4441.13	*De Eleazaro et septem pueris* (II 55 n. 20)[b]		
4460	*Ad illuminandos cat. 1* (I 87 n. 21f)		
4464	*Ad illuminandos cat. 2* (II 229 n. 5)		

* Exact number of homilies unspecified. # Listed as *De incompr. dei hom. 1-9*. The identity of the last four (presumably from among CPG 4319-4323) unspecified. a *hom. 3* not considered genuine. b Possibly. c Also assigned to Antioch.

b. *Chronology*

Table 10.b. Chronology — Baur

Year (month-season)	Homily	Cited (vol.-page)
386		
Lent	*Sermones 1-?* in Genesim* (CPG 4410)	I 259
Oct. 8	*De s. Pelagia* (CPG 4350)	I 200, 259
Oct. 17	*De s. Ignatium* (CPG 4351)	I 200, 259
Dec. 25	*In diem natalem* (CPG 4334)a	I 259
date unspecified	*De incompr. dei natura hom. 1-5* (CPG 4318) + 4 from CPG 4319-4323#	I 259 n. 3 "
	Adv. Iudaeos or. 1-3 (CPG 4327)	I 259 n. 4
387		
Jan. 6	*De baptismo Christi* (CPG 4335)	I 259
before Lent	*De s. Meletio Antiocheno* (CPG 4345)	I 259 n. 5
Lent:	*De statuis hom. 1-18,20* (CPG 4330):	I 263ff
March 3/5	*De statuis hom. 2*	I 264-265
March 14	*De statuis hom. 3*	I 266
mid March	*De statuis hom. 16*	I 180
April 25 (Easter)	*De statuis hom. 21* (CPG 4330)	I 276
Sunday before Ascension	*De statuis hom. 19* (CPG 4330)	I 285 n. 5
Ascen. - Pentecost	*De decem mill. talent. debitore* (CPG 4368)	I 285
immed. after Pentecost	*De Anna sermones 1-5* (CPG 4411)	I 285
autumn	*Adv. Iudaeos or. 4-8* (CPG 4327)	I 285
388		
Jan. 1	*In kalendas* (CPG 4328)	I 285
early January	*In Iuventinum et Maximum* (CPG 4349)	I 200 n. 63, 285
Jan. 24	*De s. hieromartyre Babyla* (CPG 4347)	I 200 n. 64, 285
Lent	*Hom. 1-32 in Genesim* (CPG 4409)	I 285
Easter	*De resurrectione mortuorum* (CPG 4340)	I 285
after Pentecost	*Hom. 33-67 in Genesim* (CPG 4409)	I 285
Dec. 25	*In diem natalem* (CPG 4334)b	I 199 n. 56
date unspecified	*De Lazaro conciones 1-7* (CPG 4329)	I 285
	De prod. Iudae hom. 1 (CPG 4336)	"
	De cruce et latrone hom. 1 (CPG 4338)	"
	In princ. Act. hom. 1-4 (CPG 4371)	"
	De mutatione nominum hom. 1-4 (CPG 4372)	"
	In illud: Vidi dominum hom. 1-4 (CPG 4417)	"
389		
390		
?	*In Matt. hom. 1-90* (CPG 4424)	I 288-289

391		
date unspecified	*In Ioh. hom. 1-88* (CPG 4425)	I 289
392		
393		
394		
395		
396		
397		
date unspecified	*In Eph. hom. 1-24* (CPG 4431)	I 299
	In I Tim. hom. 1-18 (CPG 4436)	"
	In II Tim. hom. 1-10 (CPG 4437)	"
	In Titum hom. 1-6 (CPG 4438)	"
398		
399		
April 10	*Contra ludos et theatra* (CPG 4441.7)[c]	II 238 n. 4
Paschal period	*Habita postquam presb. Gothus* (CPG 4441.9)	II 77
July 3	*Contra ludos et theatra* (CPG 4441.7)[d]	II 86-87
August	*In Eutropium* (CPG 4392)	II 112-117
autumn	*In Col. hom. 1-12* (CPG 4433)	II 93
400		
date unspecified	*In Acta apost. hom. 1-55* (CPG 4426)	II 93-94
401		
after April 14	*De regressu* (CPG 4394)	II 150-151
date unspecified	*De recipiendo Severiano* (CPG 4395)	II 160-161, 165
402		
403		
404		

* Exact number of homilies unspecified. # Not identified. [a] See the year 388 below. [b] See the year 386 above. [c] See July 3, 399. [d] See April 10, 399.

Sequence A. (Constantinople) *De s. hieromartyre Phoca* (CPG 4364); (following day) *Hom. dicta postquam reliquiae martyrum* (CPG 4441.1); (following day) *Hom. dicta praesente imperatore* (CPG 4441.2).[827]

c. *Supporting evidence*

Baur's provision of evidence in support of his assertions is minimal to say the least. He relies largely on the opinions of others, although he will occasionally offer a personal opinion when stating why one view should be accepted in preference to another. His strongest statement of conviction occurs in relation to the exegetical series. With the exception of the first eight sermons on Genesis (CPG 4410), such series, he believes,

---

[827] Baur, *Chrysostom and His Time*, II 34-37.

were almost certainly literary compositions written in the form of homilies.[828]

This belief leads Baur, despite the firm opinions expressed by Bonsdorff, to err on the side of caution when discussing the exegetical series. The sixty-seven homilies on Genesis (CPG 4409) are, he asserts, assigned by recent scholars to the year 388. He confusedly states that Bonsdorff assigns the series along with the Lazarus sermons (CPG 4329) to 389,[829] following this with an allusion to the opinion of Max Herzog zu Sachsen, who located the series on Genesis at Constantinople.[830] He concludes by stating that a clear authoritative opinion on the Genesis homilies has yet to emerge.[831] The commentary on the Psalms (CPG 4413) is dismissed as a written explanation of selected Psalms, with no mention of date or location.[832] With regard to the series on Matthew (CPG 4424), Baur considers it a written commentary and remarks that Chrysostom must have begun composing it soon after the sermons on Genesis. He further states that it is generally supposed to belong to the year 390, and that this date may be accurate.[833] In assigning the eighty-eight homilies on John (CPG 4425) to the following year (391) Baur embraces the arguments put forward by Bonsdorff.[834]

With his discussion of the series on the Pauline epistles, we arrive at some of the few explanatory comments supplied by Baur. The commentary on Romans (CPG 4427), he says, was probably the first Chrysostom attempted, possibly directly after the series on John. This naturally occurred at Antioch.[835] Although it appears more a literary work than a series of sermons, he argues that the written polemic against the Jews and Judaism was more noticeable at Antioch because of the size of the Jewish population. In Constantinople, although Jews existed among the population, their proximity to the imperial court made them less notice-

---

[828] Baur, *Chrysostom and His Time*, I 200-202.

[829] Bonsdorff (see pp. 172-175 above) was quite clear in distinguishing the two series as belonging to separate sequences. These he located in successive years, 388 (*De Lazaro*) and 389 (*In Genesim*).

[830] See n. 670 above.

[831] Baur, *Chrysostom and His Time*, I 285-286. Baur, "Chrysostomus in Genesim", ThQ 108 (1928) 229-231, had just discussed this issue with the conclusion that, regardless of other uncertainties, the series could not have been delivered before 388.

[832] Baur, *Chrysostom and His Time*, I 286.

[833] Baur, *Chrysostom and His Time*, I 288-289. In a footnote, I 289 n. 35, Baur indicates that his opinion has changed since he assigned the homilies to 386-387 in the introduction to his German translation, *Bibliothek der Kirchenväter*, NS 23 (1915) 5-6.

[834] Baur, *Chrysostom and His Time*, I 289.

[835] Baur, *Chrysostom and His Time*, I 297.

able.[836] Further, in *In Rom. hom. 25* Chrysostom speaks of monks who dwell in the mountains, which, Baur considers, could again only refer to Antioch. In the following years are to be located the commentaries on the two Letters to the Corinthians (CPG 4428-4429). These too, Baur considers, were written in homily form.[837] In the first of them (*In I Cor. hom. 21*) it is explicitly stated that the location is Antioch. In *In I Cor. hom. 7 and 27* Chrysostom also refers to the series on Matthew and John.[838] Regarding the series on I and II Timothy (CPG 4436-4437), Baur states simply that they were produced in the last year at Antioch, as proposed by Montfaucon and now confirmed by Bonsdorff.[839] This is also the case with the homilies on Titus (CPG 4438) and on Ephesians (CPG 4431).[840]

Baur goes on to state that, as a priest at Antioch, Chrysostom had twelve years in which to preach and write, in contrast to his experience at Constantinople. There John's time was taken up by his ecclesiastical duties and by external political factors to such an extent that, in the first three years at least, it was difficult to devote time to quiet continuous endeavour. That circumstance, Baur argues, justifies assigning by default to Antioch all of the exegetical series which do not contain certain reference to Constantinople.[841] This allows him, despite the consensus, to assign to Antioch with Stilting the fifteen homilies on Philippians (CPG 4432).[842] In support of that attribution he argues that the passage in *In Phil. hom. 15* is more appropriate to Theodosius than Arcadius, since only the continual difficulties are mentioned. Theodosius faced considerably more of these than Arcadius. Further, it would have been remarkable for Chrysostom to have passed over Theodosius in silence, in order to designate the emperor right by his side in Constantinople as the "one now reigning".[843]

Regarding the sermon *In martyres Aegyptios* (CPG 4363) Baur, despite declaring in the first volume that it cannot be determined with certainty whether the homily was delivered at Antioch or Constantinople,[844] appears to favour Constantinople when he comes to refer to it for a second time.[845] Again he stipulates that the location is not certain, but adds that,

---

[836] Baur, *Chrysostom and His Time*, I 297 n. 50a.
[837] Baur, *Chrysostom and His Time*, I 298.
[838] Baur, *Chrysostom and His Time*, I 298 nn. 52-53.
[839] Baur, *Chrysostom and His Time*, I 299.
[840] Baur, *Chrysostom and His Time*, I 299.
[841] Baur, *Chrysostom and His Time*, I 299.
[842] Baur, *Chrysostom and His Time*, I 300. For Stilting's opinion see p. 123 above.
[843] Baur, *Chrysostom and His Time*, I 300 n. 65.
[844] Baur, *Chrysostom and His Time*, I 200 n. 72a.
[845] Baur, *Chrysostom and His Time*, II 76 n. 14.

while on the one hand there existed various established links between Egypt and Antioch, the fact that official ecclesiastical business between Antioch and the imperial capital had been resumed in 398 speaks for Constantinople.

Concerning the series to be assigned to Constantinople, Baur states that the homilies on Colossians (CPG 4433) were without doubt published in Constantinople in autumn of 399. In this he defers to the arguments of Bonsdorff.[846] The series on I and II Thessalonians (CPG 4434-4435) belong also to that location, although Baur believes that Bonsdorff, in assigning them to 402, has been influenced more by the desire to establish a smooth chronology than by internal evidence.[847] The fifty-five homilies on Acts (CPG 4426) belong likewise to Constantinople and were probably delivered in the year 400, since Chrysostom states in one homily (unspecified) that he had been preaching there for three years.[848] Here Baur disagrees with Bonsdorff, who believed that he had found in *In Acta apost. hom. 37* a reference to the expulsion of the Goths.[849] Baur does follow Bonsdorff, however, in assigning the homilies on Philemon (CPG 4439) to Constantinople.[850] Finally, in response to the title to the series on Hebrews (CPG 4440), long used to locate the homilies in the final years of the episcopate,[851] Baur raises a number of questions, none of which he finds can be satisfactorily answered. On the basis of the information contained in the title he is inclined to locate the origin of this commentary in the years of exile, although this solution he by no means considers certain.[852]

d. *Noteworthy aspects of Baur's distribution*

The kind of integrated discussion of the homilies which Baur pursues is not without its problems. In Chapter Six of Volume One, in which he details the liturgy of Antioch, the feast of Christmas is described as having been adopted at Antioch around the year 378.[853] In the footnote to

---

[846] Baur, *Chrysostom and His Time*, II 93.

[847] Baur, *Chrysostom and His Time*, II 93 n. 29.

[848] Baur, *Chrysostom and His Time*, II 94.

[849] Baur, *Chrysostom and His Time*, II 94 n. 31. This allusion had convinced Bonsdorff (see p. 194 above) to locate the beginning of the series shortly after July 12, 400, the date of that event.

[850] Baur, *Chrysostom and His Time*, II 94.

[851] See, for instance, Bonsdorff (p. 199 above) and Lietzmann (p. 169 above).

[852] Baur, *Chrysostom and His Time*, II 94-95.

[853] Baur, *Chrysostom and His Time*, I 199.

this comment, where *In diem natalem* is mistakenly cited as occurring at PG 49,51,[854] Baur indicates that here he may be following the date assigned to the homily by Usener (Dec. 25, 388).[855] However, when he later outlines the first year of preaching at Antioch in order to set the scene for the riots of 387, Baur follows the more common view in locating this homily at the close of 386.[856] The manner in which he does so makes it clear that he has forgotten his earlier note. As for the homilies *De statuis* (CPG 4330), it is important to note that Baur follows the revised opinion of Montfaucon in detaching *De statuis hom. 19* from the series and assigning it to the Sunday before Ascension.[857]

In discussing the homilies to be assigned to the year 388, Baur makes an unusual claim when stating that it is probable that the first four of the sermons *In illud: Vidi dominum* (CPG 4417) belong to that year.[858] Four of the six homilies on Is. 6.1 are indeed commonly linked with certain of the homilies Baur allocates to this year,[859] but the four are usually identified not as *hom. 1-4* but *hom. 2,3,5* and 6.[860] In so far as can be ascertained Baur is unique in making this assertion. The identification of the homily delivered on Easter of that year is also unusual. As indicated by the reference supplied in the relevant footnote,[861] Baur has in mind *De resurrectione mortuorum* (CPG 4340), a homily not usually associated with Easter.[862] The relevant Easter homily is more commonly identified as *De resurrectione* (CPG 4341), also known as *Contra ebriosos*, on the basis of comment found in *Hom. 33 in Gen.* (CPG 4409).[863] The compression of the two sequences of homilies (CPG 4328, 4329, 4347, 4349; and 4341, 4371, 4372, 4409, 4417.1-4) into the one year is also to be remarked upon. Bonsdorff and Rauschen had both recently promoted their distinctiveness,[864] while Stilting, who managed to squeeze the first of these into the year 387, still maintained the separateness of the second and lo-

---

[854] *In diem natalem* is to be found at PG 49,351ff, a minor typographical error.

[855] Baur, *Chrysostom and His Time*, I 199 n. 56. For Usener's opinion see p. 152 above.

[856] Baur, *Chrysostom and His Time*, I 259. This is restated at I 284-285.

[857] Baur, *Chrysostom and His Time*, I 285 n. 5. See Montfaucon (p. 84 above).

[858] Baur, *Chrysostom and His Time*, I 285. From the reference supplied in I 285 n. 13, it is clear that the inclusion of *hom.1* is intended.

[859] See Montfaucon, Sequence D (p. 108 above).

[860] See Lietzmann (p. 165 above), who follows Rauschen (p. 140 above) in this matter.

[861] Baur, *Chrysostom and His Time*, I 285 n. 16.

[862] Rauschen (see p. 145 above), as also Montfaucon (p. 79 above) and Stilting (p. 114 above), assigns the homily to before Lent 387.

[863] And in *In princ. Act. hom. 1*. See Stilting, *Acta SS. Sept.*, IV 484.

[864] See Rauschen (pp. 140-142 above) and Bonsdorff (pp. 172-174 above).

cated it in the year which followed.[865] The same casual approach to sequences is displayed in the case of the homilies *Contra Anomoeos*, assigned to the first year of preaching at Antioch. Baur refers in this instance to nine sermons *De incompr. dei natura*,[866] a label which can only
be supposed to encompass the five homilies of that name (CPG 4318)
and four from the group CPG 4319-4323. Neither the number nor the title employed is common.[867]

As we have already noted, when it comes to assigning the exegetical
series to one location or another, Baur prefers to locate the series on
Philippians (CPG 4432) at Antioch, against the majority view. In an earlier chapter of the same volume, however, he confides that, in his opinion, the ninth homily on Philippians originated in Constantinople.[868] The
two statements are never reconciled.[869] A similar discrepancy occurs with
respect to the homily *Contra ludos et theatra* (CPG 4441.7). Early in Volume Two Baur declares that it was delivered on July 3, 399.[870] In this respect he follows the date proposed by Pargoire.[871] Later, however, he has
occasion to refer to a synaxis held three days earlier at a church dedicated to Sts Peter and Paul, the evidence for which is contained within
the homily in question. There the event is dated to April 7, 399,[872] a chronology which assumes that *Contra ludos et theatra* was itself preached on
April 10. In this he follows Lietzmann and Montfaucon, who assigned the
homily to Easter Sunday.[873] Once again the two conflicting assertions are
never reconciled.

It is also worthy of note that regarding the homily *De Eleazaro et septem pueris* (CPG 4441.13), one of the so-called eleven *Novæ homiliae*,
Baur is alone in stating that it may have been given long before in

---

[865] See pp. 113 and 120 above.

[866] Baur, *Chrysostom and His Time*, I 259 n. 3.

[867] For an account of the relation between the titles and numbering traditionally
applied to these homilies and the manuscript tradition see A.-M. Malingrey, "La tradition
manuscrite des homélies de Jean Chrysostome *De incomprehensibili*", StP 10 (1970) 22-28;
and more recently, ead., "Prolégomènes à une édition des homélies de Jean Chrysostome,
Contra Anomoeos", StP 22 (1989) 154-158.

[868] Baur, *Chrysostom and His Time*, I 189 n. 29. This is presumably on the basis of the
statement by the homilist that he is a "father", commonly understood to indicate that he
holds the rank of bishop. In this Baur follows Bonsdorff (see p. 189 above), Lietzmann (p.
169 above) and Montfaucon (p. 99 above), against Stilting (p. 123 above).

[869] At *Chrysostom and His Time*, I 300, Baur shows no awareness of this earlier
statement nor, in attributing the series to Antioch, is the evidence of *hom.* 9 taken into
consideration.

[870] Baur, *Chrysostom and His Time*, II 86-87.

[871] See p. 160 above.

[872] Baur, *Chrysostom and His Time*, II 238 n. 4.

[873] See pp. 166 and 95 above.

Antioch.[874] He is more representative than Bonsdorff, however, in locating the journey to Ephesus in the first half of 401.[875] Finally, with regard to *In illud: Filius ex se nihil facit* (CPG 4441.12), although his personal opinion concerning the provenance of the homily remains unclear, Baur takes to task Montfaucon "and most of those after him" for claiming that the "teacher", to whom the homilist refers when he indicates that another individual has preached immediately before him, is the bishop Flavian. On this basis the homily was assigned to Antioch.[876] Baur argues that this "teacher" must have been not a bishop but a simple priest, appealing to the rule that the bishop or person highest in rank always preached last, and arguing further that Chrysostom usually refers to Flavian as "Father and Teacher", while a simple priest could only be designated "teacher".[877]

e. *Dates of local festivals*

Baur makes no attempt to determine the status of the fixed elements in the liturgical calendar which was followed at Constantinople during the time of Chrysostom's episcopate.[878] He does, however, enter into discussion of the feasts of the local saints and martyrs at Antioch in some detail.[879] Only those festivals with which homilies are associated are discussed here.

For Baur the liturgical year at Antioch began on Jan. 7 with the feast of the martyr Lucian,[880] followed by the festival of the two soldiers Juventinus and Maximus early in the same month.[881] The feast of St

---

[874] Baur, *Chrysostom and His Time*, II 55 n. 20. The remark is made casually. Baur supplies no evidence in support of this unusual assertion.

[875] Baur, *Chrysostom and His Time*, II 145 n. 13. Cf. Tillemont (see p. 71 above) and Montfaucon (p. 88 above). Bonsdorff, *Zur Predigttätigkeit*, 106, dated the visit from winter of 401 to just after Easter 402.

[876] In fact only Montfaucon (see p. 95 above) and Stilting (p. 110 above) appear to have followed this path. Batiffol (p. 158 above), Pargoire (p. 160 above) and Bonsdorff (p. 188 above) all assign the homily to Constantinople.

[877] Baur, *Chrysostom and His Time*, I 394.

[878] See Baur, *Chrysostom and His Time*, II 72-81.

[879] Baur, *Chrysostom and His Time*, I 199-200. The confidence Baur displays here is in marked contrast to the hesitancy expressed by those before him.

[880] Baur, *Chrysostom and His Time*, I 200 n. 62. See *In s. Lucianum* (CPG 4346).

[881] Baur, *Chrysostom and His Time*, I 200 n. 63. See *In Iuventinum et Maximum* (CPG 4349). This chronology is unusual. The homily itself is consistently dated (see pp. 52, 80, 113 above) to after that of St Babylas (Jan. 24), while Rauschen (p. 142 above) and Bonsdorff (p. 172 above) both consider the festival to have occurred on Feb. 4.

Babylas occurred next on Jan. 24.[882] The next festival which is known is that of St Drosis, which fell on March 22.[883] The martyrs Berenice, Prosdoce and Domnina were honoured on April 20.[884] The feast of St Barlaam is considered to have occurred on May 31,[885] while that of the Maccabees is located on Aug. 1.[886] Oct. 8 was devoted to the martyr Pelagia,[887] while on Oct. 17 fell the festival in celebration of Ignatius, the former bishop of Antioch.[888] The feast of St Romanus occurred on Nov. 18.[889] In December fell the festival of St Philogonius (Dec. 20),[890] while that of St Julian was celebrated on the day after Christmas (Dec. 26).[891] Finally, Baur states that a festival dedicated to Saints Peter and Paul probably existed at Antioch at the time, occurring on Dec. 28.[892]

f. *Local preaching places*

In Chapter Five of Volume One, Baur sets out the topography of the city of Antioch.[893] In the course of this description he assembles a picture of the places at which regular and special synaxes were held. These preaching places, and the homilies which Baur believes to have been delivered there, are outlined in the following table. A similar discussion takes place early in Volume Two in relation to the topography of Con-

---

[882] Baur, *Chrysostom and His Time*, I 200 n. 64. See *De s. hieromartyre Babyla* (CPG 4347).

[883] Baur, *Chrysostom and His Time*, I 200. See *De s. Droside* (CPG 4362). Baur is the only scholar to assign this to a specific date. He supplies no supporting documentation.

[884] Baur, *Chrysostom and His Time*, I 200 n. 65. See *De ss. Bernice et Prosdoce* (CPG 4355) and *In quatriduanum Lazarum* (CPG 4356). Here Baur follows the date recently established by Wilmart, "Le souvenir d'Eusèbe d'Émèse. Un discours en l'honneur des saintes d'Antioche Bernice, Prosdoce et Domnine", AB 38 (1920) 254-255.

[885] Baur, *Chrysostom and His Time*, I 200 n. 66. See *In s. Barlaam martyrem* (CPG 4361). Baur, who appears to follow the opinion of Delehaye in this instance, is unique in locating it on this date. Rauschen (see p. 142 above) considers that it fell on Aug. 14. Regarding the problems associated with dating this festival see H. Delehaye, "S. Barlaam martyr à Antioche", AB 22 (1904) 136-137.

[886] Baur, *Chrysostom and His Time*, I 200 n. 67. See *De Macabeis hom. 1-2* (CPG 4354).

[887] Baur, *Chrysostom and His Time*, I 200 n. 69. See *De s. Pelagia* (CPG 4350).

[888] Baur, *Chrysostom and His Time*, I 200 n. 68. See *In s. Ignatium* (CPG 4351).

[889] Baur, *Chrysostom and His Time*, I 200 n. 70. See *In s. Romanum* (CPG 4353).

[890] Baur, *Chrysostom and His Time*, I 200 n. 72. See *De beato Philogonio* (CPG 4319).

[891] Baur, *Chrysostom and His Time*, I 200 n. 71. See *In s. Iulianum* (CPG 4360).

[892] Baur, *Chrysostom and His Time*, I 199. Baur implies, I 199 n. 59, that the homilies *De laudibus s. Pauli* (CPG 4344) may belong to this date, although this is nowhere clearly stated. Whether they are to be located at Antioch is also unclear.

[893] Baur, *Chrysostom and His Time*, I 29-44.

stantinople.[894] Further comment regarding the location of a particular homily occurs here and there throughout the course of that volume. All of these instances are likewise recorded.

Table 10.c. Topographic detail — Baur

City (preaching place)	Homily	Cited (vol.-page)
Antioch		
Great Church (magna ecclesia)	*De mutatione nominum hom. 2* (CPG 4372)	I 31 n. 5
	Hom. 6 in Genesim (CPG 4409)	"
	In Eph. hom. 10 (CPG 4431)	"
	In illud: Si esurierit inimicus (CPG 4375)	"
Old Church (palaia ecclesia)	*In princ. Act. hom. 2* (CPG 4371)	I 30
Other than Great or Old Church (unspecified)	*De incompr. dei natura hom. 1-5* (CPG 4318)	I 31 n. 6a
Church of St Babylas		
Church/Martyrium of the Maccabees	*De Macabeis hom. 1-2* (CPG 4354)	I 32-33
Common martyrium (Romanesia)	*In ascensionem domini* (CPG 4342)	I 34
Martyrium of St Ignatius	*In s. Ignatium* (CPG 4351)	I 33 n. 16
Martyrium of St Drosis	*De s. Droside* (CPG 4362)	I 33 n. 15
Memorial chapel to St Eustathius	*In s. Eustathium* (CPG 4352)	I 33
Constantinople		
Great Church (magna ecclesia)	*In Eutropium* (CPG 4392)	II 112-117 n. 24
Church of the Apostles (ecclesia apostolorum)	*Sermo post reditum 1* (CPG 4398)	II 267 n. 26
	Adversus catharos (CPG 4441.6)	II 53 n. 20
	In illud: Messis quidem multa (CPG 4441.11)	"
Church of Holy Peace (St Eirene = the old church)	*De studio praesentium* (CPG 4441.5)	II 51 n. 8
Church of the Resurrection (St Anastasia)	*Adversus eos qui non adfuerant* (CPG 4441.4)	II 53 n. 21
	Dicta in templo s. Anastasiae (CPG 4441.8)	"
Church of the Apostle (Church of St Paul = Church of the Goths)	*Habita postquam presb. Gothus* (CPG 4441.9)	II 53 n. 24, 77

---

[894] Baur, *Chrysostom and His Time*, II 47-55.

Martyrium of St Thomas (at Drypia)	*Dicta postquam reliquiae martyrum* (CPG 4441.1) *Hom. dicta praesente imperatore* (CPG 4441.2)	II 34f n. 19, 76 n. 16 "
Martyrium (in Palaia Petra)	*Quod frequenter conveniendum sit* (CPG 4441.3)	II 53 n. 25

4. 1930-2000

In spite of their lack of agreement on every point, for three or four decades after the close of the third phase Bonsdorff and Baur were considered to have provided a satisfactory solution.[895] During this period the vigorous dialogue regarding the location and sequence of the homilies dies down and interest in the relationship of these questions to the corpus as a whole ceases. There appears only the occasional response to the proposed arrangement of the exegetical series, with the exception of the general overview provided by Johannes Quasten. This desultory activity is to be balanced against the wave of new editions which at this same time slowly begin to make their appearance. The renewed investigation of the manuscripts, coupled with certain other factors, has begun in recent years to stimulate fresh interest in these questions.

1. MISCELLANEOUS WRITINGS (1930-1970)

Between 1930 and 1970 only a small number of articles appear. Three of these are concerned with the provenance and date of an exegetical series. A fourth occurs, in which the author goes beyond a broad definition of provenance by locating certain homilies at specific churches within the city of Antioch. A fifth and sixth, prompted by the discovery of certain manuscripts, are aligned with the production of new editions. Discussion of material contained in these last two articles is therefore considered separately in section 4.5 below.

---

[895] So Meyer, *Jean Chrysostome*, XXIII-XXXV, produces a synthesis of Schwartz (see p. 146 above), some elements of Rauschen (p. 135 above) and much of Bonsdorff (p. 171 above). Since Meyer relies almost entirely on the work of others, introducing little that is new, his work is not discussed here.

a. *Nägele*

In an article which appeared in 1935, Anton Nägele presents the only serious criticism of Bonsdorff's approach to the New Testament series prior to our own.[896] This important contribution to the question of methodology occurs as a tangent to the main focus of the article, which is the question of when the series on the first and second Letters to Timothy (CPG 4436-4437) were composed. Here, against the majority of opinion,[897] Nägele argues that not only do the twenty-eight homilies belong to Constantinople, but their date can in fact be fixed to the year 402.

Nägele begins by dismissing the two pieces of evidence adduced by Montfaucon in favour of the series' Antiochene provenance. In answer to Montfaucon's adduction of the mountain-based lifestyle of monks in *In I Tim. hom. 14*, he points out that the passage contains no specific detail regarding the location and that, in any case, such comment also occurs in homilies delivered with certainty at Constantinople, for instance, in those on Hebrews (CPG 4440). He finds equally weak Montfaucon's argument *ex silentio* that the homilist is not of episcopal status.[898] One could equally argue that the absence of personal reference during discussion of the passages in Timothy regarding the role of deacon and presbyter indicates that John is bishop and is therefore preaching from Constantinople. Certainly, Nägele concludes, the homilies contain none of the overt references to Flavian that might be expected if Chrysostom were still presbyter.[899]

On the other hand, more than one piece of evidence points to Constantinople. With regard to the series on I Timothy, the main proof can be found in a passage in *hom. 15*, where Chrysostom refers to the time of Christ as having occurred "four hundred years or more earlier". Taken at face value and calculating from the point of Christ's birth, this locates the series at around 400 AD, at which time the homilist was bishop of Constantinople.[900] The rest of the evidence is less explicit. Comment on the role of presbyter or bishop throughout these homilies can be interpreted in several ways and is therefore unable to sustain proof of date or location. Thus in the case of *hom. 5*, it might be thought that John refers

---

[896] Nägele, "Homilien zu d. Timotheusbriefen", in particular 132-139.

[897] Montfaucon (see p. 100 above), Stilting (p. 123 above), Lietzmann (p. 169 above), Bonsdorff (pp. 183, 185 above) and Baur (p. 208 above) assigned both series to Antioch. Savile (p. 40 above) and Tillemont (p. 164 above) preferred Constantinople, purely on stylistic grounds.

[898] See further Nägele, "Homilien zu d. Timotheusbriefen", 132-134.

[899] Nägele, "Homilien zu d. Timotheusbriefen", 126-127. Regarding monastic communities see also p. 134.

[900] Nägele, "Homilien zu d. Timotheusbriefen", 127-128.

to his role as presbyter, while a passage in *hom. 13* might be thought to indicate that the homilist is bishop. The definition of the two roles which occurs in *hom. 11*, however, places such comments in perspective. Chrysostom sees only a fine line dividing the two offices, such that every bishop is priest, even though not every priest is bishop.[901] With regard to *In II Tim. hom. 1*, Nägele finds John's comment that he has preached "a thousand times" on the same topic, more likely at Constantinople than at Antioch. He further finds it difficult to believe that the remarks regarding the unworthiness of those in episcopal office in *In II Tim. hom. 4* could have come from the mouth of a presbyter. He likewise finds that the criticism of the dress and behaviour of widows and virgins in *In I Tim. hom. 8* speaks rather for Constantinople.[902]

After extensively criticising Bonsdorff's arguments for both the location and chronology of the series,[903] Nägele turns to his own consideration of the second of these issues. He finds the solution in *In II Tim. hom. 10*. Here the homilist states that the persons of Erastus and Tychicus have become known to the audience through "the book on Acts" (ἔγνωμεν ἐν τῷ τῶν Πράξεων βιβλίῳ).[904] Nägele argues that, had only the biblical Acts been meant, the homilist would have employed the present or perfect tense, not the aorist. As a pure Atticist, the particular choice of tense means that he must here refer to a recent reading and exegesis of Acts, namely the preaching of the fifty-five homilies on the Acts of the apostles (CPG 4426).[905] The latter, on internal evidence, can be dated to the year 401, a circumstance which establishes a *terminus post quem* for the two series on Timothy.[906] Since in *In Acta apost. hom. 44* Chrysostom states that he preaches every three or seven days, it is probable that the homilies on Timothy were delivered as early as the following year, 402.[907]

b. *Eltester*

In the course of an article on the churches at Antioch in the fourth century, published in 1937, Walther Eltester linked a small number of homilies to specific preaching places in and around the city. To at least

---

[901] Nägele, "Homilien zu d. Timotheusbriefen", 128-129.

[902] Nägele, "Homilien zu d. Timotheusbriefen", 130-131.

[903] Nägele, "Homilien zu d. Timotheusbriefen", 132-139.

[904] PG 62,658 17-20.

[905] Nägele, "Homilien zu d. Timotheusbriefen", 139-141.

[906] For his acceptance of the arguments for locating the series on II Timothy immediately after that on I Timothy see Nägele, "Homilien zu d. Timotheusbriefen", 138.

[907] Nägele, "Homilien zu d. Timotheusbriefen", 141-142.

two homilies he also assigned dates for which it is difficult to find an antecedent. For both reasons, it is important to document his contribution
to the field, even though this has been minimal.

From the title to *Adv. Iudaeos or. 4* (CPG 4327), Eltester infers that the
second sequence of homilies against the Jews was delivered in the Great
Church at Antioch.[908] On the basis of the title also, he argues that *In illud:
Filius ex se nihil facit* (CPG 4441.12) was likewise delivered at that site.
This requires him to propose that Flavian had "against the rule" permitted a presbyter to preach after him.[909] However, the remainder of the
homilies *Contra Anomoeos*,[910] among which he locates the homily following the seventh (CPG 4320),[911] were preached in the Old Church, a datum
which can be derived from the title to the homily *In illud: In faciem ei restiti* (CPG 4391).[912] Other series, such as *In princ. Act. hom. 1-4* (CPG
4371) and the homilies *De statuis* (CPG 4330), were also delivered at the
Old Church.[913] Further, in the course of the same general discussion it is
confidently stated that *In illud: Filius ex se nihil facit* was preached on
Jan. 16, 387.[914] If, as appears to be the case, Eltester is following Stilting
here,[915] it is difficult to determine how he arrives at this precise date.[916]

In addition, several other preaching places receive mention. Eltester
distinguishes two sets of sites, the first associated with the cemetery situated beyond the gate leading from the west of the city to Daphne,[917] the
second with the northern or Romanesian gate.[918] At the site of the cemetery he locates a church within which are buried Ignatius and others,
while within the cemetery itself are located the remains of Domnina and

---

[908] Eltester, "Die Kirchen Antiochias", 277-278. It is unclear whether Eltester here
refers to the sequence established by Montfaucon (see p. 74 above) and subsequently
promoted by Schwartz (p. 148 above), or that established by Rauschen (p. 137 above). The
former (i.e., *or. 4-8*), however, is the most likely.

[909] Eltester, "Die Kirchen Antiochias", 277 n. 99. For a statement of this rule see p. 286
below.

[910] Presumably CPG 4318-4323.

[911] Although it is nowhere stated, Eltester is at this point following the schema
proposed by Stilting (see p. 131 above).

[912] Eltester, "Die Kirchen Antiochias", 277 n. 99.

[913] Eltester, "Die Kirchen Antiochias", 278. Eltester infers this from the beginning of
In princ. Act. hom. 2 and from the titles to *De statuis hom. 1* and *2*.

[914] Eltester, "Die Kirchen Antiochias", 277.

[915] See n. 911 above.

[916] Stilting (see p. 110 above) locates the homily in February. Schwartz (p. 147 above),
although he does not consider CPG 4441.12 to be part of the series *Contra Anomoeos*, does
situate *De consubstantiali* (CPG 4320) on Jan. 16 of this year and it may be that Eltester
has confused the two points.

[917] Eltester, "Die Kirchen Antiochias", 278-279.

[918] Eltester, "Die Kirchen Antiochias", 281.

her daughters, and Drosis and Juventinus and Maximus. Eltester explicitly associates the homilies *In s. Iulianum* (CPG 4360), *In martyres* (CPG 4359), and *De coemeterio et de cruce* (CPG 4337) with that site. He also discusses the existence of a chapel dedicated to Pelagia. He finds in the homily delivered in honour of her feast day (CPG 4350) a vague suggestion that it was located nearby.[919] At the second location, the Romanesian gate, there was situated a martyrium constructed in the time of Flavian, at which the homily *In ascensionem* (CPG 4342) was delivered, as its title indicates. Eltester, believing that this is the first homily to have been delivered at the martyrium upon its completion, informs us that it was preached on May 14, 386.[920] Once again, there is no means of determining the grounds upon which he makes such a confident assertion.[921]

Finally, there is also mention of a recently constructed Church or martyrium of St Babylas, with which the homily delivered on the festival of this martyr (CPG 4347) is associated.[922]

c. *Costanza*

In 1952 an article by H. Costanza appeared in which it is argued that the traditional view that the twenty-four homilies on Ephesians (CPG 4431) were preached at Antioch is mistaken and that the series can on the contrary be assigned to Constantinople to the period between Chrysostom's first and second exile (Advent 403-Pasch 404).[923] *Hom. 6, 10* and *11* supply the necessary evidence.[924]

In the case of *In Eph. hom. 6*, Costanza points to a passage near the close of the homily in which it is stated that the leaders of the church (ἄρχοντες) are sick, that the faithful have distanced themselves in the mountains,[925] and that wicked men have taken the church by surprise.[926]

---

[919] Eltester, "Die Kirchen Antiochias", 285.

[920] Eltester, "Die Kirchen Antiochias", 281.

[921] Tillemont (see p. 55 above), Montfaucon (p. 79 above) and Stilting (n. 417 above) were hesitant in assigning the homily to a year (392 or 388).

[922] Eltester, "Die Kirchen Antiochias", 282.

[923] Costanza, "Waar predikte Chrysostomus?", 145, further argues against Baur that the series represents a group of preached homilies, not a written commentary.

[924] The issue of these homilies had been addressed at some length by Bonsdorff (see p. 187 above), who was able to reconcile the data with an Antiochene provenance. Costanza does not take his work into consideration. The doubt regarding these homilies had first been raised by Rauschen (p. 143 above).

[925] Bonsdorff (see p. 187 above) saw in this a reference to the mountain-top monasticism considered typical of Antioch.

[926] PG 62,47 57-48 4.

Taking the second statement to refer to laity fleeing the city for refuge in
the mountains,[927] Costanza puts forward an argument against identifying
Antioch as the location.[928] On the other hand, the corrupted state of the
church leaders is entirely appropriate to the effects of Theophilus of Alexandria's machinations, while the further statement that the leaders
have been bought (ὠνηταὶ γεγόνασι αἱ ἀρχαί) brings to mind the situation
at Ephesus and the charges there of simony. The second situation evokes
for Costanza the hostility between Theophilus, the empress Eudoxia and
their supporters and the ascetics and others faithful to Chrysostom. The
third detail evokes the circumstances surrounding Chrysostom's first exile, when the church was overtaken by the opposition and surrounded by
soldiers.[929]

Concerning *In Eph. hom. 10* Costanza elicits a passage in which the
homilist compares the current situation to a fierce fire which has taken
hold of the church while all are asleep.[930] This, it is argued, can scarcely
refer to the schism at Antioch, as had been thought. By the time of
Chrysostom's presbyterate it was scarcely so immediate an issue. The
situation, however, is entirely appropriate to the period at Constantinople following John's first banishment, when the second synod had already been called and the second decree perhaps already handed
down.[931]

It is the eleventh homily, however, which sets the seal to her argument. Costanza here addresses seven points: that the division in the
church relates to power not doctrine (PG 62,85 28-29); that Chrysostom
states that he is prepared to give up his ἀρχή (PG 62,88 31-32); that he
has been personally wronged (PG 62,87 42-43); that Rauschen's concern
over PG 62,87 2-4 is unnecessary; that ἕτερος ἄρχων ἑτέρᾳ Ἐκκλησίᾳ ἐπιπηδᾷ ("one leader is attacking another church": PG 62,86 33) cannot refer to
either Paulinus or Evagrius at Antioch, but only to Theophilus and the
situation at Constantinople; that τοὺς παρανόμους ἐπὶ τὸν θρόνον ἀναβεβη-
κότας ("those who have illicitly ascended the throne": PG 62,88 34-35) refers to the judicial, not the episcopal throne, and therefore the illegal
synod; and finally, that the situation is due in large part to the enmity of
women (PG 62,87 27-37).[932] It remains only to invoke Palladius' state-

---

[927] Read in context it is difficult to interpret the passage in this way. Costanza seems
here to have been influenced by the habit of the Antiochenes to flee the city at times of
upheaval as at the time of the riots in 387. See, e.g., *De statuis hom. 21*, PG 49,218 1-6.

[928] Costanza, "Waar predikte Chrysostomus?", 149.

[929] Costanza, "Waar predikte Chrysostomus?", 149-150.

[930] PG 62,77 62-78 2.

[931] Costanza, "Waar predikte Chrysostomus?", 150-151.

[932] Costanza, "Waar predikte Chrysostomus?", 151-153.

ment that Chrysostom continued to preach for nine or ten months after his return from the initial exile to complete the picture.[933]

Costanza's argument does not, however, end there. Because of the influence of *hom. 9* and *21* in persuading scholars of the series' Antiochene provenance,[934] she considers it necessary to address that evidence. Regarding the mention of St Babylas (*hom. 9*), Costanza argues that this does not point exclusively to Antioch. As Helen, the mother of Constantine, had a shrine dedicated to the saint built at Constantinople, it can be understood that at the time of Chrysostom he was honoured there.[935] In the case of *hom. 21*, Costanza agrees that the Julian mentioned is the famed ascetic Julianus Sabas, but argues that the location cannot be Antioch. While his visit there in 362 is known to have occasioned considerable excitement, the offhand way in which it is discussed here stands out in contrast.[936]

d. *Opelt*

In a brief article which appeared in 1970, Ilona Opelt claims, contrary to the consensus, that *In Heb. hom. 14* and therefore the entire series on Hebrews (CPG 4440) was delivered at Antioch.[937] She bases her argument on the mention of the Olympic Games in *hom. 14*, showing that because of the edict of 393 in which the general Olympic Games in Greece were banned, Chrysostom cannot have used such an exemplum at Constantinople, since he only assumed the bishopric there some years after that date. The Olympics to which the homilist refers, she argues, must therefore be the local Syrian version held at Antioch. From this it follows that all of the homilies on Hebrews were delivered at that location. She further dates the series to after the earthquake of 396 and before 398 (the year in which John began preaching at Constantinople), on the basis of a reference to earthquakes in *hom. 32*.[938]

---

[933] Costanza, "Waar predikte Chrysostomus?", 153-154.

[934] See Tillemont (p. 62 above), Rauschen (p. 143 above), Lietzmann (p. 168 above) and Bonsdorff (p. 187 above).

[935] Costanza, "Waar predikte Chrysostomus?", 154.

[936] Costanza, "Waar predikte Chrysostomus?", 154.

[937] Opelt, "Das Ende von Olympia", 64-68.

[938] Opelt, "Das Ende von Olympia", 68-69.

2. QUASTEN

The brief history of the life and work of Chrysostom presented in the
third volume of *Patrology* (1960), stands on its own in the post-1930 period. With the aim of providing a convenient up-to-date survey of the
opinion and literature concerning Chrysostom, it neither introduces new
evidence, nor does it re-open debate on any of the questions under discussion. Since, as was the case with Lietzmann before him, Johannes
Quasten's summary has proved influential in that the views espoused are
thought to represent the final word, it is important to assess the source of
the arguments and opinions selected, in order to find out whether the information presented genuinely represents the common view.

Rather than pursue an integrated chronological-biographical approach, Quasten discusses the homilies and writings as a separate unit.
Here he divides the homilies into six discrete categories — exegetical;
dogmatic and polemical homilies; moral discourses; sermons for liturgical feasts; panegyrics; and occasional discourses.

a. *The exegetical homilies*

Quasten acknowledges, as did Lietzmann before him, that the greatest
difficulty associated with the exegetical series lies in determining their
chronology. Internal evidence is sparse and some series, he admits, may
only have been published in written form without ever having been delivered.[939]

Of the series on portions of the Old Testament, the two clusters of
homilies on Genesis appear to be the oldest. The first, comprising the
nine *Sermones in Genesim* (CPG 4410), Quasten asserts, was delivered at
Antioch during Lent 386.[940] This is somewhat inaccurate as it had long
been established that only the first eight of these sermons constitute a
series, and that the homily identified by Montfaucon as *Sermo 9 in Gen.*
belongs rather with the four homilies titled *De mutatione nominum* (CPG
4372).[941] Concerning the second, much longer series on Genesis (CPG
4409), Quasten follows Baur in assigning it to 388.[942] In the case of the

---

[939] Quasten, *Patrology*, III 434.

[940] Quasten, *Patrology*, III 434.

[941] This had been recognised by Montfaucon (see p. 90 above) and had in more recent
times been documented by Lietzmann (pp. 164f above) and Bonsdorff (p. 174 above), both
of whom Quasten consulted.

[942] Quasten, *Patrology*, III 434. See Baur (p. 207 above). Although Bonsdorff had
assigned the homilies to 389 and Lietzmann had abstained, this is a reasonable assertion.

discourses on the Psalms (CPG 4413), Quasten makes no attempt to assign the bulk of these to a location, pointing out that it is doubtful whether they were in fact ever delivered as homilies. He does mention in passing, however, that *Exp. in ps. 41* (CPG 4413.2) was preached in 387.[943] Of the six sermons *In illud: Vidi dominum* (CPG 4417) he states simply that some were delivered at Antioch, others at Constantinople, without attempting to distinguish which.[944] The five sermons *De Anna* (CPG 4411) and the three *De Davide et Saule* (CPG 4412) were both preached in 387.[945] To this list Quasten adds the two homilies *De prophetiarum obscuritate* (CPG 4420), composed, he claims, at Antioch in 386.[946]

Of the homilies concerned with the New Testament, Quasten states that the series on Matthew (CPG 4424) was delivered at Antioch, adducing in evidence the usual passage in *In Matt. hom. 7*. He follows Baur and Bonsdorff in assigning the ninety homilies to the year 390.[947] Quasten again relies on their work when he asserts that the series on John (CPG 4425) was delivered later than that on Matthew, probably around 391.[948] The fifty-five homilies on Acts (CPG 4426) are dated by Chrysostom himself to the third year of his episcopate, i.e., 400.[949] These, warns Quasten, are not to be confused with the four sermons *In principium Actorum* (CPG 4371) and the four *De mutatione nominum* (CPG 4372), all preached at Antioch in the paschal season of 388.[950]

As for the series on the Pauline epistles, allusions found in the thirty-two homilies on Romans (CPG 4427) point to their origin at Antioch. In *In Rom. hom. 8* Chrysostom aligns himself with the audience when he states that they are under one bishop. This proves, claims Quasten, that

---

Aside from Baur, both Rauschen (p. 141 above) and Schwartz, *Ostertafeln*, 121 n. 2, had concluded that the series probably belonged to 388.

[943] Quasten, *Patrology*, III 435.

[944] Quasten, *Patrology*, III 435-436.

[945] Quasten, *Patrology*, III 436.

[946] Quasten, *Patrology*, III 436. The source of this assertion is difficult to determine, but appears to be Stilting (see p. 115 above) by way of Bardenhewer, *Geschichte*, III 336.

[947] Quasten, *Patrology*, III 437. For the opinion of Baur and Bonsdorff see pp. 207 and 178 above.

[948] Quasten, *Patrology*, III 439.

[949] Quasten, *Patrology*, III 440. Quasten, in discussing the unfinished state of these homilies, alludes to the argument that the episcopal office brought with it a greatly reduced degree of leisure. For further discussion of this offshoot of Photius' stylistic argument see pp. 287f below.

[950] Quasten, *Patrology*, III 441. This is consistent with his dating of the longer series on Genesis (CPG 4409) to 388, the eight homilies in question and this series commonly being thought to be inseparable.

he was not yet bishop but deacon or priest at the time. *Hom. 33* provides even clearer evidence when the homilist refers to the location of his audience as the place where St Paul taught and was bound, as this is true of Antioch but not of Constantinople.[951] Quasten completes his discussion of this issue by once again relying on Baur and Bonsdorff in his assertion that the homilies on Romans were probably delivered shortly after Chrysostom had completed the series on John.[952] The series on the two Letters to the Corinthians (CPG 4428-4429) were both delivered at Antioch, the first because in *In I Cor. hom. 21* the homilist explicitly states this, the second because in *In II Cor hom. 26* Chrysostom refers to Constantinople as "there". Quasten makes no attempt to assign them a date, stating simply that in *I Cor. hom. 7* the homilist refers to his series of homilies on Matthew, while in *I Cor. hom. 27* he refers to his series on John.[953] The twenty-four homilies on Ephesians (CPG 4431) indicate their Antiochene origin through the familiar mention of St Babylas in *In Eph. hom. 9* and of St Julian in *hom. 21*. Both are favourite saints of the city and Theodoret records that the latter visited Antioch on one occasion. Further, *hom. 6* and *13* refer to monastic establishments in the neighbouring mountains, while *hom. 11* alludes to a schism which must be that of Meletius. Quasten makes no mention of date.[954]

In the case of the series on Philippians (CPG 4432), Quasten refers to the dissension caused by Baur in arguing that the homilies were preached at Antioch. Quasten himself prefers Constantinople as the location of this series, offering the common proof that John refers several times to his responsibilities as bishop, most particularly in *In Phil. hom. 9*. Quasten dismisses Baur's argument that the allusion to the reigning monarch in *hom. 15* fits Theodosius, arguing that it is more appropriate to the "weak-minded" Arcadius. The question of date receives no mention.[955] The twelve homilies on Colossians (CPG 4433) belong also to Constantinople, since at the end of *In Col. hom. 3* the homilist clearly refers to his episcopal status. As for date, they must have been delivered in 399 because Chrysostom alludes to the fall of Eutropius, which took place in summer of that year.[956] The two series on the Letters to the Thessalonians (CPG 4434-4435) are likewise to be assigned to Constantinople

---

[951] Although *In Rom. hom. 33* is cited, Quasten clearly intends *hom. 30*.

[952] Quasten, *Patrology*, III 442.

[953] Quasten, *Patrology*, III 445.

[954] Quasten, *Patrology*, III 447.

[955] Quasten, *Patrology*, III 447-448.

[956] Quasten, *Patrology*, III 448. See, however, p. 228 below, where Quasten locates the event in mid January, 399. Although Quasten supplies no reference here, he is clearly thinking of *In Col. hom. 7*.

because in *In I Thess. hom. 8* and *In II Thess. hom. 4* he refers to the duties associated with his high office.[957]

The series on the two Letters to Timothy (CPG 4436-4437) seem, on
the other hand, to belong to Antioch. Chrysostom frequently speaks of
the office of bishop without any hint that he is himself of that status. He
also praises the devotion of the large number of solitaries living in the
neighbourhood, a feature of other homilies preached at Antioch. Further,
in *In II Tim. hom. 8* he refers to the burning of the temple of Apollo at
Daphne, an event described in detail in the homily *De s. Babyla* (CPG
4347).[958] The six homilies on Titus (CPG 4438) must be located at
Antioch also, because Daphne and the Cave of Matrona mentioned in *In
Titum hom. 3* occur in the vicinity of that city. Quasten adds as an aside
that the lengthy discussion of the burden of a bishop (no reference supplied) applies to a person other than the homilist.[959] Concerning the three
homilies on Philemon (CPG 4439), Quasten states simply that they most
probably belong to the same time as those on Timothy and Titus.[960]
Finally, the thirty-four homilies on Hebrews (CPG 4440) are to be assigned to Chrysostom's last year at Constantinople (403/404) on the basis
of the title, which states that they were published after his death from
stenographic notes by Constantine, a priest of Antioch.[961]

b. *Dogmatic and polemical homilies*

The first group of homilies which Quasten discusses under this category are the twelve *Contra Anomoeos* (CPG 4318-4325). Here he makes
several claims which could scarcely be considered representative. The
twelve homilies, he states, divide into two series of which the first comprises the five homilies *De incomprehensibili dei natura* (CPG 4318).
These were delivered at Antioch around 386 to 387.[962] This first assertion
more or less represents the consensus.[963] It is the second which is somewhat strange. The second series of homilies, presumably CPG 4319-4325,

---

[957] Quasten, *Patrology*, III 449.

[958] Quasten, *Patrology*, III 449-450. This comment appears to be made *de novo*,
although it may prove to derive from a source not addressed here.

[959] Quasten, *Patrology*, III 450.

[960] Quasten, *Patrology*, III 450. In this, Quasten defers to the opinion of Lietzmann (see
p. 169 above). Bonsdorff (p. 197 above), whose view was subsequently embraced by Baur
(p. 209 above), had argued strongly for their location at Constantinople.

[961] Quasten, *Patrology*, III 450.

[962] Quasten, *Patrology*, III 451.

[963] See, for instance, Lietzmann (p. 167 above) and Baur (p. 205 above).

was, he declares, delivered at Constantinople in 397.[964] This statement involves two difficulties. Quasten himself states that Chrysostom was not consecrated bishop of Constantinople until Feb. 26, 398.[965] Further, the second series is usually thought to comprise just the two homilies (CPG 4324-4325). The remainder, CPG 4319-4323, are thought to belong to the first series and to have been delivered accordingly during the first two years at Antioch.[966]

When it comes to the baptismal catecheses, Quasten's depiction of the *status quaestionis* is more accurate.[967] He follows recent opinion in assigning the two *Catecheses ad illuminandos* first published by Montfaucon (CPG 4460 and 4464) to Lent 388.[968] The first of these is identical to the first in the series of four instructions discovered by Papadopoulos-Kerameus (CPG 4460-4462, 4467). The Antiochene provenance of those four is demonstrated by the liturgy described therein, while in the third catechesis (CPG 4462) Chrysostom refers to the bishop, numbering himself among the priests. Quasten follows both Papadopoulos-Kerameus and Wenger in stating that they were in all probability delivered during Lent of 388 also. The then recently discovered series of eight catecheses (CPG 4465-4472) is assigned with Wenger to shortly after 388.

Concerning the eight homilies *Adv. Iudaeos* (CPG 4327), it is simply stated that they were delivered at Antioch from 386 to 387.[969]

c. *Moral discourses*

Of the homilies which Quasten defines as moral discourses, *In kalendas* (CPG 4328) was delivered on Jan. 1 (the year is unspecified) at Antioch. The location is known because in the introduction Chrysostom regrets the absence of the bishop.[970] *Contra ludos et theatra* (CPG 4441.7) is assigned without explanation to the now standard date of July 3,

---

[964] Quasten, *Patrology*, III 451.

[965] Quasten, *Patrology*, III 425. Further, in the opening sentence of section 2.b, *Patrology*, III 451, he defines Chrysostom's Antiochene period as lasting from 386 to 398.

[966] See Montfaucon (p. 72 above) and Lietzmann (p. 165 above).

[967] Quasten, *Patrology*, III 452.

[968] For the conclusion drawn by Wenger see p. 233 below. Quasten may also have been influenced by the opinion of Rauschen (p. 140 above), who considers the two instructions to have been delivered in 388 or later. With the exception of Tillemont, whom Quasten does not appear to have consulted, the earlier scholars (see pp. 76 and 117 above) tend to assign the homilies to Lent 387.

[969] Quasten, *Patrology*, III 452.

[970] Quasten, *Patrology*, III 453.

399.[971] The three sermons *De diabolo tentatore* (CPG 4332) must, Quasten states, be assigned to Antioch, although he supplies no grounds for this assertion.[972] The nine homilies *De paenitentia* (CPG 4333) were delivered at different times (he makes no claim regarding place) and only later formed into the present series. Quasten follows Charles Martin in denying the authenticity of *De paen. hom. 7*.[973]

d. *Sermons delivered on liturgical feasts.*

Of the festal discourses, *In diem natalem* (CPG 4334) is stated to have been delivered on Dec. 25, 386.[974] The sermon *De baptismo Christi* (CPG 4335) was most probably given on Jan. 6, 387.[975] Quasten also discusses a number of other homilies (CPG 4336-4339, 4341-4343 and 4408). In the course of this he alludes to the Antiochene origins of *De coemeterio et de cruce* (CPG 4337), although this is never clearly stated.[976]

e. *Panegyrics*

With regard to the panegyrical sermons Quasten's mode is again more descriptive than analytical. He alludes to a number of homilies preached on saints and martyrs, among which he includes several delivered on former bishops of Antioch (CPG 4319, 4345, 4347, 4351 and 4352).[977] The fact that the encomium *Laus Diodori episcopi* (CPG 4406) was delivered in 392 is stated without further elaboration.[978] Finally, he describes the seven homilies *De laudibus s. Pauli* (CPG 4344) at some length without any attempt to locate or date them.

---

[971] Quasten, *Patrology*, III 453. This is the date proposed by Pargoire (see p. 160 above) and followed by both Bonsdorff (p. 188 above) and Baur (p. 206 above).

[972] Quasten, *Patrology*, III 453.

[973] Quasten, *Patrology*, III 453. Martin, "Une homélie De Poenitentia de Sévérien de Gabala", *Revue d'Histoire ecclésiastique* 26 (1930) 331-343, attributes the homily to Severian. For this attribution see further De Aldama, *Repertorium*, 144 (no. 395).

[974] Quasten, *Patrology*, III 454.

[975] Quasten, *Patrology*, III 455.

[976] Quasten, *Patrology*, III 455.

[977] Quasten, *Patrology*, III 456. Although Philogonius is here described as an Antiochene bishop, Quasten had earlier assigned the relevant homily (CPG 4319) to Constantinople. See Sequence B, p. 230 below.

[978] Quasten here follows the date proposed by Tillemont (see p. 55 above). Montfaucon (p. 88 above) finds no grounds on which either to accept or refute this.

f. *Occasional discourses*

Under "occasional discourses" Quasten groups the homily *Cum pres-byter ordinatus* (CPG 4317), delivered on the occasion of Chrysostom's ordination at the beginning of 386, and the twenty-one sermons *De statuis* (CPG 4330), delivered at Antioch in 387. The last of these, *De statuis hom. 21*, was preached in that year on Easter Sunday.[979] In assigning *In Eutropium* (CPG 4392) and *De capto Eutropio* (CPG 4528) to Sunday, Jan. 17, 399 and a few days later, respectively, Quasten reverts to an older chronology of these events which can scarcely be considered to reflect the current status of opinion.[980] This is further inconsistent with a prior assertion that the fall of Eutropius took place in "summer" of that year.[981] Finally, the sermons *Antequam iret in exsilium* (CPG 4396) and *Post reditum a priore exsilio 2* (CPG 4399) are assigned, as is common, to the year of the first exile, 403.[982]

g. *Summary*

Of the following two tables, the first records Quasten's distribution of the homilies between the two cities, the second outlines the particular chronology observed by him. The small number of sequences which he details are set out following Table 11.b.

Table 11.a. Provenance — Quasten

CPG no.	Antioch	CPG no.	Constantinople
4317	*Cum presbyter fuit ordinatus* (p. 457)	4319	*De beato Philogonio* (p. 451)
4318	*De incompr. dei natura hom. 1-5* (p. 451)	4320	*De consubstantiali* (p. 451)
4327	*Adv. Iudaeos orationes 1-8* (p. 452)	4321	*De petitione matris fil. Zeb.* (p. 451)
4328	*In kalendas* (p. 453)	4322	*In quatriduanum Lazarum* (p. 451)
4330	*De statuis hom. 1-21* (p. 457)	4323	*De Christi precibus* (p. 451)

[979] Quasten, *Patrology*, III 457.

[980] Quasten, *Patrology*, III 458. See Stilting (p. 126 above). This dating is also promoted by Bardenhewer, *Geschichte*, III 343. Bonsdorff (p. 189 above), who follows Seeck, art. "Arkadios", RE 3 (1895) 1146-1147, in locating the fall of Eutropius in August 399, presents a more accurate view of the *status quaestionis*.

[981] Quasten, *Patrology*, III 448.

[982] Quasten, *Patrology*, III 458-459.

4332	De diabolo tentatore hom. 1-3 (p. 453)	4324	Contra Anomoeos hom. 11 (p. 451)
4334	In diem natalem (p. 454)	4325	De Christi divinitate (p. 451)
4335	De baptismo Christi (p. 455)	4392	In Eutropium (p. 458)
4371	In princ. Act. hom. 1-4 (p. 441)	4396	Sermo antequam iret in exsilium (p. 458)
4372	De mutatione nom. hom. 1-4 (p. 441)	4399	Sermo post reditum 2 (pp. 458-459)
4406	Laus Diodori episcopi* (p. 456)	4417	In illud: Vidi dominum hom. ?-? (pp. 435f)
4409	Hom. 1-67 in Genesim (p. 434)	4426	In Acta apost. hom. 1-55 (p. 440)
4410	Sermones 1-9 in Genesim (p. 434)	4432	In Phil. hom. 1-15 (pp. 447f)
4411	De Anna sermones 1-5 (p. 436)	4433	In Col. hom 1-12 (p. 448)
4412	De Davide et Saule hom. 1-3 (p. 436)	4434	In I Thess. hom. 1-11 (p. 449)
4413	Exp. in ps. 41 (p. 435)	4435	In II Thess. hom. 1-5 (p. 449)
4417	In illud: Vidi dominum hom. ?-? (pp. 435f)	4440	In Heb. hom. 1-34 (p. 450)
4420	De proph. obscuritate hom. 1-2 (p. 436)	4441.7	Contra ludos et theatra (pp. 453)
4424	In Matt. hom. 1-90 (p. 437)	4528	De capto Eutropio (p. 458)
4425	In Ioh. hom. 1-88 (p. 439)		
4427	In Rom. hom. 1-32 (p. 442)		
4428	In I Cor. hom. 1-44 (p. 445)		
4429	In II Cor. hom. 1-30 (p. 445)		
4431	In Eph. hom. 1-24 (p. 447)		
4436	In I Tim. hom. 1-18 (pp. 449f)		
4437	In II Tim. hom. 1-10 (pp. 449f)		
4438	In Titum hom. 1-6 (p. 450)		
4439	In Philemon hom. 1-3 (p. 450)		
4460	Ad illuminandos cat. 1 (p. 452)		
4461	Catechesis de iuramento (p. 452)		
4462	Cat. ultima ad baptizandos (p. 452)		
4464	Ad illuminandos cat. 2 (p. 452)		
4465-4472	Catecheses ad illuminandos 1-8 (p. 452)		

* Implied.

Table 11.b. Chronology — Quasten

Year (month-season)	Homily	Cited (page)
386		
beginning	Cum presbyter fuit ordinatus (CPG 4317)	457
Lent	Sermones 1-9 in Genesim (CPG 4410)	434
Dec. 25	In diem natalem (CPG 4334)	454
date unspecified	De proph. obscuritate hom. 1-2 (CPG 4420)	436

387*		
Jan. 6	*De baptismo Christi* (CPG 4335)	455
- Easter	*De statuis hom. 1-21* (CPG 4330)	457
date unspecified	*De Anna sermones 1-5* (CPG 4411)	436
	De Davide et Saule hom. 1-3 (CPG 4412)	"
	Exp. in ps. 41 (CPG 4413.2)	435
388		
Lent	*Ad illuminandos cat. 1* (CPG 4460)	452
	Ad illuminandos cat. 2 (CPG 4464)	"
	Catechesis de iuramento (CPG 4461)	"
	Cat. ultima ad baptizandos (CPG 4462)	"
	Ad neophytos (CPG 4467)	"
Paschal period	*In princ. Act. hom. 1-4* (CPG 4371)	441
	De mutatione nom. hom. 1-4 (CPG 4372)	"
date unspecified	*Hom. 1-67 in Genesim* (CPG 4409)	434
389#		
390		
date unspecified	*In Matt. hom. 1-90* (CPG 4424)	437
391		
date unspecified	*In Ioh. hom. 1-88* (CPG 4425)	439
392		
date unspecified	*Laus Diodori episcopi* (CPG 4406)	456
393		
394		
395		
396		
397		
date unspecified	Sequence B (see below)	451
398		
399		
Jan. 17	*In Eutropium* (CPG 4392)	458
a few days later	*De capto Eutropio* (CPG 4528)	458
July 3	*Contra ludos et theatra* (CPG 4441.7)	453
date unspecified	*In Col. hom. 1-12* (CPG 4433)	448
400		
date unspecified	*In Acta apost. hom. 1-55* (CPG 4426)	440
401		
402		
403		
date unspecified	*Antequam iret in exsilium* (CPG 4396)	458f
	Post reditum 2 (CPG 4399)	"
403/404	*In Heb. hom. 1-34* (CPG 4440)	450

* See Sequence A below. # CPG 4465-4472 = shortly after 388.

Sequence A. (386-387) *De incompr. dei nat. hom. 1-5* (CPG 4318) ‖ *Adv. Iud. or. 1-8* (CPG 4327).

Sequence B. (397: Constantinople) *De b. Philogonio* (CPG 4319); *De consubstantiali* (CPG 4320); *De petitione matr. fil. Zeb.* (CPG 4321); *In quatrid. Lazarum* (CPG 4322); *De Christi precibus* (CPG 4323); *Contra Anom. hom. 11* (CPG 4324); *De Christi divinitate* (CPG 4325).

Sequence C. (shortly after 388) *Catecheses ad illuminandos 1-8* (CPG 4465-4472).

3. SOURCES CHRETIENNES

The reason for including the opinions expressed by those who have produced new editions of Chrysostom homilies is that the editors might be expected to have undertaken a re-examination of where and when the homilies were delivered, in the process taking the sum of previous scholarship into consideration. As it turns out, this is not always the case. Since, however, it is likely that those who consult these editions will treat the opinions expressed there as definitive, as occurred with the edition of Montfaucon, it is important that the views promoted in the introduction to each be recorded in full.

a. *SC 28bis*

The first of Chrysostom's homilies to appear in the series *Sources Chrétiennes* are the five *De incompr. dei natura* (CPG 4318). The Greek text presented in the volume of 1951 is simply a reprint of that found in Migne (= Montfaucon), and it is not until the second edition, which appeared in 1970, that a new critical text based on the collated manuscripts was substituted. The interest of Jean Daniélou, who supplied the introduction to that edition, lies mainly with the nature of the Anomoean heresy and the theological content of the homilies. However, he offers in passing that Chrysostom delivered two series on this issue, the first at Antioch in 386-387, the second after 397 at Constantinople. It is to the first series that these five homilies belong.[983] Daniélou implies that all five were delivered in 386, offering in support the statement that the allusion to the autumn festivities of the Jews in *Adv. Iudaeos or. 1* (CPG 4327), which was delivered shortly after *De incompr. dei nat. hom. 1*, allows the date of the latter to be fixed at the beginning of September, 386.[984] He shows no interest in referring to previous opinion or in substantiating any of these claims, implying that the date and location of these homilies is an established datum.

---

[983] Malingrey, *Sur l'incompréhensibilité* (SC 28bis), 9.
[984] Malingrey, *Sur l'incompréhensibilité* (SC 28bis), 9 n. 1.

b. *SC 50bis*

The first critical edition, which appeared in 1957, is that of the eight baptismal instructions (CPG 4465-4472) preserved in ms. Stavronikita 6.[985] Since these catecheses were discovered subsequent to the edition of Montfaucon and, with the exception of *Cat. 3* (CPG 4467),[986] are being presented for the first time, Antoine Wenger undertakes to determine both where and when they were delivered.[987]

In considering where the catecheses were preached, Wenger "naturally" thinks of Antioch. This leads him first to prove that they are unlikely to have been delivered at Constantinople. In the first instance the tone of the instructions is found to support this premise. There is nothing in the eight discourses which is appropriate to a bishop. On the contrary, the explicit humility and somewhat familiar tone are more suited to a presbyter of Antioch.[988] Having dismissed Constantinople from the picture, Wenger then produces decisive proof of their delivery at Antioch. *Cat. 8* (CPG 4472), preached on the Saturday following Easter, refers to the presence of indigenous persons from the country (ἀπὸ τῆς χώρας).[989] These individuals speak a foreign tongue. Wenger finds it inconceivable that in the vicinity of Constantinople the locals would have spoken a language other than Greek. He then draws upon the homilies *De ss. martyribus* (CPG 4357) and *De statuis hom. 19* (CPG 4330) to demonstrate that this conforms perfectly to the situation at Antioch.[990]

As for the date of the series, Wenger proceeds by elimination. Finding nothing in common with the eight sermons on Genesis (CPG 4410) delivered during Lent of 386, he concludes that it does not belong to that year.[991] In order to demonstrate that it does not fall either in the years 387 or 388, Wenger digresses into a discussion of the date of the four catecheses which form an independent series (CPG 4460-4462 and

---

[985] For a discussion of the contents of this manuscript and further background to the catecheses see Wenger, "La tradition des oeuvres", 5-32.

[986] See n. 551 above.

[987] Wenger, *Huit catéchèses* (SC 50bis), Intro., 59-65.

[988] This is the inverse of the argument from episcopal tone. See further pp. 283f below.

[989] The identity of these is discussed at length by van de Paverd, *Homilies on the Statues*, 255-293.

[990] Wenger alludes further, *Huit catéchèses* (SC 50bis), 63, to similarities between the liturgical formulae and practices described in these and in the catecheses first published by Papadopoulos-Kerameus (CPG 4461-4462).

[991] Wenger, *Huit catéchèses* (SC 50bis), 63.

4467).[992] These he locates in the year 388 alongside the first thirty-three of the sixty-seven homilies on Genesis (CPG 4409). *Cat. 1* (CPG 4460) was delivered after *Hom. 11 in Gen.*, thirty days before Easter. *Cat. 3* (CPG 4462) is to be located on Thursday of Holy Week that year, and *Cat. 4* (CPG 4467) on the eve of Easter. The four homilies *In principium Actorum* (CPG 4371) and a fifth now lost, in the first and third of which the neophytes are addressed in person, locate themselves in the same position during the Paschal octave, and therefore displace *Cat. 4-8* (CPG 4468-4472) of the present series as possible candidates for that year.[993] Left with the years 389 to 398, Wenger prefers to narrow the possibilities to the years immediately following 388, on the basis of the similiarity in language between this series and that on Genesis (CPG 4409).[994]

c. *SC 272*

In her introduction to the text of *Cum presbyter ordinatus fuit* (CPG 4317), published in 1980, Anne-Marie Malingrey sees no need to elaborate, beyond stating that the sermon was delivered on the day of Chrysostom's ordination.[995] Once again the implication is that this date in 386, as also the authenticity of the homily, is an established and well-known fact.[996]

d. *SC 277*

With the publication in 1981 of his critical edition of the six homilies *In illud: Vidi dominum* (CPG 4417), Jean Dumortier finally states unequivocally that the fourth homily is not a genuine work of Chrysostom, proposing rather that it be attributed to the ninth century patriarch Ni-

---

[992] Wenger, *Huit catéchèses* (SC 50bis), 63-65. Concerning this series see further pp. 236f and 247f below.

[993] Wenger, *Huit catéchèses* (SC 50bis), 42, on the basis of internal evidence locates *Cat. 4* on the Sunday or Monday of the Paschal week, *Cat. 5* on the Tuesday, *Cat. 6* on the Wednesday, *Cat. 7* on the Friday and *Cat. 8* on the Saturday following Easter.

[994] Since Wenger, *Huit catéchèses* (SC 50bis), 63, titles section 7 of the introduction "Date: Pâques de l'année 390?", a proposition which goes unmentioned in the ensuing discussion, it might be inferred that this is his final conclusion.

[995] Malingrey, *Sur le sacerdoce* (SC 272), 367.

[996] No mention is made of the charge brought by Baur, *Chrysostom and His Time*, I 180, that the homily is of doubtful authenticity.

cephorus.[997] This proposition is of major consequence as, up until now, scholars had worked hard to reconcile this sermon with the other five homilies, a feat which had always involved certain difficulties.[998]

Concerning the opinion that *In illud: Vidi dom. hom. 2, 3, 5,* and *6* alone form a series and that *hom. 1* belongs to a quite different period, this Dumortier affirms.[999] He locates *hom. 1* during the last three years at Antioch (395-398), citing Tillemont's argument that it must date to the period following the accession of Arcadius,[1000] an opinion which Dumortier finds incontestable.[1001] The remaining four homilies are assigned, also with Tillemont, to not long after Chrysostom's ordination. The tone employed in the first two (*hom. 2* and *3*) displays the lack of assurance of a beginner in the presence of his bishop. Dumortier ignores Tillemont's identification of the sermon which preceded *hom. 2* as *Cum presbyter fuit ordinatus* (CPG 4317), however, while adopting the latter's conclusion concerning the date of *hom. 6*. Preferring to keep all four homilies together, rather than distribute them over the course of a year, as Tillemont had done, Dumortier locates *hom. 2, 3, 5, 6* at the end of 386 and beginning of 387.[1002]

e. *SC 300*

In 1982 an edition of the seven panegyrics on St Paul (CPG 4344) prepared by Auguste Piédagnel appeared. In considering the question of where they were delivered, Piédagnel concludes, in much the same way as those before him, that the majority, if not all, were delivered at Antioch.[1003] This location is certain in the case of *hom. 4*. Chrysostom recounts the burning of the temple of Apollo at Daphne, the suburb of Antioch, as an event well known to his audience. Several lines later he alludes to a further catastrophe specific to the populace at Antioch. The springs which dried up in the time of the emperor Julian are, further-

[997] Dumortier, *Homélies sur Ozias* (SC 277), 13-17. This suggestion had been put forward by him as early as 1973, but with some hesitancy. See Dumortier, "Une homélie chrysostomienne suspecte", MSR 30 (1973) 185-191.

[998] In general these were resolved by assigning the piece to Constantinople. See, e.g., Tillemont (p. 50 above) and Montfaucon (p. 93 above).

[999] Dumortier, *Homélies sur Ozias* (SC 277), 9. On the basis of the ms. tradition Dumortier, "Une homélie chrysostomienne suspecte", 185, had already argued that *hom. 2, 3, 5* and *6* constitute an original group; *hom. 1* and *4* were added later.

[1000] For this see p. 49 above.

[1001] Dumortier, *Homélies sur Ozias* (SC 277), 10-11.

[1002] Dumortier, *Homélies sur Ozias* (SC 277), 11-12.

[1003] Piédagnel, *Panégyriques de S. Paul* (SC 300), 10-13.

more, referred to as being those of "our land".[1004] As for the remaining homilies, Piédagnel admits that there is little internal evidence. He draws upon a comment in *In kalendas* (CPG 4328), a homily delivered with certainty at Antioch, to demonstrate that John had preached on the subject of St Paul there with the intention of delivering further encomia in that city. He then proceeds from an analysis of the rhetorical elements of the homilies *De laudibus s. Pauli* to show that *hom. 1* is the only true encomium amongst the seven. On further comparing *hom. 1* with *hom. 4*, he is led to conclude that *hom. 1* cannot have been delivered after that homily. A thematic examination of *hom. 2* leads him to the same conclusion. This locates *hom. 1* and *2* with *hom. 4* at Antioch. Piédagnel finds in *hom. 3* a fulfilment of the intention stated in *In kalendas*, a circumstance which permits him to assign this homily likewise to Antioch. *Hom. 5-7*, like *hom. 4*, all indicate that they were delivered on the occasion of a festival honouring St Paul. Acknowledging that in all probability a feast day dedicated to St Paul also graced the liturgical calendar at Constantinople, Piédagnel nonetheless finds occasion to assign all three homilies to Antioch. In particular the majestic tone of *hom. 7*, which might be thought to indicate the episcopal office of the homilist, is discounted by pointing out the dissimilarity between the vocabulary found in this homily and in those which constitute the series on Acts (CPG 4426), which were delivered with certainty at Constantinople.

Regarding the question of date, Piédagnel investigates whether the feast day upon which *hom. 4-7* were preached can be identified.[1005] After some deliberation he concludes that there may have existed at Antioch an annual celebration on Dec. 28 devoted to the apostle Paul alone. It is also possible, however, that in accord with the usage at Jerusalem the festival on that date was dedicated to both Sts Peter and Paul. In either case, it seems that this is the festival indicated in the homilies. Piédagnel also considers whether all seven homilies were delivered over the course of a week or belong to separate years. He observes a development in style and progression in the themes treated in each which leads him to conclude that they were more likely to have been preached in separate years. *Hom. 1-6* Piédagnel situates in the first half of Chrysostom's ministry at Antioch (a little before and a little after 390). *Hom. 7*, possibly delivered a little later, is difficult to situate, leading him to propose the extremes of 387 and 397 for the series.[1006]

[1004] These same arguments were put forward as early as phase one. See Savile (p. 44 above).

[1005] Piédagnel, *Panégyriques de S. Paul* (SC 300), 13-19.

[1006] Piédagnel, *Panégyriques de S. Paul* (SC 300), 20.

f. *SC 362*

Concerning the homily *De s. Babyla* (CPG 4347), a new text of which
was published alongside that of the discourse *De s. Babyla contra Iulianum et gentiles* (CPG 4348) in 1990, Bernard Grillet and Jean-Noël
Guinot express interest only in the question of date. The link between
Babylas and Antioch is so well established that it is entirely passed over
in favour of demonstrating that the homily was delivered before an audience and therefore dates to the period following Chrysostom's ordination
in 386.[1007] Since in the course of the homily John refers to himself as
young in comparison to those who witnessed the original events surrounding the translation of Babylas' remains,[1008] it was probably preached
not long afterwards. In fact, they argue, the homily can be located
between *De Lazaro conc. 3* and *4* (CPG 4329), because in the latter
Chrysostom says that the festival of St Babylas intervened, preventing
him from fulfilling the promise made in *conc. 3*.[1009] A reference to this
interruption is found in the opening lines of *De s. Babyla*. They conclude
that the year to which these homilies belong is unknown, but that *De s.
Babyla* itself was with certainty delivered on the saint's festival, Jan. 24.
Finally, they allude to Lietzmann's proposal that the date Jan. 24, 388 or
393 is probable, although the argument for this, they state, is not convincing.[1010]

g. *SC 366*

Also in 1990, there appeared a new edition of three baptismal
catecheses (CPG 4460-4462), prepared by Auguste Piédagnel with the intention of improving upon the text of Papadopoulos-Kerameus.[1011] Since
the last of the original four catecheses (CPG 4467) had only recently been
re-edited among the eight homilies (CPG 4465-4472) presented by Wenger,[1012] Piédagnel does not undertake to re-present it. However, he does
spend some time considering the relationship of that catechesis to each
of the two series, concluding that it forms a strong bond with the first
(CPG 4460-4462). This leads him to propose that, although originally de-

---

[1007] Grillet-Guinot, *Homélie sur Babylas* (SC 362), 279.

[1008] *De s. Babyla* (SC 362,296 8-10).

[1009] This was first proposed by Tillemont (see p. 52 above).

[1010] The source cited is an article by Downey, "The Shrines of St. Babylas at Antioch
and Daphne", in *Antioch On-the-Orontes* II, 45-48.

[1011] See n. 551 above.

[1012] See p. 232 above.

livered after the third of those instructions, it later became attached to the second series (CPG 4465-4472) in the tradition.[1013]

Piédagnel firmly assigns the three catecheses which he presents to Antioch, arguing that the manner in which Chrysostom deplores the sins he has committed since his own baptism (*Cat. 3*: CPG 4462) is more appropriate to an Antiochene presbyter than the bishop of Constantinople. Moreover, towards the end of this same homily the homilist explicitly numbers himself among the priests who assist the bishop during the baptismal ceremony. In addition, Piédagnel finds the exhortations against swearing in *Cat. 1-2* (CPG 4460-4461) the same as those in the homilies *De statuis* (CPG 4330), which leads him to argue that Chrysostom is preaching before the same audience, since the vices attacked are the same.[1014] As for the date of this series, he adopts Wenger's proposal that the instructions be located in Lent 388.[1015]

In the course of his introductory comments, Piédagnel devotes several pages to considering the supposed catechesis *Ad illuminandos cat. 2* (CPG 4464). Acknowledging the concurrent work of Frans van de Paverd on the subject,[1016] he adopts the latter's proposal that Lent at Antioch lasted not seven but eight weeks, drawing the conclusion that the sermon in question is in fact not a catechesis at all, but constitutes part of the series *De statuis*.[1017]

h. *SC 396*

With her critical edition of CPG 4320-4325 in 1994, Anne-Marie Malingrey completes the series *Contra Anomoeos* presented in part in SC28[bis].[1018] No new investigation of the provenance or date of these homilies is undertaken, the editor being satisfied that consensus on these topics has been reached. As a consequence, *Contra Anom. hom. 7-8* (CPG 4320-4321) are assigned to January 387;[1019] *hom. 9* (CPG 4322) to either Lazarus Saturday or the week after Easter 387, with *hom. 10* (CPG 4323)

[1013] Piédagnel, *Trois catéchèses* (SC 366), 33-38.

[1014] Piédagnel, *Trois catéchèses* (SC 366), 38-39.

[1015] Piédagnel, *Trois catéchèses* (SC 366), 39. See p. 233 above.

[1016] Piédagnel, *Trois catéchèses* (SC 366), 23, 29. See p. 245 below.

[1017] Piédagnel, *Trois catéchèses* (SC 366), 20-32. He refers (p. 30) to van de Paverd's dating of the homily to Wednesday of Holy Week, April 21, 387.

[1018] See p. 231 above.

[1019] Malingrey, *Sur l'égalité* (SC 396), 396 n. 6, offers the opinion of both Montfaucon (see p. 72 above) and Schwartz (p. 147 above) in support.

being delivered a short time later;[1020] finally, *hom. 11* and *12* (CPG 4324-4325) are said to belong to the period immediately after Chrysostom's consecration as bishop of Constantinople. Malingrey is the first to assign *hom. 11* to a specific day (Feb. 28, 398).[1021] A chronology of the first five homilies *Contra Anomoeos* (= *De incompr. dei nat. hom. 1-5*: CPG 4318) and *De b. Philogonio* (CPG 4319) is also presented, in which the most notable feature is the fixing of *De incompr. dei nat. hom. 1* on the first Sunday in September 386.[1022] Also worthy of note is the argument that *hom. 2* locates itself at the end of October 386, since it was delivered following the homilies *De s. Pelagia* (CPG 4350) and *In s. Ignatium* (CPG 4351), delivered on Oct. 8 and 17, 386, respectively.[1023] In this, although it is nowhere stated, she follows the opinion of Schwartz.[1024]

i. *SC 433*

In 1998 an edition of the first eight of the *Sermones in Genesim* (CPG 4410) appeared, prepared by Laurence Brottier. In considering the date and provenance of these sermons Brottier differs little from her predecessors, although she approaches the question of date with slightly more caution. The sermons were delivered most likely in 386 since the large series on Genesis (CPG 4409) is commonly attributed to the years 388-389 and it is difficult to believe, she argues, that the small series postdates the longer one. Since they clearly belong to Lent[1025] and since Lent in 387 was taken up with the homilies *De statuis* (CPG 4330), the year 386 is the only remaining candidate.[1026] A provenance of Antioch for these sermons is confirmed by the two references to Flavian (*sermones 1* and *8*) as John's "father" and "master".[1027]

[1020] For the link between the two homilies Malingrey, *Sur l'égalité* (SC 396), 370 n. 1, cites Montfaucon (see p. 72 above). The use of the liturgical cycle or *lectio continua* to situate *hom. 9* was suggested to her by S. J. Voicu.

[1021] Malingrey, *Sur l'égalité* (SC 396), 370.

[1022] Malingrey, *Sur l'égalité* (SC 396), 369.

[1023] Malingrey, *Sur l'égalité* (SC 396), 369 n. 3.

[1024] See p. 147 above.

[1025] Brottier, *Sermons* (SC 433), 12-13, points out that three elements confirm this conclusion: four sermons contain references to the fast; there are numerous references to daily preaching; and *sermones 4-7* contain indications that they were delivered during the late afternoon or early evening.

[1026] Brottier, *Sermons* (SC 433), 11-12.

[1027] Brottier, *Sermons* (SC 433), 12.

4. MISCELLANEOUS WRITINGS (1980-2000)

Between 1980 and the end of the millenium several books and articles appeared in which some aspect of the date or location of a small number of homilies is addressed. Some of these respond to issues raised by the production of a new edition, others to points of historical interest.

a. *Holum, Cameron, Liebeschuetz, Kelly*

In recent years a number of scholars interested in the chronology of the reign of Arcadius have debated the date of one or more Constantinopolitan homilies. In a footnote to his 1982 investigation of the role played by the Theodosian empresses,[1028] Kenneth Holum points out that *Hom. dicta postquam reliquiae martyrum* (CPG 4441.1) situates itself between 400 and early 402, since Eudoxia is pictured wearing the diadem. This signifies that at the time she held the status of Augusta, a circumstance which dates the homily to after Jan. 9, 400. Since no mention is made of the young Theodosius, the date of his elevation to Augustus (Jan. 10, 402) can be considered a *terminus ad quem*. Had he been Augustus at the time, it is argued, the child would somehow have been involved in the ceremony.

Alan Cameron and Wolf Liebeschuetz have both made observations of significance for the chronology of the Constantinopolitan homilies.[1029] Each, in the course of his investigations, discusses individual sermons attributed to the location. In an article, Cameron further undertakes to reassess the location and date traditionally assigned to the series on Acts (CPG 4426).

Earthquakes have long been used as a means of localising the date of certain of the homilies. For the years spanning Chrysostom's episcopate two separate quakes, occurring in the years 398 and 400/402, have been proposed.[1030] In 1987 Cameron, in an attempt to establish the year in which Synesius departed Constantinople, devoted an entire article to this

---

[1028] *Theodosian Empresses. Women and Imperial Dominion in Late Antiquity* (The Transformation of the Classical Heritage III) Berkeley 1982, 56 n. 35.

[1029] The books, Liebeschuetz, *Barbarians and Bishops* (1990) and Cameron, Long & Sherry, *Barbarians and Politics* (1993), represent the culmination of their investigations. In particular Cameron, Long & Sherry, *Barbarians and Politics*, Appendix II, 405-408, present their view of Chrysostom's movements in the years 400 to 402.

[1030] Regarding the earthquake of 398 see n. 325 above. More recently, Downey, "Earthquakes at Constantinople and vicinity, A.D. 342-1454", *Speculum* 30 (1955) 597, and Grumel, *La Chronologie*, Paris 1958, 477, admit occurrences only in 402 and 403. The second is considered by Grumel to be doubtful.

issue. In order to support his argument that the 398 earthquake is ficti-
tious, the record of the quake in 402 probably a mistake for one in 403,
and that the only quakes to be established with certainty occurred in 400
and 403,[1031] Cameron is obliged to reassess the chronology of the homilies on Acts and the visit to Ephesus.[1032]

In the course of *In Acta apost. hom. 41* Chrysostom refers to an earthquake of the previous year. A further reference to an earthquake occurs
in *hom. 7*. If the date of 400/401 uniformly proposed for this series is correct, the occurrence of an earthquake in 400 coinciding with Synesius'
departure from Constantinople can be firmly established. Cameron begins by proving that the series was delivered at Constantinople.[1033] In a
number of passages the homilist is unmistakably described as bishop. In
hom. 3 the responsibilities of a bishop are within his personal experience
(PG 60,39-42); in *hom. 8* he has the power of excommunication and sits
on a throne (PG 60,74); while at the end of *hom. 9* an imaginary inter-
locutor refers to him as bishop (PG 60,84). Further, John alludes to the
emperor and palace as "conspicuous" in the experience of his audience.
In *hom. 21* it is possible to receive a personal invitation to the palace
from the emperor; in the course of this homily the protocol involved
during an audience with the *basileus* is also described (PG 60,168 and
170); the homily further refers to the emperor's *adventus* and victories
(PG 60,170), a situation also found in *hom. 11* (PG 60,99); in *hom. 3* the
palace is mentioned as well as the bishop's throne (PG 60,39); while *hom.
32* alludes to the deliberations of the emperor and his council on both
military and domestic issues (PG 60,237). Cameron dismisses as scarcely
worth comment Seeck's argument that the series belongs to Antioch,[1034]
pointing out that in *hom. 38* Theodorus' conspiracy in 372 is treated as a
distant reminiscence.[1035] He supports this with Bonsdorff's argument that
in *hom. 25* a contrast is drawn between Antioch and the present location.

[1031] Cameron, "Earthquake 400", in particular 351-355.

[1032] Cameron, "Earthquake 400", 344-351. This section of the article is repeated almost
verbatim in Cameron, Long & Sherry, *Barbarians and Politics*, 94-101. See, however, D.
Roques, "Synésios à Constantinople: 399-402", *Byzantion* 65 (1995) 419-426, where it is
argued that the earthquakes mentioned in *hom. 7* and *41* are metaphoric and the event
referred to not physical but political. Throughout the article (pp. 405-439) Roques does
not dispute the chronology that Cameron establishes for the series, merely the significance
of the reference to an earthquake in the previous year for the chronology of Synesius'
sojourn at Constantinople.

[1033] In this Cameron uniformly follows the arguments put forward by Bonsdorff (see
pp. 192f above).

[1034] See p. 154 above.

[1035] For the identification between the Theodorus of *hom. 41*, on whom Seeck's argument relies, and the events recounted in *hom. 38* see Downey, *Antioch*, 401-402.

As the series was undoubtedly preached at Constantinople, the date can be established from *hom. 44*. As Chrysostom states in this homily (PG 60,266), it is his third year at the present location. Working from the date of his consecration on Feb. 26, 398, *hom. 44* and *41* can then be assigned to early in 401. Arguing against the assertion that the series began shortly after Easter, Cameron points out that *hom. 1* cannot have been delivered around Easter and that *hom. 4* makes no indication that Pentecost is close at hand. Furthermore, *hom. 29* mentions that it is winter, while *hom. 37* clearly alludes to the expulsion and massacre of the Goths, indicating that the homily was delivered after July 12, 400. Drawing upon the parallels between *hom. 37* and *Cum Saturninus et Aurelianus* (CPG 4393), delivered probably in late summer 400,[1036] Cameron finds that *hom. 37* can have been delivered no earlier than autumn 400. If one accepts that John delivered the homilies at the rate of two a week, it must have taken at the minimum six, perhaps even eight or nine months to deliver the series. After demonstrating, contrary to Baur and Liebeschuetz,[1037] that the trip to Ephesus did not take place until November 401,[1038] Cameron concludes that the series could have been delivered uninterrupted from late summer or early autumn 400. Given the number of homilies, this would place a substantial part of the series in 401. Alternately, the whole series could be located in that year.

In the course of the excursus on the chronology of the visit to Ephesus, Cameron dates the homily *De regressu* (CPG 4394) to just past Easter (April 6) in the year 402.[1039]

In 1988 Cameron, by demonstrating that the title appended to the homily is incorrect, re-introduced *De capto Eutropio* (CPG 4528) into the corpus. As early as Savile, it had been noted that the details surrounding the capture of the asylum-seeker mentioned in this homily differ from the account of Eutropius' arrest provided by the church historians.[1040] On the strength of the manuscript title, however, it was the authenticity of the homily which came to be questioned, rather than the identity of the individual to which it refers.[1041] Cameron, arguing that there is nothing

---

[1036] Cameron, "Earthquake 400", 348. See, however, Cameron, "A misidentified homily", 36, where this homily is assigned to early summer of that year.

[1037] For Baur, see p. 206 above. Liebeschuetz, "The Fall", 5 n. 19, follows Baur in dating the return "soon after Easter 401".

[1038] This is revised to December 401 in Cameron, Long & Sherry, *Barbarians and Politics*, 407.

[1039] Cameron, "Earthquake 400", 350-351. The excursus is presented in a revised form in Cameron, Long & Sherry, *Barbarians and Politics*, Appendix II, 405-407.

[1040] See Savile, VIII 721.

[1041] See De Aldama, *Repertorium*, 64 (no.170).

in the homily to identify the fugitive as Eutropius,[1042] looks elsewhere for
a suitable candidate. This he finds in the person of Count John, who was
exiled together with Aurelian and Saturninus at the time of Gainas'
coup.[1043] Having established this identity, he proposes that the homily
was delivered not in August 399, as those who considered it genuine had
supposed, but in April 400.

In the course of this argument two other homilies from Constantinople are considered. The date of *In Eutropium* (CPG 4392), which genuinely describes the fugitive eunuch-consul, is established as August
399.[1044] The sermon *Cum Saturninus et Aurelianus* (CPG 4393), the title
of which is less than accurate, is located two months before the massacre
of the Goths which occurred in July 400.[1045] In this Cameron differs from
Liebeschuetz, who had just proposed a date for the homily in late summer or autumn of that year.[1046]

In his biography of Chrysostom (1995), J.N.D. Kelly also has something to contribute regarding a small number of miscellaneous Constantinopolitan sermons (CPG 4396-4399). Although in the main he derives
the provenance and chronology of the homilies to which he refers from
elsewhere,[1047] he does make several comments of interest regarding
authenticity. With respect to the two sermons *Antequam iret in exsilium*
(CPG 4396) and *Cum iret in exsilium* (CPG 4397) Kelly argues that the
two are in essence genuine, if in some respects garbled, and that they
represent two redactions of the same sermon, namely that which was
delivered in the three day grace period which extended from the decision
of the Synod of the Oak (late September 403) to the point at which
Chrysostom was arrested.[1048] The first of the two sermons *Post reditum a
priore exsilio* (CPG 4398) is likewise in essence genuine, if available only

---

[1042] Cameron, "A misidentified homily", 36-39.

[1043] Cameron, "A misidentified homily", 39-45.

[1044] Cameron, "A misidentified homily", 34.

[1045] Cameron, "A misidentified homily", 36. This point is argued in greater detail in
Cameron, Long & Sherry, *Barbarians and Politics*, 173-175.

[1046] Liebeschuetz, review of G. Albert, *Goten in Konstantinopel* (Paderborn 1984),
Classical Review NS 36 (1986) 157. Twelve months earlier Cameron, "Earthquake 400",
348, had himself accepted this dating.

[1047] So, for instance, with regard to the sermons of the first and second year at Antioch
(excluding those on the statues) Kelly, *Golden Mouth*, 55-71 follows Schwartz (see p. 146
above); the homilies on the statues (pp. 72-82) and series of eight catecheses (p. 88) van de
Paverd (see p. 245 below); the exegetical series (excluding Acts) (pp. 87-92, 132-133) Bonsdorff (p. 171 above); the series on Acts (pp. 166-168) Cameron (pp. 240f above). It should
be noted, however, that the claim (p. 67) that *De s. pentecoste hom. 1* (CPG 4343) was
delivered in 386 does not derive from Schwartz and, so far as I can discover, is unprece-
dented.

[1048] Kelly, *Golden Mouth*, 229-231.

in Latin translation, and was delivered in the Church of the Apostles early in October 403. The second of these two sermons (CPG 4399) was delivered, he asserts, in the Great Church on the following Sunday. Since the reference to bloodshed in the baptistery which this sermon contains can now be shown to refer to an event which occurred just prior to the homilist's return from exile, there are no longer any grounds for doubting its authenticity.[1049] While none of these points is startling in itself, collectively they contribute to a reappraisal of the value of these sermons, leading to minute adjustments in their chronology.

b. *Wenger, Aubineau*

Two articles have appeared as the result of preparation for a new edition of the *Novae homiliae* (CPG 4441) first published by Montfaucon. As his contribution to a collection of essays published in 1987 in honour of Marcel Richard, Antoine Wenger restores a substantial passage and supplies the conclusion to *De Eleazaro et septem pueris* (CPG 4441.13).[1050] The conclusion was missing in the manuscript used by Montfaucon, while Montfaucon failed to notice that the passage which constitutes PG 63,528D-529D in Migne is an interpolation. Wenger identifies it correctly as belonging to the as yet unpublished *In illud: Quia quod stultum est Dei* (CPG 4441.14).[1051] Wenger makes no new claim as to the date of the homily, preferring to rely on the conclusion drawn by Pargoire.[1052] He adds, however, that on the basis of the newly restored ending in which the homilist exhorts his listeners to flock to the sanctuary of the Maccabees on the following day after crossing (διαπερῶντες) the strait, we can identify the church with that of the Maccabees situated, according to the *Chronicon Paschale*, just beyond the Golden Horn.[1053]

Michel Aubineau, in an article of 1992, takes Montfaucon to task over his attribution to Antioch of the two homilies *In illud Isaiae: Ego dominus deus feci lumen* (CPG 4418) and *In illud: Filius ex se nihil facit* (CPG 4441.12) on the basis of the manuscript titles.[1054] In the course of consid-

---

[1049] Kelly, *Golden Mouth*, 236-237.

[1050] Wenger, "Restauration", 599-604.

[1051] Wenger, "Restauration", 600-601.

[1052] For Pargoire's argument that the homily was delivered on Sunday, July 31, 399 see p. 161 above.

[1053] Wenger, "Restauration", 601. Although he gives no indication of the fact, this was argued also by Pargoire, "Les homélies en juillet 399", 160.

[1054] Aubineau, "Restitution", 528-544, in particular 533-535. In the case of CPG 4418 I cannot see that Montfaucon attributes this to Antioch. While Tillemont (see p. 66 above),

ering the first, Aubineau shows Montfaucon's emendation of the title of the second to προειρηκότος [ἐπισκόπου] ὀλίγα ("a [bishop] having spoken a few words beforehand"), in which the latter wished to see a reference to Flavian, to be entirely conjectural. The manuscript tradition supports the readings προειρηκότος ὀλίγα ("a person having spoken a few words beforehand"), ἑτέρου προειρηκότος ὀλίγα ("another having spoken a few words beforehand") and, in the case of Stav. 6, ἑτέρου ἐπισκόπου προειρηκότος ("another bishop having spoken beforehand").[1055] In accepting a Constantinopolitan provenance in this instance, Aubineau promotes the conclusion drawn by Pargoire that the homily was delivered in the Great Church at Constantinople on July 24, 399. Aubineau's main interest, however, lies with the first homily (CPG 4418). Here he produces fresh evidence in the form of the Jerusalem codex *Photius 47* to show that the title appended to the homily in the manuscript used by Savile, and consequently Montfaucon, is abbreviated. The full title: Τοῦ αὐτοῦ, ἐν τῇ ἐκκλησίᾳ τῇ ἐπὶ εἰρήνην, ἑτέρου προειπόντος ὀλίγα, ἐλέχθη ὁμιλία εἰς τὴν ῥῆσιν... ("Homily of the same, preached in the church dedicated to Peace on the lection ... another having said a few words beforehand"), found in more than one manuscript, indicates that the homily was delivered in the church of St Eirene, a discovery which definitively indicates that the homily belongs to Constantinople.[1056]

Aubineau's attempt to locate further the year or time of year during which the homily was delivered fails to result in a conclusion.[1057] In passing, however, he reaffirms Montfaucon's assertion that the three homilies on marriage (CPG 4377-4379) belong to Constantinople, because in the third Chrysostom mentions an episcopal colleague, possibly Maximus of Seleucia, who has preached in his absence.[1058] He also has cause to date the only other homily known to have been delivered in St Eirene (*De studio praesentium*: CPG 4441.5). Since CPG 4441.1 and 2 can, he believes, be located in 398,[1059] and CPG 4441.6 is to be located on Jan. 17, 399,[1060]

---

as Aubineau observes, would prefer to attribute the homily to Constantinople, Montfaucon himself (p. 94 above) avoids drawing a conclusion.

[1055] Aubineau, "Restitution", 533.

[1056] Aubineau, "Restitution", 534.

[1057] Aubineau, "Restitution", 536-541.

[1058] Aubineau, "Restitution", 538 n. 30.

[1059] Aubineau, "Restitution", 540, bases this almost entirely on Batiffol's proposal (see p. 157 above) that the homilies must be early in the piece because of the positive light in which the empress is portrayed. One suspects that Aubineau locates them in 398 more from an *a priori* desire to establish a chronological arrangement for the series than on the basis of any real evidence. He appears unaware of Holum's recent assertion (p. 239 above) that the first of the two homilies was delivered after Jan. 9, 400.

he is tempted to situate CPG 4441.5 in between. The probable chronological arrangement of the homilies is strengthened when one takes into
consideration the sequence established by Pargoire for CPG 4441.7,10,12
and 13 (July 3, 17, 24 and 31, respectively).[1061] In the end this notion is
enough to convince Aubineau to locate *De studio praesentium* in the last
months of 398 or at the beginning of January 399.[1062]

c. *Van de Paverd*

In addition to the articles of Wenger and Aubineau a further work deserves attention. In 1991 the results of Frans van de Paverd's meticulous
investigation of the sequence and precise date of the homilies *De statuis*
(CPG 4330) appeared in print.[1063] While the attribution of these homilies
to the year 387 at Antioch is one of the rare fixed points in the provenance and chronology of the Chrysostomic corpus, and a recovery of the
original sequence and date of this series is therefore of little consequence
to the remainder of the homilies, in the course of his book van de Paverd
nonetheless touches on several issues of significance, most notably the
reliability of manuscript titles,[1064] the transmission of homiletic series[1065]
and the character of Syrian monasticism.[1066] Of importance to the eventual reassessment of the chronology of the homilies which belong to
Antioch is his determination that the duration of Lent at that location
was not six or seven weeks, as had been variously argued, but eight.[1067]
Of equal value is his painstaking reconstruction of the daily lives of the
citizens of Antioch throughout the Lenten period, and of the character
and frequency of the liturgical synaxes.[1068]

[1060] The argument for this is not entirely clear either. Again he relies on Batiffol (see p.
155 above), whom he has just quoted, "Restitution de quatorze folios", 540, as saying that
the homily is to be located in 399 *at the earliest* (emphasis added). A paragraph later the
homily is firmly located on Jan. 17, 399.

[1061] See pp. 158-161 above. Aubineau, "Restitution", 540, finds this particularly
convincing. For the original suggestion that the manuscript arrangement is chronological
see Montfaucon (p. 102 above). See, however, Mayer, "Pargoire's sequence", where the
validity of Pargoire's sequence is challenged and the argument for the chronological
arrangement of the series is dismissed.

[1062] Aubineau, "Restitution", 540-541.

[1063] Van de Paverd, *Homilies on the Statues*.

[1064] Van de Paverd, *Homilies on the Statues*, 228-230.

[1065] Van de Paverd, *Homilies on the Statues*, 322.

[1066] Van de Paverd, *Homilies on the Statues*, 255-293.

[1067] Van de Paverd, *Homilies on the Statues*, 250-254.

[1068] Van de Paverd, *Homilies on the Statues*, 161-201.

As for the homilies themselves, van de Paverd establishes once and for all that they were delivered in a sequence other than that presented in the manuscripts, in the process restoring *hom. 19* to the period before Easter.[1069] In brief, he concludes that *De statuis hom. 1* was delivered on Sunday, Feb. 21, 387, a full week before the beginning of Lent.[1070] *Hom. 2* and *3* were delivered on the following Saturday and Sunday (Feb. 27-28), the riots having occurred some time during the intervening week.[1071] Chrysostom continued to preach every day until the following Saturday (*hom. 4-8* = Monday, March 1-Friday, March 5; on the Saturday, March 6, not *hom. 9* but *hom. 15* was delivered).[1072] There is then a break of a week, after which Chrysostom resumes his preaching with *hom. 16*. This was delivered on either the Saturday or Sunday, March 13 or 14.[1073] It is now the end of the second week of Lent. Sermons are preached on the following Monday (*hom. 9* = March 15) and Tuesday (*hom. 10* = March 16), coinciding with the arrival of the judges and further arrests.[1074] As a result of the legal proceedings John does not preach again till the following Monday (*hom. 11* = March 22).[1075] It is now the beginning of the fourth week of Lent. He proceeds to preach every day of this week, ending on the Sunday (*hom. 11-13* = Monday, March 22-Wednesday, March 24; a homily now lost = Thursday, March 25; *hom. 14* = Friday, March 26; *hom. 17-18* = Saturday and Sunday, March 27-28).[1076] There is then a gap of almost two weeks before Chrysostom preaches again on the Friday of the sixth week of Lent (*hom. 20* = April 9).[1077] A martyrial festival intervenes, after which he preaches on the following Monday (*hom. 19* = April 12).[1078] It is now the seventh week of Lent. The final homily in the series (*hom. 21*) was delivered on Easter Sunday, April 25.[1079] To the Wednesday of Holy Week, April 21, 387, van de Paverd assigns *Ad illuminandos cat. 2* (CPG 4464) which, he argues, is erroneously labelled a bap-

----

[1069] Montfaucon (see n. 195 and p. 84 above), followed by Baur (p. 210 above), had assigned the homily to the Sunday before Ascension on the basis of the title. For a more detailed discussion see van de Paverd, *Homilies on the Statues*, 233-240.

[1070] Van de Paverd, *Homilies on the Statues*, 293-297.

[1071] Van de Paverd, *Homilies on the Statues*, 297 and 316-317.

[1072] Van de Paverd, *Homilies on the Statues*, 297-315.

[1073] Van de Paverd, *Homilies on the Statues*, 317-324.

[1074] Van de Paverd, *Homilies on the Statues*, 341-345.

[1075] Van de Paverd, *Homilies on the Statues*, 332-333.

[1076] Van de Paverd, *Homilies on the Statues*, 328-333 and 348-357.

[1077] Van de Paverd, *Homilies on the Statues*, 254-255.

[1078] Van de Paverd, *Homilies on the Statues*, 254-255.

[1079] Since van de Paverd's interest lies with the other homilies in the series, this is explicitly stated only in the table on p. 364. For a discussion of the date on which Easter was celebrated at Antioch in 387 see van de Paverd, *Homilies on the Statues*, 360-361.

tismal instruction and is shown by the manuscripts to be a part of the series *De statuis*.[1080]

In addition, van de Paverd has occasion to discuss *Cat. 8* (CPG 4472) which, along with the other seven baptismal instructions edited by Wenger (CPG 4465-4471), was, he concludes, most probably delivered at Antioch in the year 391.[1081] This conclusion is reached by arguing that *De statuis hom. 19* and *Cat. 8* refer to the same occasion, that is, a specific martyrial festival during which a group of rural ascetic-priests assemble at Antioch; and that this two-day festival is fixed and, as a consequence of the newly determined date of *De statuis hom. 19*, can be located on April 10 and 11. Since, as Wenger had already demonstrated, *Cat. 7* (CPG 4471) was delivered on the Friday after Easter and, as its theme indicates, on one of the two days of that festival, and since *Cat. 8*, delivered on the Saturday after Easter, reflects back on this festival, Easter in the year in which the two catecheses were delivered fell on April 6. The only year during Chrysostom's presbyterate in which the various circumstances coincide is 391.[1082]

d. *Devos*

Further to the question of the baptismal instructions and acting in response to Piédagnel's edition of three of the catecheses (CPG 4460-4462),[1083] in 1991 Paul Devos produced an article discussing these and a fourth baptismal instruction (CPG 4463=4467).[1084] A new edition of the fourth homily had earlier been published in *Sources Chrétiennes*, where it appears as the third in a series of eight catecheses (CPG 4465-4472).[1085] It is found also associated with the above three catechetical instructions,

---

[1080] Van de Paverd, *Homilies on the Statues*, 227-230. This same thesis had been proposed some months earlier by Piédagnel (see p. 237 above).

[1081] Van de Paverd, *Homilies on the Statues*, 255-293. For Wenger's dating of this series see p. 233 above.

[1082] Van de Paverd, *Homilies on the Statues*, 290-291. This view has recently been challenged by Arthur Shippee in his review of R. Kaczynski's German translation of Chrysostom's baptismal catecheses (Freiburg 1992). Shippee, JECS 3 (1995) 73, draws an association between the staged animal hunts mentioned in *Cat. 1* (CPG 4465) and the κυνήγιον staged at Antioch by Argyrius, the preparations for which are recorded by Libanius in his correspondence of 390. Arguing that the preparations are unlikely to have stretched into 391 and that another hunting spectacle will not have been staged again for some years, Shippee points to the need for further investigation of this issue.

[1083] See p. 236 above.

[1084] Devos, "Quatre homélies baptismales".

[1085] See p. 232 above.

however, in a Russian manuscript.[1086] After lamenting the circumstance
that once more the four homilies have failed to appear together in the
one publication, Devos proceeds to attempt to date *Cat. 2* (CPG 4461)
and *3* (CPG 4462) more precisely. *Cat. 3* was, he determines, delivered
not on the Wednesday of Holy Week, as Piédagnel argues,[1087] but on the
vigil of Good Friday, i.e., Maundy Thursday. *Cat. 2* was delivered not
twenty days before Easter, as might be calculated from the statement
that the ten-day period for giving up the swearing of oaths allotted in *Cat.
1* (CPG 4460) has expired, but the day before *Cat. 3*, i.e., the Wednesday
of Holy Week. *Cat. 1* and the fourth instruction (CPG 4467) were, he concurs with Piédagnel and Wenger, delivered at Antioch thirty days before
Easter and on Easter morning respectively.[1088] Devos then attempts to
demonstrate once and for all that CPG 4467 was delivered immediately
following, and therefore forms a discreet series with, Piédagnel's three
catechetical homilies. Its location among the eight catecheses found in
Stav. 6 is, he argues, the result of a later development.[1089] If, he concludes, the year 388 proposed by both Wenger and Piédagnel for this
four-homily series is correct, the catecheses can be located on Friday,
March 10; Wednesday, April 5; Maundy Thursday, April 6; and Easter
Sunday, April 9, respectively.[1090]

e. *Zincone*

In an article preparatory to his edition of the two homilies *De prophetiarum obscuritate* (CPG 4420), which appeared in 1998,[1091] Zincone differs little from previous scholarship when it comes to assessing the
homilies' provenance and date. The same arguments are repeated without alteration in the introduction to his edition.[1092] The two were delivered at Antioch because in the second John speaks of the prayers of the
faithful on behalf of the bishop in a manner that indicates that he himself does not hold that position.[1093] Zincone similarly follows the consen-

---

[1086] For a discussion of this and the edition from this manuscript of CPG 4461-4462
and 4467 in 1909 by Athanasius Papadopoulos-Kerameus see Devos, "Quatre homélies
baptismales", 137-138.

[1087] See p. 237 above. This claim does not appear in the introduction to SC 366.

[1088] Devos, "Quatre homélies baptismales", 140-147.

[1089] Devos, "Quatre homélies baptismales", 147-149.

[1090] Devos, "Quatre homélies baptismales", 153.

[1091] Zincone, "Le omelie".

[1092] Zincone, *Omelie sull'oscurità*, 14-15.

[1093] Zincone, "Le omelie", 395. Cf. Tillemont (see p. 54 above) and Montfaucon (pp. 77
and 94 above).

sus when he argues that *De proph. obsc. hom. 1* was delivered a little be-fore *hom. 2*, and that *hom. 2* was delivered on a Sunday, as indicated by the opening to *De diabolo tent. hom. 1*.[1094] He adds, moreover, that the manuscript tradition is of interest in this respect since in many codices *De diabolo tent. hom. 1* immediately follows *De proph. obsc. hom. 2*.[1095] Regarding the date, however, he avoids going into a discussion of the place of the sequence *De proph. osbc. hom. 1, hom. 2, De diabolo tent. hom. 1* within Chrysostom's Antiochene oeuvre. Apart from stating that there are no decisive elements within the homilies which permit a pre-cise dating,[1096] he simply notes the divergent opinions of Tillemont and Baur in this instance,[1097] and adds an unsupported claim by Marguerite Harl that the homilies were delivered in 386.[1098]

5. OTHER

Since all attempts to group historical devlopments into patterns are in themselves artificial, there remain one or two items that do not fit neatly into the schema employed in this fourth section.

In an article of 1956, Antoine Wenger, noting the arrangement of cer-tain homilies in the Athonite codex Stav. 6, pointed out that not only does the manuscript support the inclusion of *Sermo 9 in Gen.* (CPG 4410) among the sequence of homilies *De mutatione nominum* (CPG 4372), but that it also points to an association between that group and the sermon *In illud: Si esurierit inimicus* (CPG 4375). On examining the contents of the latter homily and *De mutatione nom. hom. 4*, he concludes that there is clear internal evidence that the first was preached directly following the second and that this firmly locates *In illud: Si esurierit inimicus* at Antioch and not at Constantinople, as had previously been supposed.[1099]

This same opinion was reached independently by Robert Wilken. In a footnote to his book on Chrysostom's anti-Jewish rhetoric, he argues that there is nothing in the text of *In illud: Si esurierit* which supports a Con-stantinopolitan provenance. On the contrary, the references to people staying away from church, to the heat, the agora, the size of the church, the Jews, and John's use of the term ἄκαιρος (untimely) with respect to

---

[1094] Zincone, "Le omelie", 395-396.

[1095] Zincone, "Le omelie", 396.

[1096] Zincone, "Le omelie", 396.

[1097] Tillemont see pp. 53f above. Baur in fact makes no comment.

[1098] M. Harl, "Origène et les interprétations patristiques grecques de l"obscurité' bibli-que", VC 36 (1982) 336.

[1099] Wenger, "La tradition des oeuvres", 45.

Jewish observance of the law are all features which he considers characteristic of the Antiochene homilies.[1100]

In an article of 1961, Wenger made available for the first time the
Greek text of the homily *De regressu* (CPG 4394), previously known only
from a Latin translation, in the process finally establishing its authenticity. In the course of his introductory comments Wenger follows Baur in
assigning to 401 the journey to Ephesus, the return from which gave occasion to this sermon.[1101] The homily indicates that Chrysostom was absent from Constantinople during the Paschal festival that year and that
the absence itself lasted a little more than a hundred days.

6. SUMMARY

The sporadic nature of the investigations carried out during this
phase makes it difficult to obtain a perspective. Since in the later stages
of this phase the provenance of the homilies under consideration is
largely considered to have been definitively established, and since
throughout the phase as a whole only a small number of homilies is considered on any one occasion, a presentation from the viewpoint of either
location or date is not particularly meaningful. An attempt has been
made to overcome this difficulty in the form of the following table. The
information is presented according to the sequence in which the homilies appear in CPG. The opinion of Quasten, an overview of whose work
has been presented at the close of section 4.2, is not included.

Table 12. Overview of Phase Four

CPG no.	Place	Date	Proposed by
4317	A	day of ordination (386)	Malingrey
4318	A	386 (*hom. 1* - beginning of September)	Daniélou
4318	A	386 first Sunday in Sept. (*hom. 1*), end of Oct. (*hom. 2*), November-December (*hom. 3-5*)	Malingrey
4319	A	Dec. 20, 386	Malingrey
4320	A	January 387	"
4321	A	January 387	"
4322	A	Lazarus Sat./Paschal week, 387	"
4323	A	after Laz. Sat./Paschal week, 387	"

[1100] Wilken, *Chrysostom and the Jews*, 66 n. 1.

[1101] Wenger, "Homélie «à son retour»", 111. See earlier Wenger, *Huit catéchèses* (SC
50bis), 59. It has more recently been argued that the journey, and consequently the
homily, took place a year later, in 402. See Cameron (p. 241 above).

4324	CP	Feb. 28, 398	"
4325	CP	a little after Feb. 28, 398	"
4329 (3)	A	before Jan. 24 (see 4347)	Grillet-Guinot
4329 (4)	"	just after Jan. 24 (see 4347)	"
4330 (1)	A	Sunday, Feb. 21, 387	van de Paverd
4330 (2)	"	Saturday, Feb. 27, 387	"
4330 (3)	"	Sunday, Feb. 28, 387	"
4330 (4)	"	Monday, March 1, 387	"
4330 (5)	"	Tuesday, March 2, 387	"
4330 (6)	"	Wednesday, March 3, 387	"
4330 (7)	"	Thursday, March 4, 387	"
4330 (8)	"	Friday, March 5, 387	"
4330 (9)	"	Monday, March 15, 387	"
4330 (10)	"	Tuesday, March 16, 387	"
4330 (11)	"	Monday, March 22, 387	"
4330 (12)	"	Tuesday, March 23, 387	"
4330 (13)	"	Wednesday, March 24, 387	"
4330 (14)	"	Friday, March 26, 387	"
4330 (15)	"	Saturday, March 6, 387	"
4330 (16)	"	Sat./Sun., March 13/14, 387	"
4330 (17)	"	Saturday, March 27, 387	"
4330 (18)	"	Sunday, March 28, 387	"
4330 (19)	"	Monday, April 12, 387	"
4330 (20)	"	Friday, April 9, 387	"
4330 (21)	"	Easter Sunday, April 25, 387	"
4344	A	between 387 and 397	Piédagnel
4347	A	Jan. 24, year unknown	Grillet-Guinot
4350	A	Oct. 8, 386	Malingrey
4351	A	Oct. 17, 386	"
4375	A "		Wenger Wilken
4377	CP		Aubineau
4378	CP		"
4379	CP		"
4392	CP	August 399	Cameron
4393	CP "	late summer/autumn 400 late summer 400; c. April 400	Liebeschuetz Cameron
4394	CP "	post Easter 401; April 402	Wenger; Cameron
4396- 4397	CP	late September 403	Kelly
4398	CP (Eccl. apost.)	early October 403	Kelly
4399	CP (Magn. eccl.)	Sunday, early October 403	Kelly
4410.1-8	A	Lent 386	Brottier
4417 (1)	A	between early 395 and late 397	Dumortier
4417 (2-3)	A	late 386	"
4417 (4)	-	9th century (of spurious authenticity)	"
4417 (5-6)	A	late 386-early 387	"
4418	CP (S. Eirene)	unknown	Aubineau
4420	A		Zincone
4426	CP	late summer/early aut. 400-401 or 401	Cameron
4431	CP	Advent 403-Easter 404	Costanza

4436	CP	402	Nägele
4437	CP	402	"
4440	A	396-397	Opelt
4441.1	CP	400-early 402	Holum
	"	398	Aubineau
4441.2	CP	398	Aubineau
4441.5	CP	last months 398 or beg. of January 399	"
4441.6	CP	Jan. 17, 399	"
4441.7	CP	July 3, 399	"
4441.10	CP	July 17, 399	"
4441.12	CP (Magn. eccl.)	July 24, 399	"
4441.13	CP	Sunday, July 31, 399	Wenger
		July 31, 399	Aubineau
4460	A	388, Lent, following 4409 (11)	Wenger
	"	388	Piédagnel
	"	Friday, March 10, 388	Devos
4461	A	388	Wenger
	"	388	Piédagnel
	"	Wednesday (H.W.), April 5, 388	Devos
4462	A	Thursday (H.W.), 388	Wenger
	"	388	Piédagnel
	"	Thursday (H.W.), April 6, 388	Devos
4464	A	Wednesday (H.W.), April 21, 387	Piédagnel
	"	Wednesday (H.W.), April 21, 387	van de Paverd
4465	A	390?	Wenger
	"	391	van de Paverd
4466	A	390?	Wenger
	"	391	van de Paverd
4467	A	Easter eve, 388; Easter morn, 390?	Wenger
	"	391	van de Paverd
	"	Easter Sunday, April 9, 388	Devos
4468	A	Easter Sunday/Monday, 390?	Wenger
	"	391	van de Paverd
4469	A	Tuesday (Easter week), 390?	Wenger
	"	391	van de Paverd
4470	A	Wednesday (Easter week), 390?	Wenger
	"	391	van de Paverd
4471	A	Friday after Easter, 390?	Wenger
	"	Friday, April 11, 391	van de Paverd
4472	A	Saturday after Easter, 390?	Wenger
	"	Saturday, April 12, 391	van de Paverd
4528	CP	April 400	Cameron

Summary

At the beginning of Part One we asked whether the chronological and geographic distribution of the homilies currently being promoted is definitive, free from error and comprehensive. In short, has the case been closed? The answer to this must now be a resounding "no!".

Firstly, there is no single complete and consistent schema currently available. The work of Quasten, Baur, Bonsdorff and Lietzmann, not always precise, diverges in more than one detail. Individually not one of these authors covers every homily within the corpus and, even when consulted collectively, still fail to do so. Indeed, not since 1753 and the efforts of Stilting has the entire corpus been carefully and systematically investigated with respect to these issues.

Secondly, at almost no point in the history of the literature on these topics have the conclusions drawn been error-free. This is understandable, given the sheer number of homilies with which the scholars have been required to work and the complexity of their textual history. Nonetheless, while a single error in the work of a single scholar is unfortunate, the net effect is disturbing and casts serious doubt upon the results produced in each successive century.

Thirdly, a point which is of significance to the present investigation, the distribution of the homilies between the cities of Antioch and Constantinople has predominantly been determined by chronological concerns, with the perceived links between homilies (i.e., the place of a homily within a sequence or series) overwhelmingly being accorded precedence over internal evidence.

Also of note is the strength of the bias towards Antioch in the various distributions. In the cases of Montfaucon and Stilting in particular, the number of homilies assigned to Antioch, as opposed to Constantinople, is in the order of between 3.5:1 and 4:1 — significantly higher than the base ratio of 2:1, predicated on the number of years spent at each location. The question must be asked to what degree this bias reflects the real state of affairs — since political factors contributed to the interruption of John's preaching in Constantinople at certain points[1102] — or is a consequence of the assumptions brought to bear in analysing the provenance of the corpus. Factors which may have been of influence are the expectation of a sharp distinction between the role and duties of bishop and presbyter at this time; and the weight of detail available concerning life at Antioch in the late fourth century as a result of the writings of Libanius, as opposed to the relative paucity of evidence for Constantinople.

[1102] Regarding John's three to four month absence in Asia Minor dealing with ecclesiastical affairs see *De regressu* (CPG 4394), Wenger, "Homélie «à son retour»", 114 sec. 2 ll.3-4. Concerning the termination of his preaching duties some four months prior to his final exile see Liebeschuetz, "The Fall", 20; recently confirmed by Kelly, *Golden Mouth*, 243. In late 403, although the time between his departure for exile and his recall was of short duration, John spent an undefined period at a suburban estate negotiating the conditions of his return before finally agreeing to enter the city (Socr., HE 6.16 [GCS NF 1,339 3-8]; Soz., HE 8.18 [GCS NF 4,374 1-2]). The Gainas-led sedition in 400 seems also to have taken John away from his preaching duties for a time (*Cum Saturninus et Aurelianus* [CPG 4393] PG 52,413 2 a.i.-415 12).

A number of other concerns relate to the dominance exerted over the subsequent literature by certain points of view. In the most obvious case, the opinion of Montfaucon has enjoyed a greater degree of influence and been less subjected to criticism than it perhaps deserves, purely by virtue of its collocation with the most widely consulted text of the Chrysostomic corpus. The opinion of Stilting, on the other hand, has never been given adequate consideration. It is only on the rare occasion that his work is taken into account in the subsequent literature.[1103] In more recent times, Pargoire's efforts with respect to the chronology of the *Novae homiliae* (CPG 4441) have been deferred to as definitive, even though the constituent elements of his argument had yet to be subjected to critical evaluation.[1104] The work of Schwartz regarding the schema developed for the years 386-387 also raises concern, in that it casually dismisses the thesis of Usener, while drawing heavily upon the conclusions of Montfaucon. Lietzmann's subsequent uncritical promotion of Schwartz's view, over that of Rauschen, glosses over the true *status quaestionis* at the beginning of this century, particularly when he presents the case as closed. In fact, there has never been a satisfactory solution to this problem.

To sum up, then, the very least that the investigation of the literature just undertaken suggests is this: that at present any scholar who wishes to state the provenance or date of a particular homily of Chrysostom with any accuracy would be wise to review the literature carefully and methodically as far back as Montfaucon, and to weigh the merit of each scholar's conclusions for themselves.

To assist the reader who wishes to gain an overview of the major opinions detailed in this chapter, particularly for purposes of comparison, a synthesis of the views of Savile, Tillemont, Montfaucon, Stilting, Rauschen, Lietzmann, Bonsdorff, Baur and Quasten is provided on the following pages. Table 13.a outlines the view of those scholars with regard to the provenance of the homilies of Chrysostom, Table 13.b in respect of their chronology.

A third table (Table 14) presents an overview of the most significant opinion from Phase Three regarding the years 386-387. The views of Usener, Rauschen and Schwartz have been placed side by side in order to make it easier to observe the genuine divergence of opinion in light of the perceived consensus for these first two years. The table further illustrates the schemas available to Lietzmann, who remains the main modern reference for the chronology of these years. By comparing the schema which he offers with those presented in Table 14, it can be seen that he has essentially adopted Schwartz's view, with little real consideration of the other two.

[1103] With minor exceptions Martin (see n. 2) based his chronology on Stilting.

[1104] See now, however, Mayer, "Pargoire's sequence", where Pargoire's conclusions are challenged and a different sequence and chronology for the *Novae homiliae* proposed.

Table 13.a. Overview (Savile-Quasten) — Location

– = Unable to decide. A shaded box indicates that at the time the homily/series was not available.

CPG no.	SAVILE	TILLEMONT	MONTFAUCON	STILTING	RAUSCHEN	LIETZMANN	BONSDORFF	BAUR	QUASTEN
4317		A	A	A	A	A	A		A
4318		A	A	A	A	A	A	A	A
4319		A	A	A	A	A	A	A	CP
4320		A	A	A	A	A	A		CP
4321		A	A	A	A	A	A		CP
4322			A	A	A	A	A		CP
4323		A	A	A	A	A	A		CP
4324		CP	CP	CP	CP		CP	CP	CP
4325		CP	CP	CP	CP		CP		CP
4327	A	A	A	A	A	A	A	A	A
4328		A	A	A	A	A	A	A	A
4329	A^a	A^{f},_u	A	A	A	A	A	A	
4330	A	A	A	A	A	A	A	A	A
4332		A	A	A	A^p			A^c	A
4333	CP^b	A^n	A^f	A				A^i	
4334	A	A	A	A	A	A	A	A	A
4335		A	A	A	A	A	A	A	A
4336	CP^c	A^d,_c	A	A,^{d} CP^c	A^c		A	A^d	
4337			A	A	A			A	
4338		A	A	A				A^d	
4339			A	CP	A		A		
4340		A	A	A	A	A		A	
4341	A	A	A	A	A	A	A		
4342	A	A	A	A			A	A	
4343	A^d	A^d,_c	A^d	A^r				A	
4344	A	A	A	A	A	A			
4345		A	A	A	A	A		A	
4346		A	A	A	A	A		A	
4347	A	A	A	A	A	A	A	A	

CPG no.	SAVILE	TILLEMONT	MONTFAUCON	STILTING	RAUSCHEN	LIETZMANN	BONSDORFF	BAUR	QUASTEN
4349		A	A	A	A	A		A	
4350		A	A	A	A	A	A	A	
4351		A	A	A	A	A		A	
4352		A	A	A	A			A	
4353		A	A	A	A			A	
4354		A^m	A	A^m				A^m	
4355		A	A	A	A			A	
4356			A	A				A	
4357		A	A	A				A	
4358		A	A	A					
4359		A	A	A					
4360	A	A	A	A	A			A	
4361		A	A	A	A			A	
4362		A	A	A				A	
4363		CP	–	CP				CP	
4364		CP	CP	CP	A				
4365		–	–	–				A	
4366	A	CP	A	CP^r	A			A	
4367		–							
4368		A	A	A	A	A		A	
4369		–	A	CP					
4370		CP	CP	CP					
4371	A^e, Cp^d	A	A	A	A	A	A	A	A
4372		A	A	A	A	A	A	A	A
4373		–	–	–					
4374	CP	–	CP	CP					
4375		CP	CP	A, CP				A	
4376		–	A	A					
4377		CP	CP	CP					
4378		CP	CP	CP					
4379		CP	CP	CP					
4380		A	A	A	A				

CPG no.	SAVILE	TILLEMONT	MONTFAUCON	STILTING	RAUSCHEN	LIETZMANN	BONSDORFF	BAUR	QUASTEN
4381		–	–						
4382		A	A	A				A	
4383		A	A	A					
4384		–	–	A					
4385		A	A	A		A			
4386	A	A	A	A	A	A	A		
4387		–	–						
4388		A	A	–					
4389		–	–						
4390		–	–	A					
4391		A	A	A		CP	CP	CP	CP
4392		CP	CP	CP		CP			
4393		CP	CP	CP				CP	
4394		CP	CP	CP					CP
4396			CP	CP		CP			
4397			CP			CP			
4398			CP	CP		CP		CP	CP
4399			CP	CP		CP			A
4406		A	A	A	A				
4408		A							
4409	CP	A	A	A	A	A	A	A	A
4410	A^d	A	A	A	A	A	A	A^j	A
4411	A	A	A	A	A	A	A	A	A
4412		A	A	A	A	A	A		A°
4413	A	A,q A°	A	A	A	A		A^d	
4414	CP	CP	CP	CP					
4415		A	A^r	–					
4417	A^f	A^s, CP^b	A^h CP^b	A^h, CP^b,d	A^h CP^b,d	A^h	A^h	A^k	A + CP*
4418		CP^r	–						
4419		A	A	A	A				
4420		A	A	A					A
4423			A^r	A					

CPG no.	SAVILE	TILLEMONT	MONTFAUCON	STILTING	RAUSCHEN	LIETZMANN	BONSDORFF	BAUR	QUASTEN
4424	A#	A	A	A	A	A	A	A	A
4425		A	A	A	A	A	A	A	A
4426	CP	CP	CP	CP	CP	CP	CP	CP	CP
4427	A	–	A	A	CPq	A	A	A	A
4428	A		A	A	A	A	A	A	A
4429	CP	A	A	A	A	A	A	A	A
4431	CP	A, CPt	A	A	Aq	A	A	A, CPl	A
4432	CP	CP	CP	CP		CP	CP	CP	CP
4433	CP	CP	CP	CP		CP	CP	CP	CP
4434	CP, Ag	CP	CP	CP		CP	CP	CP	CP
4435	CP	CP	CP	A		CP	CP	A	A
4436	CP	CPr	Ar	A		A	A	A	A
4437	CP	CPr	Ar	A		A	A	A	A
4438	A	A	A	Ar	A	A	A	A	A
4439	CP	CPr	–	Ar		A	CP	CP	A
4440	CP	CP	CP	CP		A	CP		CP
4441.1			CP	CP		CP	CP	CP	
4441.2			CP	CP		CP	CP	CP	
4441.3			CP	CP		CP	CP	CP	
4441.4			CP	CP		CP	CP	CP	
4441.5			CP	CP		CP	CP	CP	
4441.6			CP	CP		CP	CP	CP	
4441.7			CP	CP		CP	CP	CP	CP
4441.8			CP	CP		CP	CP	CP	
4441.9			CP	CP		CP	CP	CP	
4441.10			CP	CP		CP	CP	CP	
4441.11			CP	A		CP	CP	CP	
4441.12			A	CP			CP		
4441.13			CP	A		CP	CP		
4460		A	A	A	A			A	A
4461									A
4462									A

4464+	A	A	A	A	A	A
4467						A
4528	CP	CP	CP	CP	CP	CP

a *hom. 6 only* b *hom. 4 only* c *hom. 2 only* d *hom. 1 only* e *hom. 1-3 only* f *hom. 1-5 only* g *hom. 8 only* h *hom. 2,3,5,6 only* i *hom. 5 only* j *At least hom. 1-8* k *hom. 1-4 only* l *hom. 9 only* m *hom. 1-2 only* n *hom. 1-8 only* o *Exp. in ps. 41 only* p *hom. 2-3 only* q *Probably* r *Possibly* s *hom. 1-3,6 only* t *hom. 13 only* u *hom. 7 only* # *If series accepted as homogeneous* * *Doesn't specify* + CPG 4465-4466 and 4468-4472 are excluded from consideration as they became available only at the close of the time period represented.

Table 13.b. Overview (Savile-Quasten) — Date

A shaded box indicates that at the time the homily/series was not available.

CPG no.	SAVILE	TILLEMONT	MONTFAUCON	STILTING	RAUSCHEN	LIETZMANN	BONSDORFF	BAUR	QUASTEN
4317		early 386	beginning 386	c. beginning 386	beginning 386	beginning 386	386		beginning 386
4318		c. September - 386	386	August 386,° November-December 386y	end Aug./beg. Sept. - before Dec. 20 386	autumn 386- c. February 387	autumn 386	386	386-387
4319		Dec. 20 386	Dec. 20 386	Dec. 20 386	Dec. 20, 386	autumn 386- c. February 387	autumn 386	Dec. 20	397
4320		Jan. 3 387	Jan. 5 387	February 387	Jan. 1 387	autumn 386- c. February 387	before Lent 387		397
4321		Jan. 4 387	Jan. 6 387	February 387	Jan. 2 387	autumn 386- c. February 387	before Lent 387		397

CPG no.	SAVILE	TILLEMONT	MONTFAUCON	STILTING	RAUSCHEN	LIETZMANN	BONSDORFF	BAUR	QUASTEN
4322			early 387	February 387	after Jan.6- before end Jan. 387	autumn 386- c. February 387	before Lent 387		397
4323		latter half 387	early 387	after mid-Feb. (before Lent) 387	after Jan.6- before end Jan. 387	autumn 386- c. February 387	before Lent 387		397
4324		after Feb. 26 398	398	after Feb. 26 398			398		397
4325		after Feb. 26 398	398	after Feb. 26 398			398		397
4327		c. mid Sept.- 386,[e] before Lent 387,[f] c. mid Sept.- 387[g]	c. late August- September 386,[k] second half 387[g]	c. late Aug.- Sept. 386,[e] late Feb./early March 387,[f] Sept.-c. mid Oct. 387[g]	early - mid Sept. 386,[v] Jan. 387,[f] late Aug.-mid Sept. 387[r]	autumn 386,[e] Jan.31 387,[f] autumn 387[g]	autumn 386,[e] pre Lent 387,[f] autumn 387[g]	386,[k] autumn 387[g]	386-387
4328		Jan. 1 387	Jan. 1	Jan. 1 387	Jan. 1 388 or later	388 (most prob.)/ 393	Jan. 1 388	Jan. 1 388	Jan. 1
4329		Jan. 2-before Lent 387aa	Jan. 2 -[w]	Jan. 2 - Feb. (before Lent) 387	Jan. 2 - 388 or later	388 (most prob.) or 393	Jan. 2-before Jan. 24 388;[k] post Feb.4 388[r]	388	
4330		before Lent - April 25 (Easter) 387	before Lent - Easter 387, Sunday before Ascen. 387[n]	early March - April 25 (Easter) 387	Jan. 24-March 21 (Easter),[l,m] Sunday before Ascen.[n] 387	Lent 387	Lent 387	Lent 387,[l] April 25 387,[m] before Ascen. 387[n]	- Easter 387

CPG no.	SAVILE	TILLEMONT	MONTFAUCON	STILTING	RAUSCHEN	LIETZMANN	BONSDORFF	BAUR	QUASTEN
4332		Lent 388		Lent 386					
4333		Feb. 24-after March 19 396g	395 or later[x]	386[u,x,s]					
4334		Dec. 25 386	Dec. 25 386	Dec. 25 386	Dec. 25 386	Dec. 25 386	Dec. 25 386	Dec.25 386, Dec.25 388	Dec. 25 386
4335		Jan. 6 387	Jan. 6 387	Jan. 6 387	Jan. 6 387	Jan. 6 387	Jan. 6 387	Jan. 6 387	Jan. 6 387
4336	401[b]	Maundy Thursday 395°	Maundy Thursday 388[b,s]		Maundy Thurs. 388-396[b]		March 29 (Maundy Thurs.) 389s	388°	
4337		March 26 (Good Friday) 392	March 26 (Good Friday) 392		April 4 (Good Friday) 391				
4338		Good Friday 395	Good Friday year unknown					388	
4339			Good Friday year unknown		Good Friday 388-396		March 30 (Good Friday) 389s		
4340		latter half 387	early 387	February 387	after Jan.6 - before end Jan. 387	387		Easter 388	
4341		March 27 (Easter Sunday) 395	Easter Sunday 388s	April 9 (Easter Sunday) 388	Easter Sunday 388-396		April 1 (Easter Sunday) 389		
4342		Ascension 392							

CPG no.	SAVILE	TILLEMONT	MONTFAUCON	STILTING	RAUSCHEN	LIETZMANN	BONSDORFF	BAUR	QUASTEN
4343									
4344						Dec. 28 387/ 392j			
4345		c. end of May or later 386	after May 386; or early 387	May 386	end of May 386	387		before Lent 387	
4346		Jan. 7 387	Jan. 7 387	Jan. 7 387	Jan. 7 387	Jan. 7 387		Jan. 7 (year unspec.)	
4347		Jan. 24 387	Jan. 24	Jan. 24 387	Jan. 24 388 or later	Jan. 24 388	Jan. 24 388	Jan. 24 388	
4349		Jan. 25 387		late Janurary 387	Feb. 4 388 or later	388 (most prob.)/ 393	Feb. 4 388	early January 388	
4350		Jan. 9			Oct. 8	Oct. 8 386		Oct. 8 386	
4351		Dec. 20	Dec. 20		Oct. 17	Oct. 17 386		Oct. 17 386	
4352				c. 386-388					
4353				c. 386-388	Nov. 18			Nov. 18	
4354		Aug. 1-2e		c. 386-388e				Aug. 1e	
4355		Apr. 14 392	Apr. 14 392		Apr. 20 391			Apr. 20	
4356			Apr. 15					Apr. 20	

CPG no.	SAVILE	TILLEMONT	MONTFAUCON	STILTING	RAUSCHEN	LIETZMANN	BONSDORFF	BAUR	QUASTEN
4357									
4358									
4359									
4360		June 21			March 16s			Dec. 26	
4361					Aug. 14s			May 31	
4362								March 22	
4363									
4364			end of 403 / beginning of 404s	398 or 399					
4365					Friday after Pentecost				
4366				398z					
4367									
4368		after Pent. 387	prior to Sunday before Ascen. 387	c. end of July 387	before Pentecost 387	387		Ascen. - Pent. 387	
4369			late 386 / early 387s	398					

CPG no.	SAVILE	TILLEMONT	MONTFAUCON	STILTING	RAUSCHEN	LIETZMANN	BONSDORFF	BAUR	QUASTEN
4370		398	398	Lent 398					
4371		after Easter 395	after Easter 388s	April 16-before Pent. 388	after Easter 388-396		April 5-15 389	388	paschal period 388
4372		after Easter 395	after Easter 388s	mid Pent.-after Pent. 388	after Easter 388-396		April 21-May 13 389	388	paschal period 388
4373									
4374				398					
4375				summer 387; 398-403					
4376				after Sept./Oct. 388s					
4377									
4378									
4379									
4380					Aug. 15s				
4381									

CPG no.	SAVILE	TILLEMONT	MONTFAUCON	STILTING	RAUSCHEN	LIETZMANN	BONSDORFF	BAUR	QUASTEN
4382				Oct. 387 - before Lent 388					
4383				Oct. 387 - before Lent 388					
4384				Oct. 387 - before Lent 388					
4385		Dec. 26/27 386	after Dec. 25 386	Dec. 26-31 386		386			
4386		before Lent 387		February 387	after Feb. 4 388 or later	388 (most prob.)/ 393	after Feb. 4 388		
4387									
4388									
4389				December 386					
4390				December 386					
4391				c. 386-388					
4392		399	c. August 399	January 399		399	c. Aug. 17 399	August 399	Jan. 17 399
4393		400, 403	early 400	after July 399		2nd half 400			
4394		c. end of April 401	after Easter 401	summer-late summer 400				post April 14 401	
4396			403	c. September 403		after 400 - before end 403			403

CPG no.	SAVILE	TILLEMONT	MONTFAUCON	STILTING	RAUSCHEN	LIETZMANN	BONSDORFF	BAUR	QUASTEN
4397						after 400 - before end 403			
4398			403	403		after 400 - before end 403			
4399			403	403		after 400 - before end 403			403
4406		392			before 393				392
4408									
4409	399c & 401d	Feb. 6-end Lent 395,c after Pent. 395d	388s	Feb. 26- April 5 388	Lent,c week 3 of Easter -d 388-396		Lent 389,c after Pent. 389d	Lent 388,c after Pent. 388d	388
4410		Lent (Feb. 16-) 386,h after Easter 395t	early Lent 386,h 388t.s	Lent 386,h mid-Pent.- Pent. 388t	Lent 386,h after Easter 388-396t	Lent (Feb. 16-) 386h	Lent 386,h April 29 389t	Lent 386p	Lent 386
4411		c. May - June 20 (Sunday after Pent.) 387	Monday before Ascen. - after Pent. 387	May - June 20 (Sunday after Pent.) 387	before - just after Pentecost 387	387	c. Pentecost 387	immed. after Pentecost 387	387
4412		after Pent. 387	387	late July-early August 387	2nd half (after Pent.) 387	387	after Pentecost 387		387
4413		October? 387i	after Sept. 387i	c. 394/5-397, after mid-Oct. 387i	391 or later, after Sept.13 387i	387i			387i
4414		402,o after exile 403b	c. 400b	July or later 399					

CPG no.	SAVILE	TILLEMONT	MONTFAUCON	STILTING	RAUSCHEN	LIETZMANN	BONSDORFF	BAUR	QUASTEN
4415		Holy week c. 396							
4417		c. 396°, before Lent 386a,b,f	395 or later°, before Lent 388u,s	Feb. (before Lent) 386u	before Lent 388-396u		before Lent 389u	388q	
4418									
4419				c. 386-388					
4420		388		Lent 386					386
4423									
4424		c. 391 or later	388 & 390	late 389/early 390 - late 390/early 391	391 or later	after 388- before Nov. 20 393	390	390 ?	390
4425		394z	between 391 and 394/395	late 388/early 389 - 2nd half 389	391 or later		391	391	c. 391
4426		after Easter 400	after Easter 400 - 401	after Easter 401 - early 402		401	shortly after July 12 400 - first few weeks 401	400	400
4427			after 388	391			after Easter 392		
4428				c. 392	391 or later		autumn-winter 392-393		

CPG no.	SAVILE	TILLEMONT	MONTFAUCON	STILTING	RAUSCHEN	LIETZMANN	BONSDORFF	BAUR	QUASTEN
4429				c. 392	391 or later		first half 393		
4431		before 392, poss. after 388		c. 393	395 or later[s]		396/397	397	
4432		after 400		393/394			spring/early summer 399		
4433		latter months 399	399	late 398 - first few months 399		summer 399	autumn 399	autumn 399	399
4434				400			after Easter 402		
4435		a little before first exile[s]		400			after Easter 402		
4436				c. 394 - 397			394	397	
4437				c. 394 - 397			394	397	
4438					391 or later			397	
4439							after Easter 402		
4440	403-404	c. 403-404	not long before his death	402		403/404	2nd half 402 - 1st half 403		403/404
4441.1			398 - before Aug. 399	398 or 399		late 398 - early 399	398		
4441.2			398 - before Aug. 399	398 or 399		late 398 - early 399	398		
4441.3			398	Feb. 399		late 398 - early 399	mid September 399		

CPG no.	SAVILE	TILLEMONT	MONTFAUCON	STILTING	RAUSCHEN	LIETZMANN	BONSDORFF	BAUR	QUASTEN
4441.4			398 - before Aug. 399	early 399		late 398 - early 399	398/399		
4441.5			398 - before Aug. 399	early 399		late 398 - early 399	398/399		
4441.6			Jan. 17 399	399z		late 398 - early 399	Jan. 19 399		
4441.7			Easter 399; c. June 399	April 10 (Easter) 399		April 10 (Easter) 399	July 3 399	April 10 399, July 3 399	July 3 399
4441.8			Paschal week 399	before Easter or a bit after 399		late 398 - early 399	398/399		
4441.9			Paschal week 399	Pasch - Pent. 399		late 398 - early 399	398/399	paschal period 399	
4441.10			second Sunday after Easter 399	Pasch - Pent. 399		late 398 - early 399	July 17 399		
4441.11			398 - before August 399	399		late 398 - early 399	(c. July?) 399		
4441.12			not 386 or 387	February 387			July 24 399		
4441.13			feast of the Maccabees 398/399	399		late 398 - early 399	July 31 399		
4460		Lent 388	week 3 of Lent 387	early week 2 of Lent (late March) 387	Lent 388/later				Lent 388
4461									Lent 388

4462						Lent 388
4464+	Lent 388					Lent 388
4467		Lent 387s	early April 387	Lent 388/389		Lent 388; shortly after 388
4528	399	c. August 399	January 399	399	mid August 399	a few days after Jan. 17 399

a hom. 6 only b hom. 2 only c hom. 1-32 only d hom. 33-67 only e hom. 1-2 only f hom. 3 only g hom. 4-8 only h hom. 1-8 only i Ps. 41 only j One of the seven only, identity unknown k hom. 1-3 only l hom. 1-18,20 only m hom. 21 only n hom. 19 only o hom. 1 only p At least hom. 1-8, exact no. unspecified q hom. 1-4 only r hom. 4-7 only s Probably t sermo 9 only u hom. 2,3,5,6 only v hom. 1,2,8 only w conc. 1-5,7 x hom. 4 only y hom. 2-5 only z Possibly aa hom. 1-5 only + CPG 4465-4466 and 4468-4472 are excluded from consideration as they became available only at the close of the time period represented.

Table 14. The first years at Antioch — Usener, Rauschen and Schwartz

Year (month-season)	USENER	RAUSCHEN	SCHWARTZ
386			
beginning		Sermo cum presbyter (CPG 4317)	Sermo cum presbyter (CPG 4317)
Feb. 16			Sermo 1 in Genesim (CPG 4410)
day before Lent	Sermo 1 in Genesim (CPG 4410)		
Lent	Sermones 2-8 in Genesim	Sermones 2-8 in Genesim	Sermones 2-8 in Genesim
end of May		De s. Meletio (CPG 4345)	
date unspecified			De incompr. dei natura hom. 1 (CPG 4318)
end August / beg. September	De incompr. dei nat. hom. 1 (CPG 4318)		

Year (month-season)	USENER	RAUSCHEN	SCHWARTZ
Sept. 2			Adv. Iudaeos or. 1 (CPG 4327)
early September		Adv. Iudaeos or. 1 (CPG 4327)	
Sept. 13			Adv. Iudaeos or. 2
mid September		Adv. Iudaeos or. 2	
shortly after Sept. 19		Adv. Iudaeos or. 8	
Oct. 8			De s. Pelagia (CPG 4350)
Oct. 17			In s. Ignatium (CPG 4351)
c. late Sept.–before Dec. 20		De incompr. dei natura hom. 2-4 De anathemate (CPG 3430) De incompr. dei natura hom. 5	
(Oct. 17 - Dec. 20)			De incompr. dei natura hom. 2-5 De profectu evangelii (CPG 4385)
Dec. 20		De beato Philogonio (CPG 4319)	De beato Philogonio (CPG 4319)
Dec. 25		In diem natalem (CPG 4334)	In diem natalem (CPG 4334)
387			
Jan. 1		De consubstantiali (CPG 4320)	
Jan. 2		De petitione matris fil. Zeb. (CPG 4321)	
Jan. 6		De baptismo Christi (CPG 4335)	De baptismo Christi (CPG 4335)
Jan. 7		In s. Lucianum (CPG 4346)	In s. Lucianum (CPG 4346)
Jan. 16			De consubstantiali (CPG 4320)
Jan. 17			De petitione matris fil. Zeb. (CPG 4321)
387 after Jan. 6 – before end Jan.		Adv. Iudaeos or. 3 (CPG 4327) In quatriduanum Lazarum (CPG 4322) De Christi precibus (CPG 4323) De resurrectione mortuorum (CPG 4340)	

Year (month-season)	USENER	RAUSCHEN	SCHWARTZ
Jan. 24	Adv. Iudaeos or. 3 (CPG 4327)		
Jan. 31			Adv. Iudaeos or. 3
February			In quatrid. Lazarum (CPG 4322) De resurr. mortuorum (CPG 4340) De Christi precibus (CPG 4323) De s. Meletio (CPG 4345) De statuis hom. 1-2 (CPG 4330)
March 7			De statuis hom. 3
Jan. 24 - March 21		De statuis hom. 1-18, 20-21 (CPG 4330)	
date unspecified			Remainder of CPG 4330
Sunday before Ascension		De statuis hom. 19	
before Pentecost		De decem mill. talent. deb. (CPG 4368) De Anna sermones 1-4 (CPG 4411)	
after Pentecost		De Anna sermo 5	
Aug. 15	De incompr. dei nat. hom. 1 (CPG 4318)		
Aug. 22	Adv. Iudaeos or. 1		
c. Aug. 29		Adv. Iudaeos or. 4 (CPG 4327)	
Sept. 4	Adv. Iudaeos or. 2		
Sept. 7		Adv. Iudaeos or. 5	
Sept. 8		Adv. Iudaeos or. 6	
Sept. 11	Adv. Iudaeos or. 8		
Sept. 8-13		Adv. Iudaeos or. 7	
after Sept. 13		Expositio in ps. 41 (CPG 4413.2)	

Year (month-season)	USENER	RAUSCHEN	SCHWARTZ
autumn			Adv. Iudaeos or. 4-7; Expositio in ps. 41 (CPG 4413.2); Adv. Iudaeos or. 8
date unspecified		De Davide et Saule hom. 1-3 (CPG 4412)	
388			
Jan. 6	De baptismo Christi (CPG 4335)		
Jan. 7	In s. Lucianum (CPG 4346)		
Sept. 28-30	Adv. Iudaeos or. 5-6		
Oct. 1	Adv. Iudaeos or. 7		
Dec. 20	De beato Philogonio (CPG 4319)		
Dec. 25	In diem natalem (CPG 4334)		
389			
Sept. 2	Adv. Iudaeos or. 4		

PART TWO

THE CRITERIA ON THE BASIS OF WHICH HOMILIES HAVE BEEN ASSIGNED TO ANTIOCH OR CONSTANTINOPLE

CHAPTER TWO

THE CRITERIA

With the issue of chronology placed to one side for the remainder of the investigation, the next step is to see whether the individual criteria used to distribute the homilies between the two cities are sound, justifying the faith that has been placed in them, or whether some are in fact suspect, bringing into question the conclusions that have been drawn on the basis of them.

As observed at the close of Chapter One, the predominant mechanism for distributing the homilies between the two cities has been determining that a sermon constitutes part of a sequence or series in which at least one of the homilies contains evidence of the point of origin. In this approach, chronological factors dictate the global application of evidence contained in a single homily or a small number of homilies. The argument from context — sequence X/series Y stems from A because in homily Z, delivered with certainty at A, the homilist makes reference to material treated in sequence X/series Y[1] — is simply a broader application of this same criterion. Once this is recognised, it can be seen that the criteria used to determine provenance separate into two main types — those that originate from purely chronological concerns, and those that relate to issues of location proper. For instance, the assertion that the series on Hebrews belongs to Constantinople because of its post-mortem publication from stenographic notes is an example in which provenance is determined on strictly chronological grounds; the identification of famous people and events or natural disasters can impinge upon both categories;[2] while in the case of monks who are situated on mountains provenance is determined strictly with reference to location.

The second group of criteria itself falls into two main classes: those that are specific and irrefutable, such as a comment by the homilist as-

---

[1] See, e.g., the argument promoted by Tillemont (Chapter One, p. 61) and others with respect to the series on John (CPG 4424).

[2] So, e.g., in the case of Philippians (CPG 4432) the identification of the emperor mentioned in *In Phil. hom. 15* has generally dictated the location to which the series has been assigned; whereas any reference to the burning of the temple of Apollo at Daphne is considered to localise a homily or series to Antioch.

sociating certain events in the book of Acts with the current location; and, by far the majority, those that are in essence conjectural but have acquired a strong aura of certainty through repetition. Some from this second category, such as the Photian stylistic criterion, are now transparently invalid, although their inadequacies have, of course, not always been so obvious. It is this second group of criteria — those that relate to location, not chronology — with which Part Two is primarily concerned and which forms the basis of the remainder of this investigation.[3]

Before we can assess the soundness or otherwise of these criteria, they must first be brought under some sort of control. In this chapter the criteria are sorted and grouped according to the type of evidence adduced and any underlying assumptions made explicit. The resultant categories and subcategories are then summarised in the form of a table, allowing the resultant labels for each type of criterion to be used in the following chapters as a means of referring to the different criteria in brief. When assembled, the criteria can be seen to fall into nine main categories.

1. MANUSCRIPT TITLES

In addition to criteria based on internal data, arguments for the place of delivery of certain homilies have been based on the information contained in the titles appended to those homilies in the manuscripts. The type of detail to be found divides into four classes: the identification of topographic features (e.g., "the martyrium at Romanesia", "the Church of the Apostles"); indication of the status of the homilist; the mention of famous people and/or events; and reference to the manner in which the original homily/series has been transmitted.[4] Detail derived from this source has been of special importance for localising homilies which do not belong to an exegetical series, most notably with respect to Constantinople.

The detail afforded by titles which identify topographic features ranges from the explicit,[5] to the more common naming of a church or

---

[3] It is to be stressed that throughout Part Two all previous suppositions regarding the sequentiality of homilies or the homogeneity of series are scrupulously ignored. Investigation is undertaken strictly on a case-by-case basis.

[4] Such information falls squarely within the range of criteria predicated on the basis of internal evidence. Cf. sections 2.e (order of preaching), 2.f.iii (transmission history), 3.e.i (topography — churches) and 9 (famous people and events) below.

[5] Identification of the city, as in the title to *In illud: Ne timueritis hom. 2* (CPG 4414) PG 55,511-512: ...ὁμιλία λεχθεῖσα ἐν Κωνσταντινουπόλει ἐν τῇ ἐκκλησίᾳ τῇ μεγάλῃ..., is rare. Cf. the title to *De statuis hom. 1* (CPG 4330): Ὁμιλία λεχθεῖσα ἐν Ἀντιοχείᾳ, πρεσβυτέρου

district, whose location must then be inferred.[6] Evidence of the status of the homilist is not infrequently found in conjunction with this first class of information.[7] The third category of data, reference in the title to a famous person or event, is rarely explicitly mentioned in the literature, the focus of such elements being considered so patent as to obviate the need for discussion.[8] The final type of evidence, detail concerning the manner in which the original homily/series has been transmitted, occurs only in the case of the collection of thirty-four homilies on Hebrews (CPG 4440).[9] The information that the series was published only after Chrysostom's death and from stenographic notes has led to the assumption that it was the last work to have been undertaken and that it therefore derives from Constantinople.

2. PERSONAL STATUS

The argument from the status of the homilist is simple: the career of Chrysostom divides neatly between the cities of Antioch and Constantinople; for the duration of his presbyterate he was situated at Antioch, for the duration of his episcopate, at Constantinople. The two are mutually exclusive. Therefore, if it can be determined that the homilist is of pres-

---

αὐτοῦ ὑπάρχοντος, ἐν τῇ παλαιᾷ ἐκκλησίᾳ... (PG 49,15-16), where the strength of the connection drawn on internal grounds between this homily and the remainder of the series *De statuis* has made it unnecessary to call upon this information.

[6] So, e.g., in the titles to *In princ. Act. hom. 2* (CPG 4371): Συνάξεως διὰ χρόνου ἐν τῇ παλαιᾷ ἐκκλησίᾳ γενομένης... (PG 51,77-78); *In ascensionem* (CPG 4342): ...ἐλέχθη δὲ ἐν τῷ μαρτυρίῳ τῆς Ῥωμανησίας... (PG 50,441-442); and the majority of the *Novae homiliae* (CPG 4441.1-6,8-12,14-15).

[7] So, e.g., in the fuller version of the title to *In illud Isaiae: Ego Dominus Deus feci lumen* (CPG 4418): ...ἐν τῇ ἐκκλησίᾳ τῇ ἐπὶ εἰρήνην, ἑτέρου προειπόντος ὀλίγα... See Aubineau, "Restitution", 534. Cf. *In illud: Ne timueritis hom. 2*, where the portion of the title cited above (n. 5) is prefaced by the words "after another had spoken first" (προειρηκότος ἑτέρου); *In illud: Filius ex se nihil facit* (CPG 4441.12) PG 56,247-248; and the title to *In illud: In faciem ei restiti* (CPG 4391), which provides evidence of Chrysostom's status of a different kind: Τῇ προτέρᾳ συνάξει ἐν τῇ ἐκκλησίᾳ τῇ καινῇ συναχθεὶς μετὰ τοῦ ἐπισκόπου, ταύτην ἐν τῇ παλαιᾷ εἶπεν... (PG 51,371-372). See, however, the title to *De Eleazaro et septem pueris* (CPG 4441.13): ...ὁμιλία λεχθεῖσα, ἑτέρου προειρηκότος σφόδρα πρεσβύτου... (PG 63,523-524), where such detail is the only useful information supplied.

[8] Such is the case with the homilies *De statuis* (CPG 4330) and the cluster of homilies delivered in response to specific events at Constantinople (CPG 4392-4399, 4528). Cf. also *Quales ducendae sint uxores* (CPG 4379), where the mention of Maximus in the title has had some influence on the determination of Chrysostom's status, and *Laus Diodori* (CPG 4406), where it has uniformly been assumed, not unreasonably, that the Bishop Diodore of the title has been visiting Antioch.

[9] PG 63,9-10: Εἰς τὴν πρὸς Ἑβραίους Ἐπιστολήν, ἐκτεθεῖσα ἀπὸ σημείων μετὰ τὴν κοίμησιν αὐτοῦ, παρὰ Κωνσταντίνου πρεσβυτέρου Ἀντιοχείας.

byteral or at least non-episcopal status, the homily must have been delivered at Antioch. Conversely, if it can be shown that he is of episcopal rank, the homily must automatically stem from Constantinople.

Over the centuries several means of distinguishing the homilist's status have been proposed. Aside from the rare direct comment, mention by the homilist that he is seated upon a θρόνος (throne) or is a figure of authority has been taken as an indication that he is of episcopal rank. Information that another person has preached before him at the same synaxis has also been seen in this light. Conversely, mention that another individual is due to preach after him or that another person is bishop have both been taken as indication of the homilist's non-episcopal and therefore presbyteral status. Arguments based on the relative duties and time constraints of the office of bishop and presbyter have also been introduced.

a. Direct evidence

Under the category of direct evidence three aspects present themselves. The first is a clear statement by the homilist of his status, employing the terms ἐπίσκοπος (bishop) or πρεσβύτερος (presbyter); the second is mention of bishops or presbyters, where the homilist alludes to his inclusion amongst the former or latter group; and the third is where the homilist has the opportunity to indicate that he is a bishop but fails to do so.

While no definite statement of his presbyteral status on the part of Chrysostom has so far been found, two instances have been elicited in which John openly asserts that he is bishop. In *In Acta apost. hom. 9* (CPG 4426) the homilist anticipates the audience's objection that he is "archon and bishop",[10] while in *In Col. hom. 3* (CPG 4433) he evokes the term in order to stress the distinction between the office-holder (himself) and the office.[11] The weight of this evidence has been such that in the case of the series on Acts several scholars have considered it unnecessary to probe any further.[12]

When Chrysostom is not explicit but alludes to his status, the interpretation to be drawn from the statement is not always clear and is usually subject to confirmation by other evidence. An instance in which he appears to number himself among the presbyters (*Cat. ultima ad bapti-*

---

[10] PG 60,84 27-28: 'Αλλὰ σύ, φησίν, ἄρχων εἶ καὶ ἐπίσκοπος.

[11] PG 62,324 46-49: Εἰ δὲ πρόσαντες ὑμῖν τοῦτο, οὐχ ἡμεῖς, ἀλλ' αὕτη ἡ ἐπισκοπή· οὐχὶ ὁ δεῖνα, ἀλλ' ὁ ἐπίσκοπος. Μηδεὶς ἐμοῦ ἀκουέτω, ἀλλὰ τοῦ ἀξιώματος.

[12] See Montfaucon (Chapter One, p. 97) and Lietzmann (p. 169).

zandos: CPG 4462),[13] has been supported by the argument that the homilist speaks in a manner inappropriate to a bishop, while in the same homily it is indicated that another person occupies the episcopal office.[14] By contrast, in the context of the series on Titus (CPG 4438), it is argued that the apparent inclusion by Chrysostom of himself among the bishops who are criticised in *In Titum hom. 1* is purely rhetorical, since evidence in *hom. 3*, indicative of an Antiochene provenance, is of greater weight.[15]

The claim that the homilist must by default be presbyter when he fails to mention in the course of discussion of the episcopal office and its duties that he is himself bishop, has generally been used in support of the Antiochene provenance of certain of the series which are lacking in more concrete evidence. It is argued that in these series John refers to bishops and other leaders in an impersonal way.[16]

b. *Occupation of throne*

On a practical level, the criterion based on the occupation of a throne is derived entirely from *In Col. hom. 3* where two separate statements by John, that he occupies a throne and that he is bishop, are found in the course of the one homily.[17] Therefore, it is reasoned, when the homilist indicates elsewhere that he occupies such a seat, it is to be presumed that he is the supreme figure of authority. As an argument it has been adduced only rarely, usually in conjunction with other evidence.[18]

---

[13] SC 366,240 17-21: Δεήθητε ... ὑπὲρ τοῦ ἀρχιερέως δι᾽ οὗ τῶν χειρῶν καὶ τῆς φωνῆς τῶν ἀγαθῶν τούτων τυγχάνετε. Ὑπὲρ τῶν συνεδρευόντων ἡμῖν ἱερέων...

[14] See Piédagnel (Chapter One, p. 237). Regarding the latter two criteria see further pp. 283 and 284 below.

[15] See, e.g., Montfaucon (Chapter One, p. 101). Stilting, *Acta SS. Sept.*, IV 496 is less cautious in his rejection.

[16] See, e.g., Montfaucon (Chapter One, p. 100) regarding the series on I and II Timothy, and Bonsdorff (p. 183) with respect to *In II Cor. hom. 14-15.*

[17] PG 62,324 13-18 and 46-49. In this context, the equation of occuption of the θρόνος with προεδρία (ll.16-17) is also of significance.

[18] See Savile (Chapter One, p. 39) concerning *In Col. hom. 3* itself and Bonsdorff (p. 192) with respect to *In Acta apost. hom. 8* (PG 60,74 21-26), where the association of the term "archon" with "thronos" is considered significant. Cf. *In Acta apost. hom. 9* (PG 60,84 27-28).

c. *Relationship with audience*

Various aspects of the relationship perceived to exist between the homilist and his audience have been evoked in the course of determining whether Chrysostom is of presbyteral or episcopal status. Metaphors used of himself by the homilist which denote leadership have been considered a firm indication that he is of the rank of bishop. In a similar vein, when John states that he has authority (*prostasia*) or bears full responsibility for the salvation of his audience, this has likewise been considered proof of his episcopal status. Finally, when Chrysostom speaks in a manner which is authoritative or fails to do so, this has been thought to be an effective means of identifying whether he is bishop or presbyter.

i. Metaphoric

The assumption which underpins the first of the three criteria based on the homilist's relationship with his audience derives its authority from the metaphors which Chrysostom uses when referring to a priest who is of higher status than himself (see 2.d.i below). Certain of the metaphors which the homilist uses when referring to another cleric, it is argued, indicate that that person is of episcopal rank. Therefore, when these same expressions are applied by John to himself, this must indicate that he is himself of the status of bishop. Of the metaphors commonly used by the homilist, the terms "father" and "shepherd" have been found particularly persuasive.[19] On an analogy with these expressions, which denote a headship or authority over the audience associated with a responsibility for care, the argument has been extended by Bonsdorff to include comments denoting a maternal relationship to the audience[20] and an indication by Chrysostom that he stands as "head" in relation to the audience as "body".[21]

ii. Prostasia

From metaphoric expressions denoting leadership or parental care the argument moves to explicit statement by Chrysostom that he pos-

---

[19] Regarding the term "father" see, e.g., Montfaucon (Chapter One, pp. 99, 101) with respect to *In Phil. hom. 9* and *In Heb. hom. 23*. For "shepherd" see, e.g., Tillemont (p. 64) concerning *In illud: Ne timueritis hom. 1* (CPG 4414) and Rauschen (p. 143) with regard to *In Rom. hom. 29*.

[20] See Chapter One, pp. 192 and 196 with regard to *In Acta apost. hom. 11* (PG 60,98 60-61) and *In II Thess. hom. 4* (PG 62,492 36-41).

[21] See Chapter One, p. 195 with respect to *In I Thess. hom. 5* (PG 62,427 25-27).

sesses authority (προστασία). This is assumed to exclude the possibility that he is presbyter.[22] Comments that he is an archon (ἄρχων),[23] president (προεστώς),[24] or leader (ἡγούμενος)[25] and terms that indicate that he is of some rank (ἀξίωμα), has power (αὐθεντία)[26] or is alone in his status[27] have also been seen in this light. Conversely, the statement that he has no ἀρχή has been interpreted as excluding the possibility that he is bishop.[28]

iii. Responsibility

A further aspect of the argument based on the homilist's status as indicated by the nature of his relationship with his audience rests on the concept of responsibility. The presumption here is that responsibility is attached to authority and that authority indicates episcopal status. Therefore, it is argued, when John states that he is responsible or accountable for the welfare of the audience, he must be bishop and situated at Constantinople.[29]

iv. Episcopal tone

The argument from episcopal tone posits that only a bishop would have the authority to threaten the audience with excommunication or to speak on certain subject matters. Therefore, when Chrysostom speaks in an authoritative manner or tone, the possibility that he is presbyter is excluded and the homily in which this occurs is assigned to Constantinople.[30]

---

[22] See, e.g., Savile and Bonsdorff (Chapter One, pp. 40 and 195) with respect to In I Thess. hom. 11.

[23] See, e.g., Bonsdorff (Chapter One, p. 192) regarding In Acta apost. hom. 3 and 8.

[24] See Savile (Chapter One, p. 39) with respect to In Col. hom. 3.

[25] See, e.g., Savile and Tillemont (Chapter One, pp. 40 and 65) concerning In II Thess. hom. 4 (PG 62,490 5-7).

[26] For adduction of this and the previous term see Bonsdorff (Chapter One, p. 191) regarding In Col. hom. 8.

[27] In Heb. hom. 30: ἐγὼ μὲν εἷς εἰμι (PG 63,211 10). See Bonsdorff (Chapter One, p. 198).

[28] See Lietzmann (Chapter One, p. 168) with regard to In Eph. hom. 11.

[29] See, e.g., Bonsdorff (Chapter One, pp. 192 and 196) regarding In Acta apost. hom. 11, 18, 24, 27 and 30 and In II Thess. hom. 4.

[30] See, e.g., Tillemont and Bonsdorff (Chapter One, pp. 65 and 191) with respect to In Col. hom. 7, and Bonsdorff (p. 198) concerning In Heb. hom. 4. With regard to In II Tim. hom. 4 Nägele (see p. 217) argues for episcopal status on the basis of subject matter (the unworthiness of those in episcopal office).

The inverse of this argument is presbyteral tone. Adduced less commonly in the literature, this covers comments or modes of speaking considered inappropriate to a bishop. If a bishop speaks with authority, a presbyter speaks in a manner which demonstrates humility or greater familiarity, that is, in a manner appropriate to a person of lesser status. This thesis has been introduced in more recent times to account for the provenance of the two series of baptismal catecheses.[31]

d. *Indication that another is of higher ecclesiastical status*

The argument which informs the criterion associated with an indication that another person is higher ranked than the homilist is quite simple. Since the highest ranking person is always the local bishop, if Chrysostom indicates in a sermon that another person is of higher rank than himself, he cannot have been the local bishop at that time. As Constantinople is therefore excluded, this leads one to infer that he is a presbyter at Antioch. Failure to indicate that another person is bishop in an instance where this might be expected, on the other hand, has been taken as an indication that he is himself bishop and therefore preaching at Constantinople.

Figures of higher status who have been elicited in the literature include the local bishop (Flavian), visiting bishops (*proedroi*) and more senior presbyters ("the common fathers").

i. Bishop

A selection of the metaphors which the homilist uses of another person have been understood to refer to the local bishop and therefore to Flavian, the incumbent at Antioch at the time of Chrysostom's presbyterate.[32] The terms which have been interpreted in this manner include: "another Peter",[33] "father",[34] "teacher",[35] "the high priest" (ὁ ἀρχιερεύς),[36] and

---

[31] See Wenger (Chapter One, p. 232) with regard to CPG 4465-4472 and Piédagnel (p. 237) concerning CPG 4460-4462.

[32] In some instances, interpretation has been influenced by Chrysostom's statement that the individual in question is about to preach next. See further p. 286 below.

[33] See, e.g., Savile and Bonsdorff (Chapter One, pp. 42 and 174) with respect to *In princ. Act. hom. 2* (CPG 4371): Ἀλλ' ἐπειδὴ Πέτρου ἐμνήσθην, εἰσῆλθέ μοι καὶ ἑτέρου Πέτρου μνήμη, τοῦ κοινοῦ πατρός, καὶ διδασκάλου... (PG 51,86 45-47).

[34] See, e.g., *De Anna sermo 1* (CPG 4411): Καὶ γὰρ ἐλθόντος τοῦ πατρὸς ἀπὸ τῆς μακρᾶς ἀποδημίας... (PG 54,634 9-10), adduced by Savile (Chapter One, p. 41).

[35] See, e.g., *De s. pentecoste hom. 1* (CPG 4343): τῷ κοινῷ τούτῳ πατρὶ καὶ διδασκάλῳ (PG 50,458 47-48), adduced by Savile (see p. 42 above) and *De Macabeis hom. 2* (CPG 4354):

"shepherd".[37] These are found employed by the homilist either on their own, in conjunction with the adjectives κοινός or αὐτός, or in various combinations. Although the connection is not made explicit, Bonsdorff's assertion that *In I Cor. hom. 36* demonstrates its Antiochene provenance because in this homily Chrysostom indicates that another person is "president of the assembly" (προεστώς),[38] can be considered to constitute a further example. By the time of Baur, the association between such terms and Flavian is so strong that that scholar feels it necessary to make fine distinction between a reference on the part of the homilist to "Father and Teacher" (Flavian) and to mere "teacher" (a presbyter).[39]

The argument is taken to its opposite extreme by Tillemont, who claims that the absence of any reference to another as bishop on the part of Chrysostom, when he describes in *De terrae motu* (CPG 4366) the litanies celebrated at the time of an earthquake, indicates that that homily was delivered at Constantinople.[40]

ii. Proedroi

By definition, the term πρόεδρος implies that the person to whom it refers is of high standing in the local community.[41] Thus, it is argued, when John requests the prayers of the *proedroi* on his own or his audience's behalf, he cannot himself be preeminent,[42] with the result that a Constantinopolitan provenance is excluded.[43] Bonsdorff, regarding a similar appearance of the term in *De mutatione nom. hom. 1-2* (CPG 4372), speculates that the persons referred to are visiting Syrian bishops.[44] For Tillemont's part, the conviction that the term refers specifically

---

Ἀλλ' ὥρα λοιπὸν καταπαῦσαι τὸν λόγον, ὥστε πλειόνων αὐτοὺς ἀπολαῦσαι τῶν ἐγκωμίων παρὰ τῷ κοινῷ διδασκάλῳ (PG 50,626 20-22), where the "teacher" is commonly understood to be Flavian. For adduction of this latter example see, e.g., Tillemont and Montfaucon (Chapter One, pp. 58 and 81).

[36] See, e.g., *Cat. ultima ad baptizandos* (CPG 4462): Δεήθητε ... ὑπὲρ τοῦ ἀρχιερέως... (SC 366,240 17-18), adduced by Piédagnel (Chapter One, p. 237).

[37] See *In Rom. hom. 8*: ὁρᾷς πάντας ἡμᾶς ... ὑπὸ τῷ αὐτῷ ποιμένι κοινῇ βοῶντας... (PG 60,464 42-45), adduced by Tillemont and Montfaucon (Chapter One, pp. 61 and 98) among others.

[38] Bonsdorff, *Zur Predigttätigkeit*, 40.

[39] See Baur, *Chrysostom and His Time*, I 394.

[40] See Chapter One, p. 63.

[41] LSJ s.v. πρόεδρος. In non-ecclesiastical circles this term commonly refers to persons of the status of city councillor or a presiding officer of the βουλή or ἐκκλησία.

[42] Cf. LSJ s.v. προεδρία.

[43] See Tillemont (Chapter One, p. 59) with respect to *In d. Pauli: Nolo vos ignorare* (CPG 4380).

[44] Bonsdorff, *Zur Predigttätigkeit*, 13 n. 2.

to bishops was so strong that, in the case of the first of those same two homilies, it led him to assert that some of these "bishops" were due to preach afterwards at the same synaxis.[45]

iii. "The common fathers"

Montfaucon, noting that in *In illud: Salutate Priscillam et Aquilam hom. 2* (CPG 4376) Chrysostom refers to "the common fathers" in the context of criticism of the local clergy, and assuming this to indicate persons of greater seniority, speculated that the so-called "common fathers" are to be identified as the senior presbyters at Antioch.[46]

e. *Order of preaching*

The argument from the order in which John preaches is also simple. On certain occasions more than one homily was preached at a synaxis. It is a long-established liturgical dictum that on such occasions, regardless of the number of presbyters or visiting bishops who also spoke, it was the bishop of highest status who preached last.[47] Since at Antioch Flavian is the only person who qualifies, while at Constantinople the candidate is Chrysostom himself, when the homilist indicates that another person is yet to preach, he cannot be the highest ranking cleric present and must therefore be situated at Antioch.[48] Conversely, when the homilist or the title indicates that someone else has preached beforehand, this must signify that Chrysostom is bishop and that the sermon was therefore delivered at Constantinople.[49]

This rationale appears also to have been of influence in cases where a person has preached not before or after Chrysostom, but has substituted for him at the preceding synaxis. There is a general presumption that if *locum tenens* and homilist are of equal status, then both must be bishops and the homilist situated at Constantinople.[50] Support for this conclusion

---

[45] See Chapter One, pp. 56f.

[46] See Chapter One, p. 85.

[47] See Bingham, *Antiquities*, XIV.iv.6; and Olivar, *La predicación*, 554-560. For a statement of this principle in the literature itself see Baur, *Chrysostom and His Time*, I 394 and Aubineau, "Restitution", 533.

[48] See, e.g., Tillemont (Chapter One, pp. 49 and 57) on *In illud: Vidi dom. hom. 2* (CPG 4417) and *De paen. hom. 5* (CPG 4333).

[49] See, e.g., Montfaucon (Chapter One, p. 92) on *In illud: Ne timueritis hom. 2* (CPG 4414) and Aubineau (p. 244) regarding *In illud: Filius ex se nihil facit* (CPG 4441.12).

[50] See Stilting, *Acta SS. Sept.*, IV 560, regarding *Quales ducendae sint uxores* (CPG 4379).

is drawn from the title to *In illud: Pater meus usque modo operatur* (CPG 4441.10).[51]

f. *Duties of office*

Distinctions in the nature and volume of the work attached to the offices of bishop and presbyter have been thought to provide an effective means of determining the provenance of series which contain little other useful evidence. Even though the arguments developed to deal with these cases have been applied to series as a whole, in contradiction to the present investigation, which adopts a case-by-case approach as its basis, it is important to review this group of criteria in order to gain a full perspective of the issue of provenance.

The areas considered to have been affected by Chrysostom's change in status from presbyter to bishop are frequency of preaching and level of output (workload), preparation time (style) and the level of personal involvement at the stage of publication (transmission).

i. Workload

The assumption which informs all three subcategories of the criterion based on the homilist's perceived workload proceeds as follows. As presbyter, Chrysostom had greater leisure in which to prepare and polish work for publication. This resulted in more frequent preaching and greater output. As bishop, he was much pre-occupied with affairs of state and with wider church affairs. This led to reduced productivity and less frequent preaching.

The first implication of this assumption is that, given the 2:1 ratio in the number of years spent at Antioch versus Constantinople, one would expect a vastly reduced number of homilies to have been produced at Constantinople. This expectation is clearly reflected in the literature.[52] A second inference to be drawn is that the larger of the series, since they involve considerable time in the preparation and in the delivery, must be excluded from Constantinople.[53] On this basis, the series on Genesis (CPG 4409), Psalms (CPG 4413) and John (CPG 4425) have commonly

---

[51] PG 63,511: ...λυπήσας αὐτούς, εἶτα τῇ συνάξει τῇ μετ᾽ ἐκείνην τὴν κυριακὴν παραχωρήσας εἰπεῖν ἐπισκόπῳ ἀπὸ Γαλατίας ἀφιγμένῳ, καὶ σιγήσας...

[52] Cf. Tables 1.a (p. 45), 2.a (p. 66), 3.a (p. 103), 4.a (p. 128), 9.a (p. 199), 10.a (p. 203) and 11.a (p. 228).

[53] This assertion was first put forward by Photius, *Bibl.* 172-174 (119a-b) = Henry, II (1960) 170, with respect to the larger of the two series on Genesis (CPG 4409).

been located at Antioch.[54] As an extension of both inferences, it has been the practice that where a homily or series contains no identifying features, that homily or series is assigned to Antioch by default.[55] Finally, there is at least one instance in which a homily has been directly assigned to this city on the assumption that as presbyter John's main focus and occupation was preaching.[56]

ii. Style

In an extension of the argument from workload, Photius claimed that the responsibilities attached to the episcopal office interfered with the amount of time which Chrysostom was able to devote to the preparation of his homilies. The homiletic series which are most elegant and polished, he concluded, were therefore delivered at Antioch, while those which are less smooth and finished originate from Constantinople.[57] As observed in Chapter One, this criterion enjoyed considerable popularity in the early stages of investigation. The enthusiasm with which it was embraced led to it being applied to a broad range of series. However, by the time of Montfaucon its influence was beginning to wane with the recognition that the conclusion drawn on this basis could as often as not be contradicted from a careful sifting of the internal evidence. For Montfaucon's own part the criterion is not discarded, but is accorded less weight, with its value seen to be in confirming provenance rather than actively determining it. As a consequence, it is invoked largely in the context of Constantinopolitan series (Acts, Colossians, I and II Thessalonians), in order to explain the poor quality of the homilies or the fact that they appear to be extemporaneous or less polished.[58] While use of the criterion to establish provenance effectively ceases with Tillemont, traces of its secondary role persist in the case of the fifty-five homilies on Acts, where it is still invoked to explain "the uncharacteristically disorganised and unpolished nature of the text".[59]

---

[54] See, for instance, Montfaucon (Chapter One, p. 92) with regard to the series on Psalms.

[55] See, e.g., Stilting, *Acta SS. Sept.*, IV 505, with respect to *De ss. martyribus* (CPG 4365); and, in particular, Baur, *Chrysostom and His Time*, I 299-300. Stilting (see Chapter One, p. 123) assigned the series on II Timothy to Antioch on the grounds that there is ample space for its delivery in the latter years at Antioch, whereas at Constantinople Chrysostom was too preoccupied.

[56] See Tillemont (Chapter One, p. 57) with regard to *De paen. hom. 1* (CPG 4333).

[57] For the full statement of this proposition see Photius, *Bibl.* 172-174 (119a-119b) = Henry, II (1960) 169-170.

[58] See Montfaucon, IX *Praef.*, v and XI 424.

[59] Devine, "Manuscripts", 112.

iii. Transmission history

In a further extension of the argument based on the workload which Chrysostom took on as bishop, it is assumed that at Antioch the homilist personally reviewed all texts prior to publication, but that due to the pressing nature of other commitments this was not always the case at Constantinople. In particular, where there is evidence that a series was published directly from stenographic notes, there is an automatic presumption that it stems from Constantinople.[60] In recent times this argument has also been introduced to account for the homilist's lack of involvement in the writing of the titles to certain of the Constantinopolitan homilies.[61]

3. THE CITY

In addition to evidence contained in manuscript titles and distinction drawn on the basis of the presumed status of the homilist, characteristics considered unique to the one city or the other have provided a major means of distinguishing the homilies delivered at each location. Aside from the rare explicit comment, criteria of several different kinds have been adduced. For instance, the role played by Antioch in the missionary activity of the apostles is such that, where such events are mentioned, the Antiochene origin of the homily is ensured. By contrast, since Constantinople was the site of imperial residence for the duration of Chrysostom's presbyteral as well as episcopal career, if the homily demonstrates familiarity with the emperor or his household a Constantinopolitan derivation is to be assumed. Arguments from the relative peculiarities of the cities' topography, both Christian and secular, have also been introduced.

a. *Direct evidence*

In the literature only a single instance in which Chrysostom explicitly states that he is preaching at Antioch has been elicited. This occurs in *In*

---

[60] See, e.g., Montfaucon, Stilting and Quasten (Chapter One, pp. 101f, 127 and 225) with regard to the series on Hebrews. Savile, VIII 3-4, adduces this evidence in support of the Constantinopolitan provenance of the larger of the two series on Genesis (CPG 4409). Devine, "Manuscripts", 112, proposes that this was also the case with the series on Acts.

[61] See Cameron, "A misidentified homily", 35-36, with respect to CPG 4392-4399 and 4528.

I Cor. hom. 21.[62] The force of the statement is such that it has effectively closed discussion regarding the provenance of this series.

b. *Linked to apostolic times*

Antioch's history as a Christian community is of such long standing that it receives explicit mention at several places in the New Testament, most particularly within the Acts of the Apostles. The Christian community at Constantinople, on the other hand, is of far more recent derivation. Thus when on occasion John cites events from the apostolic period which are associated with the city of Antioch, this has been taken as definitive proof that the homily is of Antiochene derivation.

Five different facets of this association have been evoked in the literature.

i. "The first city to be honoured with the name 'Christian'"

In Acts 11.26 it is stated that, because of the resounding success of Barnabas and Paul's missionary activity there, the disciples at Antioch were the first to be identified as "Christians". Several instances where Chrysostom directly associates this honour with the present location have been elicited. In one such case the city of Antioch is mentioned explicitly.[63]

ii. Source of humanitarian aid during famine

Acts 11.28-30 records that, on hearing prediction of a wide-spread famine, the community at Antioch organised a collection, the proceeds of which were sent to Jerusalem courtesy of Paul and Barnabas. As noted by Montfaucon,[64] the audience is reminded of this event from their city's past in the course of the homily *De eleemosyna* (CPG 4382).[65]

---

[62] PG 61,178 40-41: καὶ ταῦτα ἐν Ἀντιοχείᾳ...

[63] *In Matt. hom.* 7: πρώτη ἡ πόλις ἡμῶν τὸ τῶν Χριστιανῶν ἀνεδήσατο ὄνομα· (PG 57,81 23-24); *In princ. Act. hom.* 2: Ἐν γὰρ καὶ τοῦτο πλεονέκτημα τῆς ἡμετέρας πόλεως ... Ἔδει γὰρ τὴν πρὸ τῆς οἰκουμένης ἁπάσης τὸ τῶν Χριστιανῶν ἀναδησαμένην ὄνομα ... (PG 51,86 49-52); *In I Cor. hom. 21*: καὶ ταῦτα ἐν Ἀντιοχείᾳ, ἐν ᾗ πρῶτον ἐχρημάτισαν Χριστιανοί ... (PG 61,178 40-42).

[64] See Chapter One, p. 86.

[65] PG 51,270 11-18: Καὶ γὰρ ποτε λιμοῦ μέλλοντος εἰς τὴν γῆν ἐμβαλεῖν ἅπασαν, οἱ τὴν πόλιν ταύτην οἰκοῦντες τοῖς ἐν Ἱεροσολύμοις καθημένοις, αὐτοῖς δὲ τούτοις, περὶ ὧν ἡμῖν οὗτος ὁ λόγος ἅπας κεκίνηται, διὰ χειρὸς Βαρνάβα καὶ Σαύλου χρήματα ἔπεμψαν οὐκ ὀλίγα. Τίνος οὖν ἂν εἴημεν ἡμεῖς συγγνώμης ἄξιοι ... ὅταν οἱ μὲν πρόγονοι οἱ ἡμέτεροι...

iii. Site of disagreement between Peter and Paul

At Gal. 2.1-14 Paul talks of his various visits to Jerusalem and tells the Galatians of his confrontation with Peter at Antioch regarding the issue of table fellowship with gentile Christians. Certain events associated with the dispute, such as the visit by Paul to Jerusalem, as also the main elements of the debate, are outlined in Acts 15.1-35. As noted by Tillemont and Stilting,[66] in the homily *In illud: In faciem ei restiti* (CPG 4391) Gal. 2.11 is cited by the homilist and the confrontation to which it refers directly associated with the present location.[67]

iv. Peter as founder of church

At Acts 12.17 it is stated that, upon his release from prison, the apostle Peter departed Jerusalem for another place. When reconciled with Gal. 2.11-14, where Peter is found at Antioch, and with Acts 11.19-26, where the Hellenist dispersion from Jerusalem to Antioch upon the stoning of Stephen is described, it is possible to construe that on leaving Jerusalem Peter made his way to Antioch, where he was responsible for establishing and leading its first Christian community. Whether the tradition that Peter founded the Antiochene church is rooted in historical fact or not,[68] in *In princ. Act. hom. 2* Chrysostom firmly states that it was fitting that "our city", the city first "honoured with the name Christian", should receive Peter, the head of the apostles, as its first teacher.[69]

v. Site where Paul was detained

It is clear from numerous passages in the book of Acts that the apostle Paul spent some considerable time among the Antiochene Christians. In *In Rom. hom. 30* (CPG 4327) the homilist poses the following question: "If after so long a period of time, when we enter the place where Paul stayed, where he was in chains, where he sat down and talked with oth-

---

[66] See Chapter One, p. 58 and Stilting, *Acta SS. Sept.*, IV 449.

[67] PG 51,373 29-374 20: Ὅτε γὰρ ἦλθε Πέτρος, φησίν, εἰς Ἀντιόχειαν, κατὰ πρόσωπον αὐτῷ ἀντέστην. Ἆρα οὖν οὐ θορυβεῖ ἕκαστον τῶν ἀκουόντων τοῦτο ... Ἀλλὰ καὶ τῆς πόλεως ὑμῶν ἐγκώμιον τὰ ῥηθησόμενα. Αὕτη γὰρ τὸν ἀγῶνα ἐδέξατο, αὕτη τὴν μάχην...

[68] O. Cullmann, *Peter. Disciple-Apostle-Martyr*, trans. F. V. Filson, London 1962², 49-54, rates this as possible, but improbable. However, he points out (p. 54) that this belief was espoused by a number of Fathers from the third and fourth centuries, including Origen, Jerome and Eusebius.

[69] See PG 51,86 45-53. Since the homily contains other, more compelling evidence, this criterion has only rarely been adduced. For examples see Savile (Chapter One, p. 42) and Bonsdorff (p. 174).

ers, we are uplifted and sent back by those places to the memory of that
day, what is it likely that those who generously offer hospitality to
strangers will feel when the events are still fresh?"[70] This has in the main
been understood to refer to places local to Antioch.[71]

c. *Site of imperial residence*

The movements of the Eastern emperors in the latter half of the
fourth century allow for a further distinction to be drawn between Constantinople and Antioch. The argument upon which this criterion is
based proceeds as follows. Valens is the last emperor known to have resided for any part of the year at Antioch. He ceased to do so in AD 378.[72]
Since Chrysostom's career as a preacher at Antioch began some years after this event (386), the only contact between himself and the imperial
household during his years of preaching must have occurred during his
sojourn at Constantinople. Thus, for instance, when a homily demonstrates familiarity with the emperor and the palace, it must have been
delivered at Constantinople. Conversely, comments of a general nature
are most likely to be found in homilies which stem from Antioch. More
frequent reference to the emperor and his court has also been considered
a feature typical of Constantinopolitan homilies.

Over the centuries several types of evidence of imperial residence or
the absence of it have been put forward. For the sake of convenience
these have been grouped into two categories — data which are concrete
and material pertaining to the emperor and palace life which is presented in the form of an exemplum.

i. Direct evidence

Only a single instance of the provenance of a homily being established
on the basis of a direct reference by Chrysostom to the emperor occurs in
the literature. With respect to *De s. Phoca* (CPG 4364), Montfaucon
pointed out that the personal involvement of the emperor in the stational
liturgy described placed the Constantinopolitan provenance of the hom-

---

[70] PG 60,666 22-27.

[71] See, e.g., Tillemont, Montfaucon, Stilting and Quasten (Chapter One, pp. 61, 98,
122, 224). See, however, Rauschen (p. 143), who argues that John could as easily be
referring to places at Jerusalem or Rome.

[72] See Petit, *Libanius*, 167; Dagron, *Naissance*, 78-85, esp. 84; Liebeschuetz, *Antioch*,
129.

ily beyond doubt.[73] In a different vein, Savile found proof of the same location in the homilist's characterisation of the city as "imperial" (βασιλευούσῃ) in *In Acta apost. hom. 8.*[74] Arguing from the negative, Tillemont claimed that *De futurae vitae deliciis* (CPG 4388) could not have been delivered at Constantinople on the grounds that the particular comparison between church and palace which is drawn in that homily would have been inappropriate at that location. Further, although in the same homily John talks of the cream of the city being present, no mention is made of the emperor.[75]

ii. Imperial exempla

Stilting presents an embryonic version of the argument based on imperial exempla when, concerning the provenance of the series *In Philemon* (CPG 4439), he says that he prefers to locate it at Antioch, since in the Constantinopolitan material Chrysostom often alludes to the emperor or the imperial court.[76] It is Bonsdorff, however, who formalises the argument and develops it into a more finely-tuned instrument. His most explicit statement of it occurs with respect to the series on Romans (CPG 4427). There he argues that, since no emperor made a personal visit to Antioch during the entire time of John's presbyterate, while for the course of his episcopate the emperor Arcadius mostly stayed in Constantinople, the homilist's knowledge of imperial affairs can only have been acquired during the latter period, through personal experience. On this basis, if the series in question had been delivered in the imperial capital, Chrysostom could scarcely have avoided betraying this fact when discussing matters pertaining to the emperor, empress or palace.[77] In

---

[73] See Chapter One, p. 83.

[74] See Chapter One, p. 39. However, no trace of this adjective is found in the text presented by Montfaucon (see PG 60,69-76). The considerable divergence between the "rough" and "smooth" texts of Chrysostom's homilies on Acts and the consequently large number of variant readings prohibits discussion of this point at present. One awaits the new critical edition of the text of Acts promised on the one hand by Francis Gignac, on the other by Albert Devine. See Devine, "Manuscripts", and Gignac, "The New Critical Edition of Chrysostom's *Homilies on Acts*: A Progress Report", in *Texte und Textkritik. Eine Aufsatzsammlung* (TU 133) Berlin 1987, 165-168; and id., "Evidence for Deliberate Scribal Revision in Chrysostom's *Homilies on the Acts of the Apostles*", in J. Petruccione (ed.), *Nova & Vetera. Patristic Studies in Honor of Thomas Patrick Halton*, Washington, DC 1998, 209-225.

[75] See Chapter One, p. 60.

[76] See Chapter One, p. 123.

[77] Bonsdorff, *Zur Predigttätigkeit*, 35. Reference to officials associated with the emperor and therefore situated at Constantinople also impinges upon this criterion. See further pp. 300-302 below.

other words, exempla centred upon imperial matters, which reveal "personal knowledge" of these affairs, demonstrate a homily's Constantinopolitan origins. Conversely, imperial exempla which fail to demonstrate such familiarity indicate that the homily which contains them belongs to the period of Chrysostom's presbyterate at Antioch. In addition to exempla which reveal personal knowledge, as opposed to those which are general in nature and lack such character, Bonsdorff adduces a second type of exemplum. In this second category it is the physical proximity to or geographic distance from the palace demonstrated by the exemplum that enables one to distinguish between homilies delivered at the one or the other location.[78]

The chief proponent of the criterion in either form is Bonsdorff, who used it as a means of arguing for or against Constantinopolitan provenance in regard to a number of the exegetical series.[79] Prior to that point in time, it had only occasionally been adduced. In a rare application of the criterion to a miscellaneous homily, Tillemont, Montfaucon and Stilting all argued that Chrysostom's comments concerning the imperial court in *In illud: Si esurierit inimicus* (CPG 4375) demonstrate that he is preaching in Constantinople.[80] Stilting reached the same conclusion with respect to the homilist's remarks about the emperor in *In Acta apost. hom. 11*.[81]

d. *Topography — general*

Certain features unique to the topography of one city or the other have led scholars to propose that where allusion or reference to one of these appears in a homily, this provides certain evidence of the homily's location. For instance, if it is apparent that the city is coastal, then Chrysostom must be preaching at Constantinople. If, on the other hand, the city has a suburb of some reputation, that suburb must be Daphne and the sermon was therefore delivered at Antioch.[82]

---

[78] See Bonsdorff, *Zur Predigttätigkeit*, 64-65. This point is not as clearly stated as the first.

[79] See Chapter One, pp. 180, 182-185, 187, 190, 192-196, and 198.

[80] See Chapter One, pp. 65, 85 and 118 n. 404.

[81] Stilting, *Acta SS. Sept.*, IV 557.

[82] The proximity of the city to mountains (the situation at Antioch) is a feature also noted in the literature. However, since this peculiarity is usually evoked in the context of the style of monasticism practised locally, treatment of it is reserved until sec. 6 below.

i. Coastal v. non-coastal

The fact that Constantinople is surrounded by water on three sides, while Antioch is situated on a river-plain some eighteen kilometers in-land, has given rise to two small and quite specific arguments. Tillemont, puzzling over the interrelationship of the six homilies *In illud: Vidi dominum* (CPG 4417), found it difficult to reconcile John's exhortation in *hom. 5*: "Don't you see this sea?" with a provenance of Antioch.[83] Al-though he never carries this thought to its logical conclusion, he clearly believed that for such a question to be addressed to the audience greater proximity to the sea was required than that enjoyed by the Syrian capital. The second instance in which an exclusively coastal situation is required is seen in the proposition put forward by Pargoire and later restated by Wenger.[84] In *De Eleazaro et septem pueris* (CPG 4441.13) the homilist an-ticipates the stational liturgy to be celebrated on the festival of the Mac-cabees the following day, describing the effort of reaching the site of sy-naxis as involving the traversal of a few stades (ὀλίγους σταδίους δια-περῶντες).[85] Pargoire argues that the verb διαπεράω implies the crossing of an open body of water, a situation which can only refer to Constantino-ple.

ii. Suburban environs

In at least two instances the suburb Daphne or certain of its more dis-tinctive features has provided the means for distinguishing homilies de-livered at Antioch. In the case of *In Titum hom. 3*, the mention of Daphne in conjunction with the cave of Matrona has been seen as a persuasive argument for that location.[86] The reference to events at Daphne in *In s. Iulianum* (CPG 4360) has likewise been considered convincing proof of the homily's provenance.[87]

e. *Topography — Christian*

Since they were delivered on the festivals of saints and martyrs, a number of homilies contain reference to liturgical movement within and

---

[83] Tillemont, *Mémoires*, XI 562.

[84] See Chapter One, pp. 161 and 243.

[85] PG 63,530 53-54.

[86] See, e.g., Savile, Tillemont, Montfaucon and Bonsdorff (Chapter One, pp. 39, 62f, 101, 186).

[87] See Montfaucon (Chapter One, p. 82).

around the city, and therefore to sites of significance to the local Christian community. Certain other homilies, for various reasons, contain similar information. Brought together, these references allow us to construct a spiritual map, superimposed upon the regular urban and suburban topography. Since the identity and location of churches and martyria are more or less unique to each city, such evidence has been considered a particularly effective means of determining a homily's location.

i. Churches

On the basis of manuscript titles and other evidence,[88] Baur and Eltester both assembled an overview of the churches and martyria they believed existed at Antioch in Chrysostom's day. The common picture which emerges is of a Great Church (the "cathedral" church, located on the island in the Orontes),[89] the Old Church (situated in the old district), the Church of St Babylas (a recent construction, sited across the river), a church or martyrium dedicated to the Maccabees (located in the Jewish quarter), a common martyrium (situated at the Romanesian Gate), and various martyria or memorial chapels (possibly in the cemetery beyond the gate which led to Daphne).[90] The basic elements of this understanding of the Christian topography of Antioch are implicit in much of the earlier literature. For Constantinople, Batiffol provides a general overview of the sites, supplemented at some points by Pargoire.[91] This is derived entirely from the contents of the *Novae homiliae* (CPG 4441) and their titles. The overall picture arrived at is as follows: within the city itself, the Great Church (the "cathedral" church), the Church of Eirene (the former episcopal church, situated close to the Great Church), the Church of the Apostles (the burial site of Constantine and repository of the remains of Sts Andrew, Luke and Timothy), the Church of St Paul (named after a former bishop and probable meeting place of an orthodox

---

[88] On reference to preaching places in manuscript titles see pp. 278f above.

[89] There is some doubt as to whether the distinction cathedral/non-cathedral is valid for the situation which pertained at Constantinople and Antioch in the late fourth century. In a private communication of Oct. 27, 1995, Frans van de Paverd expressed the view that at this period in larger cities where there existed more than one church it is likely that all churches were "cathedral" churches, in that every basilica contained a thronos. It is now his opinion (contra *Messliturgie*, 15 and 410-411) that use of the term with respect to these cities in the late fourth century should be avoided. See W. Mayer, "Cathedral Church or Cathedral Churches? The situation at Constantinople c.360-404 AD", OCP 66 (2000) 49-68, where it is argued that "episcopal church" may be a more useful label.

[90] See Baur (Chapter One, p. 214) and Eltester, "Die Kirchen Antiochias", esp. 285-286. Kelly, *Golden Mouth*, 2-3, mentions "a small church in the old town" used at the time by the Eustathians, which he appears to derive from Eltester, "Die Kirchen Antiochias", 285.

[91] See Chapter One, pp. 154-161.

congregation of Goths); beyond the walls, at least two churches or martyria, one dedicated to St Thomas;[92] across the Bosporus in Chalcedon, a
church dedicated to Sts Peter and Paul (used by the Constantinopolitans
for stational purposes); and across the Golden Horn, a church or martyrium dedicated to the Maccabees.

These details have in large part been gleaned from the manuscript titles, the very existence of such data in the title usually being considered
sufficient to secure the provenance of the homily concerned.[93] In addition to information derived in this way, two instances of internal evidence of the city's Christian topography have been adduced. Montfaucon, assuming that at Constantinople the episcopal residence was close
to the major churches, argued in the case of *De eleemosyna* (CPG 4382)
that the distance between John's point of residence and the church of synaxis excluded Constantinople.[94] Savile, with respect to *In II Cor. hom.
26*, interpreted the homilist as saying that the city in which he was located held the Church of the Apostles, the burial site of Constantine. This
led him to situate the series on II Corinthians (CPG 4429) at Constantinople.[95]

ii. Martyr burials

In addition to the more prominent religious sites, places made holy by
the burial of the remains of martyrs also played an important role in the
spiritual landscape. Since such sites had in the main developed naturally
at Antioch, but were artificially created at Constantinople, this has been
seen as another important means of distinguishing between the two locations. In the literature evidence relating to these has been applied in several different ways. Certain saints and martyrs bear a strong association
with Antioch, either as former clergy of the city or through their act of
martyrdom. When combined with the assumption that the veneration of
martyrs is at this point in its early stages, and that the geographic spread
of the cult of individual saints is still relatively contained,[96] this has led to
the automatic assignment to Antioch of homilies known to have been
preached on the festival of a local martyr. Montfaucon, for instance, lo-

[92] The church or shrine of St Acacius receives mention in the titles of the two unedited
Novae homiliae (CPG 4441.14-15).

[93] Thus Tillemont (see Chapter One, p. 55) and Montfaucon (p. 89), for instance, were
both convinced of the Antiochene provenance of an entire sequence as the result of a
reference to the Old Church in the title to *In princ. Act. hom. 2*.

[94] See Chapter One, p. 86.

[95] From Tillemont onwards this interpretation has been reversed. See further 3.f.ii, p.
299 below.

[96] See, e.g., Tillemont's argument regarding the cult of St Barlaam, p. 306 below.

cates the sermon *De s. Pelagia* (CPG 4350) there, not on the basis of any
internal evidence, but because Pelagia is known to have been martyred in
that city.[97] Seeck, relying on the localised state of the cult of martyrs at
that time, claims that the reference to Babylas in *In Acta apost. hom. 41*
argues for Antioch, since a Constantinopolitan audience would have had
little knowledge of a local Antiochene saint.[98]

A further distinction between the location of such sites at Antioch and
Constantinople has been raised, which admits of another means of applying this criterion. Although it is seldom stated, it is universally assumed that at the first location such sites were exclusively extra-urban.[99]
Since they existed there in large numbers, when Chrysostom describes a
situation which involves the customary visitation of such sites by the local populace, this is thought to indicate that the homily is of Antiochene
derivation. Both Tillemont and Montfaucon raised this point with respect
to *In s. Barlaam* (CPG 4361).[100] Repetition of this conviction in the literature has led to the belief that, when there is no distinctive evidence of location, a homily involving an extra-urban synaxis belongs by default to
Antioch.[101]

The lack of local martyrs and saints at Constantinople due to its short
history as a centre of Christianity, coupled with the knowledge that remains were imported in order to remedy this deficiancy, admit of another proposition.[102] Since the cult sites at Antioch exist as the result of a
natural process, while the translation of relics is characteristic of Constantinople, when a homily with little other means of distinguishing its
provenance refers to the second process, it must stem from Constantinople. This is the argument put forward by Tillemont with respect to *In
martyres Aegyptios* (CPG 4363).[103]

f. *Features*

Various physical aspects of Constantinople or Antioch have been considered distinctive of that city, providing another means of establishing
the place at which a homily was delivered. Arguments in the literature

---

[97] See Chapter One, pp. 80f.

[98] See Chapter One, p. 154.

[99] For a rare statement of the principle see Eltester, "Die Kirchen Antiochias", 271.

[100] See Chapter One, pp. 59 and 82.

[101] See, e.g., Montfaucon (Chapter One, p. 83) with respect to *De terrae motu* (CPG
4366) and id., II 667 regarding the provenance of *Hom. in martyres* (CPG 4359).

[102] The underlying principle is outlined by Eltester, "Die Kirchen Antiochias", 272.

[103] See Chapter One, p. 63.

have been based on the presence of features which are considered characteristic and upon the absence of such features or upon evidence that the city is not x, leading one to infer that it must therefore be y. For the sake of convenience, the latter two propositions have been grouped together under the category of features that are negative.

i. Characteristic

Only one instance of a feature which is characteristic of Constantinople has been adduced. Savile, commenting on *In Acta apost. hom. 42*, points out that the city is described as "large" (μεγάλη), an adjective which Bonsdorff considered more than applicable to the imperial capital.[104] As for Antioch, Montfaucon found the comment that the city is adorned with suburbs (*De paenitentia hom. 3*: CPG 4333) persuasive of such a provenance.[105] Wilken, arguing for the Antiochene provenance of *In illud: Si esurierit* (CPG 4375), more or less employs this criterion when he claims that references to heat, the agora and the size of the church in which the homilist is preaching are all characteristic of the Antiochene homilies.[106]

ii. Negative

As for the negative side of the argument, Stilting took the opposite tack to Montfaucon with respect to the last mentioned homily (*De paen. hom. 3*), arguing that it must have been delivered at Antioch since, if the homilist had been preaching at Constantinople, he would have adduced features such as the senate as the city's distinguishing marks.[107] The argument that the location must be y, because x is excluded, is a more direct statement of this approach. The clearest example of this reasoning is the assertion by Tillemont and others, in contradiction of Savile, that in the case of *In II Cor. hom. 26* John is speaking from Antioch, since he discusses Constantinople in a way that indicates that he is not there.[108]

---

[104] PG 60,302 34-35: ἰδοὺ ἡλίκη πόλις ἡμῖν ἐστιν ἡ μεγάλη αὕτη. See Chapter One, pp. 39 and 193.

[105] See Chapter One, p. 77. Meyer, *Jean Chrysostome*, XXVIII, was in part convinced of the Antiochene provenance of *In illud: Vidi dom. hom. 4* (CPG 4417) by mention of the city's colonnades.

[106] See Chapter One, p. 249.

[107] See Stilting, *Acta SS. Sept.*, IV 502-503.

[108] See Chapter One, p. 61; also Lietzmann (p. 168), Bonsdorff (p. 182) and Quasten (p. 224).

Bonsdorff in the same way excludes Antioch in order to confirm the Constantinopolitan provenance of Acts (CPG 4426).[109]

g. *Status*

In several instances the status of the city has been adduced as a means of distinguishing location. In general, this criterion has been applied with the intent of proving that a homily stems from Constantinople. Thus in the case of *In Acta apost. hom. 8* Savile found the adjective "imperial" (βασιλευούση) persuasive of such a provenance, while for Bonsdorff it was the fact that the city is held up as an example for the rest of the world.[110] That the city is comparable to Rome, in that it contains the senate and consuls, was sufficient to persuade Montfaucon of the Constantinopolitan provenance of *In illud: Vidi dom. hom. 4*,[111] although the mention of its colonnades and metropolitan status led Meyer to infer that Chrysostom was preaching at Antioch.[112] Taking a slightly different approach with respect to *In Col. hom. 9*, Bonsdorff argues that the description of the present urban Christian community as the head and the rural communities as its body is an image better suited to the imperial capital.[113]

h. *Administration*

As a complement to the criterion used to establish whether the city is the seat of the emperor and his household,[114] the type of administrative officials mentioned by the homilist has been seen as an indirect means of determining the city's status, through assessing the form of government which operates locally. If it can be shown that an official belongs to the echelon which functions in direct association with the emperor or is known to form part of his court, the location must be Constantinople. If, on the other hand, the panoply of state is based around archons, with no suggestion that the emperor is directly involved, the mechanisms are those of a provincial government and the location therefore Antioch. The

---

[109] See Chapter One, p. 193.

[110] See Chapter One, pp. 39 and 193.

[111] See Chapter One, p. 93.

[112] See n. 105 above.

[113] See Chapter One, p. 191.

[114] See p. 292 above.

presence or otherwise of a military detachment is a feature which has also been considered important.

i. Officials directly associated with emperor

Since some aspect relating to the emperor or palace not uncommonly receives mention in the course of a passage in which such officials are named, the line between exempla of this type and those that indicate imperial residence is less distinct than in the case of officials of other kinds (3.h.ii below). Thus Bonsdorff suggested that, although the exemplum of the relationship between the emperor and the *hyparch* adduced in *In Phil. hom. 6* is general in nature, it could possibly be considered to speak for Constantinople, while in *In Acta apost. hom. 3* he found the fact that the bishop is described as frequenting the palace, in conjunction with the comment that no-one takes precedence over the archon of the church, not even the *hyparchs* and *toparchs*, a convincing demonstration of that homily's provenance.[115] The reference in *In Heb. hom. 13* to the range of officials associated with the palace, also noted by Bonsdorff,[116] is a further instance where the detail aligns with both categories. The general tendency, however, is to argue that where a specific *hyparch* receives mention, this figure must be the *praefectus praetorio per Orientem* and the location therefore Constantinople.

ii. Other high officials

In contrast to the previous category, information which has been taken to indicate that the city operates under a provincial government is more distinct. Where an archon is singled out by the homilist and it is implied that that person is the highest available official, the individual has generally been understood to be the *comes Orientis*, indicating a provenance of Antioch.[117] In a different vein, since the Eastern emperors at the time of Chrysostom's preaching career were both Christian, Bonsdorff argued that when the homilist refers in *In Rom. hom. 23* to the possibility of the archon being pagan, the person intended by "archon" cannot be the emperor and therefore must be some official, such as the *comes Orientis*, at Antioch.[118] The fact that the army is at the service of

---

[115] See Chapter One, pp. 190 and 192.

[116] See Chapter One, p. 198.

[117] See, e.g., Tillemont (Chapter One, p. 60) with respect to *Hom. in martyres* (CPG 4359); and Bonsdorff (p. 184) with respect to *In I Tim. hom. 14*.

[118] See Chapter One, p. 180.

the archons and not the emperor in *In II Cor. hom. 9* is likewise taken by Bonsdorff to indicate that John is preaching at Antioch.[119]

iii. Military

The use as a distinguishing feature of the presence of a military detachment and its level of activity is exclusive to Bonsdorff. In the case of *In I Thess. hom. 3*, he argues that the fact that the army is engaged in daily exercises and marches suggests a provenance of Constantinople.[120]

4. DEMOGRAPHY

The composition and character of the local population are aspects which have also been drawn upon in the effort to establish provenance. In particular, the racial mix, as manifested in the language groups and the prominence or otherwise of the Jewish community, has been adduced as a feature able to effect distinction. Various characteristics of the local Christian population have also been put forward.

a. *Language*

Under the category of language, reference to members of the audience who have knowledge of a particular language, or to the division between the urban Greek-speaking population and a rural population which is non-Greek-speaking, are the main criteria which have been adduced. For instance, it is argued that if Chrysostom assumes a knowledge of Syriac amongst his audience, he must be preaching at Antioch. This same provenance is thought to be indicated if it is clear that the rural population do not speak Greek.

i. Syriac

On the assumption that a facility with the Syriac language was not common among the population of Constantinople, while it would be natural for a percentage of the inhabitants of Antioch to possess this ability, it is argued by Bonsdorff that when the homilist alludes to Syriac-

---

[119] See Chapter One, p. 183.
[120] See Chapter One, p. 195.

speakers amongst his audience,[121] this indicates that the homily was delivered at Antioch.[122]

ii. Non-Greek-speaking rural population

Finding in *Cat. 8* (CPG 4472) reference to non-Greek-speaking individuals who have come into the city from the surrounding rural areas, Wenger argued that this must indicate a provenance of Antioch, since the individuals referred to are indigenous and it is inconceivable that in the areas surrounding Constantinople the populace spoke a language other than Greek.[123]

b. *Prominent Jewish sector*

The prominence and influence of the Jewish community at Antioch is a feature also noted in the literature.[124] On the basis that its proximity to the imperial court made the Jewish community at Constantinople less noticeable, Baur argued that overt anti-Jewish polemic of the kind found in the homilies on Romans (CPG 4427) is a feature typical of material which stems from Antioch.[125] Wilken's argument that reference to the Jews is a characteristic of Antiochene homilies appears to be based on the inverse of this assumption, namely that the size of the Jewish community at Antioch made it more prominent.[126]

c. *Characteristics of Christian population*

Various characteristics of the Christian communities at both cities have been adduced as a means of supporting a claim for Antiochene or Constantinopolitan provenance. These include the size of the Christian population, its propensity for observing Jewish festivals and its enthusiasm for various heterodox teachings.

---

[121] The examples adduced are *Hom. 4 in Gen.* (PG 53,43 12-16); *Sermo 9 in Gen.* (PG 54,624 57-625 2); and *In Matt. hom. 7* and *16* (PG 57,74 27-28; 248 45-49).

[122] Bonsdorff, *Zur Predigttätigkeit*, 10 n. 4, 15.

[123] See Chapter One, p. 232.

[124] See also 4.c.ii below.

[125] Baur, *Chrysostom and His Time*, I 303 n. 50ᵃ.

[126] See Chapter One, p. 249.

i. General

In the case of *In Acta apost. hom. 11*, the size of the Christian community referred to, some one hundred thousand, confirmed for Savile that the homily stems from Constantinople.[127] Montfaucon, on the other hand, became convinced in the case of certain of the miscellaneous homilies that assiduity in attending worship is a feature characteristic of the Antiochene Christians. In at least one instance he cites this as a reason for excluding Constantinople in favour of Antioch.[128]

ii. Judaizing tendencies

Due to the prominence of the Jewish community at Antioch and to the existence of the group of homilies *Adversus Iudaeos* (CPG 4327),[129] which constitute polemic not against the Jews but against those Christians who persist in keeping Jewish observances, the issue of Judaizing Christians has been thought to be a problem peculiar to that city. As a consequence, whenever a reference to Judaizers appears in a homily, this has been considered a sure sign that it stems from Antioch.[130]

iii. Heterodox tendencies

The arguments based on the proclivity of the Christian community toward heterodox teachings have been various. The prominence of the Anomoean heresy at Antioch, as inferred from the ten homilies *Contra Anomoeos* (CPG 4318-4323),[131] constitutes one of two grounds upon which Montfaucon assigned *In illud: Filius ex se nihil facit* (CPG 4441.12) to that location.[132] The novel appearance of Apollinaris amongst a list of heresiarchs in *In Phil. hom. 6*, on the other hand, was taken by Bonsdorff as an indication that John is preaching at Constantinople. This is supported by the remark that nowhere is Apollinaris so described among the writings from Antioch.[133]

---

[127] See Chapter One, p. 39.

[128] See Chapter One, p. 77 regarding *De paen. hom. 3* (CPG 4333).

[129] Regarding the unanimous location of these homilies at Antioch see Table 13.a.

[130] This is the main proof for assigning the sixty-seven homilies on Genesis (CPG 4409) to Antioch. See Tillemont (Chapter One, p. 55) on *hom. 12* of that series. It is also one of the main proofs for situating the series on Titus (CPG 4438) at that location. See, e.g., Tillemont (Chapter One, p. 62) and Montfaucon (p. 101).

[131] With one exception, all ten have consistently been assigned to Antioch. See Table 13.a.

[132] See Chapter One, p. 95.

[133] See Chapter One, p. 190.

In addition to the mixture of heterodox beliefs peculiar to each location, the incidence of division within the orthodox Christian community has also been considered useful. Since the example best documented for this period is the split within the orthodox church at Antioch initiated by the followers of Eustathius,[134] whenever Chrysostom refers to schismatic tendencies amongst his listeners or to an ecclesiastical division which is local, it is assumed that he must be preaching at Antioch.[135]

5. GEOGRAPHY

Various means of distinguishing the location at which the homilist is preaching have also been derived from the broader geographic context which attaches to the cities of Constantinople and Antioch. Criteria in this category have been based upon an assessment of whether John is preaching from a Syrian or a Constantinopolitan perspective, whether specific sites or regions appear to be close to or distant from the point of preaching and the type of vegetation considered native to each region.

a. *Geographic focus*

The thesis that certain of Chrysostom's comments betray the geographic perspective from which he is preaching is an argument put forward initially by Tillemont and later expanded by Bonsdorff. Both use it to assist in locating those of the exegetical series, such as Romans (CPG 4427), Psalms (CPG 4413) and John (CPG 4425), that contain scant evidence and whose provenance is as a consequence more difficult to determine. The range of material adduced is varied, in all cases with the intention of demonstrating that the homilist is viewing the world from Syria, and is therefore located at Antioch.

i. Lists of exotic locations

Bonsdorff noted that in *In Rom. hom. 13* John compares the local situation to that pertaining to the "Scythians, Thracians, Indians, Persians and many other foreign nations".[136] This statement, he argues, could not have been made at Constantinople, which is next door to

---

[134] See M. Simonetti, art. "Antioch III. Schism", EEC I 49-50.

[135] See, e.g., Tillemont (Chapter One, pp. 61f) regarding *In Matt. hom. 72/73* and *In Eph. hom. 11*.

[136] PG 60,517 17-21.

Thrace, since the passage implies that the latter is so distant that monasticism has reached even there. He further points out that on the four other occasions within Romans that the Thracians receive mention (*hom. 1, 7, 16,* and *30*) it is always in conjunction with the Scythians, a situation parallelled in other Antiochene homilies, namely those on Matthew (CPG 4424).[137]

ii. Other

Apart from lists of exotic locations, a variety of other examples thought to reveal the homilist's point of focus have also been adduced in the literature. Tillemont, for instance, saw in *Exp. in ps. 110* (CPG 4413) an Antiochene focus, since the majority of the disasters described have a direct link with that location.[138] In the case of *In Ioh. hom. 12,* Bonsdorff found Chrysostom's identification of "here" as Syria incontrovertible proof that he was preaching at Antioch.[139] Elsewhere this same scholar argued that reflection on the apostle Paul's command of Syriac, and upon the fact that it was Syrian men who spread the gospel to Rome, resulted from the homilist's geographic situation.[140] A slightly different aspect is demonstrated by *In Rom. hom. 26.* Here Bonsdorff claimed that the manner in which the cities and countryside are juxtaposed by John reflects a specifically Antiochene point of view.

b. *Proximity*

Indication by Chrysostom that a particular site or a specific region is either distant from or relatively close to the city in which he is situated has also been evoked as a means of ascertaining the location at which he is preaching. Thus Savile and Stilting have cited the story of the Phoenician actress famed "not just in our city, but even as far as Cilicia and Cappadocia" (*In Matt. hom. 67/68*) as evidence of the homily's Antiochene provenance.[141] In a similar vein, Tillemont argued with respect to *In s. Barlaam* (CPG 4361) that the proximity of the city to Caesaria in Cappadocia, where the saint was martyred, accounts for the celebration

---

[137] Bonsdorff, *Zur Predigttätigkeit,* 37.

[138] See Chapter One, p. 59.

[139] See Chapter One, p. 178.

[140] See Chapter One, p. 185 (re *In II Tim. hom. 2*) and p. 180 (*In Rom. hom. 2*). John's emphasis on the relationship between Syriac and Hebrew (*In II Tim. hom. 4, 8* and *10*) is likewise seen in this light.

[141] PG 58,636 54-55. See Chapter One, pp. 38 and 121 n. 425.

of his festival at Antioch.[142] Conversely, Bonsdorff suggested that the homilist's doubt in *In I Thess. hom. 8* as to whether any member of the audience had visited Palestine was an indication of its distance from the present location, confirming a provenance of Constantinople.[143]

c. *Native vegetation*

The argument that certain types of animals or flora are typical of one region and not the other is brought up only once in the context of *Hom. in s. pascha* (CPG 4408). Here, in the absence of other distinguishing features, Tillemont adduces the lilies and roses mentioned by the homilist,[144] arguing that they are a feature of Antioch and not Constantinople.[145]

6. MONKS AND MONASTIC PRACTICES

Chrysostom's experiences with monks throughout his years at Antioch and Constantinople and the diverse lifestyles which they are thought to have practised have given rise to a criterion considered particularly effective in distinguishing between the two locations. The assumptions which inform it proceed as follows. At Antioch the monks lived outside of the city in the neighbouring mountains, while this was not at all the case at Constantinople.[146] Moreover, John both admired and deeply respected the Antiochene monks with whom he had spent some time as a young man, while the Constantinopolitan monks, led by Isaac, were somewhat hostile and constantly causing him trouble.[147] Therefore, the argument goes, when the homilist talks of monks in a positive way, holding them up as an example, or refers to monks who live on mountains or exhorts his listeners to go visit them, he is preaching at Antioch. Such references,

---

[142] See Chapter One, p. 59. Stilting (p. 124) puts forward a similar argument in support of locating the homily *In martyres Aegyptios* (CPG 4363) at Antioch.

[143] See Chapter One, p. 195. Bonsdorff is particularly fond of this criterion. For further examples see p. 186 (re *In II Tim. hom. 8, 10*) and 000 (*In Titum hom. 6*).

[144] In the text presented by Montfaucon Chrysostom singles out not lilies and roses but roses and violets (ῥόδα καὶ ἴα: PG 52,771 1).

[145] See Chapter One, p. 60.

[146] Implicit in the literature, the essential difference between the Antiochene and Constantinopolitan forms of monasticism is carefully defined by Dagron, "Les moines et la ville", 253-254.

[147] This view is implicit in the biographies. See, e.g., Baur, *Chrysostom and His Time*, I 138-139 and II 63-66; Kelly, *Golden Mouth*, 34 and 123-125.

it is further claimed, are almost entirely lacking in the homilies which stem from Constantinople.[148]

7. OLYMPIC GAMES

Opelt's argument regarding the mention of Olympic games in *In Heb. hom. 14* is effective, if simple. The Olympics referred to could be the games of ancient derivation held in Greece or a local version, such as those held every four years at Antioch in Syria. In the above homily Chrysostom reminds his audience that many of them have been spectators at the games and not just once but on several occasions.[149] Since the emperor Theodosius passed a decree in 393 banning the Greek Olympics, and since Chrysostom only arrived at Constantinople in 398, some years after the decree had been effected, the possibility that he is addressing a Constantinopolitan audience is excluded. The Olympics referred to must therefore be the local Syrian version and the homily therefore delivered at Antioch.[150]

8. LITURGY

The value of the liturgical cycle and of the general rhythms which the worship of the Christian community followed as a means of distinguishing between the two locations is a feature which has been touched upon rarely and only in passing. Two aspects have been considered useful — the local nature of the cults of certain martyrs and the frequency of the observance of synaxes.

---

[148] Put forward by Tillemont with respect to the three homilies *In illud: Habentes eundem spiritum* (see Chapter One, p. 59), the criterion receives its earliest consistent application with Montfaucon (pp. 92, 99f), after which it rapidly becomes a datum in the literature. For more recent statements see, e.g., Bonsdorff (Chapter One, p. 176) and Quasten (p. 225). R. Kaczynski, *Das Wort Gottes in Liturgie und Alltag der Gemeinden des Johannes Chrysostomus*, Freiburg 1974, 340, goes so far as to say that at Constantinople Chrysostom could not adduce monastic practices as an exemplum because the audience there lacked close experience of them.

[149] PG 63,116 23-26: Ὀλύμπια πολλοὶ πολλάκις ὑμῶν ἐθεάσαντο· καὶ οὐκ ἐθεάσαντο μόνον, ἀλλὰ καὶ σπουδασταὶ καὶ θαυμασταὶ τῶν ἀγωνιζομένων ἐγένοντο....

[150] Opelt, "Das Ende von Olympia", 64-68.

a. *Liturgical calendar*

With respect to a point where the liturgical calendar may have differed at Antioch and Constantinople, Montfaucon argued that *In d. Pauli: Nolo vos ignorare* (CPG 4380) belongs to the first location because of a comment by the homilist that they had recently celebrated the festival of St Barlaam.[151]

b. *Frequency of synaxes*

With regard to the frequency with which Chrysostom preached at each location, Tillemont regarded a circumstance where this is restricted to Sundays as a situation peculiar to Antioch.[152]

9. FAMOUS PEOPLE AND EVENTS

The occurrence in a homily of reference to events or persons associated exclusively with the one location has been considered a particularly effective means of establishing provenance. The range of material which has been adduced in the literature includes events from Antioch's immediate past, such as the various occurrences at Daphne during the emperor Julian's residency at Antioch and the visit by Julianus Sabas; well-known incidents which occurred at that city during the time of Chrysostom's presbyterate, such as the riots which took place in 387; and notable events which occurred at Constantinople during his episcopate, such as the misfortunes experienced by the consul-eunuch Eutropius. In determining the importance to be attached to the appearance of such a reference, the manner in which it is described by the homilist has been considered significant.

a. *Eutropius*

Although in most cases reference to the fall of Eutropius has been used to establish the chronology of a homily rather than its provenance,[153] in at least two instances it is evoked explicitly for the purpose of

---

[151] See Chapter One, p. 82.

[152] See Chapter One, p. 57 with respect to *De paen. hom. 3*.

[153] See, e.g., Montfaucon (Chapter One, p. 100) with respect to *In Col. hom. 7* and Stilting (p. 125) with regard to *Quod frequenter conveniendum* sit (CPG 4441.3).

establishing location. With regard to *In Col. hom. 7* Tillemont mentioned the allusion to this event as grounds for allocating that homily to Constantinople.[154] Montfaucon drew a direct connection between John's assertion in *In illud: Ne timueritis hom. 1* (CPG 4414) — that the audience knows many current examples of individuals who have lost their wealth — and the description of the reversal suffered by Eutropius which John supplied in *In Eutropium* (CPG 4392), the homily preached in Constantinople at the time of the event.[155] In all of the cases where this particular criterion has been adduced, whether for the purpose of establishing date or provenance, the mere allusion in a homily to an individual who has suffered a sudden fall from power or wealth has led to the suspicion that it describes the Eutropius incident.

b. *Riots of 387 AD*

Following the same lines as comment regarding the fall of Eutropius, reference to the Antiochene riots has tended to be used as a chronological yardstick, rather than as a means of determining provenance. In the case of *In Col. hom. 7*, however, the "remote" manner in which Chrysostom refers to this episode has been taken as an indication that he is preaching not at Antioch, but at Constantinople.[156]

c. *Current emperor*

Within the literature, the view of the character and effectiveness of the two emperors who were in power at the time when Chrysostom was presbyter and bishop has tended toward polarisation. Theodosius is seen as a strong and effective ruler, who was able to keep the borders of the empire under control, while Arcadius is seen as weak and ineffective, struggling constantly against the threat of war, civil as well as external.[157] Thus, it is argued, if the homilist refers to an emperor who suffers from constant difficulties, as in *In Phil. hom. 15*, he cannot be referring to Theodosius and the homily must therefore have been delivered at Constantinople.[158] Taking a different approach, however, Stilting and Baur both argued that, given the fact that the last emperor to receive mention

---

[154] See Chapter One, p. 64.
[155] See Chapter One, p. 92.
[156] See Tillemont and Bonsdorff (Chapter One, pp. 64 and 191).
[157] See, e.g., Bonsdorff, *Zur Predigttätigkeit*, 79 and Quasten, *Patrology*, III 447-448.
[158] See Bonsdorff (Chapter One, pp. 189f).

prior to discussion of the present ruler is Valens, logic dictates that the present emperor must be his successor, Theodosius, and the homily therefore delivered at Antioch. War and the other difficulties mentioned, they asserted, are experiences common to the reigns of both emperors.[159]

d. *War*

As a direct consequence of the distinction drawn between the two emperors and their reigns, a further assumption has arisen within the literature with respect to war. When the homilist mentions that the empire is currently experiencing or has recently experienced attack, or that there is an ongoing war, this has been taken in some cases to refer to the difficulties with the Huns led by Alaric which Arcadius experienced on succeeding to the imperial throne early in 395.[160] Although the appearance in a homily of a reference to war has usually influenced chronological decisions, in one instance John's allusion to a series of disasters (plague, famine, drought, hail, fires and enemy incursion), which are stated to have occurred at a time when he was endowed with the office of preaching, is adduced as direct proof of the homily's Antiochene provenance.[161]

e. *Julianus Sabas*

On one occasion John refers to a famed, uneducated monk named Julianus, about whom the audience has heard and whom some have actually seen.[162] This figure has commonly been identified as Julianus Sabas,[163] a Syrian ascetic who is known to have visited Antioch in 365.[164]

---

[159] See Chapter One, pp. 123 and 208.

[160] See, e.g., Montfaucon's and Dumortier's comments (Chapter One, pp. 93 and 234) regarding *In illud: Vidi dom. hom. 1* (CPG 4417).

[161] See Montfaucon (Chapter One, p. 77) re *De paen. hom. 4.*

[162] *In Eph. hom. 21* (PG 62,153 18-27).

[163] See, e.g., Rauschen, Lietzmann and Bonsdorff (Chapter One, pp. 143, 168, 187).

[164] See Festugière, *Antioche païenne et chrétienne*, 247-252.

f. *Plot against Valens of 372 AD*

On another occasion the homilist refers to a shocking event that happened to a certain Theodorus.[165] Seeck identified this figure as the Theodorus involved in a supposed assassination attempt against Valens in 372,[166] as a consequence of which he claimed that *In Acta apost. hom. 41* was delivered at Antioch.[167] Cameron countered this argument with the observation that in *In Acta apost. hom. 38* the same conspiracy is referred to as a distant reminiscence, a factor which he believed supported a provenance of Constantinople.[168]

g. *Events of 361-362 AD*

Chrysostom refers in several places to certain events which occurred at Antioch during the reign of the emperor Julian. The most distinctive of these are the burning of the temple of Apollo at Daphne, an event associated with the translation of the remains of St Babylas from Daphne to the common cemetery at Antioch, and a drought so severe that the springs at Daphne, source of the Antiochene water-supply, dried up.[169] Arguments for the Antiochene provenance of a homily based on the appearance of such a reference have ranged from the explicit (the event is stated to have occurred at the present location)[170] to an appeal to the familiar (the homilist assumes familiarity with the happenings on the part of his audience).[171]

---

[165] *In Acta apost. hom. 41* (PG 60,291 37-40).

[166] Regarding this event see Downey, *Antioch*, 401-402.

[167] See Chapter One, p. 154.

[168] See Chapter One, p. 240.

[169] For detail concerning the events of this period see Downey, *Antioch*, 383-388 and 595-596.

[170] See Savile, Tillemont, and Piédagnel (Chapter One, pp. 44, 59, 234) regarding *De laudibus s. Pauli hom. 4* (CPG 4344) and the failure of the springs at Daphne.

[171] See, e.g., Tillemont (Chapter One, p. 62) regarding the mention of St Babylas in *In Eph. hom. 9* and Piédagnel (p. 234) on the reference to the burning of the temple of Apollo in *De laudibus s. Pauli hom. 4*. Seeck's argument regarding the familiar reference to St Babylas in *In Acta apost. hom. 41* (see Chapter One, p. 154) also impinges upon this category.

Summary

The following table presents a summary of all of the established categories and subcategories of criteria. The third column of the table provides an indication of the provenance which each is thought to support. When the criteria are viewed together in this fashion, it can be seen that the bulk of the criteria revolves around the personal status of the homilist and the features peculiar to each city.

Table 15. Types of criteria used to establish provenance

No.	DESCRIPTION	City
1	**Manuscript titles** (see also 2.e, 2.f.iii, 3.e, 9)	A, CP
2	**Personal status**	A, CP
2.a	Direct evidence	A, CP
2.b	Occupation of throne	CP
2.c	Relationship with audience	A, CP
2.c.i	Metaphoric (opposite of 2.d.i)	CP
2.c.ii	Prostasia	A, CP
2.c.iii	Responsibility	CP
2.c.iv	Episcopal tone	A, CP
2.d	Indication that another is of higher ecclesiastical status (opp. of 2.c.i)	A, CP
2.d.i	Bishop	A, CP
2.d.ii	Proedroi	A
2.d.iii	"The common fathers"	A
2.e	Order of preaching (see also 1)	A, CP
2.f	Duties of office	A, CP
2.f.i	Workload	A
2.f.ii	Style	A, CP
2.f.iii	Transmission history (see also 1)	CP
3	**The city**	A, CP
3.a	Direct evidence	A, CP
3.b	Linked to apostolic times	A
3.b.i	"The first city to be honoured with the name 'Christian'"	A
3.b.ii	Source of humanitarian aid during famine	A
3.b.iii	Site of disagreement between Peter and Paul	A
3.b.iv	Peter as founder of church	A
3.b.v	Site where Paul was detained	A
3.c	Imperial residence	A, CP
3.c.i	Direct evidence	CP
3.c.ii	Imperial exempla	A, CP
3.d	Topography — general	A, CP
3.d.i	Coastal v. non-coastal	CP
3.d.ii	Suburban environs	A
3.e	Topography — Christian (see also 1)	A, CP
3.e.i	Churches	A, CP
3.e.ii	Martyr burials	A, CP

3.f	Features	A, CP
3.f.i	Characteristic	A, CP
3.f.ii	Negative	A, CP
3.g	Status	A, CP
3.h	Administration	A, CP
3.h.i	Officials directly associated with emperor	CP
3.h.ii	Other high officials	A
3.h.iii	Military	CP
4	**Demography**	A, CP
4.a	Language	A
4.a.i	Syriac	A
4.a.ii	Non-Greek-speaking rural population	A
4.b	Prominent Jewish sector	A
4.c	Characteristics of Christian population	A, CP
4.c.i	General	A, CP
4.c.ii	Judaizing tendencies	A
4.c.iii	Heterodox tendencies	A,CP
5	**Geography**	A, CP
5.a	Geographic focus	A
5.a.i	Lists of exotic locations	A
5.a.ii	Other	A
5.b	Proximity	A, CP
5.c	Native vegetation	A
6	**Monks and monastic practices**	A, CP
7	**Olympic Games**	A
8	**Liturgy**	A
8.a	Liturgical calendar	A
8.b	Frequency of synaxes	A
9	**Famous people and events** (see also 1)	A, CP
9.a	Eutropius	CP
9.b	Riots of 387 AD	A, CP
9.c	Current emperor	A, CP
9.d	War	A
9.e	Julianus Sabas	A
9.f	Plot against Valens of 372 AD	A
9.g	Events of 361-362 AD	A

CHAPTER THREE

THE VALIDITY OF THE CRITERIA

With the criteria neatly defined, the next step is to determine whether the individual criteria are based on valid assumptions and whether the way in which each has been applied is consistent with internal evidence. In this chapter each category is examined separately and the validity of each criterion determined. On the basis of this analysis the criteria are then separated into three lists — those criteria that are invalid; criteria which require further investigation before their validity can be either disproved or asserted; and those which survive scrutiny. The results are presented at the end of the chapter in the form of a table. A second table is provided in which the status quaestionis with respect to the provenance of the individual homilies referred to in the course of the analysis is reviewed.

1. MANUSCRIPT TITLES

As established in Chapter Two, the titles to homilies record data which have been considered of relevance to the assessment of provenance. The data they contain divides into four types — 1) the identification of topographic features; 2) indication of the status of the homilist; 3) the mention of famous people and/or events; and 4) reference to the manner in which the original has been transmitted.

At first glance, those titles which contain detail extraneous to the homily or series to which they are attached afford information that is not only on the face of it helpful but which also appears to carry the weight of authority. Indeed, as we have seen in Part One, much reliance has been placed upon such data in the literature. For the information to merit this degree of confidence, however, a direct relationship between the production of the homily itself and the title appended to it is required. In other words, if the data are to be trustworthy, it is essential that the title was penned by someone who had first-hand knowledge of the circumstances under which the homily was delivered — either Chrysostom himself or a contemporary (perhaps a stenographer, who was privy to such information). It is imperative that the data not be inferred from the contents of the homily. Even if it is suspected that these conditions have been met, there is always the possibility that human error has occurred, either in the penning of the title or in the course of its transmission.

With regard to this issue, it has in recent years been demonstrated that the relationship between homily and title is much less straightforward than has previously been thought. Cameron argues that in the case of both *De capto Eutropio* (CPG 4528) and *Cum Saturninus et Aurelianus* (CPG 4393) the titles cannot have been authored by the homilist, but are instead chronological labels attached by an editor.[1] In the latter case, he concludes that the title was added early enough for accurate identification of the individuals involved but not by a contemporary, who would not have made the chronological error which it preserves.[2] The misidentification involved in the title to the first homily — Cameron has shown that the homily refers to events of at least one year later[3] — has led him to suggest that the publication of the cluster of homilies to which they belong (CPG 4392-4399, 4528) was not undertaken until after Chrysostom's rehabilitation, some twenty or more years after they were delivered.[4] Speculative as this proposal is, the fact remains that both titles contain information inconsistent with events described in the homily and which demonstrates a lack of first-hand knowledge on the part of the author.

These are not the only instances in which the accuracy of a title has been brought into question. Van de Paverd has demonstrated that in the case of *Ad illuminandos cat. 2* (CPG 4464=4331) the title is a summary which is "clearly not from the hand of Chrysostom".[5] The wording of this "summary" had led historically to the homily being considered a catechesis and becoming detached from its rightful place in the series *De statuis* (CPG 4330). In support of his own scepticism regarding the information to be found in manuscript titles, van de Paverd cites the opinion of Wenger, who proposed that they generally have nothing to do with the homilist, but are the work of contemporary stenographers or editors, or of later scribes.[6] Certainly, although Wenger identifies the terms used

---

[1] Cameron, "A misidentified homily", 35-36.

[2] Cameron, Long & Sherry, *Barbarians and Politics*, 173-175.

[3] Cameron, "A misidentified homily", 39-48.

[4] Cameron, "A misidentified homily", 36.

[5] Van de Paverd, *Homilies on the Statues*, 228-230. This doubt had been raised only a few months previously by Piédagnel, *Trois catéchèses* (SC 366), 20-32, on the basis of a an earlier suggestion by van de Paverd.

[6] Wenger, *Huit catéchèses* (SC 50bis), 133 n. 1. He does suggest, however, that where an editor is involved one cannot rule out the possibility that the homilist had provided the title.

in the title to *Cat. 2* (CPG 4466) as germane to the homilist,[7] a casual glance at the vocabulary employed in the label attached to *Cat. 8* (CPG 4472) reveals that much of it is not typical of Chrysostom.[8]

The titles appended to the various *Novae homiliae* (CPG 4441) have been considered particularly authoritative. Batiffol, excited by the mention in each of the location at which the homily was delivered, proposed that initially the titles contained this information alone and that it was only later that a summary of the contents, not always accurate, was included.[9] Aubineau, who has been investigating the issue with some thoroughness preparatory to a new edition of the series, points out that the mention of the place of preaching, found in the more primitive codices, disappears from the title when the context is changed in a later collection, a circumstance which confirms the antiquity of this detail.[10]

If it is genuinely the case that the record of the location in the title is independent of the homily and therefore contemporaneous, as Batiffol had hoped, then it is unfortunate that not even this is above suspicion.[11] The label attached to *In illud: Messis quidem multa* (CPG 4441.11) in both Ottob. gr. 43 and Stav. 6 indicates that it was delivered in "the Church dedicated to the Apostle".[12] Montfaucon and Batiffol both expressed confidence in the accuracy of this information, the latter identifying the church in question as that of St Paul, which had been handed over to a congregation of orthodox Goths at Constantinople.[13] Internal evidence, however, indicates that the sermon was preached at a location which held the remains of the apostle Andrew and Timothy, the disciple of Paul.[14] Since it is known from external sources that their remains were

---

[7] Ibid.

[8] SC 50bis,247, in particular τοὺς ἀπὸ τῆς περιοικίδος (ll.1-2). Χώρα and ἀγροικία are the terms commonly used by Chrysostom in association with the rural community. See, e.g. *Cat. 8*, SC 50bis,247 5-6; *De ss. martyribus* (CPG 4357) PG 50,646-647; *De Anna sermo 1* (CPG 4411) PG 54,634 22.

[9] Batiffol, "Quelques homélies", 566, 572.

[10] Aubineau, "Restitution", 543-544.

[11] As a consequence of his theory, Batiffol had been quite happy to question the accuracy of other information in the titles, while upholding the integrity of the data concerning the site of the homily. See, e.g., "Quelques homélies", 569, with regard to CPG 4441.11.

[12] See PG 63,515 3-6 *a.i.*: ...ῥηθεῖσα ἐν τῇ ἐκκλησίᾳ τῇ ἐπὶ τοῦ Ἀποστόλου...

[13] Batiffol, "Quelques homélies", 569. See also Montfaucon, XII 322. Regarding the church itself see Janin, *Géographie ecclésiastique*, 394-395.

[14] PG 63,518 33-42: Εἰς ἀποστόλων παραγινόμεθα θήκας· ὁρῶμεν ... τὸν Παύλου μαθητὴν μετὰ Παύλου πανταχοῦ περιτρέχοντα, καὶ τῷ διδασκάλῳ παρισούμενον ... τὸν τοῦ πρώτου τῶν ἀποστόλων ἀδελφόν, τὸν ἁλιέα τὸν σαγήνην ἁπλώσαντα καὶ ἀνθρώπους ἀντὶ ἰχθύων ἁλιεύσαντα, τὸν τοῦ Εὐαγγελίου κήρυκα· The import of this passage was noted by Matthaei, *Ioannis Chrysostomi homiliae IV ex omnibus ejus operibus selectae graece et latine*, Misenae 1792, II.2 n. 1

placed with some ceremony in a quite separate church, the Church of the Apostles,[15] one can only conclude either that a mistake has been made in the penning of the title or its transmission, or that the title in this instance preserves an alternative, possibly earlier version of the church's name, still current among the general populace.[16] A minute examination of the manuscript tradition may possibly resolve this.[17]

The problems which have been identified thus far relate largely to those titles which name the place of preaching or in which famous individuals or events are identified (types 1 and 3). A separate set of difficulties attaches to those titles which allude to the status of the homilist or refer to the means by which the original homily or series has been transmitted (types 2 and 4). In these cases it is not necessarily the data which are at fault, but rather the assumptions which have been brought to bear in their interpretation.

A compelling example is the almost unanimous allocation to Constantinople of the series on Hebrews (CPG 4440), primarily on the basis of the title in the manuscripts.[18] In more recent times, Opelt has argued on the basis of internal evidence (the Olympic Games mentioned in *In Heb. hom. 14*) that the series belongs not to Constantinople, but to Antioch.[19] Acknowledging the validity of her conclusions with respect to *hom. 14*, but disagreeing with her global application of the data to the remainder of the homilies, in an article published in 1995 Pauline Allen and I argued that the "series" is most likely not even homogeneous, but contains

---

and 21 n. 62. He identifies the first of the two figures as Peter rather than Andrew (II.23 n. 70).

[15] For discussion of this event see D. Woods, "The date of the translation of the relics of SS. Luke and Andrew to Constantinople", VC 45 (1991) 286-292.

[16] An analogy may perhaps be drawn with the so-called "New Church", which is named in at least two titles. See *Contra Anom. hom. 11* (CPG 4324), mss D, G, O and P: ἐρρέθη ἐν τῇ καινῇ ἐκκλησίᾳ (SC 396,89 and 286), which Malingrey assumes to be a mistaken reference to the Great Church at Antioch but could in fact refer to the Great Church at Constantinople (St Eirene, its predecessor as episcopal church, was also known as "the old church"; see p. 379 below); and *In illud: In faciem ei restiti* (CPG 4391): Τῇ προτέρᾳ συνάξει ἐν τῇ ἐκκλησίᾳ τῇ καινῇ συναχθεὶς μετὰ τοῦ ἐπισκόπου, ταύτην ἐν τῇ παλαιᾷ εἶπεν... (PG 51,371-372), where it appears to constitute an alternative means of referring to the Great Church at Antioch. See, however, van de Paverd, *Messliturgie*, 14-15, who considers that at Antioch the Great Church and the "New Church" are separate edifices.

[17] See the announcement of a new edition by Aubineau, "Publication des *Undecim novae homiliae* de saint Jean Chrysostome (PG 63,461-530): édition critique, comblement des lacunes, addition de deux inédits", StP 22 (1989) 83-88.

[18] So Savile, Tillemont, Montfaucon, Stilting, Lietzmann, Bonsdorff and Quasten. See Chapter One, pp. 39, 65, 102, 128, 169, 197 and 225. For an outline of the rationale behind the interpretation of this title see Chapter Two, p. 279.

[19] See Chapter One, p. 221.

sermons which derive from both locations.[20] As a consequence of Opelt's findings and our own, it can no longer be claimed that the knowledge that the homilies were published after Chrysostom's death from steno-graphic notes bears any significance for their provenance.

The different interpretations which have been placed upon one par-ticular title containing evidence of the homilist's status raise an entirely different concern. Whereas in cases where the information in the title and the internal evidence are in accord, such as that of *In illud: In faciem ei restiti* (CPG 4391),[21] the provenance can be considered patent and no difficulty is involved, problems do arise when the internal evidence which might verify or assist in interpreting such information is weak or non-existent. Such is the case with *In illud: Filius ex se nihil facit* (CPG 4441.12).[22] Even allowing for the fact that it was only in the late 1800s that it was proposed that the homily belonged among the *Novae homiliae*,[23] and for the assumption that the term διδάσκαλος = bishop,[24] Montfaucon should by his own rules have argued that the fact that a bishop had preached beforehand confirmed the episcopal status of the homilist.[25] Instead, persuaded by the attack upon the Anomoeans which forms the subject of the homily, and which he selectively associates in this instance with Antioch,[26] he finds no difficulty in re-interpreting an otherwise hard and fast dictum. In support of the Constantinopolitan provenance of the homily, Aubineau, who has had access to a greater number of manuscripts, presents three versions of the title of which the

---

[20] Allen-Mayer, "Hebrews: The Last Series?".

[21] The Antiochene provenance suggested by the mention of the bishop and the Old and New Churches in the title (see n. 16 above) is supported by the clear indication within the homily that another is bishop (PG 51,371 13 *a.i.*-372 9 *a.i.*) and that the city is directly linked to events which took place in the book of Acts (PG 51,373 26-374 20). For the valid-ity of these criteria see pp. 337-342 and 367-369 below.

[22] The title offered by Montfaucon (PG 56,247-248) reads: Ἐν τῇ μεγάλῃ ἐκκλησίᾳ, προειρηκότος (ἐπισκόπου) ὀλίγα... In the following discussion, consideration of the validity of the argument based on the order of preaching itself is avoided. For discussion of this criterion see pp. 351-360 below.

[23] See Batiffol (Chapter One, p. 157).

[24] It appears that the opening words of the homily: Πεπληρωμένην τὴν φιάλην ἔχων ὁ διδάσκαλος προειρηκώς (PG 56,247 1-2) persuaded him to emend the title. For a discussion of this equation see pp. 337-342 below.

[25] For an outline of this argument see Chapter Two, p. 286.

[26] Montfaucon here ignores the evidence of CPG 4324-4325 that Chrysostom preached likewise against this heresy at Constantinople. The same selectivity is demonstrated in his identification of the διδάσκαλος as Flavian. He is quite happy in another case to accept Til-lemont's identification of "the wise and noble teacher" who had recently preached from the θρόνος (PG 52,761 1-8) as Diodore, bishop of Tarsus. See further Chapter One, p. 88 with respect to *Laus Diodori* (CPG 4406).

third (ἑτέρου ἐπισκόπου προειρηκότος) is particularly persuasive.[27] But how
do we know that this information is not itself conjectural, this time not
on the part of a modern editor, but on the part of a person involved in
the transmission process? Given that the other two versions of the title
are non-prescriptive (προειρηκότος ὀλίγα; ἑτέρου προειρηκότος ὀλίγα), a
situation which accords well with the vagueness of the internal evidence,
one cannot avoid the suspicion that the title favoured by Aubineau is
perhaps not the most primitive. Whatever the case, it is clear that without adequate internal evidence to provide a guide, data in the title concerning the status of the homilist are vulnerable to more than one interpretation.

To sum up, we have seen that while the titles which preface the homilies in the manuscripts can on occasion provide data of great significance
for determining provenance, difficulties attach to both the accuracy and
the interpretation of such information. In the one example of type 4
(transmission), the interpretation placed upon the data is not borne out
when the provenance of the individual homilies in the series is elicited
from internal evidence. In the case of type 3 (famous people and events)
at least two titles involve leaps of intuition on the part of their author, in
the one instance leading to an inaccurate identification. In the case of
type 2 (status of the homilist), while the accuracy of at least one title can
be shown from internal evidence, in another example the lack of
adequate internal data has led to different assumptions being brought to
bear, resulting in opposing interpretations of the evidence. The identification of the place of preaching which occurs in type 1 titles provides the
greatest promise of information which is genuinely independent of the
homily, contemporaneous and therefore accurate. Unfortunately, this too
is not entirely free of suspicion.

What are the implications of these findings for our future use of such
information? At the beginning of this discussion we stated that for the
data contained in titles to be given weight, the title must be contemporaneous with the homily, in that it originates with the homilist (Chrysostom) or with a stenographer or similar individual with first-hand knowledge of the information described. This requirement is very difficult to
prove. When the entire corpus is considered, it is certainly *not* true in
every case. Even if proven, moreover, it does not remove the possibility
that a slip of the pen or a mistake in memory has occurred on the part of
the author. Given these circumstances, the burden of proof must now be
shifted from the contents of the homily, where it has been located firmly
in the past, onto the title.

In this light, I propose the following rules of thumb:

---

[27] See Chapter One, p. 244.

1. In cases where the internal evidence and the data contained in the title are entirely in accord, the information can be accepted as valid,
and the derived provenance definitive.
2. In cases where the internal evidence and the data contained in the title are in conflict, greater confidence is to be placed in the contents of
the homily, and the information supplied by the title dismissed or
subjected to re-interpretation.
3. In cases where there is no conflict and the data in the title are genuinely independent, i.e., the data cannot have been inferred from the
contents of the homily, then such information is probably reliable, but
there is no ultimate certainty. An open mind should be kept in such
cases.
4. In cases where the internal evidence is inadequate and the information in the title open to interpretation, a ruling should be avoided altogether and the mind of the investigator kept open.

In all cases, the primacy of the internal data over those contained in
the title should be maintained and each manuscript title treated with a
degree of suspicion unless internal evidence supports the attribution.

Finally, it must be said that the issue of the titles appended to individual homilies and homiletic series in the manuscript tradition leads us
into the difficult area of the transmission of homilies and the question of
the relationship between the form or context in which the homily has
been transmitted and its original delivery. Even when this issue is set
aside, with the exception of those provided in recent editions the titles
currently available do not necessarily canvass the full range of alternatives, nor do they necessarily provide us with the version which is the
most primitive. As Aubineau's own efforts make clear, there are numerous manuscripts yet to be examined before we can be certain of each title's authority.

2. PERSONAL STATUS

While the argument from personal status itself is valid (that is, if it
can be shown that John is of presbyteral status, the city is Antioch; if it
can be shown that he is a bishop, the city is Constantinople), many of the
criteria derived from it are not. The problems begin with how one determines the attributes of a presbyter and a bishop in the late fourth century. They continue when one brings the homilist's personal perspective
into consideration.

a. *Direct evidence*

Of the three categories which come under the criterion based on personal status (direct use of the term bishop or presbyter; allusion; failure
to mention that one is bishop) the first, when it is patent that the homilist is in that instance referring to himself, is the only one which can be
considered to provide a secure indication of provenance. With respect to
the two examples adduced in the literature (*In Acta apost. hom. 9* and *In
Col. hom. 3*) there can be no doubt that Chrysostom's comments relate
directly to his own person,[28] that therefore he is a bishop, and that consequently the two homilies were preached before an audience at Constantinople.

If the implication of such overt statements is clear, the conclusion to
be drawn from comments of a less direct nature is not. Since Chrysostom
is well aware of his own status, as is his audience,[29] it is more common
for him to allude to his position than to openly state this. As there is no
requirement for him to make himself clear under such circumstances,
and since the modern reader lacks the advantage enjoyed by homilist and
audience, this means that the interpretation to be placed upon such allusory comments is itself almost always open to question. Allusory evidence of Chrysostom's status is therefore inconclusive, unless substantiated by other data within the same homily.

Detail which more or less fills this requirement exists in the case of
Cat. ultima ad baptizandos (CPG 4462). Here, in addition to a request for
those about to undergo baptism to pray "for the priests who sit with us"
and "for the high-priest through whose hands and voice you receive these
benefits",[30] the homilist states that he will leave the required explanation
of faith for "the teacher", while setting aside "for ourselves what can be
said at another time, when the uninitiated are present".[31] While the first
phrase could perhaps be used with equal facility by a bishop,[32] while it

---

[28] See Chapter Two, nn. 10-11.

[29] It is significant that in more than eight hundred homilies only two occurrences of
explicit statement have been found, although it should be noted that in the apologetic
treatise *De sacerdotio* (CPG 4316) direct use of the terms bishop and presbyter is likewise
rare. For the statistics see C. Jacob, "Zur Amtsterminologie des Johannes Chrysostomus.
Die ἀρχή des ἱερεύς nach *De sacerdotio*", *Trierer theologische Zeitschrift* 100 (1991) 312.

[30] See Chapter Two, n. 13.

[31] SC 366,226 4.1-3: Ἀλλὰ τὸν μὲν περὶ πίστεως λόγον τῷ διδασκάλῳ παραχωρήσομεν...

[32] Chrysostom's use of the term ἱερεύς tends to be generic, indicating the class of those
ordained to the office of preaching (both presbyters and bishops) without reference to
status. While in the present context it has been assumed that the persons indicated are
presbyters, see, e.g., *In I Thess. hom. 10* (PG 62,455 6-456 44), *In Acta apost. hom. 3* (PG
60,39 55-57) and *Cat. ultima ad bapt.* (SC 366,236 8.1-3), where the referent is more likely
to be a bishop. Despite the confidence of Piédagnel, *Trois catéchèses* (SC 366) 240 n. 38,

cannot be excluded that the impersonal reference to the "high-priest" is used by Chrysostom of himself,[33] and while the reference to "the teacher" is in itself inconclusive,[34] the passages in combination tend to suggest that John's status at the time of delivering the catechesis was that of presbyter. In the absence of further evidence and without an exhaustive investigation of his use of each of the above expressions, however, this conclusion should not be treated as definitive. On the weight of the present evidence it can at best be considered probable.

In the case of *In Titum hom. 1*, evidence of a kind which might support or contradict the passage adduced is entirely lacking. Since the relationship between *hom. 1* and *hom. 3* of this series has yet to be proven, data contained in the latter cannot reliably be adduced to clarify the situation.[35] The passage itself occurs in the midst of a frank discussion of the difficulties attached to the episcopal office.[36] Chrysostom refers to these trials in a quite impersonal way, until he makes the following comment:

> Is this power? He [*sc.* the bishop] cannot even be avenged, since the vital organs are his own. Just as we dare not take revenge, even if our guts swell with fluid, even if they cause trouble for the head and the rest of the body — for we do not grab a sword and run them through —, so, even if any of those under our authority are like that, causing us trouble and despair as a result of those accusations, we do not dare defend ourselves. For that is far from a father's mind. Rather, it is necessary to put up with the trouble until that person is restored to good health.[37]

In isolation, the remarks are suggestive of John's personal experience of the situation. The fact that the majority of the comment in this homily is expressed in a manner which is impersonal, while the shift from the impersonal to the personal is brief and only momentary, does not speak against this. The same approach is taken by the homilist in *In Col. hom.*

---

the inference to be drawn from the circumstance of these priests being seated with the homilist is also not entirely certain. The seating arrangements for presbyters and visiting bishops is touched on briefly on pp. 330f below.

[33] For an example of impersonal reference to himself by Chrysostom when bishop see the discussion regarding *In Titum hom. 1* and *In Col. hom. 3* in the following paragraph.

[34] The qualifying adjective κοινός is required for there to be reasonable certainty that the metaphor refers to a person of episcopal status. Cf. *In diem natalem* (CPG 4334): ἐν δὲ λοιπὸν εἰπών, καταπαύσω τὸν λόγον, τῷ κοινῷ διδασκάλῳ τῶν μειζόνων παραχωρήσας (PG 49,358 53-54). For further discussion see pp. 337-342 below.

[35] There is in any case some doubt as to whether the evidence for the Antiochene provenance of *hom. 3* is conclusive. See further pp. 377f below.

[36] For the full context see PG 62,667 2-670 46.

[37] PG 62,669 12-21.

3, where, after speaking at some length of the role of the president of the church (ὁ τῆς Ἐκκλησίας προεστώς) in the third person,[38] he suddenly indicates that he has been talking about himself: "Surely it is not I who give the peace? It is Christ who bestows honour by speaking through us."[39] Prior to that point there is little to connect John with the situation which he describes. It has also been suggested that in *In Titum hom. 1* the point of reference of the plural form of the first person, as exemplified in the passage quoted above (ἡμῖν, τολμῶμεν), is less than patent.[40] It is often difficult to determine in such cases whether the homilist is referring to himself, as in the example from *In Col. hom. 3*, or is employing the first-person plural as a rhetorical device.[41] This is no basis for dismissing the evidence out of hand, however. Just as there is at present no way of proving that in this instance Chrysostom is indeed talking from the stance of bishop, there is also no way of proving conclusively that he is not bishop, but presbyter. The data are equivocal and the homily's status as regards provenance should rather be treated as uncertain.

The equivocal nature of such allusions is further seen in the case of *In Heb. hom. 4*. Until recently this homily has been located firmly at Constantinople,[42] with the result that the data about to be adduced have been overlooked. In the midst of a discussion of pagan versus Christian funeral practices Chrysostom, appearing to number himself among the presbyters, states:

> Tell me, to what purpose do you summon presbyters and those who chant psalms? Isn't it so that they might provide comfort? Isn't it so that they might honour the deceased? Why then do you insult him? Why do you make a spectacle of him? Why do you act it up, as if on a stage? We come presenting arguments about the resurrection, through the honour we accord the departed

---

[38] PG 62,322 17-323 9. See in particular the last few lines of this passage, where Chrysostom arrives at the point: "How is it not ridiculous if, after hearing so many times that we have peace, we war against one another; that, although we are on both the receiving and on the returning end, we war with the one who gives the peace (τῷ διδόντι τὴν εἰρήνην)? You say, 'And with your spirit', and you slander him (αὐτόν) outside?".

[39] PG 62,323 20-22.

[40] See Chapter Two, n. 15. Tillemont (Chapter One, p. 62) raised this same issue with respect to *In Eph. hom. 11*, although it should be noted that in both cases some bias is involved, since an Antiochene provenance had already been predicated on the basis of other evidence.

[41] In the passage from *In Titum hom. 1* quoted above John uses the first-person plural to identify with the audience, even though we later learn that the person about whom he has been speaking in the third person is himself.

[42] For the dismissal of the evidence previously adduced in support of the Constantinopolitan provenance of *In Heb. hom. 4*, as also that of the other homilies on Hebrews, see Allen-Mayer, "Hebrews: The Last Series?", 311-333. The argument which follows was first presented there on pp. 336-339.

educating everyone, particularly those not yet touched by death, to bear it nobly if ever such a thing should happen. And yet you introduce those who, as is their lot, completely ruin our effect?[43]

The "we" clearly refers back to the presbyters and psalmodists summoned to attend the funeral, but again we encounter the problem of how to interpret it. Is the first-person plural here inclusive ("I, my fellow presbyters and the psalmodists") or collective ("we the class of priests and psalmodists in general" or even "we the Christian element", as opposed to the hired female mourners)?

The supporting evidence is equally difficult to interpret. The authoritative tone which John employs and his repeated threats to ban from synaxis those who persist in such practices have commonly been interpreted as an indication of his episcopal status.[44] Yet, as we demonstrate later, such a tone is as often used by the homilist when presbyter as bishop.[45] Included amongst those who demonstrate their grief in a pagan manner, and whom Chrysostom finds particularly offensive, are men and women who profess to pursue a monastic life.[46] The fact that banning them from regular synaxis for some time might be an effective punishment, as also the insinuation that they furnish an especially poor example for passing pagans, suggests that these ascetic men and women are urban and therefore Constantinopolitan, since they are not withdrawn from the world in the manner considered typical for Antioch.[47] This evidence is counterbalanced, however, by John's request that the "leaders" (οἱ πρόεδροι) and the entire audience make a certain prayer their own.[48] This expression has usually been thought to denote a lack of authority on the homilist's part and has regularly been interpreted as an indication that he is presbyter.[49]

Since in this case the supporting data pull us in both directions, ultimately we are none the wiser. They do suggest, however, that there are problems with one or more of the above criteria, if such supposedly conflicting evidence can be found in one and the same homily. This further

---

[43] PG 63,44 19-28.

[44] See, e.g., Tillemont, Montfaucon and Bonsdorff (Chapter One, pp. 65, 101 and 198).

[45] See pp. 331-336 below.

[46] PG 63,43 23-29: Πλὴν ἀλλ᾽ οὐχ οὕτω δεινὸν τοῦτο· ὅταν δέ τις, ἢ γυνή, ἢ ἀνὴρ ἐσταυρῶσθαι τῷ κόσμῳ λέγων, ὁ μὲν τρίχας τίλλῃ, ἡ δὲ κωκύῃ μεγάλα, τί τούτου ἀσχημονέστερον; Πιστεύσατέ μοι λέγοντι· εἴγε ὡς ἐχρῆν ἐγίνετο, πολὺν ἔδει χρόνον τοὺς τοιούτους εἴργεσθαι τῶν οὐδῶν τῶν τῆς ἐκκλησίας.

[47] This is discussed further in section 6 (pp. 426-434 below).

[48] PG 63,44 5-8: Γένοιτο μὲν οὖν τοῦτο, καὶ τοῦτο εὔχομαι, καὶ τοὺς προέδρους δὲ καὶ πάντας ὑμᾶς ὑπὲρ ἀλλήλων παρακαλῶ δεηθῆναι τοῦ Θεοῦ, καὶ κοινὴν ποιήσασθαι ταύτην εὐχήν·

[49] See pp. 342-346 below.

suggests that either certain criteria are valid under certain conditions, but can safely be accorded secondary status or negated under others — the practice pursued in the past — or one or more of the above criteria must be reassessed as invalid. Which of the alternatives proves the more responsible has yet to be determined. Whatever the case, the situation which has been exposed in this homily underlines the uncertainty which attaches to an allusion made by the homilist with regard to his status. It also points out the danger which can attach to placing too great a reliance on one piece of evidence, without first minutely sifting the homily for other potentially significant data.

The third proposition associated with this criterion, the argument *ex silentio*, is to be dismissed out of hand. As Nägele pointed out in his discussion of the two series on the Letters to Timothy, the argument, though attractive, is flawed. If, when the episcopal office is under discussion, one can argue that a failure on the part of the homilist to equate himself with it indicates that he is not a bishop and is therefore preaching at Antioch, one ought with equal validity to be able to argue that, when the office of deacon or presbyter are under discussion, John's failure to equate himself with either indicates that he does not hold the office of deacon or presbyter and is therefore preaching at Constantinople.[50] As Nägele further points out, if Chrysostom is genuinely preaching at Antioch in the cases adduced in the literature, in the place of personal reference one ought to expect not just impersonal reference to the episcopacy, but an allusion in that context to Flavian, the incumbent of the office at Antioch. Neither of these conditions has been required of the evidence, even though each is a logical extension of the original argument.[51]

In fact when one examines all of the homilies with respect to which the argument *ex silentio* has been invoked,[52] in very few of these can the

---

[50] Nägele, "Homilien zu d. Timotheusbriefen", 126-127.

[51] Nägele's inclusion of reference to the diaconal office, however, can scarcely be considered useful, since logically this would only exclude the possibility that he is deacon. This option is in any case excluded, since the fact that the information appears in a homily indicates that John is ordained to the office of preaching, a duty restricted to the rank of presbyter or higher. See Bingham, *Antiquities*, XIV.iv.2; and Olivar, *La predicación* , 546-547 and 529-537. This argument, of course, assumes that the homily in question was preached and is not a piece of commentary written in a homiletic style.

[52] I.e., *In II Cor. hom. 14, 15, 18; In I Tim. hom. 5, 10, 11, 15; In II Tim. hom. 2, 4;* and *In Titum hom. 1, 2.* In the case of *In Titum hom. 1*, although some scholars have acknowledged the personal reference and have argued for Antioch on the basis that the remark is rhetorical, Lietzmann, "J. Chrysostomos", 1818 ll.47-53, implies that Chrysostom in this instance refers to the episcopal office in an impersonal way. Bonsdorff, *Zur Predigttätigkeit*, 62-63, relies upon both arguments, adducing the first with respect to *hom. 1*, the second with regard to *In Titum hom. 2*.

discussion of the episcopal office be said to be explicit, ensuring that it is the only office to which the homilist refers,[53] while not all of the examples fulfill the requirement that the office be discussed in an impersonal way.[54] Indeed in only four of the eleven homilies adduced (*In II Cor. hom. 18, In I Tim. hom. 11, In Titum hom. 1-2*) is the office of bishop clearly mentioned. The remaining examples are to be held in suspicion since in the second of the above four homilies Chrysostom, explicitly using the terms presbyter and bishop, states that there is essentially no difference between the two offices. Presbyters too, he says, have received the office of preaching and authority over the church. Only in the power to ordain do bishops exceed them.[55] Therefore when Chrysostom discusses ecclesiastical office without making it patent that his focus is the episcopal office, as in many of these passages, there is no certainty that the discussion is not inclusive of the office of presbyter or that under the gloss of a general label such as ἱερεύς (priest) his focus does not shift back and forth from the one office to the other.[56] Certainty that the episcopal office alone is under discussion is required, if the criterion is to be effective.

The questionable nature of the argument can be demonstrated from another angle. For an argument *ex silentio* to have any validity a clearly established rule must first exist. The standard which is implicit in this instance reads: if *x* is the case (i.e., the homilist is bishop), then every time that condition *a* (a discussion of episcopal office) occurs, condition

---

[53] One must distinguish here between discussion of the office which is explicit, that is, where the term ἐπίσκοπος is used or where ἀρχή or another term denoting authority is linked to the power to ordain, and that which has been perceived to refer to the episcopal office, that is, where less specific terms such as "teacher", "shepherd", "priest" or "father" are used. For further discussion of this point see pp. 331-342 below.

[54] *In II Cor. hom. 15* is to be removed from the list since John, after an extensive discussion of ἀρχή in the church (PG 61,507 43-510 26), draws distinction between his own and secular ἀρχή in the first and second persons, indicating authority of a kind usually considered sufficient for assigning a homily to Constantinople: ἐγὼ δὲ οὐχ οὕτως, ἀλλὰ τὸ νόσημα ἀποτέμνω· καὶ εἴργω μὲν αὐτὸν μυστηρίων καὶ ἱερῶν περιβόλων ... ἐγὼ δὲ οὔτε ἀφίημι ἀτιμώρητον, οὔτε κολάζω, ὡς σύ, ἀλλὰ καὶ δίκην ἀπαιτῶ τὴν ἐμοὶ πρέπουσαν, καὶ διορθοῦμαι τὸ γεγενημένον (PG 61,510 29-42).

[55] *In I Tim. hom. 11* (PG 62,553 41-46 a.i.): Καὶ γὰρ καὶ αὐτοὶ διδασκαλίαν εἰσὶν ἀναδεδεγμένοι, καὶ προστασίαν τῆς Ἐκκλησίας· καὶ ἃ περὶ ἐπισκόπων εἶπε, ταῦτα καὶ πρεσβυτέροις ἁρμόττει. Τῇ γὰρ χειροτονίᾳ μόνῃ ὑπερβεβήκασι, καὶ τούτῳ μόνῳ δοκοῦσι πλεονεκτεῖν τοὺς πρεσβυτέρους.

[56] It is noteworthy that wide-ranging and explicit discussion of the kind associated with the episcopal office rarely occurs in conjunction with the office of presbyter. Even when presbyters are mentioned, this not infrequently occurs in the context of comment upon the role of bishops. See, e.g., *In Acta apost. hom. 3* (PG 60,40 10-13); *In Phil. hom. 1* (PG 62,183 13-35); *In I Tim. hom. 13* (PG 62,565 38-41). For an example where presbyters are mentioned on their own see the passage from *In Heb. hom. 4* quoted (p. 324) above.

b (personal reference) is also met. Only when this rule is first shown to
be consistent and true under all conditions can it be argued that if condition *b* is not satisfied, then situation *x* is not the case. The argument *ex
silentio* in question, however, derives its authority not from a well-established rule, verified over many examples, but from a single occurrence.[57]
This scarcely constitutes the secure basis required. Moreover, when the
original rule is tested against other evidence it is neither consistent nor
true. In *In Acta apost. hom.* 3 Chrysostom attempts to point out the essential undesirability of the episcopal office at some length and in considerable detail,[58] yet, although it is universally assumed that this homily
was preached at Constantinople, the issue is discussed in an entirely impersonal way and at no point does the homilist openly state that the
opinion expressed derives from personal experience.[59]

Thus of the three types of data which fall under this category only the
first, where Chyrsostom explicitly uses the title "bishop" or "presbyter"
and clearly applies this to himself, is valid under all circumstances. In
the case of the second, where such titles are used but the relation to the
person of the homilist is allusory rather than direct, the conclusion to be
drawn from the data is usually open to question and therefore uncertain.
If, however, the homily in which such an allusion occurs contains further
useful data, this uncertainty may eventually be either removed or the
conclusion upgraded to probable. The third, the argument *ex silentio*, is
invalid and is therefore to be removed from the list of criteria.

b. *Occupation of throne*

Although it is never openly stated in the literature, at the basis of the
criterion associated with the question of whether or not John occupies a
throne lies the assumption that the θρόνος is unique among the furnishings of a church and that it plays a role identical to that of the western
cathedra, in that it is understood to be synonymous with the episcopal

---

[57] *In Col. hom.* 3. In *In Acta apost. hom.* 9, the only other occasion on which John
explicitly mentions that he is bishop, the comment arises from discussion of the evils of
swearing oaths, not from a reflection on the role of bishop.

[58] PG 60,38 51-42 39.

[59] There is a vague possibility that he alludes to his episcopal status at the close of the
homily (PG 60,42 28-39), but this is by no means certain. The comment at PG 60,39 55
(Οὐκ ἄλλως λέγω, ἀλλ᾽ ὡς ἔχω καὶ διάκειμαι) should be read as referring to his personal conviction and feelings, rather than experience. See our translation in Mayer-Allen, *John
Chrysostom*, 177-183, esp. 180.

office.[60] However, although Chrysostom uses the term καθέδρα once in this very specific and symbolic sense,[61] and although there is a strong suspicion that when he employs the word thronos elsewhere the same tacit equation is effected, there is no certainty that on all occasions when the term is used the two are interchangeable in the minds of both audience and homilist.

The question here is not whether Chrysostom refers to the throne as a symbol of episcopal office, but whether the equation is so strong at this time at both Antioch and Constantinople that the thronos is associated exclusively with that office. There is no question that in certain cases where the term is employed by the homilist it is to be understood that the thronos is the seat regularly occupied by the presiding bishop. In *De statuis hom.* 3, wishing to draw attention to the absence of Flavian, he refers to the vacant state of that item of furniture.[62] Again, in his ordination homily Chrysostom alludes to the succession of Meletius by Flavian, using occupation of the thronos as shorthand for occupation of the episcopal office at Antioch.[63] On another occasion, in the course of general discussion of the character appropriate to a bishop, he explicitly associates the thronos with that office, at one point equating the term with ἀρχή, at another with the office of preaching.[64] All of these examples sit well with *In Col. hom.* 3, where John informs us that he presently occupies such a seat,[65] later stating openly that he is bishop.[66]

In all of these cases, however, we have independent evidence that the thronos in question is to be associated with the role of bishop.[67] What of

---

[60] For a discussion of the development in use and status of the episcopal throne see E. Stommel, "Die bischöfliche Kathedra im christlichen Altertum", *Münchener theologische Zeitschrift* 3 (1952) 17-32; and id., "Bischofsstuhl und hoher Thron", JbAC 1 (1958) 52-75.

[61] See *In princ. Act. hom.* 2 (PG 51,86 45-48), where the term is used to evoke the episcopal line of descent from the apostle Peter to the present bishop of Antioch.

[62] PG 49,47 2-4: Ὅταν εἰς τὸν θρόνον ἀπίδω τοῦτον ἔρημον ὄντα καὶ κενὸν τοῦ διδασκάλου ... δακρύω μέν, ὅτι παρόντα οὐχ ὁρῶ τὸν πατέρα·

[63] *Cum presbyter fuit* (CPG 4317) SC 272,414 269-416 277: Καίτοι γε ὅτε τὸν πρότερον πατέρα ἀπεβάλομεν ... ἐν ἀπορίᾳ τὰ ἡμέτερα ἦν ... ὡς οὐ προσδοκῶντες τὸν θρόνον τοῦτον ἕτερον ἄνδρα τοιοῦτον δέξεσθαι ... ἀλλ᾽ οὕτως ἀθρόον, ὡς ἂν εἰ ὁ μακάριος αὐτὸς ἐκεῖνος ἀπὸ τῆς λάρνακος ἀναστάς, ἐπὶ τὸν θρόνον ἀνέβη πάλιν τοῦτον.

[64] *In Titum hom.* 2 (PG 62,671 40-44; 672 12-16; 673 26-28).

[65] PG 62,324 13-18.

[66] PG 62,324 46-49.

[67] In *De statuis hom.* 3, the city is said to have been the first named "Christian" (see p. 368 below), making it clear that the "teacher" and "father" who occupies the thronos is the bishop of Antioch, Flavian. In *Cum presbyter fuit* Chrysostom, by referring to "the common teacher of our country" (SC 272,402 150-1 ; see 2.d.i below), can only be referring to the bishop of a see of major influence. The circumstances of that bishop's life (SC 272,404 166-9) combined with the information that his predeccessor is deceased (SC 272,416 276)

a case, such as *In Acta apost. hom. 8*, where twice the homilist indicates that he occupies a thronos but the comments stand essentially in isolation?[68] John states that he has ἀρχή, that he sits on a thronos and that he is accountable for the salvation of his subjects, all in vocabulary reminiscent of the above examples.[69] Cumulatively, the two passages strongly suggest that he is bishop. Yet in *Cum presbyter fuit* Chrysostom finds no difficulty in calling the presbyteral office an ἀρχή,[70] while the notion that accountability is a mark solely of episcopal authority can be similarly dismissed.[71] If we distance ourselves from the presumption that the occupation of a thronos is the exclusive right of bishops, even in the late fourth century, a degree of suspicion can be seen to attach to this too. As Bingham points out, there is evidence that in the east at this time in certain churches presbyters were permitted to sit on thrones alongside the bishop.[72] While these thrones are distinguished from the episcopal seat either through status or physical location,[73] the range of vocabulary used in both instances is nonetheless the same.[74] Evidence from other, if contemporary, churches is, of course, no proof that this was the case also at Constantinople or Antioch. However, since, as is demonstrated in the following section, many of the factors once considered definitive proof of Chrysostom's episcopal status prove to reflect more accurately the view of the investigating scholar than that of the homilist, without further evidence it is better to maintain an open mind in this case than to draw a premature conclusion.

Before closing this section, there is a further point which needs to be made and which may strengthen the case that occupation of a thronos is, in the experience of the homilist, exclusive to those who hold episcopal office. In the literature, consideration of the occupant of a thronos is re-

---

confirm that it is Flavian, the bishop of Antioch. For the information that the office under discussion in *In Titum hom. 2* is that of bishop see PG 62,671 28-29.

[68] The following discussion is based on Allen-Mayer, "A New Approach", 24-25.

[69] PG 60,74 21-26: Ἡ καθέλετέ με ταυτησὶ τῆς ἀρχῆς, ἢ μένοντα μὴ περιβάλλετε κινδύνοις. Οὐκ ἀνέχομαι ἐπὶ τὸν θρόνον τοῦτον ἀναβαίνειν μὴ μεγάλα κατορθῶν. Εἰ γὰρ μὴ τοῦτο δυνατόν, βέλτιον ἑστάναι κάτω. Ἄρχοντος γὰρ μηδὲν τοὺς ἀρχομένους ὠφελοῦντος οὐδὲν ἀθλιώτερον; 76 3-7: καὶ ἕως ἂν ἐν τῷ θρόνῳ καθέζωμαι τούτῳ, οὐδὲν προήσομαι τῶν αὐτοῦ δικαιωμάτων. Ἄν μέ τις καταβιβάσῃ, λοιπὸν ἀνεύθυνός εἰμι· ἕως δ' ἂν ὑπεύθυνος ὦ, οὐ δύναμαι παριδεῖν, οὐ διὰ τὴν ἐμὴν κόλασιν, ἀλλὰ διὰ τὴν ὑμετέραν σωτηρίαν·

[70] SC 272,388 5-6.

[71] See pp. 331-336 below.

[72] Bingham, *Antiquities*, II.xix.5.

[73] Bingham, *Antiquities*, II.xix.6, adduces evidence for a semicircular arrangement with the episcopal throne located in the middle.

[74] I.e., θρόνος or καθέδρα. For a more recent discussion of the evidence in relation to Constantinople see van de Paverd, *Messliturgie*, 413-420.

stricted to the local bishop. In *Laus Diodori* (CPG 4406), however, Chrysostom is preaching on an occasion at Antioch when Diodore, then bishop of Tarsus, was present. In his opening remarks John tells us that at a recent synaxis the visiting bishop ascended the thronos within the church in which he and the audience are presently situated in order to preach.[75] There is no indication on his part that Flavian is also present, although this could be due to the fact that attention is focused upon the visiting bishop. The homilist does provide a rare piece of information, however. At the point in the synaxis when Diodore was delivering his homily, the presbyter was himself seated, if at some distance from the guest homilist. This raises almost as many questions as it answers (what was John sitting on? where was he situated in relation to the apse and thronos? was this normative or a peculiarity of the church in question? what occurred when there was no visiting bishop?). However, it does suggest two things — namely that in this instance Chrysostom most probably does not consider that he is seated on a thronos; and that at Antioch there was, in the minds of both homilist and audience, a sufficiently strong association between the thronos and the episcopal office per se, that either the term was reserved not for a single item of furniture but for any seating occupied by a bishop or, if only the one thronos existed in a church, that that seat could be yielded temporarily to a bishop other than the local incumbent. Is it likely that Chrysostom would elsewhere describe himself as seated in this manner when a presbyter of Antioch, given the nature of this association? On present evidence this is unanswerable, but it does seem that it is less than likely.

In sum, contrary to the expectation that occupation of a thronos by the homilist is proof positive of his episcopal status, the equation is more reliable when inverted, and indication by Chrysostom that another occupies the thronos would appear to prove that he is not of episcopal status and is therefore presbyter. Personal occupation of a thronos on the part of the homilist, on the other hand, while likely to indicate that he is bishop, cannot, without substantiating evidence, be considered certain proof of that status.

c. *Relationship with audience*

Just as there is no doubt that in certain cases the occupation of a thronos is to be equated with episcopal authority, there is no question that when he is bishop John does refer to himself using terms such as

---

[75] PG 52,761 1-8: Ὁ σοφὸς οὗτος καὶ γενναῖος διδάσκαλος, πρώην ... ἐπὶ τὸν θρόνον τοῦτον ἀναβάς, ἐμοὶ τοῦ λόγου τῶν προοιμίων ἀπήρξατο ... ἐγὼ δὲ πόρρω καθήμενος...

προεστώς or metaphoric labels such as "father" and "shepherd";[76] that he refers to his ἀρχή, προστασία and accountability;[77] and that he uses an authoritative tone when chastising his audience.[78] There is also no doubt that the same terms are employed by him in the course of general discussion of the episcopal office.[79] These points are not at issue. For the criterion as manifested in 2.c.i-iv to be effective, however, it must be proven both that such intimations of authority occur exclusively in homilies delivered by him as a bishop, and are not to be found in sermons which he delivered as a presbyter at Antioch; and that Chrysostom never associates the level of authority denoted by these terms with the office of presbyter. When the various aspects of the criterion are assessed in this light, the whole notion that the possession of authority is a reliable indication of episcopal status steadily pales.[80]

As already noted in our discussion of criterion 2.a (direct evidence of personal status), in *In I Tim. hom. 11* Chrysostom indicates that from his own point of view, and perhaps also from the point of view of the time, there is in reality little difference between the offices of presbyter and bishop. While the latter is to be distinguished by his power to ordain, *both* have authority (προστασία) over the church.[81] If this view is a genuine reflection of his own understanding of the two offices, then the metaphors denoting headship, the use of an authoritative tone and the claims to authority assembled under this criterion should all appear in homilies delivered at Antioch. A careful sifting of the evidence shows this to be the case. In *De statuis hom. 20*, as had been recognised as long ago as Montfaucon,[82] the homilist berates his audience in a manner which, in any other homily, would have been considered definitively episcopal.[83]

---

[76] See *De regressu* (CPG 4394) REB 19 (1961) 114 3.4-6, 118 10.3-8 (church's husband, shepherd, root); *In Col. hom. 3*, PG 62,322 65-323 22 (προεστώς).

[77] See *In Acta apost. hom. 9* (PG 60,84 25-31) (ἀρχή); *In Col. hom. 3* (PG 62,324 13-18) (προεδρία); *Contra ludos et theatra* (CPG 4441.7) PG 56,270 22-23 (personally accountable for salvation of audience). For the grounds upon which this last homily is to be assigned to Constantinople see 3.d.i below.

[78] See *In Acta apost. hom. 9* (PG 60,83 49-84 8) and *Contra ludos et theatra* (PG 56,268 29-37).

[79] See, e.g., *In Acta apost. hom. 3* (PG 60,39 5-7); *In Titum hom. 1* (PG 62,667 61-668 5; 669 50; 670 10-11); *In Titum hom. 2* (PG 62,671 25-26).

[80] The following discussion develops points first raised in Allen-Mayer, "A New Approach", 25-27.

[81] See n. 55 above.

[82] Montfaucon, IX 420 (preface to the series on Romans).

[83] PG 49,204 20-23: Ἰδοὺ προλέγω, καὶ διαμαρτύρομαι, καὶ λαμπρᾷ βοῶ τῇ φωνῇ, μηδεὶς τῶν ἐχόντων ἐχθρὸν προσίτω τῇ ἱερᾷ τραπέζῃ καὶ δεχέσθω τὸ σῶμα τοῦ Κυρίου· μηδεὶς προσιὼν ἐχθρὸν ἐχέτω. See further PG 49,211 13-212 4. The provenance of this homily can be confirmed independently of the series in which it is found. Twice John refers to events associated

To this example can now be added *In Col. hom. 7* where, at a time when he is presbyter,[84] John threatens to ban the women of the congregation from the church if they do not improve.[85] In this instance he proceeds to justify the threat by pointing out that the accountability for their actions rests with himself.[86]

With regard to the various metaphors which, when they have been applied by Chrysostom to himself, have been considered to denote episcopal status, the willingness to overlook these in the case of homilies considered on other grounds to have been delivered at Antioch demonstrates the essential ambiguity which attaches to them. Thus Montfaucon saw no conflict in dismissing as insignificant the homilist's designation of himself as "shepherd" in *In Rom. hom. 29*, on the grounds that such terms could be used of ordinary priests as well as bishops,[87] while adducing this same evidence in the case of *In illud: Ne timueritis hom. 1* (CPG 4414) as proof of the homily's Constantinopolitan provenance.[88] Bonsdorff likewise noted that in certain "Antiochene" sermons (*In Matt. hom. 32, In Ioh. hom. 13*) John calls himself "father", while in the case of *In Phil. hom. 9* he admitted that the homilist calls the class of priests in general "fathers".[89] This did not stop Bonsdorff from promoting the term elsewhere as an indication of episcopal status,[90] even though he did not consider its authority sufficient to call into question the provenance of the above-mentioned Antiochene homilies. That within the scope of Chrysostom's Weltanschauung the range of persons covered by the concept "spiritual father" is in fact broader than just bishop or even presbyter can be demonstrated from *In Matt. hom. 68/69*. There the leader of an extra-urban community of monks is distinguished by this label.[91]

---

with the riots, connecting them explicitly with the city (PG 49,201 32-35; 208 12-15), while on several occasions he makes it clear that it is currently Lent (PG 49,197 19-21 *a.i.*; 208 9-14).

[84] For the proof of this claim see 9.a-b (pp. 443-445 below).

[85] PG 62,350 27-31: Ἰδοὺ προλέγω· οὐκέτι παραινῶ, ἀλλ᾽ ἐπιτάττω καὶ παραγγέλλω...ὅτι ἂν ἐπιμένητε ταῦτα ποιοῦσαι, οὐκ ἀνέξομαι οὐδὲ δέξομαι ὑμᾶς οὐδὲ ἀφήσω τῶν οὐδῶν ὑπερβῆναι τούτων. See further PG 62,350 48-52, 351 1-6.

[86] PG 62,350 52-55: Ὅταν μέλλω κρίνεσθαι ἐπὶ τοῦ βήματος τοῦ Χριστοῦ, μακρὰν ὑμεῖς ἑστήκατε, καὶ ἡ παρ᾽ ὑμῶν χάρις εἰς οὐδέν, ἐμοῦ τὰς εὐθύνας παρέχοντος.

[87] See Chapter One, p. 98. Cf. the approach taken by Nägele, "Homilien zu d. Timotheusbriefen", 133 n. 1.

[88] See Chapter One, p. 92.

[89] Bonsdorff, *Zur Predigttätigkeit*, 78.

[90] See, e.g., Chapter One, p. 196 (*In II Thess. hom. 4*) and 198 (*In Heb. hom. 23*).

[91] PG 58,644 45-46: Ἡγεῖται δὲ αὐτοῖς τῆς εὐχῆς, ὁ πατὴρ καὶ ὁ προεστηκώς. Although a number of monks were subsequently ordained bishops (e.g., Diodore of Tarsus, Flavian of Antioch, Acacius of Beroea, Theodoret of Cyrrhus), one would not at this time expect to see a person of episcopal status acting as the head of an extra-urban ascetic community in

As for ἀρχή as a province also of the presbyteral office, as we noted above,[92] in the very first sermon preached after his ordination to that office Chrysostom both applies this term and describes presbyteral rank as one of the highest positions one can hope to achieve.[93] While this comment is incorporated within a highly rhetorical flourish — the self-deprecating opening to the homily bears marked similarity to an acceptance speech at a modern awards ceremony — it nonetheless indicates that the presbyteral office could be described in this manner without pushing beyond its limits the semantic range of the term. That its use here is not an aberration but part of the homilist's wider view of the respective ministries of presbyter and bishop is illustrated by *De decem mill. tal. deb.* (CPG 4368). There John refers to the weight of responsibility attached to the role of "leader of the church", indicating that as far as he is concerned the term covers both presbyters and bishops.

> Not just the secular officials, but also the leaders of the churches will have to give an account of their particular office (the accounts these latter submit for audit are grim and weighty in the extreme). For he who has been entrusted with the service of the Word will be scrutinised there minutely as to whether through either reluctance or objection he passed over saying anything that he should have said, and through his actions demonstrated that he pronounced everything and hid nothing that was of benefit. Again, he who has attained the episcopacy, in as much as he has ascended to a greater level of importance, will have demanded of him a more extensive account, not just of his teaching and supervision of the poor but also of the worthiness of his ordinations and countless other deeds.[94]

This same essential blurring of the roles of presbyter and bishop with respect to leadership, authority and responsibility is demonstrated outside of the homiletic corpus in the treatise *De sacerdotio* (CPG 4316).[95]

To sum up thus far, it is true that in the late fourth century, as viewed from a later perspective, the main distinction between the offices of bishop and presbyter lay in the source of their authority. That of a bishop

---

Syria. Monk-bishops were at this point usually actively involved in their sees. The term in this instance is more likely to refer to a non-ordained ascetic.

[92] See p. 330.

[93] *Cum presbyter fuit* (SC 272,398 4-6): Καὶ τίς ἂν ταῦτα πιστεύσειεν, ὅτι ἡμέρας οὔσης, νηφόντων ἀνθρώπων καὶ ἐγρηγορότων, μειρακίσκος εὐτελὴς καὶ ἀπερριμμένος πρὸς ὕψος ἀρχῆς ἀνηνέχθη τοσοῦτον;

[94] PG 51,23 11-23.

[95] The analyses of the treatise's vocabulary undertaken by C. Jacob, "Zur Amtsterminologie" (see n. 29), 307-315 and M. Lochbrunner, *Über das Priestertum. Historische und systematische Untersuchung zum Priesterbild des Johannes Chrysostomus*, Bonn 1993, 162-176, highlight the complexity of the relationship.

was absolute, while that of a presbyter was entirely derived from and therefore dependent upon the authority of his bishop.[96] It is not without reason then that it has been proposed that everything that Chrysostom did as bishop must have been based on this authority and that this in turn will have been reflected in his patterns of speech. It is a short step from this to assume that a presbyter firmly under his bishop's thumb will have spoken in a manner commensurate with his status. However, as we shall see again and again as we work our way through the various criteria, it is not the objective or long-term view of the situation at Antioch or Constantinople in the late fourth century which is ultimately important. Rather it is the subjective view which must be allowed to determine how we interpret information. That is, how did John or his audience view the various political, social and ecclesiastical institutions and situations as they lived with them and through them from day to day? This does not mean that our own historical view of affairs is to be discarded in the pursuit of provenance, but rather that, when the objective view does not adequately explain the full range of evidence, the view of homilist or audience should be sought, and it should ultimately be that contemporaneous point of view which is allowed to dictate the conclusion. In the present instance it is not the concrete distinction between the authority available to John as presbyter and as bishop which adequately explains the manner in which he speaks and refers to his role, but his personal definition of the role of priest and bishop as manifested in the relationship between himself and his audience.

The next questions to arise are these. If the use of authoritative tone can be shown to be independent of status, is the converse, so-called "presbyteral tone", likewise independent? Can a bishop speak in a familiar manner to his audience? Can it be that the use of such a tone stems rather from the homilist's private view of himself or is at times dictated by the demands of rhetoric? In other words, when Chrysostom speaks in a humble and familiar manner, is this confined to homilies delivered when he was presbyter? These questions are more difficult to answer. It should be noted, however, that the argument regarding presbyteral tone has only ever been raised with respect to catechetical material. The possibility that catechetical instruction, whether conducted by bishop or presbyter, demanded a different kind of relationship from that involved in the more public homiletic sphere must be entertained here.

One wonders, moreover, to what extent the entire argument from episcopal or non-episcopal tone stems from a fundamental lack of understanding of the character of Chrysostom. The way in which John views himself appears to have been little affected by any differences in

---

[96] Bingham, *Antiquities*, II.iii.

the priestly offices which he occupied. Thus, where any other individual
elevated to the episcopacy of the imperial capital might with reason have
been expected to respond significantly to the increased power and status
which came with that office, a close and systematic reading of John's
homiletic output over both periods reveals a priest who, on the one hand,
maintained a surprising degree of humility and, on the other, was driven
by a strong sense of duty and commitment to the salvation of his various
congregations. It is likely that, had he been more self-serving in his out-
look and less committed, he would have been more diplomatic in his
preaching and his episcopal career would not have been so abruptly ter-
minated.[97] It is therefore important when presenting arguments based on
such a subjective matter as tone to distinguish carefully between the office and the person. If the person is taken into consideration it is unlikely
that expressions of humility on the one hand, and forcefulness or
authoritativeness on the other, are exclusive to any period in Chrysostom's career and can therefore be used to distinguish one location from
another. This probability is further strengthened by the rhetorical element in homiletic delivery which demands exaggerated expressions of
humility and, conversely, forcefulness, depending on the desired outcome, the audience and the occasion. When these factors are taken into
consideration, views such as those espoused by Stilting, Rauschen,
Bonsdorff and others,[98] that deference to others localises homilies in the
first year of preaching at Antioch and that the series are to be arranged
according to the increasing lack of such expressions, must now be held
in suspicion.

d. *Indication that another is of higher ecclesiastical status*

Given that we are dealing with a period which predates the development of patriarchal sees and that the bishop of Rome did not at any time
during the period in question visit either Antioch or Constantinople, it
seems safe to assert the validity of the premise which informs the criterion reliant on indication that another person is of higher ecclesiastical
status than John, namely that at both Antioch and Constantinople the local bishop took precedence over all other ecclesiastical office-holders. It
therefore holds that, if John defers to another cleric as a person of higher
status, the possibility that he is the local bishop and situated at Constantinople is eliminated. Rather, he must by default at the time of the hom-

---

[97] This internal view does much to explain the perceived faults in Chrysostom's
character described by the external sources. For these see Kelly, *Golden Mouth*, 114-127.

[98] See most recently Lochbrunner, *Über das Priestertum* (n. 95), 234-235.

ily in question be a presbyter and therefore located at Antioch. The exact status of the individual of higher rank, whether more senior presbyter, visiting or local bishop, is, for the purposes of the criterion, unimportant.

i. Bishop

If it is difficult to assess the implication with regard to John's status when he applies an "episcopal" metaphor to himself, in situations where he employs that same or a similar metaphor to describe another individual the identity of the office alluded to is more easy to determine. This is not because the ambiguity attached to the label is removed, but because in a large number of cases context and other factors allow the various possibilities to be narrowed to a single option.

The challenge posed by this type of evidence is seen by reviewing several of the instances that have been adduced in the literature. In the case of *De incompr. dei nat. hom. 1* (CPG 4318) Chrysostom opens by exclaiming: "What's this? The shepherd isn't present and the sheep are standing neatly in rank!".[99] After developing the shepherd-sheep metaphor at some length, he concludes his opening comments by underscoring the strength of the bond between that individual and the current audience: "These words the teacher speaks to you, though absent, and, wherever he may be at present, he is picturing you and your assembly and is at this moment seeing not those who are there with him and in his presence, so much as you who are absent."[100] How do we know that this shepherd-teacher is a bishop? The answer is that, strictly speaking, we do not. The title of the homily, which identifies the individual as bishop, is to be held in suspicion on the grounds that it contains no information which is independent of the text.[101] The statement "in the bishop's absence" could simply be derived from the homilist's opening remark. As for the manuscripts in which pronouns in the first-person plural are substituted for the second-person plural pronouns more commonly found in the above passage,[102] suggesting that John includes himself among the sheep under the shepherd's supervision, none of these is early and all have been disregarded by Malingrey in the preparation of her text.[103]

---

[99] SC 28[bis],92 1-2.

[100] SC 28[bis],96 27-31.

[101] SC 28[bis],92: Τοῦ ἐν ἁγίοις πατρὸς ἡμῶν Ἰω ἀρχιεπισκόπου Κωνσταντινουπόλεως τοῦ Χρυσοστόμου περὶ ἀκαταλήπτου, ἀπόντος τοῦ ἐπισκόπου, πρὸς Ἀνομοίους λόγος ἀ. See rule 4, section 1 (p. 321) above.

[102] I.e., "us...us and our assembly...we who are absent". See PG 48,701 note b.

[103] See Malingrey, *Sur l'incompréhensibilité* (SC 28bis) 84-89.

Bearing in mind that, for whatever reason, the homilist does not consider himself the spiritual carer of the present congregation, we are faced with several options. The "shepherd" is indeed the local bishop and absent on a journey beyond the confines of the city, as proposed by Malingrey.[104] Chrysostom, as presbyter, therefore, is preaching in the main church at Antioch in his bishop's absence. The possibility that the homilist is substituting for another person of equal status, just as another acts as John's locum tenens when he is called away by Flavian from normal preaching duties at the synaxis prior to *In illud: In faciem ei restiti* (CPG 4391),[105] however, is also to be entertained. Difficult as it is to imagine that John, when bishop, might speak of a presbyter in this manner, on the analogy of *Habita postquam presbyter Gothus* (CPG 4441.9) one should nevertheless consider the possibility that he is guest-preacher at another congregation.[106] In these last two situations one would expect that Chrysostom is not overly familiar with his audience. That the present occasion is not an isolated occurrence and that the homilist preaches regularly before the present congregation, however, is suggested by a remark which occurs later in the homily, namely that he has been wanting for some time to preach to this specific group on the present topic, but has been putting it off until his audience seemed more receptive.[107] If, then, Chrysostom preaches regularly before the present audience but is not their chief soul-carer nor instructor, he cannot be bishop, so that the first option is the only one which is viable. This was not obvious at first glance and could be established only through a careful consideration of the context.

An example such as *Sermo 8 in Gen.*, on the other hand, requires less scrutiny of the context. There Chrysostom refers to the presence of the "teacher" and talks of the "fatherly" love which in consequence radiates from the middle of the thronos.[108] While the teacher's occupation of this particular seat leads one to suspect that the person is a bishop, all that it is necessary to understand here is that the fact that it is occupied by another precludes the possibility that the homilist is himself seated in that position.[109] In other cases it is the existence of independent evidence of

---

[104] Malingrey, *Sur l'incompréhensibilité* (SC 28bis) 92 n. 1.

[105] PG 51,372 1 *a.i.*-373 10.

[106] While it is not absolutely certain that this homily was preached at Constantinople, the quality of the data contained in the manuscript title makes it highly likely that the information is reliable. Regarding this point see n. 205 below.

[107] SC 28bis,130 334-132 345.

[108] SC 433,346 1.2-6: ἡ δὲ παρουσία τοῦ διδασκάλου φαιδροτέραν αὐτὴν εἰργάσατο. Οὐ γὰρ οὕτως ἥλιος, ἐκ μέσης τῶν οὐρανῶν τῆς κορυφῆς τὰς ἀκτῖνας ἀφιείς, καταλάμπει τὰ σώματα ὡς ὄψις πατρικῆς φιλοστοργίας, ἀκτῖνας ἀφιεῖσα ἐκ μέσου τοῦ θρόνου...

[109] Regarding this point see pp. 328-331 above.

Antiochene provenance which permits interpretation of the metaphor. Thus in *Adv. Iud. or.* 6, when John mentions the presence of "the father",[110] or in *De statuis hom.* 3, when he talks alternately of the "teacher" and "father",[111] we know that he is speaking of the bishop only because in the first, the city is clearly identified as that in which the riots took place,[112] while in the second, that person is indicated to be the normal occupant of the thronos.[113] In this latter instance the city is also firmly linked to an event from apostolic times.[114] Other cases are more difficult to interpret. In *In illud: Vidi dom. hom.* 6 Chrysostom refers to a formula recited during the eucharistic liturgy by "this great high-priest".[115] While his use of the inclusive first-person plural in contradistinction to that individual suggests that the homilist is not himself high-priest and president of the synaxis, the discussion itself is general and there is no clear indication as to whether John is discussing the present synaxis or some other occasion. The use of the demonstrative, on the other hand, does suggest that he is referring to an individual other than himself who is also present at the synaxis, a circumstance that would confirm that Chrysostom is the cleric of lower status. In the absence of supporting evidence and a clearer context, however, this conclusion can at present be considered no more than tentative.

A reference to the homilist and audience's "common father", as seen for instance in *De b. Philogonio* (CPG 4319),[116] is slightly less problematic. In this particular homily the immediate context in which the phrase occurs implies that the person is older and has been at the present location longer, since it is said that this person is more familiar with past events. Seniority to Chrysostom is further implied by the fact that this person will be speaking later on the same topic.[117] Earlier in the homily it is intimated that the occasion is one on which several sermons are scheduled for delivery.[118] That we are at Antioch is in any case confirmed by the nature of the relationship between the Philogonius whose festival

---

[110] PG 48,904 16 *a.i.*: Αἰδοῦμαι καὶ τοῦ πατρὸς τὴν παρουσίαν...

[111] See PG 49,47 2-49 22.

[112] See pp. 443-446 below.

[113] See pp. 328-331 above.

[114] See pp. 367-369 below.

[115] See SC 277,216 9-20: Διὰ τοῦτο καὶ ὁ μέγας οὗτος ἀρχιερεύς, ἐπειδὰν ἐπὶ τῆς ἁγίας ταύτης ἑστήκη τραπέζης, τὴν λογικὴν ἀναφέρων λατρείαν ... οὐχ ἁπλῶς ἡμᾶς ἐπὶ τὴν εὐφημίαν ταύτην καλεῖ...

[116] PG 48,752 47-50: Διὰ τοῦτο τῷ κοινῷ πατρὶ καὶ ζηλωτῇ τοῦ μακαρίου Φιλογονίου ταῦτα καταλιπόντες εἰπεῖν, ἅτε ἀκριβέστερον ἡμῶν εἰδότι τὰ ἀρχαῖα πάντα, πρὸς ἑτέραν δημηγορίας ὁδὸν βαδιούμεθα.

[117] For discussion of this point see pp. 351-360 below.

[118] PG 48,748 2-3 *a.i.*: ...τοὺς δὲ συνιόντας ἡμᾶς καὶ τοὺς λέγοντας καὶ τοὺς ἀκούοντας...

is being celebrated and the location. In a roundabout way Philogonius is said to have been a bishop of that city.[119] While this conforms to the situation at Antioch, where a Philogonius presided as bishop c. 320-324,[120] prior to 398 no bishop of that name is known to have been associated with Constantinople. After the manner of *De incompr. dei nat. hom. 1*, in *In kalendas* (CPG 4328) John calls attention to the absence of a member of the clergy, in this instance designated not "shepherd" or "teacher", but "high-priest and common father".[121] However, there is no difficulty in this instance in determining that the person is bishop, since the assembly of priests who are present at the synaxis, and among whom Chrysostom numbers himself,[122] are clearly subordinate to that individual.

Are there in fact any examples of an "episcopal" metaphor, qualified by the adjective κοινός (common) where the label does not refer to a bishop or to at least a person of higher status than the homilist? While the answer cannot be a categoric "no", it seems unlikely. In *De statuis hom. 6* "our priest and common father", also described as "teacher", is absent from the city on an embassy to the emperor,[123] indicating that the present location is not the city of imperial residence.[124] With the benefit of other information about the situation which pertained at Antioch following the riots, we know that this individual is the local bishop, Flavian.[125] In *De statuis hom. 21* the return of the "common father" from the city of imperial residence is celebrated, with the relationship between this individual and the rest of the congregation, John included, being underscored by such terms as "head", "shepherd", "teacher", "commander" and "high-priest".[126] In the homily *In ascensionem* (CPG 4342) the sudden reference to "this wise shepherd and common teacher", in the context of the construction of the present site of synaxis, suggests that that figure is

---

[119] PG 48,749 32-34: Διὸ μάλιστα μακαρίζω τὸν ἅγιον τοῦτον, ὅτι εἰ καὶ μετετάξατο καὶ πόλιν ἀφῆκε τὴν παρ' ἡμῖν...; 751 7-27: Πόθεν οὖν ἡμῖν ἀρκτέον τῶν ἐγκωμίων; Πόθεν ἄλλοθεν ἢ ἀπὸ τῆς ἀρχῆς, ἣν ἡ τοῦ Πνεύματος ἐνεχείρισεν αὐτῷ χάρις...Ὅτι δὲ ἐκεῖνον ὁ Θεὸς ἐχειροτόνησε, καὶ ἀπ' αὐτοῦ τοῦ τρόπου δῆλον. Ἐκ μέσης γὰρ τῆς ἀγορᾶς ἁρπασθείς, ἐπὶ τὸν θρόνον ἤγετο τοῦτον· ... καὶ ἀπὸ βήματος δικαστικοῦ ἐπὶ βῆμα ἤγετο ἱερόν.

[120] See Grumel, *La Chronologie*, Paris 1958, 446.

[121] PG 48,953 1-4: Καθάπερ χορὸς τὸν κορυφαῖον ἐπιζητεῖ, καὶ ναυτῶν πλήρωμα τὸν κυβερνήτην, οὕτω καὶ ὁ τῶν ἱερέων τούτων σύλλογος τὸν ἀρχιερέα καὶ κοινὸν πατέρα τήμερον.

[122] See PG 48,953 7-9.

[123] See PG 49,83 24-29.

[124] Regarding this point see further pp. 369-371 below.

[125] See *De statuis hom. 3* (PG 49,47 2-49 22).

[126] See PG 49,211 6-40 *a.i.*; 214 10-12.

bishop and may also indicate that he is present among the audience.[127] The absence of any corroborative evidence, however, means that the drawing of such a conclusion can only be tentative. In *De s. Babyla* (CPG 4347) John carefully distinguishes the "common father" from the other preachers and indicates that not only that individual, but also more than one of the additional preachers, is more senior than himself.[128] All other occurrences of the label "common father/teacher/shepherd" are in a similar vein,[129] providing a strong impression overall that the expression is reserved by Chrysostom for the local bishop.

Before closing the discussion regarding references to another cleric in the singular, two other points need to be raised in brief. One is that on at least one occasion Chrysostom refers to a visiting bishop in this vein, at a time when he was himself still presbyter.[130] One should therefore not assume upon seeing such metaphors applied to another individual that, even if it is clear that the homilist intends a person of the status of bishop, he is referring to the local incumbent. The other concerns the argument *ex silentio*. As proposed by Tillemont, on the analogy of homilies such as *De s. Droside* (CPG 4362), where "this fine shepherd" and "noble father" is said to have led the procession to the martyrium,[131] this argument states that, when on similar liturgical occasions John fails to indicate that another has led the procession, this means that he himself must

---

[127] See PG 50,442 3-6 *a.i.*; 443 22-37. That the individual who initiated such a major reconstruction was most likely bishop, since it required a person of that status to seek imperial approval and to negotiate with the local civil authorities, is suggested by *De s. Babyla* (SC 362,312 18-21). Towards the conclusion of that homily some of the processes involved in the building of the church of St Babylas by the former Antiochene bishop Meletius are described. Presbyters could be involved in aspects of church construction, however. See Lassus, "L'Église cruciforme", 39-41, where an inscription records that Dorys, a presbyter under Flavian, was responsible for and may well have financed the laying of sections of the mosaic floor of the Church of St Babylas.

[128] SC 362,296 5-7: ταῦτα, καὶ τὰ τοιαῦτα, τοῖς πρεσβυτέροις τῶν διδασκάλων καὶ τῷ κοινῷ πατρὶ πάντων ἡμῶν ἀφήσομεν εἰπεῖν.

[129] In the case of *De s. pentecoste hom. 1* (PG 50,458 47-51) the "common father and teacher" is chief liturgist at the present synaxis; in *In diem natalem* (PG 49,358 53-54), *De Macabeis hom. 2* (PG 50,626 20-22) and *In illud: Vidi dom. hom. 3* (SC 277,104 19-106 12) the "common teacher" is to preach immediately after; in *De ss. martyribus* (PG 50,646 17-24) the "common shepherd and teacher" is absent from the city on official duty; in *In princ. Act. hom. 2* (PG 51,86 45-88 5) the "common father and teacher" has succeeded to the chair of Peter and is described by Chrysostom as more senior in relation to himself; while in *Sermo 1 in Genesim* (SC 433,170 262-265) the "common father and teacher" is deferred to by John and said to be seated in their midst.

[130] See *Laus Diodori* (PG 52,761 1; 763 20 and 29-32; 764 17), where Diodore of Tarsus is described as "this wise and noble teacher", "the father" and "this wise father of ours", respectively.

[131] PG 50,683 1-8; 685 12-16.

have led it and is therefore bishop. Although superficially attractive, this position is untenable since it does not allow for other possibilities, namely that on occasion at Antioch, when Flavian was absent on official duties, Chrysostom or another senior presbyter led such processions. Moreover, in the sermon with respect to which this argument has been raised, the homilist's focus is not upon the significance of the occasion or upon the clergy involved but upon the zealousness of the people.[132] In the flight of rhetoric associated with this emphasis John is quite capable of ignoring the presence of the bishop in order to focus the audience's attention upon their own behaviour.

To sum up, then, on the basis of the above investigation the following guidelines for approaching such evidence can be established.

1. If Chrysostom applies a metaphor such as "father", "teacher" or "shepherd" to another and the metaphor is in turn qualified by the adjective κοινός, then there is a high probability that that person is bishop and is of higher status than the homilist. The context should nonetheless be given careful consideration before concluding that John is therefore a presbyter at Antioch.

2. If Chrysostom applies a metaphor such as "father", "teacher" or "shepherd" to another and the metaphor is not qualified by the adjective κοινός, then the status of that individual relative to the homilist is uncertain, unless it is clarified by the context. In this situation independent evidence of provenance, if it exists, should be accorded precedence.

3. The argument *ex silentio* does not adequately address every possibility and should therefore be discarded.

ii. Proedroi

In order to understand what Chrysostom means when he uses the term *proedroi* we must turn to a formula which he employs at the opening or close of certain homilies.[133] Although constantly varied, the basic formula runs: "Trusting in the prayers of x ..." or "May it be that through the prayers of x and y ...".[134] While the term *proedroi* does not occur in all

---

[132] See *De terrae motu* (CPG 4366) PG 50,713-716.

[133] See also Allen-Mayer, "Hebrews: The Last Series?", 338-339, where the formula is discussed in brief.

[134] E.g., *Adv. Iudaeos or. 6* (PG 48,904 13-15 a.i.): Διὸ δὴ καὶ τοῖς ὑπὲρ δύναμιν ἐπιχειρῆσαι πειράσομαι, ταῖς εὐχαῖς τούτου [sc. τοῦ πατρὸς] καὶ τῇ ὑμετέρᾳ τὸ πᾶν ἐπιρρίψας ἀγάπῃ; *In kalendas* (PG 48,953 31-34): Ἐπεὶ οὖν οὐ πάρεστιν ἡμῖν ὁ πατήρ, φέρε, ταῖς εὐχαῖς ταῖς ἐκείνου θαρρήσαντες τῆς πρὸς ὑμᾶς διδασκαλίας ἀψώμεθα; *De statuis hom. 6* (PG 49,92 17-20): Ἀλλὰ μὴ γένοιτο τοῦ καλοῦ τούτου συλλόγου φανῆναί τινα ἐκεῖ ταῦτα πάσχοντα, ἀλλ' εὐχαῖς τῶν ἁγίων πατέρων ἅπαντα τὰ ἁμαρτήματα διορθωσάμεν...; *De statuis hom. 20* (PG 49,212 7-8): Γένοιτο δὲ

of the variations of the formula, with only a single exception (*De mutatione nom. hom. 1*)[135] the few occurrences of *proedroi* adduced in the literature all follow this pattern.[136] To complete the picture, it should be pointed out that a slightly different approach to the formula is taken in *In Heb. hom. 4*, where John makes a direct appeal to the audience and *proedroi*, requesting them to make a certain issue their prayer.[137] This coincidence raises several issues. If the term appears within a stylised rhetorical formula, may it not be the case that the persons targeted are being referred to in a particularly broad and general way? One thinks of expressions such as "the prayers of the saints", which could refer to any group within the general class of saints, departed or living, and as a consequence scarcely admits of closer investigation. Looking to match the term with a single group of individuals may in any case be invalid. As we shall see in 2.d.iii below, under the label "fathers" the homilist focuses upon different groups of persons at different times. It may be that his employment of the term *proedroi* will prove to be similarly fluid. Above all, it should be remembered that, if the criterion is to be effective, it must be proven that such persons are real and that they are of higher status than Chrysostom.

From the last point of view, the examples in both *De mutatione nom. hom. 2* and *In d. Pauli: Nolo vos ignorare* look suspect. In the case of the first homily, whereas in three other examples of the formula the referent for "this/that man" is "the father",[138] a person who is patently real, here the context makes it clear that "that just man" can only be the patriarch Isaac,[139] a person who is long since deceased. If John is invoking the prayers of a long-dead patriarch, who then are the *proedroi*? While the possibility that these are living persons who are present among the audi-

εὐχαῖς τῶν προέδρων καὶ τῶν ἁγίων πάντων...; *De paen. hom. 5* (PG 49,314 20-22): Γένοιτο δὲ ἡμᾶς εὐχαῖς αὐτοῦ [*sc.* τοῦ πατρὸς] καὶ τῶν συνέδρων [Sav. προέδρων] ἁπάντων δυνηθῆναι καταξιωθῆναι τῆς βασιλείας τῶν οὐρανῶν...

[135] PG 51,124 9-11: Διόπερ τὸν ἡμέτερον ἀποφράξας ῥύακα, παραπέμψω τὴν ὑμετέραν ἀγάπην πρὸς τὴν ἱερὰν πηγὴν τῶν προέδρων τούτων καὶ διδασκάλων...

[136] So *De mutatione nom. hom. 2* (PG 51,132 15-17): ἵνα εὐχαῖς ἐκείνου τοῦ δικαίου καὶ τῶν προέδρων τούτων ἁπάντων...; *In d. Pauli: Nolo vos ignorare* (PG 51,252 25-26): Γένοιτο δὲ εὐχαῖς τῶν ἁγίων, καὶ τῶν προέδρων ἁπάντων...; and *Sermo 2 in Gen.* (SC 433,178 4-6): Οὐ γὰρ οἰκείᾳ δυνάμει θαρρήσαντες, ἀλλὰ ταῖς εὐχαῖς τῶν προέδρων καὶ ταῖς ὑμετέραις τὸ πᾶν ἐπιρρίψαντες... Tillemont (p. 50 above) adduces this last example for the purposes of demonstrating the homily's early chronology.

[137] PG 63,44 5-8: Γένοιτο μὲν οὖν τοῦτο, καὶ τοῦτο εὔχομαι, καὶ τοὺς προέδρους δὲ καὶ πάντας ὑμᾶς ὑπὲρ ἀλλήλων παρακαλῶ δεηθῆναι τοῦ Θεοῦ, καὶ κοινὴν ποιήσασθαι ταύτην εὐχήν·

[138] See *Adv. Iud. or. 6, In kalendas* and *De paen. hom. 5* (cited n. 134 above).

[139] PG 51,132 12-16: ... καταπαύσομεν τὸν λόγον, παρακαλέσαντες ὑμᾶς, τοὺς γεννηθέντας κατὰ τὸν Ἰσαάκ, μιμεῖσθαι τοῦ Ἰσαὰκ τὴν πραότητα καὶ τὴν ἐπιείκειαν καὶ τὴν ἄλλην ἅπασαν φιλοσοφίαν, ἵνα εὐχαῖς ἐκείνου τοῦ δικαίου...

ence cannot be ruled out, one can also argue, on the basis of the context, that he is referring to other long-dead fathers of the church, among whom the patriarch Abraham and the apostles James, John and Peter are included.[140] This particular interpretation could be said to be supported by the second example, *In d. Pauli: Nolo vos ignorare*, where the prayers invoked are those of "the saints and all the *proedroi*".[141] The fact that the two are placed side by side seems to suggest that the two concepts are equally generic. However, since in that passage the homilist is asking for their assistance in making sure that the correctness of the dogma passed down from above and from their forebears is preserved untainted,[142] one must also admit the possibility that "the saints" are intended to cover the situation in heaven, "the *proedroi*" here on earth.

Against these examples must be placed others, where it does appear that Chrysostom is referring to persons who are real and who may well be among the audience. In *Sermo 2 in Gen.* he says that he has embarked upon his sermon confident not in his own ability but relying on the prayers of the *proedroi* and his audience; in *In Heb. hom. 4* he asks the *proedroi* and the audience to pray a certain prayer; while in *De paen. hom. 5*, depending upon the reading accepted, he invokes the prayers of the "father" and "all the *proedroi*".[143] In this latter case the existence of the variants *synedroi* and *proedroi* suggests that, at some point in the transmission of the text at least, it was assumed that the persons being referred to were the clergy who sat literally at the front of the church on the *synthronon* in company with the bishop. One can presume that it is passages such as these which led to the proposal that the term might be useful as a means of determining John's status.

The use of the expression in *De mutatione nom. hom. 1* adds a further dimension to the issue. Here, in a highly rhetorical flourish, the homilist does not call upon the prayers of the *proedroi* but rather says that he will cut himself off mid-flow and send the audience "to the holy fountain of these *proedroi* and teachers". The word "teacher" is not infrequently used

---

[140] See PG 51,132 7-10. While the desired result of the behaviour requested of the audience (ending up in the bosom of Abraham) makes the immediate concept awkward, it is only so if one restricts *proedroi* to these particular biblical figures. It is more probable that John is using them as a jumping off point for a much broader concept.

[141] Cf. *De statuis hom. 20* (n. 134 above).

[142] PG 51,252 26-28.

[143] The reading furnished by Montfaucon in this instance is *synedroi*, *proedroi* being supplied by Savile. Without the benefit of a more securely established text no pronouncement can be made in this instance, although one suspects that in the context of this particular rhetorical formula the two terms may prove to be semantically equivalent.

by Chrysostom to refer to homilists, regardless of their status,[144] in consequence of which Tillemont interpreted the comments as meaning that the group were clergy who were about to preach next at this same synaxis. If his interpretation is correct, it would prove that in at least one instance John uses the term to refer to persons who are real and present at the synaxis and who, since it is hinted that more than one of them is likely to preach after, are most probably of senior status.[145] But things are not so simple. The highly rhetorical nature of the passage makes it difficult to determine exactly what the homilist means in this instance and, since he has just said that wherever one opens the holy Scriptures many rivers flow out,[146] it is not beyond the realm of possibility that Chrysostom is calling the books which constitute the Scriptures *"proedroi* and teachers" and is in a veiled way telling the audience to investigate these issues for themselves. While it could be counter-argued that this is not a typical way for him to tell the audience to read the Scriptures,[147] neither is it typical of the manner in which he indicates that another person is about to preach after him.[148] Further, although one can speculate in a number of ways about the *proedroi* referred to in the three examples adduced in the previous paragraph,[149] without the support of this latter passage it is difficult to make any serious claims about their actuality or identity.

It may be the case, however, that this criterion has been approached from the wrong perspective. Perhaps it is pointless to look too closely at the identity of the persons invoked, in the hope of determining the homi-

---

[144] See, e.g., *In illud: Messis quidem multa* (CPG 4441.11) PG 63,517 13; *In illud: Filius ex se nihil facit* (CPG 4441.12) PG 56,247 2; *Cat. ultima ad bapt.* (CPG 4462) SC 366,226 4.1-3 (cited n. 31 above).

[145] While one could imagine that in rare instances Chrysostom might, if he were bishop, permit another bishop to preach after him, it is difficult to imagine that he might allow two or more to do so. For further discussion of this point see pp. 351-360 below.

[146] PG 51,124 4-7.

[147] Cf., e.g., *In Heb. hom. 14* and *17* (PG 63,114 11-13; 127 14-17 *a.i.*); *De Eleazaro* (CPG 4441.13) PG 63,527 46-528 3.

[148] Cf., e.g., *De paen. hom. 5* (PG 49,314 5-8); *In diem natalem* (PG 49,358 53-54); *De s. Babyla* (SC 362,296 5-7; cited n. 128 above). See, however, *In illud: Vidi dom. hom. 3* (SC 277,134 54-62), where John likens his own preaching to a turbulent torrent, the "common teacher's" to a fountain, the source of many rivers of peaceful flow.

[149] One could argue, for instance, that they must be presbyters, since in *De paen. hom. 5* they are distinguished from "the father" and the term *synedroi* is a possible substitute. One could argue equally that the term refers to visiting bishops, since the collocation of *proedroi* and audience on the one hand (*Sermo 2 in Gen.*, *In Heb. hom. 4*) parallels the collocation of the "father" and audience on the other (*Adv. Iud. or. 6*). One could also argue that just because the audience or "father" is real, it does not necessarily follow that the *proedroi* must also be real and present.

list's own status. It may in fact prove more productive to focus attention upon how and where Chrysostom uses the broad formula in which the majority of the references to *proedroi* are to be found. Of the nine examples collected so far, it is noticeable that four occur in sermons that can be shown to originate in Antioch,[150] while a fifth most probably stems also from that location.[151] In a sixth (*Sermo 2 in Gen.*), John says that the audience is full of "brothers and fathers" and implies that he has a trainer (παιδοτρίβης, διδασκάλος) who is distinct from the general audience.[152] On this basis there is some suggestion that Chrysostom is not bishop but presbyter and that this sermon too originates in Antioch. Of the three remaining examples (*De mutatione nom. hom. 2, In d. Pauli: Nolo vos ignorare, In Heb. hom. 4*), the provenance is uncertain. Where once the last of these three was thought to belong with certainty to Constantinople, on the basis of its "episcopal tone", that evidence can no longer be considered valid.[153] This does not mean that examples that were genuinely delivered in the imperial capital may not yet turn up. In the absence of any occurrences of the formula which can be linked securely to Constantinople, however, the evidence affords a strong impression that the formula under discussion was used by John exclusively at Antioch. At this point it can be considered no more than a possibility. Since a more thorough study of the manner in which he employs the formula may well demonstrate that it is a common and widely exploited rhetorical device, until such time as every single occurrence of the formula has been assessed no certain conclusion can be drawn.

iii. "The common fathers"

With regard to the effectiveness of reference to "the common fathers" as a criterion, two problems immediately spring to mind. Firstly, if in the singular the term "common father" is semantically equivalent to "bishop" in the thought-world of Chrysostom, why has it been assumed that, when he refers to more than one "common father", he is referring not to more than one bishop but to a special group of presbyters? Secondly, if it should prove that the label is exploited consistently by John as a rhetori-

---

[150] *Adv. Iud. or. 6* (for proof of provenance see pp. 443-445 below); *In kalendas* (p. 340 above), *De statuis hom. 6* (p. 340 above) and *hom. 20* (see n. 83 above).

[151] *De paen. hom. 5* (see pp. 355 below).

[152] SC 433,180 13-18 and 182 28-36. If this evidence is considered too weak, the echo (SC 433,196 165-166) of a comment made in *Sermo 1 in Gen.* (SC 433,170 261-262), a homily of certain Antiochene origin (see n. 129 above) may serve to strengthen it, although evidence of this type is itself open to question.

[153] See pp. 331-336 above and further Allen-Mayer, "Hebrews: The Last Series?", 337-339.

cal periphrasis for more than one bishop, does this in fact tell us anything about his own status? With regard to the first issue, Montfaucon,
assuming that the group in question are presbyters, argued that Chrysostom would scarcely have used the term when he was a bishop at Constantinople.[154] The premise which informs his argument is that the
homilist is using the phrase to imply seniority in relation to himself. It
should be pointed out, however, that this approach is influenced by the
assumption that the two homilies *In illud: Salutate Priscillam et Aquilam*
(CPG 4376) and the sermons *In princ. Actorum* (CPG 4371) and *De mutatione nominum* (CPG 4372) were delivered before the same audience, on
the basis of similarity of subject matter.[155] That circumstance suggests
that Montfaucon had already decided that the homily in which the
phrase occurs (*In illud: Sal. Prisc. et Aqu. hom. 2*) was delivered at
Antioch and was searching for a group of clergy to whom the label might
be attached. Such an approach does not constitute sound methodology.
Rather, given the results from the investigation into the term "common
father",[156] it seems better to begin with the premise that the term "common fathers" refers to visiting bishops and then to see whether this identification is supported by the evidence.

Before turning to the homily in which the phrase occurs, it is useful to
examine first how Chrysostom elsewhere employs the term "fathers" on
its own. On several occasions he refers to customs or laws established by
such a group, in a manner which suggests that those persons belong to
the past.[157] In one instance he states that the declining attendance at synaxis is also an insult to apostles, prophets and "fathers".[158] In this case
the "fathers" clearly have something to do with the liturgy, since reference to the apostles and prophets elsewhere consistently refers to the lections.[159] In other homilies he refers to the "prayer of fathers",[160] the

---

[154] Montfaucon, III 171.

[155] Montfaucon, III 172.

[156] See pp. 337-342 above.

[157] See, e.g., *De incompr. dei nat. hom. 4*, SC 28[bis],254 333-256 343; *In princ. Act. hom.
4*, PG 51,101 24-30 and 105 49-52; and *De coemeterio et de cruce* (CPG 4337) PG 50,393 1-
31. In these passages "the fathers" are referred to in much the same way as we refer to
"the Church Fathers" now.

[158] *De Anna sermo 4* (PG 54,660 42-45 a.i.).

[159] See, e.g., *In Acta apost. hom. 29* (PG 60,217 56-57); *In Rom. hom. 24* (PG 60,625 35-
38). The possibility that here "fathers" = "evangelists" and not living members of the
clergy, while unlikely, cannot entirely be dismissed.

[160] See, e.g., *In princ. Act. hom. 1* (PG 51,70 19-21); *De resurrectione* (CPG 4341) PG
50,438 13-14; and *Hom. in s. pascha* (CPG 4408) PG 52,770 4-6. The similarity of the last
two examples can be attributed to the fact that the two homilies duplicate much of the
same material.

"blessing/s of fathers",[161] "the preaching of the fathers"[162] or a "seated assembly of fathers"[163] as an attractive and significant feature of local synaxis. In two of these cases the "prayer of fathers" is distinguished from the "blessing of priests",[164] which might suggest that the two groups are mutually distinct. However, even if one were to claim that in these two instances the term "priests" refers exclusively to presbyters,[165] one could not immediately conclude that the first group are bishops, since the "fathers" could as easily be presbyters whose primary duties are administrative rather than liturgical.[166] One could speculate that they attend synaxis regularly and are therefore included, if in a minor way, in the proceedings. In the case of the "seated assembly of fathers" (συνέδριον πατέρων), on the other hand, one might be inclined to think of the presbyters seated on the synthronon in the apse flanking their bishop.[167] The phrase could refer equally to a group of visiting bishops, perhaps even a local synod, however, since we know from *De incompr. dei nat. hom. 2* that visitors of this status could be described as "fathers".[168] Finally, in *De statuis hom. 16*, delivered at a time when he was presbyter at Antioch and when his bishop was absent,[169] John informs us that were it not for

---

[161] See, e.g., *De Anna sermo 3* (PG 54,658 8-10); *sermo 5* (PG 54,669 50-54).

[162] See, e.g., *Adv. Iud. or. 3* (PG 48,864 18-22).

[163] See, e.g., *De mutatione nom. hom. 4* (PG 51,145 32-34).

[164] See the latter two examples in n. 160 above. Van de Paverd, *Messliturgie*, 138-154, identifies the two liturgical elements as the Litany of the Catechumens and Blessing prior to the dismissal of the catechumens.

[165] Van de Paverd, *Messliturgie*, 153, points out that for Chrysostom in some cases where the "blessing of priests" is mentioned bishops are intended, in others presbyters. It is possible that in the context of prayer the term "fathers" is equally flexible.

[166] In an inscription from the floor of the Church of St Babylas at Antioch an individual named Eusebius is said to be both presbyter and administrator (οἰκονόμος) under Flavian (the inscription is dated 387 AD). In another version of the inscription he is said to be charged with the administration of the church (διέποντος τὴν [οἰκον]ομίαν τῆς ἐκκλησίας). See Lassus, "L'Église cruciforme", 39-40.

[167] The phrase recalls similar expressions such as "the priests who sit with us" (τῶν συνεδρευόντων ἡμῖν ἱερέων: *Cat. ultima ad bapt.* [see Chapter Two, n. 13]). In *De s. Babyla* Chrysostom describes a group of clerics who were obliged to follow Meletius around as "those who sat next to him" (τῶν προσεδρευόντων αὐτῷ: SC 362,312 23). Regarding the use by Gregory Nazianzenus of the expressions οἱ δέ μοι ἀμφωτέρωθεν ὑφεδριόωντο γεραιοί and πρεσβυτέρων συνέδριον see van de Paverd, *Messliturgie*, 417 (Text 129 i) and 418.

[168] SC 28[bis],142 20-144 33. The homily stems with certainty from Antioch. Regarding the grounds for this assertion see 3.b (pp. 368f) below.

[169] The Antiochene provenance of this homily is supported by the fact that, at a time when the inhabitants of the present location thought that an army was coming to take control of the city, the archon was the administrative official of highest authority available to dampen the situation (PG 49,161 22 *a.i.*-162 4 *a.i.*); and is confirmed by a clear reference to *De statuis hom. 15*. See further pp. 397-399 below.

the urging of "the fathers" he would not have got up on that particular occasion to preach.[170] While this last example does not clarify for us the identity of the group, it does suggest that some of the absent bishop's authority has devolved upon these individuals and that they are in some respect more senior than the homilist. In sum, the term seems to be used in several different ways by Chrysostom, with the result that it is impossible to be certain about the referents of the term without the assistance of a clear context or supporting evidence.

If Chrysostom is flexible in his use of the term "fathers", does the meaning become fixed when the adjective κοινός is attached? In *In illud: Salutate Prisc. et Aqu. hom.* 2 the "common fathers" are said to be the subject of criticism both by "their own" and by "those who belong to others".[171] This suggests that the individuals in question have authority over a specific group of people, although the comments which ensue make it unclear whether these are distinct groups within the Christian community, or whether the contrast here is between Christians and non-Christians.[172] The passage does imply, however, that the criticism is local.[173] John then proceeds to describe the group in a manner which under any other circumstance would have been considered by Montfaucon as episcopal. They are said to be ἄρχοντες (administrators), "teachers", and each a "spiritual father" and "more essential and better than one's own parents".[174] The situation is compared to that which arose between Moses and his sister, which is cited as a compelling example against defaming one's leaders and judging other people's lives.[175]

From such a promising start, however, the homilist does not proceed to clarify the status of the individuals, but moves on to draw a sharp distinction between what is permitted to the office of the priesthood and forbidden to the laity, most particularly involvement of any kind in the correction or chastisement of priests.[176] By emphasising the role proper to the laity in the relationship between laity and priest he obscures any distinction which might have been drawn between these "fathers" and other ranks of the priesthood. We are told by Chrysostom that their

---

[170] PG 49,163 31-33: Εἰ μὴ πολλὴν παρὰ τῶν πατέρων ὑπέστην ἀνάγκην, οὐδ' ἂν ἀνέστην, οὐδ' ἂν διελέχθην... Cf. PG 49,161 9-11 *a.i.*

[171] PG 51,203 46-49: ... τῶν κοινῶν πατέρων, ἀλλὰ ἀκούοντες αὐτοὺς βλασφημουμένους, λοιδορουμένους κακῶς καὶ παρὰ τῶν οἰκείων καὶ παρὰ τῶν ἀλλοτρίων, οὐκ ἐπιστομίζομεν τοὺς λέγοντας...

[172] See PG 51,203 51-55.

[173] At PG 51,205 11-13 Chrysostom implies that the practice is common.

[174] PG 51,203 54-204 10. Cf. PG 51,204 61-206 28, where these terms are repeated with the addition of "priest". Twice (PG 51,203 57-58; 205 9) they are said to be "our fathers".

[175] PG 51,204 13-31.

[176] See PG 51,205 15-58.

hands are kissed and their knees clasped by the laity, that they are asked
by the laity to pray for them and are approached by the latter when they
require baptism.[177] We are also told that an individual of this rank is involved in the distribution of the eucharist.[178] It could be said, however,
that the marks of status and the duties described are common to both
bishops and presbyters.[179] As for John's own status in relation to this
group of clerics, that too is unclear. As we have seen in 2.a,[180] Chrysostom not uncommonly discusses matters pertaining to the priesthood in a
manner which is impersonal. While the fact that he consistently uses the
"us" and "them" approach in this homily might tempt one to argue that
the "common fathers" have a status distinct from his own, of this we
cannot be sure. Instead, we have before us one more example of the extreme care that must be taken when assessing Chrysostom's understanding of the priesthood and his use of priestly metaphors.

If there are no internal clues as to the precise identity of these "common fathers", then are there any practical considerations which might
allow us to draw a conclusion? Against the possibility that these individuals are presbyters, of whatever seniority, it could be argued that,
when the homilist tells the laity that it is not their concern to call the
"common fathers" to account, he does not say that that task belongs to
the bishop. Yet against the identification of the individuals as bishops, it
could be pointed out that John addresses the situation as if it is confined
to the local Christian population, and talks of the audience's relationship
with the "common fathers" in a manner which suggests that it has existed for some time. In favour once more of the possibility that they are
bishops, it could be objected that, just as the homilist moves between the
plural ("fathers") and singular ("the father") in his discussion, so his
comments are at one moment general and at another specific. Alternatively, since Antioch was second only to Alexandria among the eastern
sees and also administrative centre of the diocese of Oriens, one could
argue for a pool of semi-resident bishops who regularly collected at
Antioch and stayed for relatively long periods, in much the same manner
as they came and went at Constantinople throughout the period of John's
episcopate.[181] Under these circumstances the bishops might become inte-

---

[177] PG 51,206 13-17.

[178] PG 51,206 21: διάκονον τῆς τῶν φρικτῶν ἐκείνων μυσταγωγίας.

[179] See Bingham, *Antiquities*, II.iii.1, xix.4.

[180] See pp. 322-328 above.

[181] Regarding the situation at Constantinople see nn. 719-720 below. Although lacking
the attraction of a resident Christian emperor of orthodox persuasion, for the period from
the Council of Nicaea (325) to the First Council of Constantinople (381) Antioch held sway
as the main see of the diocese of the East. See O. Pasquato, art. "Antioch I. History", EEC I
47. The city was the site of several important councils, while the role of Antiochene dele-

grated into the liturgical life of the city. Other possibilities may yet present themselves. What this exercise is intended to highlight is that without clear internal evidence, context or independent data there is no immediate means of resolving an issue of this kind. While one might suspect that a certain alternative is the case after putting forward a range of hypotheses, one cannot arrive at a probable, far less a certain solution unless there is clear evidence across the homiletic corpus to support it. Finally, even if the identity of the "common fathers" should eventually be resolved, this still does not solve the problem of the relationship of Chrysostom to this group of individuals.

e. *Order of preaching*

When it comes to the order in which the homilists preached on occasions when more than one sermon was delivered, we are in the rare situation of possessing two contemporary liturgical sources which discuss this issue. Even more fortuitously, both describe the practice employed in churches of the east in proximity to Antioch. The one, the *Itinerarium* of Egeria, describes the situation which pertained at Jerusalem in the early 380s;[182] the other, the *Apostolic Constitutions*, presents an idealised church order of Syrian provenance and similar date.[183] The evidence presented by the two on this matter, namely that on such occasions the local bishop preached last,[184] ought therefore to be compelling.

Compelling it is, but not in the manner previously supposed. Although within the literature this pronouncement has been adopted as a univer-

---

gates in the councils of Nicaea (325) and Constantinople (381) was significant. See M. Simonetti, art. "Antioch II. Councils I. From 268 to 389", EEC I 48-49; and further N.Q. King, "The 150 Holy Fathers of the Council of Constantinople 381 A.D. Some notes on the Bishop-lists", StP 1 (1957) 637. R. Taft, *The Byzantine Rite. A Short History*, Collegeville, Minnesota 1992, 23-24, stresses the point that until 381 the see of Constantinople was under the sphere of influence of Antioch.

[182] J. F. Baldovin, *The Urban Character of Christian Worship: The Origins, Development and Meaning of Stational Liturgy* (OCA 228), Rome 1987, 56-57, dates the sojourn of the author at Jerusalem between 381 and 384.

[183] See P. F. Bradshaw, *The Search for the Origins of Christian Worship. Sources and Methods for the Study of Early Liturgy*, New York-Oxford 1992, 93. R. Taft, *Beyond East and West. Problems in Liturgical Understanding*, Washington, D.C. 1984, 64 (= R. Taft, "The frequency of the eucharist throughout history", *Concilium* 152 [1982] 15) describes the work as originating "in the environs of Antioch" c.380.

[184] *Itin.* 25.1 (SC 296,246 4-7): "Sane quia hic consuetudo sic est, ut de omnibus presbyteris, qui sedent, quanti volunt, predicent, et post illos omnes episcopus predicat..."; *Const. apost.*, II.57.9 (SC 320,314 36-39): Καὶ ἑξῆς παρακαλείτωσαν οἱ πρεσβύτεροι τὸν λαόν, ὁ καθεῖς αὐτῶν, ἀλλὰ μὴ ἅπαντες, καὶ τελευταῖος πάντων ὁ ἐπίσκοπος, ὃς ἔοικε κυβερνήτῃ.

sally applicable rule, confident application of the maxim is in reality
quite restricted. In the first instance, neither piece of evidence can be
said to have general application. Egeria's comment that "it is the custom
here" implies that it is not necessarily the custom elsewhere, while the
kind of ideal construct represented by the *Apostolic Constitutions*, though
a useful benchmark, cannot be held to describe actual or wide-spread
practice. Moreover, while both sources refer to what occurred or ought
to have occurred in locations proximate to Antioch, neither is closely associated with Constantinople. Thus, while it is reasonable to suspect that
the practice described corresponds to the situation at the first location,
there is no reason to presume that it necessarily has bearing upon what
occurred at the second.

In the second instance, the *Itinerarium* and *Apostolic Constitutions* do
supply crucial information about what occurred under normal conditions (local bishop plus presbyters), but this is only one in a range of possible scenarios which might occur at a synaxis. Egeria concentrates on
the fullest possible expression of the liturgy, the cathedral rite, at an ex-
tra-ordinary urban centre, but does not tell us what occurred there in
regularly used non-cathedral urban churches, in the rural churches in its
vicinity or even the situation at the cathedral church in Jersualem on an
occasion when more than one homily was usually preached and various
presbyters were available to perform this task, but the local bishop was
himself absent. Nor does she tell us the protocol observed there at a synaxis when one or more bishops were present as guests of the local
bishop and these visitors volunteered or were invited to preach. While
one might presume that the local bishop took precedence, it is not beyond the realm of possibility that the incumbent on occasion yielded his
position, if one of the visiting clergy was especially old and venerable.
Thus not only are we not sure about what is likely to have happened at
Constantinople, but we have no standard against which to assess what is
likely to have happened even at Antioch in any circumstance other than
that which the *Itinerarium* and *Apostolic Constitutions* record. To this
must be added the problem that Chrysostom never explicitly tells us the
status of the individual who has just preached before or after him,[185] but
always alludes to the person's position enigmatically through metaphors.[186]

---

[185] Manuscript titles do on occasion identify the status of the co-preacher. Regarding
the suspicion to be attached to such information see pp. 315-321 above.

[186] These are, of course, enigmatic only to the modern reader. The audience and
homilist were well aware of the individual's status and did not need to be told. For the
range of metaphors see Chapter Two, pp. 284f.

On the basis of the above discussion, the most that we can posit is that at Antioch Chrysostom is likely to have preached ahead of his bishop under normal conditions — that is, on an occasion when more than one homily was required; when the duty of preaching at that synaxis was being undertaken by the local bishop and one or more of his presbyters; and when John himself was one of those homilists. We may perhaps also suppose that the inverse will not necessarily prove to be the case at Constantinople (i.e., that Chrysostom as bishop preached after his presbyter/s had done so), while the outcome at either location under any other circumstance (i.e., presbyter plus presbyter, minus local bishop; presbyter plus visiting bishop, with/without local bishop; local bishop plus visiting bishop, with/without presbyters) will be uncertain. Only when we have considered all of these options can we then determine whether the order in which the homilist preached is of any use to us in determining a homily's provenance.

The first proposition, that under normal conditions at Antioch (local bishop plus presbyter/s) the bishop preached last, would seem to be supported by the evidence. In *De s. Babyla*, a sermon of certain Antiochene provenance,[187] John says that he will leave discussion of the events leading up to the martyrdom of Babylas to "the more senior teachers and our common father".[188] Since we know that Chrysostom is presbyter in this instance and there is reasonable certainty that the term "common father" is consistently used by him to refer to Flavian, it seems reasonable to assume that the "more senior teachers" are in this instance presbyters. In any case, it is clear that in this instance his ranking as preacher was lower than that of his bishop. A similar situation occurs in the Antiochene homily *De b. Philogonio*, where more than one speaker is scheduled and the homilist says that he will leave the more distant events in Philogonius' life for the "common father" to relate.[189] That visiting bishops also took precedence over presbyters at Antioch is suggested by *Laus Diodori*, where the homilist indicates that Diodore of Tarsus is to preach after him.[190] Unfortunately John does not tell us whether Flavian was also present and, if so, whether he was scheduled to preach at the synaxis. In any case, if the local bishop was present, it does not necessar-

---

[187] Babylas is said to have been a former leader of the local church (SC 362,294 2.1-2); the audience was witness to the building of the Church dedicated to this martyr (see pp. 379-382 below), said to be situated beyond the river (pp. 374-376 below); and the suburb Daphne is clearly associated with the present location (pp. 376f below).

[188] See n. 128 above.

[189] See nn. 116 and 118 above. Regarding the grounds for assigning this homily to Antioch see pp. 337-340 above.

[190] PG 52,765 2-766 1: Ἀλλ' ἵνα μὴ διὰ τῆς ἡμετέρας γλώττης, ἀλλὰ διὰ τῆς τούτου ταῦτα μάθητε, ἀναπαύσωμεν τὸν ἡμέτερον λόγον...

ily mean that he was required to deliver a homily. On more than one occasion Chrysostom indicates that Flavian is present in the audience
without suggesting that another sermon had been or was about to be
preached.[191] To sum up then, we know that on two occasions at Antioch
Chrysostom did preach a sermon before his bishop, although probably
not the sermon which immediately preceded, and that he also preached
on one occasion ahead of a visiting bishop.

Does this mean that, on all occasions on which John indicates that
another individual is to preach after him, he is necessarily of presbyteral
rank and the other person is of more senior status? Is it possible that in
some of those instances he has the status of bishop and, out of deference
to a particularly elderly or venerable visiting colleague, has yielded the
honour of preaching last to that individual? If the criterion is to be of use
to us from the point of view that not preaching last is proof of subordinate status, then we need to be certain that no other possibilities, no
matter how unlikely we might deem them to be, can be admitted. Of the
five other sermons in which Chrysostom indicates that he is not the last
to preach at the synaxis,[192] at least two speak against the second option.
In *In illud: Vidi dom. hom. 3* the homilist describes the person who is to
preach next as "the common teacher" and says that he himself will concentrate on the exegesis of Isaiah, leaving to his successor the festival
homily on the martyrs which is required by the liturgical calendar.[193] After the manner of *De b. Philogonio*,[194] he further describes the individual
as an "enthusiast of the martyrs", while at the close of the homily he refers to his own preaching as immature, indicating that that of the next
preacher has matured with old age.[195] Rhetorical exaggeration aside, the
suggestion of immaturity, combined with the particular description of
the individual and the fact that it is not John who is delivering the festival homily on this occasion, strongly suggests that the second preacher
is, if not in fact bishop, at least more senior in status.

---

[191] See *De diabolo tent. hom. 2* (CPG 4332), where "the father" is addressed directly
and compared to the patriarch Isaac (PG 49,257 2-258 3) in a passage markedly similar to
In princ. Act. hom. 2 (PG 51,86 45-88 5); *De s. pentecoste hom. 1* (see n. 129); and *Sermo 8
in Gen.* (see pp. 337f above). On the other hand, his silence does not necessarily prove that
the bishop did not preach, as will be explained in the next paragraph.

[192] I.e., *De paen. hom. 5, In diem natalem, De Macabeis hom. 2, In illud: Vidi dom. hom.
2-3.* At this point *De mutatione nom. hom. 1* cannot be included (see pp. 342-346 above).

[193] SC 277,104 1.9-106 12: Ἀλλὰ τὸν μὲν περὶ τῶν μαρτύρων λόγον ἀφήσωμεν νῦν τῷ τῶν
μαρτύρων ζηλωτῇ, τῷ κοινῷ διδασκάλῳ· αὐτοὶ δὲ τὰ κατὰ τὸν Ὀζίαν πρὸς ὑμᾶς ἐροῦμεν νῦν... Cf.
SC 277,104 1.1-9, where the bodies of these particular martyrs are said to be buried
locally.

[194] See n. 116 above.

[195] SC 277,134 54-62.

A similar contrast between the homilist's own immaturity and the maturity of the next preacher is drawn in *De paen. hom. 5*. Here John likens his own preaching to the trivial tunes played by a shepherd boy, the preaching of "the father" to the output of a professional musician.[196] In this instance there is little to assist in stripping away the rhetoric, although the fact that the homilist proceeds to invoke the prayers of this "father" after the manner of *Adv. Iud. or. 6* and *In kalendas*,[197] could be thought to indicate that he is here referring to his bishop, Flavian.[198] The degree of exaggeration employed in this case serves to strengthen the impression that Chrysostom is referring specifically to his own bishop. In *Laus Diodori*, where the person who is to preach next is not Flavian but a visiting bishop, the rhetoric is markedly low key. There, although John also compares the preaching of Diodore to music, the metaphors ("lyre", "trumpet") refer to the quality of the preaching not to the maturity or seniority of the preacher.[199] In this light, one can with reasonable confidence classify with the two examples just mentioned a third (*In illud: Vidi dom. hom. 2*), where the homilist refers to the person who is to preach next simply as "teacher", but compares his own preaching to wine just off the press, that of the other to wine that has been aged for some time.[200] Finally, in the two remaining examples (*In diem natalem* and *De Macabeis hom. 2*) John refers to the individual who is to preach next as the "common teacher",[201] a term which it seems unlikely that he would use if the person were not the local bishop but a visitor.

In the two certain occurrences where Chrysostom refers to a visiting prelate (*Laus Diodori* and *In illud: Pater meus usque modo operatur* [CPG 4441.10]),[202] in the first, although he calls Diodore "father" and "teacher" throughout, when it comes to indicating that the latter is about to preach John scrupulously avoids the use of such metaphors, referring to him eventually as "this person".[203] In the second homily, where he is apparently speaking from the stance not of presbyter but local bishop,

---

[196] PG 49,314 5-19.

[197] See n. 134 above.

[198] See pp. 342-344 above.

[199] See PG 52,764 43-765 2.

[200] SC 277,100 66-73.

[201] *In diem natalem* (PG 49,358 53-54): ἐν δὲ λοιπὸν εἰπών, καταπαύσω τὸν λόγον, τῷ κοινῷ διδασκάλῳ τῶν μειζόνων παραχωρήσας; *De Mac. hom. 2* (PG 50,626 20-22): Ἀλλ' ὥρα λοιπὸν καταπαῦσαι τὸν λόγον, ὥστε πλειόνων αὐτοὺς ἀπολαῦσαι τῶν ἐγκωμίων παρὰ τῷ κοινῷ διδασκάλῳ.

[202] In the latter case the identification of the preacher from Galatia as bishop is dependent upon proving that the homily was delivered at Constantinople. For the internal data which supports this provenance see pp. 395f below.

[203] PG 52,765 2-766 1: Ἀλλ' ἵνα μὴ διὰ τῆς ἡμετέρας γλώττης, ἀλλὰ διὰ τῆς τούτου ταῦτα μάθητε, ἀναπαύσωμεν τὸν ἡμέτερον λόγον...

Chrysostom calls the visitor not "father" but "brother".[204] While it is possible that there exist as yet unrecognised examples where the homilist did not preach last when bishop of Constantinople, it can be said with reasonable certainty that, in all of the known cases where Chrysostom was not the last to preach at a given synaxis, his status was that of presbyter.

Problems arise, however, in situations where Chrysostom indicates that another person or persons have just preached before him. In the literature it is assumed that in all such cases Chrysostom is the last to preach during the synaxis. This has led scholars to further conclude that he is the highest ranking person available and that he is therefore bishop. Yet in *De s. Babyla* John makes it clear that at Antioch there were festal occasions at which a number of persons preached in addition to the bishop. While one might expect that in the period immediately after his ordination as presbyter Chrysostom was the most junior and therefore the first person to preach on such an occasion, one might also suppose that as he matured in his presbyterate, the order in which he preached altered. Thus in the latter stages of the twelve years which he spent as a presbyter at Antioch one might expect that, although he was still preaching before his bishop, he was by that time on such occasions preaching after other presbyters. This raises an interesting possibility. What if, in the same way that there was no necessity for the homilist to spell out the status of other clergy or himself, there was also no necessity for him to inform the audience that another had preached beforehand or was due to preach after? While in none of the homilies which we have to hand is there evidence both that another person has just delivered a sermon before him and that a further homilist is about to preach also, one cannot overlook the possibility that the information supplied to us by Chrysostom in this matter is only partial.[205] Although the implication for

---

[204] PG 63,511 48-52: ... ἐπειδὴ ἀδελφὸν ἡμέτερον ἀπὸ Γαλατίας ἀφικόμενον ... παρεχωρήσαμεν αὐτῷ τοῦ λόγου...

[205] Evidence for this is perhaps supplied by the manuscript titles. Although in most cases where a title mentions that another homilist has preached at the same synaxis the information can be explained by the homilist's comments, the sermon *Hab. postquam presb. Gothus* (CPG 4441.9) provides an exception. In that instance, although the title tells us that a Gothic presbyter had preached beforehand (πρεσβυτέρου Γότθου προομιλήσαντος: PG 63,499 4-5 *a.i.*), no comment is made by John which might lend itself to such an assumption. The remark that the audience has heard evidence that the teachings of the fishermen and tentmakers have reached barbarous lands (PG 63,502 1-4) refers only to the lections in Gothic also mentioned by the title (Γότθων ἀναγνόντων: PG 63,499 5 *a.i.*). The independence of the information from the contents of the homily lends weight to the validity of the data contained in this particular title (see rule 3, p. 321 above). At the same time, were it not for the title we would be unaware that another sermon had just been delivered, since Chrysostom himself fails to draw attention to it.

cases where John indicates that another is to preach after him is negligible, where there is evidence that another has preached before him, this information can no longer be used with certainty to prove that Chrysostom is on that occasion the last and therefore most senior person to have delivered a homily.

This does not mean that in his position as bishop Chrysostom did not preach after other members of the clergy. In the sermon *In illud: Messis quidem multa* (CPG 4441.11), which, from internal evidence, we know to have been preached in the Church of the Apostles at Constantinople,[206] he alludes to the fact that a preacher of advanced age has just preceded him.[207] Unfortunately, if one is to place little reliance on detail found in the manuscript titles, this is the only published sermon containing evidence of prior preaching which can be attributed with certainty to that city. However, even if it was the custom at Constantinople for the local bishop to preach last, the situation cannot in practice have been so simple. In *In illud: Pater meus usque modo operatur* (CPG 4441.10) we are informed that it was also an established custom for the local bishop to yield his place as preacher to a visitor of equal status.[208] As a consequence, when the bishop from Galatia arrived in town John arranged for him to preach at a Sunday synaxis, on which occasion he himself remained silent.[209] Yet it is difficult to imagine that this was a hard and fast rule. Even if the adverse reaction of the congregation in this instance did not move him to modify the practice,[210] the large number of bishops who kept arriving at the imperial capital during the course of his episcopate, at times staying for lengthy periods,[211] must have rendered scrupulous adherence to such a courtesy impossible. In sum, then, we know that on one occasion at Constantinople Chrysostom did preach after another cleric, whose status is unclear, while on another, if the provenance is correct, he abstained from preaching out of deference to a visiting bishop. What we do not know is whether these practices represent the

---

[206] See pp. 317f above.

[207] PG 63,515 2 *a.i.*-517 15. The comments are so allusive that it is difficult to identify why attention has been drawn to this person. However, although there is reason to doubt the information in the title that he is bishop (ἐπισκόπου ὀλίγα προομιλήσαντος: PG 63,515 5 *a.i.*; see further pp. 318-320 above), John's comment that old age is no bar to preaching does lend support to the claim that this individual had just delivered a sermon.

[208] PG 63,511 49-52: καὶ δι᾽ αὐτὸν τῆς ἐκκλησίας τὸν νόμον τὸν τοὺς ξένους οὕτως ὑποδέχεσθαι κελεύοντα ... παρεχωρήσαμεν αὐτῷ τοῦ λόγου... We are not told whether this custom was wide-spread or local.

[209] PG 63,511 39-512 2.

[210] See PG 63,511 52.

[211] See nn. 719-720 below.

norm and whether they were strictly adhered to or were subject to variation.[212]

Against the possibility that as bishop Chrysostom always preached
last there must be balanced the prospect that on occasion, when presbyter, he delivered the last homily of the synaxis also. One could imagine
that this might happen on occasions when a festival occurred while
Flavian was absent from the city on official duties. Even if Chrysostom
was not the most senior of the Antiochene presbyters at the time, he
might have been the most senior of those presbyters who were actively
involved in preaching. While one might assume that a presbyter would
under no circumstance take precedence over a visiting bishop, and that
therefore, if it could be shown that the person who had preached before
him was a bishop, our homilist would necessarily prove to be of that
status also, that the assumption itself is valid or that there were no exceptions to the rule can at present be neither proven nor disproven.

In any case, determining the status of the previous homilist is by no
means easy. Given that the identification of such individuals as bishops
in many of the manuscript titles could be guess-work based on comments made by the homilist and that, when referring to these persons,
John uses indistinct metaphors, the evidence can usually support more
than one interpretation. In both *In illud: Ne timueritis hom. 2* (CPG 4414)
and *In illud Isaiae: Ego dominus deus feci lumen* (CPG 4418), for instance, Chrysostom tells us nothing specific beyond the bare fact that
someone else has just preached a short homily.[213] Similarly, in the case
of *In illud: Quia quod stultum est dei* (CPG 4441.14) indication that another person has preached beforehand occurs, but comment regarding
the content of the sermon is vague and no detail at all is given regarding
the preacher.[214] In *In illud: Filius ex se nihil facit* (CPG 4441.12) he calls
the preceding homilist no more than "teacher";[215] while in *Adversus
catharos* (CPG 4441.6) he tells us only that two individuals have just
preached, one young and one old.[216] In *De Eleazaro et septem pueris* (CPG
4441.13) John indicates only that an elderly person has preached beforehand and with rhetorical modesty claims that with so many elderly expe-

---

[212] Since the church historians tell us that at Constantinople Chrysostom preached
mainly from the ambo, but on occasion spoke also from the thronos, the first being other
than "the norm", there is reason to suspect that in other areas related to preaching he did
not always do what was expected. For the relevant texts and a discussion of their
significance see van de Paverd, *Messliturgie*, 442-444.

[213] PG 55,511 11 *a.i.*-512 11 *a.i.* and PG 56,141 9-19 *a.i.*, respectively.

[214] Stav. 6, f.132v a.32-b.4. Even the title is vague: ...ἑτέρου προειπόντος ὀλίγα (f.132v
a.10-11).

[215] PG 56,247 1-13.

[216] PG 63,491 4-12.

rienced preachers available at the synaxis he ought himself to have remained silent.[217] This could conform to a situation when visiting bishops
were present at either location. Without additional internal evidence
which might clarify the issue, then, the mere fact that someone else has
preached before Chrysostom tells us little about his status or location.

In sum, although it does appear that the underlying presumption that
the practice observed at that time at Jerusalem is a rule applicable to
both Antioch and Constantinople holds true for Antioch, it cannot be
proven for Constantinople, while in any case the information provided by
Egeria and the *Apostolic Constitutions* is limited and does not cover every
situation. In addition, the possibility exists that as presbyter Chrysostom
on occasion preached after others or even last at a synaxis and that,
when bishop, out of deference to a visitor of similar status he did not
necessarily preach last. The limitations of the evidence supplied by the
homilist in this respect make it difficult to exclude these options. As a result, the order in which Chrysostom preached does not constitute definitive proof of his status and therefore cannot be used on its own to determine provenance. On the other hand, while the information that another
person has preached beforehand could be relevant to either location and
is therefore of limited use, as we have seen there is a strong probability
that, when a person is about to deliver a sermon after John, the second
preacher is genuinely of higher status. Although not proof positive of
John's presbyteral status in its own right, the information can assist in
the interpretation of other evidence. However, since there is the faint
possibility that as bishop Chrysostom is permitting another to preach after him, such a conclusion can be drawn only after careful consideration
of the context.

Before closing our discussion, there is still another aspect of the criterion which requires attention — the presumption that when a person
who has substituted for the homilist at a previous synaxis appears to be
of equal rank, that person, and therefore also Chrysostom, is of episcopal
status. In the homily upon which this rationale has been brought to bear
(*Quales ducendae sint uxores*: CPG 4379),[218] John calls his locum tenens
"this teacher" and "he who drags the yoke with me".[219] The first, as we
have seen, is a priestly rather than specifically episcopal metaphor, while
the second does not necessarily imply that the individual is of equal
status.[220] While the latter expression could indeed be applied to a fellow-

---

[217] PG 63,523 12-21 *a.i.*

[218] See Tillemont and Montfaucon (Chapter One, pp. 65 and 86).

[219] PG 51,225 3 and 17.

[220] Cf. *Cum presbyter fuit*, where as presbyter John refers to his bishop (τὸν κοινὸν τῆς
πατρίδος διδάσκαλον) as "fellow servant" (ὁμοδούλος, συνδούλος: SC 272,402 142-152).

bishop, it could also be applied by the homilist to a fellow-presbyter, and
one could also imagine that it might be used by John to refer to an individual who regularly shares the office of preaching with him in a situation where he is bishop and that person presbyter. In other words, the
information supplied is open to a number of interpretations. The interpretation chosen is entirely dependent upon the assumptions which one
brings to bear. In this particular case, the analogy of *In illud: Pater meus
usque modo operatur*, where Chrysostom as bishop, if that is indeed his
status, permits a visiting bishop to substitute for him at the previous synaxis, appears to have been influential. However, this is not the only case
in which the homilist refers to a locum tenens having preached in his absence. In *In illud: In faciem ei restiti* (CPG 4391), a sermon clearly delivered at Antioch,[221] John indicates that another preacher substituted for
him at his regular place of preaching on an occasion when his bishop required his presence at the episcopal church.[222] Since we have precedent
for this situation at both Antioch and Constantinople, no conclusion regarding the status of Chrysostom can be drawn on the basis of such information, except in cases where there is clear independent evidence of
provenance contained within the homily itself.

f. *Duties of office*

The first two of the three criteria for provenance based on the duties
that attach to the offices of bishop and presbyter (style and workload)
were developed in response to the problems raised by the larger and
blander of the exegetical series. Although initially devised to deal with
the series on Genesis and the Psalms, the criteria have subsequently been
applied in one form or another to the majority of the exegetical series.
Such series have presented problems largely because of the belief that
they were produced in bulk as discrete units — in other words, that all
are homogeneous both with respect to the chronology and sequentiality
of the individual homilies, and with regard to their provenance. This assumption requires that large blocks of chronological space be available
at each location for the slotting in of such series, the space available for
such an insertion being in turn dependent upon the location of stable
homiletical fixtures predicated on the basis of internal chronological evidence.[223] The arguments regarding style and workload are thus ones in

---

[221] See n. 21 above.

[222] PG 51,371 13 *a.i.*-373 10.

[223] The methodology of Bonsdorff is based firmly upon this rationale.

which the requirements of chronology are given precedence over those of provenance.

The validity of the argument from style is not reviewed here, since the general lack of correlation between style and place has long since been demonstrated by Montfaucon and Stilting. That the argument from workload is equally unsound, however, can easily be demonstrated from a methodological point of view. Its underpinnings collapse, if it can be established that certain of the series are not in fact homogeneous or if it can be shown that more than one of the chronological fixed points upon which the argument relies is neither fixed nor certain. With respect to the first issue, it is most likely that the series on Psalms, which has played a major role in the argument from workload, is not a homogeneous composition but rather an artificial series constructed both from pieces preached before an audience, and from material written for the purpose of filling in the gaps in the exegesis or for some other reason.[224] This can be seen superficially by comparing the two *expositiones* cited in confirmation of the series' provenance. *Exp. in ps. 6* bears all the hallmarks of a preached homily. Although it begins abruptly,[225] it concludes with the trinitarian formula with which Chrysostom most typically ends his homilies,[226] it twice assumes that the audience have had the text read out to them and on several occasions implies oral delivery.[227] It is also dotted with vivid exempla from every day life,[228] which contribute to a lively and entertaining exposition of the text, and which occur in addition to a large number of exempla of a more general nature.[229] Finally, aside from the

---

[224] The construction of a series or commentary in this manner is not unknown. Augustine is said to have added to his 119 *Enarrationes in psalmos* 86 pieces which he dictated in the form of sermons. Regarding this point see Allen-Mayer, "A New Approach", 21-22 and n. 8. Socrates, HE 6.4 (GCS NF 1,316 12-13) refers to both publications released by John personally (i.e., edited by him) and those released by tachygraphers (presumably recorded during delivery). See, however, R. C. Hill, "Chrysostom's *Commentary on the Psalms*", in P. Allen et al. (edd.), *Prayer and Spirituality in the Early Church*, vol. 1, Brisbane 1998, 301-317, who believes that they were all preprepared, but still preached.

[225] This is not atypical of the exegetical homilies, where it is possible that in the editorial process an original *prooimion* has been removed.

[226] PG 55,80 11-15: ... τῶν μελλόντων ἐπιτύχωμεν, χάριτι καὶ φιλανθρωπίᾳ τοῦ Κυρίου ἡμῶν Ἰησοῦ Χριστοῦ, μεθ᾿ οὗ τῷ Πατρὶ ἅμα τῷ ἁγίῳ Πνεύματι δόξα, κράτος, τιμή, νῦν καὶ ἀεί, καὶ εἰς τοὺς αἰῶνας τῶν αἰώνων. Ἀμήν.

[227] PG 55,71 40 a.i.: Ὅταν ἀκούσῃς θυμὸν καὶ ὀργὴν ἐπὶ Θεοῦ [Ps. 6.1]...; 72 13-14: Ὥστε κἀνταῦθα, ὅταν ἀκούσῃς θυμόν...; 77 12-13: Ἴσασιν οἱ πεῖραν λαβόντες ὃ λέγω...; 77 31-32: Καὶ μή με νομίσητε πρὸς μοναχοὺς ταῦτα λέγειν μόνον᾿; 76 34: Ἀκουέτωσαν οἱ ἐν εὐτελείᾳ ζῶντες...; 77 1-2: Ἀκουέτωσαν οἱ τὰς ἀργυρᾶς κλίνας ἔχοντες...

[228] See PG 55,71 29-36 a.i.; 79 17-21; 79 60-80 3.

[229] See PG 55,72 14-15 and 17-21; 74 48-65; 75 9-12 and 21-22; 77 20-26 and 59-61; 78 4-8; 79 22-23 and 24-27; 80 6-8.

exegesis much of the latter part of the exposition is exhortatory in character,[230] while the whole incorporates several rhetorical tricks commonly employed by the homilist to maintain or direct the attention of his audience.[231]

By contrast, *Exp. in ps. 110* reads like an artificially joined series of explanations of the text. While the opening is similar, the vocabulary is more complex and, in the form in which the text is available in Migne, the expected doxology or trinitarian formula and "Amen" are missing from the end. Of the three instances of a verb of hearing, all refer not to a portion of the text being exegeted, but to a passage about to be quoted by John,[232] while the exempla employed in the exposition are entirely general in character.[233] Even the mention of St Babylas and various events under Julian, which has been seen as confirmation of the series' Antiochene provenance, and which one would consequently expect to be either specific, vivid or localised, is cast in a somewhat remote way and fails to demonstrate any association with the location of the audience/reader or homilist.[234] The circumstance which most arouses suspicion is that, despite the length of the exposition, exhortatory comment is entirely absent. While a systematic examination of the style, structure and content of every exposition in the series is required to determine how much of this is due to the character of the psalm being exegeted in each instance, on initial findings the evidence seems sufficient to indicate that the thesis that the series on the Psalms was originally preached as a unit is unlikely to prove valid. If this is indeed the case, then the stumbling block of finding a gap large enough to accommodate the series

---

[230] See PG 55,76 34- 80 12.

[231] One of these is to pose a question which he imagines his audience might ask: Ἀρκεῖ οὖν ταῦτα, φησί, πρὸς τὸ διαφυγεῖν τὴν φλόγα τῆς ἁμαρτίας... (PG 55,75 39-40); another, to address an imagined assumption (PG 55,77 31-32; see n. 227 above). Once John uses an aside to inform the audience that he is returning to a previous topic (PG 55,73 55-59). The phrase οἷόν τι λέγω, which appears twice in this exposition (PG 55,72 58; 75 29), might also be relevant to oral delivery.

[232] PG 55,280 48-49: Οὐκ ἀκούεις τοῦ Ἰὼβ αὐτὸν ἐγκωμιάζοντος, καὶ λέγοντος; 281 31-32: ἄκουσον ὁ Παῦλος πῶς ἐπιζητεῖ τοῦτο, νῦν μὲν λέγων; 286 22: Καὶ ὅτι τρέφεται ἄκουε. The first is undoubtedly metaphoric rather than literal, while it could be argued that the second and third are so typical of the delivered homily that it would be one of the first features imitated if one wished to write a piece in this style. Such verbs of hearing would in any case be relevant if the author expected the finished work to be read before an audience. The two uses of the verb λέγω (PG 55,284 23-24; 288 39) are of a similar nature.

[233] See PG 55,280 14-20; 280 57-281 1; 281 11-12; 282 51-59; 284 3-6. Compared to *Exp. in ps. 6*, the present exposition also contains a noticeably larger number of exempla from the Old and New Testament.

[234] See PG 55,285 35-50. For more detailed discussion of this passage see pp. 462f below.

as a unit is removed, and there is no reason why individual homilies from among the *expositiones* cannot have been delivered at Constantinople.

The second underpinning of the argument from workload, that certain series occupy a block of time at either Antioch or Constantinople as a matter of certainty, can be dismissed comprehensively. Scholarship which has relied on the concept of workload has worked uniformly from Constantinople, the premise being that, once the chronological vacuum at Constantinople has been filled (the duration of preaching at that location being considerably shorter than at Antioch), then everything which is left over must belong to Antioch. Between the thirteen published *Novae homiliae*, the series on Colossians, Acts, Hebrews and I and II Thessalonians, and allowing for the four months or so at Ephesus and other disruptions to preaching, the available time at Constantinople has been satisfactorily filled, even without the possible addition of the series on Philippians and Philemon.

In arranging the Constantinopolitan series, and in arguing for the order in which they were preached and therefore the amount of space left over in which to slot any further material, the universally accepted chronology of the series on Colossians, Acts and Hebrews has played a significant role. Together, the first and last of these three series constitute approximately the same bulk, and therefore occupy much the same chronological space as the second. Since most other homilies and series have been arranged relative to these supposedly fixed points, their removal from the system would have a profound affect upon the chronological schema devised for Constantinople. In the case of Colossians, we have elsewhere demonstrated that not only is the crucial piece of evidence for locating the series in autumn 399 invalid, but have also shown that of the twelve homilies only two stem with any certainty from Constantinople. At least one originates in Antioch.[235] This finding is significant because it both obviates the necessity of finding "space" at either location for the series as a whole and casts a shadow of suspicion upon the other series which have been assigned in this way. In a second article, we extended our investigations to the series on Hebrews, proving that this too is unlikely to have been delivered sequentially and *en bloc*. It contains at least one homily of certain Antiochene derivation and one of probable Constantinopolitan origin, a circumstance which negates the supposed evidence contained in the manuscript title for the chronology and provenance of these thirty-four homilies.[236] The homogeneity, provenance and

---

[235] Allen-Mayer, "A New Approach", 29-38. Further discussion of the pivotal evidence in *In Col. hom.* 7 is undertaken in 9.a-b (pp. 443-445 below).

[236] Allen-Mayer, "Hebrews: The Last Series?".

therefore chronology of the series on Philippians, which has usually been included in the calculations, have been shown by us to be likewise uncertain.[237] While it does not necessarily follow from this that all series are therefore artificially constructed and non-homogeneous, our findings create large gaps in, and therefore call for a reconfiguration of, the various schemas adopted.

If, due to the assumption of homogeneity, the mechanics of distribution based on the concept of workload are flawed, is the premise of a sharp distinction in the levels of workload and distraction attached to the offices of presbyter and bishop itself valid?[238] The calculation of workload is based on the number of opportunties for preaching which were lost due to other commitments and is again predicated from what is known of the situation at Constantinople. The problem with the conclusions drawn is that correspondingly little is known about the duties of presbyters at Antioch and, in particular, about the nature and number of the tasks assigned Chrysostom throughout his twelve-year occupation of that office.[239] There is in the literature, on the one hand, an assumption that John rose in confidence and authority throughout his preaching career at Antioch, resulting in the argument that, if a homily is assumed to have been delivered there but demonstrates the sort of authority normally associated with the office of bishop, then the homily or series must belong to the latter years at that location. This notion of a progression in style or tone at Antioch was suggested by Stilting and pervades the work of Bonsdorff.[240] There is, on the other hand, a concurrent assumption that Chrysostom's official duties at Antioch were static. This is seen in the notion that John preached with great frequency as presbyter, restrained only by the occasional bout of ill-health.[241] Whether the first premise is thought to involve a growth in responsibility commensurate with the growth in authority is never made clear, but the two premises have never been seen to be incompatible. Certainly, the requirement of personal involvement in the transmission process and of leisure in which to work upon the preparation and polishing of homilies, which is predi-

---

[237] Allen-Mayer, "A Re-examination".

[238] For a recent attempt to answer this question with specific reference to the task of preaching see W. Mayer, "At Constantinople, how often did John Chrysostom preach? Addressing assumptions about the workload of a bishop", *Sacris Erudiri* 40 (2001) 9-23.

[239] Consideration of the treatise *De sacerdotio* (CPG 4316), which forms the basis of most opinion regarding this matter, is deliberately omitted from the following discussion. The relationship between the views there expressed and the realities faced by the preacher as he lived through presbyterate and episcopate from day to day is difficult to assess.

[240] See Stilting, *Acta SS. Sept.*, IV 487, 491, 494, 499, 504; and Bonsdorff, *Zur Predigttätigkeit*, 52 and 69.

[241] See Stilting, *Acta SS. Sept.*, IV 499.

cated by this set of criteria, assumes that at Antioch Chrysostom's official duties were consistently restricted to a small range of tasks — perhaps those associated with preaching, the celebration of the liturgy and some aspects of pastoral care.[242]

That this view is simplistic and that the issue is more complex than has been supposed is implied by information contained in certain homilies which have been assigned commonly to Antioch. On the one hand, if one accepts that the Antiochene provenance of these sermons is correct, then the general assumptions concerning the light workload which Chrysostom undertook and the relatively few non-homiletic duties which he was required to perform as presbyter are brought into question. If, on the other hand, one wishes to hang on to the clear distinction between the offices of presbyter and bishop, then it is the provenance of these particular homilies which must be reassessed. In *De terrae motu* (CPG 4366) John states that, in order to participate in recent events and to preach at the present festival synaxis, he has had to overlook not just his currently poor state of health, but also "countless other impediments".[243] Under normal circumstances, aside from ill-health the factor most likely to prevent him from preaching or participating with the audience in other liturgical rites is the extra-liturgical duties attached to his office. In *De paen. hom. 1* (CPG 4333), on the other hand, Chrysostom states that he has been absent from the city for some time. For the period of his absence he has been in the countryside. He characterises his attachment to his absent flock during that time in much the same way as he describes that felt by Flavian under similar circumstances in *De incompr. dei natura hom. 1*.[244] He also makes it clear that, although he was detained for longer than expected due to ill-health, his illness was not the reason which had drawn him there.[245] What that reason was John does not actually say, although the fact that the audience had the opportunity to send him a number of letters suggests that the absence was of more than short duration.[246] If one accepts that *De paen. hom. 1* was delivered by him during his presbyterate, then it becomes clear that, even discounting the pe-

---

[242] Comments by Chrysostom on the relative duties of the two offices such as in *De decem millium talentorum debitore* (PG 51,23 11-23; quoted on p. 334 above) serve to reinforce this impression.

[243] PG 50,713 16-18: Διὰ γὰρ τοῦτο οὐ μόνον ἀρρωστίας κωλυούσης, ἀλλὰ καὶ μυρίων ἑτέρων κωλυμάτων γινομένων, οὐκ ἀπέστην τοῦ περιπλέκεσθαι ὑμῶν τῇ ἀγάπῃ.

[244] PG 49,277 2-37. Cf. SC 28bis,96 27-31. In the latter example it is implied that Flavian's reluctant absence from the city is due to official business.

[245] PG 49,277 37-38: Διὰ τοῦτο καὶ τῆς τοῦ σώματος ἀρρωστίας ἐπὶ πλέον ἐκεῖ διατρίβειν ἀναγκαζούσης...

[246] PG 49,277 49-50: Καὶ γὰρ ἐκεῖ διατρίβων ἤκουον ὑμῶν τὰ ἐγκλήματα, καὶ συνεχεῖς ἐπιστολαὶ ταῦτα ἡμῖν διεκόμιζον.

riodic bouts of illness, John did not preach at Antioch without significant
interruption. Question marks are also raised by the homilist's comments
in *In Eph. hom. 8*. Here, along with ill-health, ecclesiastical concerns are
cited as factors which tie him to the present location, preventing him
from undertaking a pilgrimage to Rome.[247] This implies a level of personal involvement in church affairs which extends beyond preaching and
its associated tasks.[248]

As for the argument concerning the homilist's participation or lack of
participation in the transmission of certain homiletic series, this draws
its authority from two sources — the same set of assumptions which inform the argument from workload; and the precedent set by the series on
Hebrews, by virtue of the interpretation placed upon the title appended
to it in the manuscripts. Since the information contained in the title in
the latter instance has been shown to bear no relation to the provenance
of the individual homilies,[249] and as the effectiveness of the concept of
workload as a criterion is doubtful, since it comes into conflict with the
evidence, the argument from transmission history has no real foundation. In any case, it is not unlikely that Chrysostom's freedom to pay attention to detail in the preparation and polishing of his homiletic material fluctuated in accord with local factors at both locations.

Conclusion (2.a-f). When the criteria relating to the personal status of
the homilist are viewed as a whole, four distinct problems can be seen to
emerge.

1. We know much less about the functions, duties and hierarchy of the
   priesthood as it functioned at Antioch and Constantinople at the time
   of Chrysostom than we would like to believe. In particular, a dispro-
   portionate amount of attention has been paid to defining the office of
   bishop, with the characteristics of a presbyter being predicated largely
   from the absence of those features.
2. Too much weight has been placed on the overt in the reading of
   expressions relating to personal status and the priesthood, and too little on the subtleties of the exploitation of such expressions for rhetorical purpose.
3. Too little effort has been put into understanding Chrysostom's own
   view of the priesthood, as manifested in the offices of presbyter and
   bishop.

---

[247] PG 62,57 44-46: εἰ τῶν ἐκκλησιαστικῶν φροντίδων ἐκτὸς ἤμην, καὶ τὸ σῶμα εὔρωστον
εἶχον, οὐκ ἂν παρῃτησάμην ἀποδημίαν τοσαύτην...

[248] In *In Matt. hom. 85/86* (PG 58,762 8-764 3) John hints at a high degree of speciali-
sation amongst presbyters, who are accorded titles appropriate to their specific administrative and commercial duties.

[249] See pp. 318-321 above.

4. Almost no attention has been paid to John's personal view of his ministry as he experienced the responsibilities of the office of presbyter or bishop on a day-to-day basis. In particular, little recognition has been given to the fact that, for at least some of the time that he was presbyter, John had no premonition that he would go on to become a bishop.

In particular, the above assessment emphasises the importance of taking the context into consideration, if one wishes to gain an accurate view of how Chrysostom uses various terms. It further underscores how crucial it is to establish what is normative, not from the perspective of history or of the modern reader, but from John's own point of view.

3. THE CITY

As in the case of the criteria associated with the homilist's personal status, those which attach to the city demonstrate a variety of degrees of reliability and validity.

a. *Direct evidence*

Direct evidence of the city's identity in the homilies is unequivocal. In the case of *In I Cor. hom. 21* the import of the homilist's statement is clear. In the lead-up to it, he roundly criticises the attitude displayed towards beggars as a fault common to both the wider community and his present audience,[250] such that the punchline "and this in Antioch" can have no other point of reference. On three other occasions Chrysostom explicitly mentions that he is preaching at Antioch.[251] These have been overlooked in the literature because they occur among the homilies *De statuis* (CPG 4330).

b. *Linked to apostolic times*

The strong link between the city of Antioch and the early missionary activity of the apostles which is recorded in Acts provides some of the

---

[250] See PG 61,176 42-178 40.

[251] *De statuis hom. 14* (PG 49,153 5-6); *hom. 17* (PG 49,175 5-8; 178 20-22); *hom. 19* (PG 49,197 3-15). In both *hom. 14* and *17*, the statement occurs in conjunction with reference to Antioch's status as the first community to be called "Christian". See 3.b below.

very few pieces of data which are unarguably unique to that location and
therefore exclusive of Constantinople. Yet it must be stressed that the
mere appearance of such information in a homily does not *ipso facto* indicate that it originates in Antioch. For the provenance to be patent, in
the evocation of the data there must be an unambiguous connection
drawn between the Antioch of New Testament times and the present
audience and/or location.

With the exception of 3.b.v (identifying the city as a location where
Paul was detained), in all of the instances where the criterion has been
evoked by scholars, this requirement has been met. In the case of *In
Matt. hom. 7* and *In princ. Act. hom. 2*, John explicitly states that being
the first community to be named Christian is an honour bestowed on
"our city".[252] With regard to *In I Cor. hom. 21* this same distinction is ex-
pressly associated with Antioch, which is in turn clearly understood to be
the current location of the homilist.[253] In *De eleemosyna* likewise, the act
of charity is said to have been committed by "those who inhabited this
city ... our forebears".[254] In the homily *In illud: In faciem ei restiti*, the
audience is told that the events of Gal. 2.11 reflect well upon "your city",
precisely because it saw the confrontation take place.[255] Finally, in *In
princ. Act. hom. 2* the assertion that Peter was "our city's" first teacher is
immediately followed by the statement that the city was first named
"Christian" (3.b.i),[256] while it is also explicitly stated that the location is
not Rome.[257]

In addition to the instances adduced in the literature, several other
examples of 3.b.i-iv occur. These instances reinforce the impression that
the homilist employed such exempla only at Antioch. In *De statuis hom.
3*, first acquiring the name "Christian" (3.b.i) is an honour bestowed
upon "our city",[258] while in the case of *De statuis hom. 14* and *17* it is not
only stated to be a feature of "our city", but the city is also identified as
Antioch.[259] Not content with mentioning this distinction alone, in *hom.
17* Chrysostom further recalls both the reputation for providing humani-
tarian aid enjoyed by the citizens of Antioch (3.b.ii) and the participation
in the council at Jerusalem of Paul and Barnabas, who were at that time

---

[252] See Chapter Two, n. 63.
[253] PG 61,178 41-42. See 3.a above.
[254] See Chapter Two, n. 65.
[255] See Chapter Two, n. 67.
[256] PG 51,86 45-53.
[257] PG 51,86 53-57.
[258] PG 49,48 49-49 28.
[259] See PG 49,153 2-11; 176 42-44, respectively.

residents of the city (associated with 3.b.iii).[260] This last exemplum, which stems from Acts 15.1-3, is found also in *De incompr. dei nat. hom. 2* (CPG 4318), where it is asserted to be a situation encountered by "your forebears ... those who inhabited your city at that time".[261] Furthermore, in *In s. Ignatium* (CPG 4351), in addition to mentioning that Ignatius was a former bishop of the city,[262] John states that God's consideration for "our city" was such that he ordained that the apostle Peter spend some considerable time there (see 3.b.iv).[263]

In all of the homilies in which examples of 3.b.i-iv occur, Chrysostom exploits Antioch's past as a means of chiding or encouraging its present-day Christian population. While it is possible that this is also the intention in *In Rom. hom. 30* (3.b.v), there is one aspect in which the employment of this exemplum differs from that which we have just seen. Although John implies that the experience is common to his audience, nowhere does he indicate that the sites in question are available at the present location.[264] Even if one sets aside consideration as to whether the details are valid for Antioch in the first instance,[265] which is in this case a complicating factor, without clear evidence that the places mentioned are local it is virtually impossible to determine whether the exemplum bears any relevance to this sermon's provenance.

In sum, in instances where reference to Antioch's apostolic past is firmly tied to the present location or audience (the majority of cases), this criterion provides a secure and important means of distinguishing homilies of Antiochene origin. However, when that relationship is missing or is expressed in terms that are ambiguous, while it is always possible that Chrysostom is preaching at Antioch, this circumstance can in no way be considered certain.

c. *Site of imperial residence*

With regard to the city as the site of imperial residence, since there is at present no reason to question the premise upon which the associated

---

[260] PG 49,176 48-177 11.

[261] SC 28[bis],144 37-45.

[262] PG 50,588 1-5.

[263] PG 50,591 41-47.

[264] This was first noted by Rauschen and later acknowledged by Bonsdorff (see Chapter One, pp. 143 and 180).

[265] The reference to a place where Paul was in chains (ἐδέθη) has caused some consternation, since nowhere in Acts is this associated with Antioch. For an ingenious attempt to resolve this problem see Stilting (Chapter One, p. 122).

arguments are based (that no emperor resided at Antioch during John's presbyterate and that therefore exposure to the emperor and his household is indicative of Constantinople), attention focuses upon whether the various propositions founded upon the premise are sound or open to dispute.

i. Direct evidence

In examples where the emperor or imperial family have been involved or are about to participate in a stational liturgy the implication is clear. In these instances the homily can only have been delivered at Constantinople. Thus in *De s. Phoca* (CPG 4364) John says that later that day the emperor and his wife will leave the palace and participate in the procession and final interment of the martyr.[266] In *Hom. dicta postquam reliquiae martyrum* (CPG 4441.1) the personal involvement of the empress in the previous night's procession is described at length;[267] it is further said that the emperor is scheduled to participate in the continuing festivities on the morrow;[268] while in *Hom. dicta praesente imperatore* (CPG 4441.2) the participation of the empress in the previous day's festivities is alluded to and the involvement of the emperor on the present occasion confirmed.[269] In cases where the emperor is said to reside elsewhere the implication would also seem to be clear. In *De s. Meletio* (CPG 4345) the place where Meletius died is said to be distant from the present location,[270] and is said to have drawn a large attendence at the synod because of its status and the presence of the *basileus*.[271] In *De statuis hom. 3* it is made clear that the emperor is not available locally,[272] an embassy to him involving a lengthy journey;[273] while in *De statuis hom. 6* a similar situation is described.[274] In these instances the fact that the emperor is firmly associated with another location is confirmation of the homilies' Antiochene provenance.

The argument *ex silentio*, on the other hand, is unconvincing. The conclusion that *De futurae vitae deliciis* (CPG 4388) cannot have been delivered in the city of imperial residence, since there the homilist speaks

---

[266] PG 50,699 23-29.

[267] PG 63,467 5 *a.i.*-471 13.

[268] PG 63,472 15-40.

[269] PG 63,473 6-16.

[270] PG 50,518 16-17. See pp. 421-425 below.

[271] PG 50,518 25-31.

[272] PG 49,47 3-6.

[273] PG 49,49 43-48.

[274] PG 49,83 24-29; 83 53-84 12.

of the cream of the city being present without explicitly referring to the emperor, does not necessarily follow from the evidence. The premise here is that the imperial family resided permanently at Constantinople throughout the course of Chrysostom's episcopate (398-404). There is evidence, however, that at this period the emperor and his court withdrew each summer to a residence at Ancyra in Galatia.[275] Since in his opening remarks John makes it clear that the homily is being delivered at a time of considerable heat,[276] it could be argued that there is no reason for him to mention the emperor or his court if he is preaching during a summer when they were absent. Since the six years which John spent in the imperial capital were particularly turbulent, one could also posit that political events may at times have affected the attendance of the imperial family at the various festivals. As for Tillemont's belief that the type of comparison drawn between church and palace would have been inappropriate at Constantinople, the homilist comments only that the present gathering is more venerable to him than the palace, because there the goings-on are full of confusion and pertain only to the present life.[277] This remark could scarcely be considered offensive even if the emperor were present, while in any case Chrysostom does not usually display concern about offending the members of his audience if it is for the good of their souls.[278] Neither of these purported pieces of evidence is in fact useful for establishing this homily's provenance.

ii. Imperial exempla

The two arguments based upon certain types of exempla relating to the emperor and his court derive their authority from a firm belief in the homogeneity of the exegetical series and from a selective consideration of the evidence. A more careful and consistent examination of Chrysostom's employment of these exempla negates the effectiveness of the two arguments and shows that they must be dismissed.

By definition, an argument based upon exempla of any kind is going to be problematic. Because the purpose of an exemplum is to illustrate a

---

[275] PLRE II, s.v. Eutropius 1, 441. See Baur, *Chrysostom and His Time*, II 108-109, where it is said that because of Eutropius and the looming threat posed by Gainas the emperor did not leave Constantinople in the summer of 399.

[276] PG 51,347 36 *a.i.*

[277] PG 51,347 13-20 *a.i.*

[278] Cf., for instance, *In Acta apost. hom. 8* (PG 60,74 17-21) where John says that he will ban anyone who continues to swear, whether that person is an *archon* or even the emperor himself. While on the basis of internal evidence it is not certain that this homily was preached at Constantinople, mention by Chrysostom that he occupies the *thronos* (see pp. 328-331 above) makes this probable.

point, many of the examples used are drawn from common rather than
specific experience. In consequence, a large body of exempla is general
in nature, presents a hypothetical scenario or offers one which is ideal
and therefore distant from the present situation. This characteristic is
exacerbated by the fact that a wide range of rhetorical exempla was
taught as part of the oratorical curriculum.[279] Since the examples had
been developed over many centuries in different regions of the Hellenistic world not all would necessarily have been relevant to the local situation, a circumstance which is nonetheless unlikely to have troubled an
audience who had been familiarised with these concepts from childhood.
To sum up, in exempla we are presented with material which is rarely
tied to the present location, which is not often specific in detail, and
which may or may not in any case be relevant to the local situation. It is
extremely difficult to construct a convincing argument for provenance on
the basis of such information.

Instead, one is forced to rely on subjective arguments of the kind proposed by Tillemont when faced with an imperial exemplum in a homily
which he wished to assign to Antioch (*De futurae vitae deliciis*), namely
that the particular exemplum employed would have been inappropriate
at Constantinople. Bonsdorff's hypotheses that certain exempla betray
"personal" or "impersonal knowledge" of the emperor and his court, or
indicate geographic proximity to the court or distance from it, fall decid-
edly into this category. They too are predicated on what the investigator
feels is appropriate or inappropriate to the situation he imagines to have
existed at Antioch and Constantinople. Such arguments fail to take into
account a number of factors. The first consideration is that, although it is
true that no emperor had been resident at Antioch since 378, both Valens
and Julian had spent lengthy periods of time in that city prior to that
date.[280] At the time of Chrysostom's presbyterate (386-397), any member
of the population of Antioch over the age of fifteen or so would have
been able to recollect the trappings and protocol attached to the emperor
and his court, while all, through the imperial icons and statues, would in
any case have been familiar with the official dress and comportment of
the emperor and empress. As a result, John could have called upon a
wide range of exempla requiring more or less specific knowledge at either location. The second consideration is that, although the study of
Ameringer does not address imperial exempla, it is likely that by this
time such material had become a standard part of the orator's stock-in-

---

[279] See Ameringer, *Stylistic Influence*, 66-69, 101.

[280] Antioch was essentially the capital of the eastern principate from mid 362 to early
364 and from 370 to 378. See Downey, *Antioch*, 380-403; Dagron, *Naissance*, 81-83.

trade. Familiarity with a certain range of imperial topoi could perhaps in any case be expected of audiences at both locations.

The consequences of applying a subjective point of view when constructing an argument from exempla, while at the same time failing to take into account both the familiarity of an Antiochene audience with such material and the possibility that the material is in any case a common topos, is readily demonstrated from the evidence.[281] As Bonsdorff himself admitted, an exemplum such as that contained in *In Phil. hom. 12*, where the homilist draws upon the emperor's practice of crowning the much-admired athletes and charioteers up in his box rather than in the stadium below,[282] is found more than once in homilies of certain or assumed Antiochene origin.[283] Yet it is a particularly concrete example which, according to his own rationale, ought to indicate that the emperor regularly attends the local athletic contests and horse races and is therefore situated locally. On the other hand, Bonsdorff's application of the criterion to homiletic series requires that the types of imperial exempla found be consistent across all of the homilies within a particular series. With respect to the series on Ephesians, he regards as more natural to Antioch than Constantinople an exemplum which focuses upon travelling to an imperial city.[284] Yet when a similar, more concrete example occurs in *In Heb. hom. 2*,[285] this is ignored, even though it ought to contradict the other imperial exempla adduced.[286] Such inconsistencies in application highlight the major failing of the approach, which is that the criterion is not tested evenly across the homilies considered to stem from Antioch and Constantinople. Although a thorough study based on this principle is still required, preliminary results show that exempla which might otherwise lead one to think that Chrysostom is in the city of impe-

---

[281] The following draws upon material presented in Allen-Mayer, "A Re-examination", 277 and eaed., "Hebrews: The Last Series?", 318-323.

[282] PG 62,272 33-36. See Bonsdorff, *Zur Predigttätigkeit*, 80.

[283] See, e.g., *Hom. 5 in Gen.* (PG 53,54 11-19); *In illud: Vidi dom. hom. 3* (SC 277,110 2.4-9); and *In II Cor. hom. 3* (PG 61,413 10-15). There is sufficient evidence to suggest that the second of these does indeed originate in Antioch (see 2.e, pp. 351-354 above), while the third specifically mentions the Olympic Games. Given that the pan-Hellenic Olympics were banned by Theodosius in 393 (see sec. 7, pp. 434-438 below) and that after 378 theoretically no emperor should have been present at the local Syrian version, the association of the *basileus* with the games suggests that either John is invoking what used to be familiar at Antioch or the exemplum itself is artificial.

[284] *In Eph. hom. 4* (PG 62,34 22-25). See Bonsdorff, *Zur Predigttätigkeit*, 64.

[285] PG 63,26 4-15.

[286] Bonsdorff, *Zur Predigttätigkeit*, 110-111.

rial residence occur in homilies of reasonably certain Antiochene provenance.[287]

d. *Topography — general*

i. Coastal v. non-coastal

Although Tillemont's hesitation concerning *In illud: Vidi dom. hom. 5*
has been met with silence in the literature, nonetheless it is important to
raise the issue, if only to lay it firmly to rest. It would appear that it was
Chrysostom's use of a verb of visualisation, in combination with the demonstrative,[288] which led Tillemont to suspect that the mention of the
sea was in this instance specific rather than rhetorical. What he failed to
notice is that a markedly similar exemplum occurs in a homily of almost
certain Antiochene provenance, *De statuis hom. 9*,[289] where not only is
the introduction identical but the deictic form of the demonstrative provides an even stronger impression of specificity.[290] Since the assumption
implicit in Tillemont's scruple regarding *In illud: Vidi dom. hom. 5* is that
it would be pointless for the homilist to exhort his audience to see the sea
from a location some way inland, the most likely conclusion is that, despite its vividness, this particular exemplum is not inspired by the local
environment but is a topos, part of the standard rhetorical stock-in-
trade.[291]

---

[287] See, e.g., *De statuis hom. 10* (PG 49,111 46-112 9), where John includes the imperial
palace among a list of places accessible to his audience; and *In Matt. hom. 7* (PG 57,79 45-
48), where the possibility of being taken from the synaxis to the palace to see the *basileus*
is suggested. The provenance of the latter sermon is confirmed by the explicit connection
between the present location and apostolic times (see 3.b, pp. 367f above), while that of
the first is supported by its connection to *De statuis hom. 9* and *15*, even though the
homily itself contains no clear evidence. See van de Paverd, *Homilies on the Statues*, 328-
345 and n. 289 below.

[288] SC 277,194 32-33: Οὐχ ὁρᾷς ταύτην τὴν θάλατταν...

[289] Even though *De statuis hom. 9* itself contains little evidence of provenance, its
recollection of material treated in *hom. 15*, among other factors, secures its place among a
series of homilies which contain explicit reference to Antioch (see pp. 367-369 above). On
the interrelationship of *hom. 15-16* and *9-13* in particular see van de Paverd, *Homilies on
the Statues*, 311-341.

[290] PG 49,109 2-3: Οὐχ ὁρᾷς ταυτηνὶ τὴν θάλατταν...

[291] On Chrysostom's use of comparisons from the sea and the categorisation of this as
a theme standard in the rhetorical schools of that time see Ameringer, *Stylistic Influence*,
68-70. There is a remote possibility that, when he uses such phrases, John is gesturing to a
mosaic representation of the sea on the walls or ceiling of a particular church. This option
is very difficult to prove because of the complete lack of evidence for the interior decora-
tion of the churches at both cities during Chrysostom's residency. In support of John's use

When he argued that the verb διαπεράω, when employed without an accompanying preposition, indicates in its primary sense the crossing of a body of water, and that in the context of a shrine of the Maccabees this must necessarily indicate the topography of Constantinople, Pargoire was already largely convinced of the Constantinopolitan provenance of the homily in question (CPG 4441.13) by virtue of its location among a collection of homilies which purportedly stem from that location. While there is no denying that διαπεράω, its stem and cognates are strongly associated with the crossing of water,[292] the verb in its simple and compound forms can also on occasion be employed in the sense of traversing a land mass or of accomplishing or completing a task.[293] Since Pargoire looked no further than the homily of interest, the question arises as to whether the interpretation which he placed upon the phrase ὀλίγους σταδίους διαπερῶντες because of the verb is the one which was intended by Chrysostom.

Without attempting an exhaustive study of this issue here, on at least one occasion John does employ the simple verb with reference to the crossing of an open expanse of water.[294] On two further occasions he uses the related adverb when referring to locations at Antioch which are across the river.[295] Certainly in other homilies which refer to movement or to the traversal of ground for the purposes of a stational synaxis the verbs tend to revolve around exiting or entering the city or reaching the prescribed site on foot.[296] If it could be proven that the verb, whether in simple or compound form, never appears in the context of stational movement at Antioch, but only at Constantinople, where the peculiar topography of the city dictates that on occasion the traversal of water is

---

of phrases introduced by "don't you see..." as a standard rhetorical device, on the other hand, see the concrete exemplum which evokes the presence of the basileus in the hippodrome during chariot races in the probably Antiochene homily *In illud: Vidi dom. hom. 3* (SC 277,110 2.4-9: οὐχ ὁρᾷς τοὺς ἡνιόχους...; see n. 283 above).

[292] LSJ s.v. διαπεράω I.1; περάω I.2; πέραν.

[293] LSJ s.v. διαπεράω I.1; περάω I.2-3.

[294] *Contra ludos et theatra* (CPG 4441.7) PG 56,265 12-13: Μετ' ἐκεῖνα, τῆς ὀργῆς λυθείσης, καὶ πέλαγος περάσαντες, καὶ κυμάτων κατατολμήσαντες... The stational liturgy which this passage describes had been delayed by a violent storm, which had whipped up the expanse of water and made it impassable.

[295] *De s. Babyla* (CPG 4347) SC 362,310 10.9-11: ἡ δὲ τοῦ Θεοῦ χάρις οὐκ εἴασεν ἐκεῖ διηνεκῶς μεῖναι, ἀλλὰ πάλιν αὐτὸν τοῦ ποταμοῦ πέραν μετέστησεν...; *Laus Diodori* (CPG 4406) PG 52,764 26-28: Καὶ οὗτος πέραν τοῦ ποταμοῦ ποτε τὴν πόλιν πᾶσαν λαβών... For a further example in which the crossing of a river is implied see the exegesis of the name Abram, *Sermo 9 in Gen.* (CPG 4410) PG 54,624 60-625 12.

[296] See, e.g., *In ascensionem* (CPG 4342) PG 50,443 10-39; *De s. Droside* (CPG 4362) PG 50,683 19-20 and 684 21-23; *Dicta postquam reliquiae martyrum* (CPG 4441.1) PG 63,468 2 a.i.-469 13.

involved, then its use here may indeed prove that the city is coastal. Before one can arrive at such a result, however, an exhaustive study of the manner in which Chrysostom uses the verb and its cognates is required. For the purpose of placing the passage in *De Eleazaro* in its full and proper context, a thorough investigation of the terminology which the homilist uses to describe the movement between various sites in the course of stational liturgies at both Antioch and Constantinople would also be helpful. Whatever the outcome, Pargoire's confidence in his reading of this verb is premature.[297]

This does not mean that evidence of coastal versus non-coastal topography is not a useful means of ascertaining or confirming a homily's provenance. In *De s. Babyla* and *Laus Diodori*, the two sermons which discuss sites "across the river", the very mention of a river in association with the present city, and with events witnessed by the audience,[298] confirms that they were preached at Antioch. In the same way, the participation of the audience in a sea-crossing in the course of a stational liturgy, as described in *Contra ludos et theatra*,[299] makes it certain that the homily was delivered at Constantinople.[300] Use of the sea for stational purposes also receives mention in *De s. Phoca* (CPG 4364), where the description of the ceremony to take place on the following day, in conjunction with the anticipated participation of the emperor and his wife,[301] confirms the Constantinopolitan provenance of that homily.

ii. Suburban environs

Although it is well known that the suburb Daphne lay in the vicinity of Antioch and played a significant role in the life of its citizens, it does not follow that, every time that Chrysostom mentions the name, he is neces-

---

[297] A more useful exercise in this instance would have been to ask whether one could talk of traversing several stades in order to reach the Church of the Maccabees at Antioch. This issue is addressed in brief in 3.e.i (pp. 380-382 below).

[298] *De s. Babyla* (SC 362,310ff sec.10): Διὸ καὶ τὴν ὑμετέραν μακαρίζω πόλιν ... Καὶ γὰρ τότε, ἡνίκα ἀπὸ τῆς Δάφνης ἐπανῄει, πᾶσα μὲν ἡμῖν ἡ πόλις ... Καὶ ὑμεῖς μὲν αὐτὸν τῷ τῶν ὁμοζήλων ἀπεδώκατε χορῷ ... Ἴστε γὰρ δήπου, καὶ μέμνησθε...; *Laus Diodori* (PG 52,764 21-28): Καὶ τούτου μάρτυρες ὑμεῖς... For a further example see *De statuis hom. 18* (PG 49,187 24-28) where John says that many who inhabit the city have resorted to bathing in the river due to the closure of the baths.

[299] PG 56,265 3-18.

[300] This evidence has largely been overlooked because of Chrysostom's statement that he has been at the present location for one year. See, e.g., Montfaucon, Pargoire and Lietzmann (Chapter One, pp. 95, 158 and 170).

[301] PG 50,699 1-29; 700 16-18. For further discussion of these passages see P. Allen-W. Mayer, "Computer and Homily: Accessing the Everyday Life of Early Christians", VC 47 (1993) 268.

sarily preaching from Antioch. For the criterion to be effective, the homilist must make it clear that Daphne is accessible to his audience or is a feature of the local topography. In cases where "the suburb" is mentioned and is said also to be local, provenance can be certain only if the locality is identified by a feature, such as the temple of Apollo, the Cave of Matrona or the sacred grove of cypresses, known to be distinctive of Daphne.[302]

Under these conditions a number of homilies can be assigned with confidence to Antioch. In *Adv. Iud. or. 1* John indicates that the Jewish festivities which draw members of the local Christian community as spectators and, in some instances, participants, take place "not just here, but also in Daphne". At Daphne there exists a site called Matrona, which is elevated in relation to the city and is considered by the homilist to be as loathsome as the temple of Apollo.[303] In the case of *De statuis hom. 17*, if the provenance of the homily were not already patent from various other data,[304] we would know that Chrysostom is situated at Antioch because Daphne is identified as a noteworthy feature of the city, along with its cypresses and springs.[305] In *De s. Babyla* (CPG 4347) the homilist talks of events which occurred after the burial of the martyr, "when he spent some time in the suburb",[306] adding later that when the martyr's body was being brought back from Daphne, the present location was vacated as the whole city poured out onto the road.[307] The provenance of *In s. Iulianum* (CPG 4360) is likewise indicated when John complains that a section of his audience will on the morrow quit the present location for Daphne, the city's suburb.[308]

In the case of *In Titum hom. 3*, on the other hand, the evidence is less clear-cut. Here the homilist raises the subject of Daphne not as a location visited by the audience, but in association with Judaizers:

---

[302] See Libanius, *Or.* 11.236-239 (Foerster, I 519-521).

[303] PG 48,852 1-8: Καὶ τοῦτο οὐ περὶ τῆς ἐνταῦθα λέγω συναγωγῆς μόνον, ἀλλὰ καὶ τῆς ἐν Δάφνῃ· πονηρότερον γὰρ ἐκεῖ τὸ βάραθρον, ὃ δὴ καλοῦσι Ματρώνης. Καὶ γὰρ πολλοὺς ἤκουσα τῶν πιστῶν ἀναβαίνειν ἐκεῖ... Ἐμοὶ καὶ τὸ Ματρώνης καὶ τὸ τοῦ Ἀπόλλωνος ἱερὸν ὁμοίως ἐστὶ βέβηλον. Cf. PG 48,855 59-61.

[304] See pp. 367-369 above.

[305] PG 49,179 8-11: Ὅταν ἐθέλῃς τῆς πόλεως εἰπεῖν ἐγκώμιον, μή μοι τὴν Δάφνην εἴπῃς τὸ προάστειον, μηδὲ τὸ πλῆθος καὶ μῆκος τῶν κυπαρίσσων, μηδὲ τὰς πηγὰς τῶν ὑδάτων...

[306] SC 362,296 9-12.

[307] SC 362,310 10.1-6.

[308] PG 50,672 36-45: Τινὲς τῶν ἐνταῦθα συλλεγομένων τήμερον ... ὑπὸ ῥαθυμίας τινὸς καὶ ἀφελείας τὴν αὔριον ἡμᾶς ἐγκαταλιμπάνοντες, πρὸς τὴν Δάφνην ἀποπηδῶσιν... Τί σπεύδεις ἐπὶ τὸ προάστειον τῆς πόλεως, εἰπέ μοι; Cf. PG 50,672 46-48.

If those [sc. Christians] who carefully watch what they eat are not healthy, but sick and weak ... what would one say about those who observe the same fasts as them [sc. the Jews], who observe the Sabbath, who go off to places hallowed by them? I mean the one in Daphne, the so-called cave of Matrona, the place in Cilicia said to be of Kronos.[309]

Although it has been argued that the locations mentioned are all in proximity to Antioch,[310] Chrysostom does not say that those who observe Jewish practices are to be found at the location at which he is preaching, nor does he do other than list a number of locations to which they typically go. While it may be clear that the Judaizers he has in mind live at Antioch, it is not clear that he is himself speaking from Antioch or addressing an audience situated at that location.

If one wishes to argue that the passage is evidence of Antiochene provenance, one is forced to resort to arguments from the familiar — for instance, that in order to make a general comment of this kind, the homilist must have preached to his audience on the same topic beforehand, for example in a sermon such as *Adv. Iud. or. 1*. There is, however, no reason why John could not have used the Judaizing Christians of Antioch as an example in an earlier sermon when preaching at Constantinople, a situation which might explain the use of the qualifying passive participle λεγόμενον ("so-called") twice, when describing the sites of Matrona and Kronos. The pleasure haunt of Daphne, being well known throughout the late antique world, would have required no qualification. One could as convincingly argue that the focus on Novatianism in *In Titum hom. 3* points to Constantinople, since one of the few other sermons in which the homilist addresses this problem (*Adv. catharos*: CPG 4441.6) purportedly stems from that location.[311] Since arguments from familiarity ultimately depend upon an *a priori* assumption of provenance, and since it should not be assumed that, just because Chrysostom mentions events which typically occur at a particular place, it is necessarily the place at which he is preaching, the significance of any reference to Daphne of the type found in *In Titum hom. 3* should be deemed uncertain.

---

[309] PG 62,679 3-11.

[310] See pp. 421-425 below.

[311] PG 62,679 31-680 50. Cf. *Adv. catharos*, PG 63,492 15-50. The provenance of the latter, which all who refer to it in the literature assume to be Constantinople, by virtue of its title and location among the *Novae homiliae*, has yet to be proven. Regarding the question of its provenance see further pp. 497f below.

e. *Topography — Christian*

i. Churches

On the face of it, information regarding the churches which formed part of the local landscape ought to form a secure basis for determining a homily's provenance. Unfortunately, this is not always the case. Rarely is distinctive detail supplied outside of the manuscript titles, while there exists the additional problem of how a particular building was labelled in the minds of the local Christian population. Just because a certain church is known to us formally as St Eirene or the Church of the Apostles, it does not mean that it did not have other tags by which it was more popularly known.[312] For instance, van de Paverd points out that St Eirene, the original episcopal church at Constantinople, was known after the construction of the Great Church as "the old church".[313] If this is indeed the case, then we have a situation where at both Antioch and Constantinople the two main churches were referred to by the same names.[314] This finding counsels caution when assessing the significance of titles which tell us merely that a certain homily was preached in the "old" or "Great" church.[315] When the probability is taken into consideration that, as at Antioch, in the vicinity of Constantinople there also existed a church dedicated to the Maccabees,[316] the number of church buildings that can be considered distinctive of either location is further narrowed.

The proposition that *De eleemosyna* (CPG 4382) must have been delivered at Antioch, since at the beginning of the homily John indicates that he had to walk some distance to reach the church,[317] is in reality a moot point.[318] However, it raises some interesting issues. Montfaucon was not wrong in assuming that the episcopal palace or *patriarcheion* was cus-

---

[312] For examples see the discussion of *In illud: Messis quidem multa* (CPG 4441.11) in section 1 (p. 317 above) and n. 16.

[313] Van de Paverd, *Messliturgie*, 411. Cf. Kelly, *Golden Mouth*, 108.

[314] This point is stressed by Baur, *Chrysostom and His Time*, II 51.

[315] In a number of cases the location can be fixed on the basis of internal evidence. So, e.g., *In princ. Act. hom. 2* and *In illud: In faciem ei restiti* (see pp. 367-369 above). The point to be made here is that the mere mention of an "old" or "Great" church in a title is in itself inconclusive. It is to the internal evidence that one must look for confirmation.

[316] For the evidence see Pargoire, "Les homélies en juillet 399", 160 esp. n. 2.

[317] PG 51,261 6-9: Παριὼν γὰρ διὰ τῆς ἀγορᾶς καὶ τῶν στενωπῶν, καὶ πρὸς τὴν ὑμετέραν σύνοδον σπεύδων, εἶτα ὁρῶν ἐν μέσοις ἀμφόδοις ἐρριμμένους πολλούς...

[318] Chrysostom firmly connects the city with events from apostolic times (see pp. 367-369 above).

tomarily situated next to the "cathedral" church.[319] He was incorrect, however, in assuming that this fact necessarily excluded Constantinople. For one thing, we do not know where the presbyters of a city commonly resided. If they were housed with their bishop, this would substantially undercut Montfaucon's argument, since there would be no distinction between the movements of a bishop and those of his presbyters. Moreover, there remains the question not of relationship between church and point of residence but of where the homilist was preaching on the particular occasion in question. Since in *De eleemosyna* there is no evidence that the occasion is other than one of ordinary synaxis, one may presume that the location is one at which Chrysostom regularly preached. While one might suppose that at both Antioch and Constantinople John preached mainly in the Great Church,[320] this view is not supported by the evidence. If the titles to the *Novae homiliae* are to be relied upon, at Constantinople Chrysostom conducted seemingly ordinary synaxes not just in the Great Church but also at St Eirene, St Anastasia and the Church of the Apostles,[321] while there is some suggestion that at Antioch John preached sermons during the course of ordinary services held at the "old church".[322] From this it can be seen that unless one is certain of the identity of the church involved, it is difficult to construct a sound argument on the basis of the distance between the homilist's destination (the church at which he is delivering the sermon) and the point from which he set out.

If the argument regarding the distance between two points in the Christian topography of the city does not work under the above condi-

---

[319] See the survey conducted by W. Müller-Wiener, "Bischofsresidenzen des 4.-7. Jhs. im östlichen Mittelmeer-Raum", in *Actes du XIᵉ Congrès International d'Archéologie Chrétienne*, Rome 1989, I 651-709. According to Mathews, *Early Churches*, 13, at Constantinople the *patriarcheion* was physically connected to the Great Church, such that the bishop had no need to set foot outdoors in order to attend synaxis.

[320] This is the view most commonly adopted in the older literature. Baur, *Chrysostom and His Time*, I 30, who attributes the delivery of *In princ. Act. hom.* 2 in the "old church" to the temporary closure of the Great Church for renovation, represents the extreme. Kelly, *Golden Mouth*, 57 and 130, while maintaining that Chrysostom preached in the main in the Great Churches at Antioch and Constantinople, presents a more balanced view.

[321] See *Adv. eos qui non adfuerant* (CPG 4441.4 = St Anastasia); *De studio praesentium* (CPG 4441.5 = St Eirene); *Hom. dicta in templo s. Anastasiae* (CPG 4441.8); *In illud: Messis quidem multa* (CPG 4441.11), delivered in "the Church of the Apostle" = Church of the Apostles; and further W. Mayer, "Cathedral Church or Cathedral Churches? The situation at Constantinople c.360-404 AD", OCP 66 (2000) 49-68, where it is argued that John probably inherited a system of regular stational synaxes in the different churches of Constantinople.

[322] See the titles to *De statuis hom. 1-2*, *In princ. Act. hom.* 2 (CPG 4371) and *In illud: In faciem ei restiti* (CPG 4391).

tions, it just may be useful when one of the points is known. With respect to *De Eleazaro et septem pueris* (CPG 4441.13), discussed in relation to the physical topography of the city in 3.d.i (p. 374 above), it may be more pertinent to examine the homilist's statement that the distance between the present point of synaxis and the Church of the Maccabees, at which the synaxis is to be held on the following day, is one of "a few stades". Since Pargoire was already convinced that John was situated at Constantinople, he did not feel it necessary to test this statement against the topography of Antioch. However, if one could eliminate as an option Antioch, where the site of the Church of the Maccabees has been determined with reasonable certainty,[323] one would have established a stronger ground for making that claim.

In the homily *De Eleazaro et septem pueris* Chrysostom supplies a further useful detail upon which to base a calculation. The church in which he is currently situated is almost certainly one of ordinary synaxis. This can be deduced from the fact that he reminds the audience of a recent sermon and indicates that under normal circumstances he would have continued the topic. He also suggests that his discussion of the Maccabees might be considered inappropriate, since their festival is not celebrated officially until the following day.[324] At Antioch this requirement would eliminate most preaching places with the exception of the "old" and "Great" churches, unless there existed other churches of regular synaxis which are at present unknown. If one accepts that the Great Church was situated close to the Tetrapylon on the island in the Orontes, the "old" church near the Seleucid Agora in the old quarter of the city and the Church of the Maccabees in the Jewish quarter near the reservoir at the base of Mt. Silpius,[325] then one can make some rough calculations. Superimposing these sites onto the more accurate topographic map derived from the excavations,[326] it can be seen that the "old" church is some nine or so stades distant from the Church of the Maccabees, while the distance between the latter location and the Great Church is some twelve or more stades. Both calculations are based on a direct line between the two sites. A more accurate picture, which takes into account the patterns of the urban layout at the time, would involve the addition of a further one or two stades. Both options therefore suit the situation described by the homilist. If one further entertains the possibility that Chrysostom is

---

[323] In the Jewish quarter of the city, called Kerateion. See Vinson, "Maccabean Martyrs", 184-185.

[324] PG 63,524 9 *a.i.*-525 23.

[325] See the map provided by Downey, *Antioch in the Age of Theodosius the Great*, Norman 1962, 23.

[326] Downey, *Antioch*, plate 11.

currently situated in the Great Church at Antioch, and that reaching the
site of the festival synaxis involves the crossing of one arm of the Orontes, albeit by bridge, then rather than eliminating Antioch from the picture, one is faced with the prospect that as the point of provenance
Antioch is now equally in contention.

This finding does not mean that information regarding the location of
churches or the name of a preaching place cannot be of use in determining a homily's provenance. For instance, the information that the final resting place of St Babylas is situated "across the river" confirms that
in *De s. Babyla* (CPG 4347) the homilist is talking of the church recently
constructed by Meletius on the other side of the Orontes, and that he is
therefore speaking at Antioch.[327] The discussion undertaken in the preceding paragraphs shows, however, that the matter is more complex than
it at first appears. It further demonstrates that one should not jump to
conclusions when presented with such evidence. Rather, great care
should be taken to explore all of the possibilities and to assess the implications of the detail provided before one proceeds to draw a conclusion.

ii. Martyr burials

To an even greater degree than the churches which characterise each
city, the burial sites of former bishops, local martyrs and imported saints
ought to constitute a spiritual landscape which is unique and distinctive.
In some respects this is indeed the case. Once again, however, it turns
out that the distinctions are not necessarily as discrete as they at first appear.

It is certainly true that, as a result of its long association with Christianity, there had accumulated in the vicinity of Antioch the tombs of a
number of bishops and martyrs. This is evident from the fact that there
exists more than one sermon preached on a festival commemorating a
former bishop of Antioch, where it is said that the person in question is
buried locally and the audience is exhorted to regularly visit his tomb.[328]
Further, in *De s. Droside* (CPG 4362) it is not only said that the remains
of St Drosis are available locally, but that the martyrium which contains

---

[327] See pp. 374-376 and n. 295 above. In the same way, when combined with the
knowledge that Meletius was buried with St Babylas (*De s. Babyla*, SC 362,310 10.8-18),
the information that the synaxis is being held at the site of Meletius' remains (PG 50,515
22-25; 520 2-4 and 24-25) confirms that *De s. Meletio* (CPG 4345) was preached in the
church of St Babylas at Antioch.

[328] So, e.g., *De s. Meletio* (see previous note); *De s. Babyla* (SC 362,294 1.1-2.2); and *In
s. Ignatium* (CPG 4351) PG 50,588 1-5; 594 29-33; 595 7-8; 596 20-21.

them is the resting place of other martyrs as well.[329] According to *De ss. martyribus* (CPG 4357), the rural areas under the supervision of the bishop of Antioch also held a significant number of martyr burials, although it is uncertain whether the Christians within Antioch considered these part of their own spiritual landscape.[330] Whatever the case, it seems clear that the tombs of individuals intimately associated with the region where they were buried dotted the landscape around Antioch in a relatively broad radius.[331]

While little attention is paid to this aspect in relation to Constantinople, its landscape too was marked by the tombs of some local martyrs and bishops. That is, contrary to the impression given in the literature, not all of the saints and martyrs venerated in that city were imported from elsewhere. One such case is that of Mocius, a priest who was martyred at Constantinople during the Diocletianic persecutions.[332] Another is that of Paul, a former bishop of Constantinople, whose remains are said to have been deposited by Theodosius in the church which subsequently bore the bishop's name.[333] It is probable that there existed at the time other sites also whose history was uniquely and exclusively Constantinopolitan, of which the vagaries of history have failed to make us aware.[334] Thus it is not entirely accurate to assume that the sites of the one city were natural, the other artificial.

---

[329] PG 50,683 29-34; 685 17-19. It is probable that the sermon was delivered at Antioch since Chrysostom does not himself lead the procession to the point of synaxis (PG 50,683 1-8; 685 12-16). Regarding this point see further pp. 337-342 above.

[330] PG 50,646 5-7; 647 1-18. That the homily was delivered at Antioch is highly probable, since John refers to the "common shepherd and teacher" as being absent presiding over a major martyrial festival in the countryside (PG 50,646 22-24; see pp. 337-342 above); the location at which the annual festival of the Maccabees is held is inside the city (as opposed to a suburban region; PG 50,647 1-3); and the language of the inhabitants of the countryside is distinct from that of the inhabitants of the city (PG 50,646 8-16; see p. 404 below).

[331] Although judgement must at this point be reserved, the comment in both *De coemeterio et cruce* (CPG 4337: PG 49,393 27-29) and *In martyres Aegyptios* (CPG 4363: PG 50,694 20-22 *a.i.*), both homilies of uncertain provenance, to the effect that the city is surrounded by the burials of saints as if by a protective wall, may reflect this situation.

[332] Janin, *Géographie ecclésiastique*, 354-358.

[333] Janin, *Géographie ecclésiastique*, 394-395. See Liebeschuetz, *Barbarians and Bishops*, 164, who argues that despite Theodosius' efforts the cult never caught on.

[334] Acacius, a Cappadocian soldier thought to have been martyred in the pre-Constantinian city c.303/4 (see Janin, *Géographie ecclésiastique*, 13-15), can no longer be included in this list. See D. Woods, "The Church of 'St.' Acacius at Constantinople", VC 55 (2001) 201-207, who argues persuasively that Acacius was on the contrary martyred at Nicomedia in 305 and that it was only by the time of Chrysostom that his remains were imported to Constantinople to validate a tradition that the church built there prior to 359 by a certain count Acacius was named for the martyr.

It is also not accurate to presume that the importation and translation of remains was a phenomenon known only at Constantinople. While it is tacitly assumed in the literature that the Antiochenes would have had no need to resort to such a practice, it is noteworthy that the body of Meletius must have been interred at Constantinople in the first instance and then later exhumed and brought back to Antioch for local burial.[335] The triple translation of St Babylas' remains — from the original point of burial to Daphne; from the martyrium at Daphne to the common cemetery; and subsequently from the common cemetery to the purpose-built church across the Orontes — is well documented by Chrysostom.[336] Although the entire process was local, it demonstrates that at Antioch the concept of formal translation was not unknown. In the sermon *In s. Iulianum* (CPG 4360), known to have been delivered at Antioch due to the mention of Daphne,[337] the homilist informs us that the city possesses the bones of the martyr even though he was a native of Cilicia and drowned at sea.[338] This latter instance, involving the translation of foreign remains, bears some resemblance to the activity considered characteristic of Constantinople.[339] In other words, both cities were familiar with the practice of translation, even though at different times each city may have been exposed to the practice under different conditions and to different degrees. Consequently, when faced with a sermon in which the homilist appears to indicate that the city has been the recipient of foreign remains, one cannot automatically assume, as did Tillemont in regard to *In martyres Aegyptios* (CPG 4363), that the homily is being preached at Constantinople.[340]

The assumption that at Constantinople the sites were largely within the city perimeters, while at Antioch they were exclusively outside, is likewise open to question. It will be remembered that, whenever the occasion involves the exiting of the city or Chrysostom comments upon the

---

[335] See *De s. Meletio* (PG 50,519 2-8). If Gregory of Nyssa's stress upon the συσκηνία (co-tenancy) of Meletius and the apostles in his funeral oration (*Oratio funebris in Meletium episcopum*; Jaeger-Langerbeck, *Gregorii Nysseni Opera* [1967] IX,441 1-10) is more than purely rhetorical, then it is probable that in 381 Meletius was interred temporarily in the Church of the Apostles.

[336] For the first and second instance see *De s. Babyla contra Iulianum et gentiles* (CPG 4348) SC 362,178 67.6-10 and 222 96.10-20. The second and third instances receive mention in *De s. Babyla* (SC 362,310 10.1-6 and 9-11).

[337] See pp. 376-378 above.

[338] PG 50,674 58-62.

[339] Cf. *De s. Phoca* (CPG 4364).

[340] In fact, as Stilting, *Acta SS. Sept.*, IV 505, subsequently demonstrated, the sermon does not commemorate martyrs whose remains were sent from Egypt, but Egyptians who were condemned to the mines for their faith and died in exile as a result of their labours.

availability of the tombs of martyrs in the local countryside, the evidence has on this basis been taken to indicate that he is preaching at Antioch. While there is no doubt that the majority of the sites at the latter location were extra-urban, the criterion can in this instance be effective only if it can also be demonstrated that extra-urban sites were not available to the Christian population of Constantinople. Even with the small amount of evidence available to us, it is patent that this was not the case. In *Hom. dicta postquam reliquiae martyrum* (CPG 4441.1) the remains in question are clearly being conveyed to a church or martyrium which is beyond the city walls.[341] A similar situation is outlined in *De s. Phoca* (CPG 4364), where the audience is exhorted to evacuate the city in order to assemble at the site chosen as the martyr's final resting place.[342] After the event, the sites would have been available, as at Antioch, both for synaxis annually on the day of the martyr's festival and for regular interim use as a place of private prayer. Since our knowledge of the status and location of martyr burials at Constantinople in the late fourth century is limited, it is possible that further extra-urban sites existed there at this time.[343] While this does not exclude the possibility that, when John exhorts his audience to visit the extra-urban tombs of martyrs, he is preaching at Antioch, it does mean that one cannot reliably assign a sermon to Antioch on this basis. In other words, since extra-urban burial sites were not exclusive to Antioch, they cannot be considered a distinctive feature of that location.

The reverse of this principle, however, may prove to be more effective. That is, as a city Constantinople was unusual at this time in that the intra-mural interment of human remains was permitted there.[344] Moreover, there is no evidence to contradict the belief that at Antioch, prior to Chrysostom's departure in 397, human burial was still conducted exclusively beyond the boundaries of the city.[345] If it could be shown that the

---

[341] The distance to the martyrium is described as lengthy (PG 63,468 2 *a.i.*); the city is said to have been emptied for the occasion (PG 63,470 10); and the procession is described as travelling "from the city" in order to arrive at the present location (PG 63,470 14-15).

[342] PG 50,699 22-23.

[343] The shrine dedicated to the protomartyr Stephen, constructed by Aurelianus opposite Isaac's monastery (*Vita Isaaci* 4.18, *Acta SS. Mai*, VII 253E) and in which Isaac was interred upon his death (c.416), may only have been built subsequent to John's second exile. See Liebeschuetz, *Barbarians and Bishops*, 141, who dates it to late in Aurelianus' life. One needs, in any case, to draw a careful distinction between sites claimed by the orthodox Christian community and those under the control of the Arians or other heterodox parties. Miller, "Sampson hospital", 110, argues that the suburban Church of St Mocius, which was associated with a cemetery and various persons' remains, had at the time been ceded to the Arians.

[344] See Miller, "Sampson hospital", 110 and n. 39.

[345] Although interested primarily with the situation which pertained in the West, in his introduction P. Ariès, *Essais sur l'histoire de la mort en Occident du Moyen Age à nos jours*,

city in question contained no urban burials of martyrs or saints, then one
might have reasonably secure grounds for assigning a homily to Antioch.
Conversely, if it could be shown that in the city in question the remains
of saints or martyrs were interred in urban churches, then one might
have reasonably secure grounds for assigning a homily to Constantinople.

The original criterion can prove effective, however, under certain
conditions — namely when the saint or martyr can be clearly identified;[346] when it is evident that the individual is buried locally; and when
there exists a close link between the person and the city in question. Only
in instances where all three requirements are satisfied can the attribution
be considered certain.[347] In the case of a martyr as well known as St
Babylas, an assumption of familiarity on the part of the audience is insufficient ground, since it must be demonstrated that the remains are
buried locally also.[348] As for identification, this can be relatively straightforward in the case of former bishops (e.g., Meletius, Ignatius and
Babylas), where the link with the city is well established and there is both
between and within the two cities no duplication of names. When one is
dealing with martyrs, however, the situation can become more complex.
The sheer numbers involved ensured that by the end of the fourth century there was more than one martyr who shared the same name. Names
themselves could become confused. Montfaucon himself mentions that
there were at least two martyrs by the name of Romanus and that the details of Pelagia's death had become confused somehow with the martyrdom of Domnina, Bernice and Prosdoce.[349] Thus in the case of *In s. Romanum* (CPG 4353) and *De. s. Pelagia* (CPG 4350), without clear indication by Chrysostom that the subject of the encomium was martyred locally or is connected with the present location in some way, the possibility that he is preaching about a martyr of the same name who had been
imported to Constantinople cannot entirely be excluded.

Paris 1975, 29, provides a neat summary of the legal prescriptions against intra-mural
burial in late antiquity. Eltester, "Die Kirchen Antiochias", 271, cites the translation of the
remains of Ignatius from the cemetery to the converted Tychaeum under Theodosius II
(408-450) as the first instance of intra-mural interment at Antioch.

[346] Identification should not be based on the manuscript title alone. Regarding this
point see pp. 371-321 above.

[347] For examples see n. 328 above.

[348] Costanza, "Waar predikte Chrysostomus?", 154, argues that the saint was equally
well known at Constantinople. Chrysostom's own publication of the tract *De s. Babyla
contra Iulianum et gentiles* (CPG 4348) ensured that the events which occurred at Antioch
before and after the death of Babylas were widely circulated. For further discussion of this
point see pp. 459-463 below. For discussion on the distinctiveness of the two liturgical
calendars at this time see pp. 438-442 below.

[349] Montfaucon, II 584, 610.

f. *Features*

i. Characteristic

For a feature which is considered characteristic of a city to be useful in eliciting which homilies were delivered at that location, it must be unique to that particular city. If this situation cannot be verified in fact, there is a second set of conditions under which the criterion can still operate in a manner which is valid. If it can be shown that the feature is so commonly associated with a specific city in Chrysostom's mind that it becomes virtually synonymous with that city and that city only, then, even if the first requirement is not met, the exclusivity generated by the homilist's own application of the feature can still make it an effective means of distinguishing between locations. In the case of the two characteristics adduced in the literature (size = Constantinople; suburbs = Antioch), the first fails to meet the above requirements, while the second is inconclusive.

The idea that size is characteristic of Constantiople in particular appears to rest on the assumption that the imperial city must inevitably be larger than Antioch by virtue of its status as the seat of imperial government.[350] Bonsdorff, on adducing John's comment in *In Acta apost. hom. 42*: "Look how large this city of ours is!",[351] without hesitation concluded that the remark obviously relates to Constantinople.[352] Since, however, in *hom. 9* of this series the episcopal status of the homilist was clearly demonstrated,[353] the only requirement which Bonsdorff placed upon the comment in *hom. 42* is that it be consistent with, that is, that it not disprove, the latter evidence. He did not test whether size is associated exclusively with Constantinople. Yet when Antioch was under threat of reprisal as a consequence of the overturning of the imperial statues, it is precisely this characteristic of the city which Chrysostom emphasised time and again.[354] In conjunction with the size of the population, it is a characteristic evoked in at least one further Antiochene homily.[355]

---

[350] This leaves aside the *a priori* assumption of Constantinopolitan provenance on the basis of a homily's appearance within a particular series.

[351] PG 60,302 34-35: ἰδοὺ ἡλίκη πόλις ἡμῖν ἐστιν ἡ μεγάλη αὕτη.

[352] Bonsdorff, *Zur Predigttätigkeit*, 89.

[353] See pp. 322-328 above.

[354] *De statuis hom. 2*: Πόλις οὕτω μεγάλη καὶ τῶν ὑπὸ τὴν ἔω κειμένων ἡ κεφαλή... (PG 49,36 48-49); *hom. 3*: ἐννόησον τὸ τῆς πόλεως μέγεθος, καὶ ὅτι οὐ περὶ μιᾶς καὶ δύο καὶ τριῶν καὶ δέκα ψυχῶν ἐστιν ἡμῖν ἡ σκέψις νῦν, ἀλλὰ περὶ μυριάδων ἀπείρων, περὶ τοῦ κεφαλαίου τῆς οἰκουμένης ἁπάσης. (PG 49,48 45-48); *hom. 6*: πόλιν οὕτω καὶ μεγάλην καὶ πολυάνθρωπον... (PG 49,91 7-8); and *hom. 17* (where the features normally considered noteworthy are described): Οὐ τὸ μητρόπολιν εἶναι, οὐδὲ τὸ μέγεθος ἔχειν καὶ κάλλος οἰκοδομημάτων, οὐδὲ τὸ πολλοὺς κίονας, καὶ στοὰς εὐρείας, καὶ περιπάτους, οὐδὲ τὸ πρὸ τῶν ἄλλων ἀναγορεύεσθαι

This does not mean that size is in fact a feature associated exclusively with Antioch in the mind of Chrysostom. In *De s. Meletio* (CPG 4345), a homily delivered at Antioch,[356] he nonetheless states that the synod at Constantinople in 381 attracted a large attendance both because of that city's size and the fact that it is the seat of the emperor.[357] Constantinople is likewise called "that great city" in *De statuis hom. 21*.[358] Thus we have examples where size is adduced as a feature characteristic of both cities. It may be, however, that in the last example and elsewhere the adjective is indicative rather of a city's status than its literal size. In *De statuis hom. 17*, in which, as already noted, John mentions Antioch's own size as of remark, another city (Constantinople or possibly Rome) is referred to simply as "the big city".[359] The fact that the homilist felt it unnecessary to comment further suggests that the epithet is one which is widely used to identify that site. In the end, regardless of whether in such instances size is literal, relative or even introduced as a topos, the concept is clearly associated with both Antioch and Constantinople in Chrysostom's mind. This circumstance negates its effectiveness as a distinguishing criterion.

The usefulness of suburbs as a characteristic of one city as opposed to the other is less easy to determine. For one thing, although the passage in regard to which they have been evoked as a feature typical of Antioch re-

---

πόλεων... (PG 49,176 32-36). The Antiochene provenance of each of these homilies is able to be proven on independent grounds: *hom. 2* (city = head of all the cities in the East [see p. 394 below]); *hom. 3* (indication that another is bishop [pp. 337-339 above], city is that which was first named Christian [p. 368 above]); *hom. 6* (indication that another is bishop); *hom. 17* (direct statement [p. 367 above], connection with events from Apostolic age [pp. 368f above]).

[355] *Cum presbyter fuit* (CPG 4317): πόλις οὕτω μεγάλη καὶ πολυάνθρωπος (SC 272,390 16-17). If one discounts the evidence of the title and sifts out the rhetorical elements, there is reasonably clear evidence that another currently holds the episcopal office at the present location (2.d.i) and that therefore it is to the presbyteral, not the episcopal office that Chrysostom is being ordained.

[356] Aside from the chronological evidence (some five years have passed since Meletius' death in 381: PG 50, 515 11-13), Meletius is said to be a former prelate of the present city (PG 50,515 3-7), Constantinople is said to be distant from the present location (PG 50,518 16-17) and the remains of Meletius are said to be buried at the site of the present synaxis (PG 50, 520 24-25). In the homily *De s. Babyla* (CPG 4347) SC 362,310 10.12-312 27, the site of burial is identified as the Church of St Babylas. This is confirmed by archaeological evidence. See Lassus, "L'Église cruciforme", 38.

[357] PG 50,518 26-27: ... διὰ τὸ τῆς πόλεως μέγεθος καὶ διὰ τὴν τοῦ βασιλέως προσεδρίαν.

[358] PG 49,214 10-12: Ὡς δὲ ἐπέβη τῆς μεγάλης πόλεως ἐκείνης, καὶ εἰς τὰς βασιλικὰς εἰσῆλθεν αὐλάς...

[359] PG 49,175 5-8: Καὶ νῦν τὰ ἐνταῦθα γεγενημένα ἀκούσεται μὲν βασιλεύς, ἀκούσεται δὲ καὶ ἡ μεγάλη πόλις, ἀκούσεται δὲ πᾶσα ἡ οἰκουμένη, ὅτι τοιοῦτοι τὴν Ἀντιοχέων πόλιν οἰκοῦσι μοναχοί...

fers to suburbs in the plural,[360] this is atypical of the manner in which the homilist speaks of that city. In homilies delivered at that location Chrysostom consistently refers to "the suburb" in the singular, at times not even bothering to name it as Daphne.[361] Although Antioch does appear to have had other suburbs,[362] it is specifically "the suburb Daphne" which the homilist singles out as a feature distinctive of it.[363] Information regarding the suburban layout of Constantinople at the turn of the fourth century, moreover, is scarce,[364] although Cyril Mango argues that the Constantinople of the fourth to seventh centuries was not described by its physical walls but was a conurbation which incorporated the suburbs of Hebdomon to the west and Sycae (Galata), across the Golden Horn.[365]

Searching for which city could characteristically be defined by its suburbs may, however, be an incorrect way of viewing the problem. Although in its singular form προάστειον is genuinely used by Chrysostom to indicate a physical suburb, it is possible that when the term appears in its plural form without a definite article, as in the instance adduced, it is being employed by him to describe not a physical area beyond the confines of the city but the dwellings or estates situated in those areas. Philostratus, who predates Chrysostom by roughly a century, twice uses the

---

[360] *De paen. hom. 3* (PG 49,291 22-24 a.i.): Τοῦτο γὰρ μέγιστον ἐγκώμιόν ἐστι τῆς ἡμετέρας πόλεως, οὐ τὸ θορύβους ἔχειν καὶ προάστεια, οὐδὲ χρυσορόφους οἴκους καὶ τρικλίνους...

[361] See, e.g., *Adv. Iud. or. 5* (CPG 4327): ... καὶ τὰς πονηρὰς φεύξωνται τῶν Ἰουδαίων διαγωγὰς καὶ συναγωγάς, τάς τε ἐν τῇ πόλει, τάς τε ἐν τῷ προαστείῳ... (PG 48,904 22-24); *In s. Iulianum* (CPG 4360): Τινὲς τῶν ἐνταῦθα συλλεγομένων τήμερον ... ὑπὸ ῥᾳθυμίας τινὸς καὶ ἀφελείας τὴν αὔριον ἡμᾶς ἐγκαταλιμπάνοντες, πρὸς τὴν Δάφνην ἀποπηδῶσιν ... Τί σπεύδεις ἐπὶ τὸ προάστειον τῆς πόλεως, εἰπέ μοι; (PG 50,672 36-45); *In princ. Act. hom. 1* (CPG 4371) ... ἐπὶ τῶν Ὀλυμπιακῶν ἀγώνων τὸ αὐτὸ τοῦτο ἔθος κρατεῖ. Μετὰ γὰρ τὰς τριάκοντα ἡμέρας τὰς ἐνταῦθα ἀναγαγόντες αὐτοὺς εἰς τὸ προάστειον περιάγουσι... (PG 51,76 4-7). For the Antiochene provenance of *Adv. Iud. or. 5* and *In princ. Act. hom. 1* see pp. 434-438 below.

[362] If one defines a suburb as a settled area which is extra-mural, then, with the exception of Daphne, not a great deal of attention has been paid to these areas in the archaeological excavations carried out at Antioch. For an overview of the excavation sites for 1932-1936 see Plans I and VIII, *Antioch On-the-Orontes* II, 215 and 222. Libanius, *Or.* 11.231 (Foerster, I 518), however, mentions large settled areas beyond the walls and Downey, *Antioch*, 16 n. 6 and 19 n. 15, identifies an excavated bath, church and villa located to the north-east and west of Antioch with his comment.

[363] *De statuis hom. 17* (PG 49,179 8-14): Ὅταν ἐθέλῃς τῆς πόλεως εἰπεῖν ἐγκώμιον, μή μοι τὴν Δάφνην εἴπῃς τὸ προάστειον, μηδὲ τὸ πλῆθος καὶ μῆκος τῶν κυπαρίσσων, μηδὲ τὰς πηγὰς τῶν ὑδάτων, μηδὲ τὸ πολλοὺς τὴν πόλιν οἰκεῖν ἀνθρώπους, μηδὲ τὸ μέχρι βαθυτάτης ἑσπέρας ἐπὶ τῆς ἀγορᾶς διατρίβειν μετὰ ἀδείας πολλῆς, μηδὲ τῶν ὠνίων τὴν ἀφθονίαν·

[364] The major studies of the urban development of Constantinople, C. Mango, *Le développement urbain de Constantinople (ive-viie siècles)*, Paris 1985, and Dagron *Naissance*, either refer in this regard to a later period or do not address the issue.

[365] Mango, "Development", 118.

term in that sense.[366] This meaning, while even less useful from the point of view of establishing provenance,[367] makes good sense in the present context. Since John goes on to mention specifics of architecture and furnishings (houses with gilded roofs and triclinia), both of which are associated with a high level of wealth, a reference to villas or estates scattered in the areas outside the city walls would be particularly appropriate. On at least one occasion Chrysostom hints at a mania among the wealthy for building in these regions,[368] while the excavations at Daphne have revealed a tradition of constructing expensive housing in that suburb spanning the second to fifth centuries.[369] In the fifth century at Constantinople there existed a great deal of open space beyond the Constantinian walls. The fact that the private estates which sprinkled the area were at that time still designated *proasteia*, despite the expansion of the city limits by the construction of a second set of land walls under the emperor Theodosius II in 413,[370] implies a tradition of building private villas in the extra-urban regions of Constantinople that was well established by the time of John's arrival there. All in all, unless it can be demonstrated that the *proasteia* mentioned are indeed the physical suburbs and that the homilist never mentions more than the one suburb (Daphne) when speaking of Antioch, *proasteia* fail as a feature which can admit of distinction. Under all other circumstances, whether as suburban regions or as suburban villas or estates, *proasteia* are to be found at both Constantinople and Antioch and, depending upon what Chrysostom wishes to emphasise at the time, could be adduced as a feature characteristic of either city.

As for Wilken's argument that references to the heat, the agora and the size of the church are characteristic of the Antiochene homilies, implying that these features are therefore distinctive of Antioch itself, the argument is sustainable only if one compares the comments to those which occur in a very restricted number of supposedly Antiochene homilies, namely the four *De mutatione nominum* (CPG 4372).[371] If the question of the validity of Wenger's proposal that *In illud: Si esurierit* (CPG 4375) follows those homilies in sequence is set aside,[372] however,

---

[366] LSJ s.v. προάστειον 2.

[367] Presumably suburban villas and estates are a feature regularly associated with any major city.

[368] See *In Phil. hom. 7* (PG 62,236 51-55). Regarding the uncertain provenance of this homily see Allen-Mayer, "A Re-examination", 273-284.

[369] See R. Stillwell, "Houses of Antioch", DOP 15 (1961) 47-57.

[370] See Mango, "Development", 118, in particular n. 3.

[371] See *De mutatione nom. hom. 1* (PG 51,113 1-9) re agora; *hom. 2* (PG 51,125 17-28) re size of church, heat.

[372] See Chapter One, p. 249.

and the individual features are examined objectively, there is little support either for the notion that reference to these features is characteristic
of Antiochene homilies in general or that the features themselves are distinctive of Antioch. Although references to heat can be found in one or
two other homilies, the homilies in question tend to be of unclear provenance, [373] while one markedly similar reference to the discomfort caused
those attending synaxis by the heat is found in a homily from Constantinople.[374] In addition, allusions to the size or height of the building in
which worship is being held are in fact rare, with the only two references
occurring in *In illud: Si esurierit* itself and in *De mutatione nom. hom.
2*.[375] With regard to the agora, mention occurs frequently in homilies
from both locations with the result that it can scarcely be considered distinctive[376]

ii. Negative features

In much the same way as arguments *ex silentio*, propositions posed
from the negative either prove to be invalid or create more problems
than they solve. In the first instance, the assumption that remote description of events necessarily reflects physical remoteness, a premise adduced with respect to *In Col. hom. 7* and *In Acta apost. hom. 38*, fails to
stand up to scrutiny.[377] As for the argument that the homilist is not at
location x because x is described as "there", although the premise is
sound in itself it has been misapplied. In *In II Cor. hom. 26* Chrysostom
does not in fact employ the adverb ἐκεῖ with reference to Constantinople;
nor, on the other hand, does he identify Constantinople with the present
location, the two conditions which would need to be fulfilled, if the argument is to be effective. A careful reading of the complex series of contrasts which occurs in the critical passage in this homily shows rather
that in the first instance the adverb "here" is applied to Constantinople
purely in contradistinction to Rome, that is, with the intention of stating

---

[373] See, e.g., *De terrae motu* (CPG 4366) PG 50,713 3-5 and 50-52; *In Phil. hom. 10* (PG
62,259 18-29).

[374] *De s. Phoca* (CPG 4364) PG 50,706 2-5.

[375] In any case, the Great Church at Constantinople, to which Krautheimer, *Three
Christian Capitals*, Berkeley 1983, 50-55, attributes a side nave must have been of comparable size to that of the Great Church at Antioch, such that the description in both
homilies could have been applied to either building.

[376] For examples from Constantinople see, e.g., *De s. Phoca* (PG 50,699 16-17); *De
regressu* (CPG 4394) REB 19 (1960) 118 10.3-5; *Contra ludos et theatra* (CPG 4441.7) PG
56,266 28-29.

[377] This is demonstrated in sections 9.a-b and 9.f (pp. 443-445 and 459-462 below).

"in this location, as opposed to that".[378] It does not refer to the present situation of audience and homilist. The second ἐνταῦθα again refers not to the present location but to the circumstances on earth, as opposed to the situation which will pertain at the last judgement when the dead are raised to eternal life.[379] The next series of adverbs draw a contrast not between the present location and the site of the imperial palace, which is said to be "there", but between the imperial palace and the tombs of the apostles within Constantinople.[380] This is made clear in the last instance, where John changes adverbs and denotes the palace by the adverb "here", in contrast to the bones of the holy apostles. Rather than convincing proof of the homily's provenance, the entire passage represents an extended, if detailed exemplum of the efficacy of holy people even after death, which requires no special knowledge on the part of the audience. While the fact that Chrysostom himself displays surprisingly detailed knowledge of the palace, imperial protocol and the layout of the Church of the Apostles at Constantinople may lead to the suspicion that he is situated at that location, it proves little, since such detail may have been well known at Antioch also.[381]

Of the other arguments put forward, the proposal that *De paen. hom. 3* cannot have been delivered at Constantinople because, had this been the case, Chrysostom must have adduced the senate as its most characteristic feature, is to be dismissed as subjective and unprovable. Since the structure of the Constantinopolitan senate was markedly different from that at Rome and its role in the administration of the eastern empire was not central,[382] there is in any case some question as to whether a person immersed in the life of the imperial capital would have considered it a feature that was either distinctive or characteristic. As for Bonsdorff's adduction of impersonal reference to Antioch as proof of the Constantinopolitan provenance of several homilies on Acts, this argument is not as straightforward as it might at first appear. Although in neither *In Acta*

---

[378] PG 61,582 19-21: Καὶ τοῦτο οὐκ ἐν τῇ Ῥώμῃ ... ἀλλὰ καὶ ἐν τῇ Κωνσταντινουπόλει. Καὶ γὰρ καὶ ἐνταῦθα...

[379] PG 61,582 30-31: Εἰ γὰρ ἐνταῦθα οὕτως ἐν τοῖς τάφοις, πολλῷ μᾶλλον ἐν τῇ ἀναστάσει...

[380] PG 61,582 36-583 1: Πολὺ γὰρ τῶν ἄλλων τάφων τῶν βασιλικῶν τὰ σήματα ταῦτα σεμνότερα· ἐκεῖ μὲν γὰρ πολλὴ ἡ ἐρημία, ἐνταῦθα δὲ πολλὴ ἡ πανήγυρις. Εἰ δὲ βούλει καὶ ταῖς βασιλικαῖς παραβαλεῖν αὐλαῖς τοὺς τάφους τούτους, πάλιν ἐνταῦθα τὰ νικητήρια. Ἐκεῖ μὲν ... ἐνταῦθα δέ ... ἐκεῖ...ἐνταῦθα ... Ἀλλὰ γλυκὺ θέαμα χρυσοφοροῦντα βασιλέα ... ἰδεῖν ... Ἀλλὰ τὰ ἐνταῦθα τοσούτῳ σεμνότερα ... Ἅμα γὰρ ἐπέβης τῶν οὐδῶν, καὶ πρὸς τὸν οὐρανὸν ὁ τόπος τὴν διάνοιαν παρέπεμψεν ... Καὶ ἐνταῦθα μὲν ὑπέταξεν ἄρχοντι ... τὰ δὲ ὀστᾶ τῶν ἁγίων...

[381] See n. 402 below.

[382] For a description of its composition and function see Jones, LRE, I 132-136. As for the role it played in administration see further LRE, I 366-410, where the Constantinopolitan senate scarcely rates a mention.

apost. hom. 25 nor *31* do we encounter comments of the kind assembled in 3.b above, at several points the homilist uses the adverb ἐνταῦθα to refer to Antioch,[383] while it is in any case difficult to say to what extent the impersonal tone which occurs arises from the exegesis. As we have seen elsewhere, Chrysostom is quite capable of discussing an issue or concept impersonally even if it has strong personal relevance.[384]

These findings do not mean that the criterion is to be dismissed out of hand. In one instance John does supply proof that he is not at Antioch, which leads to the conclusion that he must therefore be at Constantinople. In *Contra Anom. hom. 11* (CPG 4324), after claiming that he has preached at the present location only once before,[385] the homilist proceeds to draw a series of comparisons between the present and his former location. Amongst these, the information that the present location is not the one in which he was born and raised, and that the Christian community in which he was formerly situated is older than that in which he now finds himself, make it clear that he is now at a location other than Antioch.[386]

g. *Status*

Arguments based on the status of the city are not as simple as they appear. Statements by Chrysostom in this respect are rarely absolute and require careful consideration of the context, if they are to be correctly interpreted. In *In Acta apost. hom. 8* the description of the city as "imperial" will need to be assessed in this light, as well as from a textual point of view,[387] since Bonsdorff's argument that the location is Constantinople, because the city is held up as an example for the rest of the world, is unconvincing. For different reasons both cities were at the time of elevated status in the secular and Christian world, such that either could have been promoted in this manner.[388] Bonsdorff's argument with respect to *In Col. hom. 9*, namely that the homilist's depiction of the present location as "head" in relation to the rural churches (its "body") is

---

[383] PG 60,192 6-16 *a.i.*; 193 4-5; 194 14-19. This, of course, is no proof that he is situated at Antioch. It is interesting to note, however, that in the literature the adduction of the adverbs ἐνταῦθα or ἐκεῖ as proof of location has been selective.

[384] See pp. 322-328 above.

[385] SC 396,286 1-3.

[386] SC 396,288 11-15.

[387] See Chapter Two, n. 74.

[388] See PG 60,74 31-38. John does not actually state that the city is elevated over any other, only that it will receive acclaim if it is known that the citizens refrain from swearing.

more appropriate to Constantinople, is also less than persuasive. His
thoughts in this matter have apparently been influenced by Chrysostom's
statement that instruction of the rural churches and their "teachers" is
his personal responsibility,[389] since elsewhere it is made clear that
Antioch itself is a prime example of this relationship.[390] Although statements regarding the secular status of the city might be considered to offer information which is more reliable, again the significance of the data
can be less concrete than it seems. A comment to the effect that the city
is a metropolis can be interpreted as pointing to either location, since at
the time both Constantinople and Antioch were technically of that status.
A statement to the effect that the city is "head of the cities in the East",[391]
however, can point only to Antioch, which at the time held the position
of head of the diocese of Oriens and was the seat of its governor, the
comes Orientis.[392] That the title is associated firmly with the Syrian capital in Chrysostom's mind is confirmed by *De statuis hom. 3*, where there
exists independent evidence of the sermon's provenance.[393]

h. *Administration*

Not all references to an administrative official or the army are equally
useful. As with information concerning the emperor, his family and the
court, distinction must be drawn between detail supplied in *exempla*,
which are rarely specific to the location, and direct reference, where it is
clear that the person or army is real and is in some way involved in the
daily life of the city.

---

[389] PG 62,362 29-32. While this might be thought to indicate that he is bishop (see pp.
331-336 above), the duties of presbyters at this period are less than clear (pp. 360-366
above).

[390] So, for instance, in *De ss. martyribus* (CPG 4357) Flavian is said to be off in the
countryside presiding over a local martyr's festival (PG 50, 646 5-7, 17-24), while at the
recent festival of the Maccabees the whole countryside poured into the city as the centre
of celebrations (PG 50,647 1-3). In *De incompr. dei nat. hom. 2* a number of "spiritual
fathers" are said to have recently assembled at Antioch (SC 28bis,142 20-144 33).

[391] E.g., *De statuis hom. 2* (PG 49,36 48-49): Πόλις οὕτω μεγάλη καὶ τῶν ὑπὸ τὴν ἔω
κειμένων ἡ κεφαλή... Cf. PG 49,33 11-13 *a.i.*, 34 16-17 *a.i.* and 1-2 *a.i.*, where a clear link is
drawn between the city in question and the present location.

[392] Jones, LRE, I 373.

[393] *De statuis hom. 3* (PG 49,47 41-44): Ἔγνω καλῶς ἐκεῖνος, ὅτι οὐχ ὑπὲρ μιᾶς πόλεως
αὐτῷ νῦν ὁ λόγος, ἀλλ' ὑπὲρ τῆς Ἀνατολῆς ἁπάσης· τῶν γὰρ πόλεων τῶν ὑπὸ τὴν ἔω κειμένων
κεφαλὴ καὶ μήτηρ ἐστὶν ἡ πόλις ἡ ἡμετέρα (the city is said also to be the first named Christian
[see p. 368 above]). In so far as I am aware, the phrase is employed only in these two sermons.

i. Officials directly associated with emperor

The mere mention of a *hyparch*, *eparch* or *toparch* is no proof that Chrysostom is situated at Constantinople. Just as it was necessary to separate the homilist's understanding of certain metaphors or terms relating to the priesthood from our own, so there is no certainty that what we understand by *hyparch*, *eparch* and other such terms and what was understood by John and his audience is one and the same. In other words, there is no certainty that, when Chrysostom uses such terms, he is employing them in a strictly technical sense. Rather, it is possible that the semantic loading fluctuates from specific to generic depending upon the nature of the argument in hand or the particular rhetorical effect required.

On this note of warning, there is at least one instance in which we can be almost certain that the fact that Chrysostom mentions an official of this standing in association with the present location indicates that he is preaching at Constantinople. The information given is concrete, explicitly connected with the city and the context in which the official is mentioned sufficient to enable an identification. In *In illud: Pater meus usque modo operatur* (CPG 4441.10) John tells us that the murder which took place in the hippodrome on the previous day has filled the city with tragedy.[394] He further informs us that the victim was a member of the bureau of the *eparch* (ὑπὸ τὴν τάξιν τὴν τοῦ ἐπάρχου).[395] Although there is some suggestion that provincial *eparchs* did exist at this period,[396] the title was mainly attached to the prefecture of the city of Constantinople (ὁ ἔπαρχος τῆς πόλεως).[397] In this instance, the association between the *eparch* and the ceremonial of the hippodrome is particularly instructive. Whereas it is relatively certain that at Antioch a person elected to the liturgy of the *syriarch* was responsible for the production of spectacles, including chariot races,[398] at Constantinople responsibility for the contests staged at the hippodrome fell to the urban prefect.[399] When this information is matched with the fact that it is a member of his staff who was killed at the hippodrome on the previous day, one arrives at the most plausible

---

[394] PG 63,512 24-25.

[395] PG 63,512 31-32.

[396] See R. Guilland, "Études sur l'histoire administrative de l'Empire byzantin — L'Éparque II. Les éparques autres que l'éparque de la ville", *Byzantinoslavica* 42 (1981) 186-196.

[397] ODB I s.v. Eparch of the City.

[398] See Petit, *Libanius*, 131-133; Liebeschuetz, "The Syriarch in the Fourth Century", *Historia* 8 (1959) 113-126, in particular, 123.

[399] O. Pasquato, *Gli Spettacoli in s. Giovanni Crisostomo. Paganesimo e Cristianesimo ad Antiochia e Costantinopoli nel IV secolo* (OCA 201) Rome 1976, 90-91.

explanation as to why an official associated with the *eparch* was, at the time of a chariot race, exposed to risk down in the stadium of the hippo-drome.

The significance of a comment such as that which occurs in *In Acta apost. hom. 3*, on the other hand, is less easy to determine. Here Chrysos-tom, wishing to stress the lofty status of a bishop, says that not even *hyparchs* and *toparchs* enjoy the same prestige. Rather, when a bishop enters the palace or the houses of the wealthy, it is he who takes prece-dence.[400] Two difficulties need to be addressed in relation to this passage. The first is the identity of the dignitaries signified by the terms *hyparch* and *toparch*. Is John using the terms technically (i.e., to single out pre-fects and district governors),[401] or generically? Given the lack of detail, this is almost impossible to determine. The second difficulty is that the scenario itself is general. It does not necessarily refer to a specific bishop, nor does it necessarily refer to the present location. It must be borne in mind that the population of Antioch was most probably well acquainted with the protocol observed when a bishop entered the palace, through the visits to Constantinople undertaken in 381 by Meletius and in 387 by Flavian.[402] In consequence, unless it can be shown that Chrysostom is re-ferring to specific dignitaries of a type neither encountered nor known at Antioch, the comment could have been appreciated at either location and tells us little about the homily's provenance.[403]

Finally, under most circumstances information contained within an *exemplum* which is of general application is to be dismissed out of hand. The hypothetical situation involving the *hyparch* and the emperor ad-duced by the homilist in *In Phil. hom. 6* might well, as Bonsdorff pro-posed, make best sense if the hyparch is the *praefectus praetorio per Orientem*, the second-in-command to the emperor,[404] but it can only indi-

---

[400] PG 60,41 6-10: Ὕπαρχοι καὶ τοπάρχαι οὐκ ἀπολαύουσι τοσαύτης τιμῆς, ὅσης ὁ τῆς Ἐκκλησίας ἄρχων. Ἂν ἐν βασιλείοις εἰσίῃ, τίς πρῶτος; ἂν παρὰ γυναιξίν, ἂν παρὰ ταῖς οἰκίαις τῶν μεγάλων, οὐδεὶς ἕτερος αὐτοῦ προτετίμηται.

[401] LSJ s.v. τοπάρχης, ὕπαρχος 2.b.

[402] The efficiency of communication in the late antique world should not be underesti-mated. Chrysostom tells us of letters coming thick and fast when he was away in the coun-try (*De paen. hom. 1*, see n. 246 above), and of travellers passing on news when he was away from Constantinople (*De regressu* [CPG 4394] REB 19 [1961] 122 20.1-4), while, if one accepts that the homily refers to Flavian's trip to Constantinople, in *De Anna sermo 1* John tells us that on his return Flavian spent some considerable time relating what had occurred at the palace (PG 54,634 7-11). In *De statuis hom. 6* John relates to the audience information which was brought to Antioch by travellers who had passed Flavian on the road to Constantinople (PG 49,83 17-84 4).

[403] *In II Cor. hom. 26* (PG 61,582 45-47) where, among other officials who stand next to the emperor, *taxiarchs*, *phylarchs* and *hyparchs* are listed, presents similar difficulties.

[404] PG 62,221 17-22.

cate a provenance of Constantinople if one has already decided that that is where the homily was preached.[405] On rare occasions, however, an otherwise general exemplum can supply unique information described in a manner which strongly suggests that it is directed at a Constantinopolitan audience. As we have argued in relation to the series on Hebrews, in *In Heb. hom. 13* the mention of the position of *dekanos* falls under this category, since evidence associating *dekanoi* with the imperial palace first comes to light late in the fourth century, while Chrysostom appears to distinguish between this particular application of the term and another which is in more common usage.[406] Without an explicit link between the exemplum and the location of preaching this information cannot be considered proof positive of the homily's provenance. That it stems from Constantinople, however, can be considered probable.

ii. Other high officials

Just as the mention of a *hyparch* or *toparch* is in itself no proof that Chrysostom is situated at Constantinople, so is simple reference to an archon no confirmation that the local administration is provincial and that the homily in which the reference occurs was preached at Antioch. On the one hand, the homilist applies the term ἄρχων to members of the civil administration in much the same way that he employs ἱερεύς to describe members of the priesthood, that is, as a generic label which takes on more or less specific shades of meaning according to the context. On the other hand, John does not employ either of the two titles, *comes Orientis* and *consularis Syriae*, which, from a modern perspective, could be said to distinguish most clearly the administration at Antioch. It must also be remembered that just because the emperor is not mentioned, it does not mean that homilist and audience are necessarily at Antioch. In consequence, unless the detail supplied is extremely clear or the context definitive, without the assistance of contemporary external evidence it is difficult to prove that a particular archon is both the most senior administrative official available and that the office held could not be found also at Constantinople. Furthermore, this applies only to cases where the archon is clearly real and is attached to the present location. If the office is mentioned as part of an exemplum or a hypothetical scenario the task becomes more or less impossible.

The difficulties which attach to using the criterion in isolation to demonstrate provenance are exemplified by *De statuis hom. 16*. Here we are told that only the authority of the local ἄρχων, a pagan, has been suf-

---

[405] This point was first made in Allen-Mayer, "A Re-examination", 275-276.

[406] Allen-Mayer, "Hebrews: The Last Series?", 324-328.

ficient to quell the rumours circulating the city. In order to do this, the
archon has taken the unusual steps of entering the church in which John
is preaching and of addressing the assembled audience.[407] Thus we have
a situation where the archon is real, is a person of significance in the local community and is also a pagan. Although it has been suspected that
this person is the *consularis Syriae*,[408] the identification has been built
upon the assumption that the homily is Antiochene because it constitutes
part of the series *De statuis*. If it were not associated with that series and
one were forced to rely upon the information supplied within the homily
itself, there is little evidence to support this conclusion. Since the information supplied is sparse, speculation concerning the identity of the official requires prior knowledge of whether the location involved is Antioch
or Constantinople. Within the homily, only the information that the ru-
mour concerned the arrival of soldiers, who were about to encircle the
city and engage in the confiscation of property,[409] could be thought to
suggest that we are at Antioch, since it would appear that in the latter
part of the fourth century the stationing of troops there was periodic
rather than constant, in accord with the empire's needs.[410] This is no
proof, however. Instead it is the presence of a detailed summary of a recently delivered homily, incorporating the distinctive image of a flying
sickle, an allusion to Zachariah 5.1-4,[411] which provides confirmation.
The summary is of sufficient detail that it enables accurate identification
of the earlier sermon as *De statuis hom. 15*,[412] a homily of indisputable
Antiochene derivation.[413] Even with the provenance of *hom. 16* con-

---

[407] PG 49,161 8-22 *a.i.*, 166 19-25.

[408] Van de Paverd, *Homilies on the Statues*, 55. See also pp. 19-22, where he indicates
that Libanius uses the same bland term (ἄρχων) when describing the involvement of this
official in events.

[409] PG 49,162 4-16 *a.i.*

[410] Petit, *Libanius*, 177-190. Liebeschuetz, *Antioch*, 116-117, adduces evidence that a
unit was permanently garrisoned at Antioch in the 390s, suggesting that this was not the
case in the years which immediately preceded. Kelly, *Golden Mouth*, 156, however, points
out that Constantinople was in much the same situation in 400, since no military units
were at that point stationed in the capital, apart from the *scholae palatinae* (the imperial
guard).

[411] PG 49,163 44-57.

[412] For a detailed comparison of the points summarised in *hom. 16* with the contents
of *hom. 15* see van de Paverd, *Homilies on the Statues*, 317-321. Such precision is rare,
however, and a great deal of caution should be exercised when attempting to match such
summaries with the contents of extant homilies. Had Chrysostom been slightly more
vague on the present occasion, the sermon in question could as easily have been identified
as *In Acta apost. hom. 12*.

[413] For discussion of this point see pp. 443-445 below.

firmed, the preference for the office of *consularis Syriae* over that of *comes Orientis* is still open to question.[414]

If in *De statuis hom. 16* the referent of the term *archon* is unclear, even though it is patent that Chrysostom has a specific official in mind and the location is known, the circumstances under which the term is employed in *In Rom. hom. 23* negate the possibility that it might have bearing upon the provenance of that homily. Although Bonsdorff argued that the possibility that the archon could be a pagan meant that John could not be referring to the emperor and that therefore he must be discussing the administration at Antioch, this interpretation is not supported by the evidence. Bonsdorff supposed that the term refers to a person of the highest authority, i.e., emperor or provincial governor. Although that was most probably the case in *De statuis hom. 16*, in this particular homily discussion is restricted to comment relevant to the exegesis of the biblical text (Rom. 13.1ff). In consequence, the comment which does appear is general in character and does not lend itself to attempts to define the status of the archon in question. In addition, the possibility that the archon is pagan is presented as just that, a possibility.[415] If one wishes to argue that the option reflects a situation which is real rather than rhetorical,[416] then even though the audience might be more likely to encounter a pagan official at Antioch, the situation cannot have been entirely unknown at Constantinople also.[417] In any case, the force of the statement is weakened by the fact that Chrysostom assumes earlier in the homily that the majority of archons are Christian.[418]

Even so, there is at least one case where, although the provenance is not known in the first instance, mention of "the archon" does suggest that the homily was delivered at Antioch. As noted by Tillemont, in *Hom. in martyres* (CPG 4359) on the day of a martyrial festival virtually the whole city is said to have attended the celebration. Those who might

---

[414] As the name of the *comes Orientis* in 387 is unknown, there is no way of determining whether he was pagan or Christian, a factor which might have enabled distinction. See van de Paverd, *Homilies on the Statues*, 23 n. 63.

[415] PG 60,618 38-40: καὶ ὁ ἄρχων δέ σε θαυμάσεται μειζόνως, καὶ δοξάσει σου τὸν Δεσπότην ἐντεῦθεν, κἂν ἄπιστος ᾖ.

[416] Cf. *In Matt. hom. 82/83* (PG 58,744 56-58) where John instructs the priests who serve the eucharist that it is their duty to bar anyone who approaches unworthily, "even if the person is a military commander, a *hyparch* or the *basileus* himself". Few would argue that this represents a real possibility.

[417] The fact that Fl. Tatianus rose to the position of *praefectus praetorio per Orientem* under Theodosius suggests that at this early period Christian emperors were not averse to appointing non-Christians to high-ranking positions in the civil service. See PLRE I s.v. Flavius Eutolmius Tatianus 5, 877-878.

[418] PG 60,618 20-23: Εἰ γὰρ Ἑλλήνων ὄντων τότε τῶν ἀρχόντων ταῦτα ἐνομοθέτησε, πολλῷ μᾶλλον νῦν ἐπὶ τῶν πιστῶν τοῦτο γίνεσθαι χρή.

have been prevented from attending due to various constraints are said to have presented themselves regardless, no slave allowing the fear of their master to deter them, no poor person the necessity of begging, no old man the feebleness of his age, no woman the delicacy of her constitution, no rich person the conceit arising from excess, nor the archon the dementia of power.[419] The sudden introduction of the definite article suggests that there is only one archon present, while the hierarchy of description leads one to suspect that he is the best available representative of local civil authority. Tillemont's argument that at Constantinople administrative officials are not singled out in this way is unconvincing,[420] since one cannot rule out the possibility that the imperial family is absent at the present time and that, with the court removed from the city for the summer,[421] the archon mentioned is the next best administrative official available. There is also no indication by John that he is for his own part not the highest-ranking priest available, which might assist in excluding the possibility that he is situated at Constantinople.

However, towards the close of the sermon Chrysostom does supply two pieces of topographic detail which lead to the suspicion that he is indeed at Antioch and that the archon in question is genuinely the highest local administrative officer. The point of synaxis is outside the city, within walking distance,[422] and is close to a number of gardens.[423] The detail evokes the situation described by Chrysostom in *In Acta apost. hom. 38*, where he recalls an incident which occurred just outside Antioch. There he says that, after visiting a certain martyrium (probably situated in the direction of Daphne),[424] he made his way back through the gardens which bordered the river.[425] If the martyrium was situated on the road to Daphne, this could well explain the homilist's fear that the crowd will be distracted by taverns and that their behaviour will deteriorate on

---

[419] PG 50,663 23-31: Τίς γὰρ οὐκ ἂν ἀγάσαιτο σήμερον ἡμῶν τὸν σύλλογον ... Ὡς πᾶσα μὲν σχεδὸν ἡ πόλις ἐνταῦθα μεθώρμισται, καὶ οὔτε οἰκέτην δεσπότου φόβος κατέσχεν, οὔτε πένητα ἡ τῆς πτωχείας ἀνάγκη, οὔτε γηραιὸν τῆς ἡλικίας ἡ ἀσθένεια, οὔτε γυναῖκα τὸ τῆς φύσεως ἁπαλόν, οὔτε πλούσιον τῆς περιουσίας ὁ τῦφος, οὐ τὸν ἄρχοντα τῆς ἐξουσίας ἡ ἀπόνοια·

[420] See Tillemont, *Mémoires*, XI 367.

[421] See n. 275 above.

[422] PG 50,666 8-10: Οὕτω τοίνυν εἰς τὴν πόλιν ἐπανίωμεν, μετὰ τῆς προσηκούσης εὐταξίας, μετὰ εὐτάκτου βαδίσεως...

[423] PG 50,665 2-6: Ἀλλὰ κήποις ἐνδιατρίψαι βούλει, καὶ λειμῶσι καὶ παραδείσοις; Μὴ νῦν, ὅτε δῆμος τοσοῦτος, ἀλλ᾽ ἐν ἑτέρᾳ ἡμέρᾳ· σήμερον γὰρ παλαισμάτων καιρός, σήμερον θεωρία ἀγωνισμάτων, οὐ τρυφῆς, οὐδὲ ἀνέσεως. Ἦλθες ἐνταῦθα...

[424] See Libanius, *Or.* 11.234 (Foerster, I 518-519).

[425] PG 60,274 56-58: τότε ἐγὼ εἰς μαρτύριον ἀπιέναι βουλόμενος, ἐπανήειν διὰ τῶν κήπων παρὰ ποταμόν...

the way back to the city.[426] This additional detail is not conclusive, since suburban martyria at Constantinople were also within walking distance[427] and it is reasonable to suppose that the roads which exited major cities at this time commonly passed near gardens and were lined by taverns and inns. Taken together, however, the facts that the archon is singled out as the civil representative at the festival and that the topographic detail conforms with the region leading to Daphne from Antioch are suggestive, at least, of an Antiochene provenance. Whether this conclusion eventually proves correct or not, it is nonetheless clear that of itself reference to "the archon" is inadequate as a determinant of the place of delivery. It requires the assistance of other evidence to tip the scales for or against a particular location.

iii. Military

Arguments concerning military activities and the presence or otherwise of a military encampment are even more difficult, since throughout this period divisions of the army were almost continually being deployed and redeployed to handle both external and internal affairs.[428] The ability to draw a firm distinction between Antioch and Constantinople in this matter is therefore limited, with the result that any hypothesis proposed requires subtlety and needs to take a large number of variables into account. For instance, Bonsdorff's thesis that in *In II Cor. hom.* 9 the submission of the army to the authority of archons indicates Antioch, since at Constantinople the army was under the direct command of the emperor, is simplistic and does not take careful note of either the information or the manner in which it is supplied. The soldiers mentioned are not members of the regular army, but attached as a specialised police force to archons with judicial authority.[429] Their duties are constant irrespective of what occurs in the regular army and their service to the ar-

---

[426] PG 50,663 43-59.

[427] See *Hom. dicta postquam reliquiae martyrum* (CPG 4441.1), where newly translated remains are escorted from within the city to a suburban martyrium by a procession conducted on foot.

[428] See Liebeschuetz, *Barbarians and Bishops*, 7-132, in particular 26-31, 51-59 and 90-92.

[429] PG 61,466 4-8: Οὐχ ὁρᾷς τοὺς ἐνταῦθα στρατιώτας τοὺς τοῖς ἄρχουσι διακονουμένους, πῶς ἕλκουσι, πῶς δεσμοῦσι, πῶς μαστιγοῦσι, πῶς τὰς πλευρὰς διορύττουσι, πῶς λαμπάδας ταῖς βασάνοις προσάγουσι, πῶς ἀποτέμνουσιν; Cf. *De statuis hom. 13* (PG 49,137 24-35) where soldiers act as security guards at the trial, although van de Paverd, *Homilies on the Statues*, 68 n. 335, argues that this is a special case.

chons is a matter of course.[430] This does not necessarily mean that John is situated at Antioch, particularly since, even if one could prove that soldiers served in this manner only in provincial administrations, the involvement of such soldiers in torture is evoked as an exemplum, requiring only a general knowledge of this kind of activity on the part of the audience.

Similar difficulties occur in regard to the exemplum adduced as proof of the Constantinopolitan provenance of *In I Thess. hom. 3*.[431] Bonsdorff assumes that the presence of soldiers who exit the city on a daily basis to engage in exercises necessarily indicates the city of imperial residence. In making this assumption he fails to take into account several details. Exempla that begin "Don't you see these...", no matter how vivid, do not necessarily indicate that the situation described is available to the audience,[432] while divisions of the army were stationed periodically at Antioch, even in times of so-called peace.[433] Once this is recognised, one is obliged to admit that the exemplum could have been used with effectiveness at either location.

4. DEMOGRAPHY

As in the case of criteria relating to the status of the homilist and the features local to each city, those which are based on the assumed demographic make-up of each city demonstrate a variety of degrees of reliability also.

a. *Language*

i. Syriac

The argument that, when Chrysostom assumes a working knowledge of Syriac on the part of a section of the audience, he must be situated in Syria, stems from the fact that comment of this kind occurs in *In Matt.*

---

[430] It may be that Chrysostom is here thinking of a military guard, such as that attached to the person of the *comes Orientis* or *magister militum*. For the operations which these guards carried out in the days succeeding the riots at Antioch see Downey, *Antioch*, 429.

[431] PG 62,411 22-30: Οὐκ ἴστε ὅτι ἐν εἰρήνῃ τὰ τοῦ πολέμου γυμνάζεσθαι χρή; οὐχ ὁρᾶτε τοὺς στρατιώτας τούτους ... εἰς ὕπτια πεδία καὶ εὐρύχωρα καθ᾽ ἑκάστην, ὡς εἰπεῖν, ἡμέραν ἐξιόντες, τὰ τοῦ πολέμου γυμνάζονται μετὰ πολλῆς τῆς ἀκριβείας;

[432] See p. 374 above.

[433] Liebeschuetz, *Antioch*, 116-117.

hom. 7, a certifiably Antiochene homily,[434] and in *Sermo 9 in Gen.*, which has been assumed to be Antiochene by virtue of its association with the homilies *De mutatione nominum.* In both instances, after exegeting an Old Testament name John adds the comment that this information is known by those who are familiar with Syriac.[435] However, in neither is the remark other than general (i.e., he does not say "as many of *you* as know Syriac", but "all those who know Syriac") and in consequence it is difficult to say whether the comment is prompted by the fact that the homily is being delivered in the Syrian capital, where one might expect to find a certain percentage of native speakers of Syriac, or whether it is to be attributed solely to the nature of the material being exegeted.[436] Should the latter prove to be the case, the fact that such a comment appears on at least one occasion in an Antiochene homily would be coincidental. Rather, for an assumption of a knowledge of Syriac to be effective as an indication of Antiochene provenance, both explicit application of the remark to the audience and proof of a direct connection between comment and location are required.

While one might presume that a connection between such comment and Syria would be natural, matters are complicated by the suggestion that a significant ex-patriot Syrian community existed at Constantinople at the time that Chrysostom was bishop. Whether this was restricted to monks and bishops — Isaac, Severian and Acacius, for instance, were all Syrian — or included members of the laity is uncertain, but John tells us that, on an occasion when the empress led the stational procession to an extra-urban martyrium, the psalms chanted along the way were sung in not just Greek, but also Latin, Syriac and most probably Gothic.[437] Other references to Syriac are unhelpful in narrowing the options. In *In Matt. hom. 16* it is difficult to say whether the example of contemporary Syriac speech is supplied for any reason other than clarification of Ps. 4.5, since the homilist makes it clear that the Syriac idiom is other than familiar to

---

[434] See pp. 367-369 above.

[435] *In Matt. hom.* 7 (PG 57,74 26-28): ὅθεν καὶ Ζοροβάβελ ἐκλήθη, διὰ τὸ ἐκεῖ σπαρῆναι. Καὶ ὅσοι τὴν Σύρων ἴσασι γλῶτταν, ἴσασι τὸ λεγόμενον; *Sermo 9 in Gen.* (PG 54,624 57-625 2): Καὶ γὰρ Ἄβραμ ἐκαλεῖτο τὸ πρότερον, ἀλλὰ τοῦτο τὸ ὄνομα οὐκ ἔστιν Ἑλληνικόν, οὐδὲ τῇ ἡμετέρᾳ γλώττῃ ... τῇ Σύρων φωνῇ τὸ πέραν λέγεται, καὶ ἴσασιν ὅσοι τῆς φωνῆς ταύτης εἰσὶν ἔμπειροι.

[436] Cf. *Sermo 9 in Gen.* (PG 54,628 46-53), the explanation of "Noah", where Syriac is introduced as the closest contemporary cognate of Hebrew and therefore useful for clarifying the explanation. The information provided requires no knowledge on the part of the audience, being presented as a simple statement of fact.

[437] *Hom. dicta postquam reliquiae martyrum* (CPG 4441.1) PG 63,472 10-13: Καὶ γὰρ μυρίους ἡμῖν ἐξήγαγες χορούς, τοὺς μὲν τῇ Ῥωμαίων, τοὺς δε τῇ Σύρων, τοὺς δὲ τῇ βαρβάρων, τοὺς δε τῇ Ἑλλάδι φωνῇ τὰ τοῦ Δαυΐδ ἀνακρουομένους ᾄσματα·

his audience;[438] while in *Hom. 4 in Gen.* Syriac is again introduced in a general way, this time in confirmation of the plural number of the Hebrew word *shamayim* (heaven).[439] Since in no other instance than *In Matt. hom. 7* do we have certain proof of the homily's provenance from internal evidence, there is at present no way of proving whether reference to Syriac is coincidental to provenance or directly related. For the time being the status of this criterion must remain uncertain.

ii. Non-Greek-speaking rural population

Wenger's argument that the presence of a rural population that speaks a language other than Greek necessarily indicates a provenance of Antioch, on the other hand, seems reasonable when tested against the evidence. In support of this proposition Wenger himself adduces *De statuis hom. 19* and *De ss. martyribus* (CPG 4357),[440] both homilies of certain Antiochene derivation.[441] Although in *Cat. 8* itself, as well as in *De statuis hom. 19*, the influx of persons from the countryside is restricted to rural priests of some description,[442] in *De ss. martyribus* the homilist refers to a situation where "those from the country" represent a broad cross-section of the rural population.[443] Even so, in all three situations the difference in language between the rural sector and the urban population is carefully stressed. There are further striking similarities between the description of the priests supplied in *De statuis hom. 19* and *Cat. 8*

---

[438] PG 57,248 45-49: Καθάπερ γὰρ ἡμεῖς ἢ οἰκέταις, ἤ τισι τῶν καταδεεστέρων ἐπιτάττοντες λέγομεν· ¨Απελθε σύ, εἰπὲ τῷ δεῖνι σύ· οὕτω καὶ οἱ τῇ Σύρων κεχρημένοι γλώττῃ 'Ρακὰ λέγουσιν, ἀντὶ τοῦ, Σύ, τοῦτο τιθέντες.

[439] PG 53,43 12-16: Λέγουσι τοίνυν οἱ τὴν γλῶτταν ἐκείνην ἀκριβῶς ἠσκημένοι, τὸ τοῦ οὐρανοῦ ὄνομα πληθυντικῶς καλεῖσθαι παρὰ τοῖς 'Εβραίοις, καὶ τοῦτο καὶ οἱ τὴν Σύρων γλῶτταν ἐπιστάμενοι συνομολογοῦσι.

[440] *De statuis hom. 19* (PG 49,188 6-12 a.i.): 'Εορτὴν γὰρ μεγίστην εἶναι νομίζω τὴν παροῦσαν ἡμέραν, διὰ τὴν τῶν ἀδελφῶν παρουσίαν τῶν ἡμετέρων, οἱ τὴν πόλιν ἡμῖν ἐκαλλώπισαν τήμερον καὶ τὴν ἐκκλησίαν ἐκόσμησαν. Λαὸς κατὰ μὲν τὴν γλῶτταν ἡμῖν ἐνηλλαγμένος, κατὰ δὲ τὴν πίστιν ἡμῖν συμφωνῶν...; *De ss. martyribus* (PG 50,646 8-15): Πόλις μὲν γὰρ καὶ χώρα ἐν τοῖς βιωτικοῖς πράγμασιν ἀλλήλων διεστήκασι ... Μὴ γάρ μοι τὴν βάρβαρον αὐτῶν φωνὴν ἴδῃς ... τί δέ μοι βλάβος τῆς ἑτεροφωνίας, ὅταν τὰ τῆς πίστεως ᾖ συνημμένα;. Cf. *Cat. 8* (SC 50bis,247 1.5-248 2.6): οἱ ἀπὸ τῆς χώρας πρὸς ἡμᾶς συρρεύσαντες ... μὴ τοῦτο ἴδωμεν ... ὅτι βάρβαρον ἔχουσι τὴν γλῶτταν ...

[441] Wenger, *Huit catéchèses* (SC 50bis) 60-63. For the grounds for assigning each homily to Antioch see pp. 367 and 337-341 above, respectively.

[442] For a detailed discussion of their identity see van de Paverd, *Homilies on the Statues*, 260-290.

[443] PG 50,647 1-3 and 13-20. Cf. *De beato Philogonio* (CPG 4319) PG 48,750 6-8, where it is suggested that at Antioch the mingling of city-dwellers and people from the surrounding countryside on days when a major Christian festival was being celebrated was not uncommon, due to the increased commercial activity associated with such festivals.

which reinforce the conclusion that the baptismal instruction too was delivered at Antioch.[444] Our concern here, however, is with the linguistic division between χώρα (countryside) and πόλις (city). Although it has been assumed that such a division did not pertain at Constantinople, since the rural community of Thrace would have spoken Greek, the degree of association between Constantinople and the rural areas across the Bosporus near Chalcedon is less well known.[445] Even without precise knowledge of the degree of interaction between Constantinople and the neighbouring rural communities, or certainty regarding whether the latter was homophonous with the imperial capital, nonetheless the weight of the evidence does seem to favour Antioch. Pending clarification of the situation at Constantinople, it seems reasonable to accept that, in situations where it is clear that the foreign-speaking individuals are members of a rural population which exists in proximity to the city in which Chrysostom is preaching, it is probable that John is situated at Antioch.

b. *Prominent Jewish sector*

Baur argued that the Jewish sector at Antioch was more prominent because it was not overshadowed by the imperial court and that this prominence is reflected in the prevalence of anti-Jewish material in the Antiochene homilies. In particular, the appearance of such comment in the series on Romans was seen to be indicative of its Antiochene provenance. Yet, although one finds in Chrysostom's sermons a clear association between Antioch and Judaizing Christians,[446] it does not necessarily follow that therefore anti-Jewish polemic is a characteristic and distinctive feature of the homilies which stem from Antioch. The problem here is that we are dealing on the one hand (in regard to Judaizing Christians) with a real situation, on the other (with respect to anti-Jewish polemic) with rhetoric.[447] As we have seen above, arguments based on rhetorical elements, such as exempla or expressions of humility, are often unreliable and produce results that bear little relation to the real provenance of

---

[444] See van de Paverd, *Homilies on the Statues*, 256-260.

[445] Mango, "Development", 118, points out that, although officially an independent city, in practice Chalcedon constituted part of the conurbation recognised as Constantinople.

[446] Of the eight sermons *Adv. Iudaeos* three contain clear proof of Antiochene derivation (*or. 1, 5, 6*; see pp. 376-378 above and pp. 434-438 and 443-445 below), while a fourth (*or. 2*) both summarises and echoes statements made in *or. 1* (cf. PG 48,857 2-26 and 845 4-5, 856 42-45; 861 5-16 and 849 1ff; 860 55-861 3 and 846 65-847 5).

[447] For an excellent study of the anti-Jewish material from this perspective see Wilken, *Chrysostom and the Jews*.

a homily, when this is able to be established. Yet the argument that overt anti-Jewish polemic is to be equated with distance from the imperial court, and therefore a provenance of Antioch, is introduced without any recourse to an assessment of how, where and why Chrysostom introduces such material within his homilies. In particular, no attempt is made to compare the frequency of such comment in the definitively Constantinopolitan versus Antiochene homilies or to draw a distinction between exegetical and non-exegetical material. In consequence, no consideration is given to the possibility that within an exegetical series such comment might arise naturally in response to the text being exegeted, rather than reflect the prominence of Judaism in the local community.

Moreover, the very fact that the "literary war against the Jews and Jewry" was constant among the fathers of the church at this period,[448] leads to the suspicion that a statistical analysis of Chrysostom's homilies which takes all of these variables into account may prove that there is no substantial difference between the homilies delivered at Antioch and Constantinople in regard to the distribution of comment on matters Jewish. Such an analysis, however, awaits a redistribution of the entire corpus on scientific principles, particularly the sermons assembled into exegetical series. In other words, Baur's assumption that Jewish material is more common in Antiochene homilies is an impression influenced by the existence of the sermons *Adv. Iudaeos* and by various assumptions concerning the distribution and homogeneity of the exegetical series. While it may prove to have some basis, it is more likely that it will turn out to be unsustainable. In the meantime, if one accepts the premise that the Jewish community at Antioch was far more prominent than that which existed at the time at Constantinople, then one would do better to turn to an analysis of comment in the homilies which refers to the local contemporary Jewish communities and their practices. It is far more likely that, in establishing what occurred locally, one will be able to assess whether there are any distinctive differences between the role in the wider community played by the Jewish population at each location.

c. *Characteristics of Christian population*

i. General

Arguments for provenance based upon the presumed characteristics of the Christian population at each location encounter the same difficulties as those which take as their basis features assumed to be distinctive

---

[448] Baur, *Chrysostom and His Time*, I 303 n. 50[a].

of the one city or the other.[449] As regards size, the fact that in both *In Matt. hom. 85/86* and *In Acta apost. hom. 11*, the one considered to stem from Antioch, the other from Constantinople, the homilist claims that the local Christian population numbers some 100,000,[450] leads to the suspicion that this figure is rhetorically convenient rather than accurate. As for the attentiveness and assiduity of the Christian population at Antioch, there is more than one homily of Antiochene derivation in which John chides the audience for their poor attendance,[451] while there is at least one homily of Constantinopolitan provenance in which he praises the audience for their attentiveness and assiduity.[452] This does not mean that good attendance and behaviour in church can alternatively be said to be a characteristic of Constantinopolitan audiences, since the homilist at times praises the Antiochenes also for exhibiting these same characteristics. Although there is at present insufficient reliable evidence for the behaviour of the Christian population at Constantinople, it is likely that Chrysostom alternately praises and chides his audiences at both locations, depending upon the time of year, the climate and other factors which favourably or adversely affect their behaviour and attendance. Of the two characteristics of the Christian population adduced in the literature, neither is in reality of use for establishing provenance.

ii. Judaizing tendencies

That a tendency to Judaize is a characteristic exhibited exclusively by the Christian community at Antioch is probable but not provable, since one cannot exclude entirely the possibility that the fact that no evidence of this behaviour is found in Constantinopolitan homilies is due either to the current distribution of the homilies or to an accident of survival. With this in mind, there is nonetheless strong evidence for Antioch, where the problem is addressed directly in at least three sermons (*Adv.*

---

[449] See 3.f.i (pp. 387-391 above).

[450] *In Matt. hom. 85/86* (PG 58,762 59-763 2): Καὶ γὰρ τῇ τοῦ Θεοῦ χάριτι εἰς δέκα μυριάδων ἀριθμὸν οἶμαι τοὺς ἐνταῦθα συναγομένους τελεῖν; *In Acta apost. hom. 11* (PG 60,97 22-25): Εἰπὲ γάρ μοι, ἡ πόλις ἡμῖν εἰς πόσον μιγάδων ἀριθμὸν νῦν τελεῖ; πόσους βούλεσθε εἶναι Χριστιανούς; βούλεσθε δέκα μυριάδας, τὸ δὲ ἄλλο Ἑλλήνων καὶ Ἰουδαίων; Both statements occur within a similar context.

[451] See, e.g., *De statuis hom. 20* (PG 49,199 25-28; 199 59-200 3); *In princ. Act. hom. 1* (PG 51,65-67 1-22).

[452] See *Contra Anom. hom. 11* (CPG 4324) SC 396,286 5-288 18, where the assiduity and piety of the church at Antioch are said to be less than that of the church at Constantinople. For the grounds for assigning this homily to Constantinople see 3.f.ii (pp. 391-393 above).

Iud. or. 1, 5, 6).[453] The difficulty with this is that the three sermons constitute part of a cluster of eight homilies which have the problem of Judaizing as their focus, while casual reference to the problem occurs only twice elsewhere, in *Hom. 12 in Gen.* and in *In Titum hom. 3.* Had the eight sermons *Adv. Iudaeos* not survived, there would be no basis for suggesting that a reference to Judaizing among the local Christians is an indication of Antiochene provenance. Given that they did survive, why then are there so few references to Judaizing outside of this small number of homilies? While one possibility is that, subsequent to Chrysostom's ordination as presbyter, the problem persisted among only a small number of Christians for a short period of time before ceasing altogether, another more likely scenario is that, since the problem was not widespread,[454] after a short time John himself lost interest in the topic, turning his attention to other, more pressing issues. Since the majority of the eight homilies *Adv. Iudaeos* is preached in response to the proximity of a major Jewish festival,[455] a further possibility is that, aside from *Hom. 12 in Gen.*, very few of the hundreds of other extant homilies were preached at significant points in the Jewish calendar.

How then do these findings relate to the issue of provenance? Since in two of the three sermons *Adv. Iudaeos* of certain Antiochene derivation comment arises in response to the rhythms of the local Jewish calendar (*or. 1, 5*), while in all three the situation is said to be local,[456] we can posit that in other cases where these two conditions are met, there is a strong likelihood that the homilies were delivered at Antioch also. Of the two sermons to which the criterion has been applied, *Hom. 12 in Gen.* affords evidence of both, Chrysostom stating that he has recently had to divert from his current theme in order to address those of the congregation who have been causing division by adhering to Jewish practice.[457] There is some suggestion that this diversion was made more urgent by virtue of the particular time of year.[458] The comment in *In Titum hom. 3*, on the other hand, fails in both respects. The practice of fasting, celebrating the sabbath with the Jews or visiting their holy places is not said to be local, while the places listed are named in a manner which suggests that the

---

[453] See n. 446 above.

[454] That the number who participated in the Jewish festivals and fasts is small is suggested in *Adv. Iud. or. 1* (PG 48,849 12-13) and *or. 3* (PG 48,862 23-25 *a.i.*).

[455] *Adv. Iud. or. 1* (PG 48,844 25-28); *or. 2* (PG 48,857 2-3); *or. 3* (PG 48,861 22-28 *a.i.*); *or. 4* (PG 48,871 6-27 *a.i.*); *or. 5* (PG 48,883 24-26); *or. 7* (PG 48,915 13-19 *a.i.*); *or. 8* (PG 48,927 42 *a.i.*).

[456] *Adv. Iud. or. 1* (PG 48,844 28-32; 847 39-848 17; 851 38-39; 852 1-6); *or. 5* (PG 48,904 18-25); *or. 6* (PG 48,913 5-35).

[457] PG 53,98 17-31 *a.i.*

[458] PG 53,98 10 *a.i.*-99 5.

homilist does not expect local knowledge of these sites on the part of his audience.[459] The difference between the manner in which John expresses himself here and in the other examples suggests that the material introduced was in this instance chosen more for its familiarity to the homilist than its application to the audience. The comment, moreover, is prompted not by an external Jewish festival but arises entirely from the particular text being exegeted. In the case of *In Titum hom. 3*, then, the reference to Judaizing cannot be considered to have any bearing upon that homily's provenance.

iii. Heterodox tendencies

Arguments based upon the existence of a particular heresy or schism at one place or the other are problematic from the start since, of necessity, they rely upon an assessment of the evidence which is either selective or heavily coloured by assumptions. For instance, just as the existence of a series of homilies with Judaizing as their focus formed the basis for the argument that any homily which addresses that problem belongs to the same location, so the existence of a number of homilies *Contra Anomoeos* (CPG 4318, 4320-4323), which appeared to have Antioch as their point of origin, persuaded Montfaucon to assign *In illud: Filius ex se nihil facit* (CPG 4441.12) likewise to that city. The relative weight of a particular heresy at one location or another is impossible to prove, however, and the argument becomes untenable when it is seen that Chrysostom preached against the Anomoeans at Constantinople also.[460]

The opposite problem occurs in the case of *In Phil hom. 6* and the argument from Apollinarism.[461] Apparently on the basis that Apollinaris received official condemnation at the second ecumenical council at Constantinople in 381,[462] Bonsdorff assumed that the appearance of this figure among a list of heresiarchs indicated a provenance of Constantinople. He supported his claim with the argument that nowhere among the Antiochene homilies is Apollinaris labelled a heretic. This second claim has significance only if one believes that the views of Apollinaris were still being treated with sympathy at Antioch at the time of Chrysostom's presbyterate (386-397), due to the former's long association with that lo-

---

[459] PG 62,679 6-11. For discussion of this latter point see pp. 376-378 above and 421-425 below.

[460] *Contra Anom. hom. 11* (CPG 4324). For the grounds for assigning this homily to Constantinople see pp. 391-393 above.

[461] The following draws upon material presented in Allen-Mayer, "A Re-examination", 276-277.

[462] See Lietzmann, *Apollinaris*, 29-31 and 62-65.

cation.[463] Quite apart from the difficulty of positing a delay of some six-
teen or seventeen years between the official condemnation of Apollinarian christology and a wide-spread acceptance of that decision at
Antioch, there exists a further problem which effectively negates the argument. That is, it is not just in the purportedly Antiochene homilies that
reference to Apollinaris as an heresiarch fails to appear, but also among
the homilies considered to be of Constantinopolitan derivation.[464] In
other words, there is no support for the claim that condemnation of
Apollinarism is characteristically Constantinopolitan. There is, on the
other hand, reason to argue that the remark could have been made at
Antioch, and therefore at either location. As Grillmeier points out, at
Antioch suspicion of heresy had already become attached to Apollinaris
by the year 379, since at the synod held at Antioch in that year the bishops Diodore of Tarsus and Meletius openly took up a position against
him.[465] When coupled with the fact that Apollinaris directly attacked the
position of Diodore,[466] with which Chrysostom could be expected to have
some sympathy,[467] it can be seen that the homilist would have had as
much reason to label Apollinaris a heretic at Antioch as at Constantinople. On this basis, the argument that Apollinarism could be described as
a major heresy only from the perspective of Constantinople would appear to owe more to an *a priori* assumption of Constantinopolitan provenance than to any real evidence.

Since clear reference to Novatian teaching in relation to a particular
location occurs in only a single homily of possible Constantinopolitan
origin (*Adv. catharos*: CPG 4441.6),[468] an argument positing that Novatianism was a particular problem encountered at Constantinople, and that

---

[463] Lietzmann, *Apollinaris*, 13, 66, indicates that Apollinaris taught at the exegetical
school there in 373/4. For an overview of the situation between the Antiochenes and
Apollinaris after this date see Grillmeier, *Christ in Christian Tradition*, I 351ff.

[464] *In Phil. hom. 6* (PG 62,218 7 a.i.-219 1) is the sole example among the authentic
homilies. Grillmeier, *Christ in Christian Tradition*, I 418, finds it singular that Chrysostom
is unpreoccupied with the Apollinarist heresy.

[465] Grillmeier, *Christ in Christian Tradition*, I 351. A similar view is offered by N. Q.
King, "The 150 Holy Fathers of the Council of Constantinople 381 A.D. Some notes on the
Bishop-lists", StP 1 (1957) 637, who posits that Meletius of Antioch was directly involved
in the movement to have Apollinaris' views condemned.

[466] Lietzmann, *Apollinaris*, 235-236.

[467] See Grillmeier, *Christ in Christian Tradition*, I 418. For an outline of the christologi-
cal views of Diodore and Chrysostom see ibid., 351-360, 418-421.

[468] The bulk of the refutation of Novatian teaching occurs in the columns missing
from the PG text. For the full argument see Stav. 6, ff.81v-84r. Even though Novatianism
was strictly a rigorist form of Nicene Christianity, it is included in the discussion here because Chrysostom uses the term "heretics" when referring to those who practise it.

therefore a focus upon it in a homily is suggestive of Constantinopolitan provenance, would encounter much the same difficulty.

The argument that schism is a characteristic of the Christian community at Antioch demonstrates the danger attached to placing too great a weight on a famous example. The belief that only a division which history perceives as a schism could be labelled in that manner by the homilist, and that therefore, when a schism is mentioned, the identity of the location is automatically solved, can lead to a careless and selective assessment of the evidence. Nowhere is this seen more clearly than in the case of *In Eph. hom. 11*. Here, assuming that, because the split is said to have occurred among the orthodox, John must be referring to the Meletian schism at Antioch,[469] scholars have seized upon the homilist's claim that he has been chosen not for ἀρχή or αὐθεντία (office or sole authority) but for the preaching of the Word,[470] as proof that he is of presbyteral status. But this statement does not necessarily mean that John has no invested authority. He is here expressing a personal opinion that must be viewed carefully within its context.[471] Indeed, as both Rauschen and Costanza recognised, as the sermon progresses Chrysostom moves away from general discussion, drawing closer and closer to detail which is personal and highly specific. In this respect an analogy can be drawn with *In Col. hom. 3*, where it was seen that information supplied toward the end of the discussion proved to be the more reliable and contradicted the impression of distance from the episcopacy given by comments made at the beginning.[472]

A careful analysis of all of the claims made by Chrysostom in the latter half of *In Eph. hom. 11* shows that not only is the identity of the schism mentioned in this homily not patent, but that the split which so affected the church at Antioch presents as an unlikely candidate. In the first instance, when the homilist thinks of division within the church he thinks not of doctrinal differences as the root cause, but a desire for power (φιλαρχία).[473] Moreover, the reason that he has raised the issue is to address those Christians who follow or associate with persons who actively divide the church. It is bad enough when the latter hold contrary doctrine, he says, but far worse when there is no difference at all. The ex-

---

[469] PG 62,86 1-9: Ταῦτά μοι εἰρήσθω πρὸς τοὺς ἀδιαφόρως διδόντας ἑαυτοὺς τοῖς σχίζουσι τὴν Ἐκκλησίαν ... Τί λέγεις; ἡ αὐτὴ πίστις ἐστίν, ὀρθόδοξοί εἰσι κἀκεῖνοι.

[470] PG 62,87 2-4: εἰς διδασκαλίαν λόγου προεχειρίσθημεν, οὐκ εἰς ἀρχὴν οὐδὲ εἰς αὐθεντίαν.

[471] As seen in sections 2.a and c (pp. 327 and 332-334 above), comment of this kind is often misleading and should not be taken at face value.

[472] See pp. 323f above.

[473] PG 62,85 28-29: Οὐδὲν οὕτως Ἐκκλησίαν δυνήσεται διαιρεῖν, ὡς φιλαρχία. Cf. PG 62,85 36-38, where it becomes clear that he has members of the priesthood in mind.

cuse offered by those who follow the said persons is that they can see no
difficulty, since the latter are orthodox and it is all the one faith.[474] The
situation, in so far as it can be ascertained at this point, is apparently one
in which a certain group, at the prompting of members of the clergy,
have chosen to worship separately from the rest of the orthodox Christians. Judging by the final comment ("So why aren't they with us?")
John's interest in the topic appears to be more than just general, leading
to the suspicion that it has relevance locally. At this point one could dismiss the accusation of φιλαρχία as a subjective interpretation of affairs on
the part of Chrysostom and argue that the situation could yet describe
the one which pertained at Antioch. Since the Antiochene schism was of
sufficient duration for a number of bishops and priests to have been ordained by the Eustathian camp,[475] a circumstance which must have
caused offence to the Meletians, John's next comment, that the issue of
proper ordination is to be defended as fiercely as correct doctrine,[476]
would appear to support that view. As the homily progresses, however,
this position becomes less tenable.

Chrysostom continues by saying that the local pagans already criticise
the Christian community for the divisions caused by heresy. What then,
he says, will they say about this?[477] On the face of it, the comment discounts a situation which is of long duration. Again he emphasises that
the situation involves two bodies of Christians with the same doctrine
and the same worship patterns, this time adding that the situation involves "one archon assaulting another church".[478] For the first time he
makes it quite clear that the situation is local.[479] Tantalising as is the
mention of an archon attacking what one may assume is another archon's church, when it comes to eliciting details which might identify the
situation for the modern scholar, we encounter the same difficulty ob-

---

[474] PG 62,86 1-9: Ταῦτά μοι εἰρήσθω πρὸς τοὺς ἀδιαφόρως διδόντας ἑαυτοὺς τοῖς σχίζουσι τὴν
Ἐκκλησίαν. Εἰ μὲν γὰρ καὶ δόγματα ἔχουσιν ἐναντία, καὶ διὰ τοῦτο οὐ προσῆκεν ἐκείνοις
ἀναμίγνυσθαι· εἰ δὲ τὰ αὐτὰ φρονοῦσι, πολλῷ μᾶλλον. Τί δήποτε; Ὅτι φιλαρχίας ἐστὶν ἡ νόσος ...
Τί λέγεις; ἡ αὐτὴ πίστις ἐστίν, ὀρθόδοξοί εἰσι κάκεῖνοι. Τίνος οὖν ἕνεκεν οὐκ εἰσὶ μεθ' ἡμῶν;

[475] Although the most thorough discussion of the schism is still that provided by F.
Cavallera, Le schisme d'Antioche, Paris 1905, for a useful summary see M. Simonetti, art.
"Antioch III. Schism", EEC I 49-50.

[476] PG 62,86 13-18: Ἀρκεῖν τοῦτο ἡγεῖσθε, εἰπέ μοι, τὸ λέγειν, ὅτι ὀρθόδοξοί εἰσι, τὰ τῆς
χειροτονίας δὲ οἴχεται καὶ ἀπόλωλε; ... Ὥσπερ γὰρ ὑπὲρ τῆς πίστεως, οὕτω καὶ ὑπὲρ ταύτης
μάχεσθαι χρή.

[477] PG 62,86 29-32: Πῶς οἴσομεν τὸν παρὰ τῶν Ἑλλήνων γέλωτα; Εἰ γὰρ ὑπὲρ τῶν αἱρέσεων
ἐγκαλοῦσιν ἡμῖν, ὑπὲρ τούτων τί οὐκ ἐροῦσιν;

[478] PG 62,86 32-33: Εἰ τὰ αὐτὰ δόγματα, εἰ τὰ αὐτὰ μυστήρια, τίνος ἕνεκεν ἕτερος ἄρχων
ἑτέρᾳ Ἐκκλησίᾳ ἐπιπηδᾷ;

[479] PG 62,86 38-39: Βούλεσθε εἴπω ἃ περὶ τῆς πόλεως λέγουσι τῆς ἡμετέρας;

served at the beginning of 2.a (p. 322 above). Added to the fact that both homilist and audience are well aware of the situation under discussion, enabling John merely to allude to what is happening rather than state matters openly, it would appear that in this instance he is treading upon particularly delicate ground. At the close of this fifth section he tells us that his concern over the current situation is such that he is compelled to do what is inappropriate.[480] Since he immediately attempts to justify his stance with reference to his authority,[481] it can be inferred that by "inappropriate" he means something that is either outside the authority attached to his office, that is, criticism of a bishop by a presbyter, or something which contravenes an unwritten code, for instance criticism of a visiting bishop by the local incumbent. To do either openly would have placed him in a difficult position.

It is from this point onward that we draw close to the crux of the matter. As Chrysostom proceeds to argue that he is not trying to control his audience's faith in this respect, merely to give them good advice,[482] we receive the strong impression that he has been caught in an awkward situation. It would seem that the issue is not entirely straightforward, as it would be if he were discussing a situation of long standing, as with the Eustathians at Antioch. Rather, it appears to involve a situation where the audience's argument that, if both groups are identical what does it matter, is at least as defensible as John's claim that the behaviour of the "other group" is schismatic. In other words, it is unlikely that the division that the homilist is addressing is a schism by modern definition, even though he himself views it in that light.[483] It is also not beyond possibility that Chrysostom is guilty of a certain degree of exaggeration for the purpose of underlining his point.

After stating this with some force,[484] he adduces an exemplum which is intended to summarise the issue at hand. If one doesn't give one's loyalty to a rival emperor, but takes the purple cloak of one's own emperor, ripping it into many fragments, is that a lesser crime than transferring one's loyalty to another? What if one then took the emperor by the throat

---

[480] PG 62,86 50-54: Ἀλγῶ ... ὡς οἰκείου μέλους ἀποστερούμενος· πλὴν ἀλλ᾽ οὐχ οὕτως ἀλγῶ ὡς ἀναγκάζεσθαί τι, διὰ τὸν φόβον τοῦτον, τῶν μὴ προσηκόντων ποιεῖν.

[481] See n. 470 above.

[482] PG 62,87 1-7: Οὐ κυριεύομεν ὑμῶν τῆς πίστεως, ἀγαπητοί, οὐδὲ δεσποτικῶς ταῦτα ἐπιτάττομεν ... συμβούλων τάξιν ἐπέχομεν παραινούντων. Ὁ συμβουλεύων λέγει τὰ παρ᾽ ἑαυτοῦ, οὐκ ἀναγκάζων τὸν ἀκροατήν, ἀλλ᾽ αὐτὸν ἀφίησι τῆς τῶν λεγομένων αἱρέσεως κύριον.

[483] See PG 62,87 8-12, where John takes pains to point out that he is advising the audience for their own benefit, so that none of them can complain on Judgement Day that no-one had told them that their current behaviour was a sin.

[484] PG 62,87 12-14: Διὰ τοῦτο λέγω καὶ διαμαρτύρομαι, ὅτι τοῦ εἰς αἵρεσιν ἐμπεσεῖν τὸ τὴν Ἐκκλησίαν σχίσαι οὐκ ἔλαττόν ἐστι κακόν.

and killed him, ripping the body apart limb from limb, what penalty
could one pay that would be worthy of that action? There is no punishment, says the homilist, which could match it. What then of those who
murder Christ and rip his limbs apart? Aren't they worthy of gehenna?
They deserve far worse, says John, and you women who are present,
make sure that you relate this exemplum to those who are not. For by far
the greatest exhibitors of this failing are women.[485] This is a statement of
some significance. For the first time it becomes clear not just that it is
the orthodox Christian community which is suffering division, but that it
is largely women who are at fault in attending the rival services.[486] For
the first time it also becomes clear that their actions are directed personally at John. If you think that you are causing me grief and getting
vengeance on me by doing this, he continues, think again. It is yourselves
whom you are hurting. It would be more direct and less harmful for you
to beat me and spit at me in public.[487] These are strong words, which
have seemingly no connection with the long-standing schism at Antioch.
Rather, it would appear from this that the women and a smaller number
of men are attending services directed by some other member of the
clergy as a public statement intended to indicate their personal displeas-
ure with Chrysostom.[488]

This is the clearest glimpse of the situation which Chrysostom permits
us, the remainder of his comments being somewhat obscure. But there is
sufficient reason to be suspicious of an identification of Antioch as the
scene of events, and to speculate that John is situated instead at Constantinople. It is hard to imagine why Chrysostom would be so concerned
about a noticeable sector of a formerly faithful audience having defected
to another church at the same location,[489] and why ill-feeling would be so
strongly and personally directed against him, if he were a presbyter. This
is, of course, no proof that he is not presbyter, but certain other details
supplied by John suggest that this is indeed the case. The affair, he says,
is a matter of adultery.[490] That is, it is analogous to forsaking a legal partner for communion with a partner who is not one's lawful spouse. Of the
two, it is not the audience's relationship with himself, but with the other

---

[485] PG 62,87 14-30.

[486] PG 62,87 28-29: ὡς γὰρ ἐπὶ τὸ πολὺ γυναικῶν τοῦτο τὸ ἐλάττωμα...

[487] PG 62,87 30-37: Εἴ τινες ἡμᾶς λυπεῖν καὶ ἀμύνασθαι τούτῳ νομίζουσιν, εὖ εἰδέτωσαν, ὅτι
ταῦτα μάτην ποιοῦσιν. Εἰ γὰρ ἡμᾶς ἀμύνασθαι βούλει, ἐγώ σοι δίδωμι τρόπον, καθ᾽ ὃν χωρὶς τῆς σῆς
βλάβης ἀμύνασθαι δυνήσῃ· ... ῥάπισον, ἔμπτυσον ἐντυχοῦσα δημοσίᾳ, καὶ πληγὰς ἔντεινον.

[488] Cf. PG 62,87 42-88 6, esp. 87 50-88 2: ἕκαστον τῶν σὺν ὑμῖν λυπουμένων πρὸς ἡμᾶς, καὶ
διὰ ταύτην τὴν λύπην βλαπτόντων ἑαυτούς, καὶ ἀλλαχοῦ πορευομένων...

[489] See PG 62,88 17-23: Τῶν γὰρ εἰς τὴν Ἐκκλησίαν ταύτην τελούντων ... οἱ δὲ δῆθεν
σπουδάζειν δοκοῦντες, οὗτοί εἰσιν οἱ τὴν συμφορὰν ταύτην ἐργαζόμενοι.

[490] PG 62,88 28: Μοιχεία τὸ πρᾶγμά ἐστιν.

party which has come about illegally.[491] Confident of his own legitimate election, John throws out the following challenge: "If you entertain these suspicions about us, I'm prepared to give up my office (ἀρχή) to whomever you wish. Just let the church be one. But if it's we who've come about by legal process, convince those who've ascended the throne illegally to put it aside."[492] Although, as we have seen, a reference to ἀρχή carries with it a certain ambiguity, in this context the implication that it is he who has ascended the throne legally strongly suggests that Chrysostom is telling us that he holds episcopal office.[493]

How then do we explain the allusion to "those who've ascended the throne illegally"? If the location really is Constantinople, as it seems, it is possible that John is referring not to bishops who have been illegally elected to office, as might be inferred if he were referring to the schism at Antioch, but to visiting bishops who have taken to acting out the role of presiding bishop in front of a congregation in another church in Constantinople. This might explain why the laity who attend such services find it hard to perceive that they are doing anything which might be construed as sinful. When all of the details provided are taken into consideration, the following scenario presents itself as a possibility. The sources claim that John alienated a number of wealthy women at Constantinople.[494] It is also said that Chrysostom handed over to Severian of Gabala the role of principal homilist for the duration of his absence at Ephesus.[495] It is suggested by the sources that Severian spent the time cultivating personal support amongst various sectors of Constantinopolitan society, including the disaffected women, with the intention of causing detriment to Chrysostom's own standing.[496] From that it is only a small step to suppose that he continued to hold services, albeit at another church, on John's return and that he may eventually have begun to flout convention and the latter's authority by openly preaching and presiding from the thronos. If one considers the reference to *"those* who have ascended the throne illegally" to be literal, one could speculate that it was not just

---

[491] PG 62,88 28-31: Εἰ δὲ οὐ δέχῃ περὶ ἐκείνων ταῦτα ἀκούειν, οὐκοῦν οὐδὲ περὶ ἡμῶν· τῶν γὰρ δύο τὸ ἕτερον παρανόμως γεγενῆσθαι δεῖ.

[492] PG 62,88 31-35.

[493] For the limitations of this criterion see pp. 328-331 above.

[494] Palladius, *Dial.* 4, 8 (SC 341,94 89-98, 162 76-79); Socr., HE 6.15 (GCS NF 1,336 10-18). Despite the mistrust expressed by Liebeschuetz, "The Fall", 10-12, it is possible that these claims contain some grain of truth.

[495] Soz., HE 8.10 (GCS NF 4,363 2-8).

[496] Socr., HE 6.11 (GCS NF 1,329 13-17); Soz., HE 8.10 (GCS NF 4,363 2-5). For the view of Severian's activities portrayed in the *Vita* attributed to Martyrius see F. van Ommeslaeghe, "Que vaut le témoignage de Pallade sur le procès de saint Jean Chrysostome?", AB 95 (1977) 395.

Severian who presided from the thronos at that particular church, but some of the other semi-permanently visiting bishops hostile to Chrysostom, for instance Acacius of Beroea or Antiochus of Ptolemais, also.[497]

This scenario may not necessarily be accurate. The true identity of the figures involved may be different and there may yet prove to be a better explanation of these events.[498] The fact remains, however, that a selective assessment of the evidence can support almost any interpretation, particularly when Chrysostom's statements are accepted at face value and one is guided by an *a priori* identification of the event. A more careful and systematic examination shows that it is highly unlikely that the schism described has anything in common with that which persisted at Antioch, while there is every likelihood that John is bishop and that we have described for us a situation which existed at one point at Constantinople.

5. GEOGRAPHY

In comparison to the criteria based on demographic factors, which exhibit diverse degrees of reliability, those which relate to geographic factors are largely untenable.

a. *Geographic focus*

i. Lists of exotic locations

Superficially, Bonsdorff's proposition that, when the homilist includes the Thracians in a list of races intended to describe the limits of the known world, he is preaching from Syria, is quite attractive. In *De incompr. dei nat. hom. 2*, a sermon of secure Antiochene derivation,[499] Chrysostom, in listing all the races of the world, certainly starts with the Syrians and works his way west around the northern edge of the Mediterranean to the British Isles, before returning to the Sauromatians, In-

---

[497] See n. 719 below.

[498] Costanza's interpretation of events, "Waar predikte Chrysostomus?", 153, which places the homily at the time between the first and second exiles and identifies the illegal ascendants of the throne as Theophilus and his synod and the "women" with the conflict with Eudoxia, although based on a selective assessment of the evidence and therefore questionable, presents another possibility. For a further option, namely that John is referring to the Novatian bishop Sisinnius, see Mayer-Allen, *John Chrysostom*, 60.

[499] See pp. 367-369 above.

dians and Persians.[500] When compared with this particular passage, the example from *In Rom. hom. 13* appears to support the same view of the world, simply presenting it in a much abbreviated form.[501] The weakness of this argument lies, however, in the failure of Bonsdorff to test the reverse side of the proposition — namely that if the orientation arises strictly from the homilist's location, and the nations listed are chosen because they are typically distant, then in homilies which stem from Constantinople not only will such a list be oriented differently, but it certainly ought not to include a reference to Thracians.

Had he examined this side of the argument, Bonsdorff would have discovered markedly similar lists in at least two homilies, one of certain, the other of almost certain Constantinopolitan derivation. In the homily *Hab. postquam presbyter Gothus* (CPG 4441.9) Chrysostom, referring to the now wide-spread use of the New Testament in the vernacular, lists as a selection of those to whom this is available "Scythians, Thracians, Sauromatians, Maurians and Indians",[502] while in *In illud: Messis quidem multa* (CPG 4441.11) he chooses a similar catalogue to describe those who once worshipped idols.[503] Although in these examples explicit comparison to the present location is lacking, the persistence of this form at Constantinople does suggest that the structure of such lists is to some extent independent of location. For instance, if Bonsdorff's argument is taken to its logical conclusion, the absence of Thracians from such a list ought to suggest a change of perspective, that is, that John is possibly preaching from Constantinople. Yet in the case of *De laudibus s. Pauli hom. 4* (CPG 4344), where an example of this kind occurs,[504] there is no doubt that the sermon belongs to Antioch.[505]

In sum, while a greater number of examples needs to be elicited from other securely located homilies before the suspicion can be confirmed, there is sufficient evidence to suggest that the constituent elements of

---

[500] SC 28bis,164 258-264: ἀναλόγισαι πάντα τὰ ἔθνη, Σύρους, Κίλικας, Καππαδόκας, Βιθυνούς, τοὺς τὸν Εὔξεινον πόντον οἰκοῦντας, Θρᾴκην, Μακεδονίαν, τὴν Ἑλλάδα πᾶσαν, τοὺς ἐν ταῖς νήσοις, τοὺς ἐν τῇ Ἰταλίᾳ, τοὺς ὑπὲρ τὴν καθ᾽ ἡμᾶς οἰκουμένην, τοὺς ἐν ταῖς νήσοις ταῖς Βρεττανικαῖς, Σαυρομάτας, Ἰνδούς, τοὺς τὴν τῶν Περσῶν οἰκοῦντας γῆν, τὰ ἄλλα τὰ ἄπειρα γένη καὶ φῦλα, ...

[501] PG 60,517 17-21: Καὶ οὐ παρ᾽ ἡμῖν μόνον, ἀλλὰ καὶ παρὰ Σκύθαις, καὶ Θρᾳξὶ καὶ Ἰνδοῖς καὶ Πέρσαις, καὶ ἑτέροις δὲ βαρβάροις πλείοσι...

[502] PG 63,501 4-7: καὶ Σκύθαι καὶ Θρᾷκες καὶ Σαυρομάται καὶ Μαῦροι καὶ Ἰνδοὶ καὶ οἱ πρὸς αὐτὰς ἀπῳκισμένοι τὰς ἐσχατιὰς τῆς οἰκουμένης... Regarding the provenance of this homily see p. 356 n. 205 above.

[503] PG 63,519 54-57: Σκύθαι μὲν γὰρ καὶ Θρᾷκες καὶ Μαῦροι καὶ Ἰνδοὶ καὶ Πέρσαι καὶ Σαυρομάται, καὶ οἱ τὴν Ἑλλάδα καὶ οἱ τὴν Ἤπειρον οἰκοῦντες, καὶ πᾶσα, ὡς εἰπεῖν, ἡ ὑφ᾽ ἡλίῳ... Regarding the provenance of this homily see pp. 317f above.

[504] See SC 300,202 10.5-11.

[505] See p. 462 below.

such lists of exotic tribes have little or no bearing upon the location of Chrysostom. On the contrary, an example such as that which occurs in *In Rom. hom. 30*, used by John to impress the audience with the spread of Christianity and seen by Bonsdorff as demonstrating Syrian perspective,[506] serves to fuel the suspicion that such lists have a standard structure, the content of which is open to variation. Whether this results from the fact that such lists form a standard part of the rhetorical repertoire (at least among Antiochene-trained orators), or whether they genuinely derive from a habitual way of viewing the rest of the world as a result of spending the majority of one's life in Syria (i.e., the view is so deeply ingrained as to be unaffected by a substantial change in location), the fact remains that they are not exclusive to homilies which stem from Antioch. As a consequence, the mere appearance of such a list within a homily can no longer be considered of value for fixing its provenance.[507]

ii. Other

The major difficulty with Bonsdorff's perception of a definably Syrian perspective is that it is in the first instance subjective and therefore open to interpretation, while in the second it does not necessarily follow that a bias of this kind arises as a result of being physically situated in Syria. Rather, it is equally possible that it derives from the fact that Chrysostom was born, raised and had spent the majority of his adult life in that country. That is, he had spent so much of his life viewing the world from that point that it is likely that this viewpoint had become habitual and independent of location. A perspective reinforced over such a long period of time is hard to break. In any case, immigrants under most conditions maintain a strong and instinctive loyalty to their country of origin, which can become stronger rather than weaker as the cultural and functional differences are reinforced. With these points in mind, it is somewhat unreasonable to expect that John will have confined comments which betray a Syrian loyalty or perspective to the homilies preached at Antioch. Indeed, even if he were aware of this tendency, and therefore able to make a conscious attempt to overcome it, one would expect that at best comments of this nature would either occur sporadically throughout his time at Constantinople or occur with some frequency in the first year, gradually decreasing to the point of tapering off. Abrupt cessation is the least likely of the possible scenarios.

---

[506] PG 60,665 32-33: καὶ Πέρσαι καὶ Σκύθαι καὶ Θρᾷκες, καὶ οἱ τὰς ἐσχατιὰς οἰκοῦντες...

[507] Although the passages cited have yet to be investigated, one suspects that the collocation of Thracians and Scythians, also suggested as a sign of Syrian perspective by Bonsdorff, will prove likewise to be a topos.

On this basis, most of the evidence adduced under the category of geographic perspective can be dismissed. The argument that *Exp. in ps. 110* betrays an Antiochene focus, because most of the disasters mentioned occurred at that location, bears questionable significance for the provenance of the exposition if one takes into account the fact that the disasters are described in general terms, that at no point are they associated with the present location,[508] and that the whole is prefaced by the statement that the events about to be discussed are widely known and a matter of public record.[509] The bias towards Antioch in this instance can be considered a reflection rather of Chrysostom's personal background, there being a natural tendency in reflecting upon the past to select for events which, through experience or hearsay, have impinged upon one's own life. This does not, of course, remove the possibility that the exposition may have been intended in some form for an Antiochene audience.[510] The point here is simply that this circumstance cannot be proven on the basis of such evidence.

The significance of the cluster of passages adduced by Bonsdorff, because in them the homilist focuses upon Syria or its language, is likewise open to question. One of the examples adduced relates to the role which Syria played in the missionary activity of the apostles.[511] Another points out the connection between Hebrew and Syriac,[512] while another refers to a specific Septuagint translator as "the Syrian".[513] In these cases it could as easily be argued not that Chrysostom is playing upon the audience's nationalistic sympathies, but that his comments reflect a natural personal pride in the Christian heritage of his native country. In any case, John could simply be expanding upon information for the edification of his audience since all of the comments are purely factual. The fact that in *In Ioh. hom. 2* Syrians are listed first among those who have received the Gospel of John in their own language,[514] is equally equivocal. As we have seen in the previous sub-section (5.a.i), such lists are in any case something of a topos and it is only his belief that the entire series on

---

[508] That the events associated with Babylas occurred at Daphne (PG 55,285 42) is stated as a matter of fact.

[509] PG 55,285 34-35: Ἀλλὰ τέως τὰ καθολικά, καὶ ἅπασι δῆλα καὶ γνώριμα, ἃ καθ᾽ ἑκάστην γίνεται γενεάν, ἴδωμεν. The subsequent refinement of this statement (PG 55,285 38-39: Εἰ δὲ βούλεσθε καὶ τὰ ἐπὶ τῆς γενεᾶς συμβάντα τῆς ἡμετέρας...) restricts only the chronology, not the character of the events. For further discussion of this passage see p. 462 below.

[510] For the argument that *Exp. in ps. 110* was most probably never delivered as a homily see pp. 360-363 above.

[511] *In Rom. hom. 2*, PG 61,401 37-41 (ἄνδρες Σύροι evangelised the Romans).

[512] *In II Tim. hom. 4* (PG 62,622 30-37).

[513] *In II Cor. hom. 3* (PG 61,413 41-42).

[514] PG 59,32 19-23.

John stems from Antioch that prevented Bonsdorff from arguing that the inclusion of Syrians indicates geographic distance and a provenance of Constantinople.

There exists one further group of examples which falls loosely under this category and whose significance is more difficult to assess. Bonsdorff adduces several examples where Chrysostom appears to indicate that he is situated in Syria. In the case of *In Rom. hom. 26*,[515] in which Bonsdorff observed a Syrian point of view in the juxtaposition of cities and countryside, the remark appears in conjunction with a reference to extra-urban monasticism.[516] Although one might consider the proximity of πόλις (city) and ἔρημος (wilderness) in this instance to be evocative of Syria,[517] particularly since the homilist speculates that a pagan would question the necessity of "walking to the mountains and seeking out the wilderness areas",[518] the monastic context complicates matters. References to extra-urban monasticism of the kind elicited here are often tinged with an idealised nostalgia, bordering upon the rhetorical, a circumstance which makes them particularly difficult to interpret.[519] Although John appears to suggest in this instance that the monks are within walking distance of the city, the situation is not stated to be real but is posed as one which is hypothetical. At this point in our investigation there is no means of establishing whether such a scenario may or may not bear significance for provenance.

The case of *In Ioh. hom. 12/11*, on the other hand, is much clearer. Here, as Bonsdorff was the first to note, Chrysostom claims that the good news of Christ's birth was spread to "us" not just by "shepherds, widows or old men, but by the very nature [*al.* voice] of the happening, proclaiming itself louder than any trumpet ... such that the echo of it was immediately heard here".[520] Since John proceeds to cite Matt. 4.24 ("For his fame spread into Syria...") there can be no doubt that the comment applies to the homilist's current physical location. If Bonsdorff's observation regarding the previous example was accurate, his application of a similar argument to *In II Cor. hom. 8* is less so. Here Chrysostom re-

---

[515] See PG 60,642 15-19.

[516] PG 60,643 9-10: Πάντως ἐρεῖς, ὅτι Δείξω σοι ἑτέρους ποιοῦντας, μοναχοὺς ἐν ἐρημίαις καθημένους.

[517] Brown, "Rise and function", 83, stresses this aspect of Syrian geography as significant in shaping the styles of asceticism which took hold there.

[518] PG 60,643 13-15: Καὶ γὰρ καὶ ἐκεῖνος εὐθέως ἐρεῖ· Οὐκοῦν ποία μοι ἀνάγκη βαδίζειν ἐπὶ τὰ ὄρη, καὶ τὰς ἐρημίας διώκειν;

[519] See pp. 426-434 below.

[520] PG 59,83 7-11: Οὐκ ἔτι γὰρ ποιμένες μόνον, οὐδὲ χῆραι γυναῖκες, οὐδὲ ἄνδρες πρεσβῦται ἡμᾶς εὐαγγελίζονται, ἀλλὰ καὶ αὐτὴ τῶν πραγμάτων ἡ φύσις [*al.* φωνή], πάσης σάλπιγγος λαμπρότερον βοῶσα, καὶ οὕτω γεγονός, ὡς καὶ ἐνταῦθα αὐτῆς εὐθέως ἀκουσθῆναι τὸν ἦχον.

marks that the apostles introduced the angelic life "in our land, in that of *barbaroi*" and at "the very ends of the earth".[521] In this Bondsorff wished to see a reference to Syria, presumably because of the missionary activity undertaken by various of the apostles there. In contrast to the previous example, however, the context is not clear and, given the progression from the present country to that of *barbaroi* to the ends of the earth, it is to be suspected that the remark refers to the spread of the Gospels rather than any activity undertaken by the apostles. If this view is adopted, there is no reason to exclude the possibility that John is here referring to Constantinople.

In sum, the significance of the mere mention of Syria or Syriac within a homily, that is, where either is included in a statement of fact without any claim being made that this is of relevance to the present location or audience, is entirely neutral. The reasons which may have prompted its inclusion are impossible to determine. In consequence, such statements cannot be of use in determing provenance and any argument based upon them should be discarded. Comments where Chrysostom supplies detail which might be thought to apply to Syria or where he appears to indicate that he is situated in that country are another matter. Each of these requires careful assessment on its own merits before a conclusion can be drawn.[522]

b. *Proximity*

Despite its attractions, the argument based on a calculation of geographic proximity to or distance from various locations is difficult to prove. Some examples admit of other explanations, some are persuasive of a particular provenance but fail to provide adequate means of proving or disproving the suspicion, while in the case of others it is only a prior assumption of provenance which affords them significance. Few are a reliable indicator of provenance. For instance, Bonsdorff's argument that the remarks intended to clarify points of geography in *In II Tim. hom. 8* and *10* would have been less necessary at Constantinople than at Antioch,[523] is of little use, since he himself admits that the same remarks

---

[521] PG 61,459 4-7: οὗτοι δὲ ἀγγέλων ἡμῖν εἰσηγήσαντο πολιτείαν· οὐκ εἰσηγήσαντο δὲ μόνον, ἀλλὰ καὶ κατώρθωσαν, ἐν τῇ ἡμετέρᾳ, ἐν τῇ τῶν βαρβάρων, ἐν αὐταῖς τῆς γῆς ταῖς ἐσχατιαῖς.

[522] For instance, *In Matt. hom. 32/33*, in which Bonsdorff saw an indication that John was still in the country of his birth, contains a large amount of apparently conflicting evidence and requires a detailed assessment on its own.

[523] PG 62,645 31-32: Ἀντιόχειαν δὲ τὴν τῆς Πισιδίας ἐνταῦθά φησι...; PG 62,659 12-13: Ἡ Μίλητος τῆς Ἐφέσου ἐγγὺς οὖσα τυγχάνει.

could have been made at Constantinople.[524] In any case, while in the second instance the comment does appear to be intended to fill in an assumed deficiency in the knowledge of the audience, the first may have little to do with real geography. It could be surmised that most members of the laity with a general knowledge of the travels of St Paul, irrespective of where they were situated, would naturally assume that Antioch was the Syrian capital, since this is where St Paul spent much of his time. It may be that the distinction is drawn by Chrysostom solely for the purposes of negating such an assumption. The similar argument adduced with respect to *In Titum hom. 6*,[525] namely that the homilist would not have used such an expression at Constantinople,[526] can be countered on the grounds that claims as to whether John would or would not have used a certain expression are indefensible. Since it is a simple statement of fact, there is no reason why Chrysostom could not have made this remark at Constantinople.

The argument concerning the Phoenician actress of *In Matt. hom. 67/68*, on the other hand, is more plausible. The events described are real and clearly connected to the present location,[527] the woman derives from Phoenicia,[528] while her fame is said to have been considerable, spreading beyond the present city as far as Cilicia and Cappadocia.[529] The nature of the information and the proximity of all of these sites to Antioch strongly suggest that that is the point of origin. One further detail may weight the scales in favour of probability. Although it appears that the actress is now dead,[530] the events are said to have occurred "within our generation". This and similar phrases are used elsewhere to refer to the various disasters which occurred in the time of the emperor Julian, some twenty to thirty years earlier.[531] While in the present instance the phrase may re-

---

[524] Bonsdorff, *Zur Predigttätigkeit*, 61.

[525] PG 62,696 10-11 *a.i.*: Ἡ δὲ Νικόπολις τῆς Θρᾴκης ἐστί.

[526] Bonsdorff, *Zur Predigttätigkeit*, 62 n. 6.

[527] PG 58,636 48-55: Ἢ οὐκ ἠκούσατε ... τὴν ἐπὶ τῆς γενεᾶς τῆς ἡμετέρας ... Καὶ γὰρ αὕτη πόρνη ποτὲ παρ' ἡμῖν ἦν ... ἐν τῇ πόλει τῇ ἡμετέρᾳ ...

[528] PG 58,636 51-52: ... τὴν ἐκ Φοινίκης τῆς παρανομωτάτης πόλεως.

[529] PG 58,636 53-55: ... πολὺ τὸ ὄνομα αὐτῆς πανταχοῦ, οὐκ ἐν τῇ πόλει τῇ ἡμετέρᾳ μόνον, ἀλλὰ καὶ μέχρι Κιλίκων καὶ Καππαδοκῶν.

[530] PG 58,637 16-18: Αὕτη μυστηρίων καταξιωθεῖσα τῶν ἀπορρήτων, καὶ τῆς χάριτος ἀξίαν ἐπιδειξαμένη σπουδήν, οὕτω τὸν βίον κατέλυσεν...

[531] See, e.g., *Exp. in ps. 110* (ἐπὶ τῆς γενεᾶς τῆς ἡμετέρας: events from 361-363 AD) PG 55,285 38-50); *In Matt. hom. 4* (ἐν τῇ γενεᾷ τῇ ἡμετέρᾳ: events c.361-363) PG 57,41 2-13; *In Acta apost. hom. 41* (ἐπὶ τῶν καιρῶν τῶν ἡμετέρων: events c.361-363) PG 60,291 29-31. By contrast, in *In Phil. hom. 15* events in the imperial households from the time of Constantine to the present are described as "old, but still preserved in memory, seeing that they happened in our time" (ἐπὶ τῶν χρόνων τῶν ἡμετέρων) PG 62,295 15-18.

fer to a different set of years, it does suggest that Chrysostom is thinking not of the immediate past but of a period somewhere between the reigns of Constantine and Valens. With this established, the statements that the actress at one point ensnared the brother of an empress and that the *hyparch* was approached and soldiers mobilised to secure her return,[532] accord well with the period in question. All of these factors suggest that the imperial court and its administrative machinery were at the time situated locally.[533] However, persuasive as these details might be, there is nothing here that actively speaks against Constantinople. Without further evidence, that the homily stems from Antioch can be considered no more than probable.[534]

Other examples of this kind are less persuasive. Bonsdorff's proposition that the fact that Chrysostom has to ask his audience if anyone has ever visited Palestine in *In I Thess. hom. 8* suggests distance,[535] and therefore a provenance of Constantinople, relies more on a conviction that the homily stems from that location than a careful reading of the evidence. For one thing, the homilist replies to his own question in the affirmative, proceeding to ask those who have been there to confirm what he has to say for those who have not.[536] The question of proximity is in fact irrelevant, since one would hardly expect that the entire Christian population of Antioch would have had the opportunity to visit Palestine, no matter how close at hand.[537] Tillemont's suggestion that the Antiochene provenance of *In Titum hom. 3* is confirmed by the reference to a site in Cilicia is suspect for another reason.[538] In this instance the manner in which the site is mentioned calls into question whether the information is intended to be other than factual.[539] This same scholar's argument that proximity to Caesarea in Cappadocia, where St Barlaam was martyred, accounts

---

[532] PG 58,637 3-4: Εἷλέ ποτε καὶ βασιλίδος ἀδελφὸν αὕτη ἡ πόρνη; 637 12-16: Ταύτης ἕνεκεν καὶ ὕπαρχος ἠνωχλήθη, καὶ στρατιῶται ὡπλίσθησαν...

[533] Both Julian and Valens treated Antioch as the imperial capital (see n. 280 above), while in most of the years between 337 and 361 Constantius or Gallus resided there for a period. See Downey, *Antioch*, 355-373; Dagron, *Naissance*, 79-83.

[534] Identification of the Phoenician actress with the Antiochene actress/prostitute named Pelagia, converted to Christianity and asceticism at Antioch at the time of a small conference of bishops, among whom was one called Nonnus, is possible, but difficult to establish. For the *vita* of the actress Pelagia see P. Petitmengin et al. (edd.), *Pélagie la pénitente. Métamorphoses d'une légende* I. *Les textes et leur histoire*, Paris 1981, 77-93.

[535] PG 62,442 33-38: ... Ἐπεδήμησεν οὖν ὑμῶν τις τῇ Παλαιστίνη ποτέ;

[536] PG 62,442 38-40: ἔγωγε οἶμαι. Τί οὖν; Μαρτυρήσατέ μοι ὑμεῖς οἱ τοὺς τόπους ἑωρακότες πρὸς τοὺς οὐ γενομένους ἐκεῖ.

[537] In so far as we know, John himself was among those who had never been.

[538] PG 62,679 6-11. See Tillemont (Chapter One, pp. 62f).

[539] For discussion of this point see pp. 376-378 above.

for the celebration of that saint's festival at Antioch is interesting but unprovable, since the spread of the commemoration of a saint from one
place to another at this time was undoubtedly complex and the details
are largely unknown. In other words, while one might assume that the
celebration had spread to Antioch, there is at present no way of proving
that it had not been adopted at Constantinople also. Stilting's proposition
that the homily *In martyres Aegyptios* (CPG 4363) was delivered at
Antioch because of that city's proximity to the mines in Asia Minor, also
falls into difficulty, since it could be said that the mining industry which
operated at the time in the Balkans was in relatively the same proximity
to Constantinople.[540] The suggestion, first put forward by Tillemont, that
the comparison of prices at the present location with those in Cappadocia in *In I Tim. hom. 17* better suits Syria than Thrace,[541] is also not without difficulty. Chrysostom refers in his example to a number of locations
in addition to Cappadocia, namely a region called Ser, the source of
silken clothing, and Arabia and India, the source of aromatics.[542] It is
hard to see why one should single out Cappadocia as being proximate,
unless it is to be inferred that Cappadocia purchases the fruit in question
from the city at which John is presently located. This does not necessarily follow from the text. Rather, it would appear that we have before us
one further example of a proposal which has its basis in a desire to find
evidence to support a particular provenance rather than the quality of
the particular evidence itself.

  This does not mean that the argument from proximity is itself invalid.
There are at least two examples where it provides a secure indication of
provenance. In *De s. Meletio* (CPG 4345) the location to which the former
bishop was summoned is said to be "not near or close, but as far as
Thrace itself",[543] while it is later made clear that that site (Constantinople) is geographically distinct from the present location.[544] In *In s. Eusta-*

---

[540] See S. Vryonis, "The Question of the Byzantine Mines", *Speculum* 37 (1962) 1-17
and in particular p. 11, where reference is made to an edict of 370 in which the activities
of Thracian miners is addressed.

[541] Tillemont, *Mémoires*, XI 376 n. I. Cf. Bonsdorff, *Zur Predigttätigkeit*, 57, where the
exemplum is described as not particularly appropriate to Constantinople, but natural at
Antioch.

[542] PG 62,596 34-39: εἰσὶν καρποὶ παρ' ἡμῖν εὐτελεῖς, ἐν δὲ τῇ Καππαδοκῶν χώρᾳ τίμιοι, καὶ
τῶν παρ' ἡμῖν τιμίων πολυτελέστεροι πάλιν ἐν τῇ Σηρῶν χώρᾳ ἕτεροι, ὅθεν τὰ ἱμάτια ταῦτα. Ἐν δὲ
τῇ ἀρωματοφόρῳ Ἀραβίᾳ καὶ Ἰνδίᾳ, ἔνθα εἰσὶν οἱ λίθοι, πολλὰ τοιαῦτα ἔστιν εὑρεῖν.

[543] PG 50,518 16-17: ... οὐκ ἐγγύς που οὐδὲ πλησίον, ἀλλ' εἰς τὴν Θρᾴκην αὐτήν.

[544] PG 50,518 49-50: Ἐγίνετο δὲ τοῦτο [*sc.* Meletius' death] καὶ διὰ φειδὼ τῆς πόλεως τῆς
ἡμετέρας. Εἰ γὰρ ἐνταῦθα τὴν ψυχὴν ἀφῆκεν...

thium (CPG 4352) likewise, Thrace is clearly stated to be distinct from the present location and situated some distance away.[545]

In sum, the criterion can provide a reliable solution only if the region named is Thrace or Syria and this is said to be distinct from the present location. Only under these circumstances can the alternative be securely excluded. In cases where regions are named and discussed in relation to the present location, the conclusion drawn can at best be probable, at worst uncertain. In cases where there is no clear reference to the present location or the information is supplied in a manner which is entirely factual, no conclusion regarding the provenance of the homily should be drawn, since it is not certain that the material has any bearing upon provenance and is in any case open to subjective interpretation.

c. *Native vegetation*

There may well be some merit to Tillemont's claim that roses and lilies are flora indigenous to Antioch. In his famous encomium on the city Libanius mentions roses growing on either side of the road to Daphne,[546] while Downey, on the authority of Pliny, states that lilies were specifically associated with Antioch and Laodicea, the oil of which (used for medicinal purposes) was a local export.[547] It is unfortunate that the text of *In s. pascha* (CPG 4408) presented by Montfaucon names not lilies but violets (ἴα), which are probably not to be equated with the flowers used in the manufacture of this product.[548] This, however, is only one side of the issue. Even if it should prove possible to establish that lilies or roses are a feature of Antioch and not of Constantinople,[549] if the criterion is to be useful it is important also to determine whether the flowers are mentioned exclusively in Antiochene homilies or whether reference to them is introduced indiscriminately. It is unfortunate that at present there are

---

[545] PG 50,601 5-7: Τὸ μὲν γὰρ σῶμα τοῦ μάρτυρος κεῖται ἐν Θρᾴκῃ, ὑμεῖς δὲ οὐκ ἐν Θρᾴκῃ διατρίβοντες, ἀλλὰ πολὺ τῆς χώρας ἐκείνης ἀφεστηκότες...

[546] *Or.* 11.234 (Foerster, I 518-519).

[547] Downey, *Antioch*, 21.

[548] Pliny, *Nat. hist.*, 21.11-14 (Jones, VI 176-180) distinguishes the term κρίνον as being associated with a type of lily found in the east, while the medicinal uses of the flower known as ἴον are discussed in a passage separate from that (21.74; Jones, VI 252-254) in which he states that the juice extracted from the flower of the lily is known as *sirium*.

[549] That there is a clear connection with the one city and not the other is unlikely. Pliny, *Nat hist.*, 21.1 (Jones, VI 160) states that roses and lilies are regularly used in wreaths in Italy, suggesting that they were probably commonly encountered — whether as a native plant, a cultivar or an import — throughout much of the Mediterranean.

insufficient homilies of certain attribution which incorporate such a reference to enable us to make even a tentative determination.

Furthermore, all of these questions become irrelevant if it is only within generalised exempla that the flowers receive mention, where no link is drawn between flora and place. In the case of *In s. pascha*, the comments seem to have aroused Tillemont's interest precisely because they are expressed in a manner which is direct and do not appear within the context of an exemplum. While the connection between the flowers and the present location cannot be said to be explicit, it could be considered to be implied.[550] It must be stressed, however, that this situation is rare. More commonly the season of spring, meadows and a combination of roses, lilies and violets are for Chrysostom essential elements in a range of comparisons and metaphors.[551] At least two of these examples are listed by Ameringer in his study of the influence of the second sophistic upon Chrysostom's oratorical style, one of them being characterised as "a comparison of undoubted sophistic origin".[552] Although a methodical investigation of all of the references to roses, lilies and such flowers is required before any firm conclusion can be drawn, one strongly suspects that in most, if not all of the examples located, these will turn out to be not a reflection of the vegetation native to Antioch, useful to us in determining the provenance of the homilies which contain them, but non-distinctive rhetorical topoi.

6. MONKS AND MONASTIC PRACTICES

The criterion relating to the manner in which Chrysostom refers to monks, which is based on the belief that there was a sharp distinction between the styles of monasticism supposed to have been practised at each city (extra-urban v. urban) and that John markedly favoured the one form over the other, is superficially attractive. That the criterion is by no

---

[550] PG 52,770 65-771 3: Ἡ μὲν οὖν γῆ κατὰ τὸν καιρὸν τοῦτον τοῦ ἔαρος ῥόδα καὶ ἴα καὶ ἄλλα ἡμῖν ἐκδίδωσιν ἄνθη· τὰ μέντοι ὕδατα σήμερον τῆς γῆς τερπνότερον ἡμῖν λειμῶνα ἀνέδειξε. Matters are complicated, however, by the fact that much of *In s. Pascha* is a doublet of much of *De resurrectione* (CPG 4341), such that this passage is found repeated there word for word (PG 50,439 28-30).

[551] See, e.g., *De statuis hom.* 6: καὶ καθάπερ πολλοὶ πολλάκις ἐκ λειμῶνος ἀναχωροῦντες, ῥόδον ἢ ἴον ἤ τι τῶν τοιούτων ἀνθῶν λαβόντες... (PG 49,90 46-50); *In s. Ignatium* (CPG 4351): Καὶ ταὐτὸν πάσχομεν, οἷον ἂν εἴ τις εἰς λειμῶνα εἰσελθών, καὶ πολλὴν μὲν τὴν ῥοδωνιὰν ἰδών, πολὺ δὲ τὸ ἴον, καὶ τὸ κρίνον τοσοῦτον, καὶ ἕτερα δὲ ἠρινὰ ἄνθη ποικίλα τε καὶ διάφορα... (PG 50,587 42-47); *De ss. martyribus* (CPG 4357): Οὐχ οὕτω λειμῶνές εἰσι τερπνοί, ῥόδα καὶ ἴα παρεχόμενοι τοῖς θεωμένοις... (PG 50,649 45-47). A more extended series of images is presented at *In Acta apost. hom.* 6 (PG 60,61 7-30).

[552] Ameringer, *Stylistic Influence*, 74.

means as straightforward as it at first seems, however, is evident from the fact that Montfaucon saw no difficulty, in one instance, in citing the appearance of various references to monks as the basis for attributing an entire series to Antioch,[553] in another, in claiming that the same type of comment was not indicative of Antiochene provenance, but merely a reminiscence expressed at Constantinople.[554] With regard to the latter case (the series on Hebrews: CPG 4440), Auf der Maur has more recently attempted to reconcile the evidence with a provenance of Constantinople by distinguishing different types of references to monks. He argues that although in this series Chrysostom mentions monks with some frequency, nowhere does he tell his audience to go visit them, but contents himself with pointing out the similarities between secular and monastic life.[555] Although this solution neatly avoids the problem of the number of references to monks contained in the series,[556] frequent reference being considered characteristic of Antioch, this approach is itself not without difficulty. The homilist may not tell the audience to visit such persons, but he does on two occasions (*In Heb. hom.* 10, 17) characterise the latter by the phrases "those situated on mountains" (τοὺς ἐν ὄρεσι καθημένους) and "those situated in the *eremos* (wilderness)" (τοὺς ἐν τῇ ἐρήμῳ καθεζομένους), phrases elsewhere considered descriptive of Antiochene-style monasticism.[557] To add to the difficulty, in neither instance can John be reminiscing about an alien form of monasticism, since he indicates that his audience interacts with these individuals and that the latter share, if infrequently, in the eucharist.[558] If one persists in locating the two homi-

---

[553] Montfaucon, V *Praef.* p. 3, with respect to the expositions on the psalms (CPG 4413). See, e.g., *Exp. in ps. 6* (PG 55,77 31-32).

[554] Montfaucon, XII *Praef.* v, with respect to *In Heb. hom. 10* (PG 63,87 53-88 14).

[555] Auf der Maur, *Mönchtum*, 48.

[556] Auf der Maur, *Mönchtum*, 48, cites five occurrences (*hom. 7, 10, 22, 25, 34*). If one broadens the definition of "monk" to include persons of either gender who pursue an ascetic lifestyle, the number is in fact closer to ten. See *In Heb. hom. 4* (PG 63,43 21-29); *hom. 7* (PG 63,67 6-17); *hom. 10* (see n. 558); *hom. 11* (PG 63,96 9-27); *hom. 15* (PG 63,122 5-7); *hom. 17* (PG 63,131 57-61); *hom. 22* (PG 63,158 50-57); *hom. 25* (PG 63,177 4-14); *hom. 28* (PG 63,199 18-20); *hom. 34* (PG 63,236 33-37).

[557] So Montfaucon, V 534 and Stilting, *Acta SS. Sept.*, IV 497-498, with regard to *In ps. 145* (CPG 4415) PG 55,526 36-37 (τῶν ἐν ὄρεσι καθημένων μοναχῶν); Baur, *Chrysostom and His Time*, I 303 n. 50a, concerning *In Rom. hom. 25* (PG 60,635 60-61: οἱ τὰ ὄρη κατειληφότες μοναχοί); and Bonsdorff, *Zur Predigttätigkeit*, 37, regarding *In Rom. hom. 26* (PG 60,643 5-644 5: μοναχοὺς ἐν ἐρημίαις καθημένους; τοὺς κατειληφότας τὰ ὄρη).

[558] *Hom. 10* (PG 63,87 59-64): μὴ πρὸς τοὺς ἐν ὄρεσι μόνον καθημένους ὦμεν σπουδαῖοι· ἅγιοι μὲν γὰρ ἐκεῖνοι καὶ βίῳ καὶ πίστει, ἅγιοι δὲ καὶ οὗτοι τῇ πίστει, πολλοὶ δὲ καὶ βίῳ. Μή, ἐὰν ἴδωμεν μοναχὸν εἰς φυλακήν, τότε εἰσέλθωμεν· ἐὰν δὲ κοσμικόν, μὴ εἰσέλθωμεν·; *hom. 17* (PG 63,131 57-61): Πρὸς οὖν ἅπαντας ἡμῖν ὁ λόγος ἐστίν, οὐ πρὸς τοὺς ἐνταῦθα δὲ μόνον, ἀλλὰ καὶ πρὸς τοὺς ἐν τῇ ἐρήμῳ καθεζομένους· ἐκεῖνοι γὰρ ἅπαξ τοῦ ἐνιαυτοῦ μετέχουσι, πολλάκις δὲ καὶ διὰ δύο ἐτῶν.

lies at Constantinople, then Chrysostom's claim in *hom. 10* that his audience are enthusiastic supporters (σπουδαῖοι) of "the monks on the mountains" is further irreconcilable with the suggestion that provision by the urban laity of assistance for those in the *eremos* is a factor which points firmly to Antioch.[559]

Since we ourselves have argued that the series on Hebrews is not in fact homogeneous,[560] it may be that the difficulties just highlighted stem from the current distribution of the homilies, rather than a failure of the original premise. In other words, it may be that the distinctions drawn in the literature — that monks are presented in a positive light at Antioch, in a negative light at Constantinople; that Antiochene monasticism is strictly extra-urban, Constantinopolitan urban — still hold and can provide an effective means of distinguishing material delivered at the two locations. Whatever the case may prove to be, however, one aspect of the criterion can immediately be dismissed, namely the argument that John mentions monks with some frequency in the Antiochene homilies, rarely at Constantinople. Such an argument relies upon the homogeneity of series, and consequently upon a distribution of the homilies which is no longer tenable.

As for the material distinction which has been drawn between the forms of monasticism practised, there is no question that monks did live on the mountains which surround the city of Antioch and that certain of these ascetics rarely entered the city.[561] Conversely, it seems certain that at the time that Chrysostom resided at Constantinople, there existed in that city communities of ascetics of some kind,[562] possibly separate from the group of monks led by Isaac.[563] That certain of these ascetics involved themselves in various ways in the affairs of the city is reasonably well documented.[564] The question that must be asked is whether these were

---

[559] See R. Kaczynski, *Das Wort Gottes in Liturgie und Alltag der Gemeinden des Johannes Chrysostomus*, Freiburg 1974, 210 n. 688, with regard to *In Phil. hom. 1* (PG 62,184 53-185 21).

[560] Allen-Mayer, "Hebrews: The Last Series?".

[561] *De statuis hom. 17* (PG 49,172 7 a.i.-173 4): οἱ τὰς ἀκρωρείας τῶν ὀρῶν κατοικοῦντες μοναχοὶ τὴν οἰκείαν ἐπεδείξαντο φιλοσοφίαν. Ἔτεσι γὰρ τοσούτοις ἐν ταῖς αὐτῶν καλύβαις συγκεκλεισμένοι ... ἐπειδὲ τοσοῦτον νέφος εἶδον τὴν πόλιν περιιστάμενον, καταλιπόντες αὐτῶν τὰς σκηνὰς καὶ τὰ σπήλαια, πάντοθεν συνέρρευσαν... For the grounds for assigning the homily to Antioch see pp. 367-369 above.

[562] Miller, *Birth of the Hospital*, 74-84 (cf. id., "Sampson Hospital", 110-113), persuasively argues that these urban ascetics, involved in the charitable institutions of the city, had mild Arian leanings.

[563] Palladius, *Dial. 6* (SC 341,126 15-128 19). See further Dagron, "Les moines et la ville".

[564] See Dagron, "Les moines et la ville", 262-265.

the only forms of monasticism practised at the two locations. If it can be shown that this is not the case, then it will prove difficult to demonstrate that the monastic lifestyles practised in or near each city were mutually exclusive and therefore distinctive.

In attempting to answer this question, it is instructive to examine the evidence supplied by the homilist in the above-mentioned homilies on Hebrews.[565] Bearing in mind that we now do not know for certain where all but a few of these sermons were delivered, do the data conform to the two extremes that have been posited in the literature? The ten passages which occur in this series cover a wide range of terms and practices. For instance, in *In Heb. hom. 4* Chrysostom refers to "solitaries" (μονάζοντες) and "perpetual virgins" (ἀειπαρθένοι), whom he considers to be part of the urban community, in that a ban on their attending church would have a disciplinary effect.[566] According to the criterion, the presence of male and female ascetics who participate regularly in the liturgical life of the city would immediately suggest a provenance of Constantinople. However, there is little in the homily to support this conclusion. On the one hand, the argument that the tone of the homilist is episcopal can instantly be dismissed;[567] on the other, Chrysostom appears to include himself among the presbyters who preside at Christian funerals,[568] while he also invokes the prayers of the *proedroi*. This last practice can be seen to occur in more than one Antiochene homily, but is as yet unobserved in sermons preached at Constantinople.[569] While neither of these latter pieces of data is conclusive, the evidence for Constantinople is even less convincing and the possibility that these ascetics formed part of the community at Antioch cannot be excluded.

In *hom. 11* we find a more explicit reference to urban monks. Here Chrysostom chides the audience for refusing to give not just to the beggars who wander the streets but also ἐπὶ μοναζόντων ἀνδρῶν ("to men who live a monastic life").[570] The latter, he says, ask for nothing more than sustenance. In giving them bread it is not you, the audience, who gives, but who receives. But, he continues, if these men should claim that they are also of clerical rank or call themselves priests, do not associate with them without interrogating them first. There is considerable risk in such

---

[565] The following discussion derives in large part from that presented in Allen-Mayer, "Hebrews: The Last Series?", 342-347.

[566] PG 63,43 21-29.

[567] See pp. 331-336 above.

[568] See pp. 332-325 above.

[569] See pp. 342-346 above.

[570] PG 63,96 9-12.

involvement.[571] The presence of monks who find it necessary to beg in order to eat would usually be considered to reflect the situtation at Constantinople. Monastic communities of the kind situated in the vicinity of Antioch were apparently able to provide for themselves in this respect,[572] while, in the case of ascetic individuals or holy men, the rigor of their askesis appears to have prevented them from soliciting alms.[573] Rather, there is an expectation that the laity will seek out the holy man and provide him with food and clothing as an act of piety.[574] By contrast, Constantinople appears at this period to have attracted a large number of visiting clergy and monks, many of whom stayed on for extended periods.[575] The resources available for feeding and housing such visitors and the number which these could accommodate at any one time is uncertain.[576] That the homilist further adjures the audience to treat with suspicion any monastic mendicant who claims also to be a priest might be thought further to support this conclusion. Much has been made of the hostility that developed between Chrysostom and the monastic community at Constantinople,[577] while Timothy Miller has also recently pointed out that some of the more established monastic communities in and around the imperial city had Arian leanings.[578] Either of these circumstances might have led Chrysostom to warn against accepting the claims of monks at face value, and to highlight for his audience the risks involved in such an association.

---

[571] PG 63,96 22-27.

[572] See, e.g., In Matt. hom. 69/70 (PG 58,653 19-21); and hom. 72/73 (PG 58,671 9-22).

[573] In In I Tim. hom. 14 (CPG 4436) PG 62,574 55-58, such holy men are characterised as "those unable to beg" (τοὺς οὐ δυναμένους ἐπαιτεῖν).

[574] See In Phil. hom. 9 (PG 62,250 33-50), and our comments on this passage in Allen-Mayer, "A Re-examination", 281-283. For the general relationship between the holy man and society in Syria see Brown, "Rise and function"; and his reappraisal, id., "The Rise and Function of the Holy Man in Late Antiquity, 1971-1997", JECS 6 (1998) 353-376. Brown's analysis assumes, however, that the Syrian "holy man" was a strictly rural (i.e., village) phenomenon.

[575] Among these were the fifty Nitrian monks who arrived in the autumn of 400 and stayed for some two years or more. See Liebeschuetz, "The Fall", 7-8; and Kelly, Golden Mouth, 191-202.

[576] On the operation of xenones at Constantinople see Miller, Birth of the Hospital, 22 and 26-27. Visiting bishops and monastic leaders were generally housed at the episcopal palace. See Baur, Chrysostom and His Time, II 137, 187; and Kelly, Golden Mouth, 196. But see Palladius, Dial. 7 (SC 341,150 87-91), where, as a politically expedient alternative, the Tall Brothers are said to have been housed in a xenon attached to St Anastasia and their needs supplied by a number of wealthy women.

[577] See, e.g., Liebeschuetz, Barbarians and Bishops, 210-214; and T. E. Gregory, "Zosimus 5,23 and the People of Constantinople", Byzantion 43 (1973) 61-83.

[578] See n. 562 above.

Until recently all of these factors would have led one to conclude that the homily was delivered at Constantinople. Now, in the light of *hom. 4*, we ought also to entertain the possibility that the monks described in *hom. 11* are part of the experience at Antioch. As van de Paverd has recently demonstrated, there is evidence that a group of ascetics from the Syrian countryside, who served the rural communities as priests, gathered at Antioch once a year or so to consult with the bishop.[579] Although these Syriac-speaking monk-priests provided for themselves by their own agricultural labours when at home, it appears that they were relatively poor. Van de Paverd dates the two homilies in which he finds evidence of these visitors to the years 387 and 391. While in those years Chrysostom speaks of the visiting ascetics with his usual enthusiasm, it is not impossible that in others a poor crop yield, coupled with the costs of such a journey, might have reduced them to soliciting food on their arrival. Further, although we are informed that the monk-priests are not native speakers of Greek, the formulae employed by the beggars of Antioch are exactly the sort of phrase that a tourist might be exposed to constantly, and as a consequence pick up and imitate.[580] Doubtless there are other possible explanations for the comments made by John in this respect, which remain as yet unrecognised.[581] Thus as far as *hom. 11* is concerned, until the various forms of monasticism reflected elsewhere in the homilies and writings of Chrysostom have been more thoroughly investigated, it seems best that we reserve our judgement.

In *hom. 10* mention is made of local monks (μοναχοί) who "sit on mountains". John also suggests that there is a well-established custom of the laity providing such individuals with support.[582] As already noted, these details would normally be considered proof that the homily was delivered at Antioch. Yet the form of monasticism posited for that location requires that interaction with the laity take place in the mountains outside of the city, with the monks rarely, if ever, involved in civil affairs. It is curious then that Chrysostom adduces as an example of his audi-

---

[579] *Homilies on the Statues*, 260-293.

[580] See, e.g., *In Phil. hom. 15* (PG 62,290 25-26): ... ἅπερ οἱ προσαιτοῦντες λέγουσιν, Ὡς ἔθος ἔχεις διδόναι; *In I Thess. hom. 9* (PG 62,454 38-39): Πόσοι καθ' ἑκάστην ἡμέραν προσέρχονται λέγοντες, Ἐλέησόν με... While there is no certainty as to where either of these two sermons was delivered, the concise and stereotypical character of the phrases they record is likely to be typical of those employed by beggars at both locations.

[581] It is not only the information contained in the homilies that requires reappraisal. Neil Adkin, "The date of St. John Chrysostom's treatises on 'subintroductae'", *Revue Bénédictine* 102 (1992) 255-266, has recently shown that the arguments which Dumortier had put forward for assigning the two treatises on *subintroductae* (CPG 4311-4312) to the years 381/2 of Chrysostom's diaconate are invalid.

[582] PG 63,87 53-88 14.

ence's zealousness towards these individuals assistance given to monks who are "in custody".[583] If one accepts that the location is Antioch, the implication that it is not unusual for the local monks to fall foul of the law is incompatible with the somewhat idealistic view of their activities which forms the foundation of the criterion.[584] If one wishes to argue for Constantinople, on the other hand, on the basis that this last circumstance does not conform with Antioch, then one must reassess the value of phrases such as "those seated on the mountains" or "those situated in the wilderness". These can no longer be seen as literal, and therefore indicative of place, but must now be viewed as rhetorical. This suggests that the picture of the form of monasticism local to each location which has been promoted in the literature is simplistic and somewhat less than adequate.

In *hom. 15* a male monastic is singled out from the audience and chided for succumbing to the laughter that has been rippling through the church during the course of the synaxis.[585] This is of particular interest since, as we have already noted, the monks of Antioch are generally supposed to have kept to themselves. As there is no indication that the homily was delivered on a festal occasion, at which time people from outside of the city who did not normally attend may have been present,[586] we are led to ask if this indicates a more regular and direct interaction between monk and community of the kind proposed for Constantinople. The context in which the comment appears may in this instance prove to be instructive. Chrysostom speaks here in a veiled manner that suggests that he has turned and is looking directly at the offenders. These are not just βιωτικοὶ ἄνδρες ("lay men"); they are also seated.[587] It may be that he is referring directly to members of the priesthood, even bishops, who are seated on the synthronon around or behind him and that certain of these also happen to be monks.[588] Certain of the bishops resident at Constan-

---

[583] PG 63,87 62-64 (cited n. 558 above).

[584] In fact both Julian and Libanius present a view of the monks of Antioch which is less than positive. For an assessment of their polemic see D. H. Raynor, "Non-christian attitudes to monasticism", StP 18/2 (1989) 267-273.

[585] PG 63,122 5-7.

[586] For the increase in attendance which occurred at Antioch at the time of the major Christian festivals see De b. Philogonio (PG 48,755 8-40); In princ. Act. hom. 1 (PG 51,65-67 1-19); and De ss. martyribus (CPG 4357) PG 50,647 1-3. It is possible that certain of the Antiochene monks also made a rare appearance in the city on these occasions in order to partake of the eucharist, after the manner of the situation described in In Heb. hom. 17 (PG 63,131 57-61).

[587] PG 63,121 52-54.

[588] On the number of clergy of monastic persuasion associated with the church at Constantinople see Auf der Maur, Mönchtum, 118-123.

tinople at the time, most notably Acacius of Beroea, were also ascetics.[589] One could imagine Chrysostom being particularly upset by members of the priesthood openly chatting and laughing during the synaxis, since they were probably in full view of the laity.[590] One could also imagine that he might feel constrained to avoid openly mentioning this group if there were bishops among them. This is not conclusive proof of Constantinopolitan provenance, of course, since it is probable that at the time of Chrysostom's presbyterate Antioch also regularly drew a large body of visiting clergy, if not from elsewhere, at least from the surrounding churches in Syria. A proportion of these individuals were undoubtedly practising ascetics also.[591] Once again one is led to suspect that the picture of monasticism drawn in the literature bears a less than close resemblance to the evidence. It seems likely that a more thorough and systematic investigation of the issue will prove that the distinctions between the monastic lifestyles which existed at Antioch and Constantinople at the close of the fourth century are less clear than is commonly supposed.[592]

These difficulties do not mean that it will prove impossible to draw any useful distinction. Although much, if not all, of the criterion in its present form must be discarded, more subtle differences between the forms of monasticism found at each location may yet emerge. For instance, little attention has been paid to the ascetic lifestyles of women as described in the homilies and as manifested at each location.[593] In addition, as we have argued elsewhere, it may be that under certain conditions the term ἅγιος is employed by Chrysostom in a technical sense, that is, to refer to a holy man, requiring a common and possibly Syrian understanding of this concept on the part of the audience.[594] Also, there is

---

[589] See Baur, *Chrysostom and His Time*, II 186-187.

[590] On the open character of the churches at Constantinople see Mathews, *Early Churches*, 105-106.

[591] See the comments regarding *In Heb. hom. 11*, this section above, and n. 586.

[592] For a preliminary investigation which supports this case see W. Mayer, "Monasticism at Antioch and Constantinople in the Late Fourth Century. A case of exclusivity or diversity?", in *Prayer and Spirituality*, vol. 1 (n. 224 above), 275-288.

[593] The studies which do exist tend to concentrate on John's ascetic treatises, particularly those on the *subintroductae*, or on the monastic community founded by Olympias. See, e.g., E. A. Clark, "John Chrysostom and the *Subintroductae*", *Church History* 46 (1977) 171-185; ead., "Authority and Humility: A Conflict of Values in Fourth-century Female Monasticism", *Byzantinische Forschungen* 9 (1985) 17-33; S. Elm, *'Virgins of God'. The Making of Asceticism in Late Antiquity*, Oxford 1994; and B. Leyerle's forthcoming book on the *subintroductae*.

[594] See Allen-Mayer, "A Re-examination", 281-283, with regard to *In Phil. hom. 1* and 9. On the problems which attach to an argument based on "Syrian perspective", however, see pp. 418-421 above.

no question that the mountainous topography inhabited by a certain sector of the monks of Antioch is unique to that location. If it can be proved in a particular instance that the monks or ascetics whom John describes are situated on real mountains or in real caves, and that the community or individuals in question are local, then the basis for assigning that homily to Antioch is secure. Thus, for instance, when in *In illud: Vidua eligatur* (CPG 4386) the fathers in the audience are accused of running off to the "holy men" and harrassing those on the peaks of the mountains for help whenever their sons suffer mental illness, there are strong grounds for suspecting that the situation described is local to Antioch.[595] In most cases, however, the evidence is not so clear and there is some difficulty involved in teasing out the rhetoric from the reality.

To sum up then, while there is evidence that extra-urban forms of monasticism existed at Antioch and urban forms at Constantinople, it is likely that these were not mutually exclusive. It is also likely that phrases such as "those seated on mountains" or "those situated in the *eremos*" are not to be interpreted literally, but are rhetorical in character. These factors considerably diminish the effectiveness of the criterion as posited. Suggestions that an exhortation to visit monks or that an assumption that the laity provide for the needs of ascetics is an indication that Chrysostom is preaching at Antioch, are at present unable to be proven or disproven. As for the arguments which rely on the frequency of monastic reference or whether such reference is positive or negative, these are based upon a distribution of the homilies which can no longer be sustained. They are therefore to be discarded. The only secure use of the criterion in its present form occurs when it is clear that the monks or ascetics in question live on mountains or in caves that are real, and that those monks or ascetics are also local.

7. OLYMPIC GAMES

With respect to *In Heb. hom. 14* Ilona Opelt's argument regarding the Olympic Games is relatively sound and convincing. Although she fails to address the question of the availability to an Antiochene audience of alternative Olympics prior to the year 393, due to her conviction that the series dates to 396 or later,[596] the information that a large number of the audience have attended the Olympics in question on repeated occasions

---

[595] PG 51,331 18-21: Πάλιν ἂν μὲν ὑπὸ δαίμονος ἐνεργῆται, πρὸς πάντας τοὺς ἁγίους τρέχεις, καὶ τοὺς ἐν ταῖς κορυφαῖς τῶν ὀρέων ἐνοχλεῖς, ὥστε αὐτὸν τῆς μανίας ἀπαλλάξαι ἐκείνης.
[596] See Opelt, "Das Ende von Olympia", 68-69.

strongly suggests that the games are local.[597] This conclusion is supported by the level of detail provided, which extends beyond that of a mere topos.[598] Even if it should prove subsequently that the Greek Olympics did continue to take place after the ban in 393, the fact that attendance is within the repeated and common personal experience of the audience certainly indicates in this instance that the homily was preached at Antioch.

The question arises, however, whether this argument is equally useful in all cases where Olympic games are adduced as an exemplum. Taken to its logical conclusion, Opelt's analysis of the historical evidence implies that there would have been little point in Chrysostom using examples from the Olympics in sermons preached to a Constantinopolitan audience. This suggests that what we may have here is a criterion which points exclusively to Antioch.

Certainly in the case of *In princ. Act. hom. 1* (CPG 4371) the connection between the Olympics mentioned and Antioch is clear cut. "After the thirty days spent here", says the homilist, "the competitors are taken up to the suburb and led around".[599] That the Syrian Olympics lasted forty-five days and were staged partly in Antioch itself and partly at Daphne is known from independent historical sources.[600] In the case of *Adv. Iud. or. 5* (CPG 4327) the evidence would seem to be equally clear. Here, it is not the direct association between the present location and the staging of the games but the audience's experience as spectators which Chrysostom invokes.

> It's ridiculous that, when sitting at the Olympic games, you have the stamina to hang around from midnight until the very middle of the day, the hot sun bearing down on your naked head, waiting to see upon whom the wreath will be placed, and won't leave until the contest has been decided. Yet now, when our contest is about not this kind of wreath but that which is imperishable, you tire easily and are exhausted.[601]

The significance of other references to the Olympics, however, is less easy to determine. In *De baptismo Christi* (CPG 4335) there is no explicit connection between the games and the present city nor is the audience's experience as spectators invoked. The level of detail is high, however,

---

[597] See Chapter Two, n. 149.

[598] See PG 63,116 26-32.

[599] PG 51,76 4-7.

[600] See Downey, "The Olympic Games of Antioch in the Fourth Century A.D.", *Transactions of the American Philological Association* 70 (1939) 438; Petit, *Libanius*, 126; Liebeschuetz, *Antioch*, 136-137.

[601] PG 48,897 26-34.

and the reverent behaviour exhibited by those in the agora as the *agono-thetes* passes through is presented with the intention of causing the audience to reflect upon their own poor behaviour when receiving the eucharist.[602] Despite the manner in which the exemplum is introduced,[603] the strong contrast which is evoked and the manner in which the two behaviours are juxtaposed leads to the firm impression that church and agora are situated at the one location. This cannot be considered proof that the homily was delivered at Antioch, however.[604] Until such time as other evidence of a more convincing nature can be located and adduced, that it is Antiochene is technically no more than a possibility.

In the case of *In Heb. hom. 17* the link between exemplum and place is not entirely obvious, although the way in which the exemplum is introduced does perhaps suggest that the homilist is addressing an audience familiar with the procedure which he describes.[605] "Tell me, I ask, in the Olympic games doesn't the herald stand and cry out in a loud and resonant voice, 'Is there anyone accuses this person of being a slave, a thief, or of wicked character?'?"[606] That this is the formula recited by the herald when introducing contestants at the games of Antioch is intimated by John's comments in *In princ. Act. hom. 1*:

> No slave competes, no servant does military service. Rather, if he's caught out as a slave he's struck from the military register with a penalty. The same custom prevails not just in the case of military service, but also with respect to the Olympic games. For after the thirty days spent here they take them [*sc.* the contestants] up to the suburb and lead them around, and when the entire theatre is seated the herald cries out, "Does anyone accuse this person?", so that he might set foot in the contests unencumbered by the suspicion of slavery.[607]

---

[602] PG 49,370 20-28: Οὐχ ὁρᾶτε ἐπὶ τῶν Ὀλυμπίων ἀγώνων, ὅταν ἀγωνοθέτης διὰ τῆς ἀγορᾶς βαδίζῃ, στέφανον ἐπὶ τῆς κεφαλῆς ἔχων, στολὴν ἀναβεβλημένος, ῥάβδον ἐν τῇ χειρὶ κατέχων, ὅση ἡ εὐταξία, τοῦ κήρυκος βοῶντος ἡσυχίαν εἶναι μετ' εὐκοσμίας; ... Ἐν ἀγορᾷ ἡσυχία, καὶ ἐν ἐκκλησίᾳ κραυγή;

[603] Questions which begin: "Don't you see..?" have a strong rhetorical flavour. On this point see p. 374 above.

[604] Although it is universally assumed that *De baptismo Christi* stems from Antioch, the assumption has been based on chronological grounds and is not derived from any evidence of provenance. For the main proponents of this approach see Tillemont, Montfaucon, Rauschen and Schwartz (Chapter One, pp. 51f, 78, 137 and 147).

[605] The following argument is adapted from that presented in Allen-Mayer, "Hebrews: The Last Series?", 339-341.

[606] PG 63,133 9-12.

[607] PG 51,76 1-10.

Since Chrysostom is not always scrupulous about citing formulae in full,[608] and since he expects the congregation in this second instance to supply a clause referring to slavery for themselves, it seems reasonable to assume that the two formulae are essentially one and the same. Further, by mentioning in *In Heb. hom. 17* that the herald grabs the contestant by the head and leads him past the spectators,[609] John makes an allusion to the formal parading of the contestants in a way which is slightly more detailed than that mentioned in *In princ. Act. hom. 1*. This may add weight to the possibility that Chrysostom is addressing an audience for whom spectatorship at the Olympic games is a regular and intimate part of their cultural experience. One could argue, however, that the formula exploited in this exemplum could be equally well known to the citizens of other cosmopolitan cities, particularly if the ritual is common to all such games and had for centuries been characteristic of the Greek Olympics. With this in mind, and in the absence of any association between exemplum and audience or place, one cannot rule out the possibility that the exemplum could have been used before a congregation at Constantinople.

Other exempla taken from the games are introduced in a matter-of-fact way and offer information or snapshots of a general character.[610] With the exception of perhaps *De mutatione nom. hom. 2*, where it is specified that the wreath striven for by the athlete is of laurel,[611] none of these contain information specific to a particular Olympics nor do they require any special knowledge on the part of the audience. If one sets aside the chronological issue raised by Opelt and the fact that a particu-

---

[608] As is the case, for instance, with the renunciation formula recited prior to baptism. Cf. *In Col. hom. 6* (PG 62,341 61-342 1; 342 42-45). See further P. W. Harkins, "Pre-Baptismal Rites in Chrysostom's Baptismal Catecheses", StP 8 (1966) 228-234. It is noteworthy that any truncation of the formula cited in *In Heb. hom. 17* would cause the initial εἰ to be converted to μή, as occurs in *In princ. Act. hom. 1*.

[609] PG 63,133 18-19: ... τῆς κεφαλῆς ἕκαστον κατέχων καὶ παράγων...

[610] See, e.g., *De resurr. mortuorum* (CPG 4340) PG 50,421 62-422 5; *In s. Romanum* (CPG 4353) PG 50,606 4-8 a.i.; *De Macabeis hom. 1-2* (CPG 4354) PG 50,621 62-64 and 624 17-19; *De mutatione nom. hom. 2* (PG 51,125 11-17); *In illud: Vidi dom. hom. 6* (SC 277,218 42-44); *In Matt. hom. 13* and *hom. 33/34* (PG 57,216 2-3 and 395 18-28); *In II Cor. hom. 3* (PG 61,413 10-14); and *Cat. 3* (CPG 4467) SC 50bis,155 9.1-4. The list includes only exempla in which the Olympics are explicitly identified.

[611] Although C. Millon and B. Schouler, "Les jeux olympiques d'Antioche", *Pallas* 34 (1988) 66, assume that in the Syrian, as in the pan-Hellenic Olympics, the victor's wreath was composed of olive, there is evidence that laurel was associated specifically with the Syrian games. Libanius, *Or.* 11.269 (Foerster, I 533-534), mentions a laurel wreath in connection with the *hellanodikes*. Downey, *Antioch*, 231-232, refers to evidence that both the *grammateus* and *amphithales* wore crowns of laurel, one constructed of natural leaves, the other simulated in gold. That the final events in the games were staged at Daphne (Gr. δάφνη = laurel) strengthens the suspicion that the choice was deliberate.

lar version of the games is local to Antioch, there is nothing in any of
these to suggest that they are other than part of the standard repertoire
of a classically-trained orator. As Ameringer points out, such metaphors
and exempla derive from a tradition of long standing, absorbed into the
Christian literature through the writings of St Paul.[612] While there is a remote possibility that John restricts the use of such exempla to material
delivered at Antioch,[613] the fact that such images and allusions are a
widely-used rhetorical device must be kept in mind.

To answer our original question, then, not all of the exempla based on
the Olympic games are of equal use. In cases where there is an expectation that the audience have been frequent spectators and are intimate
with the formalities and details of the games, or where it is clear that a
version of the Olympics is held locally, we can be certain that Chrysostom is speaking at Antioch. In cases where either circumstance is implied
but not made explicit, we can suspect that this is the case but cannot be
certain. If, on the other hand, the exemplum is entirely general in character or presented as a simple statement of fact, the mere fact that it appears in a homily cannot be taken as an indication of provenance. Unless
it can be proven in future that Olympic exempla, regardless of quality,
are used by John exclusively at Antioch, the suspicion that an exemplum
from this last category is a rhetorical topos of indiscriminate use must
always attach.

8. Liturgy

Of the two arguments adduced under the category of liturgical practice the one is difficult to prove, the other is easily dismissed. The first
(that the festivals of certain martyrs were celebrated at one city and not
the other) relies on two factors: one, that the cult of the saints and martyrs was still relatively localised at this time; and two, that the calendar
of non-mobile festivals observed at each location was therefore in the
main distinct. The first of these two factors in turn relies on the assumption that the original cult of a saint or martyr is strongly associated with
a particular place, namely the site where the remains are buried or a
place sanctified by some detail of the individual's martyrdom or life.[614]

---

[612] Ameringer, *Stylistic Influence*, 60.

[613] Of the homilies listed in n. 610, probably *De Macabeis hom. 2* and possibly *In illud: Vidi dom. hom. 6* can be attributed to Antioch on independent grounds. See further pp. 339 and 355 above. At this point, no exemplum of this kind has been found in a demonstrably Constantinopolitan homily.

[614] This is not necessarily incorrect. Thus Eustathius is commemorated at Antioch because he served it as bishop, even though, as Chrysostom tells us, his remains lie in

From this premise stems the associated belief that the cult spreads from its point of origin in a relatively uniform manner, that is, that in the initial stages it is more likely to be taken up and adopted by urban centres in proximity to the point of origin. Hence the argument that the commemoration of St Barlaam must be local to Antioch since the city is not far from Caesarea, the site of that individual's martyrdom.[615] From this conclusion it is a short step to argue that the festival of St Barlaam was a feature of the Antiochene calendar, such that when in another homily (*In d. Pauli: Nolo vos ignorare*: CPG 4380) it is indicated that the festival of St Barlaam was recently celebrated,[616] this is taken as evidence that that homily too was delivered at Antioch.

In the specific case of St Barlaam the argument is in fact based on a misreading of the evidence. For once, however, this error does not undercut the value of the conclusions, since, although it turns out that the evidence for the origin of the cult at Caesarea is unreliable, the role of the city of Antioch, on the other hand, is more prominent than Tillemont supposed. As Delehaye points out, amongst the confusion of possible mutiple saints of that name, the martyr Barlaam is closely associated with Antioch, such that the bulk of the evidence points in that direction.[617] In particular, the Syriac Martyrology discovered by Wright, which Aigrain dates to before 411 AD and possibly even as early as 360,[618] locates the festival of a Barlaa[s] martyred at Antioch on August 14.[619] By the same token, while there is strong reason to associate the martyr firmly with Antioch, there is no evidence that the festival of a St Barlaam was ever celebrated at Constantinople.[620] Thus, even though in the homily *In s. Barlaam* (CPG 4361) itself John fails to draw any direct connection between the events in the life of the martyr in question and the city in which he is preaching or between the martyr's burial site and the same, the simple fact that he is preaching on a festival dedicated to the martyr

---

Thrace. See *In s. Eustathium* (CPG 4352) PG 50,600 27-32; 601 5-7; 602 7-8; 604 10-13. For an analysis of the complex relationship between the cult of the martyrs and the interest in "holy places" which burgeoned in the fourth century see R. A. Markus, "How on Earth Could Places Become Holy? Origins of the Christian Idea of Holy Places", JECS 2 (1994) 257-271 and literature.

[615] See further pp. 421-425 above.

[616] PG 51,242 21-26 *a.i.*

[617] H. Delehaye, "Saint Barlaam martyr à Antioche", AB 22 (1904) 129-136.

[618] R. Aigrain, *L'hagiographie. Ses sources, ses méthodes, son histoire*, Poitiers 1953, 23-25.

[619] See H. Lietzmann, *Die drei ältesten Martyrologien* (Kleine Texte 2), Bonn 1911², 13.

[620] See P. Maraval, *Lieux saints et pèlerinages d'orient. Histoire et géographie des origines à la conquête arabe*, Paris 1985, 401-410, who lists the holy places that were associated with pilgrimage at Constantinople. No location dedicated to a Barlaam is among them.

in this instance is strongly indicative of an Antiochene provenance. The fact that the sermon *In d. Paul: Nolo vos ingorare* indicates that a festival of St Barlaam took place on the previous day, and that on that occasion the audience participated in a synaxis at a site specifically associated with the saint,[621] serves to strengthen the conclusion, as well as suggesting that this second sermon, too, was delivered at Antioch. Unfortunately, without a direct link between the martyr's life or resting place and the city in which John is preaching these conclusions cannot be accepted as definitive. Nonetheless, because of the apparent uniqueness of the cult to Antioch and the weight of the external sources there attaches to them a high degree of probability.

The case of St Barlaam and the apparent uniqueness of his celebration at Antioch, however, is rare. More usually, given the scarcity of local contemporary liturgical documents and the abridged nature of the Syriac Martyrology it is very difficult to ascertain the status of the non-mobile festivals at either Constantinople or Antioch at this time.[622] For an argument based on the presence of a particular festival in the local calendar to be effective, one must be able to demonstrate both that the festival was celebrated at the location posited and that it was not celebrated also at the other location. Evidence from one or two centuries later can be of assistance in this matter but not definitive,[623] since there is always the possibility that a festival which is listed was introduced subsequent to the time of Chrysostom or that one which was celebrated at the time that he was resident at Antioch or Constantinople fails to appear because it was subsequently dropped from that city's liturgical calendar. The latter could have occurred due to any number of reasons, such as a charge of heresy later attaching to the individual commemorated or to the person who had introduced the festival.[624] In addition, a strong association be-

---

[621] PG 51,242 21-26 *a.i.*: Καὶ τούτων ἁπάντων μάρτυρες ὑμεῖς, οἱ τοῖς ἄθλοις τοῦ μακαρίου Βαρλαὰμ χθὲς εντρυφήσαντες...καὶ κοῦφοι οἴκαδε ἀπὸ τῶν ἐκείνου διηγημάτων ἀναχωρήσαντες.

[622] The two ground-rules laid down by Mathews in the introduction to his analysis of the early churches of Constantinople — 1) that liturgical and other evidence must geographically coincide; 2) that the evidence must be more or less contemporary — here apply. See Mathews, *Early Churches*, 5. Regarding the status of the Syriac Martyrology see Aigrain, *L'hagiographie*, 23.

[623] For instance, the fact that a little more than a century later Severus had occasion to preach on the feast of St Barlaam at Antioch (*Hom. 73*, PO 57,90-96) can be adduced to support the suspicion that the festival mentioned in CPG 4380 was also held at that location, but does not in itself allow one to draw that conclusion.

[624] Markus, "How on Earth?" (see n. 614), 259-260, points out that in the late fourth century opinion regarding holy places and the transplanting of relics and the cult associated with them was still mixed. A less than enthusiastic reception on the part of the Christian populace or clergy could have led also to the place of a festival within the local calendar being short-lived.

tween an individual and a specific location, whether through origin or through possession of a martyr's remains, is not the only possible reason for the adoption of a particular festival. The movement of clergy at this time may also have been of influence. Since each brought to the new place to which he was assigned a set of liturgical norms shaped by the old, it would be surprising if bishops such as Gregory Nazianzenus, a Cappadocian, and John Chrysostom, a Syrian, did not effect some changes to Constantinopolitan liturgical practice.[625] Under these circumstances, separation of what is uniquely Constantinopolitan and uniquely Antiochene becomes somewhat difficult. Ultimately, unless, as in the case of St Barlaam, there is strong evidence that a festival is unique to one of the two locations or the homilist makes reference to two or more clearly identifiable festivals and these are of sufficient rarity to narrow the odds, the best result that can at present be obtained is a strong suspicion that one or the other of the two cities is the point of origin.

As for the second argument (that preaching on Sundays only is indicative of a particular city), care must be taken to distinguish the frequency with which synaxes were held at each location from the frequency with which Chrysostom preached. This is essential, since the homilist's comments regarding how often he has been preaching do not necessarily correspond to the number and frequency of the synaxes that are being held. Other priests may have been rostered to preach on certain days of the week, a fact upon which John may have found no need to remark, while he himself may have been preaching in the interim in other churches. This does not take into account other discontinuities in preaching caused by the intervention of non-homiletic duties. In consequence, the frequency with which Chrysostom preached at each location is unlikely to have been constant, but is liable rather to have fluctuated under the influence of a number of factors.[626]

As for the frequency with which synaxes were held at each city (a more constant determinant), the rate at which these occurred also varied throughout the year in accord with the liturgical season. Since we do not know enough about the liturgical rhythms at Antioch and Constantinople at this time,[627] an assessment of the frequency of synaxes is almost en-

---

[625] This has been suggested by R. Taft, *The Byzantine Rite. A Short History*, Collegeville, Minnesota 1992, 23-24. See further id., "The authenticity of the Chrysostom anaphora revisited. Determining the authorship of liturgical texts by computer", OCP 56 (1990) 5-51.

[626] The survey of frequency of preaching provided by Olivar, *La predicación*, 641-645 and 651-662, would appear to support this conclusion. See further Mayer, "At Constantinople" (n. 238 above).

[627] For instance, if one posits that after Pentecost the number of synaxes should have reverted to the "usual" one or two per week, it is difficult to explain why Chrysostom indicates in the latter half of the homilies on Genesis (*hom. 33-67*) that he is at times

tirely dependent upon an investigation of the evidence contained in the homilies themselves. This inquiry is in turn reliant upon the conclusions which have been drawn regarding the homilies' sequence and chronology. As should be clear by now, the sequencing and chronology formerly applied to the homilies themselves require radical reassessment and can no longer be considered reliable.[628] Consequently, rather than being a factor which admits of distinction between the two locations, the frequency with which synaxes were held and the frequency with which Chrysostom preached at each city are factors which must wait upon a complete overhaul of chronology as well as provenance for their elucidation.

9. FAMOUS PEOPLE AND EVENTS

While on the surface reference to a famous person or event ought to provide compelling evidence of a homily's point of delivery, particularly since such figures and events are unique and therefore exclusive, several difficulties are exposed when one examines the way in which the data have been interpreted in the literature. In the same way that Chrysostom is well aware of his own status and this is also well known to the audience, making explicit statement unnecessary, so in the case of a well-known individual or event we are unlikely to encounter explicit information. If the event or person is as famous as is generally supposed, then there is certainly no need for John to do more than allude to it for the benefit of those who are contemporaneous with the event or person, who have perhaps been personally involved, or who are familiar with received details concerning them. Allusion, as we have seen elsewhere,[629] is

---

preaching every day. See, e.g., *hom.* 33-35 and *hom.* 36 (PG 53,332 19-21 *a.i.*): Ἰδοὺ γὰρ σχεδὸν ἐφ᾽ ἑκάστης ἡμέρας ἐκ τῆς κατ᾽ αὐτὸν ἱστορίας προθέντες ὑμῖν τὴν διδασκαλίαν... Either the issue of the frequency of extra-Lenten synaxes is more complex than has previously been supposed or one is forced to question the homogeneity of the latter part of the series on Genesis.

[628] An exception to this is van de Paverd's investigation of the duration of Lent at Antioch and the frequency of preaching at this period (*Homilies on the Statues*, 161-201), which is in turn based on a detailed reassessment of the sequence and chronology of the homilies *De statuis*. The value of both liturgical analysis and chronology lies precisely in the well-defined parameters of the survey and the painstakingly scientific methodology employed. Note, however, that even this exemplary study is compromised by the fact that some early manuscripts of the series contain in fact not twenty-two homilies, but twenty-four, as established recently by Andrius Valevicius, "Les 24 homélies 'de Statuis' de Jean Chrysostome. Recherches nouvelles", *Études augustinennes* 46 (2000) 83-91. The established sequence and chronology now needs to be adjusted to include *De decem mill. tal. deb.* (CPG 4368) and *In ps. 145* (CPG 4415).

[629] See pp. 322-328 above.

particularly vulnerable to misinterpretation. Moreover, of the two (event and person), events are associated not just with a place but with a specific point in time. As a result of this additional focus it has not infrequently been the chronological aspect of the data which has been allowed to determine the place to which a homily is allocated. This circumstance has led to a failure to question whether the suggested provenance is consistent with other internal evidence and, at times, even to a neglect of the immediate context in which reference to the person or event is found. Although not always acknowledged, the manner in which Chrysostom refers to the data is also of significance in determining whether the conclusion reached is trustworthy.

a-b. *Eutropius and the riots of 387 AD*

A clear-cut example of both the difficulty posed by allusory evidence and the danger of ignoring the context in which it appears is provided by *In Col. hom.* 7.[630] The homily contains two passages, both of which have been understood to refer to a famous person and event. The first mentions an individual, recently in a position of some power and influence, who is now stripped of everything and in a state of poverty.[631] The figure has consistently been identified as the consul-eunuch Eutropius. The second recalls the blow to Antioch's pride suffered at the time of the riots, a wound which still rankles.[632] Although the two sets of data are essentially incompatible, since the first, if the identification is correct, points firmly to Constantinople, the second to Antioch, an *a priori* assumption that the homily stems from Constantinople[633] has led to considerable weight being placed upon the first, while the second has been treated as a reminiscence expressed not at the site of the event but from a stance involving both temporal and geographic distance. Yet the first is far less specific and ought therefore to be given less weight than the second. Indeed careful consideration of the thought process which prompts both *exempla* shows that this is the proper way to proceed.

The one feature which distinguishes Eutropius from other office-holders in the east at this time is that he is a eunuch. By the same token

---

[630] The argument which follows is an abbreviated version of that which appears in Allen-Mayer, "A New Approach", 30-35.

[631] PG 62,347 8-13.

[632] PG 62,347 56-348 6.

[633] Due in part to Chrysostom's indication in *In Col. hom. 3* that he is of episcopal status (see p. 322 above) and to the perceived episcopal tone which occurs later in *hom. 7* (see pp. 331-333 above).

it is widely assumed in the literature that his spectacular downfall is the
only example of that kind to occur over the span of Chrysostom's presbyterate and episcopate, and that it is therefore the only one which fits the
characteristics of the first exemplum. Yet as a candidate Eutropius can
be disqualified on both accounts. Immediately before launching into the
exemplum, Chrysostom reflects: "To whom are they [sc. those in high of-
fice] not subject? To their lovers, the eunuchs, those who do everything
for the sake of money, a whim of the people, fits of rage of those more
powerful."[634] It would be less than effective for John then to call to his
audience's attention a person who was himself both exempt from the in-
trigues of lovers and who was the most powerful contemporary example
of a manipulative eunuch. Indeed there is little justification for leaping to
the conclusion that the exemplum refers to a specific individual. Although the homilist refers to an office-holder with judicial authority and
a few heralds in his service,[635] these characteristics are common to more
than one administrative office and could elicit an official at either
Antioch or Constantinople in possession of a consular position, major
prefecture or provincial governorship.[636] As Liebeschuetz points out in
his study of the court of Arcadius, the period in question is particularly
rich in examples of individuals in high office at Constantinople who suffered sudden and marked reversals in their fortunes.[637] We ourselves
have elicited a further two cases germane to Antioch.[638]

The second exemplum, on the other hand, is far more specific. No-one
has doubted that it refers to Antioch, only that it is addressed to an Antiochene audience. With the evidence of the first exemplum discounted,
however, one can begin to view the second in a more balanced light. The
point that Chrysostom wishes to make here is that to be held in esteem
on account of persons or objects that are worthless is worse than to be
held in no honour at all. In this context he turns upon his listeners the
very argument which they use when referring to the city, namely that at
the time of the riots they would have preferred that the entire city be destroyed than that it be saved as a result of the representations of their

[634] PG 62,347 5-8.

[635] PG 62,347 8-9: Ὁ χθὲς ἐπὶ τοῦ βήματος ὑψηλός, ὁ κήρυκας ἔχων λαμπρᾷ τῇ φωνῇ
βοῶντας...

[636] The praetorian prefects, the urban prefect at Constantinople, the proconsuls, and
the comites provinciarum all held imperial appellate jurisdiction. See Jones, LRE, I 481.

[637] Liebeschuetz, Barbarians and Bishops, 89-92 and 105-116.

[638] Allen-Mayer, "A New Approach", 31-33. See further Asterius of Amaseia, In
kalendas 9 (C. Datema, Asterius of Amasea. Homilies I-XIV. Text, Introduction and Notes,
Leiden 1970, 43 13-33), preached in 400, where the dramatic falls of Rufinus, Timasius,
Abundantius and Tatianus are adduced along with that of Eutropius as recent compelling
examples of the instability of power.

coastal neighbour.[639] This argument is powerful in an Antiochene context but ineffective and of little relevance to an audience at Constantinople. Moreover, the expression "our city", which occurs twice in the course of the exemplum, regularly refers to the present location in other instances in which we have seen it employed by the homilist.[640] To read it as a purely rhetorical use of the first-person plural ("our personal city", i.e., "the city where I used to live") is to distort the evidence.

This does not mean that all references to the riots of 387 are equally useful, nor does it mean that all purported allusions to the sudden fall of Eutropius are equally false. To continue with the Antiochene riots, even at the time of the event and in the period immediately following it reference to the actual overturning of the imperial statues, the one distinctive feature in the episode, is rare. Only twice in the course of the twenty-two sermons currently associated with that period[641] does Chrysostom explicitly mention it, although in both instances he makes it clear that the event is within the personal experience of the audience.[642] Mention of the overturning of the statues occurs in one further homily not immediately associated with the event. Here again the homilist indicates that the episode is well known to his audience, tying it firmly to the present location.[643] As a consequence of the clarity of the description and the patent connection between event and place, there can be no doubt that all three homilies stem from Antioch.

---

[639] PG 62,347 56-348 5: Ὅπερ δὲ περὶ τῆς πόλεως πρὸς ἀλλήλους λέγετε, βούλομαι πρὸς ὑμᾶς εἰπεῖν. Προσέκρουσέ ποτε τῷ κρατοῦντι ἡ πόλις ἡ ἡμετέρα ... Ἡ δὲ γείτων πόλις, αὕτη ἡ ἐπιθαλάσσιος, ἐλθοῦσα παρεκάλεσε τὸν βασιλέα ὑπὲρ ἡμῶν· οἱ δὲ τὴν πόλιν οἰκοῦντες τὴν ἡμετέραν ἔλεγον τοῦτο χεῖρον εἶναι τοῦ κατασκαφῆναι τὴν πόλιν.

[640] See the examples presented in 3.b (pp. 367-369 above).

[641] I.e., De statuis hom. 1-21 (CPG 4330) and Ad illum. cat. 2 (CPG 4464). See further van de Paverd, Homilies on the Statues, 205-364. Neither of the two homilies which should now be added to this number (see n. 628 above) makes explicit reference to the event.

[642] De statuis hom. 5 (PG 49,73 1-13): ... ἀλλ᾿ οἴκοθεν καὶ ἐξ αὐτῶν τῶν συμβεβηκότων ἡμῖν ἐν τοῖς ἡμέραις ταύταις πειράσομαι ποιῆσαι φανερόν. Ἐπειδὴ γὰρ ἦλθε παρὰ βασιλέως τὰ γράμματα τὴν εἰσφορὰν ταύτην τὴν ἀφόρητον εἶναι δοκοῦσαν κελεύοντα καταθεῖναι ... Μετὰ ταῦτα, ἐπειδὴ συνέβη τὰ τολμηθέντα, καί τινες μιαροὶ καὶ παμμίαροι τοὺς νόμους καταπατήσαντες, τοὺς ἀνδριάντας καθεῖλον...; hom. 15 (PG 49,154 2-14 a.i.): Μὴ τοίνυν ἀλγῶμεν, ἀγαπητοί, μηδὲ καταπίπτωμεν ἐπὶ τῇ παρούσῃ θλίψει ... ὁ μὲν γὰρ διάβολος ἐνέπνευσέ τισι παρανόμοις ἀνθρώποις, καὶ εἰς τοὺς τῶν βασιλέων ὕβρισαν ἀνδριάντας ... Ἡ γὰρ πόλις ἡμῶν ....

[643] Adv. Iud. or. 6 (CPG 4327): Ἴστε δήπου πάντες καὶ μέμνησθε, ὅτε τοὺς ἀνδριάντας καθεῖλον παρ᾿ ἡμῖν μιαροί τινες ἄνθρωποι καὶ γόητες, πῶς οὐκ ἐκεῖνοι μόνον οἱ τολμήσαντες, ἀλλὰ καὶ ὅσοι παρόντες ἁπλῶς τοῖς γενομένοις ἐφάνησαν, εἰς δικαστήριον ἀναρπασθέντες καὶ συναπαχθέντες ἐκείνοις, τὴν ἐσχάτην ἔδωκαν δίκην; (PG 48,913 23-28).

In the case of *Ad illuminandos cat. 2* (CPG 4464), however, where a
further reference to the riots has been perceived to occur,[644] the description and therefore its significance is less than clear.[645] Although there are
strong grounds for believing that "those deemed to have committed an
outrage against the emperor" are the same individuals who were arrested
in connection with the riots in 387, since the behaviour and dress of the
women at the courthouse reflect those described in *De statuis hom. 13*,[646]
and since it is reasonably certain that *Ad illuminandos cat. 2* belongs in
the company of the homilies *De statuis*,[647] the passage itself is somewhat
bland and cannot in itself effect a determination on provenance. The
situation is described entirely in the third person, it is set in the context
of a general contrast between the day of Judgement and the present and,
most importantly, lacks the crucial direct association with the place or
audience that we have seen elsewhere. If the other homilies *De statuis*
had failed to survive, we would be hard put to identify the event in question.[648]

Part of the difficulty for the modern scholar attempting to identify the
events or persons to which Chrysostom refers in such passages is that the
way in which he presents these is dictated by the aspect which he wishes
to emphasise for the moral edification of his listeners. It is rarely in his
interest to give us the whole picture. Thus in the case just mentioned,
since his point is that, if rich women are capable of modifying their dress
through a very real fear of the present judicial system, they ought also to
be able to tone it down in fear of the judgement to come, it is the behaviour of the female relatives of the defendants which is the point of focus.
The charges which led to the trial are alluded to simply as a means of setting the scene. As we have seen in the case of *In Col. hom. 7* above, in
such instances it is the context which becomes the controlling factor. It
is only by giving the context careful consideration that one can test the
various possibilities against the information provided. However, given
the peculiarities of the medium and the knowledge-base shared by

---

[644] The passage in question has consistently been used to argue for the date of the
homily, rather than its location at Antioch. See Montfaucon, Stilting and Rauschen
(Chapter One, pp. 76, 117 and 140).

[645] PG 49,238 25-35: Καὶ τί χρὴ λέγειν τὴν ἡμέραν ἐκείνην, ἐξὸν καὶ ἀπὸ τῶν παρόντων ταῦτα
ἀποδεῖξαι πάντα; Ὅτε γοῦν οἱ δόξαντες εἰς τὸν βασιλέα ὑβρικέναι, εἰς τὸ δικαστήριον εἵλκοντο καὶ
περὶ τῶν ἐσχάτων ἐκινδύνευον, τότε αἱ μητέρες καὶ αἱ γυναῖκες ... πρὸ τῶν θυρῶν τοῦ δικαστηρίου
κυλινδούμεναι, οὕτω τοὺς δικάζοντας ἐπέκαμπτον.

[646] See PG 49,137 29-138 25.

[647] See van de Paverd, *Homilies on the Statues*, 227-255.

[648] Presumably similar scenarios occurred at Antioch in 372 at the time of the
conspiracy against Valens, and at Constantinople in 400 or 401 following the coup
instigated by Gainas.

homilist and audience, to which we ourselves are not privy, it is not to be expected that on every occasion it will be possible to make an accurate identification.

Perhaps it is not even reasonable to expect that Chrysostom always has a single person or instance in mind. To return to Eutropius, in the sermon *In Eutropium* (CPG 4392), although the main proof of the identity of the individual upon which the homily focuses is taken from the title,[649] John does provide sufficient detail to enable us to be certain that it is indeed Eutropius who is described. The individual was formerly consul,[650] there is definitely only one person involved,[651] the person in question is a eunuch,[652] he had been responsible for the passing of laws denying the right of asylum in church,[653] and the events have taken place in the city of imperial residence.[654] In combination, this information is decisive. In the case of *Quod frequenter conveniendum sit* (CPG 4441.3), where the upheaval cited has been identified as the fall of Eutropius,[655] detail of the kind just seen is lacking, although it is clear that a specific event and person are being evoked.[656] The metaphoric tremor,[657] also referred to as a "shipwreck",[658] a "blow", a "storm", a "catastrophe" and a "reversal",[659] has occurred recently,[660] in fact not quite thirty days before.[661] The aftermath of the event personally affects the present location[662] and can be viewed by the audience,[663] while the populace in general was witness to the original event.[664] The mysterious reversal affects

---

[649] PG 52,391-392: Ὁμιλία εἰς Εὐτρόπιον εὐνοῦχον πατρίκιον καὶ ὕπατον.

[650] PG 52,391 2-3; 393 19-22.

[651] PG 52,393 1-7. This is of significance in the case of *De capto Eutropio* (CPG 4528) where, despite the title and the mention of an individual who has sought asylum, it is hinted that more than one person is involved (PG 52,400 28-30; 401 35-40).

[652] PG 52,394 53-58.

[653] PG 52,394 27-28.

[654] PG 52,393 36-39; 395 32-51.

[655] See Stilting and Bonsdorff (Chapter One, pp. 125 and 188f).

[656] If the evidence is examined carefully, the argument that the σεισμός refers to an actual earthquake cannot be sustained. For the most recent statement of that view see Lietzmann (Chapter One, p. 170).

[657] PG 63,461 31.

[658] PG 63,461 25-27.

[659] PG 63,462 2-3.

[660] PG 63,461 22-23 and 30-31.

[661] PG 63,462 4-5.

[662] PG 63,461 25-27: Πᾶσα ἡ πόλις ἡμῖν τῶν λειψάνων τοῦ ναυαγίου ἐκείνου ἐμπέπλησται·

[663] PG 63,461 23-24: οὐ πρὸ τῶν ὀφθαλμῶν ὑμῶν ἐστι τὰ ὑπομνήματα;

[664] PG 63,462 4-5: ... τὴν πρὸ τῶν ὀφθαλμῶν φαινομένην, τὴν πρὸ τριάκοντα οὐδ' ὅλως γεγενημένην ἡμερῶν...

one person only[665] and is specifically associated with confiscation, exile and a broad redistribution of the individual's property and wealth.[666] However, if the presupposition that all of the *Novae homiliae* date to the first two years at Constantinople and that they were all delivered at that one location is removed,[667] the detail provided is insufficient for the identification of the person involved. The comment that the individual is in exile is perhaps useful, although the confusion between the cases of Eutropius and Count John that occurs in the title to *De capto Eutropio* (CPG 4528)[668] demonstrates the potential difficulties involved. With regard to confiscation, in *In Heb. hom. 32* Chrysostom himself states that the loss of houses and property to one's enemies is a not uncommon phenomenon, such that he could have named more than one victim who was still alive.[669]

In the case of *In illud: Ne timueritis hom. 1* (CPG 4414), however, there is no indication that the homilist is discussing a specific instance. Indeed it is scarcely even likely that he has the example of Eutropius in mind. In the context of discussing the folly of placing great value on wealth he says: "For often it [*sc.* wealth] doesn't come to an end after the person, but it even comes to an end before the person. Indeed you know countless examples in this city of the untimely end of wealth, and you have learnt that while the possessor lives, the possessions perish. For a change into poverty is the end of wealth."[670] Irrespective of whether Chrysostom goes on to talk about wealth in terms familiar from the homily *In Eutropium*, as has been argued,[671] he is clearly emphasising here the contrast between former wealth and current poverty. Unless this statement was made shortly after the fall of Eutropius, in which case one would expect comment of a less general nature, it is scarcely appropriate to the known situation. Rather, this remark, combined with the note that

---

[665] PG 63,461 35-44: Καὶ ὁ μὲν ... ἕτεροι δὲ ... καὶ οἱ πρὸ τούτου κολακεύοντες αὐτόν ...

[666] PG 63,461 30-39: οὕτω δὴ καὶ τοῦ πρώην ἐντεῦθεν ἐπενεχθέντος σεισμοῦ, ὁ μὲν τὴν οἰκίαν, ὁ δὲ τοὺς ἀγρούς, ὁ δὲ τὰ ἀνδράποδα, ὁ δὲ τὸ ἀργύριον, ὁ δὲ τὸ χρυσίον διανειμάμενοι ... Καὶ ὁ μὲν ... ἄοικος, ἄπολις πρὸς τὴν ὑπερορίαν φυγὰς γέγονε, καὶ τῆς ἀναγκαίας ἀπορεῖ τροφῆς·

[667] Both assumptions are common throughout the literature. See in particular Montfaucon and Aubineau (Chapter One, pp. 102 and 244f).

[668] See Cameron, "A misidentified homily", 34-48.

[669] PG 63,222 43-54. There is no certainty that this homily was itself delivered at Constantinople, although this is perhaps immaterial, since the comment is general in nature and claims that the phenomenon is wide-spread. Regarding the provenance of the homilies on Hebrews in general see Allen-Mayer, "Hebrews: The Last Series?".

[670] PG 55,502 37-42.

[671] See Montfaucon (Chapter One, p. 92). The image of wealth as a murderous slave is a favourite topos for Chrysostom. For other examples see Cameron, "A misidentified homily", 37-38.

there are numerous such examples available at the present location, suggests only that John is thinking of a wide range of candidates, if he has any specific examples in mind at all. As we have argued above with regard to the perceived Eutropius exemplum in *In Col. hom.* 7, at Antioch as well as Constantinople there were more than a few instances of the sudden loss of both wealth and power upon which the homilist could call. Indeed the passage is markedly similar to that which occurs in *In Heb. hom.* 32,[672] although no-one has felt obliged to suggest that Chrysostom is referring to Eutropius in that context.

In the course of the above discussion we have seen that a perceived reference to a famous individual or event is one thing, while its significance for establishing the provenance of the homily in which it occurs is another. Not all of the identifications that have been made have proven to be accurate, a situation which arises in part from the nature of the evidence itself and in part from overzealousness on the part of the modern scholar, often due to an *a priori* assumption of provenance. In the case of Eutropius and the Antiochene riots of 387, we have identified several levels at which problems can occur. First, Chrysostom and his audience share knowledge to which we are not privy. This results in different levels of detail being provided, depending upon the point which John at the time wishes to highlight. If the information is not only specific but encompasses details which are unique to a particular person or event, it is possible to make an accurate identification. If, while the information is specific, the details provided are not unique but could apply to a number of known situations, the context becomes crucial for determining the specific incident or person to which the homilist refers. The identification in this instance can range from probable to uncertain.

In either case, the second point is that an accurate identification is unhelpful unless it is accompanied by an explicit and definite connection between the event and the audience or present location. Where this is lacking, there is always the possibility that the event or person is so well known that Chrysostom is able to use it as an exemplum at more than one location. The third area of difficulty attaches to exempla where the required explicit connection with the present location exists, but specific detail is entirely lacking. In such cases there is no certainty that John has a particular and therefore identifiable incident or person in mind. If the exemplum is entirely general in nature and could cover a wide range of possibilities, it can be of no use for establishing the place of preaching. If

---

[672] PG 63,222 43-55: πολλάκις δὲ καὶ εἰς ἐχθροὺς ἦλθεν ὁ κλῆρος, οὐκ ἀπελθόντων μόνον ἡμῶν, ἀλλὰ καὶ ζώντων ... καὶ τούτου τὰ ὑποδείγματα πολλὰ ἐν ταῖς πόλεσιν ὁρᾶται· ... εἶπον ἂν ὀνομαστὶ καί τινας ἐξ αὐτῶν, καὶ πολλὰ εἶχον διηγήματα εἰπεῖν ... οὐκ οἰκίαι δέ, ἀλλὰ καὶ ἀνδράποδα καὶ ἅπας ὁ κλῆρος πολλάκις εἰς τοὺς ἐχθροὺς περιῆλθε. Τοιαῦτα γὰρ τὰ ἀνθρώπινα.

the range of possibilities is restricted, its significance can at best be uncertain. In cases where both explicit connection to the audience or location and specific detail is lacking, the exemplum can never be of use in
establishing provenance and should be removed from the body of evidence. It remains to be seen whether the rules which have been established here apply equally to the rest of the types of evidence that have
been adduced.

c-d. *War and the current emperor*

Since the criteria relating to both war and the current emperor rest
upon the same set of assumptions, it is inevitable that in considering the
one, we will also encounter issues relevant to the other. For this reason
references to the presiding emperor and to war are examined here together. The key point made in the use of such allusions is that, upon the
death of Theodosius early in 395, his successor Arcadius almost immediately began to experience difficulty in maintaining the stability of the
eastern half of the empire. In 395 itself Alaric and his supporters
marched upon Constantinople, at which time the threat was only nar-
rowly averted.[673] The activities of Tribigild in 398 and the mounting
threat posed by Gainas in 399, leading to the coup of 400, are well documented.[674] From these events two suppositions have been drawn — that
Arcadius had continuing problems with war, especially in 395 and 400,
and that he had particular difficulty with certain tribes, both externally
and internally, most notably the Huns and Goths. These premises are
counterbalanced by the assumption that Theodosius, at least for the period of Chrysostom's presbyterate (386-early 395), was in firm control of
both situations.[675] Hence, when in *In Phil. hom. 15* Chrysostom asks:
"Hasn't this current ruler been involved in episodes of trouble, danger,
grief, despondency, disaster and intrigue from the moment he put on the

---

[673] PLRE I, s.v. Flavius Rufinus 18, 779-780; Liebeschuetz, *Barbarians and Bishops*, 55-
59. Alaric's activities continued into 397.

[674] PLRE I, s.v. Gainas, 379-380. See further Liebeschuetz, *Barbarians and Bishops*,
256-260.

[675] This appears to be based on the assumption that the treaty signed with the
Visigoths in 382 effectively put an end to all such activity. On the nature of the treaty see
Liebeschuetz, *Barbarians and Bishops*, 26-31.

crown?",[676] Bonsdorff, Quasten and others have thought that the person referred to must of necessity be Arcadius.[677]

But is this necessarily the case? In particular, is it impossible that Chrysostom can be describing Theodosius here? Arguing that the homilist is unlikely to have jumped from Valens to Arcadius in a list of emperors in recent history, passing over Theodosius in silence, neither Stilting nor Baur found difficulty with identifying Theodosius as the current ruler, the latter going so far as to assert that Theodosius experienced the greater share of ongoing problems.[678] A careful consideration of the period from 386 to the close of 394 at least confirms that Theodosius continued to be troubled by the threat of war and political instability. In 386 itself a group of Goths under Odotheus crossed the Danube; in 387 Theodosius was obliged to deal with the threat posed internally by Maximus; throughout 388-391 the same Alaric who later threatened the equanimity of Arcadius waged a guerilla campaign in Macedonia, leading to a direct confrontation with Theodosius and his army in 391-392; while in 394 Theodosius set out with his army for the West to deal with the usurper Eugenius.[679] Regardless of whether Theodosius was able to control each of these situations,[680] his reign at this period can scarcely be said to have been free from trouble and anxiety. As for the period prior to the homilist's presbyterate, Chrysostom himself documents this as being particularly wretched for both emperor and family.[681] In fact, if for the moment we leave aside the question of the sequence in which the emperors are cited in this homily, we arrive at the same dilemma seen elsewhere. Although the homilist says that he is discussing the current emperor, the features of that emperor's reign which he evokes are too general to admit of distinction. Indeed so general are they in character that it is difficult to say whether John has any specific examples in mind. Moreover, the argument from sequentiality, although logical, is itself not necessarily useful. The desire to achieve rhetorical effectiveness can at times override the claims of logic. Ultimately, in the absence of any fur-

---

[676] PG 62,295 44-46.

[677] Bonsdorff (see Chapter One, pp. 189f); Quasten (p. 224). See further Allen-Mayer, "A Re-examination", 271-272, 274-275, which presents an earlier version of the argument which follows.

[678] See Chapter One, pp. 123 and 208.

[679] See Liebeschuetz, *Barbarians and Bishops*, 30-53.

[680] The view that Theodosius had force of character, while Arcadius was weak, if decent, as espoused by Jones, LRE, I 173, has developed with the benefit of hindsight. The point at issue here is not how history viewed the reigns of the two emperors, but how they were viewed by Chrysostom and by the general public as they lived through them from day to day.

[681] *Ad viduam iuniorem* (CPG 4314) SC 138,138 289-140 309.

ther evidence within the homily, it is impossible to make a determination.

As for references to a current or recent state of war, the evidence that this was an almost unremitting occurrence throughout the reigns of both Theodosius and Arcadius leads to the suspicion that such data are going to be less than useful. Unless the detail is so precise as to permit the identification of a particular campaign, the localisation of such exempla to a specific point in time, and therefore a specific place, is at best going to be difficult, at worst unachieveable. Since only a single instance of war as an indication of provenance has been adduced, such references more commonly being used to establish chronology, in order to round out the discussion we include in our examination one or two examples from the latter category. With regard to *In Eph. hom. 6*, it has been argued that the allusion to the existence of a current state of war points to the year 395 or later.[682] As we have already seen, the assumption that the years 386-394 were free of troubles with Germanic and Turkish tribes or from enemy incursion is invalid. Moreover, regardless of the eventual outcome, at the time that it occurred each incursion or uprising must have seemed equally alarming and momentous to the citizens of the East. While Chrysostom here describes the wars as happening "even now", and tells us that peoples and entire cities have been overrun and destroyed, while countless individuals have been taken as slaves by the barbarians,[683] these events appear to be remote to the present location. It is also not beyond possibility that a number of separate occurrences have been conflated by the homilist for rhetorical effect. If the details do fit the circumstances of Alaric's activities between 395 and 397, it is possible that they are also appropriate to the activities of Tribigild in 389-399 or even to a conflict between nations external to the empire.[684] The reality is that our knowledge of the details of these events is less than adequate, making the identification of the war or wars in question uncertain.

In the case of *In illud: Vidi dom. hom. 1* (CPG 4417), the homily has consistently been assigned to the period after 395, both due to a reference to the incompetence of those in power and to the perception that

---

[682] See Stilting and Bonsdorff (Chapter One, pp. 122f and 188). Rauschen (p. 143) firmly asserts that this circumstance excludes the years 386-395.

[683] PG 62,48 44-54: ... οἷον ἐπὶ τῶν πολέμων τῶν ἔτι καὶ νῦν συμβαινόντων ... Οὐχ ὁρᾶτε τοὺς πολέμους; οὐκ ἀκούετε τὰς συμφοράς; ... Ἔθνη καὶ πόλεις ὁλόκληροι κατεποντίσθησαν καὶ ἀπώλοντο, μυριάδες τοσαῦται παρὰ τοῖς βαρβάροις δουλεύουσιν... Μεγάλην ἐκεῖνοι τὴν δίκην ἔδωκαν...

[684] Chrysostom states only that the wars are contemporary, not that they are of concern to the emperor. Neither does he locate the wars geographically. Indeed the point which he wishes to emphasise here, that the punishment for sin can be extreme, is of little assistance in determining whether the comments are specific to the empire or general.

Chrysostom alludes to a time of war.[685] There are several problems with this identification. Firstly, although the current state of affairs is considered to be negative, with mention of a state of turmoil, disaster, war and even defeat,[686] this is attributed popularly to the poor decision-making of "those in power" (ἡ τῶν κρατούντων ἀβουλία).[687] It is uncertain whether in the minds of the general populace οἱ κρατοῦντες refers to the emperor and his western counterpart, to powerful officials who are second only to the emperor, such as the consuls or *praefectus praetorio per Orientem*, or to more localised officials, such as the *comes Orientis* and *consularis Syriae*, if the people discussing the disastrous state of affairs are situated at Antioch. The homilist himself tends to use phrases in the singular when referring to the current emperor.[688] Moreover, it is difficult to say at what point the current state of affairs might have been characterised as a defeat, since history tends to emphasise eventual success rather than interim failure. Admittedly the situation could well reflect the disturbance caused by the Hun invasion of Syria in 395/6,[689] but it could also mirror the situation in the late 380s, when Antioch appears to have been put under considerable economic strain due to the campaign against Maximus.[690] It is also possible that it reflects events in 399, leading up to the deposition of Eutropius and the occupation of Constantinople by the troops under Gainas.[691] Again, however, the problem faced is that the information provided is veiled and open to a number of interpretations. While there might be grounds for favouring one hypothesis over another, the level of detail is insufficient to permit a positive identification.

---

[685] See in particular Tillemont (Chapter One, p. 490). Dumortier (p. 234) wholeheartedly embraces his assertions.

[686] SC 277,66 62-68 70: Ἀλλὰ κακῶς, φησί, τὰ τῶν πραγμάτων, καὶ τὰ τῆς πολιτείας διάκεινται ... Ἐκείνη τὰ ἄνω κάτω πεποίηκεν, ἐκείνη πάντα τὰ δεινὰ εἰσήγαγεν, ἐκείνη τοὺς πολέμους ἐξώπλισεν, ἐκείνη τὴν ἧτταν ἐνήργησεν. Οὐκ ἄλλοθεν ἡμῖν ὁ τῶν ἀνιαρῶν ἐσμὸς ὑπερεχέθη ...

[687] SC 277,66 65-66.

[688] E.g., *In Heb. hom. 6* (PG 63,59 34): τὸν βασιλεύοντα νῦν; and *In Phil. hom. 15* (PG 62,295 44): ὁ νῦν κρατῶν; but compare *In viduam iuniorem* (SC 138,138 289), where τοῖς νῦν βασιλεύουσι refers to the concurrent emperors Theodosius and Gratian.

[689] See Downey, *Antioch*, 437-438. One of the current talking points is affairs in the army (SC 277,66 48-51). For evidence that a garrison was stationed at Antioch at this period see Liebeschuetz, *Antioch*, 116-117.

[690] For the various pieces of evidence see Petit, *Libanius*, 121; Liebeschuetz, *Antioch*, 129 and 164-165. It is around this period (388) that the citizens of Antioch sent an embassy to Constantinople to complain about the then *consularis Syriae*, Lucianus (Petit, *Libanius*, 187; PLRE I, s.v. Lucianus 6).

[691] For an overview of the chronology and character of these events see Liebeschuetz, *Barbarians and Bishops*, 264-268.

This brings us to the one instance where mention of the threat of war (ἐπανάστασις ἐχθρῶν) has been adduced as grounds for establishing provenance. In *De paen. hom. 4* John evokes the threat as a past event, but one which occurred at least in 386 or later, since at the time he was endowed with the office of preaching.[692] It is not an isolated happening, moreover, but is one of a list of major disasters (famine, plague, hail, drought and large-scale fires),[693] every one of which in the short term has had a marked chastening effect upon the local Christian population. Admittedly the sort of threat posed by hostile forces required to provoke the level of fear suggested must have been immediate and directed at the city concerned, hence the conclusion that the situation referred to is the Hun invasion of Syria in 395/6. But this is not the only occasion on which one of the two cities in question was under direct threat of invasion at a time when Chrysostom was present. The occupation of Constantinople for several months by military forces in 400 must have occasioned considerable fear among its inhabitants.[694]

The other disasters, each of which one must confirm for the city to which one wishes to attribute the homily, further complicate the issue. While drought and famine are a common enough occurrence at Antioch, the documented examples all occur in the period before Chrysostom began preaching.[695] In addition, although one could imagine that hail might have fallen on occasion at Antioch, Libanius in his encomium upon the city is adamant that the local climate in winter is so congenial that this is never the case.[696] As for plague and fire, wide-spread outbreaks of disease are commonly associated with major earthquakes,[697] although it is inter-

---

[692] PG 49,302 15-16.

[693] PG 49,301 60-302 12.

[694] Reading the phrase in this sense will depend upon whether Chrysostom could be supposed to have used the term ἐχθρός of imperial forces engaged in a civil coup. Given, however, that he elsewhere calls Novatians, who are technically orthodox Nicene Christians, "heretics" (*Adv. catharos*, Stav. 6, f.81v a.2-7), it is quite likely that he would have had no qualms about employing the term "enemy" here for rhetorical effect.

[695] For references to a famine at Antioch in 333 and anticipated famine in 354 see Downey, *Antioch*, 365. For the sources which refer to a drought during the winters of 361-362 and 381-382, leading to failure of the local wheat crop and subsequent grain shortages, see ibid., 383-384 and 419-421. In the latter case, the resultant famine persisted into 384.

[696] *Or.* 11.216 (Foerster, I 511-512). Although at this point Libanius is discussing the effectiveness of the stoas in protecting the inhabitants of Antioch against the elements, his claim extends to the mildness of the winter season.

[697] Earthquakes of a significant magnitude are documented for the year 396 (affecting both Antioch and Constantinople) and the years 400 and 403 (Constantinople). Regarding these dates see Grumel, *La Chronologie* (n. 120 above), 477 and Cameron, "Earthquake 400", 351-355. Times of increased population and overcrowding, such as the situation at

esting that these are not mentioned among the disasters,[698] while fires of varying magnitude were doubtless a periodic occurrence in any crowded urban centre.[699] The disasters listed are so common that in all probability an example of one or more of them occurred at some point during Chrysostom's residency at each location. Indeed if one wished to argue that the homily was delivered not at Antioch but at Constantinople, one could cite the violent storm which severely damaged the local crops just prior to harvest in 399 and which presumably led to subsequent difficulties with the food supply (famine),[700] the threat to Constantinople posed by Gainas (hostile menace) and the associated conflagration of the church of the Goths (fires).[701] Thus, although we have a situation where the homilist is referring to events specifically associated with the present location, the events themselves (war and natural disasters) are not uncommon and therefore cannot be shown to be unique to the one city or the other. This does not entirely disqualify war and natural disaster as criteria useful for making a determination, since it is possible that the manner in which they are combined by John might turn out to be a deciding factor. Our patchy knowledge of what occurred throughout this period at Antioch and Constantinople, however, at present prevents us from arriving at even the most tentative of conclusions.

e. *Julianus Sabas*

The intervention of the ascetic Julianus Sabas in the dispute between the pro- and anti-Nicene factions at Antioch, which led him to visit the city briefly in 365, is reliably documented by Theodoret.[702] The latter claims as his source Acacius of Beroea, who had himself been a disciple

---

Antioch alluded to in *De eleemosyna* (CPG 4382), may also have been a contributing factor. For the grounds for attributing that homily to Antioch see pp. 367-369 above.

[698] The dramatic effect of a decent-sized tremor upon the local populace is well attested to by Chrysostom. See *In Acta apost. hom.* 7 (PG 60,66 16-20); *In Acta apost. hom. 41* (PG 60,291 3-10); *De Lazaro concio 6* (CPG 4329) PG 48,1027 1-27; and *De terrae motu* (CPG 4366) PG 50,713-716.

[699] References to domestic fires are scattered throughout the homilies. For a particularly dramatic example see *In Eph. hom. 10* (PG 62,77 19-57).

[700] *Contra ludos et theatra* (CPG 4441.7) PG 56,265 3-7. It is noteworthy that the violence of the storm provokes an immediate and wide-spread liturgical response (PG 56,265 7-12).

[701] See A. M. Schneider, "Brände in Konstantinopel", *Byzantinische Zeitschrift* 41 (1941) 382. In *De capto Eutropio* (CPG 4528), when describing the relevant events (PG 52,399 9-12), John claims that the city itself was aflame.

[702] HR 2.18-20 (SC 234,237-241).

of the renowned ascetic.[703] That this Julianus was known at Antioch is therefore reasonably certain. With regard to the mention of an ascetic named Julianus in *In Eph. hom. 21*, however, it is not the existence of a link between Julianus Sabas and Antioch which is at issue, but questions relating to the degree of detail in which the event and person are described and the precise relationship between event and location or audience. Is the detail provided by the homilist sufficient to identify positively the Julianus mentioned and, even if the answer to that question is yes, the person in question indeed being Julianus Sabas, is the link drawn between event and audience of such clarity that all possibilities, other than that Chrysostom is preaching before an audience situated at Antioch, can be excluded?

Once again it is important to take note of the context in which the exemplum occurs. Chrysostom's main interest in this sermon is to argue that the reading of the Scriptures by the young is an activity that should not be restricted to those who pursue monastic practices, but should also be enjoined upon the laity. This discipline, he claims, equips the young with an ability to reason and argue more powerful than an education in secular philosophy and rhetoric. And yet, he says, one cannot find a single lay person with this skill.[704] It is at this point that he contrasts the situation with the one which pertains among monastics. One could, he says, mention any number of monks skilled in this manner, but he will name just one as an example. That particular ascetic is known and has been heard of by the audience. Some, presumably not a large sector of the audience, have even seen him in the flesh.[705] His name is Julian, he came from a rural background, his parents were humble and he himself was of similar status.[706] He lacked formal education[707] and led an extra-urban existence, since his visits to urban communities were infrequent.[708] Nonetheless his fame is wide-spread at the present point in time.[709] From what little we know of Julianus Sabas such detail fits the circumstances

---

[703] On this point see Festugière, *Antioche païenne et chrétienne*, 247. According to Theod., HR 2.16 (SC 234,230), Acacius was a resident of Antioch at the time of these events.

[704] PG 62,151 62-153 13.

[705] PG 62,153 18-19: Ἴστε δήπου, καὶ ἀκηκόατε, οἱ δὲ καὶ ἐθεωρήσατε τὸν ἄνδρα, ὃν μέλλω νῦν ἐρεῖν·

[706] PG 62,153 19-21: Ἰουλιανὸν λέγω τὸν θαυμάσιον. Οὗτος ἦν ἀνὴρ ἄγροικος, ταπεινὸς καὶ ἐκ ταπεινῶν·

[707] PG 62,153 21: οὐδὲ ὅλως τῆς ἔξωθεν παιδείας ἔμπειρος...

[708] PG 62,153 22-23: Τούτου εἰς τὰς πόλεις ἐμβάλλοντος (σπανιάκις δὲ τοῦτο ἐγίνετο)...

[709] PG 62,153 26-27: οὐχὶ πάντων βασιλέων καὶ τὸ ὄνομα αὐτοῦ λαμπρότερον ᾄδεται ἔτι καὶ νῦν; From this it can perhaps be inferred that Julianus is no longer alive.

of his life.[710] As a note of warning, however, the detail is also common to any number of ascetics, particularly those of fourth-century Syria. Many led an extra-urban existence, were of rural background, poorly educated and yet exerted some degree of influence.[711] In the last quarter of the fourth century the fame of such Syrian and Mesopotamian ascetics was already wide-spread,[712] and doubtless there was more than one Julian among them. Even so, given the fact that Julianus Sabas was involved, if briefly, in the affairs of the church at Antioch, and given that a number of the monastic communities in the district governed by Antioch were founded by or associated with that monk's disciples,[713] there is a reasonable probability that it is this particular Julianus whom Chrysostom has in mind.

Even if this is the case, and bearing in mind that this identification cannot be proven conclusively, there is no certainty that John is describing the ascetic to an audience at Antioch. The type and degree of knowledge which he expects of the audience is in this instance crucial. Elsewhere, when referring to a person or event directly associated with the city in the past, Chrysostom commonly speaks of "our city", "your city", "your forebears"[714] or employs phrases such as "which you yourselves experienced", "you are witnesses", or "for you know and remember".[715] It is therefore somewhat surprising in this instance that he does not say "For you know and remember the man ... when he visited our city", but "You know and have heard of and some have even seen the

---

[710] Theodoret in fact tells us nothing of his background, education or verbal skills, concentrating instead on his miracles and ascetic habits. He states that through his reputation for piety he attracted more than a few followers. See Theod., HR 13 (SC 234,222 1-2). Aside from the above-mentioned visit to Antioch, Theodoret characterises Julianus as spending most of his time in various wilderness locations.

[711] See Brown, "Rise and function", 82-84, 87.

[712] See A. Vööbus, *History of Asceticism in the Syrian Orient* II (CSCO 197) Louvain 1960, 123. He describes as trustworthy the comment in the life of Alexander Akoimetos that it was at Constantinople that Alexander heard about the monks of Syria.

[713] P. Canivet-A. Leroy-Molinghen, *Théodoret de Cyr. Histoire des moines de Syrie* I (SC 234) Paris 1977, 32-33.

[714] See pp. 368f above.

[715] See, e.g., *De s. Meletio* (CPG 4345): ὃ δὴ καὶ ὑμεῖς ἐπάσχετε. Καθήμενοι γὰρ ἐνταῦθα καὶ τῇ πόλει περιγραφόμενοι... (PG 50,517 38-40), referring to the period of Meletius' exile from Antioch in Armenia (361-362); *Laus Diodori* (CPG 4406): Καὶ τούτου μάρτυρες ὑμεῖς, πῶς τὸν ἅπαντα χρόνον... (PG 52,764 21-22), referring to the period of Diodore's residency at Antioch (prior to 372); and *De s. Babyla* (CPG 4347): Ἴστε γὰρ δήπου καὶ μέμνησθε, πῶς κενὴ μὲν ἦν ὠνίων ἡ ἀγορά... (SC 362,302 22-23) and Ἴστε γὰρ δήπου, καὶ μέμνησθε, ὅτι μὲν θέρους τῆς ἀκτῖνος μέσης κατεχούσης τὸν οὐρανόν... (SC 362,312 21-22), the first of which recalls the famine and drought at Antioch under Julian (361-362), the second the construction of the church of St Babylas at Antioch prior to 381.

man" and "when he would betake himself to the cities...".[716] This peculiarity is of particular interest since Theodoret, on the report of Acacius, states that the visit of Julianus Sabas to Antioch was a widely observed affair.[717] Even allowing for exaggeration on the part of Theodoret and generalisation in this instance on the part of the homilist, one would at least have expected Chrysostom to call upon his audience to recollect Julianus had he been speaking before a congregation at Antioch. Instead he expects the majority of his audience to be familiar with the individual not personally but from hearsay, while only a minority appears to have seen him in person. If it really is Julianus Sabas who is under discussion, this would accord better with the situation at Constantinople, especially since it is known that Acacius of Beroea, an eyewitness to the visit and a close associate of the monk,[718] was resident at Constantinople for periods throughout Chrysostom's episcopacy and is likely on occasion to have been among the bishop's audience.[719] Among the large number of bishops who came and went at Constantinople throughout this period,[720] there were doubtless others who had encountered the renowned ascetic.

This is all speculative, however. On the evidence supplied, it can at best be argued that it is probable that the Julianus mentioned is Julianus Sabas and that, if this solution is adopted, it is likely that the homily was not preached at Antioch. At worst, it could be argued that the ascetic is a Julianus entirely unknown to us and who never had any direct association with the city of Antioch. Under that condition, the manner in which the person is introduced to the audience would be appropriate at either location and the mention of Julianus would therefore be of little use to us in establishing the provenance of this homily.

---

[716] This point has been noted by Costanza, "Waar predikte Chrysostomus?", 154.

[717] HR 2.18 (SC 234,236 2-3): πάντες δὲ πανταχόθεν συνέθεον, ἰδεῖν τε ποθοῦντες τὸν τοῦ θεοῦ ἄνθρωπον...; 238 9-10: Ἀκακίου δὲ τοῦ μεγάλου τὸ μὲν πλῆθος τῶν συνειλεγμένων ὁρῶντος...

[718] See n. 703 above.

[719] Baur, *Chrysostom and His Time* , II 187, points out that Acacius was invited to Constantinople for the consecration of Chrysostom in 398 and again sought hospitality at the episcopal palace c.402. Liebeschuetz, "The Fall", 12, states that at this time Acacius seems to have resided almost permanently at Constantinople.

[720] Palladius, *Dial.* 13 (SC 341,274 150-156), states that twenty-two bishops had gathered in the capital by the early part of the thirteenth year of indiction (Sept. 399-Sept. 400). There were some forty bishops available to support Chrysostom and a further thirty-six present in support of Theophilus at the time of the Synod of the Oak (autumn 403). See Palladius, *Dial.* 8 (SC 341,172 176-180).

f. *Plot against Valens of 372 AD*

The reference to the Antiochene-based plot against Valens in *In Acta apost. hom.* 38 and the perceived allusion to that event in *hom. 41* of the same series present us with some difficulties. Cameron's argument is that in the first of the two sermons the event is described as a distant reminiscence, indicating that Chrysostom is no longer at the site at which the incident took place.[721] This proposition is directed by an *a priori* assumption of Constantinopolitan provenance based upon the requirement of homogeneity, however, and can be countered by the example of *In Col. hom.* 7. There the riots of 387 are described in an equally remote way,[722] even though it is patent that the discussion is taking place at Antioch.[723] If one accepts that the comments in that homily are made after the death of the emperor involved,[724] that is, after January 395, then the period which has elapsed since the riots is at most some eight to ten years. Based on this calculation, and bearing in mind that, if *In Col. hom.* 7 was not preached after the death of Theodosius, the time lapse would be even shorter, it would be reasonable for Chrysostom to describe events which occurred in 372 in a remote manner at any point after his ordination as presbyter.

Furthermore, there is the small matter of the expression "our city".[725] As observed in discussion of comments linking the city and apostolic times (3.b) and also pointed out in the previous section (9.e), in a number of cases where Chrysostom adopts this expression he intends it to be taken literally and is speaking in the city in which the event occurred. There is no question that in *In Acta apost. hom.* 38 he is talking about Antioch, since he says that he was a young man at the time[726] and that, upon visiting a certain martyrium, he made his way back through the gardens which bordered the river.[727] As pointed out, the common view that John is in this instance using the first-person plural rhetorically, that is, that he intends the audience to understand that he is talking not about their own city but the city of his birth, is strongly influenced by the as-

---

[721] Cameron, "Earthquake 400", 345.

[722] PG 62,347 57-58: Προσέκρουσέ ποτε τῷ κρατοῦντι ἡ πόλις ἡ ἡμετέρα... Cf. *In Acta apost. hom.* 38: Ἐκινήθη ποτε τυράννων ὑποψία ἐν τῇ πόλει τῇ ἡμετέρᾳ... (PG 60,274 49-50).

[723] See pp. 443-445 above.

[724] This suggestion is put forward by us in Allen-Mayer, "A New Approach", 35.

[725] See n. 722.

[726] PG 60,274 50: ... τότε δὲ ἔτι μειράκιον ἤμην.

[727] PG 60,274 56-58: τότε ἐγὼ εἰς μαρτύριον ἀπιέναι βουλόμενος, ἐπανήειν διὰ τῶν κήπων παρὰ ποταμόν... The river plays a major role in the story which unfolds. For the significance of this point see pp. 374-376 above.

sumption that the series on Acts is homogeneous. That is, since *hom. 9* was with certainty delivered at Constantinople, it has been required that every other piece of evidence conform to that location. Without the requirement of homogeneity, indeed had this sermon not been transmitted as part of a series, scholars are as likely to have read "our city" in its literal sense, arguing that the story is more pointed and effective if recounted to an audience at Antioch. This is not to say that the homily necessarily originated at that location, since this one phrase is the only suggestion that there might be any common link between the homilist, the audience and the incident in question. However, it is sufficient to point out that on the basis of the evidence presented there is no reason why Chrysostom should of necessity have been speaking from Constantinople. Rather, in the manner in which we find them recounted in *hom. 38*, the homilist's personal experiences at the time of the plot against Valens could have been related with facility at either location.

As for Seeck's identification of the Theodorus of *In Acta apost. hom. 41* with the ring-leader in the plot against Valens, we find here a timely warning against rushing in to match names against known historical figures. The information provided by Chrysostom in this instance is exceedingly sparse, the event apparently being so familiar to the audience that there is no need to elaborate. This is unfortunate from our point of view, but once again highlights the difficulties for the modern scholar posed by the body of knowledge tacitly shared by homilist and audience. The only detail supplied is that the subject of the event was a certain Theodorus, that the incident occurred in the previous year and that at the time its repercussions were widely felt and shocked the majority into sobriety.[728] Despite Seeck's conviction that Chrysostom could have been making these remarks at a time when he was lector, it is to the period after his ordination as presbyter that one must look, if one accepts that the homily in question was preached and not merely written.[729] On chronological grounds this rules out the Theodorus involved in the plot against Valens as a candidate.

---

[728] PG 60,291 37-40: Τὰ κατὰ Θεόδωρον ἐκεῖνον γεγενημένα πέρυσι, τίνα οὐκ ἐξέπληξε; Καὶ ὅμως οὐδὲν πλέον γέγονεν, ἀλλὰ πρὸς καιρὸν γενόμενοι εὐλαβεῖς, πάλιν ἐπανῆλθον ὅθεν γεγόνασιν εὐλαβεῖς.

[729] Irrespective of style, a written commentary implies a work which is intended to be less of the moment and more general, such that it can appeal to a range of readers or audiences and be read on more than a single occasion. If one accepts this argument, then it is unlikely that in such a work one would find an appeal to events of the previous year, as twice occurs in the course of this homily. This tends to suggest that *hom. 41* was in the first instance preached before an audience. For the point that the office of preaching was at the time restricted to presbyters and bishops see n. 51 above.

Candidates for the period from 386 to early 404, on the other hand, are thin on the ground. Indeed, despite the implication that what occurred to Theodorus was of considerable moment to those cognisant of the event, the external sources are, in so far as one can tell, silent on the matter.[730] In any case, even if it were possible to identify positively the individual and event in question, John tells us no more than that the event occurred in the previous year and that it shocked those aware of it. He does not say that it occurred in the city in which he and his audience are situated,[731] nor does he intimate that the audience were witnesses to the event. It is possible, as we have argued elsewhere, that administrative officials formerly of influence in the one city and later elevated to the other maintained influence at their former place of residence through building programmes or legislation, such that, when sudden misfortune befell them, it is likely that this had profound repercussions at both locations.[732] The other events described in the homily are equally unhelpful. An earthquake, said to have occurred in the previous year, is recalled to the audience's memory as having shaken the entire city.[733] In the last quarter of the fourth century, however, tremors were a not uncommon occurrence at both locations.[734] The events surrounding St Babylas, Jerusalem and the destruction of the temples, items certainly known to an audience at Antioch but possibly also familiar to a congregation at Constantinople,[735] are said simply to have occurred "in our time".[736] Once

---

[730] Among the twenty or so persons of this name listed in PLRE I, only one, Theodorus 17 (p. 899), presents as a possible candidate. Known to Libanius at Antioch, he was influential at court in Constantinople from 388 to 390 and then mysteriously lost influence in 390/1. Information regarding the cause and nature of that reversal is unfortunately unavailable. See, however, Mayer, "Pargoire's Sequence", 293, where the possibility that the event took place in 400 and was subsequently overshadowed by Gainas' activities is raised.

[731] An earthquake which occurred in the previous year, the first of several events recalled by Chrysostom, is introduced under the topic of "what has happened to us" (PG 60,291 3-4). It is uncertain, however, whether this extends to the Theodorus episode, particularly since less recent events which did not occur locally (τὰ κατὰ τὰ Ἱεροσόλυμα, PG 60,291 30) are described in between.

[732] Allen-Mayer, "A New Approach", 33.

[733] PG 60,291 4-8.

[734] It appears that at least three earthquakes of note occurred during Chrysostom's career as a preacher, one at Antioch (396) and two at Constantinople (400, 403). See n. 697 above. This does not account for tremors of a lesser severity, such as that recalled in De statuis hom. 2 (PG 49,35 38-40), which may have been alarming at the time but were quickly forgotten. There is, moreover, always the possibility that Chrysostom is referring here not to a literal but a metaphoric shaking of the city, as is the case in Quod frequenter conveniendum sit (CPG 4441.3). See further pp. 447f above.

[735] Cf. Exp. in ps. 110 (PG 55,285 34-55), where it is implied that these events are widely known. For further discussion see pp. 362f and 419 above.

again, although Chrysostom refers to a number of specific events, the lack of an unambiguous connection between event and audience in the case of those events which are specific in a geographic rather than chronological sense, leads to an outcome which is uncertain.

g. *Events of 361-362 AD*

With regard to the various happenings in and around Antioch at the time of the emperor Julian, the manner in which these are mentioned in *De laudibus s. Pauli hom. 4* (CPG 4344) provides us with a rare instance where the clarity with which the events are described and the explicit nature of the connection between one of these events and the present location combine to produce a provenance which can be considered certain. Although neither emperor, locale nor martyr is identified, the affair of the lightning strike on the temple of Apollo is described in some detail,[737] while the springs that dried up at the time are said to be local.[738] This is in marked contrast to *Exp. in ps. 110*, where a majority of the same occurrences are presented without the crucial appropriating link,[739] with explicit identification of Julian, Babylas and Daphne[740] and in a context which suggests that the events are widely known beyond their original geographic locus.[741] A comparable list, similarly described, occurs in *In Matt. hom. 4*.[742] While all three passages refer in essence to the same events, the majority of which are known to have occurred at Antioch, in the latter two cases it is not sufficient to draw an analogy from the first and to argue that the two originate at Antioch because the subject matter is germane or familiar to the inhabitants of that location. The more offhand and less detailed mode of description could as easily be attributed

---

[736] PG 60,291 29-31.

[737] SC 300,192 5-12. That the audience knows that the emperor in question is Julian, that the location is Daphne and that the martyr is Babylas is assumed throughout.

[738] SC 300,192 16: Πάλιν αἱ πηγαὶ αἱ παρ' ἡμῖν...

[739] See PG 55,285 35-55. For further discussion see p. 419 above.

[740] PG 55,285 41-45: τοῦ ἁγίου μάρτυρος Βαβύλα τοῦ ἐν Δάφνῃ ... αὐτοῦ τοῦ Ἰουλιανοῦ...

[741] PG 55,285 34-39: Ἀλλὰ τέως τὰ καθολικά, καὶ ἅπασι δῆλα καὶ γνώριμα, ἃ καθ' ἑκάστην γίνεται γενεάν, ἴδωμεν. Πόσα ἐπὶ Ἰουλιανοῦ ... Εἰ δὲ βούλεσθε καὶ τὰ ἐπὶ τῆς γενεᾶς συμβάντα τῆς ἡμετέρας... This reading is likely, since the details of most of the events listed were readily available in the tract *De s. Babyla contra Iulianum et gentiles* (CPG 4348). See SC 362,216-218 (sec. 92-93).

[742] See PG 57,41 1-13. The allusion to events associated with St Babylas, the proposed rebuilding of the temple at Jerusalem and the destruction of pagan temples in *In Acta apost. hom. 41* (PG 60,291 29-32) constitutes this same list in an even more abbreviated form.

to Chrysostom's own familiarity with the material, causing it to be exploited as something of a topos, as to a special knowledge of the events on the part of the audience.

Before closing discussion of the various persons and events that have been adduced, an allusion to the conflagration of pagan temples in the latter part of *In II Tim. hom. 8* deserves attention.[743] Despite Quasten's conviction that John here alludes to the burning of the temple of Apollo at Daphne,[744] the detail supplied does not match what is known of that event. In both the tract *De s. Babyla contra Iulianum et gentiles* (CPG 4348) and the encomium upon the martyr (CPG 4347) Chrysostom is careful to state that only the temple of Apollo was affected by the lightning strike and that the damage which occurred was isolated.[745] The occasion alluded to in the above homily involves the destruction by fire of more than one pagan temple or shrine, with a concomitant loss of life.[746] The point which John makes here is that the same pagan priests to whom his parishioners are resorting for advice as to the whereabouts of lost animals were unable to predict an event of such devastating consequence to themselves.[747] This suggests that the event in question is local and, if identified, might enable us to pinpoint the location of the homily.[748]

Summary of 9.a-g

At the conclusion of 9.a-b we outlined three areas in which difficulty was seen to occur and asked whether these applied equally to the rest of the adduced types of evidence. As it turns out, they are useful in assessing types 9.e-g, where a specific and geographically localised event or series of events and/or persons is involved. They are less useful in the case of 9.c-d, where the persons and events tend to be localised not geographically but chronologically and where evidence of place must generally be inferred. Even so, several rules of thumb for approaching the full

---

[743] PG 62,648 65-649 2: ἀλλὰ χρημάτων μὲν ἕνεκεν οὐδὲ εἰπεῖν ἐδύναντο, ὅταν οἱ ναοὶ αὐτῶν οἱ εἰδωλικοὶ ἐπίμπραντο, καὶ πολλοὶ συναπώλλυντο.

[744] See Chapter One, p. 225.

[745] See SC 362,250 (sec. 114) and 308 (sec. 8-9).

[746] This may help elucidate the cryptic "destruction of the temples", mentioned by John in *In Acta apost. hom. 41* (PG 60,291 29-31).

[747] See PG 62,648 44-650 20.

[748] Downey, *Antioch*, 396, mentions that during the brief period of Jovian's principate (late 363) a temple to the deified Trajan at Antioch was the target of arson. Given the general dislike of his predecessor Julian and of that emperor's promotion of pagan practices at Antioch, it may be that this was not an isolated event.

range of such data can be established. These principles should also hold true for any evidence pertaining to famous persons and events as yet unrecognised.

Two main axiomata apply, from which all subsequent rules governing the interpretation of individual exempla derive.

1. It does not necessarily follow that, because an event occurred at a particular place, mention of that event or persons associated with it can only have been made to persons situated at that same location. A healthy scepticism regarding the nature of the relationship between event/person and audience should be maintained at all times.
2. Two criteria must be satisfied in order for an attribution of provenance made on the basis of such evidence to be certain.

   i) The event/person must be accurately identified.
   ii) There must be a direct and clearly defined link between event/person and the present location or audience.

If only one of these conditions is met, then the attribution made on the basis of the evidence is open to question.

From these, the following refinements to the rules proposed at the conclusion of 9.a-b can be made. Regarding 2.i (accurate identification of the event/person):

a. An identification can be made with confidence only if the information provided by Chrysostom is specific and encompasses detail which is unique, whether in isolation or in combination (i.e., administrative title, gender, personal name, place name, other such information).
b. If the information provided is specific, but the detail supplied is not unique but could apply to a number of known situations, the context may permit the elimination of certain of the possibilities, enabling identification. A result derived in this way can at best be considered probable. If the context does not assist in narrowing the field of candidates, the result must remain uncertain.
c. If the information provided does not necessarily refer to a specific instance or individual, it is irresponsible to attempt an identification. Rather, the information should be withdrawn from the repertoire of material used to establish provenance and discarded.

With regard to the requirement specified in 2.ii (the existence of a nexus between person/event and present location or audience):

a. If the homilist states that a majority of the audience were witnesses, that the audience is personally affected by the event, that it occurred in "our city" and impinged upon the lives of the audience, or that persons or locations that played a role in the event are local, then a se-

cure link can be considered to exist. If the event is said to have occurred in "our city" and to have affected the homilist but indication
that it also affected the audience is lacking, a direct link is possible
but the conclusion regarding it should at this point be treated as uncertain.
b. Arguments from familiarity are subjective and should be dismissed.

Summary

The following tables provide an overview of the current status quaestionis with regard to the criteria and the provenance derived from them,
in light of the results obtained in Chapter Three. In Table 16 the various
arguments collected under each criterion are separated out into three
categories — those that can be considered valid; those that may eventually prove valid or invalid, but which at present require further investigation; and those which are patently invalid.

Table 16. The status of the criteria

No.	Description	VALID	UNCERTAIN	INVALID
1	Manuscript titles	(Types 1-3) If supported by internal evidence	(Types 1-3) Under all other circumstances	Type 4
2.a	Personal status (direct statement)	If terms ἐπίσκοπος or πρεσβύτερος clearly associated with self	Mention of bishops or presbyters where connection to self alluded to (unless confirmed by other evidence)	Failure to mention personal status during discussion of episcopal office, impersonal discussion thereof
2.b	Occupation of θρόνος	Indication that another occupies this seat	Mention that he himself occupies θρόνος (unless supported by other data)	
2.c	Relationship with audience			i. Metaphoric ii. Prostasia iii. Responsibility iv. Episcopal tone
2.d.i	"Episcopal" metaphors (applied to another)	If qualified by the adjective κοινός + status of the individual supported by context	Metaphors not qualified by κοινός (unless clarified by context or confirmed by other data)	Argument ex silentio
2.d.ii-iii	Proedroi, "Common fathers"		Both	

2.e	Order of preaching		• Preaching before or after another person (the first may, however, assist in interpreting other evidence, e.g., 2.d.i) • Homilist substituted for by *locum tenens* of equal status (unless supported by other data)	
2.f	Duties of office			i. Workload ii. Style iii. Transmission history
3.a	Name of city	If firmly associated with present location		
3.b	City = linked to apostolic times	If firmly associated with present location	If no firm association with present location	
3.c.i	Imperial residence	If emperor or empress firmly associated with present location, or clear that emperor and court reside in another city		• Argument *ex silentio* • Inappropriateness of a comparison with palace to city of imperial residence
3.c.ii	Imperial exempla			All
3.d.i	Coastal v. non-coastal topography	If firmly associated with present location	Use of the verb διαπεράω	Exemplum starting: "Don't you see the sea?"
3.d.ii	Suburban environs	Daphne, if clearly assoc. with present location	Daphne, if not clearly linked to present location	
3.e.i	Christian topography — churches		Reference to churches, unless clearly identifiable on basis of internal evidence and unique to location.	
3.e.ii	Martyr burials	Local burial of saint or martyr where individ. clearly identifiable and directly involved in history of city	City does or does not contain urban burial sites	• Translation of martyr/saint's remains • Extra-urban sites
3.f.i	Characteristic features of the city		Suburbs/suburban estates	Size, agora, heat, size of church building
3.f.ii	Negative features	That the location is not x and must therefore be y, if evidence for x clear	Arguments based solely on ἐνταῦθα ... ἐκεῖ	

3.g	Status	"Head of the cities in the east", if firmly assoc. with present location	"Imperial"	• Metropolitan status • Head-body metaphor • Being held up as example to the world
3.h.i	Administration (assoc. with emperor)	*Eparch*, if clearly associated with hippodrome and both associated with present location	Mention of *hyparchs*, *toparchs*, *eparchs* or similar officials, if not clearly associated with present location	Exempla not containing unique information and with no connection to present location
3.h.ii	Administration (local)		If *archon* real and attached to present location, may suggest Antioch (requires assistance of other data)	Exempla
3.h.iii	Military		Direct reference	Exempla
4.a-b	Demography (Language, Jewish population)		•Reference to Syriac • Non-Greek-speaking rural population • Prominence of Jewish sector	
4.c	Christian community		•Judaizing tendencies amongst local Christians • Schism	• Size thereof • Assiduousness and attentiveness • Ref. to Judaizing with no indication that local • Preaching against Anomoeans • Reference to Apollinaris as heretic
5.a	Geographic focus	Here = Syria, where connection clearly drawn	*Polis* close to *eremos*	• Lists of exotic locations • Factual references to Syria or Syriac
5.b	Geographic proximity	If present location distinct and distant from Syria or Thrace	If proximate region/s associated with present location	• Factual information • Information supplied without clear reference to present location
5.c	Native vegetation		Roses and lilies/violets	
6	Monks	If mountains/caves real and monks/ascetics local	"those seated on mountains", "those situated in the *eremos*"	• Frequent/infrequent reference to monks • Urban v. extra-urban • Positive v. negative ref.
7	Olympic Games	If clearly held at the present location or audience spectators	• If relationship between games and place or audience not clear • General exempla	

8	Liturgy	Fixed liturgical calendar, if festival directly assoc. with the city and unique to it	Fixed liturgical calendar, under all other conditions	Frequency of synaxes or preaching
9.a	Eutropius	If clearly identifiable and clearly associated with present location	If refers to specific event involving single individual, but no specific or unique detail supplied	If comments general and do not refer to a specific incident
9.b	Riots of 387	If clearly identifiable and clearly associated with present location	If not clearly identifiable or not clearly associated with present location	
9.c	Current emperor		Unless specific and unique detail supplied	
9.d	War		Unless specific and unique detail supplied	
9.e	Julianus Sabas		Unless clearly identifiable and clear understanding of relationship to present location	
9.f	Plot against Valens		If clearly identifiable but relationship to present location uncertain	If misidentified
9.g	Events of 361-362	If clearly identifiable and clearly associated with present location	If events not clearly identifiable, but situation described as local	If identifiable, but presented as a list said to have occurred in "our time"

In Table 17 every homily to which a criterion for provenance has been applied in the literature is listed,[749] along with an indication of the specific criteria applied and the provenance obtained on that basis. A further two columns update the information according to the results obtained in the above investigation, restricting this to homilies whose provenance is directly addressed by us in the course of Chapter Three and the three articles on the series on Colossians, Philippians and Hebrews previously published.[750] In this manner, the identity of the homilies yet to be investigated can be seen at a glance, as also the instances

---

[749] *In illud: Vidi dom. hom. 4* (CPG 4417) is excluded because of the doubt raised concerning its authenticity. See the Introduction, pp. 26f.

[750] Allen-Mayer, "A New Approach"; eaed., "A Re-examination"; and eaed., "Hebrews: The Last Series?".

where the current attribution differs from that which had been previously obtained.

It should be noted that Table 17 covers only those homilies which have been assigned a provenance on the basis of their own title or internal evidence. Although the number of homilies which have not been included may appear surprising at first view, the exclusion of a homily is an indication that it has been assigned provenance not on the basis of any internal evidence but on chronological grounds or by virtue of its place within a particular sequence or series. In the same manner, the criteria which apply to a series as a whole (i.e., those included under 2.f — style, workload and transmission) are not included. In the third and fifth columns of the table the numbers assigned to the criteria in Chapter Two are used for ease of reference. For a summary of these see Table 15. In the fourth column of the table brackets are used to indicate the consensus in cases where the opinion offered differs substantially from it. The shaded areas in the last two columns indicate instances where the provenance of the homily has not been assessed substantially in the present chapter and a reassessment has yet to be undertaken.

Table 17. The status of the homilies individually assigned provenance

CPG no.	Homily	Criteria (former)	Place (former)	Criteria (current)	Place (current)
4318	*De incompr. dei natura hom. 1*	2.d.i	A	2.d.i	A
4319	*De beato Philogonio*	2.d.i,e	A	2.d.i,e	A
4327	*Adv. Iudaeos or. 4*	1	A		
"	*Adv. Iudaeos or. 6*	2.d.i	A	9.b	A
4328	*In kalendas*	2.d.i	A	2.d.i	A
4332	*De diabolo tentatore hom. 2*	2.d.i	A		
4333	*De paenitentia hom. 1*	2.f.i	A		
"	*De paenitentia hom. 3*	3.f.i, 4.c.i, 8.b	A		
"	*De paenitentia hom. 4*	9.d	A		—
"	*De paenitentia hom. 5*	2.d.i,e, 6	A	2.d.i,e	A*
4334	*In diem natalem*	2.d.i,e	A	2.d.i,e	A*
4342	*In ascensionem*	1, 2.d.i	A	2.d.i	A*
4343	*De s. pentecoste hom. 1*	2.d.i	A	2.d.i	A
4344	*De laudibus s. Pauli hom. 4*	9.g	A	9.g	A
4350	*De s. Pelagia*	3.e.ii	A		
4354	*De Macabeis hom. 1*	3.e.ii	A		
"	*De Macabeis hom. 2*	2.d.i,e	A	2.d.i,e	A*
4357	*De ss. martyribus*	2.d.i	A	2.d.i	A
4359	*Hom. in martyres*	3.e.ii,h.ii	A	3.e.ii,h.ii	A[+]
4360	*In s. Iulianum martyrem*	3.d.ii,e.ii	A	3.d.ii	A
4361	*In s. Barlaam*	3.e.ii, 5.b	A	8.a	A*
4362	*De s. Droside martyre*	2.d.i	A	2.d.i	A*
4363	*In martyres Aegyptios*	3.e.ii, 5.b	CP,A		—

4364	*De s. Phoca*	3.c.i	CP	3.c.i,d.i	CP
4365	*De ss. martyribus*	2.f.i	A?		
4366	*De terrae motu*	2.d.i, 3.e.ii	CP,A		
4371	*In princ. Act. hom. 2*	1, 2.d.i, 3.b.i,b.iv	A	2.d.i, 3.b.i,b.iv	A
4372	*De mutatione nom. hom. 1*	2.d.ii,e	A		
"	*De mutatione nom. hom. 2*	2.d.ii	A		
4375	*In illud: Si esurierit inimicus*	3.c.ii,e.i,f.i, 4.b	CP,A		
4376	*In illud: Sal. Pr. et Aqu. hom. 2*	2.d.iii	A		—
4379	*Quales ducendae sint uxores*	2.c.i,e	CP		
4380	*In d. Pauli: Nolo vos ignorare*	2.d.ii, 3.e.ii, 8.a	A	8.a	A*
4382	*De eleemosyna*	3.b.ii,e.i	A	3.b.ii	A
4383	*In illud: Hab. eundem spir. hom. 1*	6	A		
4388	*De futurae vitae deliciis*	3.c.i,e.ii	A		
4391	*In illud: In faciem ei restiti*	1, 2.d.i, 3.b.iii	A	2.d.i, 3.b.iii	A
4393	*Cum Saturninus et Aurelianus*	1	CP		
4408	*In s. pascha*	5.c	A		—
4409	*Hom. 4 in Genesim*	4.a.i	A		—
"	*Hom. 12 in Genesim*	4.c.ii	A	4.c.ii	A⁺
4410	*Sermo 1 in Genesim*	2.d.i	A	2.d.i	A
"	*Sermo 8 in Genesim*	2.d.i	A	2.b,d.i	A
"	*Sermo 9 in Genesim*	4.a.i	A		—
4411	*De Anna sermo 1*	2.d.i	A		
4413	*Exp. in psalmum 6*	6	A		
"	*Exp. in psalmum 110*	5.a.ii, 9.g	A		—
4414	*In illud: Ne timueritis hom. 1*	2.c.i, 9.a	CP		
"	*In illud: Ne timueritis hom. 2*	1, 2.e	CP		
4415	*In psalmum 145*	6	A		
4417	*In illud: Vidi dom. hom. 2*	2.d.i,e	A	2.d.i,e	A*
"	*In illud: Vidi dom. hom. 3*	2.d.i,e	A	2.d.i,e	A*
"	*In illud: Vidi dom. hom. 5*	3.d.i	CP? (A)		—
"	*In illud: Vidi dom. hom. 6*	2.d.i	A		
4418	*In illud Isaiae: Ego dominus deus*	1, 2.e	CP		
4420	*De proph. obscuritate hom. 2*	2.d.i	A		
4424	*In Matt. hom. 7*	3.b.i, 4.a.i	A	3.b.i	A
"	*In Matt. hom. 16*	4.a.i	A		—
"	*In Matt. hom. 17*	2.c.iv	CP (A)		
"	*In Matt. hom. 32*	5.a.ii	A		
"	*In Matt. hom. 40*	2.c.iv	CP (A)		
"	*In Matt. hom. 55*	6	A		
"	*In Matt. hom. 67/68*	5.b, 6	A	5.b	A*
"	*In Matt. hom. 70*	6	A		
"	*In Matt. hom. 72/73*	4.c.iii, 6	A		

"	*In Matt. hom. 82*	2.c.iv	CP (A)		
"	*In Matt. hom. 85*	2.c.iv, 2.d	CP,A		
4425	*In Ioh. hom. 2*	5.a.ii	A	—	
"	*In Ioh. hom. 12*	5.a.ii	A	5.a.ii	A
4426	*In Acta apost hom. 3*	2.c.i, 3.c.i,h.i	CP		
"	*In Acta apost. hom. 8*	2.b,c.i,c.iv, 3.c.i-ii,g	CP		
"	*In Acta apost. hom. 9*	2.a,c.i,c.iv	CP	2.a	CP
"	*In Acta apost. hom. 11*	2.c.iv, 3.c.ii, 4.c.i	CP		
"	*In Acta apost. hom. 18*	2.c.iv	CP		
"	*In Acta apost. hom. 21*	3.c.ii	CP		
"	*In Acta apost. hom. 24*	2.c.iv	CP		
"	*In Acta apost. hom. 27*	2.c.iv	CP		
"	*In Acta apost. hom. 30*	2.c.iv	CP		
"	*In Acta apost. hom. 32*	3.c.ii	CP		
"	*In Acta apost. hom. 38*	3.f.ii, 9.f	CP	—	
"	*In Acta apost. hom. 40*	3.f.ii	CP		
"	*In Acta apost. hom. 41*	3.e.ii, 9.f-g	A (CP)	—	
"	*In Acta apost. hom. 42*	3.f.i	CP	—	
4427	*In Rom. hom. 2*	5.a.ii	A		
"	*In Rom. hom. 8*	2.c.i, 2.d.i	CP,A		
"	*In Rom. hom. 13*	5.a.i	A	—	
"	*In Rom. hom. 23*	3.h.ii	A	—	
"	*In Rom. hom. 24*	3.c.ii	A		
"	*In Rom. hom. 25*	6	A		
"	*In Rom. hom. 26*	5.a.ii, 6	A		
"	*In Rom. hom. 29*	2.c.i, 5.b	CP,A		
"	*In Rom. hom. 30*	3.b.v, 5.a.i	A	—	
4428	*In I Cor. hom. 21*	3.a,b.i	A	3.a,b.i	A
"	*In I Cor. hom. 36*	2.d.i	A		
4429	*In II Cor. hom. 3*	5.a.ii	A		
"	*In II Cor. hom. 8*	5.a.i	A		
"	*In II Cor. hom. 9*	3.c.ii,h.ii-iii	A	—	
"	*In II Cor. hom. 10*	3.c.ii	A		
"	*In II Cor. hom. 12*	3.c.ii	A		
"	*In II Cor. hom. 14*	2.a	A		
"	*In II Cor. hom. 15*	2.a	A	—	
"	*In II Cor. hom. 18*	2.a	A		
"	*In II Cor. hom. 26*	3.a, 3.f.ii	CP,A	—	
4431	*In Eph. hom. 4*	3.c.ii	A		
"	*In Eph. hom. 6*	6	A		
"	*In Eph. hom. 9*	3.c.ii,e.ii, 9.g	A,CP		
"	*In Eph. hom. 10*	4.c.iii	A,CP		
"	*In Eph. hom. 11*	2.c.ii, 4.c.iii	A,CP	other	CP*
"	*In Eph. hom. 13*	6	A		
"	*In Eph. hom. 21*	9.e	A,CP	—	
4432	*In Phil hom. 1*	6	A? (CP)	—	
"	*In Phil. hom. 6*	3.c.ii,h.i, 4.c.iii	CP	—	
"	*In Phil. hom. 9*	2.c.i-ii,c.iv	CP	—	
"	*In Phil. hom. 15*	3.c.ii, 9.c	A,CP	—	
4433	*In Col. hom. 2*	3.c.ii	CP		
"	*In Col. hom. 3*	2.a-b,c.ii	CP	2.a	CP
"	*In Col. hom. 7*	2.c.iv, 9.a-b	CP	9.b	A

"	*In Col. hom. 8*	2.c.ii,c.iv	CP		
"	*In Col. hom. 9*	3.g	CP		
"	*In Col. hom. 10*	3.c.ii	CP		
4434	*In I Thess. hom. 3*	3.h.iii	CP		—
"	*In I Thess. hom. 5*	2.c.i, 3.c.ii	CP		
"	*In I Thess. hom. 6*	3.c.ii	CP		
"	*In I Thess. hom. 8*	2.c.ii-iv, 3.c.ii, 5.b	CP		
"	*In I Thess. hom. 9*	2.c.ii-iii, 3.c.ii	CP		
"	*In I Thess. hom. 10*	2.c.ii-iv, 3.c.ii	CP		
"	*In I Thess. hom. 11*	2.c.ii-iii, 3.c.ii	CP		
4435	*In II Thess. hom. 3*	2.c.ii, 3.c.ii	CP		
"	*In II Thess. hom. 4*	2.c.i-iv, 3.c.ii	CP		
4436	*In I Tim. hom. 5*	2.a	A		
"	*In I Tim. hom. 8*	2.c.iv	CP (A)		
"	*In I Tim. hom. 10*	2.a	A		
"	*In I Tim. hom. 11*	2.a	A		
"	*In I Tim. hom. 12*	3.c.ii	A		
"	*In I Tim. hom. 14*	3.c.ii,h.ii, 6	A		
"	*In I Tim. hom. 15*	2.a	A		
"	*In I Tim. hom. 17*	5.b	A		—
4437	*In II Tim. hom. 2*	2.a, 3.c.ii, 5.a.ii	A		
"	*In II Tim. hom. 3*	2.a	A		
"	*In II Tim. hom. 4*	2.a,c.iv, 5.a.ii	CP,A		
"	*In II Tim. hom. 8*	5.b, 9.g	A		
"	*In II Tim. hom. 10*	5.b	A		
4438	*In Titum hom. 1*	2.a	A		—
"	*In Titum hom. 2*	2.a	A		
"	*In Titum hom. 3*	3.d.ii, 4.c.ii, 5.b	A		—
"	*In Titum hom. 6*	5.b	A		
4440	*In Heb. hom. 4*	2.c.ii,c.iv	CP	2.a,d.ii, 6	—
"	*In Heb. hom. 6*	3.c.ii	CP		—
"	*In Heb. hom. 7*	6	CP		—
"	*In Heb. hom. 9*	3.c.ii	CP		—
"	*In Heb. hom. 10*	6	CP		—
"	*In Heb. hom. 13*	3.c.ii,h.i	CP	3.h.i	CP*
"	*In Heb. hom. 14*	7	A (CP)	7	A
"	*In Heb. hom. 15*	3.c.ii	CP		—
"	*In Heb. hom. 22*	6	CP		—
"	*In Heb. hom. 23*	2.c.i	CP		—
"	*In Heb. hom. 25*	6	CP		—
"	*In Heb. hom. 27*	3.c.ii	CP		—
"	*In Heb. hom. 28*	3.c.ii	CP		—
"	*In Heb. hom. 30*	2.c.i-ii	CP		—
"	*In Heb. hom. 32*	3.c.ii	CP		—
"	*In Heb. hom. 34*	6	CP		—
4441.9	*Habita postquam presbyter Gothus*	1	CP	1	CP*
4441.10	*In illud: Pater meus usque modo op.*	1	CP	3.h.i	CP*
4441.11	*In illud: Messis quidem multa*	1	CP	3.e.i	CP

4441.12	*In illud: Filius ex se nihil facit*	1, 2.e, 4.c.iii	A,CP		—
4441.13	*De Eleazaro et septem pueris*	3.d.i	CP		—
4462	*Cat. ultima ad baptizandos*	2.a,c.iv,d.i	A	2.a,d.i	A*
4472	*Catechesis 8*	2.c.iv, 4.a.ii	A	4.a.ii	A*
4528	*De capto Eutropio*	1	CP		

— = Insufficient grounds for making a determination. * Probably. [+] Possibly.

PART THREE

TOWARDS AN IMPROVED METHODOLOGY

CHAPTER FOUR

A MORE CAUTIOUS APPROACH

On the basis of the conclusions reached at the end of Part One, in Part Two we undertook to ascertain whether the criteria that have been used to distribute Chrysostom's homilies between the cities of Antioch and Constantinople merit the reliance that has been placed upon them. As a result of the investigation undertaken in Part Two it can be seen that not only are the criteria *not* beyond question, but only a minority stand firm when subjected to critical examination. Further, it is evident that the failure in the past to recognise the difficulties associated with the criteria being employed owes as much to the assumptions that have been brought to bear when developing the original criteria, as to the selective manner in which they have subsequently been applied.

Before we can proceed towards a more reliable methodology, then, the various kinds of difficulty encountered need to be clearly identified, brought together and summarised. The problems encountered in the search for provenance can be grouped into three areas: those that arise from a failure to apply basic investigative principles, those that relate to the manner in which the criteria are applied, and those that arise from the medium in which the data are found. These categories are examined here in section one. In section two a revised method for arriving at a more nuanced result is outlined. In section three this method is applied to a specific group of homilies as a test case, and the results analysed. A table of homilies whose provenance was determined in Chapters Three and Four to be certain is assembled for future use as a test base. Finally, the main implications of the findings in Parts Two and Three are outlined.

1. Addressing the deficiencies

1. RESTORING BASIC INVESTIGATIVE PRINCIPLES

At its broadest, the range of methodological problems uncovered in Chapter Three can be summarised as follows:

1. A failure to test each criterion against the evidence for consistency —
   that is, a failure to ask: has the argument been applied from every
   possible angle to see if it holds true? Is the evidence upon which the
   argument is posited genuinely exclusive? If the proposition can be
   demonstrated to apply to the one city, does the converse, i.e., that it
   does not apply to the other, also hold true?
2. The interpretation of evidence according to an *a priori* assumption of
   provenance. This approach, which includes arguments from familiarity, is associated with a tendency to search selectively for data which
   support the hypothesis, with a concomitant failure to view such data
   in context. In the process, conflicting or supplementary data have
   tended to be overlooked.
3. The adduction of arguments *ex silentio*. For an argument *ex silentio* to
   work, a clearly established and verifiable rule must first exist (if *x* is
   the case, then every time that *a* occurs, *b* is the case also), in order to
   be able to claim that if *a* occurs, but not *b*, then *x* is not the case. Such
   rules rarely prove to be true under all conditions.
4. The prioritisation of chronological evidence. This bias has led to an
   inconsistent application of the criteria. That is, data indicative of
   provenance that have been considered true and reliable under any
   other circumstance have been held to be not true when "contradicted"
   by chronological evidence.
5. A failure to take the rhetorical character of the medium into account.
   This neglect has given rise to the naïve acceptance of certain statements made by the homilist. It has also resulted in the placement of a
   greater reliance on data contained in exempla than may be warranted.

Fixing these problems is the first step in moving towards a more reliable methodology. The correction of areas 1-4 (examining the data from
every possible angle, being consistent in the application of criteria, ignoring suspicions about chronology, being self-critical about implicit assumptions, examining data with an open mind, and always paying attention to the full context in which the data appear), in particular, restores
the application of general investigative principles which are essential to
the achievement of a valid result.

2. APPLYING THE CRITERIA

   A restoration of the consistent application of basic scientific principles, however, solves only one of a number of problems. A second area of
concern identified in Chapter Three is the need for a clear understanding
of the conditions under which a valid criterion can be held to produce a

valid result. Such clarity is essential, if we are to become more rigorous in our application of each criterion.

As became clear in Chapter Three, even if the associated criterion is valid, the mere existence of a certain type of data in a homily does not guarantee that the data are indicative of a particular provenance. Rather, the manner in which the detail is presented and the context in which it occurs are both critical when assessing its implications. Thus, for instance, in the case of reference to an historical person or event a number of conditions must be satisfied before the conclusion drawn on the basis of that reference can be considered reliable. As we pointed out at the end of Chapter Three, section 9, the event or person must be clearly identifiable (that is, there must be detail that is unique), and the event or person must be clearly linked by the homilist to the present location and/or audience.[1] Only when both conditions are met can the outcome of application of the criterion be considered secure. Similarly, in the case of topographical features, it is not enough for Chrysostom to mention a particular locale or building by name. That feature must also be unique to one of the two cities and it must be clear that the audience has ready access to that landmark or that it is part of the local topography.[2] In the case of martyr burials, for the criterion to be effective the individual must be clearly named or the details of that person's life unique; it must be evident that the individual is buried locally; and there must exist a close link between the martyr or saint and one of the two cities.[3] Similar requirements occur in the case of references to the Olympics,[4] monks,[5] geographic proximity,[6] martyr festivals,[7] and events associated with Antioch from the apostolic era.[8] Conditions of these kind in fact apply in varying numbers in the case of all valid criteria.

All of the conditions attached to a criterion must be met, if the result derived from applying that criterion is to be positive as well as valid.

---

[1] See pp. 463-465.

[2] See Chapter Three, p. 377.

[3] See Chapter Three, p. 386.

[4] Either it must be clear that the audience have been frequent spectators or are familiar with the protocol and detail of the games; or it must be clear that a version of the games is held locally. See Chapter Three, p. 438.

[5] It must be clear that the monks or ascetics live on mountains or in caves that are real; and that they are local. See Chapter Three, p. 434.

[6] The location named must be either Thrace or Syria; and it must be clearly distinct from the present location. See Chapter Three, p. 425.

[7] Reference must occur to two or more festivals; and the festivals named must be sufficiently rare to be distinctive. See Chapter Three, p. 441.

[8] There must be an unambiguous connection drawn between the Antioch of the New Testament and the present audience/location. See Chapter Three, p. 368.

When one or more of the specific conditions are not met the degree to
which a result can be achieved and the conclusion can be relied upon
varies. Thus, for example, in the case of *In Titum hom. 3*, where there occurs a direct reference to the suburb Daphne, but no connection is drawn
between that location and the location at which John is preaching, and
where the manner in which he refers to the suburb is such that the
comment could have been made to an audience at either location, the result derived from applying the criterion is uncertain.[9] In the case of *De
baptismo Christi*, where one finds a reference to the Olympic games, but
it is neither indicated that the audience regularly attends nor that a version of the games is held locally, yet the comment is more specific than
general and there exists what appears to be a tacit connection to the
audience, the result can be considered possible but accorded no higher
degree of certainty.[10] On the other hand, in the case of *In Eph. hom. 11*,
where John refers to the illegal ascension of the thronos by others in contradistinction to his own legal possession of that particular piece of ecclesiastical furniture, the lack of direct reference to his status and the
allusory nature of his comments fall short of allowing us to consider a
provenance of Constantinople certain. Rather the best that can be
achieved is a result that is probable.[11] Thus being clear about the conditions under which a criterion produces a positive result is only part of
the solution. If a valid result is to be achieved in all instances, it is also
necessary that the implications of a failure to meet one or more of those
conditions are recognised and understood.

3. READING THE DATA

Again, eliminating the deficiencies in the way criteria have been applied in the past solves only the second of a number of problems. In the
previous section the difficulties addressed related to the use of criteria
that have been shown to be valid. In order to determine whether a criterion is valid in the first instance we need to be sure that the data have
been interpreted correctly. As became evident in the analysis of many of
the criteria in Chapter Three, the act of interpretation presents us with a
third and final area of difficulty. Even when we operate with valid criteria alone and are scrupulously scientific in our analysis the result can
still be badly skewed, if the data have been read at face value rather than
with sensitivity and attention to the constraints placed upon them by the

[9] See Chapter Three, p. 378.
[10] See Chapter Three, pp. 435f.
[11] See Chapter Three, pp. 411-416.

demands of genre, rhetoric, authorial intent and the homilist's perspective. Paying careful attention to the context in which the data occur is also an important corrective.

a. *Genre and intent*

The key aspect of the homiletic medium that moulds the data embedded within it is the fact that the homily is didactic in intent.[12] Whether it is the intention of the homilist to educate the audience by explicating scripture, to alter the audience's beliefs by engaging in polemic against the dogma of other religious groups, to encourage new behaviours or excise those that are ingrained, or simply to inspire the audience to greater devotion of the martyrs and saints, everything within a homily is directed towards a particular end. That goal, which changes from homily to homily, gives the homilist license to be selective with information according to the particular point that he wishes to make. Thus in relation to the riots of 387 we find different aspects elicited in a number of different homilies, which provide markedly different perspectives on the event. In *In Col. hom. 7*, John talks about the shame of having a neighbouring inferior city intercede with the emperor on Antioch's behalf,[13] when in *De statuis hom. 3* and *21* he is at pains to imply that it is Flavian's audiences with the emperor which are the key to averting destruction.[14] Yet in *De statuis hom. 17* and *18* it is the intercession of the Antiochene monks at the trial of the decurions that is said to win the day.[15] All three explanations are contradicted by Libanius, *Or. 21*, where the *magister officiorum* Caesarius is said to have been the one successful in swaying the emperor.[16] Van de Paverd documents several other instances in relation to the riots where Chrysostom gives events a particular slant or presents information selectively in order to support a particular argument.[17] The point to be made here is not that John consciously misrepresents the

---

[12] F. Siegert, "Homily and panegyrical sermon", in *Handbook of Classical Rhetoric*, 420, defines a "sermon" as the "'public explanation of a sacred doctrine or a sacred text', with its *Sitz im Leben* being worship", and argues that of all the religious cults in antiquity only Jewish synagogue worship and Christianity demanded the application of rhetorical skill to teaching within the context of worship.

[13] PG 62,347 56-348 6.

[14] PG 49,47-50; 211-222.

[15] PG 49,171-180; 186 38-61.

[16] Foerster, II 449-466.

[17] *Homilies on the Statues*, 60, 64-65, 72, 137-156. Van de Paverd, 18-19, points out that Chrysostom's overall concern within the homilies *De statuis* is to prove the superiority of Christian over pagan philosophy.

course of events, but that he has a particular agenda on each occasion and that the version of events recorded by him in each instance is trimmed, packaged, and at times even embroidered to support a particular case.

The pressure of the educational agenda upon the way in which information is presented is not just restricted to historical events. It is a constant factor throughout John's homilies.[18] The overall focus of the individual homily, the nature of the message being conveyed at the point at which the data appear, and the immediate context within which the detail is presented must therefore all be taken into account, if one is to be able to assess the reliability and significance of an individual piece of evidence.

b. *Rhetoric*

If the homily is a result of the coalescence of teaching and rhetoric within a worship environment,[19] then the second factor which needs carefully to be taken into consideration when interpreting data is the manner in which the educational message is delivered. In the context of the Christian homily classical rhetoric may constitute a means to an end rather than an end in itself,[20] but it is nonetheless a means that is significant. This is especially the case with the homilies of John Chrysostom.[21] The difficulties associated with this factor were made clear in Chapter Three when assessing the criteria associated with determining John's status (2.a-f). There we observed the semantic elasticity of terms such as "the fathers" and "proedroi", which covered a range of meanings according to context.[22] We observed the fine and often difficult to draw line between a simple metaphor and a rhetorical topos. We observed John deliberately drifting between the impersonal and the personal when discussing different aspects of the priesthood. Indeed, in regard to virtually all of the criteria in that section it proved difficult to determine John's status objectively, except in those rare cases where he is explicit.

---

[18] See, e.g., the problems that relate to data thought to be indicative of the status of the city (Chapter Three, pp. 393f). The demands of rhetoric also contribute. See the discussion in 3.b below.

[19] See Siegert (n. 12).

[20] See Kinzig, "Greek Christian Writers", 636-641.

[21] For a bibliography of the literature on Chrysostom's exploitation of classical rhetorical forms see Kinzig, "Greek Christian Writers", 646 n. 58.

[22] Cf. the discussion regarding the terms *hyparch*, *eparch* and *toparch* etc (Chapter Three, 3.h.i, pp. 395-397).

Exempla, a fundamental part of the orator's toolbox, were seen to present another difficulty. As observed,[23] they tend to have a life of their own within the rhetorical domain and determining the extent to which information contained within them reflects an objective external reality is problematic. Even those exempla that appear to be more direct, such as those that begin "Don't you see...", were shown to be misleadingly so, and the information which they contain exploitable at either location. Careful study of formulae, exempla and terminology across the whole corpus, as demonstrated in Chapter Three, offers a means of grasping whether detail is generic or specific and whether an exemplum is a standard topos or contains information which is able to be relied upon.

That consideration of the constraints of rhetoric is as important as recognition of the educational agenda for interpreting the data is demonstrated by one final assumption implicit in the literature, but not directly addressed in Chapter Three, namely that the appearance of directness and simplicity in John's sermons is to be equated with openness.[24] The necessary consequence of this assumption is the casual dismissal of the influence of rhetoric and a belief that it is valid to interpret the data largely at face value. While it may well be the case that on some occasions what John said and what he felt or believed were in accord, it is also patently the case that on others the educational impact of a particular message was greatly assisted by resort to classical rhetorical forms with their own freedoms and constraints. Thus, as Wilken demonstrates,[25] in the case of the orations *Adv. Iudaeos* (CPG 4327), Chrysostom takes advantage of the traditional *psogos* (invective), with its license for exaggerated forms of abuse, to push his case against those Christians who persist in participating in the festivals of the Jews. At the same time he exploits the exaggerated flattery appropriate to the encomium in other homilies such as *Hom. dicta postquam reliquiae martyrum* (CPG 4441.1) and *De regressu* (CPG 4394).[26] Within sermons of these kinds it would be

---

[23] See Chapter Three (3.c.ii), pp. 371-374.

[24] This assumption finds support in Socrates' various claims that John was frank and reckless, with a freedom of speech that overstepped polite bounds (HE 6.3, GCS NF 1,315 10-11), that he upset those in office by rebuking them unacceptably (HE 6.5, GCS NF 1,316 17-19); and that his public invective against women, in which the majority saw veiled reference to the empress, was attributable to his hot temper and ready speech (HE 6.15, GCS NF 1,336 11-14). All of these comments imply a bluntness and readiness to speak before thinking that belie artifice. See, however, Kinzig, "Greek Christian Writers", 639-640, where it is pointed out that the ideal of ἀφέλεια (simplicity) is taken directly from pagan rhetorical theory and that, despite his championing of it, in practice Chrysostom exploited a variety of rhetorical styles.

[25] Wilken, *Chrysostom and the Jews*, 95-127.

[26] See Mayer-Allen, *John Chrysostom*, 27.

incautious to accept that the opinions expressed limpidly mirrored
John's own. When we consider the distortions produced by the application of hyperbole and other general rhetorical techniques within the
course of ordinary homilies, for instance the exaggerated expressions of
humility combined with flattery which John exploits at the opening to
Sermo 2 in Gen. (CPG 4409) and *De Eleazaro* (CPG 4441.13),[27] the notion
of reading what is said within a homily at face value and without consideration for the rhetorical filter through which it is expressed becomes untenable.

c. *Perspective*

In Chapter Three it became apparent that beyond educational agenda
and rhetoric a third factor with the capacity to affect our reading of the
data needs also to be taken into consideration. That factor is the various
perspectives from which the data are presented. Of these the primary filter is the homilist's own Weltanschauung or world view. A secondary filter is the contemporary society and world within which the homilist and
audience operate. A tertiary filter is the perspective of the faction of
Christianity to which the homilist and his audience belong.
    Examples which highlight the existence of this third filter are cases
where John refers to other Christian groups as heretics, such as the Novatians, who strictly speaking had an equal claim to being Nicene Christians and were accorded equal tolerance under imperial law.[28] It is also
here that we see how the various influences (educational agenda, rhetoric and perspective) can overlap, since there is both a lesson in calling a
rival Christian faction heretical as well as an element of rhetorical exaggeration in employment of the term. An example of crossover between
this third filter and the first lies in John's employment in *In Eph. hom. 11*
of the label "schism", when referring to the actions of a rival bishop.
Here, as demonstrated in Chapter Three, the schism cannot objectively
be termed a schism but is labelled thus because in John's eyes, which are
also those of a bishop trying to preserve the integrity of Nicence Christianity in his see, the actions of the anonymous bishop are in essence split-
ting his church.[29] The first perspective is also exemplified in the case of
determining what evidence points characteristically to the offices of
presbyter and bishop in Chrysostom's writings. As rapidly became clear,
criteria which might objectively be thought to signify a particular status

---

[27] SC 433,178 4-182 35 and PG 63,523 12-21 *a.i.*
[28] See Chapter Three, p. 410 n. 468.
[29] See Chapter Three, pp. 411-416.

are compromised and the assumed lines blurred by the less distinctive view of the two offices which John himself holds.[30] An example which demonstrates the significance of the second perspective is the problems associated with objectively identifying the church to which a title might refer. Labels such as the Great Church and the Old Church were apparently a common way of referring to the latest episcopal church and its antecedent at both locations, just as the New Church might be a popular way of referring to the Great Church or to another recently constructed building known more formally by another label. The problems encountered when trying to identify a famous individual or event, where the knowledge shared by preacher and audience obviate the necessity to provide conclusive detail, further demonstrate the need to approach the data from a contemporary viewpoint.

2. A modified approach

With the main deficiencies in the previous approach identified and summarised, the next question to be addressed is: where do we go from here? Simple correction of the deficiencies of the old methodology produces a more reliable result, but that result, as indicated in Tables 16-17, is largely negative. In the case of many homilies a provenance that was thought to be certain must now be treated as uncertain and few of the original criteria have been found to be completely reliable. The introduction of a number of modifications to the broader methodology, however, offers the possibility of an improved outcome with a more nuanced result. The first two modifications to the approach which are proposed in this section arise in part from the analysis of the criteria in Chapter Three and in part from an understanding of the deficiencies outlined above in section 1. The third modification is introduced into discussion for the first time, but arises naturally from a consideration of the question of how one determines which homilies genuinely belong together in a so-called sequence or series.[31] A number of such putative sequences were outlined in Chapter One.

---

[30] See Chapter Three, pp. 322-327.

[31] See the Introduction, p. 25, where it is argued that an examination of sequence is the natural next step in the investigative process.

1. DEGREES OF CERTAINTY

If a consequence of the findings established in Part Two is that one can no longer attribute the bulk of John's homilies to the cities of Antioch or Constantinople with certainty, this result is not as pessimistic as it might at first appear. To conclude that because a homily cannot be attributed with certainty, nothing can be said about its provenance at all, is too strict a response. As pointed out when discussing the valid application of criteria above, a clear understanding of and scrupulous attention to the conditions which guarantee the validity of the outcome when a particular criterion is being employed allows for a range of outcomes in addition to a certain or uncertain result. If, when applying a criterion, not all of the conditions are met, it may be that a particular provenance can nonetheless be assessed as probable. In other cases it may be that the one condition which is met cannot support a probable result but will sustain at least the possibility that the homily stems from a particular location, provided that no other evidence within the homily speaks against that conclusion. By allowing for varying degrees of certainty, where the degree of certainty is determined on the basis of a careful weighing of the relative merits of individual pieces of evidence, a more nuanced result than a simple either/or is obtained.

Grading the results along a scale that stretches from certain to uncertain allows the information contained within every homily in the corpus to be used, while maintaining clarity as to the amount of weight that can be placed upon it. This is a marked improvement on the old system with its numerous false positives and false assumptions, or the corrected system with its large number of negative results.

2. THE PRIORITISATION OF EVIDENCE

Homilies which contain more than one piece of evidence which may be indicative of provenance present a challenge to the current system. In the past scholars have tended to give priority to one, dismissing the significance of the others. In Chapter Three it became clear that, on the contrary, each piece must be examined on its own merits if a reliable result is to be achieved. Precisely how one determines the weight to be placed on each item and how one deals with apparently conflicting data are the questions that are addressed here.

In some cases determining the weight that can be placed on each piece of evidence and therefore which data have priority is simple. In the case of a homily such as *In Col. hom.* 7, where episcopal tone and reference to a famous person and to a famous event have been adduced, episcopal tone is an invalid criterion and can be dismissed, the supposed ref-

erence to Eutropius fails to meet any of the required conditions and
proves to be too generic to bear any weight, while the reference to the riots of 387, assumed to be a remote reiminiscence and therefore unreliable, on the contrary meets the required conditions and in fact produces
a positive result. The procedure in cases where data are contained in
both the body of the homily and the title is also straightforward. As established in Chapter Three, priority is always to be given to the internal
evidence.[32]

In cases where no data which might produce a certain result occur,
but there exist several pieces of evidence which have some slight bearing
in a particular direction, resolution is more difficult. In the case of a
homily such as *In Heb. hom. 4*, where episcopal tone and Chrysostom's
allusion to his leadership and authority have been adduced, but there
also exist references to urban male and female ascetics, to *proedroi*, and a
possible indication that John is of presbyteral status,[33] the relative weight
of the different pieces of evidence is hard to determine. While episcopal
tone and indications of leadership and authority are all invalid and readily dismissed, of the remaining three items the ascetics are clearly real
and local, since John threatens to ban them from synaxis, the call for the
prayers of the audience and *proedroi* suggests that the *proedroi* too are
real and in attendance, and the reference to the attendance of presbyters
and psalmodists at funerals also clearly refers to a local practice. The
problem here lies with how one interprets each piece of information. The
presence of urban ascetics who regularly attend synaxis might indicate
Constantinople, but it is also probable that the assumption that monasticism at Antioch was strictly extra-urban is false and that the situation described in this homily may be non-distinctive. If that is the case, then the
other two pieces of evidence, which ostensibly point to a provenance of
Antioch would no longer be contradicted. Unfortunately, neither of the
two remaining pieces of evidence is conclusive either. The formula which
calls for the prayers of the *proedroi* and others may be used exclusively by
John at Antioch, but it may also be the case that it is not. The fact that he
appears to include himself among the presbyters who conduct Christian
funerals may also be an artifact of rhetoric rather than intended to con-
vey concrete detail. In this instance, then, no resolution is possible, even
though we might suspect that the evidence leans slightly towards
Antioch. What is important for our methodology, however, is that the
ambiguous data in a case like this are kept in view to one side. There are
many homilies yet to be investigated in a systematic way with careful at-

---

[32] For a more detailed outline of how to proceed see the rules established at the
conclusion to Chapter Three (sec.1), pp. 320f.

[33] See Chapter Three, pp. 324-326.

tention to all of the relevant pieces of data. Over time it is likely that certain assumptions will be verified or dismissed conclusively and that the weighting of the evidence in this homily will shift, allowing a firmer conclusion.

The methodology which we have just described can be summarised as follows:

1. Set out all of the evidence which may be indicative of provenance within the homily.
2. Assess each item for validity.
3. Discard those that are patently invalid.
4. Carefully assess the relative weight of the remaining items.
5. Determine whether any are ostensibly in conflict.

A6.1 If there is no conflict, determine whether the evidence points collectively in a particular direction.

A6.2 Assess the degree of certainty and draw a conclusion.

B6.1 If there is conflict, determine whether there is a heavier weighting in one direction.

B6.2 If there is a heavier weighting, then re-examine the evidence for the other direction to see if there are invalid assumptions. Also assess for validity of assumption the evidence which appears to take priority.

B6.3 If necessary, realign the weightings.

B6.4 When satisfied that exploration of the data cannot be carried any further, assess the degree of certainty and draw a conclusion.

7. Hold ambiguous data in reserve.
8. When a new criterion is developed, or an assumption verified or dismissed, re-examine the ambiguous data to see whether the ambiguity is resolved in any instance.
9. In instances where ambiguity is removed and the data takes on a particular weighting, go back to those homilies which contain the data and repeat steps 5-6.

This process is painstaking but, if carefully observed, has the potential not only to increase the reliability of the results obtained, but also to increase our understanding of John Chrysostom, the cities of Antioch and Constantinople and late fourth-century church and society by resolving the validity or otherwise of a number of key assumptions.

3. Sequence and the Assessment of Provenance

While provenance must always have priority over chronology, as argued in the introduction, verification of the sequence in which two or more homilies were delivered can be used to further improve the quality of the results obtained by introducing the first two modifications. It can be employed as a check against results obtained from internal data. It can also be used to upgrade them.

In practice, however, this is not as simple as it sounds. Just as a range of problems relating to the old methodology for determining provenance were uncovered, so also sequence has been determined on the basis of less than reliable criteria.[34] Developing a methodology for determining the sequence of homilies reliably, moreover, is likely to require the same differentiation of degrees of certainty that we have proposed here. If the connection between one homily and another is neither certain nor uncertain, but proves to be probable or possible, then we are likely to end up with an even more complexly nuanced result. With that caveat in place, however, and if we consider initially only those sequences that can be determined with near certainty, the addition of sequence to the methodology provides a useful augment to the assessment and correction of provenance.

At its simplest, in cases where an apparently secure link can be demonstrated between a homily of unknown provenance and a homily of known provenance, the known provenance and its degree of certainty can be extended to the first homily. A straightforward example is that of *In Col. hom. 2* and *3*. *In Col. hom. 3* stems with certainty from Constantinople,[35] while *In Col. hom. 2*, the provenance of which has yet to be reviewed, contains no data indicative of provenance beyond a vague reference to current disasters.[36] Verification of the connection between the two is threefold. Firstly, John repeats in *hom. 3* Col. 1.15, which in *hom. 2* he says is used as a proof text by heretics and is therefore better left until the listeners are refreshed on the morrow.[37] In *hom. 3* it is the first verse exegeted.[38] Secondly, he consciously echoes at the opening of *hom.*

---

[34] See Mayer, "Pargoire's sequence", 276-286, where the problem with Pargoire's sequence of CPG 4441.7,10,12,13 is discussed, and Table 14, where the difficulty of determining the sequence of the homilies delivered by John in 386-early 388 is demonstrated. To complicate matters in relation to the latter group of homilies, Wendy Pradels now proposes a fourth schema in the introduction to the forthcoming Brändle-Pradels edition of the series *Adv. Iudaeos* (CPG 4327), which she has kindly permitted me to view.

[35] See Chapter Three, p. 322.

[36] See PG 62,315 6-8.

[37] PG 62,313 49-53.

[38] PG 62,317 12-14 *a.i.*

3 the language he used when leaving aside the verse in *hom.* 2,[39] and, thirdly, the temporal adverbs in both homilies ("tomorrow", "today ... yesterday") match precisely. Even though his preliminary comments about the implications of Col. 1.15 in *hom.* 2 do not match the approach he takes in *hom.* 3,[40] that is not a secure ground for doubting the connection. Since the connection seems secure, *hom.* 2 and 3 can be said to have been delivered at the same location and *hom.* 2 therefore takes on a provenance of Constantinople. *Contra Anomoeos hom. 11* (CPG 4324) and *De Christi divinitate* (CPG 4325), where the first was delivered with certainty at Constantinople[41] and the connection between the two appears secure,[42] constitute a similar example.

The straightforwardness of the above examples lies in the fact that in neither case did the homilies of previously unknown or unproven provenance contain data that was indicative of provenance. Had they done so, the secure connection between the two homilies alone would have been insufficient to permit the automatic extension of the provenance of the one homily in the sequence to the other. This leads us to extend the process outlined when discussing the prioritisation of evidence. In cases where there appears to be a verifiable sequence and both homilies contain data indicative of provenance, the data in each homily must first be assessed independently and given an independent weighting. Only then, can the weight of the data in the one homily be assessed against the weight of the data contained in the other. The key here is the avoidance of a misreading of the evidence due to a presupposition that all the data will necessarily point in the same direction or that the conclusion drawn regarding the security of the link between the two homilies is unshakeable. Using sequence as a corrective thus works in both directions. It allows one to check the security of the apparent sequence, while at the same time allowing for the challenging of underlying assumptions in cases where the data contained in the two homilies appear to be in conflict. If, after independent assessment, the internal evidence for provenance in each homily supports or fails to contradict the evidence for sequentiality, then both provenance and sequence can be considered secure. If, however, the data indicative of provenance in the one homily is apparently in conflict with the data in the other, then not only must the

---

[39] PG 62,317 14-16 *a.i.*: Τήμερον ἀποδοῦναι ἀναγκαῖον τὸ ὄφλημα, ὅπερ χθὲς ἀνεβαλόμην, ὥστε ἀκμαζούσαις ὑμῶν προσβαλεῖν ταῖς διανοίαις. Cf. PG 62,313 51-53: διὸ σήμερον ἀναβαλλομένους αὔριον τοῦτο προσθεῖναι δεῖ, ἀκμαζούσαις ὑμῶν ταῖς ἀκοαῖς προσβάλλοντας.

[40] PG 62,313 53-59; cf. PG 62,317 12 *a.i.*-318 4 *a.i.*

[41] See Chapter Three (3.f.ii), p. 393.

[42] See SC 396,320 29-322 35 which recalls SC 396,292 61-67 and 294 92-296 98; and SC 396,352 436-438 which recalls 306 228-230.

assumptions informing the criteria applied be re-examined, but the basis for determining sequence must also carefully be reassessed.

3. Testing the modified approach

In order to demonstrate how the modified approach produces more nuanced results, we turn to a case study of a particular set of homilies, until now assigned with complete certainty to Constantinople. As we shall see, when a careful study of the internal evidence indicative of provenance is conducted according to the steps outlined above, even in a case where there has existed a high degree of certainty as regards provenance a less confident, but more reliable outcome is obtained.

1. CASE STUDY OF THE *NOVAE HOMILIAE*

As noted in Part One, the primary basis on which the *Novae homiliae* (CPG 4441.1-15) have been assigned to Constantinople is the topographical information contained in the majority of the titles appended to the homilies in the series. Although not one hundred per cent reliable,[43] in combination with the assumption that series that present as series in the manuscripts are homogeneous this data has been persuasive of a common provenance. Because of the high degree of certainty qua provenance which has attached to this particular series little attention has been paid to the data contained within the individual homilies. A careful examination of the internal data is required, if we are to determine whether the degree of reliance which has been placed in the manuscript titles is justified.

a. *Certainty*

Five of the homilies in this series contain explicit evidence of their point of origin. For instance, the presence of the empress and then the emperor at the festivities described *in Hom. dicta postquam reliquiae martyrum* (CPG 4441.1) and *Hom. dicta praesente imperatore* (CPG 4441.2) situates both homilies firmly within the period of John's episco-

---

[43] See Chapter Three, pp. 317-320.

pate at Constantinople.[44] Likewise, although it is not certain whether the
emperor is himself present on that occasion, in the course of *In martyres
omnes* (CPG 4441.15) Chrysostom makes it clear that the emperor characteristically visits the present location before and after military cam-
paigns and on other important occasions,[45] a sign that the shrine is local
to the city in which the emperor currently resides. In the case of *Contra
ludos et theatra* (CPG 4441.7), the features of the local topography described in the course of the sermon,[46] as well as the information that it is
a year since John has arrived at the location,[47] guarantee the homily's
Constantinopolitan provenance.[48] In the case of *In illud: Messis quidem
multa* (CPG 4441.11) it is the disparity between the information in the
title and within the body of the homily which highlights the latter detail
and firmly points us towards Constantinople. While the title tells us that
it was delivered in "the church dedicated to the apostle",[49] John himself
mentions that he and his audience are in an environment where the
tombs of more than one apostle are in fact present.[50] More specifically,
the apostles to be viewed are Paul's disciple (Timothy) and the brother of
the first of the apostles (Andrew).[51] This circumstance convincingly
eliminates Antioch as an option, since no tomb of an apostle was located
there during the period of John's residency. If we turn our attention to
Constantinople, the information is further consistent not with the

---

[44] PG 63,469 5-471 15; 473 6-23. See Chapter Three (3.c.i), pp. 370f where the argument for the equation of imperial presence with Constantinopolitan provenance is af-
firmed.

[45] Stav. 6, f.142r b.11-142v a.14: ...καὶ βασιλεύς· καὶ ὕπατοι· καὶ στρατηλάται· καὶ πάντες
κατὰ τὴν ἡμέραν αὐτῶν συντρέχουσιν. ἐν τῷ τάφῳ τῶν μαρτύρων ... Καὶ βασιλεὺς διάδημα
ἀποτίθεται· καὶ δορυφόροι καὶ ὑπασπισταί. λόγχας καὶ δόρατα καὶ ἀσπίδας ἔξω ῥίψαντες οὕτω τῷ
σηκῷ [142v] τῶν μαρτύρων ἐπιβαίνουσι· καὶ πάντα εἴκει καὶ παραχωρεῖ τῷ φόβῳ τῶν ἁγίων
τούτων· καὶ ὁ τὴν πορφυρίδα περιβεβλημένος καὶ πάντα σείων τῷ νεύματι· πρηνὴ πολλάκις ἑαυτὸν
ῥίψας πρὸς τὸν τάφον τοῦ μάρτυρος. καλεῖ τὰς εὐχὰς τὰς ἐκείνου· κἂν εἰς πόλεμον ἐξίῃ σύμμαχον
αὐτὸν λαβὼν ἄπεισι· κἂν ἀπὸ νίκης ἐπανέλθῃ. κοινωνὸν αὐτὸν τῆς πρὸς τὸν δεσπότην εὐχαριστίας
καλεῖ· καὶ συνεφάψασθαι παρακαλεῖ τῆς ἐπὶ τοῖς γεγενημένοις εὐφημίας.

[46] PG 56,265 8-12 (a local church associated with Sts Peter, Paul, Andrew and Timothy) and 12-18 (a transmarine crossing to a church associated specifically with Sts Peter
and Paul).

[47] PG 56,268 47-48.

[48] For a more detailed argument see Chapter Three, pp. 374-376 and 385f.

[49] PG 63,515 5-6 *a.i.*: Τοῦ αὐτοῦ ὁμιλία, ῥηθεῖσα ἐν τῇ ἐκκλησίᾳ τῇ ἐπὶ τοῦ Ἀποστόλου... See
further Chapter Three, pp. 317f.

[50] PG 63,518 33-34.

[51] PG 63,518 37-42.

vaguely described church of the title, but with the Church of the Apostles, situated near the Constantinian wall to the north of the Mese.[52]

b. *Probability*

Of the fifteen homilies in the series it is only the above five (CPG 4441.1-2,7,11,15) which contain internal evidence of their provenance which is definitive. Of the remaining ten, however, there are three which contain internal evidence or independent detail in the title that is suggestive of a Constantinopolitan origin. In these instances, while one cannot state categorically that the homilies stem from Constantinople, there are sufficient grounds for accepting that such a provenance is in each case probable.

The first sermon in this category is *Hom. habita postquam presbyter Gothus* (CPG 4441.9). In the title we are informed that it was preached in the church named after Paul, after Goths had read the lessons and a presbyter, also a Goth, had delivered a preliminary homily.[53] What distinguishes this sermon from the other *Novae homiliae* is the absence of any reference in the opening lines to the sermon which the title claims has just been preached. In all other instances in the series where this category of data occurs in the title the same information is reflected in the opening or body of the sermon.[54] In those cases the detail in the title cannot be considered reliable, since it could as easily represent guesswork based on data internal to the homily. In this case, however, the detail is quite concrete (it is not just a presbyter, but a presbyter of Gothic nationality who has just preached), with so little to support it in the body of the sermon, that we are able to say that it is genuinely independent. This independence encourages us to place some weight upon the details supplied in the title. The question remains, however, as to whether this confidence is justified. The presence of a Gothic community at Constantinople and the assignment of a church to the orthodox among them for na-

---

[52] On the history of this church and the translation of these apostles' relics see most recently C. Mango, "Constantine's Mausoleum and the Translation of Relics" and "Constantine's Mausoleum: Addendum", *Byzantinische Zeitschrift* 83 (1990) 51-61 and 434; and D. Woods, "The date of the translation of the relics of SS. Luke and Andrew to Constantinople", VC 45 (1991) 286-292.

[53] PG 63,499 4-6 *a.i.*: Τοῦ αὐτοῦ ὁμιλία λεχθεῖσα ἐν τῇ ἐκκλησίᾳ τῇ ἐπὶ Παύλου, Γότθων ἀναγνόντων, καὶ πρεσβυτέρου Γότθου προομιλήσαντος.

[54] CPG 4441.6 (PG 63,491 1-12); 4441.11 (PG 63,515 6 *a.i.*-517 15); 4441.12 (PG 56,247 1-4 and title); 4441.13 (PG 63,523 12-24 *a.i.*); and 4441.14 (f.132v a.1-33).

tive-language worship needs little comment.[55] But what if the reference
to lections read in a language other than Greek prompted an editor, who
knew of these facts, to assume that the language was Gothic? It is also
not beyond the realm of possibility that subsequent to that leap of intuition, the reference to a sermon preached by a presbyter crept in on analogy with other homilies in the series. While detailed analysis of the
manuscripts may prove to be decisive on this point, at this present stage
our only resort is to assess the degree of conformity between title and internal evidence. Before we can embrace the title we must therefore ask
whether evidence internal to the homily supports the title's assertion that
the language is Gothic. After all, a number of homilies make it clear that
mixed-language audiences, at least, were also on occasion a feature at
Antioch.[56]

The sermon in fact tells us very little on this point. It is clear that the
scriptures have just been read in a language other than Greek.[57] The
phrase used to characterise the language ("the tongue of barbarians"),
however, is undistinctive and, while it does appear to be used to describe
the Gothic language in the Constantinopolitan *Hom. dicta postquam
reliquiae martyrum*,[58] it is used equally in an Antiochene homily to describe those who speak Syriac.[59] The only other reference of substance is
to the mixed character of the audience, where "the most barbaric of all
people" are said to be standing side by side with "the sheep of the
church".[60] This circumstance is not inconsistent with the mixed-language
audience already described at Antioch, although the emphasis on the degree of barbarism does give pause. Nowhere in homilies which describe
citizens of Antioch rubbing shoulders with Syriac-speaking individuals

[55] *Ep.* 207 (PG 52,726-727): care of church of the Goths enjoined upon monks on the
estate of Promotus; Theod., HE 5.30 (GCS NF 5,330): John appoints church with native-
language clergy for Goths; Soz., HE 8.4 (GCS NF 4,356 14-17): Goths harrassed and
church of the Goths burned to the ground at time of coup led by Gainas.

[56] See *De statuis hom. 19* (CPG 4330) PG 49,188 8-9 *a.i.* (κατὰ μὲν τὴν γλῶτταν ἡμὶν
ἐνηλλαγμένος); and *Cat. 8* (CPG 4472) SC 50[bis],248 2.2-6 (βάρβαρον ἔχουσι τὴν γλῶτταν). The
reference in both these instances is to Syriac-speaking visitors who are most probably rural monk-priests. See van de Paverd, *Homilies on the Statues*, 260-292.

[57] PG 63,499 3 *a.i.*-501 4: Ἐβουλόμην παρεῖναι Ἕλληνας τήμερον, ὥστε τῶν ἀνεγνωσμένων
ἀκοῦσαι ... Ποῦ τὰ τῶν ἁλιέων καὶ σκηνοποιῶν; οὐκ ἐν Ἰουδαίᾳ μόνον, ἀλλὰ καὶ ἐν τῇ τῶν βαρβάρων γλώττῃ, καθὼς ἠκούσατε σήμερον...

[58] PG 63,472 11-12: ... τοὺς μὲν τῇ Ῥωμαίων, τοὺς δὲ τῇ Σύρων, τοὺς δὲ τῇ βαρβάρων, τοὺς δὲ
τῇ Ἑλλάδι φωνῇ...

[59] See *Cat. 8*, n. 56 above.

[60] PG 63,502 9-11: Καὶ τοῦτο σήμερον ἐωράκατε, τοὺς πάντων ἀνθρώπων βαρβαρικωτέρους
μετὰ τῶν τῆς Ἐκκλησίας προβάτων ἐστῶτας...

do we find the latter characterised in quite this way.[61] One other point which may speak in favour of accepting that the ethnicity of the non-Greek speakers is Gothic is the absence in the homily of any reference to the temporary status of that section of the audience. In the case of Antioch the existence of a permanent native-language-worshipping Syrian community is unknown and John makes it clear in both instances where reference to Syriac-speakers occurs, that their participation in worship is extraordinary and their stay in the city of short duration.[62] While none of these considerations confirms the identity of the non-Greek language in question, neither do they undermine the possibility that it is Gothic. Rather, there is a slight bias in that language's favour. There being no overt grounds for rejecting the information in the title and some slight basis for accepting it, it can be accepted for the time being that the title contains information independent of the body of the sermon precisely because the author was cognisant of the circumstances of its delivery.

The degree of probability of Constantinopolitan provenance in the case of *In illud: Pater meus usque modo operatur* (CPG 4441.10) is somewhat higher. In this instance, the burden of proof rests not with the title, but with information provided in an exemplum located in the prooimion of the homily. On the day prior to the homily a terrible accident had occurred at the local hippodrome in which a young man had been killed. That person had been down on the floor of the stadium while a race was in progress as a result of his duties on the staff of the *eparch*.[63] The connection between the bureau of the *eparch* and official duties at the hippodrome may in this instance point directly to Constantinople. Although there is some suggestion that provincial *eparchs* did exist at this period, the title was associated more particularly with the prefecture of the city of Constantinople (ὁ ἔπαρχος τῆς πόλεως). It is also reasonably certain that at Antioch responsibility for the production of spectacles, including chariot races, fell to an official known as the *syriarch*. At Constantinople, on the other hand, the task of staging the contests at the hippodrome fell within the duties of the urban prefect or *eparch*. The cir-

---

[61] Syriac-speakers are described variously as: ἐπιχώριοι (*De b. Philogonio* [CPG 4319], PG 48,750 7-8); οἱ ἀπὸ τῆς χώρας, distinctive in σχῆμα and τῆς γλώττης τὴν διάλεξιν, ἄγροικον (*Cat. 8*, SC 50bis,247 1.5-6; 249 4.1-2; 250 6.1). Cf. *De statuis hom. 19* (PG 49,188 11 a.i.-190 55).

[62] *De statuis hom. 19* (PG 49,188 9-12 a.i.; 190 56-58); *Cat. 8* (SC 50bis,247-248 1.4-16).

[63] PG 63,512 24-36: ὑπὸ τὴν τάξιν τὴν τοῦ ἐπάρχου τελῶν. See Chapter Three (3.h.i), pp. 395f, for the full argument and supporting evidence.

cumstances described in the exemplum fit more neatly into place, then, if we posit that the event took place at Constantinople.[64]

The degree of probability in the case of *De studio praesentium* (CPG 4441.5) is similar. The homily contains several references to the emperor, the palace and the imperial administration, of which one, at least, implies that they are not just real but local. Any potentially conflicting evidence (promotion of the mother of the Maccabees as a role model,[65] reference to women who practice a distinctive extreme form of asceticism,[66] the chiding of rich members of the audience for being stingy in giving to ascetics[67]) is in this context neutral. The implications of references to the emperor, empress and palace, other than those which are explicit, as in the case of those that occur in CPG 4441.1-2, are difficult to assess. Here, however, the existence of a direct connection between the comments and the location is at least possible since in the prooimion to the homily John talks at length about those among the audience who have failed to attend because they have given priority to financial concerns. In the course of his argument he claims that on the day of Judgement there will be no discrimination in regard to status, in particular there will be no person wearing the imperial diadem or purple, and no person conveyed on a chariot with countless lictors chasing people out of their path in the marketplace.[68]

This exemplum is in itself non-distinctive, but the addition of the emperor to mention of those in high office prepares us for the reference to the emperor which occurs shortly after, namely in the context of an argument that those who are absent are covered in ulcers and wounds, but have no idea that they are ill.[69] Furthermore, says John, no-one is likely to tell them since everyone they associate with is distracted by their own worldly concerns. The list begins with their wives, moves to their household slaves, continues on to the jurors (δικασταί), whom John says are absorbed in political concerns, and culminates with the imperial majesties (οἱ βασιλεῖς).[70] The list assumes that the places normally frequented by

---

[64] The other data which might be thought to offer a clue as to the homily's provenance, namely that John ceded his place as preacher to an elderly visiting colleague at the preceding synaxis (PG 63,511 48-52), is difficult to interpret without an *a priori* assumption that John is bishop and therefore at Constantinople.

[65] PG 63,488 30-40.

[66] PG 63,488 62-489 13.

[67] PG 63,490 47-52.

[68] PG 63,486 1-8.

[69] PG 63,486 15-18.

[70] PG 63,486 19-30. What is meant by the plural in this context is difficult to determine, but in the Constantinopolitan homily *De s. Phoca* (CPG 4364) John mentions that the βασιλεῖς will be joining in the celebrations at the martyrium (PG 50,699 23-27), which,

those who are absent (in this case clearly men) are the home, the law-courts and the palace. The fact that John then goes on to draw a distinction between the silence observed by senior administrative officials in the palace in the presence of the seated emperor and the lack of silence which occurs when the psalms are chanted in church,[71] in this context suggests that he adduces the exemplum precisely because the situation is familiar and readily understood.

The lack of an explicit connection between the palace and the present location, despite the implicit association between palace and audience, means that a Constantinopolitan provenance cannot be said to be certain. That *De studio praesentium* was delivered in that city can nonetheless be considered probable. It is important to note in this instance, however, that without the assumption on the part of the homilist that the palace is a place regularly frequented by those who have failed to attend, neither the last exemplum nor the very first could be considered significant. It is only after a probable connection between palace and location has been established that their number, quality and proximity to the key passage can be considered to lend any weight.

c. *Possibility*

The homily *Adversus catharos* (CPG 4441.6), on the other hand, which might be considered to belong to Constantinople on circumstantial grounds, is less easy to assign, if all of the evidence is considered separately. The title itself must be treated with suspicion, since the information contained within it could easily represent the results of an informed guess based on data internal to the homily.[72] Here the information that John "owes a debt" to Theodosius, whose God-assisted deeds John then goes on to describe, might lead one to suspect that the day on which the homily was delivered is the anniversary of Theodosius' death, but there is no explicit proof of this fact. In either case, the anniversary of Theodosius' death could as readily be celebrated in any major eastern city of the empire as at Constantinople. Moreover, John does not point toward the

on the analogy of CPG 4441.1-2, leads one to suspect that in that instance he means the emperor and empress.

[71] PG 63,487 3-5.

[72] PG 63,491 1-3. It is clear from the opening of the homily that two persons of indeterminate status have preached before John and that it is a day associated with the dead emperor Theodosius, and from the body of the homily that John is addressing the Novatian heresy. It is a short step for an editor who assumes the homily was delivered at Constantinople to identify the two preachers as bishops and locate the sermon in the Church of the Apostles, the resting place of Theodosius' remains.

tomb as he might have done were he preaching in the Church of the Apostles, nor does he in any other way exploit the venue. This does not mean that he is not situated in that church at the time, since one of the two earlier preachers might have played upon the connection, but it does give pause, seeing that John is so ready to exploit the visual and mental associations of particular sites or their role in the local spiritual landscape on other occasions.[73]

A second piece of evidence, the circumstance that two other persons preached before John on that occasion, cannot be considered proof of the fact that he is the most senior person present and therefore the local bishop. Such evidence is by no means as patent as it might at first appear, especially since the episcopal status of the two preachers itself cannot be assumed, and seeing that the scenario can admit of other explanations.[74] A third aspect of the homily is slightly more persuasive. The presence of a significant and long-established Novatian community at Constantinople is well attested, as is the fact that, after the edict of Gratian and the ceding of the Constantinopolitan churches to the Nicene Christians by Theodosius in late 380, the Nicene Christian community was obliged to tolerate the co-tenancy of the city precincts by the Novatians.[75] No such community is attested for Antioch, although this does not mean that such a community did not exist there. It may simply have been overshadowed by the struggles for power between the Arian, Anomoean, Apollinarian and two Nicene communities. Even so, the idea that John's focus in this particular homily upon those who call themselves "pure" (καθαρός) is sparked by the licit competition between the less rigorous Nicene comunity over which he has oversight and the rigorist Novatians led by Sisinnius is attractive and, while *Adversus catharos* contains no specific internal evidence which is other than equivocal, the suspicion that it was delivered at Constantinople is not unreasonable and has some slight weight in its favour.

A homily which contains minimal evidence that may perhaps point to Constantinople is *De Eleazaro et septem pueris* (CPG 4441.13). Up to this point the argument for provenance has rested upon a single word.[76] Pargoire, noting the verb διαπεράω in the midst of John's instructions to his

---

[73] As in *In illud: Messis quidem multa* and various homilies on martyrs or delivered at martyria. See, e.g., *In ascensionem* (CPG 4342) PG 50,443 22-37; *De s. Meletio* (CPG 4345) PG 50,515 22-25; *De s. Babyla* (CPG 4347) SC 362, 294 1.1-2.2; *In s. Ignatium* (CPG 4351) PG 50,594 29-33 and 595 7-8. Cf. *In Eutropium* (CPG 3492), where John spends much of the sermon exploiting the physical presence of the cowering fugitive.

[74] See the discussion below in relation to *De Eleazaro et septem pueris* (CPG 4441.13) and, further, Chapter Three (2.e), pp. 351-360.

[75] See Socr., HE 5.10, 6.22 (GCS NF 1,284 18-30; 346 11-17).

[76] See Chapter Three (3.d.i), pp. 375f.

audience at the close of the homily,[77] argued that it most commonly denotes the crossing of a sea or strait. In other words, when John urges his audience to attend the celebration of the Maccabees on the following day he is asking them to cross a body of water in order to reach the appropriate site. That location Pargoire identifies as the Church of the Maccabees mentioned in the *Chronicon Paschale*, a structure which was situated across from the city of Constantinople on the opposite shore of the Golden Horn.[78]

This proposal is extremely neat. Two difficulties attach to the argument, however. Firstly, when he interprets διαπεράω in this light, Pargoire already believes that the sermon was preached at Constantinople by virtue of its location among a group of homilies that, he says, were without exception delivered in that city.[79] Secondly, despite Pargoire's assertion that the homily is homogeneous with the rest of the series, it is one of just two homilies among the fifteen that bear a title in which the "characteristic" topographic detail is absent.[80] Given the importance which Batiffol and Aubineau attach to this feature, the very lack of such detail in this instance ought to lead one to suspect the homily's place within the series.[81] As a further consequence, unlike the thirteen cases in which information in the title can be tested against data contained in the body of the sermon and vice versa, in this instance we are reliant solely upon internal evidence for proof of the homily's provenance. Before we can proceed any further, the questions that must therefore be asked are whether, in the absence of any mention of the medium to be traversed, it can be determined that the crossing of a body of water is in fact precisely what John and his audience understood when he used διαπεράω; and, should this prove to be the case, whether this geographical particularity is consistent with the topography of Antioch also or is exclusive to Constantinople.

---

[77] PG 63,530 53-55: ... ὀλίγους σταδίους διαπερῶντες ὑπὲρ τῆς θεωρίας τῶν παλαισμάτων ἐκείνων.

[78] Pargoire, "Les homélies en juillet 399", 160.

[79] Pargoire, "Les homélies en juillet 399", 160.

[80] The other instance is *Contra ludos et theatra* (CPG 4441.7). Thorough analysis of the manuscript tradition is awaited for confirmation of this point. In Stav. 6, however, in neither instance does there appear in the title additional information of this kind.

[81] In the case of *Contra ludos et theatra*, however, Constantinopolitan provenance is nonetheless readily established. It is to be concluded that the mere absence of topographic detail in the title does not disqualify a homily from inclusion. It must also be said that the presence of topographic detail in the title is not exclusive to Constantinopolitan homilies but is a feature of certain homilies delivered at Antioch also. See, e.g., *De statuis hom. 1* and *2* (CPG 4330) PG 49,15-16; 33-34; and *In illud: In faciem ei restiti* (CPG 4391) PG 51,371-372.

There is no denying that the verb διαπεράω is almost always employed
by Chrysostom in the context of crossing water. Most commonly it is to
be found employed in relation to the sea.[82] On one occasion John uses it
metaphorically to describe the passage accross the strait of this present
life.[83] In one other instance it alludes to the Old Testament crossing of
the river Jordan into the promised land.[84] The question that must be answered in the present instance is whether the association between the
verb and water is so strong in the minds of John and his audience that,
when no mention is made of the medium, the crossing of water is automatically to be understood. On the basis of the above survey of John's
use of the term, it seems that the association was strong and that it is
likely that the traversal of water is to be assumed. This finding is perhaps
supported by a review of the range of verbs of motion employed elsewhere by John in association with the unit of distance, the stade. Examples are few, but in the three cases which can be located he uses verbs
which imply general movement on land (τρέχω, βαδίζω).[85] The point to be
made here is that John could easily have selected one of these verbs or
their compounds had he been describing a brief journey of whatever nature on land. Rather, his avoidance of these common words implies that
in this case he required a verb with a meaning that was specific. In this
light, his choice of διαπεράω appears deliberate.

If then, as seems probable, διαπεράω does in this instance indicate that
the location to be reached was across a body of water, the next issue to
be resolved is whether this feature was unique to Constantinople. It is
indeed peculiar to that city, if the water in question was either the sea itself or open to the sea. At Antioch the only immediately available body of
water was the river Orontes. The frequency with which John uses the
verb to describe traversal of the sea is persuasive of this option. It must
not be forgotten, however, that the verb can also be employed to indicate
the crossing of a river, and it is this second possibility, coupled with the
knowledge that in the fourth century there existed a strong association
between the Maccabean martyrs and Antioch,[86] which prevents us from

---

[82] See, e.g., *De b. Philogonio* (CPG 4319) PG 48,755 1-2; *Hom. 1 in Gen* (CPG 4409) PG
53,25 11-15; *hom. 6* (PG 53,59 14-16; 60 1-4); and *hom. 17* (PG 53,144 19-20); *In Ioh. hom.
33* (CPG 4425) PG 59,187 8-9 a.i.; *In ep. I ad Cor. hom.7* (CPG 4428) PG 61,53 7-8 a.i. Cf.
Hom. 2 in Gen. (PG 53,32 25).

[83] *Exp. in ps. 119* (CPG 4413) PG 55,343 1-2 (τὸν εὔριπον τοῦ παρόντος ... βίου). Cf., however, *Hom. 1 in Gen.* (PG 53,25 15: τὸ πέλαγος τοῦ παρόντος βίου).

[84] *Hom. 39 in Gen.*, PG 53,365 2-5.

[85] *Ad viduam iuniorem* (CPG 4314) SC 138,140 298-299; *De statuis hom. 11* (PG 49,124
42-46); *In Acta apost. hom. 18* (CPG 4426) PG 60,148 24-27.

[86] See Vinson, "Maccabean Martyrs", 178-186 and literature. Vinson herself assumes
(p. 186 n. 61) that the homily *De Eleazaro et septem pueris* was delivered at Antioch.

dismissing that city from the picture altogether. It is fairly certain that the Christian site of the Maccabean cult at Antioch was situated within the Theodosian Walls in the quarter called Kerataion. This district was located at the southern end of the city, possibly stretching from the Gate of the Cherubim towards Mt Silpius.[87] If, at the time that John was exhorting his listeners to traverse a few stades on the morrow, he was in fact preaching in the Great Church, situated within Antioch on the island in the Orontes, or even in the Church of St Babylas, across the Orontes,[88] it is not impossible that the term διαπεράω might have been considered by John to be topographically appropriate. A traversal of water, even by bridge, might be thought to warrant a verb other than τρέχω or βαδίζω.

On the other hand, John's insistence that the reason for that traversal is to view the sufferings of the martyrs and to gain inspiration from that sight may possibly dictate against this reading.[89] Martha Vinson draws careful distinction between two cultic sites at Antioch. The Christian site, situated within the boundaries of the city, is only explicable, she asserts, if no human remains were buried there.[90] Rather, she argues, the alleged remains of the father and mother and their seven sons were located in the suburbs at Daphne in a crypt associated with the cave of Matrona.[91] While John's use of verbs of sight can be rhetorical,[92] and it may in any case be that he is here referring to illustrations of the martyrdom of the Maccabees rather than to any sarcophagi or other signs of physical remains, the repeated emphasis on the visual, coupled with the prominence given by John to the mother of the Maccabees, is more suggestive of the cave of Matrona than of the church in Antioch itself.[93] The fact that Chrysostom suspects that his listeners might be wearied by the length of the journey to the site is consistent with this possibility and suggests that he is conveniently glossing over the real figure when he

---

[87] Vinson, "Maccabean Martyrs", 181-185.

[88] That this church was used for more than just festival synaxes is suggested by the opening to De s. Babyla (SC 362,294 1.1-3).

[89] PG 63,530 52-55 and Stav. 6 f.132r: Διὰ δὴ τοῦτο παρακαλῶ ... ὥστε παραγενέσθαι ἅπαντας, πρεσβύτιδας μὲν ἵνα τὴν ὁμήλικα θεάσωνται, νέας δὲ ἵνα διδάσκαλον λάβωσι τὴν πρεσβῦτιν, ἄνδρες δὲ ἵνα τὴν γυναῖκα ἴδωσι στεφανουμένην ... καὶ γὰρ ἑκατέρᾳ τῇ φύσει καὶ ἡλικίᾳ πάσῃ ὑποδείγματα παλαισμάτων καὶ ἀγωνισμάτων καὶ νίκης καὶ τροπαίων καὶ στεφάνων ἔστιν ἰδεῖν. Ἵν' οὖν τῆς καλῆς ἀπολαύσωμεν θεωρίας μετὰ πολλῆς ἀπαντήσωμεν προθυμίας ἵν' ἴδωμεν παλαίοντας νικῶντας στεφανουμένους ἀνακηρυττομένους ... (emphasis added). The text is supplied by Wenger, "Restauration", 603-604.

[90] "Maccabean Martyrs", 182 and 185-186.

[91] "Maccabean Martyrs", 179-181.

[92] See Chapter Three, p. 374.

[93] For the particular association between the cave at Daphne and the mother of the Maccabees see Vinson, "Maccabean Martyrs", 179-180.

subsequently asserts that the distance is only "a few" stades.[94] The problem with this identification of the locality is that the cave of Matrona was
apparently firmly associated in the Antiochene mind with Jewish rather
than Christian practice,[95] and is therefore unlikely to have been a
destination sought out by the Christian community at Antioch on the day
of the martyrs' celebration. Indeed, as Vinson points out, it is clear from
the homily *De ss. martyribus* (CPG 4357) that at Antioch the festival of
the Maccabees was celebrated within the boundaries of the city.[96]

The question marks which hang over both Antiochene locations do
not automatically point us to Constantinople, however. There are a few
other details within the homily which must also be considered. Firstly,
we must ask to what degree the fact that another individual has just
preached a sermon before him is indicative of John's own status.[97] After
all, *De Eleazaro et septem pueris* is one of a cluster of six sermons among
the fifteen *Novae homiliae* in which it is indicated, either in the prooi-
imion of the homily or the title or both, that he is preaching after one or
more persons have already done so.[98] Moreover, the only comparable examples outside of this series are two homilies whose titles locate them at
Constantinople.[99] These circumstances encourage the suspicion that
John's preaching after others have done so is an artifact of his episcopal
status. If we could be certain that this was the case, then we would finally have clear proof that *De Eleazaro et septem pueris* was delivered at
Constantinople. Unfortunately, as already argued in Chapter Three, the
evidence concerning the order in which clergy of different status
preached on occasions when more than one homily was delivered is not
so readily interpreted.[100] In only one of the examples cited (*In illud: Messis quidem multa*) is it clear from independent internal evidence that the
homily was delivered at Constantinople. While we may suspect, on the
basis of this sermon, that in the other instances Chrysostom is the last

---

[94] PG 63,530 47-50: καθάπερ μέλισσαι τῶν σίμβλων ἐκπηδήσατε ... μηδὲν πρὸς τὸ τῆς ὁδοῦ
κατοκνήσαντες μῆκος.

[95] Vinson, "Maccabean Martyrs", 183-184.

[96] "Maccabean Martyrs", 186 n. 61.

[97] PG 63,523 12-21 *a.i.*; 524 13-14 *a.i.*

[98] *Adv. catharos* (PG 63,491 1-12); *Hom. habita postquam presbyter Gothus* (PG 63,499
4-6 *a.i.*); *In illud: Messis quidam multa* (PG 63,515 5 *a.i.*-517 15); *In illud: Filius ex se nihil
facit* (CPG 4441.12) PG 56,247 1-10; and *In illud: Quia quod stultum est dei* (CPG 4441.14)
Stav. 6 f.132v a.1-33.

[99] *In illud: Ne timueritis cum dives factus fuerit hom. 2* (CPG 4414) and *In illud Isaiae:
Ego dominus deus feci lumen* (CPG 4418). Regarding the version of the title to the latter in
which it is stated that the homily was delivered in the church of Eirene see Aubineau,
"Restitution", 534-535.

[100] See pp. 351-360.

person to preach on that day and that this indicates that he is of more senior status, certain other possibilities cannot be negated. It is conceivable, for instance, that at Antioch he became in time the most popular presbyter available and that public pressure dictated that he preach after other presbyters, regardless of seniority.[101] This circumstance would be particularly relevant if he were preaching not in the church where Flavian, his bishop, customarily presided, but at another church in the same city which had a separate complement of clergy.[102] Allowing for the exaggeration natural to a modesty topos, in *De Eleazaro et septem pueris* John's opening praise for the elderly person who has just preached and his comment that, with so many elderly experienced preachers present, he, a relatively young person, should stay silent and listen are not inconsistent with this option.

Secondly, we must ask to what extent John's defense of the status of the Maccabees as martyrs against what he says is a significant number of people who do not believe that they should be included in the local martyrology[103] is indicative of local opinion. It could be argued, given the long-standing devotion to the Maccabees on the part of the inhabitants of Antioch, that the fact that John finds it necessary to defend celebration of the martyrs by Christians in this instance is suggestive of Constantinople, particularly if we accept Vinson's argument that veneration of the Maccabees by Christians at Antioch had its origins in the reign of Julian (c. 363).[104] Direct reference to the likely reaction of a Jew in the course of his argument in support of the martyrs' status neither supports nor counteracts this conclusion,[105] since it is likely that there was a Jewish community at Constantinople also and, in any case, the comment is probably rhetorical.

The first point to be made in relation to the above findings is that the emphasis placed on the single piece of evidence previously adduced (a verb presumed to indicate the crossing of water) has obscured two other equally valid pieces of evidence (that another person has preached first, and that the local audience has some difficulty with accepting that the Maccabees can be celebrated as martyrs by Christians). Whether these

---

[101] In the homily *In illud: Filius ex se nihil facit*, for example, John indicates that the prior homilist was obliged to terminate his sermon prematurely due to the pressure of public sentiment in John's favour. However, the homily *In illud: Pater meus usque modo operatur*, if delivered at Constantinople, indicates that public fervour for his preaching was strong at that location (PG 63,511 39-512 2).

[102] See W. Mayer, "John Chrysostom and His Audiences. Distinguishing different congregations at Antioch and Constantinople", *Studia Patristica* 31 (1997) 80-85.

[103] PG 63,525 33-41.

[104] "Maccabean Martyrs", 187-188.

[105] PG 63,526 51-56.

other pieces of data support the first has thus never been subjected to examination. When all of the data are weighed equally, however, we see
that, while none of them is in obvious contradiction and all of them
might possibly point to Constantinople, the first two are essentially
equivocal, while it is only the last that points with any conviction towards the imperial capital. Without a firmer means of determining the
significance of the second piece of data, we are unable to say more at this
point than that, while the homily could nonetheless have been preached
at Antioch, it is perhaps more likely that it was delivered at Constantinople.

d. *Uncertainty*

Of the remaining five homilies, one has been assigned to Constantinople on dubious grounds, while the other four are relatively bland and,
if separated from their titles, could as readily be assigned to Antioch. The
sermon which has dubiously been attributed to Constantinople is *Quod
frequenter conveniendum sit* (CPG 4441.3). The basis for this attribution
is an exemplum in the prooimion, in which John refers to an event which
occurred in the city some thirty or so days earlier. A very wealthy man,
unnamed, was stripped of all his assets and is currently a fugitive, in fear
for his life.[106] A number of scholars argue that the individual in question
is the notorious consul-eunuch Eutropius.[107] Others, simply assuming
that the homily belongs to Constantinople because of its location in the
series, interpret the metaphoric σεισμός literally and concentrate instead
on ascertaining its date.[108] Neither approach is convincing. Upon a careful reading of the exemplum the earthquake argument is readily dismissed.[109] As for the Eutropius position, as Batiffol has been the only one
to point out, there is nothing in the exemplum to identify the man of
wealth with a political office; nor, in his opinion, do the individual's current circumstances match the experience of Eutropius.[110] His is an
intelligent observation. A quick glance at the years immediately before
and after John's arrival at Constantinople reveals, in addition to Eutropius' own case, a surpisingly large number of examples of high-profile

---

[106] PG 63,461 22-44.

[107] See Stilting (Chapter One, p. 125); Migne, PG 63,462 n.(a); Bonsdorff (p. 189);
Meyer, *Jean Chrysostome*, XXXIV.

[108] So Montfaucon and Lietzmann (Chapter One, pp. 102 and 170).

[109] See Chapter Three (9.a-b), pp. 447f.

[110] Batiffol, "Quelques homélies", 570-571.

men of wealth whose fortunes underwent similarly public reversals.[111] Eutropius was personally responsible for the downfall of several such individuals.[112] In sum, not only are the circumstances of the exemplum not unique to Eutropius,[113] but, if we ignore the title for the present, the case presented in the exemplum is as likely to point us away from Constantinople towards Antioch.

Of the four homilies (CPG 4441.4,8,12,14) which have yet to be assessed, all have specific topographical information in their titles which points to Constantinople.[114] If the titles are ignored, there is little within the homilies that is distinctive of location. In the case of *In illud: Filius ex se nihil facit* (CPG 4441.12) we are informed that another member of the clergy has just attempted to preach but was cut short by an audience anxious to hear Chrysostom.[115] The status of that individual is not indicated. As we have already established, such information could possibly point to Constantinople but is not necessarily distinctive. The subject matter of the homily, correction of Anomoean teaching regarding the inequality of Father and Son, is likewise neutral, since we know that John was obliged to address the heresy at both locations.[116] Similarly in the case of *In illud: Quia quod stultum est dei* (CPG 4441.14) it appears that another person has just preached. Here John gives a brief summary of the preceding sermon and then moves onto an exegesis of the epistle lection since, as he says, he wishes to avoid being accused of lack of taste for explaining another person's words.[117] Again the comments are too

---

[111] Regarding Rufinus, Aurelian, Saturninus and Count John at Constantinople see Liebeschuetz, *Barbarians and Bishops*, 89-82 and 105-116. Concerning Lucianus and Flavius Tatianus in relation to Antioch see Allen-Mayer, "A New Approach", 31-33.

[112] See PLRE I, s.v. Flavius Abundantius and Flavius Timasius.

[113] In a homily delivered in 400 AD Asterius of Amaseia alludes to the fate of Eutropius only after that of Rufinus, Timasius, Abundantius, and Tatianus and his son Proclus, confirming Eutropius' place in contemporary thought as only one of a number of such exempla. See Chapter Three, n. 638. Cf. Jerome, *Ad Heliodorum*, *Ep.* 60.16, CSEL 4^2 (1996) 570 1-9, where the cases of Abundantius, Rufinus and Timasius are cited as exempla.

[114] *Quod frequenter conveniendum sit* is said to have been delivered in St Anastasia, *Hom. dicta in templo s. Anastasiae* in the same, *In illud: Filius ex se nihil facit* in the Great Church, and *In illud: Quia quod stultum est dei* in the Church of St Acacius.

[115] PG 56,247 1-10.

[116] For proof that *De incompr. dei nat. hom. 1-2* were preached at Antioch see Chapter Three, pp. 337f and 368f; for proof of the Constantinopolitan provenance of *Contra Anom. hom. 11* see p. 393. The topic is also addressed in *In illud: Pater meus usque modo operatur* (CPG 4441.10), which, as established above, was probably delivered likewise at Constantinople.

[117] Stav. 6, f.132v a.33-b.16: ὃ δὴ καὶ νῦν πεποίηκεν ὁ καλῶς εἰρηκώς· τήν τε πανήγυριν ταύτην ἀνυμνήσας τὴν πνευματικὴν· καὶ τῶν τῷ οὐνῷ πρεπόντων φορτίων τὰ σύμβολα διηγησάμενος· καὶ πῶς ἐν τῇ πανηγύρει ταύτῃ οὐχὶ τοῖς πλουτοῦσι μόνον. ἀλλὰ πολλῷ μᾶλλον τοῖς πένησιν εὔκολος τῷ βουλομένῳ ἡ κτῆσις γίνεται· Ἀλλ' ἵνα μὴ δόξωμεν ἀπειροκαλίας ἔγκλημα ὑπομένειν·

vague to determine the status of the individual relative to John. The
homilies *Quod frequenter conveniendum sit* (CPG 4441.4) and *Hom. dicta
in templo s. Anastasiae* (CPG 4441.8), on the other hand, are entirely
lacking in detail which might be of assistance.

e. *Sequentiality*

Does evidence that certain homilies were preached in sequence alter
the conclusions drawn from a case by case study of internal data? If Pargoire's thesis that CPG 4441.7,10,12 and 13 were all preached in sequence in the same month and year were to hold true,[118] then, since CPG
4441.7 is of certain Constantinopolitan provenance (CPG 4441.10 being
of probable, 4441.13 of possible and 4441.12 of uncertain status), the
provenance of homilies 10, 12 and 13 would take on the same degree of
certainty. Unfortunately the arguments which support his thesis do not
withstand careful scrutiny,[119] and, while it remains possible that homilies
7, 10 and 12 do form a sequence, it is more likely that they do not. It
would therefore be incautious to upgrade the status of homilies 10 and
12 on that basis. On the other hand, it is possible to demonstrate that the
link between homilies 10 and 12 is firm, with the result that the provenance of hom. 12 can be upgraded with confidence from uncertain to
probable.

In CPG 4441.12 John begins his explanation of the day's topic by recalling the subject matter of the previous synaxis. The focus on that occasion was Jn 5.17: "My father is working still, and I am working", which
Chrysostom used to demonstrate the equality of the Son with the Father.[120] While this detail suggests CPG 4441.10, where that same verse
and the topic of the equal status of Christ were indeed the focus of much
of the homily, it is a third piece of information which permits us to ce-
ment the relationship. As he embarks upon the topic of the day proper,
the counter-arguments of the Anomœans,[121] John makes the point that
the statement that Christ was setting himself up as equal to God is a reflection of Christ's own understanding of the situation and definitely not
a conjecture of the Jews. This matter, he informs his audience, is one
which he himself explained in the clearest possible way in the previous

τὰ ἑτέρων ἐκ δευτέρου διηγούμενοι· φέρε δὴ τῶν σήμερον ἀνεγνωσμένων μίαν ῥῆσιν μεταχειρισά-
μενοι. τὸ σύνηθες ὑμῖν καταβάλωμεν ὄφλημα·

[118] For a summary of Pargoire's argument see Part One, pp. 158-161.

[119] See Mayer, "Pargoire's sequence".

[120] PG 56,247 28-32.

[121] PG 56,247 36-38; 248 31-33.

sermon, to which the listener who wishes to take the matter further is referred.[122] Since precisely this explanation occupies the latter section of CPG 4441.10,[123] it seems certain that that homily and the one which is said to have preceded CPG 4441.12 are one and the same.

The only other case within the series where evidence of two homilies having been preached in sequence occurs, that of CPG 4441.1 and 2,[124] serves to support the conclusion that both were delivered with certainty at Constantinople, since it indicates that both were delivered at the same location.

2. ANALYSIS OF RESULTS

As the above case study has demonstrated, when the provenance of a group of homilies is assessed objectively, individually, and on the basis of internal data alone, the results are inevitably less certain than previously supposed. They are, on the other hand, more honest, they discourage unsustainable assumptions of certainty of provenance, and, in relation to those homilies where provenance has been assessed as other than certain, they allow for the possibility that the findings from the re-analysis of other homilies may subsequently alter the conclusions drawn. In the case study just conducted thirteen of the fifteen homilies have titles attached which contain topographical data specific to Constantinople. The two homilies whose titles are devoid of such detail are *Contra ludos et theatra* (CPG 4441.7) and *De Eleazaro et septem pueris* (CPG 4441.13). Of these two, Constantinopolitan provenance is demonstrated in the case of the first on the basis of internal data. In the case of the second, internal evidence is weak and the bias towards Constantinople is slight, allowing one to conclude only that Constantinopolitan provenance is possible. Of the remaining thirteen, a further four demonstrate certain Constantinopolitan provenance (CPG 4441.1,2,11,15), which supports the implication of the topographical detail found in the title. Of the remaining nine, internal data contained in three (CPG 4441.5,9,10) and firm evidence of a link between the last and a fourth homily (CPG 4441.12) permit one to conclude that Constantinopolitan provenance is probable. A further homily contains weak evidence which may point to Constantinople (CPG 4441.6), while the data contained in a final four homilies are either equivocal or too bland to admit of distinction (CPG 4441.3,4,8,14).

---

[122] PG 56,248 45-249 3.

[123] PG 63,516 12-32.

[124] See PG 63,473 1-6, which picks up PG 63,472 15-40, the concluding comments of CPG 4441.1.

The question which remains is how much credence can be given to the specific topographical information found in the titles, since this is necessarily independent of the contents of the homily (nowhere does Chrysostom explicitly state within a homily that he is preaching at such and such a location). As in the case of the data about a Gothic presbyter having preached first (CPG 4441.9), which proved to be uninferrable from the contents of the homily, such detail, if genuinely able to be attached to a particular city, ought to lend some weight to the conclusion derived from internal data. Before we can proceed to apply the topographical information to the findings based on the homilies' contents, however, it must be pointed out that not all of the churches and martyria mentioned are verifiably Constantinopolitan. The martyrium of St Thomas at Drypia, mentioned in the titles to CPG 4441.1 and 2,[125] is otherwise unknown,[126] as is the martyrium at Palaia Petra, mentioned in the title to CPG 4441.3.[127] In the case of CPG 4441.1-2 this creates no difficulty, since the homilies are certifiably Constantinopolitan due to the participation on those occasions of the emperor and empress. In the case of CPG 4441.3, however, where the internal data is equivocal, the specific topographical detail in the title must also be treated as equivocal and can therefore be of no assistance.

In the case of the Great Church, mentioned in the titles to CPG 4441.1,10 and 12,[128] this location is non-distinctive, since the episcopal church was labelled in that manner at both cities, and therefore is also unhelpful. In the case of CPG 4441.6, it must also be remembered that once it is assumed that the homily is preached on the anniversary of Theodosius' death the assumption that it was delivered in the Church of the Apostles naturally follows, and therefore the latter information is unreliable and should not be used to assist in determining the homily's provenance. In the case of CPG 4441.11 the information in the title, that it was preached in the Church of the Apostle, is patently wrong and, as demonstrated, it can be determined from internal comment that the homily was in fact preached in the Church of the Apostles.[129] The provenance of the homily is thus in this instance patent in spite of the detail in the title. In the case of CPG 4441.9, where the detail about a Gothic presbyter in the title already serves to point to a probable provenance of Constantinople, the information that the homily was preached in the Church

---

[125] See PG 63,467 9-15 *a.i.* (the martyrium is said to be in Drypia, but not identified) and PG 63,473 1-6 (held in the martyrium of the apostle and martyr Thomas in Drypia).

[126] See Janin, *Géographie ecclésiastique*, 251.

[127] PG 63,461-462.

[128] See PG 63,511 1-8 and PG 56,247-248.

[129] See Chapter Three, p. 317.

of St Paul,[130] à church demonstrably located at that city, adds weight to the conclusion. In the case of CPG 4441.5, which likewise demonstrates a probable provenance of Constantinople, the information that it was preached in the Church of St Eirene,[131] a location distinctive of that city, again serves to reinforce the conclusion. This leaves CPG 4441.4,8,14 and 15, the first two preached in St Anastasia,[132] the last two in St Acacius.[133] Both churches are unique to Constantinople. Since CPG 4441.15 has already been shown to be of certain Constantinopolitan provenance, the information simply confirms the conclusion. CPG 4441.4,8 and 14, however, were deemed of uncertain provenance on initial examination. The specific and unique topographical detail in the titles in these instances can be used to upgrade the conclusion regarding their provenance from uncertain to possible.

Adding in the data in the titles thus does little to alter the conclusions drawn from a detailed examination of the internal evidence. There is a slight increase in the probability of Constantinopolitan provenance in relation to two of the homilies (CPG 4441.5 and 9), while three homilies previously of uncertain provenance are now included among those that were possibly delivered at Constantinople (now CPG 4441.4,6,8,13,14). Only one homily (CPG 4441.3) remains of indeterminate provenance. The results can be summarised as follows.

Table 18. Status of the *Novae homiliae*

CPG no.	Homily	Criteria (current)	Degree of certainty	Place (current)
4441.1	*Hom. dicta postquam reliquiae mart.*	3.c.i	certain	CP
4441.2	*Hom. dicta praesente imperatore*	3.c.i	certain	CP
4441.3	*Quod frequenter conveniendum sit*		uncertain	—
4441.4	*Adversus eos qui non adfuerant*	1, 3.e.i	possible	CP
4441.5	*De studio praesentium*	1, 3.c.i,e.i	probable	CP
4441.6	*Adversus catharos*	4.c.iii	possible	CP
4441.7	*Contra ludos et theatra*	3.d.i	certain	CP
4441.8	*Hom . dicta in templo s. Anastasiae*	1, 3.e.i	possible	CP
4441.9	*Hom. dicta postquam presbyter Gothus*	1, 3.e.i, 4	probable	CP
4441.10	*In illud: Pater meus usque modo operatur*	3.h.i	probable	CP
4441.11	*In illud: Messis quidem multa*	3.e.i	certain	CP
4441.12	*In illud: Filius ex se nihil facit*	sequence	probable	CP
4441.13	*De Eleazaro et septem pueris*	8.a	possible	CP

---

[130] PG 63,499 4-6 *a.i.*

[131] PG 63,485 1-5.

[132] See PG 63,477 35-38 *a.i.* and PG 63,493 46 *a.i.*

[133] See Stav. 6, f.132v a.1-4 and f.138v b.1-5.

4441.14	*In illud: Quia quod stultum est dei*	1, 3.e.i	possible	CP
4441.15	*In martyres omnes*	3.c.i	certain	CP

These results allow us to examine further the question of the significance of another person having preached before John (criterion 2.e). It will be remembered that six of the *Novae homiliae* contain an indication that another person or persons has just preached a sermon at the same synaxis. In only one of those instances is the provenance of the homily certain (CPG 4441.11). Now, however, a futher two examples can be seen to occur in homilies of probable Constantinopolitan provenance (CPG 4441.9,12), while the remaining three occur in homilies of at least possible Constantinopolitan provenance (CPG 4441.6,13,14). While this finding does not prove that when John preaches after another individual he is necessarily bishop and therefore situated at Constantinople, it does increase the probability that this is the case.

3. PRODUCING A TEST BASE: HOMILIES OF CERTAIN PROVENANCE

With the effectiveness of the corrections and modifications to the approach established, the final step is to establish a reliable body of material against which data, criteria and hypotheses can in the future be tested. In Chapter Three the means of testing the validity of the interpretation of data or of the assumptions which underlie the criteria was consistently to check the interpretation or hypothesis against data contained in homilies where the provenance could be determined with certainty. Here we gather together the homilies of certain provenance as a resource for future investigation. Additions to the collection will occur as the investigation of the provenance of the homilies progresses and the number of homilies of certain provenance is increased.

In the course of Chapters Three and Four the provenance of an initial fifty-one sermons has been proven on the basis of existing criteria or established on the basis of secure connection to a homily of certain provenance. Table 19 provides a list of those homilies by CPG number and title, side by side with the conclusion drawn and the criteria upon which the determination was made. It is noteworthy that a significant number do not appear in Table 17. Their provenance had not been formally proven before this point because of tacit assumptions relating to chronology or homogeneity.

Table 19. Homilies of certain provenance

CPG no.	Homily	Criteria (current)	Place (current)
4317	*Cum presbyter fuit ordinatus*	2.d.i	A
4318	*De incompr. dei natura hom. 1*	2.d.i	A
"	*De incompr. dei natura hom. 2*	3.b	A
4319	*De beato Philogonio*	2.d.i,e	A
4324	*Contra Anomoeos hom. 11*	3.f.ii	CP
4325	*De Christi divinitate*	sequence	CP
4327	*Adv. Iudaeos or. 1*	3.d.ii	A
"	*Adv. Iudaeos or. 5*	7	A
"	*Adv. Iudaeos or. 6*	9.b	A
4328	*In kalendas*	2.d.i	A
4330	*De statuis hom. 2*	3.g	A
"	*De statuis hom. 3*	2.b, 3.b.i,c.i,g	A
"	*De statuis hom. 5*	9.b	A
"	*De statuis hom. 6*	2.d.i, 3.c.i	A
"	*De statuis hom. 14*	3.a,b.i	A
"	*De statuis hom. 15*	9.b	A
"	*De statuis hom. 17*	3.a,b.i-iii,d.ii	A
"	*De statuis hom. 18*	3.d.i	A
"	*De statuis hom. 19*	3.a	A
"	*De statuis hom. 20*	9.b	A
"	*De statuis hom. 21*	2.d.i, 3.c.i	A
4343	*De s. pentecoste hom. 1*	2.d.i	A
4344	*De laudibus s. Pauli hom. 4*	9.g	A
4345	*De s. Meletio*	3.e.i-ii, 5.b, 9	A
4347	*De s. Babyla*	2.d.i, 3.d.i-ii,e.i	A
4351	*In s. Ignatium*	3.b.iv,e.ii	A
4352	*In s. Eustathium*	5.b	A
4357	*De ss. martyribus*	2.d.i	A
4360	*In s. Iulianum martyrem*	3.d.ii	A
4364	*De s. Phoca*	3.c.i,d.i	CP
4371	*In princ. Act. hom. 1*	7	A
"	*In princ. Act. hom. 2*	2.d.i, 3.b.i,iv	A
4382	*De eleemosyna*	3.b.ii	A
4391	*In illud: In faciem ei restiti*	2.d.i, 3.b.iii	A
4392	*In Eutropium*	3.c.i, 9.a	CP
4406	*Laus Diodori*	2.e, 3.d.i	A
4410	*Sermo 1 in Genesim*	2.d.i	A

"	*Sermo 8 in Genesim*	2.b,d.i	A
4424	*In Matt. hom. 7*	3.b.i	A
4425	*In Ioh. hom. 12/11*	5.a.ii	A
4426	*In Acta apost. hom. 9*	2.a	CP
4428	*In I Cor. hom. 21*	3.a,b.i	A
4433	*In Col. hom. 2*	sequence	CP
"	*In Col. hom. 3*	2.a	CP
"	*In Col. hom. 7*	9.b	A
4440	*In Heb. hom. 14*	7	A
4441.1	*Hom. dicta postquam reliquiae mart.*	3.c.i	CP
4441.2	*Hom. dicta praesente imperatore*	3.c.i	CP
4441.7	*Contra ludos et theatra*	3.d.i	CP
4441.11	*In illud: Messis quidem multa*	3.e.i	CP
4441.15	*In martyres omnes*	3.c.i	CP

Summary

When we began this investigation, we set out to determine why there were inconsistencies in the literature and whether a consensus concerning the provenance of John Chrysostom's homilies had ever been reached. In Parts One and Two we showed that not only had a consensus never been reached regarding the provenance of every homily within the corpus, but that a large number of the findings that had been recorded were invalid and the underlying assumptions informing those conclusions false. In Part Three we set out to repair the deficiencies in the previous approach and to use the corrected methodology to develop a more rigorous approach. The key to the modified approach is a scrupulous avoidance of placing greater weight on the evidence than it can bear. Testing every part until it breaks or holds firm is an important element in achieving a reliable outcome. Equally vital is a willingness to adjust the findings each time a new result or new piece of evidence is slotted into place or the weighting of data changes.

The implications of these findings and the proposed modifications to the general approach are several. Firstly, the findings counsel considerable caution when approaching smaller corpora of homilies. It would appear from the investigation in Chapter Three that the influence of the genre, rhetoric and varied perspectives upon the data contained in homilies is greater than usually allowed for and the potential for a false reading high. In a case where there is not a large body of homilies across which to test an interpretation, hesitation concerning the validity of a reading is necessarily increased. Secondly, in the course of establishing the validity or otherwise of the criteria a number of key assumptions were either challenged or disproved. Among them are the distinctions between the offices of bishop and presbyter, particularly in relation to duties, status and workload; the discreteness of monastic forms between the two cities; and the distinctiveness of the liturgical calendars and practice. In many more cases assumptions about various aspects of Antiochene and Constantinopolitan society rest on data contained in homilies whose provenance is now reduced to uncertain. A fresh examination of many of these aspects, taking into account the revised provenance, is now required. Thirdly, analysis of the current methodology for determining sequence, development of a more reliable methodology, and revision of the sequences which currently appear in the literature are desiderata, particularly in light of the usefulness of sequence for extending provenance and of the profound implications of the dismissal of the assumption of the homogeneity of series. Only when a more cautious and reliable evaluation of the provenance of Chrysostom's homilies and of the web of connections that exist between them has been completed can a final desideratum, a sound chronology of the corpus, be achieved.

INDEX OF GREEK TERMS

INDEX OF REFERENCES TO CHRYSOSTOM

Homilies of definite provenance are labelled ^A and ^CP, respectively; ? indicates that a provenance is probable, but not definite.

1. By CPG number

Contra eos qui subintroductae (CPG 4311) 431^581

Quod regulares fem. (CPG 4312) 431^581

Ad viduam iuniorem (CPG 4314) 451^681, 453^688, 500^85

De sacerdotio (CPG 4316) 322^29, 334, 364^239

Sermo cum presbyter fuit ordinatus^A (CPG 4317) 49, 72, 114, 147, 175^673, 228, 233-4, 329^63, 330, 334, 359^220, 388^355

De incomprehensibili dei natura hom. 1-5 (CPG 4318) 51, 72, 79, 84, 95, 109, 136, 138, 147, 153, 165, 167, 178, 211, 218, 225, 230-1, 238, 304, 409

   1:^A 52, 72-3, 107, 137, 153, 231, 238, 337, 340, 365, 505^116

   2:^A 73, 107, 147^540, 238, 348, 369, 394^390, 416, 505^116

   3: 75, 112, 147^541

   4: 72, 347^157

   5: 87, 112-13, 125

De beato Philogonio^A (CPG 4319) 51-2, 72, 78, 87, 95, 110, 112-13, 135^480, 136-8, 147, 152, 154, 165, 167, 178, 211, 213^890, 218, 225-7, 230, 238, 304, 339, 353-4, 404^443, 409, 432^586, 495^61, 500^82

De consubstantiali (CPG 4320) 52, 72, 95, 110, 114, 125, 136, 138, 147, 165, 167, 178, 211, 218^916, 225-6, 230, 237-8, 304, 409

De petitione matris filiorum Zebedaei (CPG 4321) 52, 72, 78^208, 95, 110, 114, 136, 138, 147, 165, 167, 178, 211, 218, 225-6, 230, 237-8, 304, 409

In quatriduanum Lazarum (CPG 4322) 27, 53^92, 72, 95, 110, 114, 136, 138, 147, 165, 167, 178, 211, 218, 225-6, 230, 237-8, 304, 409

De Christi precibus (CPG 4323) 27, 53, 72, 95, 110-11, 114, 136, 138, 147, 165, 167, 178, 211, 218, 225-6, 230, 237-8, 304, 409

Contra Anomoeos hom. 11^CP (CPG 4324) 63, 73, 125, 225-6, 230, 237-8, 318^16, 319^26, 393, 407^452, 409^460, 490, 505^116

De Christi divinitate^CP (CPG 4325) 63, 73, 84, 125, 225-6, 230, 237-8, 319^26, 490

Contra Iudaeos et gentiles qod Christus sit deus (CPG 4326) 178

Adv. Iudæos or. 1-8 (CPG 4327) 43, 51^79, 72^177, 73-4, 136-8, 146-8, 151-3, 168, 178, 226, 230, 304, 405-6, 408, 483, 489^34

   1:^A 42, 51, 73, 78, 107, 109, 111, 231, 377-8, 405, 408

   2: 51, 73, 78, 107, 109, 111, 405, 408^455

   3: 52, 73, 74^184, 78, 89, 109^347, 111, 138, 348^162, 408^454-5

   4: 53, 74, 111-12, 118, 140, 218, 408^455

   5:^A 53, 74, 111-12, 118, 140, 389^361, 405, 408, 435

   6:^A 53, 74, 111-12, 118, 140, 151, 339, 342^134, 343^138, 345^149, 346^150, 355, 405, 408, 445^643

2. Alphabetically by title

3. By location in PG, SC *et al.*

PG 49,153 2-11 368[259]

15:[A] PG 49,154 2-14 *a.i.* 445[642]

  PG 49,179 8-11 377[305]

16: PG 49,161 8-22 *a.i.* 398[407]

  PG 49,161 22 *a.i.*-162 4 *a.i.* 348[169]

  PG 49,162 4-16 a.i. 398[409]

  PG 49,163 31-3 349[170]

  PG 49,163 44-57 398[411]

  PG 49,166 19-25 398[407]

17:[A] PG 49,172 7 *a.i.*-173 4 428[561]

  PG 49,175 5-8 367[251], 388[359]

  PG 49,176 32-6 387[354]

  PG 49,176 42-4 368[259]

  PG 49,176 48-177 11 369[260]

  PG 49,178 20-2 367[251]

  PG 49,179 8-14 389[363]

18:[A] PG 49,186 38-61 481[15]

  PG 49,187 24-8 376[298]

19:[A] PG 49,188 6-12 *a.i.* 404[440], 494[56], 495[62]

  PG 49,188 11 *a.i.*-190 55 495[61]

  PG 49,190 56-8 495[61]

  PG 49,197 3-15 367[251]

20:[A] PG 49,197 19-21 *a.i.* 333[83]

  PG 49,199 25-8 407[451]

  PG 49,199 59-200 3 407[451]

  PG 49,201 32-5 333[83]

  PG 49,204 20-3 332[83]

  PG 49,208 9-15 333[83]

  PG 49,211 13-212 4 332[83]

  PG 49,212 7-8 342[134]

21:[A] PG 49,211 6-40 *a.i.* 340[126]

  PG 49,211-12 481[14]

  PG 49,214 10-12 340[126], 388[358]

  PG 49,218 1-6 220[927]

Ad illuminandos cat. 2
  PG 49,238 25-35 446[645]

De diabolo tentatore hom. 1-3
2: PG 49,257 2-258 3 354[191]

De paenitentia hom. 1-9
1: PG 49,277 2-37 365[244]

  PG 49,277 37-8 365[245]

  PG 49,277 49-50 365[246]

3: PG 49,291 22-24 *a.i.* 389[360]

4: PG 49,301 60-302 12 454[693]

  PG 49,302 15-16 454[692]

5:[A?] PG 49,314 5-19 345[148], 355[196]

  PG 49,314 20-22 343[134]

In diem natalem[A?]
  PG 49,358 53-4   323[34], 341[129], 345[148], 355[201]

De baptismo Christi
  PG 49,370 20-8 436[602]

De coemeterio et de cruce
  PG 50,393 1-31 347[157]

  PG 50,393 27-9 383[331]

De resurrectione mortuorum
  PG 50,421 62-422 5 437[610]

De resurrectione
  PG 50,438 13-14 347[160]

  PG 50,439 28-30 426[550]

In ascensionem[A?]
  PG 50,441-2 279[6]

  PG 50,442 3-6 *a.i.* 341[127]

  PG 50,443 22-37 341[127], 498[73]

  PG 50,443 10-39 375[296]

De s. pentecoste hom. 1-2
1:[A] PG 50,458 47-51 284[35], 341[129]

De s. Meletio[A]
  PG 50,515 3-7 388[356]

  PG 50,515 11-13 388[356]

  PG 50,515 22-5 382[327], 498[73]

  PG 50,517 38-40 457[715]

  PG 50,518 16-17   370[270], 388[356], 424[543]

PG 56,247 1-13   358[215], 502[98], 505[115]

PG 56,247 28-32 506[120]

PG 56,247 36-8 506[121]

PG 56,248 31-3 506[121]

PG 56,248 45-249 3 507[122]

Contra ludos et theatra[CP] (CPG 4441.7)

PG 56,265 3-18   376[299], 455[700-1], 492[46]

PG 56,265 12-13 375[294]

PG 56,266 28-9 391[376]

PG 56,268 29-37 332[78]

PG 56,268 47-8 492[47]

PG 56,270 22-3 332[77]

In Matt. hom. 1-90

4: PG 57,41 1-13 422[531], 462[742]

7:[A] PG 57,74 25-8 176[679], 303[121], 403[435]

PG 57,79 45-8 374[287]

PG 57,81 23-4 38[17], 290[63]

13: PG 57,216 2-3 437[610]

16: PG 57,248 45-9 303[121], 404[438]

33/34: PG 57,395 18-28 437[610]

67/68:[A?] PG 58,636 48-55 306[141], 422[527-9]

PG 58,637 3-4 423[532]

PG 58,637 12-16 423[532]

PG 58,637 16-18 422[530]

68/69: PG 58,644 45-6 333[91]

69/70: PG 58,653 19-21 430[572]

72/73: PG 58,671 9-22 430[572]

82/83: PG 58,744 56-8 399[416]

85/86: PG 58,762 8-764 3 366[248]

PG 58,762 59-763 2 407[450]

In Ioh. hom. 1-88

2: PG 59,32 19-23 419[514]

12:[A] PG 59,83 7-11 420[520]

33: PG 59,187 8-9 a.i. 500[82]

In Acta apost. hom. 1-55

1: PG 60,22 16-20 193[786]

PG 60,24 28-31 193[788]

PG 60,24 56-63 193[788]

3: PG 60,38 51-42 39 240, 328[58]

PG 60,39 5-7 332[79]

PG 60,39 55-7 322[32], 328[59]

PG 60,40 10-13 327[56]

PG 60,41 6-10 396[400]

6: PG 60,61 7-30 426[551]

7: PG 60,66 16-20 455[698]

8: PG 60,74 17-21 371[278]

PG 60,74 21-6 240, 281[18], 330[69]

PG 60,74 31-8 393[388]

9:[CP] PG 60,83 49-84 8 332[78]

PG 60,84 25-31 240, 280[10], 281[18], 332[77]

11: PG 60,97 22-5 407[450]

PG 60,98 60-1 282[20]

PG 60,99 240

18: PG 60,148 24-7 500[85]

21: PG 60,168 240

PG 60,170 240

25: PG 60,192 6-16 a.i. 393[383]

PG 60,193 4-5 393[383]

PG 60,194 14-19 393[383]

29: PG 60,217 56-7 347[159]

32: PG 60,237 240

38: PG 60,274 49-50 459[722,726]

PG 60,274 56-8 400[425], 459[727]

41: PG 60,291 3-10 455[698], 461[731,733]

PG 60,291 29-32 422[531], 461[731], 462[736,742], 463[746]

PG 60,291 37-40 312[165], 460[728]

42: PG 60,302 34-5 299[104], 387[351]

44: PG 60,266 241

In Rom. hom. 1-32

2: PG 60,401 37-41 180[710], 419[511]

8: PG 60,464 42-5 179[700], 285[37]

PG 60,465 27-35 179[701]

13: PG 60,517 17-21 305[136], 417[501]

23: PG 60,618 17-40 180[708], 399[415,418]

24: PG 60,625 35-8 347[159]

25: PG 60,635 60-1 427[557]

26: PG 60,642 15-19 420[515]

PG 63,643 5-664 5 427[557]
PG 60,643 9-10 420[516]
PG 60,643 13-15 420[518]
29: PG 60,660 55-8 180[703]
30: PG 60,665 32-3 418[506]
PG 60,666 22-7 292[70]

In I Cor. hom. 1-44
7: PG 61,53 7-8 *a.i.* 500[82]
21:[A] PG 61,176 42-178 40 367[250]
PG 61,178 40-2 39[23], 290[62-3], 368[253]

In II Cor. hom. 1-30
3: PG 61,413 10-15 373[283], 437[610]
PG 61,413 41-2 183[726], 419[513]
8: PG 61,459 4-7 183[726], 421[521]
9: PG 61,466 4-8 183[723], 401[429]
15: PG 61,507 43-510 26 327[54]
PG 61,510 29-42 327[54]
26: PG 61,582 19-21 392[378]
PG 61,582 30-1 392[379]
PG 61,582 36-583 1 392[380]
PG 61,582 45-7 396[403]

In Eph. hom. 1-24
4: PG 62,34 22-5 373[284]
6: PG 62,47 57-48 4 219[926]
PG 62,48 44-54 452[683]
8: PG 62,57 44-6 366[247]
10: PG 62,77 19-57 455[699]
PG 62,77 62-78 2 220
11:[CP?] PG 62,85 28-9 220, 411[473]
PG 62,86 1-9 411[469], 412[474]
PG 62,86 13-18 412[476]
PG 62,86 29-32 412[477]
PG 62,86 32-3 220, 412[478]
PG 62,86 38-9 412[479]
PG 62,86 50-4 413[480]
PG 62,87 1-7 413[482]
PG 62,87 2-4 220, 411[470]
PG 62,87 8-12 413[483]
PG 62,87 12-14 413[484]
PG 62,87 14-30 414[485-6]

PG 62,87 27-37 220, 414[487]
PG 62,87 42-3 220
PG 62,87 42-88 6 414[488]
PG 62,88 17-23 414[489]
PG 62,88 28 414[490]
PG 62,88 28-31 415[491]
PG 62,88 31-5 220, 415[492]
21: PG 62,151 62-153 13 456[704]
PG 62,153 18-27 311[162], 456[705-9]

In Phil. hom. 1-15
1: PG 62,183 13-35 327[56]
PG 62,184 53-185 21 428[559]
6: PG 62,218 7 *a.i.*-219 1 410[464]
PG 62,221 17-22 396[404]
7: PG 62,236 51-5 390[368]
9: PG 62,250 33-50 430[574]
10: PG 62,259 18-29 391[373]
12: PG 62,272 33-6 190[767], 373[282]
15: PG 62,290 25-6 431[580]
PG 62,295 15-46 189[765], 422[531], 451[676], 453[688]

In Col. hom. 1-12
2:[CP] PG 62,313 49-53 489[37]
PG 62,313 53-9 490[40]
PG 62,315 6-8 489[36]
3:[CP] PG 62,317 14-16 *a.i.* 490[39]
PG 62,317 12-14 *a.i.* 489[38]
PG 62,317 12 *a.i.*-318 4 *a.i.* 490[40]
PG 62,322 17-323 9 324[38]
PG 62,322 65-323 22 332[76]
PG 62,323 20-2 324[39]
PG 62,324 13-18 281[17], 329[65], 332[77]
PG 62,324 46-9 280[11], 281[17], 329[66]
6: PG 62,341 61-342 1 437[608]
PG 62,342 42-5 437[608]
7:[A] PG 62,347 5-8 444[634]
PG 62,347 8-13 443[631], 444[635]
PG 62,347 56-348 6 443[632], 445[639], 459[722], 481[13]
PG 62,350 27-31 333[85]
PG 62,350 48-52 333[85]

GENERAL INDEX

Abraham (OT patriarch) 344

Abundantius 444[638], 505[113]

Acacius, bishop of Beroea 333[91], 403, 416, 433, 455, 456[703], 458

Acacius, *comes* 383[334]

Acacius (saint) 383[334]

agonothetes 436

agora 249, 299, 390-1, 436

Alaric 311, 450-2

Alexander Akoimetos 457[712]

Alexandria 350

ambo 358[212]

amphithales 437[611]

Ancyra 371

Andrew (apostle) 317, 492

animal hunt 247[1082]

Anomoean heresy 84, 95-6, 110-11, 115, 125, 231, 304, 319, 409, 498, 505-6

Anonymous
  vita Chrysostomi 38

Antioch 55, 290-2, 393-4
  administration 60, 301-2, 397-401, 444
  cemetery 81, 218, 296, 312, 384
  churches of 55-6, 58, 60, 79, 83, 89, 95, 214, 218-19, 296-7, 338, 379-86, 400
  characteristic features of 55, 59-60, 62, 77, 82, 87, 101, 174[670], 176, 187, 298-9, 302-5, 307, 387-93, 405-16
  topography of 294-7, 374-86, 388-90, 400-1, 459, 500-1

Antiochene riots
  see riots of 387 CE

Antiochene schism 61-2, 99, 122, 168, 220, 224, 305, 411-16

Antiochus, bishop of Ptolemais 416

Antoninus, bishop of Ephesus 194

Apollinaris of Laodicea 190, 304, 409-10

Apollo, temple of (Daphne) 44[59], 80, 91, 225, 234, 277[2], 312, 377, 462-3

Arabia 424

Arcadius 49, 93, 189-90, 192, 194, 208, 224, 234, 239, 293, 310-11, 444, 450-2

archon 192, 300-2, 348[169], 371[278], 397-400-1

Argyrius 247[1082]

Arians 385[343], 428[562], 430, 498

Armenia 457[715]

army 301-2, 348[169], 394, 398[410], 401-2, 451

Ascension 76[195], 84, 90, 117, 140, 210

asceticism 220, 247, 306, 325, 333[91], 420[517], 423[534], 428-34, 456-7, 479[5], 487, 496
  Antiochene 38, 59, 78, 86, 92, 176, 180, 184, 187, 208, 219[925], 225, 245, 307, 481, 487
  see also monks

Asterius, bishop of Amasea 444[638], 505[113]

Augustine, bishop of Hippo 361[224]
  Enarrationes in psalmos 361[224]

Aurelianus 88, 242, 385[343], 505[111]

autumn 182, 192, 195, 209, 231, 241, 363

Baarlam 423, 439-41

Babylas 62, 80, 91, 143, 154, 168, 187, 193[783], 221, 224, 236, 298, 312, 353, 362, 377, 382, 384, 386, 419[508], 461-3

baptism 196, 237, 350

MODERN AUTHOR INDEX